THIRD EDITION

INTRODUCTION TO FUTURES AND OPTIONS MARKETS

THIRD EDITION

INTRODUCTION TO FUTURES AND OPTIONS MARKETS

John C. Hull

University of Toronto

 Prentice Hall, Upper Saddle River, New Jersey 07458

Acquistions Editor: Paul Donnelly
Editorial Director: James C. Boyd
Assistant Editor: Gladys Soto
Marketing Manager: Patrick Lynch
Production Editors: Evyan Jengo/Louise Rothman
Associate Managing Editor: David Salierno
Managing Editor: Dee Josephson
Manufacturing Buyer: Ken Clinton
Manufacturing Supervisor: Arnold Vila
Manufacturing Manager: Vincent Scelta
Design Manager: Patricia Smythe
Cover Design Manager: Jayne Conte
Composition: Publication Services
Cover Design: Rosemarie Votta
Cover Photo: Glen Gyssler Computer Art

Copyright © 1998, 1995, 1991 by Prentice-Hall, Inc.
A Simon & Schuster Company
Upper Saddle River, New Jersey 07458

Library of Congress Cataloging-in-Publication Data

Hull, John C.
    Introduction to futures and options markets / John C. Hull. — 3rd ed.
        p.   cm.
    Includes bibliographical references and index.
    ISBN 0-13-889148-6
        1. Futures market.   2. Options (Finance).   3. Futures market — Problems, exercises, etc.   4. Options (Finance) — Problems, exercises, etc.   I. Title.
        HG6024.A3H84   1997   97-26191
        332.64'5 — dc21   CIP

Prentice-Hall International (UK) Limited, London
Prentice-Hall of Australia Pty. Limited, Sydney
Prentice-Hall Canada, Inc., Toronto
Prentice-Hall Hispanoamericana, S.A., Mexico
Prentice-Hall of India Private Limited, New Delhi
Prentice-Hall of Japan, Inc., Tokyo
Simon & Schuster Asia Pte. Ltd., Singapore
Editora Prentice-Hall do Brasil, Ltda., Rio de Janeiro

Printed in the United States of America

10 9 8 7 6 5 4 3 2 1

**To
My Family**

Contents

Preface

This book has been written for undergraduate and graduate elective courses in business and economics. Many practitioners who want to acquire a working knowledge of futures and options markets will also find the book useful.

I was persuaded to write this book by colleagues who liked my other book, *Options, Futures, and Other Derivatives,* but found the material a little too advanced for their students. *Introduction to Futures and Options Markets* covers some of the same ground as *Options, Futures, and Other Derivatives*—but in a way that readers who have had limited training in mathematics will find easier to understand. One important difference between this book and my other is that this one does not contain any calculus.

The book can be used in a number of different ways. Instructors who like to focus on one- and two-step binomial trees when valuing options may wish to cover only the first 10 chapters. Instructors who feel that swaps are adequately covered by other courses can choose to omit chapter 6. Instructors who feel the material in chapters 17 and 18 is too specialized can skip these chapters. Some instructors may choose to devote relatively more time to futures and swaps markets (Part 1); others may choose to structure their course mostly around options markets (Part 2).

Chapter 1 provides an introduction to futures and options markets and outlines the different ways in which they can be used. Chapter 2 describes the mechanics of how futures and forward contracts work. Chapter 3 shows how forward and futures prices can be determined in a variety of different situations using pure arbitrage arguments. Chapter 4 discusses how futures contracts can be used for hedging. Chapter 5 deals with the special problems associated with interest-rate futures contracts. Chapter 6 covers swaps. Chapter 7 describes the mechanics of how options markets work. Chapter 8 develops some relationships that must hold in options markets if there are to be no arbitrage opportunities. Chapter 9 outlines a number of different trading strategies involving options. Chapter 10 shows how options can be priced using one- and two-step binomial trees. Chapter 11 discusses the pricing of stock options using the Black–Scholes analysis. Chapter 12 extends the ideas in chapter 11 to cover options on stock indices and currencies. Chapter 13 deals with futures options. Chapter 14 provides a detailed treatment of hedge parameters such as delta, gamma, and vega. It also discusses scenario analysis and portfolio insurance. Chapter 15 explains how to calculate and use the value-at-risk measure. Chapter 16 explains the use of binomial trees to value American options. Chapter 17 discusses what happens when the assumptions underlying Black–Scholes do not hold. It also explains how the Black–Scholes model is used in practice and reviews empirical research. Finally, chapter 18 covers interest rate options.

At the end of each chapter there are seven quiz questions that students can use to test their understanding of the key concepts. The answers are at the end of the book. Additional questions and problems are provided at the end of each chapter.

Changes in this Edition

The most significant change in this edition is the inclusion of a new chapter on Value at Risk (chapter 15). Value at Risk has become an extremely important risk management tool in the last few years and we have now reached the stage where no discussion of derivatives is complete without some time being devoted to it.

Other changes in this edition reflect the feedback I have had from both students and instructors. The material on swaps in chapter 6 has been revised to reflect the use of swaps for asset management as well as liability management. Day count conventions are discussed in chapter 5. Scenario analysis is covered in chapter 14. Chapter 17 has been rewritten to focus on the volatility smiles that are observed for equity options and currency options and how they are used in practice. Chapter 18 has been rewritten to provide background information on mortgage-backed securities and to explain the standard market models that are used to value European bond options, interest-rate caps and floors, and European swap options. Improvements have been made throughout the text in the presentation of the algebra and accompanying examples. New end-of-chapter problems are included. A glossary of terms has been added.

New Windows®-based software, DerivaGem, is included with this book. The software has been specially designed to complement the material in the text. It allows readers to calculate prices, implied volatilities, and hedge statistics for European call and put options, six different types of exotic options, and three different types of interest-rate options. The software can be used to:

1. Display the binomial tree used to value an option
2. Plot any one of option price, delta, gamma, vega, theta, and rho *against* any one of asset price, strike price, interest rate, volatility, and time to maturity

Several hundred Powerpoint slides have been included with the Instructor's Manual. Regular updates of both the Powerpoint slides and DerivaGem software can be found on the Prentice Hall Web site:

ftp://www.prenhall.com/pub/be/finance.d-006/hull

and on the author's Web site:

http://www.mgmt.utoronto.ca/~hull

Acknowledgments

Many people have played a part in the production of this book. Colleagues who have made excellent and useful suggestions are Farhang Aslani, Emilio Barone, Giovanni Barone-Adesi, George Blazenko, Laurence Booth, Phelim Boyle, Peter Carr, Don Chance, J.-P. Chateau, Jerome Duncan, Steinar Ekern, Robert Eldridge, David Fowler, Louis Gagnon, Mark Garman, Dajiang Guo, Bernie Hildebrandt, Jim Hilliard, Basil Kalymon, Elizabeth Maynes, Izzy Nelken, Paul Potvin, Edward Robbins, Gordon Roberts, Chris Robinson, John Rumsey, Klaus Schurger, Eduardo Schwartz, Michael Selby, Piet Sercu, Yochanan Shachmurove, Bill Shao, Yisong Tian, Stuart Turnbull, Ton Vorst, George Wang, Zhanshun Wei, Bob Whaley, Alan White, and Qunfeng Yang.

I am particularly grateful to Jerome Duncan, John Rumsey, and Alan White. Jerome Duncan (Hofstra University) made many suggestions as to how the presentation could be improved, and corrected some of the institutional details in the first draft. John Rumsey (Dalhousie University) read the early chapters very carefully and made many detailed suggestions for improvements. I would also like to thank Bernie Hildebrandt for excellent research assistance.

Alan White is a colleague at the University of Toronto with whom I have been carrying out joint research in the options and futures area for the last 15 years. During that time we have spent many hours discussing different issues concerning options and futures markets. Many of the new ideas in this book, and many of the new ways used to explain old ideas, are as much Alan's as mine.

Special thanks are due to my editor at Prentice Hall, Paul Donnelly, for his enthusiasm, advice, and encouragement. I am also grateful to Scott Barr, Leah Jewell, and Evyan Jengo, who at different times have played key roles in the production of this book.

I welcome comments on the book from readers. My e-mail address is

hull@mgmt.utoronto.ca

John C. Hull
University of Toronto

THIRD EDITION

INTRODUCTION TO FUTURES AND OPTIONS MARKETS

CHAPTER 1

Introduction

In recent years futures and options markets have become increasingly important in the world of finance and investments. That world has now reached the stage where it is essential for all finance professionals to understand how these markets work, how they can be used, and what determines prices in them. This book addresses all three issues.

In this opening chapter we take a first look at futures and options markets. We examine their history and provide an overview of how they are used by hedgers, by speculators, and by arbitrageurs. Later chapters will give more details and elaborate on many of the points made here.

Futures Contracts

A *futures contract* is an agreement to buy or sell an asset at a certain time in the future for a certain price. The two largest exchanges on which futures contracts trade are the Chicago Board of Trade (CBOT) and the Chicago Mercantile Exchange (CME). We will examine how a futures contract comes into existence by considering the corn futures that trade on the Chicago Board of Trade.

In March an investor in New York might call a broker with instructions to buy 5,000 bushels of corn for July delivery. The broker would immediately pass these instructions on to a trader on the floor of the Chicago Board of Trade. At about the same time, another investor in Kansas might instruct a broker to sell 5,000 bushels of corn for July delivery. These instructions would also be passed on to a trader on the floor of the Chicago Board of Trade. The two floor traders would meet, agree on a price to be paid for the corn in July, and the deal would be done.

The investor in New York who agreed to buy has what is termed a *long futures position;* the investor in Kansas who agreed to sell has what is termed a *short futures position*. The price agreed to by the two traders on the floor of the exchange is known as the *futures price*. We will suppose the price is 170 cents per bushel. This price, like any other price, is determined by the laws of supply and demand. If at a particular time more floor traders wish to sell July corn than buy July corn, the price will go down. New buyers will then enter the market so that a balance between buyers and sellers is maintained. If more floor traders wish to buy July corn than to sell July corn, the price goes up—for similar reasons.

Issues such as margin requirements, daily settlement procedures, trading practices, commissions, bid-ask spreads, and the role of the exchange clearinghouse are discussed in chapter 2. For the time being, we can assume that the result of the events just described is that the investor in New York has agreed to buy 5,000 bushels of corn for 170 cents per bushel in July and the investor in Kansas has agreed to sell 5,000 bushels of corn for 170 cents per bushel in July. Both sides have entered into a binding contract.

History of Futures Markets

Futures markets can be traced back to the Middle Ages. They were originally developed to meet the needs of farmers and merchants. Consider the position of a farmer in April of a certain year who will harvest grain in June. There is uncertainty about the price the farmer will receive for the grain. In years of scarcity it might be possible to obtain relatively high prices—particularly if the farmer is not in a hurry to sell. On the other hand, in years of oversupply the grain might have to be disposed of at fire-sale prices. The farmer and the farmer's family are clearly exposed to a great deal of risk.

Consider next a merchant who has an ongoing requirement for grain. The merchant is also exposed to price risk. In some years an oversupply situation may create favorable prices; in other years scarcity may cause the prices to be exorbitant. It clearly makes sense for the farmer and the merchant to get together in April (or even earlier) and agree on a price for the farmer's anticipated production of grain in June. In other words, it makes sense for them to negotiate a type of futures contract. The contract provides a way for each side to eliminate the risk it faces because of the uncertain future price of grain.

We might ask what happens to the merchant's requirements for grain during the rest of the year. Once the harvest season is over, the grain must be stored until the next season. In undertaking this storage, the merchant does not bear any price risk but does incur the costs of storage. If the farmer or some other person stores the grain, the merchant and the storer both face risks associated with the future grain price, and again there is a clear role for futures contracts.

THE CHICAGO BOARD OF TRADE

The Chicago Board of Trade (CBOT) was established in 1848 to bring farmers and merchants together. Initially its main task was to standardize the quantities and qualities of the grains that were traded. Within a few years the first futures-type contract was developed. It was known as a *to-arrive contract*. Speculators soon became interested in the contract and found trading the contract to be an attractive alternative to trading the grain itself. The Chicago Board of Trade now offers futures contracts on many different underlying assets, including corn, oats, soybeans, soybean meal, soybean oil, wheat, Treasury bonds, and Treasury notes.

THE CHICAGO MERCANTILE EXCHANGE

In 1874 the Chicago Produce Exchange was established, providing a market for butter, eggs, poultry, and other perishable agricultural products. In 1898 the butter and egg dealers withdrew from the exchange to form the Chicago Butter and Egg Board. In 1919 this was renamed the Chicago Mercantile Exchange (CME) and was reorganized for futures trading. Since then, the exchange has provided a futures market for many commodities, including pork bellies (1961), live cattle (1964), live hogs (1966), and feeder cattle (1971). In 1982 it introduced a futures contract on the Standard & Poor's (S&P) 500 Stock Index.

The International Monetary Market (IMM) was formed as a division of the Chicago Mercantile Exchange in 1972 for futures trading in foreign currencies. The currency futures traded on the IMM now include the British pound, the Canadian dollar, the Japanese yen, the Swiss franc, the German mark, and the Australian dollar. The IMM also trades a one-month LIBOR futures contract, a Treasury bill futures contract, and a Eurodollar futures contract.

OTHER EXCHANGES

Many other exchanges throughout the world now trade futures contracts. Among them are Bolsa de Mercadorias y Futuros (BM&F) in São Paulo, the London International Financial Futures Exchange (LIFFE), the Swiss Options and Financial Futures Exchange (SOFFEX), the Tokyo International Financial Futures Exchange (TIFFE), the Singapore International Monetary Exchange (SIMEX), and the Sydney Futures Exchange (SFE). (For a more complete list, see the table at the end of this book.) Most of the contracts traded on the various world exchanges can be categorized as either *commodity futures contracts* (in which the underlying asset is a commodity) or *financial futures contracts* (in which the underlying asset is a financial instrument such as a bond or a portfolio of stocks). New contracts are being proposed all the time. There can be little doubt that futures markets are one of the most successful financial innovations ever.

Options Contracts

Options contracts have been traded on exchanges for a far shorter period of time than futures contracts. Nevertheless, they too have been remarkably popular with investors. There are two basic types of options: calls and puts. A *call option* gives the holder the right to buy an asset by a certain date for a certain price. A *put option* gives the holder the right to sell an asset by a certain date for a certain price. The price in the contract is known as the *exercise price* or the *strike price;* the date in the contract is known as the *expiration date,* the *exercise date,* or the *maturity.* A *European option* can be exercised only on the maturity date; an *American option* can be exercised at any time during its life.

It should be emphasized that an option gives the holder the right to do something. The holder does not have to exercise this right. This fact distinguishes options from futures contracts. The holder of a long futures contract is committed to buying an asset at a certain price at a certain time in the future. By contrast, the holder of a call option has a choice as to whether to buy the asset at a certain price at a certain time in the future. It costs nothing (except for margin requirements, which will be discussed in chapter 2) to enter into a futures contract. By contrast, an investor must pay an up-front fee or price for an options contract.

The largest exchange for trading stock options is the Chicago Board Options Exchange (CBOE). To illustrate how an options contract gets initiated, we suppose an investor instructs a broker to buy one call option contract on IBM stock with a strike price of $100 and a maturity date in October. The broker will relay these instructions to a trader on the floor of the CBOE. This trader will then find another trader who wants to sell one October call contract on IBM with a strike price of $100. A price will be agreed upon and the deal will be done. Suppose the agreed-upon price is $6. This is the price for an option to buy one share. In the United States, one stock option contract is a contract to buy or sell 100 shares. Therefore, the investor must arrange for $600 to be remitted to the exchange through the broker. The exchange will then arrange for this amount to be passed on to the party on the other side of the transaction. Note that the stock price does not have to equal the exercise price. The price of IBM stock in this example could be, say, $102 at the time the deal is done.

In our example the investor has obtained at a cost of $600 the right to buy 100 IBM shares for $100 each. The party on the other side of the transaction has received $600 and has agreed to sell 100 shares for $100 per share if the investor chooses to exercise the option. There are four types of participants in options markets:

1. Buyers of calls
2. Sellers of calls
3. Buyers of puts
4. Sellers of puts

Buyers are referred to as having *long positions;* sellers are referred to as having *short positions.* Selling an option is also known as *writing the option.*

History of Options Markets

The first trading in puts and calls began in Europe and in the United States as early as the eighteenth century. In the early years the market got a bad name because of certain corrupt practices. One of these involved brokers being given options on a certain stock as an inducement for them to recommend the stock to their clients.

PUT AND CALL BROKERS AND DEALERS ASSOCIATION

In the early 1900s a group of firms set up the Put and Call Brokers and Dealers Association. The aim of this association was to provide a mechanism for bringing buyers and sellers together. Investors who wanted to buy an option would contact one of the member firms. This firm would attempt to find a seller or writer of the option from either its own clients or those of other member firms. If no seller could be found, the firm would undertake to write the option itself in return for what was deemed to be an appropriate price. A market created in this way is known as an *over-the-counter market,* because traders do not physically meet on the floor of an exchange.

The options market of the Put and Call Brokers and Dealers Association suffered from two deficiencies. First, there was no secondary market. The buyer of an option did not have the right to sell it to another party prior to expiration. Second, there was no mechanism to guarantee that the writer of the option would honor the contract. If the writer did not live up to the agreement when the option was exercised, the buyer had to resort to costly lawsuits.

THE FORMATION OF OPTIONS EXCHANGES

In April 1973 the Chicago Board of Trade set up a new exchange, the Chicago Board Options Exchange, specifically for the purpose of trading stock options. Since then options markets have become increasingly popular with investors. The American Stock Exchange (AMEX) and the Philadelphia Stock Exchange (PHLX) began trading options in 1975. The Pacific Stock Exchange (PSE) did the same in 1976. By the early 1980s the volume of trading had grown so rapidly that the number of shares underlying the option contracts sold each day exceeded the daily volume of shares traded on the New York Stock Exchange.

In the 1980s markets developed in the United States for options in foreign exchange, options on stock indices, and options on futures contracts. The Philadelphia Stock Exchange is the premier exchange for trading foreign exchange options. The Chicago Board Options Exchange trades options on the S&P 100 and the S&P 500 stock indices, the American Stock Exchange trades options on the Major Market Stock Index, and the New York Stock Exchange trades options on the NYSE Index. Most exchanges offering futures contracts now also offer options on these contracts. Thus, the Chicago Board of Trade offers options on corn futures, the Chicago Mercantile Exchange offers options on live cattle futures, and so on. Options exchanges now exist all over the world. (See the table at the end of this book.)

OVER-THE-COUNTER MARKETS

The 1980s and 1990s have also seen the development of active over-the-counter markets for options. *Over-the-counter options* are typically agreed to over the phone rather than on the floor of an exchange. One party to the transaction is usually an investment bank that maintains a portfolio of option positions and hedges its risk using procedures that will be described later in this book. The other party is a client of the investment bank such as a fund manager or the treasurer of a large corporation.

One advantage of options traded in the over-the-counter market is that they can be tailored to meet the particular needs of the investment bank's client. For example, a corporate treasurer who wants a European call option to buy 1.6 million pounds sterling on May 3, 1999, at an exchange rate of 1.5125, will not find exactly the right product trading on an exchange. However, it is likely that a number of investment banks would be pleased to provide a quote for an over-the-counter contract that meets the treasurer's precise needs.

TYPES OF TRADERS

Both options and futures markets have been outstandingly successful. One reason is that they have attracted many different types of traders. Three broad categories of traders can be identified: hedgers, speculators, and arbitrageurs. In the next few sections, we consider the activities of each of these.

Hedgers

As already mentioned, futures markets were originally set up to meet the needs of hedgers. Farmers wanted to lock in a guaranteed price for their produce. Merchants wanted to lock in a price they would pay for this produce. Futures contracts enabled both sides to achieve their objectives.

AN EXAMPLE OF HEDGING USING FUTURES

Commodity futures are still widely used for hedging by producers and users of commodities. Financial futures can also be used for hedging purposes. Suppose that it is now July and company A, based in the United States, knows that it will have to pay £ 1 million in September for goods it has purchased from a British supplier. The current exchange rate is 1.6920, and the September futures price for CME contracts on the British pound is 1.6850. This means that, ignoring commissions and other transactions costs, the exchange rate for immediate delivery is

$$\$1.6920 = £1$$

and the exchange rate for delivery in September is

$$\$1.6850 = £1$$

Company A could hedge its foreign exchange risk by taking a long position in £ 1 million worth of September futures contracts. (Each contract traded on the CME is for the delivery of £ 62,500, so that a total of 16 contracts would have to be purchased.) Ignoring commissions and other transactions costs, the contracts have the effect of fixing the price to be paid to the British exporter at $1,685,000.

Consider next another U.S. company, which we will refer to as company B. This company is exporting goods to the United Kingdom and in July knows that it will receive £ 3 million in September. Company B can hedge its foreign exchange risk by shorting September futures. (In this case, 48 contracts would be required so that the company's total short position would be 48 × £62,500, or £ 3 million.) The company would have fixed the U.S. dollars to be realized for the sterling at $5,055,000 (= 3 × $1,685,000).

Table 1.1 summarizes the hedging strategies for company A and company B. Note that if the companies choose not to hedge, they might do better than if they do hedge. Alternatively, they might do worse. Consider company A. If the exchange rate is 1.6600 in September and the company has not hedged, the £ 1 million that it has to pay will cost $1,660,000, which is less than $1,685,000. On the other hand, if the exchange rate is 1.7100, the £ 1 million will cost $1,710,000—and the company will wish it had hedged! The position of company B if it does not hedge is the reverse. If the exchange rate in

TABLE 1.1 Use of Futures for Hedging

From the Trader's Desk—July
> Company A—must pay £ 1 million in September for imports from Britain
> Company B—will receive £ 3 million in September from exports to Britain
> Quotes:
>> Current exchange rate   1.6920
>> September futures price   1.6850
> Size of futures contract:
>> £ 62,500

Company A's Hedging Strategy
> A long position in 16 futures contracts locks in an exchange rate of 1.6850 for the £ 1 million the company will pay.

Company B's Hedging Strategy
> A short position in 48 futures contracts locks in an exchange rate of 1.6850 for the £ 3 million the company will receive.

September proves to be less than 1.6850, company B will wish it had hedged; if the rate is greater than 1.6850, the company will be pleased it has not done so.

This example illustrates a key aspect of hedging with futures contracts. The cost of, or price received for, the underlying asset is ensured. However, there is no assurance that the outcome with hedging will be better than the outcome without hedging.

AN EXAMPLE OF HEDGING USING OPTIONS

Options can also be used for hedging. Consider an investor who in August owns 500 IBM shares. The current share price is $102 per share. The investor is concerned that the share price may decline sharply in the next two months and wants protection. The investor could buy October put options on the Chicago Board Options Exchange to sell 500 shares for a strike price of $100. Since each put contract on the CBOE is for the sale of 100 shares, a total of five contracts would be purchased. If the quoted option price is $4, each option contract would cost $100 \times \$4 = \$400$, and the total cost of the hedging strategy would be $5 \times \$400 = \$2,000$.

This strategy is summarized in Table 1.2. The strategy costs $2,000 but guarantees that the shares can be sold for at least $100 per share during the life of the option. If the market price of IBM stock falls below $100, the options can be exercised so that $50,000 is realized for the whole holding. When the cost of the options is taken into account, the amount realized is $48,000. If the market price stays above $100, the options are not exercised and expire worthless. However, in this case the value of the holding is always above $50,000 (or above $48,000 when the cost of the options is taken into account).

A COMPARISON

A comparison of Tables 1.1 and 1.2 reveals a fundamental difference between the use of futures and options for hedging. Futures contracts are designed to neutralize risk by fixing the price that the hedger will pay or receive for the underlying asset. Options

---

TABLE 1.2 Hedging Strategy Using Options

From the Trader's Desk—August
    An investor owns 500 IBM shares and wants protection against a possible decline in the share price over the next two months.
        Quotes:
                Current IBM share price $102
                IBM October 50 put $4

The Investor's Strategy
    The investor buys five put option contracts for a total cost of $5 \times 100 \times \$4 = \$2{,}000$.

The Outcome
    The investor has the right to sell the shares for at least $500 \times \$100 = \$50{,}000$.

---

contracts, by contrast, provide insurance. They offer a way for investors to protect themselves against adverse price movements in the future while still allowing them to benefit from favorable price movements. Unlike futures, options involve the payment of an upfront fee.

Speculators

We now move on to consider how futures and options markets can be used by speculators. Whereas hedgers want to avoid an exposure to adverse movements in the price of an asset, speculators wish to take a position in the market. Either they are betting that the price will go up or they are betting that it will go down.

AN EXAMPLE OF SPECULATION USING FUTURES

Consider a U.S. speculator who in February thinks that the pound sterling will strengthen relative to the U.S. dollar over the next two months and is prepared to back that hunch to the tune of £ 250,000. One thing the speculator can do is simply purchase £ 250,000 in the hope that the sterling can be sold later at a profit. The sterling once purchased would be kept in an interest-bearing account. Another possibility is to take a long position in four CME April futures contracts on sterling. (Each futures contract is for the purchase of £ 62,500.) Table 1.3 summarizes the two alternatives on the assumption that the current exchange rate is 1.6470 and the April futures price is 1.6410. If the exchange rate turns out to be 1.7000 in April, the futures contract alternative enables the speculator to buy in April for $1.6410 an asset worth $1.7000, so that a profit of $(1.7000 - 1.6410) \times 250{,}000 = \$14{,}750$ is realized. The cash market alternative leads to an asset being purchased for 1.6470 in February and sold for 1.7000 in April, so that a profit of $(1.7000 - 1.6470) \times 250{,}000 = \$13{,}250$ is made. If the exchange rate falls to 1.6000, the futures contract gives rise to a $(1.6410 - 1.6000) \times 250{,}000 = \$10{,}250$ loss, whereas the cash market alternative gives rise to a loss of $(1.6470 - 1.6000) \times 250{,}000 = \$11{,}750$. The alternatives appear to give rise to slightly different profits and losses. But these calculations do not reflect the interest that is earned or paid. It will be shown in

TABLE 1.3   Speculation Using Futures

From the Trader's Desk—February
An investor feels that sterling will strengthen relative to the U.S. dollar over the next 2 months and would like to take a speculative position.
Quotes:

Current exchange rate	1.6470
April futures price	1.6410

Alternative Strategies

1. Buy £ 250,000 for $411,750, deposit the sterling in an interest-earning account for two months, and hope that it can be sold at a profit at the end of the two months.

2. Take a long position in four April futures contracts. This commits the investor to purchase £ 250,000 for $410,250 in April. If the exchange rate in April proves to be above 1.6410, the investor will realize a profit.

Possible Outcomes

1. Exchange rate is 1.7000 in two months. The investor makes $13,250 using the first strategy and $14,750 using the second strategy.

2. Exchange rate is 1.6000 in two months. The investor has a loss of $11,750 using the first strategy and $10,250 using the second strategy.

chapter 3 that when the interest earned in sterling and the interest paid in dollars are taken into account, the profit or loss from the two alternatives is the same.

What then is the difference between the two alternatives? The first alternative of buying sterling requires an up-front investment of $411,750. By contrast, the second alternative requires only a small amount of cash—perhaps $25,000—to be deposited by the speculator in what is termed a margin account. The futures market allows the speculator to obtain leverage. With a relatively small initial outlay, the investor is able to take a large speculative position.

AN EXAMPLE OF SPECULATION USING OPTIONS

We consider next an example of how a speculator could use options. Suppose that in September a speculator wants to go long in Exxon stock. In other words, the speculator wants to be in a position to gain if the stock price increases. Suppose that the stock price is currently $78 and that a December call with an $80 strike price is currently selling for $3. Table 1.4 illustrates two possible alternatives, assuming that the speculator is willing to invest $7,800. The first alternative involves the straight purchase of 100 shares. The second involves the purchase of 2,600 call options (i.e., 26 call option contracts) on Exxon.

Suppose that the speculator's hunch is correct and the price of Exxon's shares rises to $90 by December. The first alternative of buying the stock yields a profit of

$$100 \times (\$90 - \$78) = \$1,200$$

TABLE 1.4 Speculation Using Options

From the Trader's Desk—September

A speculator with $7,800 to invest thinks that the price of Exxon will increase in the next three months and has obtained the following quotes:

Current stock price	$78
Exxon December call with an $80 strike price	$3

The speculator has $7,800 to invest.

Alternative Strategies

1. Buy 100 shares of Exxon.
2. Buy 2,600 December call options (or 26 December contracts) on Exxon with an $80 strike price.

The cost of each alternative is $7,800.

Possible Outcomes

1. Exxon rises to $90 by December. The investor makes a profit of $1,200 using the first strategy and $18,200 using the second strategy.
2. Exxon falls to $70 by December. The investor loses $800 with the first strategy and $7,800 with the second strategy.

However, the second alternative is far more profitable. A call option on Exxon with a strike price of $80 gives a profit of $10, since the option enables something worth $90 to be bought for $80. The total value of all the options that have been purchased is

$$2,600 \times \$10 = \$26,000$$

Subtracting the original cost of the options yields a net profit of

$$\$26,000 - \$7,800 = \$18,200$$

The options strategy is, therefore, over 15 times more profitable than the strategy of buying the stock.

Options also give rise to a greater potential loss. Suppose the stock price falls to $70 by December. The first alternative of buying stock yields a loss of

$$100 \times (\$78 - \$70) = \$800$$

Since the call options expire without being exercised, the options strategy would lead to a loss of $7,800—the original amount paid for the options. These results are summarized in Table 1.5.

It is clear from Table 1.5 that options like futures provide a form of leverage. For a given investment, the use of options magnifies the financial consequences. Good outcomes become very good, while bad outcomes become very bad!

A COMPARISON

Futures and options are similar instruments for speculators in that they both provide a way in which a type of leverage can be obtained. However, there is an important dif-

TABLE 1.5   Comparison of Profits (Losses) from Two Alternative Strategies for Using $7,800 to Speculate on Exxon Stock

Investor's Strategy	December Stock Price	
	$70	$90
Buy shares	($800)	$1,200
Buy call options	($7,800)	$18,200

ference between the two. In the futures example in Table 1.3, the speculator's potential loss as well as the potential gain is very large. In the options example in Table 1.4, no matter how bad things get, the speculator's loss is limited to the $7,800 paid for the options.

Arbitrageurs

Arbitrageurs are a third important group of participants in futures and options markets. Arbitrage involves locking in a riskless profit by simultaneously entering into transactions in two or more markets. In later chapters we will see how arbitrage is sometimes possible when the futures price of an asset gets out of line with its cash price. We will also examine how arbitrage can be used in options markets. This section illustrates the concept of arbitrage with a very simple example.

Consider a stock that is traded on both the New York Stock Exchange and the London Stock Exchange. Suppose that the stock price is $172 in New York and £ 100 in London at a time when the exchange rate is $1.7500 per pound. An arbitrageur could simultaneously buy 100 shares of the stock in New York and sell them in London to obtain a risk-free profit of

$$100 \times [(\$1.75 \times 100) - \$172]$$

or $300 in the absence of transactions costs. The strategy is summarized in Table 1.6. Transactions costs would probably eliminate the profit for a small investor. However, a large investment house faces very low transactions costs in both the stock market and the foreign exchange market. It would find the arbitrage opportunity very attractive and would try to take as much advantage of it as possible.

Arbitrage opportunities such as the one just described cannot last for long. As arbitrageurs buy the stock in New York, the forces of supply and demand will cause the dollar price to rise. Similarly, as they sell the stock in London, the sterling price will be driven down. Very quickly the two prices will become equivalent at the current exchange rate. Indeed, the existence of profit-hungry arbitrageurs makes it unlikely that a major disparity between the sterling price and the dollar price could ever exist in the first place. Generalizing from this example, we can say that the very existence of arbitrageurs means that in practice only very small arbitrage opportunities are observed in the prices that are quoted in most financial markets. In this book most of the

TABLE 1.6 Arbitrage

From the Trader's Desk

A stock is traded on both the New York Stock Exchange and the London Stock Exchange. The following quotes have been obtained:

New York Stock Exchange $172 per share
London Stock Exchange   £ 100 per share
Value of £ 1 $1.7500

The Trader's Arbitrage Strategy

1. Buy 100 shares in New York.

2. Sell the shares in London.

3. Convert the sale proceeds from pounds to dollars.

The Profit

$$100 \times [(\$1.75 \times 100) - \$172] = \$300$$

arguments concerning futures prices and the values of option contracts will be based on the assumption that there are no arbitrage opportunities.

Derivatives

Options and futures contracts are examples of *derivatives*. These are instruments whose values depend on the prices of other, more basic variables. An IBM stock option is a derivative because its value depends on the price of IBM stock, a wheat futures contract is a derivative because its value depends on the price of wheat, and so on.

In recent years investment banks have been very imaginative in designing new derivatives to meet the needs of clients. These are usually sold in the over-the-counter market by financial institutions to their clients, or they are added to bond or stock issues to make these issues more attractive to investors. Some of these derivatives are similar to the futures and options contracts traded on exchanges. Others are far more complex. The possibilities for designing interesting new derivatives seem to be virtually limitless. In this section we look at a few examples of derivatives that have been designed by investment banks.

INTEREST-RATE CAPS

An interest-rate cap is a very popular derivative that is traded in the over-the-counter market. When it is sold by financial institutions to corporate borrowers, it provides protection against the rate of interest on a floating-rate loan, on which the interest rate is reset periodically, going above some level. This level is known as the *cap rate*. If the rate of interest on the loan does go above the cap rate, the seller of the cap provides the difference between the interest on the loan and the interest that would be required if the cap rate applied. Suppose that the loan is for $10 million, the cap rate is 12 percent per annum, and that for a particular three-month period during the life of the cap, the floating rate applicable to the loan turns out to be 14 percent per annum. The seller of the interest-rate cap would provide $50,000 (one-fourth of 2 percent of $10 million) at the end of the three months to bring interest payments for the three-month period down to 12 percent. Interest-rate caps are discussed further in chapter 18.

STANDARD OIL'S BOND ISSUE

An example of a derivative added to a bond issue is provided by Standard Oil's issue of zero-coupon bonds in 1986. Some of these bonds matured in 1990. In addition to the bond's $1,000 maturity value, the company promised to pay an amount based on the price of oil at maturity of the bond. This additional amount was equal to the product of 170 and the excess (if any) of the price of a barrel of oil at maturity over $25. However, the maximum additional amount paid was restricted to $2,550 (which corresponds to a price of $40 per barrel). The bonds provided holders with a stake in a commodity that was critically important to the fortunes of the company. If the price of the commodity went up, the company was in a good position to provide the bondholder with the additional payment.

OTHER EXAMPLES

As mentioned earlier, there is virtually no limit to the innovations that are possible with derivatives. The variables underlying derivatives are usually stock prices, stock indices, interest rates, exchange rates, and commodity prices. However, other variables can be and are occasionally used. For example, ski slope operators have been known to issue bonds where the payoff depends on the total snow falling at a certain resort, and banks have been known to create deposit instruments on which the interest paid depends on the performance of the local football team.

THOSE BIG LOSSES

In the early 1990s organizations such as Gibson Greetings, Procter & Gamble, Kidder Peabody, Orange County, and Barings experienced huge losses trading derivatives. The losses received a great deal of publicity and made many people very wary of derivatives. Some nonfinancial corporations have announced plans to reduce their use of derivatives. The level of interest in some of the more exotic products offered by financial institutions has declined.

The stories behind the losses emphasize the point made in this chapter that derivatives can be used for either hedging or speculation; that is, they can be used either to reduce risks or to take risks. The losses occurred because derivatives were used inappropriately. Employees who had an implicit or explicit mandate to hedge their company's risks decided instead to speculate.

The lesson to be learned from the losses is the importance of *internal controls*. Senior management within a company should issue a clear and unambiguous policy statement about how derivatives are to be used and the extent to which it is permissible for employees to take positions on movements in market variables. Management should then institute controls to ensure that the policy is carried out. It is a recipe for disaster to give one or two people complete authority to trade derivatives without a close monitoring of the risks being taken.

Summary

In this chapter we have taken a first look at futures and options markets. A futures contract involves an obligation to buy or sell an asset at a certain time in the future for a certain price. There are two types of options: calls and puts. A call option gives the holder the right to buy an asset by a certain date for a certain price. A put option gives the holder the right to sell an asset by a certain date for a certain price. Futures and options are now traded on a wide range of different assets.

Options and futures markets have been very successful innovations. Three main types of participants in the markets can be identified: hedgers, speculators, and arbitrageurs. Hedgers are in the position of facing risk associated with the price of an asset. They use futures or options markets to reduce or eliminate this risk. Speculators wish to bet on future movements in the price of an asset. Futures and options contracts can give them extra leverage; that is, the contracts can increase both the potential gains and potential losses in a speculative venture. Arbitrageurs are in business to take advantage of a discrepancy between prices in two different markets. If, for example, they see the futures price of an asset getting out of line with the cash price, they will take offsetting positions in the two markets to lock in a profit.

Options and futures are examples of derivatives. These are instruments whose prices depend on the values of other, more basic underlying variables. For example, the price of a stock option depends on the value of the underlying stock. Investment bankers have become increasingly imaginative in devising new derivatives in recent years. Most of these securities are not traded on exchanges. Either they are sold by financial institutions to their corporate clients or they are added to new issues of bonds and stocks in order to make the latter more attractive to investors.

Quiz

1. What is the difference between a long futures position and a short futures position?
2. Explain carefully the difference between (a) hedging, (b) speculation, and (c) arbitrage.
3. What is the difference between (a) entering into a long futures contract when the futures price is $50 and (b) taking a long position in a call option with a strike price of $50?
4. An investor enters into a short cotton futures contract when the futures price is 50 cents per pound. One contract is for the delivery of 50,000 pounds. How much does the investor gain or lose if the cotton price at the end of the contract is (a) 48.20 cents per pound and (b) 51.30 cents per pound?
5. Suppose that you write a put contract on IBM with a strike price of $40 and an expiration date in three months. The current price of IBM stock is $41. What have you committed yourself to? How much could you gain or lose?
6. You would like to speculate on a rise in the price of a certain stock. The current stock price is $29, and a three-month call with a strike of $30 costs $2.90. You have $5,800 to

invest. Identify two alternative strategies. Briefly outline the advantages and disadvantages of each.

7. Suppose you own 5,000 shares worth $25 each. How can put options be used to provide you with insurance against a decline in the value of your holding over the next four months?

Questions and Problems

1.1. A stock when it is first issued provides funds for a company. Is the same true of a stock option? Discuss.

1.2. Explain why a futures contract can be used for either speculation or hedging.

1.3. A pig farmer expects to have 90,000 pounds of live hogs to sell in three months. The live-hogs futures contract on the Chicago Mercantile Exchange is for the delivery of 30,000 pounds of hogs. How can the farmer use the contract for hedging? From the farmer's viewpoint, what are the pros and cons of hedging?

1.4. It is now July 1997. A mining company has just discovered a small deposit of gold. It will take six months to construct the mine. The gold will then be extracted on a more or less continuous basis for one year. Futures contracts on gold are available on the New York Commodity Exchange. There are delivery months every two months from August 1997 to April 1999. Each contract is for the delivery of 100 ounces. Discuss how the mining company might use futures markets for hedging.

1.5. Suppose that a March call option with a strike price of $50 costs $2.50 and is held until March. Under what circumstances will the holder of the option make a gain? Under what circumstances will the option be exercised?

1.6. Suppose that a June put option with a strike price of $60 costs $4 and is held until June. Under what circumstances will the holder of the option make a gain? Under what circumstances will the option be exercised?

1.7. An investor writes a September call option with a strike price of $20. It is now May, the stock price is $18, and the option price is $2. Describe the investor's cash flows if the option is held until September and the stock price is $25 at this time.

1.8. An investor writes a December put option with a strike price of $30. The price of the option is $4. Under what circumstances does the investor make a gain?

1.9. Interest-rate caps are described in the section on derivatives. Is a cap on the average rate of interest during the life of a loan worth more or less than a cap on the rate at any given time? Explain your answer.

1.10. Show that the Standard Oil bond described in the section on derivatives is a combination of a regular bond, a long position in call options on oil with a strike price of $25, and a short position in call options on oil with a strike price of $40.

1.11. Discuss how foreign currency options can be used for hedging in the situation described in Table 1.1.

1.12. The price of gold is currently $500 per ounce. The futures price for delivery in one year is $700. An arbitrageur can borrow money at 10 percent per annum. What should the arbitrageur do? Assume that the cost of storing gold is zero.

1.13. The Chicago Board of Trade offers a futures contract on long-term Treasury bonds. Characterize the investors likely to use this contract.

1.14. An airline executive has argued: "There is no point in our using oil futures. There is just as much chance that the price of oil in the future will be less than the futures price as there is that it will be greater than this price." Discuss the executive's viewpoint.

1.15. The current price of a stock is $94, and three-month call options with a strike price of $95 currently sell for $4.70. An investor who feels that the price of the stock will increase is trying to decide between buying 100 shares and buying 2,000 call options (20 contracts). Both strategies involve an investment of $9,400. What advice would you give? How high does the stock price have to rise for the option strategy to be more profitable?

1.16. "Options and futures are zero-sum games." What do you think is meant by this statement?

CHAPTER **2**

Mechanics of Futures and Forward Markets

This chapter covers the details of how futures markets work. We examine issues such as the specification of contracts, the operation of margin accounts, the organization of exchanges, the regulation of markets, the way in which quotes are made, and the treatment of futures transactions for accounting and tax purposes. We also look at forward contracts. These are in some respects similar to futures contracts. They involve an agreement to buy or sell an asset on a certain date for a certain price. However, there are important differences between the two types of contracts. Futures contracts are traded on an organized exchange, and the contract terms are standardized by that exchange. By contrast, forward contracts are private agreements between two financial institutions or between a financial institution and one of its corporate clients.

Closing Out Futures Positions

As discussed in chapter 1, a futures contract is an agreement to buy or sell an asset for a certain price at a certain time in the future. The reader may be surprised to learn that the vast majority of the futures contracts that are initiated do not lead to delivery. The reason is that most investors choose to close out their positions prior to the delivery period specified in the contract. Making or taking delivery under the terms of a futures contract is often inconvenient and in some instances quite expensive. This is true even for a hedger who wants to buy or sell the asset underlying the futures contract. Such a hedger usually prefers to close out the futures position and then buy or sell the asset in the usual way.

Closing out a position involves entering into an opposite trade to the original one. For example, an investor who buys five July corn futures contracts on May 6 can close out the position on June 20 by selling (i.e., shorting) five July corn futures contracts. An investor who sells (i.e., shorts) five July contracts on May 6 can close out the position on June 20 by buying five July contracts. In each case, the investor's total gain or loss is determined by the change in the futures price between May 6 and June 20.

In spite of the fact that delivery is so unusual, we will spend part of this chapter reviewing the delivery arrangements in futures contracts. It is the possibility of final delivery that ties the futures price to the cash price. An understanding of delivery procedures is essential to a full understanding of the relationship between cash and futures prices.

The Specification of the Futures Contract

The exchanges in the United States that trade futures contracts are listed in Table 2.1.[1] Other futures exchanges throughout the world are listed at the end of this book. When developing a new contract, the exchange must specify in some detail the exact nature of the agreement between the two parties. In particular, it must specify the asset, the contract size (exactly how much of the asset will be delivered under one contract), where delivery will be made, and when delivery will be made. Sometimes alternatives are specified for the grade of the asset that will be delivered or for the delivery locations.

As a general rule, it is the party with the short position (the party that has agreed to sell the asset) that chooses what will happen when alternatives are specified by the exchange. When the party with the short position is ready to deliver, it files a *notice of intention to deliver* with the exchange. This notice indicates selections it has made with respect to the grade of asset that will be delivered and the delivery location.

THE ASSET

When the asset is a commodity, there may be quite a variation in the quality of what is available in the marketplace. When the asset is specified, it is therefore important that the exchange stipulate the grade or grades of the commodity that are acceptable. The New York Cotton Exchange has specified the asset in its orange juice futures contract as

> U.S. Grade A, with Brix value of not less than 57 degrees, having a Brix value to acid ratio of not less than 13 to 1 nor more than 19 to 1, with factors of color and flavor each scoring 37 points or higher and 19 for defects, with a minimum score 94.

The Chicago Mercantile Exchange in its random-length lumber futures contract has specified that

> Each delivery unit shall consist of nominal 2 × 4s of random lengths from 8 feet to 20 feet, grade-stamped Construction and Standard, Standard and Better, or #1 and

---

[1]The exchange abbreviations in Table 2.1 are the abbreviations used by the exchanges themselves. Newspapers sometimes use other abbreviations. For example, the *Wall Street Journal* uses CMX instead of COMEX and CBT instead of CBOT.

TABLE 2.1   U.S. Exchanges That Trade Futures

Chicago Board of Trade (CBOT)
141 West Jackson Boulevard
Chicago, IL 60604
312-435-3500
Grains and oilseeds, metals, financials, chemicals, insurance

Chicago Mercantile Exchange (CME)
30 South Wacker Drive
Chicago, IL 60606
312-930-1000
Divisions: International Monetary Market (IMM), Index and Option Market (IOM)
Livestock, meat, financials, wood

Coffee, Sugar, and Cocoa Exchange (CSCE)
4 World Trade Center
New York, NY 10048
212-938-2800
Food and fiber

Commodity Exchange, Inc. (COMEX)
4 World Trade Center
New York, NY 10048
212-938-2900
Metals, financials

New York Futures Exchange (NYFE)
20 Broad Street
New York, NY 10005
212-656-4949
Financials

New York Mercantile Exchange (NYMEX)
4 World Trade Center
New York, NY 10048
212-938-2222
Metals, petroleum

Kansas City Board of Trade (KCBT)
4800 Main Street, Suite 303
Kansas City, MO 64112
816-753-7500
Grains, financials

MidAmerica Commodity Exchange (MidAm)
444 West Jackson Boulevard
Chicago, IL 60604
312-435-3500
Grains and oilseeds, livestock, meat, metals, financials

Minneapolis Grain Exchange (MGE)
400 South Fourth Street
Minneapolis, MN 55415
612-338-6212
Grains, food, and fiber

New York Cotton Exchange (NYCE)
4 World Trade Center
New York, NY 10048
212-938-2702
Division: Financial Instruments Exchange (FINEX)
Food and fiber, financials

Chicago Rice and Cotton Exchange (CRCE)
444 West Jackson Boulevard
Chicago, IL 60604
312-341-3078
Food and fiber

Philadelphia Board of Trade (PBOT)
1900 Market Street
Philadelphia, PA 19103
215-496-5165
Subsidiary of Philadelphia Stock Exchange (PHLX)
Financials

#2; however, in no case may the quantity of Standard grade or #2 exceed 50 percent. Each delivery unit shall be manufactured in California, Idaho, Montana, Nevada, Oregon, Washington, Wyoming, or Alberta or British Columbia, Canada, and contain lumber produced from grade-stamped Alpine fir, Englemann spruce, hem-fir, lodgepole pine, and/or spruce pine fir.

For some commodities a range of grades can be delivered, but the price received is adjusted according to the grade chosen. For example, in the Chicago Board of Trade corn futures contract, the standard grade is "No. 2 Yellow," but substitutions are allowed at differentials established by the exchange.

The financial assets in futures contracts are generally well defined and unambiguous. For example, there is no need to specify the grade of a Japanese yen. However, there are some interesting features of the Treasury bond and Treasury note futures contracts traded on the Chicago Board of Trade. The underlying asset in the Treasury bond contract is any long-term U.S. Treasury bond that has a maturity of greater than 15 years and is not callable within 15 years. In the Treasury note futures contract, the underlying asset is any long-term Treasury note with a maturity of no less than 6.5 years and no more than 10 years from the date of delivery. In both cases, the exchange has a formula for adjusting the price received according to the coupon and maturity date of the bond delivered. Treasury futures are discussed in chapter 5.

THE CONTRACT SIZE

The contract size specifies the amount of the asset that has to be delivered under one contract. This is an important decision for the exchange. If the contract size is too large, many investors who wish to hedge relatively small exposures or who wish to take relatively small speculative positions will be unable to use the exchange. On the other hand, if the contract size is too small, trading may be expensive because there is a cost associated with each contract traded.

The correct size for a contract clearly depends on the likely user. Whereas the value of what is delivered under a futures contract on an agricultural product might be $10,000 to $20,000, it is much higher for some financial futures. For example, under the Treasury bond futures contract traded on the Chicago Board of Trade, instruments with a face value of $100,000 are delivered.

DELIVERY ARRANGEMENTS

The place where delivery will be made must be specified by the exchange. This is particularly important for commodities that involve significant transportation costs. In the case of the Chicago Mercantile Exchange's random-length lumber contract, the delivery location is specified as

> On track and shall either be unitized in double-door boxcars or, at no additional cost to the buyer, each unit shall be individually paper-wrapped and loaded on flatcars. Par delivery of hem-fir in California, Idaho, Montana, Nevada, Oregon, and Washington, and in the province of British Columbia.

When alternative delivery locations are specified, the price received by the party with the short position is sometimes adjusted according to the location chosen by that party. For example, in the case of the corn futures contract traded by the Chicago Board of Trade, delivery can be made at Chicago, Burns Harbor, Toledo, or St. Louis. However, deliveries at Toledo and St. Louis are made at a discount of 4 cents per bushel from the Chicago contract price.

DELIVERY MONTHS

A futures contract is referred to by its delivery month. The exchange must specify the precise period during the month when delivery can be made. For many futures contracts, the delivery period is the whole month.

The delivery months vary from contract to contract and are chosen by the exchange to meet the needs of market participants. For example, currency futures on the International Monetary Market have delivery months of March, June, September, and December; corn futures traded on the Chicago Board of Trade have delivery months of March, May, July, September, and December. At any given time, contracts trade for the closest delivery month and a number of subsequent delivery months. The exchange specifies when trading in a particular month's contract will begin. The exchange also specifies the last day on which trading can take place for a given contract. Trading generally ceases a few days before the last day on which delivery can be made.

PRICE QUOTES

The futures price is quoted in a way that is convenient and easy to understand. For example, crude oil futures prices on the New York Mercantile Exchange are quoted in dollars per barrel to two decimal places (i.e., to the nearest cent). Treasury bond and Treasury note futures prices on the Chicago Board of Trade are quoted in dollars and thirty-seconds of a dollar. The minimum price movement that can occur in trading is consistent with the way in which the price is quoted. Thus, it is $0.01 per barrel for the oil futures and one thirty-second of a dollar for the Treasury bond and Treasury note futures.

DAILY PRICE MOVEMENT LIMITS

For most contracts, daily price movement limits are specified by the exchange. If the price moves down by an amount equal to the daily price limit, the contract is said to be *limit down.* If it moves up by the limit, it is said to be *limit up.* A *limit move* is a move in either direction equal to the daily price limit. Normally, trading ceases for the day once the contract is limit up or limit down. However, in some instances the exchange has the authority to step in and change the limits.

The purpose of daily price limits is to prevent large price movements from occurring because of speculative excesses. However, limits can become an artificial barrier to trading when the price of the underlying commodity is advancing or declining rapidly. Whether price limits are, on balance, good for futures markets is controversial.

POSITION LIMITS

Position limits are the maximum number of contracts that a speculator may hold. In the Chicago Mercantile Exchange's random-length lumber contract, for example, the position limit is 1,000 contracts with no more than 300 in any one delivery month. Bona fide hedgers are not affected by position limits. The purpose of the limits is to prevent speculators from exercising undue influence on the market.

Convergence of Futures Price to Spot Price

As the delivery month of a futures contract is approached, the futures price converges to the spot price of the underlying asset. When the delivery period is reached, the futures price equals—or is very close to—the spot price.

To see why this is so, we first suppose that the futures price is above the spot price during the delivery period. Traders then have a clear arbitrage opportunity:

1. Short a futures contract.
2. Buy the asset.
3. Make delivery.

These steps are certain to lead to a profit equal to the amount by which the futures price exceeds the spot price. As traders exploit this arbitrage opportunity, the futures price will fall. We next suppose that the futures price is below the spot price during the delivery period. Companies interested in acquiring the asset will find it attractive to enter into a long futures contract and then wait for delivery to be made. As they do so, the futures price will tend to rise.

The result is that the futures price is very close to the spot price during the delivery period. Figure 2.1 illustrates the convergence of the futures price to the spot price. In Figure 2.1a the futures price is above the spot price prior to the delivery month. In Figure 2.1b the futures price is below the spot price prior to the delivery month. The circumstances under which these two patterns are observed are discussed later in this chapter and in chapter 3.

FIGURE 2.1 Relationship between Futures Price and Spot Price as the Delivery Month Is Approached (a) futures price above spot price; (b) futures price below spot price.

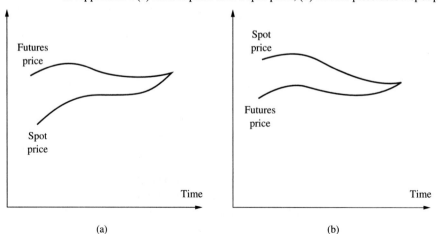

The Operation of Margins

If two investors get in touch with each other directly and agree to trade an asset in the future for a certain price, there are obvious risks. One of the investors may regret the deal and try to back out. Alternatively, the investor simply may not have the financial resources to honor the agreement. One of the key roles of the exchange is to organize trading so that contract defaults are avoided. This is where margins come in.

MARKING TO MARKET

To illustrate how margins work, we consider an investor who contacts his or her broker on Thursday, June 5, 1997 to buy two December 1997 gold futures contracts on the New York Commodity Exchange (COMEX). We suppose that the current futures price is $400 per ounce. Because the contract size is 100 ounces, the investor has contracted to buy a total of 200 ounces at this price. The broker will require the investor to deposit funds in a *margin account.* The amount that must be deposited at the time the contract is entered into is known as the *initial margin.* We suppose this is $2,000 per contract, or $4,000 in total. At the end of each trading day, the margin account is adjusted to reflect the investor's gain or loss. This practice is referred to as *marking to market* the account.

Suppose, for example, that by the end of June 5 the futures price has dropped from $400 to $397. The investor has a loss of $600 (= 200 × $3) because the 200 ounces of December gold, which the investor contracted to buy at $400, can now be sold for only $397. The balance in the margin account would therefore be reduced by $600 to $3,400. Similarly, if the price of December gold rose to $403 by the end of the first day, the balance in the margin account would be increased by $600 to $4,600. A trade is first marked to market at the close of the day on which it takes place. It is then marked to market at the close of trading on each subsequent day.

Note that marking to market is not merely an arrangement between broker and client. When there is a decrease in the futures price so that the margin account of an investor with a long position is reduced by $600, the investor's broker has to pay the exchange $600 and the exchange passes the money on to the broker of an investor with a short position. Similarly, when there is an increase in the futures price, brokers for parties with short positions pay money to the exchange and brokers for parties with long positions receive money from the exchange. Later we will examine in more detail the mechanism by which this happens.

The investor is entitled to withdraw any balance in the margin account in excess of the initial margin. To ensure that the balance in the margin account never becomes negative, a *maintenance margin*, which is somewhat lower than the initial margin, is set. If the balance in the margin account falls below the maintenance margin, the investor receives a *margin call* and is expected to top up the margin account to the initial margin level the next day. The extra funds deposited are known as a *variation margin.* If the investor does not provide the variation margin, the broker closes out the position by selling the contract. In the case of the investor considered earlier, closing out the position would involve neutralizing the existing contract by selling 200 ounces of gold for delivery in December.

TABLE 2.2 Operation of Margins for a Long Position in Two Gold Futures Contracts

The initial margin is $2,000 per contract, or $4,000 in total, and the maintenance margin is $1,500 per contract, or $3,000 in total. The contract is entered into on June 5 at $400 and closed out on June 26 at $392.30. The numbers in the second column, except the first and the last, represent futures prices at the close of trading.

Day	Futures Price ($)	Daily Gain (Loss) ($)	Cumulative Gain (Loss) ($)	Margin Account Balance ($)	Margin Call ($)
	400.00			4,000	
June 5	397.00	(600)	(600)	3,400	
June 6	396.10	(180)	(780)	3,220	
June 9	398.20	420	(360)	3,640	
June 10	397.10	(220)	(580)	3,420	
June 11	396.70	(80)	(660)	3,340	
June 12	395.40	(260)	(920)	3,080	
June 13	393.30	(420)	(1,340)	2,660	1,340
June 16	393.60	60	(1,280)	4,060	
June 17	391.80	(360)	(1,640)	3,700	
June 18	392.70	180	(1,460)	3,880	
June 19	387.00	(1,140)	(2,600)	2,740	1,260
June 20	387.00	0	(2,600)	4,000	
June 23	388.10	220	(2,380)	4,220	
June 24	388.70	120	(2,260)	4,340	
June 25	391.00	460	(1,800)	4,800	
June 26	392.30	260	(1,540)	5,060	

Table 2.2 illustrates the operation of the margin account for one possible sequence of futures prices in the case of the investor considered earlier. The maintenance margin is assumed for the purpose of the illustration to be $1,500 per contract, or $3,000 in total. On June 13 the balance in the margin account falls $340 below the maintenance margin level. The drop triggers a margin call from the broker for an additional $1,340. Table 2.2 assumes that the investor does in fact provide this margin by close of trading on June 16. On June 19 the balance in the margin account again falls below the maintenance margin level, and a margin call for $1,260 is sent out. The investor provides this margin by close of trading on June 20. On June 26 the investor decides to close out the position by shorting two contracts. The futures price on that day is $392.30 and the investor has a cumulative loss of $1,540. Note that the investor has excess margin on June 16, 23, 24, and 25. Table 2.2 assumes that the excess is not withdrawn.

FURTHER DETAILS

Some brokers allow an investor to earn interest on the balance in a margin account. The balance in the account does not, therefore, represent a true cost, providing the interest rate is competitive with that which could be earned elsewhere. To satisfy the initial margin requirements (but not subsequent margin calls), an investor can sometimes deposit securities with the broker. Treasury bills are usually accepted in lieu of cash at about 90 percent of their face value. Shares are also sometimes accepted in lieu of cash—but at about 50 percent of their face value.

The effect of the marking to market is that a futures contract is settled daily rather than all at the end of its life. At the end of each day, the investor's gain (loss) is added to (subtracted from) the margin account, bringing the value of the contract back to zero. A futures contract is in effect closed out and rewritten at a new price each day.

Minimum levels for initial and maintenance margins are set by the exchange. Individual brokers may require greater margins from their clients than those specified by the exchange. However, they cannot require lower margins than those specified by the exchange. Margin levels are determined by the variability of the price of the underlying asset. The higher this variability, the higher the margin levels. The maintenance margin is usually about 75 percent of the initial margin.

Margin requirements may depend on the objectives of the trader. A bona fide hedger, such as a company that produces the commodity on which the futures contract is written, is often subject to lower margin requirements than a speculator. The reason is that there is deemed to be less risk of default. Day trades and spread transactions often give rise to lower margin requirements than do hedge transactions. In a *day trade* the trader announces to the broker an intent to close out the position in the same day. Thus, if the trader has taken a long position, the plan is to take an offsetting short position later in the day; if the trader has taken a short position, the plan is to take an offsetting long position later in the day. In a *spread transaction* the trader simultaneously takes a long position in a contract on an asset for one maturity month and a short position in a contract on the same asset for another maturity month.

Note that margin requirements are the same on short futures positions as they are on long futures positions. It is just as easy to take a short futures position as it is to take a long one. The cash market does not have this symmetry. Taking a long position in the cash market involves buying the asset and presents no problems. Taking a short position involves selling an asset that you do not own. This is a more complex transaction that may or may not be possible in a particular market. It is discussed further in the next chapter.

THE CLEARINGHOUSE AND CLEARING MARGINS

The *exchange clearinghouse* is an adjunct of the exchange and acts as an intermediary in futures transactions. It guarantees the performance of the parties to each transaction. The clearinghouse has a number of members, all with offices close to the clearinghouse. Brokers who are not clearinghouse members themselves must channel their business through a member. The main task of the clearinghouse is to keep track of all the transactions that take place during a day so that it can calculate the net position of each of its members.

Just as an investor is required to maintain a margin account with a broker, a clearinghouse member is required to maintain a margin account with the clearinghouse. This is known as a *clearing margin*. The margin accounts for clearinghouse members are adjusted for gains and losses at the end of each trading day in the same way as are the margin accounts of investors. However, in the case of the clearinghouse member, there is an original margin but no maintenance margin. Every day the account balance for each contract must be maintained at an amount equal to the original margin times the number of contracts outstanding. Thus, depending on transactions during the day and price movements, the clearinghouse member may have to add funds to its margin account at the end of the day. Alternatively, it may find it can remove funds from the account at this time. Brokers who are not clearinghouse members must maintain a margin account with a clearinghouse member.

In determining clearing margins, the exchange clearinghouse calculates the number of contracts outstanding on either a gross or a net basis. The *gross basis* simply adds the total of all long positions entered into by clients to the total of all the short positions entered into by clients. The *net basis* allows these to be offset against each other. Suppose a clearinghouse member has two clients: one with a long position in 20 contracts, the other with a short position in 15 contracts. Gross margining would calculate the clearing margin on the basis of 35 contracts; net margining would calculate the clearing margin on the basis of 5 contracts. Most exchanges currently use net margining.

It should be stressed that the whole purpose of the margining system is to reduce the possibility of market participants sustaining losses because of defaults. Overall the system has been very successful. Losses arising from defaults in contracts at major exchanges have been almost nonexistent.

Newspaper Quotes

Many newspapers carry futures quotations. The *Wall Street Journal*'s futures quotations can currently be found in the Money and Investing section. Table 2.3 shows the quotations for commodities as they appeared in the *Wall Street Journal* of Wednesday, September 25, 1996. The quotes refer to the trading that took place on the previous day (i.e., Tuesday, September 24, 1996). The quotations for index futures and currency futures are given in chapter 3. The quotations for interest-rate futures are given in chapter 5.

The asset underlying the futures contract, the exchange that the contract is traded on, the contract size, and how the price is quoted are all shown at the top of each section in Table 2.3. The first asset is corn, traded on the Chicago Board of Trade. The contract size is 5,000 bushels and the price is quoted in cents per bushel. The months in which particular contracts are traded are shown in the first column. Corn contracts with maturities in December 1996, March 1997, May 1997, July 1997, September 1997, and December 1997 were traded on September 24, 1996.

PRICES

The first three numbers in each row show the opening price, the highest price achieved in trading during the day, and the lowest price achieved in trading during the day. The opening price is representative of the prices at which contracts were trading immediately after the opening bell. For December 1996 corn on September 24, 1996, the opening price was $312\frac{3}{4}$ cents per bushel, and during the day the price traded between 313 cents and $309\frac{3}{4}$ cents.

TABLE 2.3 Commodity Futures Quotes from the *Wall Street Journal* on September 25, 1996

FUTURES PRICES

Tuesday, September 24, 1996.

Open interest Reflects Previous Trading Day.

	Open	High	Low	Settle	Change	Lifetime High	Lifetime Low	Open interest

GRAINS AND OILSEEDS

CORN (CBT) 5,000 cu.; cents per bu.

	Open	High	Low	Settle	Change	Lifetime High	Lifetime Low	Open interest
Dec	312¾	313	309¾	310½	− 2¾	389	239	189,154
Mr97	319¾	319¾	316½	317	− 2¾	394½	279¼	62,588
May	326½	326½	322¾	323	− 3¼	394	306	26,557
July	328	328	324½	325	− 3	393	284	19,643
Sept	308	308	306½	306½	− 2½	335	298	2,526
Dec	298¾	298¾	296½	298	− 1¾	249¾	310	13,722

Est vol 45,000; vol Mon 50,970; open int 316,376, +7,345.

OATS (CBT) 5,000 bu.; cents per bu.

Dec	166¼	169	165½	167¾	+ 1	257¼	160	8,883
Mr97	173½	175¾	173	174	+ ¼	258½	169¼	2,296
May	178½	179	177½	178½	+ ½	250	173¾	260

Est vol 750; vol Mon 507; open int 11,499, − 161.

SOYBEANS (CBT) 5,000 bu.; cents per bu.

Nov	795	796	788	791¼	− 7½	825	585	121,578
Ja97	804½	804½	796	798¼	− 8¼	824	650	29,460
Mar	807	808¼	801	803¼	− 8¼	830	695	15,770
May	802	805½	800	803	− 6¾	828	735	14,786
July	804	806	800	803¼	− 7½	828	611	12,092
Nov	732	734½	729½	732¾	− 4¾	749	597½	5,345

Est vol 45,000; vol Mon 42,338; open int 199,390, −2,371.

SOYBEAN MEAL (CBT) 100 tons; $ per ton.

Oct	260.80	260.80	258.20	260.00	− .80	265.70	190.00	20,076
Dec	257.70	257.70	255.00	255.90	− 1.90	262.00	178.00	43,742
Ja97	256.00	256.00	254.20	254.60	− 2.40	260.00	215.00	8,420
Mar	253.30	253.40	251.60	251.70	− 2.90	258.00	226.50	11,055
May	249.00	249.50	248.50	248.50	− 2.10	256.00	224.50	6,493
July	249.50	249.50	247.70	248.30	− 2.30	256.00	199.20	3,011
Aug	247.00	247.00	245.00	246.40	− 1.90	251.50	227.00	591

Est vol 17,000; vol Mon 20,836; open int 94,192, +87.

SOYBEAN OIL (CBT) 60,000 lbs.; cents per lb.

Oct	25.00	25.09	24.88	24.94	− .24	29.10	23.82	12,487
Dec	25.42	25.45	25.28	25.33	− .24	29.30	24.45	47,028
Ja97	25.67	25.68	25.55	25.58	− .20	29.28	24.82	7,775
Mar	25.97	26.03	25.88	25.90	− .24	29.25	25.12	9,422
May	26.20	26.28	26.11	26.18	− .19	29.25	25.38	6,124
July	26.40	26.48	26.30	26.40	− .15	29.10	25.70	1,666

Est vol 11,000; vol Mon 9,257; open int 85,256, +60.

WHEAT (CBT) 5,000 bu.; cents per bu.

Dec	425	433½	425	429½	+ 3	632¾	362	46,526
Mr97	418	424½	417½	420½	+ 2¼	618½	409	13,361
May	403	408½	402	404¾	+ 2¾	547	395	1,148
July	386	389½	386	388	+ 3	465	365	5,279

Est vol 12,000; vol Mon 10,870; open int 67,625, −324.

WHEAT (KC) 5,000 bu.; cents per bu.

Dec	434½	442	433	437¼	+ 2½	667	421	19,384
Mr97	426	431	425	426¾	+ 1	650	415½	8,228
May	407½	411	406	406	− 1	575	401	822
July	391	393	389	389½	+ 1¾	499	381	2,709

Est vol 6,862; vol Mon 3,608; open int 31,230, +358.

WHEAT (MPLS) 5,000 bu.; cents per bu.

Dec	411	420	411	419	+ 6¼	634	403	15,396
Mr97	413	419	413	416	+ 2¾	632	406	5,855
May	413	415	412	412	+ 1½	591	406½	415

Est vol 4,134; vol Mon 2,592; open int 22,002, −230.

CANOLA (WPG) 20 metric tons; Can. $ per ton

Nov	442.00	442.00	4338.5	440.60	− 1.70	455.00	361.00	26,845
Ja97	446.00	446.00	442.30	444.20	− 1.90	456.00	371.50	10,645
Mar	445.00	445.10	442.40	444.20	− 2.30	457.30	395.00	6,147
May	444.50	444.50	442.10	443.60	− .90	451.50	427.00	2,202
July	442.50	443.50	442.00	443.50	− 1.50	446.50	422.00	1,859
Nov	387.00	388.00	387.00	388.00	− 9.00	410.00	387.00	225

Est vol 8,005; vol Mn 3,194; open int 47,939, +2,663.

WHEAT (WPG) 20 metric tons; Can. $ per ton

Oct	200.30	200.50	199.80	199.80	− 2.10	228.50	170.00	2,130

Dec	186.00	186.00	185.40	186.00	− .40	216.00	179.00	4,644
Mr97	181.00	181.20	180.60	180.90	− .60	217.00	178.50	3,756
May	181.70	182.00	181.50	181.50	− 1.00	209.00	180.00	496

Est vol 925; vol Mn 836; open int 11,106, +355.

BARLEY-WESTERN (WPG) 20 metric tons; Can. $ per ton

Nov	150.00	150.50	149.80	150.20	− .70	177.20	162.00	8,776
Fb97	154.00	154.50	154.00	154.50	− .90	182.00	151.50	6,998
Mar	155.50	155.80	155.10	155.10	− .90	181.00	152.40	1,085
May	....	....	157.50	157.50	− .50	182.00	155.80	239

Est vol 500; vol Mn 621; open int 17,170, − 199.

LIVESTOCK AND MEAT

CATTLE-FEEDER (CME) 50,000 lbs.; cents per lb.

Sept	63.50	63.70	63.45	63.60	+ .05	64.85	50.95	1,483
Oct	63.15	64.05	63.15	63.60	+ .45	65.55	52.30	6,545
Nov	63.92	64.65	63.85	64.35	+ .50	65.90	54.60	2,871
Ja97	64.00	64.82	64.00	64.52	+ .55	65.75	55.70	1,843
Mar	63.40	64.15	63.40	64.02	+ .57	65.20	56.15	1,114
Apr	63.60	64.20	63.60	64.17	+ .57	65.25	57.75	726
May	63.87	64.35	63.87	64.30	+ .50	65.50	59.80	647
Aug	65.70	66.10	65.70	66.10	+ .60	66.70	64.05	207

Est vol 2,758; vol Mn 2,185; open int 15,436, −174.

CATTLE-LIVE (CME) 40,000 lbs.; cents per lb.

Oct	71.65	72.87	71.55	72.72	+ 1.12	73.52	59.90	28,150
Dec	67.05	67.77	66.85	67.62	+ .77	68.95	59.40	32,401
Fb97	64.60	64.82	64.30	64.72	+ .27	66.02	60.15	16,288
Apr	66.17	66.30	65.90	66.20	+ .12	67.90	62.65	7,751
June	64.02	64.20	63.85	64.10	+ .10	66.75	61.00	3,554
Aug	64.10	64.22	64.00	64.02	− .02	66.75	62.65	3,950
Oct	66.00	66.00	65.90	66.00	+ .10	66.90	65.90	332

Est vol 18,643; vol Mn 13,434; open int 92,426, −225.

HOGS (CME) 40,000 lbs.; cents per lb.

New contract prices begin with Feb97

Oct	56.95	57.45	56.65	57.22	+ .05	57.45	41.00	8,078
Dec	56.75	57.35	56.42	57.15	+ .42	57.50	41.90	15,524
Fb97	76.95	76.95	76.50	76.60	− .07	78.70	63.15	4,937
Apr	73.70	73.75	73.20	73.47	− .07	76.50	61.15	1,805
June	78.00	78.20	77.70	77.70	− .55	80.40	67.60	2,011
July	75.50	75.75	75.00	75.12	− .67	77.00	67.40	444
Aug	70.55	70.65	70.20	70.37	− .02	71.60	66.00	201
Oct	....	....	....	67.95	....	67.95	62.00	109

Est vol 7,044; vol Mn 4,706; open int 33,163, −896.

PORK BELLIES (CME) 40,000 lbs.; cents per lb.

Feb	77.00	77.60	75.67	77.50	+ .85	89.75	60.82	4,666
Mar	77.00	77.50	75.75	77.30	+ .52	89.35	60.60	842
May	78.40	79.22	77.25	79.22	+ .32	87.80	60.50	305
July	58.55	79.47	77.50	79.47	+ .27	88.00	63.00	119

Est vol 2,177; vol Mn 1,426; open int 5,955, − 128.

FOOD AND FIBER

COCOA (CSCE)-10 metric tons; $ per ton.

Dec	1,357	1,368	1,357	1,366	+ 7	1,578	1,290	31,624
Mr97	1,392	1,401	1,391	1,400	+ 6	1,518	1,322	17,441
May	....	....	1,420	+ 6	1,526	1,335	8,126
July	1,434	1,434	1,434	1,440	+ 15	1,502	1,375	6,091
Sept	1,450	1,451	1,450	1,457	+ 15	1,512	1,430	5,516
Dec	....	....	1,482	+ 11	1,540	1,453	676
Mr98	....	....	1,503	+ 3	1,569	1,472	3,797
May	....	....	1,518	+ 3	1,584	1,488	4,486

Est vol 2,383; vol Mn 3,458; open int 77,759, +427.

COFFEE (CSCE)-37,500 lbs.; cents per lb.

Dec	105.50	106.50	104.90	106.00	+ 1.45	148.90	91.00	14,321
Mr97	102.75	103.20	102.00	102.70	+ 1.25	127.25	91.50	5,087
May	102.50	103.25	102.00	102.65	+ 1.10	124.00	93.00	2,063
July	102.50	103.25	102.90	102.55	+ 1.55	124.00	95.00	723
Sept	102.50	102.50	102.50	102.55	+ 1.55	116.50	95.00	219
Dec	102.50	102.50	102.50	103.00	+ 1.55	113.40	97.00	294

Est vol 6,600; vol Mn 5,630; open int 22,707, +184.

SUGAR-WORLD (CSCE)-112,000 lbs.; cents per lb.

Oct	11.35	11.43	11.16	11.17	− .13	12.50	9.51	24,128
Mr97	11.28	11.30	11.02	11.04	− .23	11.76	9.48	57,745
May	11.23	11.24	10.98	11.01	− .23	11.55	9.64	22.022

(continued)

TABLE 2.3 (cont.)

	Open	High	Low	Settle	Change	Lifetime High	Lifetime Low	Open Int
July	11.02	11.02	10.85	10.85 −	.18	11.20	9.40	14,6165
Oct	10.90	10.90	10.75	10.76 −	.14	11.08	9.43	10,191
Mr98	10.77	10.73	10.65	10.66 −	.17	10.93	10.13	1,887
May			....	10.56 −	.17	10.82	10.20	212

Est vol 40,469; vol Mn 17,578; open int 140,813, −463.

SUGAR-DOMESTIC (CSCE)-112,000 lbs.; cents per lb.

	Open	High	Low	Settle	Change	Lifetime High	Lifetime Low	Open Int
Nov	22.42	22.42	22.35	22.39 −	.03	22.98	21.25	2,478
Ja97	22.51	22.54	22.51	22.51	....	22.64	22.00	4,766
Mar				22.54 −	.02	22.72	21.90	3,015
May	22.70	22.80	22.70	22.77 −	.01	22.94	21.95	2,164
July	22.70	22.90	22.90	22.90 −	.05	22.99	22.00	2,491
Sept	22.70	22.89	22.89	22.89 −	.03	22.99	22.37	2,028
Nov				22.55		22.58	22.20	471
Ja98				22.31 −	.15	22.51	22.30	181

Est vol 372; vol Mn 55; open int 17,594, +38.

COTTON (CTN)-50,000 lbs.; cents per lb.

	Open	High	Low	Settle	Change	Lifetime High	Lifetime Low	Open Int
Oct	77.40	75.74	74.20	75.72 +	1.10	86.50	69.08	1,619
Dec	75.90	77.24	75.75	77.22 +	1.12	84.40	70.50	28,437
Mr97	77.05	78.25	76.95	78.23 +	1.08	85.15	72.00	9,035
May	77.70	78.97	77.70	78.89 +	.84	85.40	73.10	6,665
July	78.20	79.60	78.40	79.50 +	.90	85.40	73.75	4,754
Oct	77.90	78.85	78.70	78.75 +	.20	81.30	74.60	982
Dec	77.65	78.10	77.60	78.02 +	.37	80.10	74.30	3,588
Mr98				78.80 +	.30	81.00	75.50	111
May				79.30 +	.15	81.00	76.25	130

Est vol 11,000; vol Mn 5,417; open int 55,374, −793.

ORANGE JUICE (CTN)-15,000 lbs.; cents per lb.

	Open	High	Low	Settle	Change	Lifetime High	Lifetime Low	Open Int
Nov	105.50	106.00	104.80	105.60 +	.75	135.25	103.00	8,745
Ja97	105.40	105.60	105.00	105.30 +	.30	135.50	104.10	6,095
Mar	107.25	107.50	107.00	107.50 +	.50	136.00	106.0	2,657
May	109.10	109.40	109.25	109.45 +	.50	131.00	108.50	649
July				111.20 +	.40	128.50	110.00	213
Sept				112.50 +	.40	121.30	112.00	234

Est vol 600; vol Mn 1,103; open int 18,684, +250.

METALS AND PETROLEUM

COPPER-HIGH (Cmx.Div.NYM)-25,000 lbs.; cents per lb.

	Open	High	Low	Settle	Change	Lifetime High	Lifetime Low	Open Int
Sept	89.00	90.20	89.00	89.90 +	1.65	121.30	82.70	2,556
Oct	88.50	89.80	88.50	89.65 +	1.70	119.00	85.00	2,172
Nov	88.00	89.50	88.00	89.45 +	1.50	116.90	85.00	1,539
Dec	88.05	89.60	88.05	89.15 +	1.50	118.80	82.80	25,693
Ja97	88.80	88.80	88.70	88.90 +	1.50	115.00	84.20	1,189
Feb				88.65 +	1.45	112.90	84.20	833
Mar	87.70	88.80	87.70	88.45 +	1.45	115.30	83.00	8,541
Apr	88.50	88.50	88.50	88.45 +	1.45	112.50	83.50	500
May	88.30	88.60	88.30	88.45 +	1.45	113.70	83.50	2,824
June				88.45 +	1.45	112.50	82.50	667
July				88.45 +	1.45	113.65	83.00	2,811
Aug				88.45 +	1.45	112.50	84.10	486
Sept				88.45 +	1.45	113.70	83.00	3,881
Oct				88.60 +	1.45	112.00	84.50	430
Nov				88.75 +	1.45	112.00	84.50	399
Dec	89.00	89.30	89.00	88.85 +	1.45	110.80	83.75	2,217
Ja98				89.00 +	1.45	95.00	85.20	79
Feb				89.15 +	1.45	94.80	85.50	113
Mar				89.25 +	1.45	113.00	85.00	874
July				89.60 +	1.45	88.00	86.00	238

Est vol 8,500; vol Mn 4,701; open int 56,202, −825.

GOLD (Cmx.Div.NYM)-100 troy oz.; $ per troy oz.

	Open	High	Low	Settle	Change	Lifetime High	Lifetime Low	Open Int
Sept				382.60 +	1.30	389.00	383.10	1
Oct	382.70	382.70	381.70	382.80 +	1.20	432.20	380.70	6,139
Dec	384.80	385.80	384.80	385.70 +	1.30	447.50	379.60	105,980
Fb97	387.70	388.30	387.20	388.10 +	1.30	428.00	385.70	13,662
Apr	390.10	390.10	389.70	390.40 +	1.20	428.00	388.20	8,154
June	392.30	392.30	392.30	392.90 +	1.10	456.00	391.40	11,665
Aug				395.50 +	1.10	414.50	395.00	4,748
Oct				398.20 +	1.10	426.50	396.30	404
Dec	400.80	401.30	400.80	400.90 +	1.00	477.00	399.50	10,451
Fb98				403.80 +	1.00	424.00	402.00	577
Apr				406.40 +	1.00	408.40	402.40	1,354
June				409.30 +	1.00	489.50	407.50	4,883
Dec	418.00	418.00	418.00	417.90 +	.90	505.00	416.30	5,295
Ju99				426.30 +	.80	520.00	425.40	5,663
Dec				434.70 +	.70	506.00	437.40	3,604
Ju00				443.30 +	.60	473.50	442.50	3,700
Dec				451.90 +	.50	474.50	450.50	5,054
Ju01				460.60 +	.40			1,155

Est vol 27,000; vol Mn 11,528; open int 192,489, +15.

PLATINUM (NYM)-50 troy oz.; $ per troy oz.

	Open	High	Low	Settle	Change	Lifetime High	Lifetime Low	Open Int
Oct	389.50	390.40	388.50	390.00 +	1.30	441.00	388.00	10,650
Ja97	392.00	392.50	390.70	392.00 +	1.30	442.00	389.60	11,744
Apr	395.00	395.00	393.80	394.70 +	1.40	426.00	392.80	5,980
July				397.70 +	1.40	418.00	396.90	626

Est vol 2,890; vol Mn na; open int 29,025, −580.

SILVER (Cmx.Div.NYM)-5,000 troy oz.; cnts per troy oz.

	Open	High	Low	Settle	Change	Lifetime High	Lifetime Low	Open Int
Sept	492.0	492.0	492.0	488.2 +	4.1	602.0	480.5	106
Dec	489.0	494.0	489.0	493.5 +	4.0	670.0	454.0	70,377
Mr97	500.0	501.0	497.0	501.1 +	4.0	611.0	492.5	11,706
May	503.0	504.0	503.0	506.1 +	4.0	606.0	498.0	6,398
July	510.0	510.0	508.0	511.2 +	4.0	655.0	503.0	4,907
Sept				516.3 +	4.0	576.0	513.0	3,075
Dec	523.0	527.0	521.0	524.3 +	4.0	695.0	502.0	1,716
Mr98				532.4 +	4.0	573.0	529.0	106
July				543.1 +	4.0	700.0	590.0	381
Dec	559.0	559.0	559.0	556.7 +	4.0	734.0	550.0	709
Jl99				576.2 +	4.0	660.0	588.0	350
Dec				591.3 +	4.0	720.0	585.0	117

Est vol 11,000; vol Mn 8,206; open int 100,062, +527.

CRUDE OIL, Light Sweet (NYM) 1,000 bbls.; $ per bbl.

	Open	High	Low	Settle	Change	Lifetime High	Lifetime Low	Open Int
Nov	23.39	24.10	23.34	24.07 +	.70	24.64	16.68	85,660
Dec	22.88	23.55	22.85	23.53 +	.69	23.83	16.65	62,184
Ja97	22.32	22.95	22.31	22.92 +	.61	23.10	16.70	40,670
Feb	21.82	22.31	21.82	22.35 +	.55	22.50	16.72	25,708
Mar	21.40	21.75	21.40	21.87 +	.51	21.87	16.75	18,144
Apr	21.03	21.30	21.01	21.49 +	.48	21.40	16.74	13,081
May	20.68	20.95	20.68	21.12 +	.46	20.95	16.92	9,169
June	20.34	20.55	20.34	20.78 +	.43	20.55	16.71	26,312
July	20.10	20.30	20.10	20.52 +	.42	20.30	16.80	9,812
Aug	19.84	20.07	19.84	20.28 +	.40	20.07	16.88	7,049
Sept	19.66	19.85	19.63	20.05 +	.38	19.85	16.71	7,835
Oct	19.45	19.74	19.45	19.85 +	.37	19.74	16.84	5,277
Nov	19.27	19.47	19.23	19.65 +	.36	19.47	16.90	5,518
Dec	19.05	19.35	19.05	19.46 +	.35	19.35	16.80	23,449
Ja98	18.94	19.15	18.94	19.31 +	.34	19.15	17.04	7,879
Feb				19.20 +	.33	18.77	17.15	3,320
Mar				19.09 +	.32	18.14	17.30	1,602
Apr	18.57	18.57	18.57	18.98 +	.31	18.57	17.38	591
May				18.88 +	.31	17.90	17.39	860
June	18.40	18.40	18.40	18.78 +	.31	18.70	17.17	7,630
July				18.70 +	.30	17.70	17.60	1,271
Aug				18.65 +	.27			98
Sept				18.62 +	.25	18.06	17.94	1,011
Oct				18.62 +	.25	18.00	17.75	158
Nov				18.62 +	.25			170
Dec	18.20	18.20	18.20	18.63 +	.25	19.10	17.05	8,346
Ja99				18.65 +	.25	17.85	17.85	3,005
June				18.69 +	.24	18.15	17.80	3,603
Dec	18.40	18.40	18.40	18.75 +	.24	19.82	17.62	7,655

Est vol na; vol Mon na; open int 388.307, −8.516

HEATING OIL NO. 2 (NYM) 42,000 gal.; $ per gal.

	Open	High	Low	Settle	Change	Lifetime High	Lifetime Low	Open Int
Oct	.6755	.6980	.6744	.6969 +	.0221	.7015	.4975	25,160
Nov	.6785	.6960	.6724	.6947 +	.0223	.7000	.4870	33,045
Dec	.6690	.6880	.6690	.6887 +	.0208	.6935	.4945	32,060
Ja97	.6580	.6745	.6580	.6757 +	.0183	.6795	.4975	21,769
Feb	.6395	.6535	.6395	.6552 +	.0158	.6575	.4960	11,029
Mar	.6095	.6250	.6095	.6252 +	.0138	.6275	.4850	5,268
Apr	.5850	.5915	.5845	.5937 +	.0128	.5930	.4745	3,478
May	.5625	.5690	.5625	.5702 +	.0118	.5690	.4660	2,457
June	.5450	.5560	.5450	.5582 +	.0113	.5560	.4620	2,562
July	.5460	.5475	.5460	.5542 +	.0108	.5520	.4595	2,055
Aug	.5544	.5544	.5544	.5572 +	.0108	.5500	.4860	1,784
Sept	.5530	.5560	.5530	.5612 +	.0108	.5570	.4940	1,557
Oct	.5614	.5614	.5614	.5652 +	.0108	.5614	.5050	853
Nov	.5654	.5654	.5654	.5692 +	.0108	.5654	.5075	549
Dec	.5725	.5725	.5660	.5732 +	.0108	.5725	.5179	1,792
Ja98				.5747 +	.0108	.5655	.5240	512

GASOLINE-NY Unleaded (NYM)) 42,000 gal.; $ per gal.

	Open	High	Low	Settle	Change	Lifetime High	Lifetime Low	Open Int
Oct	.6000	.6300	.6000	.6283 +	.0276	.6700	.5050	19,085
Nov	.6020	.6270	.6020	.6260 +	.0259	.6570	.4915	19,159
Dec	.5995	.6220	.5990	.6210 +	.0229	.6450	.4850	10,196
Ja97	.5985	.6180	.5985	.6180 +	.0214	.6325	.4870	7,499
Feb	.5995	.6145	.5990	.6210 +	.0214	.6260	.4910	2,155
Mar	.6065	.6085	.6065	.6220 +	.0214	.6200	.5290	1,472
Apr				.6410 +	.0214	.6365	.5550	1,630
May				.6365 +	.0214	.6330	.5575	566
June				.6250 +	.0214	.6240	.5550	353

Est vol na; vol Mon na; open int 60,295, +535.

(continued)

TABLE 2.3 (cont.)

NATURAL GAS, (NYM) 10,000 MMBtu.; $ per MMBtu's

Month	Open	High	Low	Settle	Chg	Lifetime High	Lifetime Low	Open Int
Oct	1.872	1.905	1.810	1.828	− .045	2.840	1.730	18,202
Nov	2.068	2.115	2.010	2.055	− .017	2.840	1.800	27,272
Dec	2.264	2.295	2.210	2.262	− .004	2.865	1.868	19,689
Ja97	2.320	2.345	2.275	2.312	− .004	2.860	1.882	15,552
Feb	2.265	2.285	2.215	2.255	− .005	2.730	1.815	9,164
Mar	2.170	2.175	2.125	2.145	− .005	2.530	1.749	7,377
Apr	2.035	2.040	1.995	2.023	+ .003	2.330	1.701	4,950
May	1.970	1.990	1.960	1.973	− .002	2.235	1.710	4,161
June	1.955	1.955	1.920	1.933	− .002	2.200	1.717	3,970
July	1.940	1.940	1.910	1.920	− .005	2.185	1.775	3,234
Aug	1.940	1.940	1.910	1.920	− .005	2.160	1.850	3,089
Sept	1.940	1.940	1.910	1.920	− .005	2.150	1.731	3,463
Oct	1.930	1.930	1.920	1.925	− .005	2.140	1.880	2,869
Nov	1.995	1.995	1.975	1.983	− .007	2.200	1.945	1,282
Dec	2.090	2.095	2.075	2.083	− .007	2.300	1.915	3,410
Ja98	2.100	2.100	2.080	2.085	− .015	2.280	2.080	2,973
Feb	2.045	2.045	2.015	2.020	− .020	2.215	2.015	1,110
Mar	1.970	1.970	1.955	1.950	− .015	2.105	1.930	939
Apr	1.915	1.915	1.915	1.910	− .010	1.980	1.825	705
May	1.920	1.915	1.910	1.910	− .010	2.000	1.830	715
June	1.915	1.915	1.915	1.910	− .010	1.980	1.745	1,203
July	1.915	1.915	1.915	1.910	− .010	1.980	1.852	560
Aug	1.915	1.915	1.915	1.910	− .010	1.960	1.845	486
Sept	1.915	1.915	1.915	1.910	− .010	1.980	1.850	464
Oct	1.915	1.915	1.910	1.910	− .010	1.985	1.840	600
Nov	....	....	....	1.975	− .010	2.050	1.915	667
Dec	....	....	....	2.075	− .010	2.175	1.950	1,847
Ja99	....	....	....	2.080	− .010	2.180	2.085	1,092
June	....	....	....	1.885	− .010	1.965	1.860	362

Est vol na; vol Mon na; open int 146,973, +921.

BRENT CRUDE (IPE) 1,000 net bbls.; $ per bbl.

Month	Open	High	Low	Settle	Chg	Lifetime High	Lifetime Low	Open Int
Nov	22.34	22.97	22.32	22.96	+ .70	23.60	15.40	62,635
Dec	21.85	22.40	21.85	22.39	+ .65	22.81	15.43	37,971
Ja97	21.30	21.79	21.30	21.76	+ .58	22.08	15.43	21,895
Feb	20.76	21.14	20.75	21.15	+ .51	21.37	16.45	12,289
Mar	20.25	20.53	20.17	20.54	+ .44	20.74	16.35	10,915
Apr	19.72	20.07	19.72	20.06	+ .39	20.10	16.30	4,666
May	19.30	19.64	19.30	19.64	+ .38	19.64	15.99	1,891
June	18.95	19.30	18.94	19.25	+ .34	19.30	16.05	6,482
July	18.69	18.97	18.69	18.97	+ .33	18.97	16.40	925
Aug	18.57	18.76	18.45	18.74	+ .34	18.76	16.75	435
Sept	18.39	18.55	18.33	18.53	+ .31	18.55	17.60	1,445

Est vol 53,388; vol Mn 30,530; open int 161,549, 1,266.

GAS OIL (IPE) 100 metric tons; $ per ton

Month	Open	High	Low	Settle	Chg	Lifetime High	Lifetime Low	Open Int
Oct	220.00	223.50	220.00	223.25	+ 5.00	225.00	147.00	25,145
Nov	211.75	215.00	211.25	215.00	+ 7.00	215.00	146.50	15,239
Dec	205.75	208.25	205.75	208.25	+ 5.75	211.00	150.00	15,415
Ja97	199.75	202.00	199.75	210.75	+ 5.00	204.50	152.00	12,178
Feb	192.75	194.50	192.75	194.25	+ 4.75	197.00	154.25	2,695
Mar	186.50	186.75	186.50	186.75	+ 4.50	189.50	157.25	3,718
Apr	179.50	179.75	179.50	179.25	+ 4.00	181.25	155.5	3,342
May	....	....		175.00	+ 4.25	171.50	153.00	1,210
June	171.50	172.00	171.50	171.25	+ 4.75	173.25	152.00	4,697
Sept	....	....		169.50	+ 4.75	171.50	152.00	235
Dec	169.00	169.00	169.00	168.75	+ 5.25	169.00	160.50	686

Est vol 19,604; vol Mn 15,188; open int 84,838, +1,012.

EXCHANGE ABBREVIATIONS
(for commodity futures and futures options)

CBT-Chicago Board of Trade; CME-Chicago Mercantile Exchange; CSCE-Coffee, Sugar & Cocoa Exchange, New York; CMX-COMEX (Div. of New York Mercantile Exchange); CTN-New York Cotton Exchange; DTB-Deutsche Terminboerse; FINEX-Financial Exchange (Div. of New York Cotton Exchange); IPE-International Petroleum Exchange; KC-Kansas City Board of Trade; LIFFE-London International Financial Futures Exchange; MATIF-Marche a Terme International de France; ME-Montreal Exchange; MCE-MidAmerica Commodity Exchange; MPLS-Minneapolis Grain Exchange; NYFE-New York Futures Exchange (Sub. of New York Cotton Exchange); NYM-New York Mercantile Exchange; SIMEX-Singapore International Monetary Exchange Ltd.; SFE-Sydney Futures Exchange; TFE-Toronto Futures Exchange; WPG-Winnipeg Commodity Exchange.

Source: Reprinted by permission from the *Wall Street Journal,* September 25, 1996. Copyright ©Dow Jones & Company, Inc. All rights reserved.

SETTLEMENT PRICE

The fourth number is the *settlement price.* This is the average of the prices at which the contract traded immediately before the bell signaling the end of trading for the day. The fifth number is the change in the settlement price from the previous day. In the case of the December 1996 corn futures contract, the settlement price was $310\frac{1}{2}$ cents on September 24, 1996, down $2\frac{3}{4}$ cents from September 23, 1996.

The settlement price is important, because it is used for calculating daily gains and losses and margin requirements. In the case of the December 1996 corn futures, an investor with a long position in one contract would find his or her margin account balance reduced by $137.50 (= 5,000 × 2.75 cents) between September 23, 1996 and September 24, 1996. Similarly, an investor with a short position in one contract would find that the margin balance increased by $137.50 between September 23, 1996 and September 24, 1996.

LIFETIME HIGHS AND LOWS

The sixth and seventh numbers show the highest futures price and the lowest futures price achieved in the trading of the particular contract over its lifetime. The December 1996 corn contract had traded for over a year on September 24, 1996. During this period the highest and lowest prices achieved were 239 cents and 389 cents.

OPEN INTEREST AND VOLUME OF TRADING

The final column in Table 2.3 shows the *open interest* for each contract. This is the total number of contracts outstanding. The open interest is the number of long positions or, equivalently, the number of short positions. Because of the problems in compiling the data, the open-interest information is one trading day older than the price information. Thus, in the *Wall Street Journal* of September 25, 1996 the open interest is for the close of trading on September 23, 1996. In the case of the December 1996 corn futures contract, the open interest was 189,154 contracts.

At the end of each section, Table 2.3 shows the estimated volume of trading in contracts of all maturities on September 24, 1996 and the actual volume of trading in these contracts on September 23, 1996. It also shows the total open interest for all contracts on September 23, 1996 and the change in this open interest from the previous trading day. For all corn futures contracts, the estimated trading volume was 45,000 contracts on September 24, 1996, and the actual trading volume was 50,970 contracts on September 23, 1996. The open interest for all corn futures contracts was 316,376 on September 23, 1996, up 7,345 from the previous trading day.

Sometimes the volume of trading in a day is greater than the open interest at the end of the day. This is indicative of a large number of day trades.

PATTERNS OF FUTURES PRICES

A number of different patterns of futures prices can be picked out from Table 2.3. The futures price of gold on the New York Commodity Exchange and the futures price of oats on the Chicago Board of Trade increase as the time to maturity increases. This is known as a *normal market*. By contrast, the futures price of wheat on the Chicago Board of Trade is a decreasing function of the time to maturity. This is known as an *inverted market*. For live cattle the pattern is mixed. The futures price first decreases, then increases, then decreases, and then increases as the time to maturity increases.

Keynes and Hicks

As the maturity of the futures contract is approached, the futures price of an asset converges toward its spot price. An interesting question is whether the futures price is above or below the expected future spot price. If the futures price is above the expected future spot price, there is an expectation that the futures price will decline. Similarly, if the futures price is below the expected future spot price, there is an expectation that the futures price will rise. Economists John Maynard Keynes and John Hicks argued that if hedgers tend to hold short positions and speculators tend to hold long positions, the futures price will be below the expected future spot price. This is because speculators require compensation for the risks they are bearing. They will trade only if there is an expectation that the futures price will rise over time. If hedgers tend to hold long positions while speculators hold short positions, Keynes and Hicks argued that the futures price must be above the expected future spot price. The reason is similar. To compensate speculators for the risks they are bearing, there must be an expectation that the futures prices will decline over time.

When the futures price is below the expected future spot price, the situation is known as *normal backwardation;* when the futures price is above the expected future spot price, the situation is known as *contango.* In the next chapter we will examine in more detail both the determinants of futures prices and the relationship between futures prices and expected future spot prices.

Delivery

As mentioned earlier in this chapter, very few of the futures contracts that are entered into lead to delivery of the underlying asset. Most are closed out early. Nevertheless, it is the possibility of eventual delivery that determines the futures price. An understanding of delivery procedures is therefore important.

The period during which delivery can be made is defined by the exchange and varies from contract to contract. The decision on when to deliver is made by the party with the short position, whom we shall refer to as investor A. When investor A decides to deliver, investor A's broker issues a *notice of intention to deliver* to the exchange clearinghouse. The notice states how many contracts will be delivered and, in the case of commodities, also specifies where delivery will be made and what grade will be delivered. The exchange then chooses a party with a long position to accept delivery.

Suppose that the party on the other side of investor A's futures contract when it was negotiated on the floor of the exchange was investor B. It is important to realize that there is no reason to expect that it will be investor B who takes delivery. Investor B may well have closed out his or her position by taking a short position in a contract with investor C, investor C may have closed out his or her position by taking a short position in a contract with investor D, and so on. The usual rule chosen by the exchange is to pass the notice of intention to deliver on to the party with the oldest outstanding long position. Parties with long positions must accept delivery notices. However, if the notices are transferable, long investors have a short period of time, usually half an hour, to find another party with a long position that is prepared to accept the notice from them.

In the case of a commodity, taking delivery usually means accepting a warehouse receipt in return for immediate payment. The party taking delivery is then responsible for all warehousing costs. In the case of livestock futures, there may be costs associated with feeding and looking after the animals. In the case of financial futures, delivery is usually made by wire transfer. For all contracts the price paid is usually based on the settlement price immediately preceding the date of the notice of intention to deliver. Where appropriate, this price is adjusted for grade, location of delivery, and so on. The whole delivery procedure from the issuance of the notice of intention to deliver to the delivery itself generally takes two to three days.

There are three critical days for a contract. These are the first notice day, the last notice day, and the last trading day. The *first notice day* is the first day on which a notice of intention to make delivery can be submitted to the exchange. The *last notice day* is the last such day. The *last trading day* is generally a few days before the last notice day. To avoid the risk of having to take delivery, an investor with a long position should close out his or her contracts prior to the first notice day. Table 2.4 provides examples of how

TABLE 2.4	First Notice Day, Last Notice Day, and Last Trading Day for a Number of Different Contracts			
Exchange	*Asset*	*First Notice Day*	*Last Notice Day*	*Last Trading Day*
CBOT	Corn	Last business day prior to delivery month	Second-to-last business day of delivery month	Eighth-to-last business day of delivery month
CME	Cattle (live)	Sixth calendar day of delivery month	Second-to-last business day of delivery month	Twentieth calendar day of delivery month
CSCE	Cocoa	Seven business days prior to first business day of delivery month	Last trading day	Eighth-to-last business day of delivery month
COMEX	Gold	Second-to-last business day of month prior to delivery month	Second-to-last business day of delivery month	Third-to-last business day of delivery month

the first notice day, last notice day, and last trading day are set for a number of different contracts.

CASH SETTLEMENT

Some financial futures, such as those on stock indices, are settled in cash because it is inconvenient or impossible to deliver the underlying asset. In the case of the futures contract on the S&P 500, for example, delivering the underlying asset would involve delivering a portfolio of 500 stocks. When a contract is settled in cash, it is simply marked to market at the end of the last trading day, and all positions are declared closed. To ensure that the futures price converges to the spot price, the settlement price on the last trading day is set at the closing spot price of the underlying asset.

One exception to the rule that the settlement price on the last trading day equals the closing spot price is the S&P 500 futures contract. Here the final settlement price is based on the opening price of the index the morning after the last trading day. This procedure is designed to avoid some of the problems connected with the fact that stock index futures, stock index options, and options on stock index futures all expire on the same day. Because arbitrageurs often take large offsetting positions in these three contracts, there may be chaotic trading and significant price movements toward the end of an expiration day as they attempt to close out their positions. The media have coined the term *triple witching hour* to describe trading during the last hour of an expiration day.

The Trading Pit

Futures trading usually takes place in *trading pits*. These are polygonal-shaped rings with steps descending to the center. Each pit is generally dedicated to the trading of a particular asset. The traders interested in trading a certain contract month tend to meet at a particular place in the pit. Trading currently takes place by what is known as *open-outcry auction.* A trader announcing a *bid* (i.e., a proposal to buy) will shout "*n* at *p*," where *n* is the number of contracts and *p* is the price. A trader announcing an *offer* (i.e., a proposal to sell) will shout "*p* for *n*." The price is usually abbreviated. Thus, a trader wanting to buy four contracts of December gold at $403.20 might shout "4 at 20." The 20 would refer to 20 cents, with $403 being understood. A complicated system of hand signals is also used to signal bids and offers.

A trader who announces a bid or offer must trade with the first trader who signals acceptance. Each trader then records the number of contracts, the contract type, the delivery date, the price, the name of the clearing firm on the other side of the transaction, and the initials of the other trader.

Recently, there has been a great deal of discussion on the viability of automated futures trading systems. Under an automated system, buyer and seller are matched by computer. A potential buyer sits at a computer terminal and indicates the price at which he or she is willing to buy. This price is relayed throughout the system. Another trader, also sitting at a computer terminal and logged into the system, can signal a willingness to sell at the buyer's price by pressing the appropriate keys. Some of the major North American exchanges currently use this type of system outside normal trading hours, and some European exchanges use it for all trading. It is possible that all exchanges will eventually eliminate the open-outcry auction.

PIT REPORTING

Reporters employed by the exchange record the times and prices of bids and offers. These are usually displayed on a large board above the trading floor. Prices are also communicated via ticker tape and in other ways to investors who are not on the floor of the exchange. Within a matter of seconds, the prices on a futures exchange are known throughout the world.

For each contract month, the board shows

1. The range of opening prices
2. The highest price (trade or bid) achieved during the day
3. The lowest price (trade or offer) achieved during the day
4. The estimated trading volume
5. The most recent seven prices before the last recorded price, with an indication as to whether they are bids, offers, or trades
6. The last recorded price, with an indication as to whether it is a bid, offer, or trade
7. The difference between the last price and the previous trading day's settlement price
8. The previous trading day's settlement price
9. Lifetime high
10. Lifetime low

TYPES OF TRADERS

There are two main types of traders on the floor of the exchange: commission brokers and locals. *Commission brokers* execute trades for other people and charge a commission for doing so. *Locals* are individuals who add liquidity to the market by trading on their own accounts.

When an investor places an order with a broker, the broker relays the order by telephone to its trading desk on the floor of the exchange. The order is then sent by messenger to the commission broker for action. When the order has been filled, the information is sent back to the trading desk, and a confirmation of the trade eventually reaches the investor. The total commission, charged when a contract is initiated, is usually a round-trip commission that covers both the purchase and sale of the contract. The same commission is charged regardless of whether the contract is ultimately closed out. Commissions vary significantly. One investor might pay only $25 per contract, while another pays $200 per contract.

Participants in futures markets, whether locals or those away from the floor of the exchange, can be categorized as hedgers, speculators, or arbitrageurs, as discussed in chapter 1. Speculators can be classified as scalpers, day traders, or position traders. *Scalpers* are watching for very short term trends and attempt to profit from small changes in the contract price. They usually hold their positions for only a few minutes. *Day traders* hold their positions for less than one trading day. They are unwilling to take the risk that adverse news will occur overnight. *Position traders* hold their positions for much longer periods of time. They hope to make significant profits from major movements in the markets.

SEATS ON EXCHANGES

To trade on the floor of the exchange, an individual must buy or rent a seat on the exchange. Seats are frequently bought and sold, and their price depends on the volume of trading activity. Seats on the Chicago Board of Trade, the Chicago Mercantile Exchange, and the International Monetary Markets cost several hundred thousand dollars, whereas those on smaller exchanges are significantly less expensive. Owners of seats are exchange members. However, not all exchange members are clearinghouse members. An exchange member must maintain an account with a clearinghouse member for the purpose of clearing trades.

TYPES OF ORDERS

The simplest type of order placed with a broker is a *market order*. It is a request that a trade be carried out immediately at the best price available in the market. However, there are many other types of orders. We will consider those that are more commonly used.

A *limit order* specifies a particular price. The order can be executed only at this price or at one more favorable to the investor. Thus, if the limit price is $30 for an investor wanting to take a long position, the order will be executed only at a price of $30 or less. There is of course no guarantee that the order will be executed at all, because the limit price may never be reached.

A *stop order* or *stop-loss order* also specifies a particular price. The order is executed at the best available price once a bid or offer is made at that particular price or a less favorable price. Suppose a stop order to sell at $30 is issued when the market price is $35. It becomes an order to sell when and if the price falls to $30. In effect, a stop order becomes a market order as soon as the specified price has been hit. The purpose of a stop order is usually to close out a position if unfavorable price movements take place. It limits the loss that can be incurred.

A *stop-limit order* is a combination of a stop order and a limit order. The order becomes a limit order as soon as a bid or offer is made at a price equal to or less favorable than the stop price. Two prices must be specified in a stop-limit order: the stop price and the limit price. Suppose that at the time the market price is $35, a stop-limit order to buy is issued with a stop price of $40 and a limit price of $41. As soon as there is a bid or offer at $40, the stop-limit becomes a limit order at $41. If the stop price and the limit price are the same, the order is sometimes called a *stop-and-limit order.*

A *market-if-touched order* (MIT) is executed at the best available price after a trade occurs at a specified price or at a price more favorable than the specified price. In effect an MIT becomes a market order once the specified price has been hit. An MIT is also known as a *board order.* Consider an investor who has a long position in a futures contract and is issuing instructions that would lead to closing out the contract. A stop order is designed to place a limit on the loss that can occur in the event of unfavorable price movements. By contrast, a market-if-touched order is designed to ensure that profits are taken if sufficiently favorable price movements occur.

A *discretionary order* or *market-not-held order* is traded as a market order except that execution may be delayed at the broker's discretion in an attempt to get a better price.

Some orders specify time conditions. Unless otherwise stated, an order is a day order and expires at the end of the trading day. A *time-of-day order* specifies a particular period of time during the day when the order can be executed. An *open order* or a *good-till-canceled order* is in effect until executed or until the end of trading in the particular contract. A *fill-or-kill order,* as its name implies, must be executed immediately on receipt or not at all.

Regulation

Futures markets in the United States are currently regulated federally by the Commodity Futures Trading Commission (CFTC), which was established in 1974. This body is responsible for licensing futures exchanges and approving contracts. All new contracts and changes to existing contracts must be approved by the CFTC. To be approved, the contract must have some useful economic purpose. Usually this means that it must serve the needs of hedgers as well as speculators.

The CFTC looks after the public interest. It is responsible for ensuring that prices are communicated to the public and that futures traders report their outstanding positions if they are above certain levels. The CFTC also licenses all individuals who offer their services to the public in futures trading. The backgrounds of these individuals are investigated, and there are minimum capital requirements. The CFTC deals with complaints brought by the public and ensures that disciplinary action is taken against individuals when appropriate. It has the authority to force exchanges to take disciplinary action against members who are in violation of exchange rules.

With the formation of the National Futures Association (NFA) in 1982, some of the responsibilities of the CFTC were shifted to the futures industry itself. The NFA is an organization of individuals who participate in the futures industry. Its objective is to prevent fraud and ensure that the market operates in the best interests of the general public. The NFA requires its members to pass an exam. It is authorized to monitor trading and take disciplinary action when appropriate. The agency has set up an efficient system for arbitrating disputes between individuals and its members.

From time to time other bodies such as the Securities and Exchange Commission (SEC), the Federal Reserve Board, and the U.S. Treasury Department have claimed jurisdictional rights over some aspects of futures trading. These bodies are concerned with the effects of futures trading on the spot markets for securities such as stocks, Treasury bills, and Treasury bonds. The SEC currently has an effective veto over the approval of new stock or bond index futures contracts. However, the basic responsibility for all futures and options on futures rests with the CFTC.

TRADING IRREGULARITIES

Most of the time futures markets operate efficiently and in the public interest. However, from time to time trading irregularities do come to light. One type of trading irregularity occurs when an investor group tries to "corner the market."[2] The investor group takes a huge long futures position and also tries to exercise some control over the supply of the underlying commodity. As the maturity of the futures contracts is approached, the investor group does not close out its position, so that the number of outstanding futures contracts may exceed the amount of the commodity available for delivery. The holders of short positions realize that they will find it difficult to deliver and become desperate to close out their positions. The result is a large rise in both futures and spot prices. Regulators usually deal with this type of abuse of the market by increasing margin requirements, imposing stricter position limits, prohibiting trades that increase a speculator's open position, and forcing market participants to close out their positions.

Other types of trading irregularities can involve the traders on the floor of the exchange. These received some publicity early in 1989 when it was announced that the FBI had carried out a two-year investigation, using undercover agents, of trading on the Chicago Board of Trade and the Chicago Mercantile Exchange. The investigation was initiated because of complaints filed by a large agricultural concern. The alleged offenses included overcharging customers, not paying customers the full proceeds of sales, and traders using their knowledge of customer orders to trade first for themselves.

Accounting and Tax Treatment

The full details of the accounting and tax treatment of futures contracts are beyond the scope of this book. An investor who wants detailed information should consult experts. This section provides some general background information.

---

[2]Possibly the best known example involves the activities of the Hunt brothers in the silver market in 1979–1980. Between the middle of 1979 and the beginning of 1980, their activities led to a price rise from $9 per ounce to $50 per ounce.

ACCOUNTING

FASB Statement No. 52, Foreign Currency Translation, established accounting standards in the United States for foreign currency futures. FASB Statement No. 80, Accounting for Futures Contracts, established accounting standards in the United States for all other contracts. The two statements require changes in market value to be recognized when they occur unless the contract qualifies as a hedge. If the contract does qualify as a hedge, gains or losses are generally recognized for accounting purposes in the same period in which the gains or losses from the item being hedged are recognized.

Consider an investor who in September 1996 takes a long position in a March 1997 corn futures contract and closes out the position at the end of February 1997. Suppose that the futures prices are 317 cents per bushel when the contract is entered into, 337 cents per bushel at the end of 1996, and 347 cents per bushel when the contract is closed out. One contract is for the delivery of 5,000 bushels. If the investor is a speculator, the gains for accounting purposes are

$$5,000 \times \$0.20 = \$1,000$$

in 1996 and

$$5,000 \times \$0.10 = \$500$$

in 1997. If the investor is hedging the purchase of 5,000 bushels of corn in 1997, the entire gain of $1,500 is realized in 1997 for accounting purposes.

This example is shown in Table 2.5. The treatment of hedging gains and losses is sensible. If the investor in our example is a company that is hedging the purchase of 5,000 bushels of corn at the end of February 1997, the effect of the futures contract is to ensure that the price paid is close to 317 cents per bushel. The accounting treatment reflects that this price is paid in 1997. The 1996 accounting calculations are unaffected by the futures transaction.

TABLE 2.5   Accounting Treatment of a Futures Transaction

From the Trader's Desk—February 1997

September 1996:	Investor takes a long position in one March 1997 futures contract to buy 5,000 bushels of corn. Futures price is 317 cents per bushel.
End of 1996:	Futures price is 337 cents per bushel.
February 1997:	The contract is closed out. Futures price is 347 cents per bushel.

If Investor Is a Speculator

Accounting gain in 1996 $= 5,000 \times 20$ cents $= \$1,000$
Accounting gain in 1997 $= 5,000 \times 10$ cents $= \$500$

If Investor Is Hedging a Purchase of Corn in 1997

The transaction has no impact on the reported results in 1996
Accounting gain in 1997 $= 5,000 \times 30$ cents $= \$1,500$

TAX

Under the U.S. tax rules, two key issues are the nature of a taxable gain or loss and the timing of the recognition of the gain or loss. Gains or losses are classified either as capital gains/losses or as part of ordinary income. A noncorporate taxpayer can deduct capital losses only to the extent of capital gains plus ordinary income up to $3,000. A noncorporate taxpayer can carry forward a net capital loss for an unlimited period of time. For a corporate taxpayer, capital losses are deductible only to the extent of capital gains. A corporation may carry back a capital loss three years. Any excess can be carried forward five years.

Generally, positions in futures contracts and foreign currency contracts are treated as if they are sold on the last day of the tax year. Any gains or losses on contracts other than foreign currency contracts are treated as capital gains/losses. Gains or losses on foreign currency contracts are treated as ordinary income/losses.

Hedging transactions are exempt from the foregoing rule. A hedging transaction is defined under the tax regulations as a transaction entered into in the normal course of business primarily for one of the following reasons:

1. To reduce the risk of price changes or currency fluctuations with respect to property that is held or to be held by the taxpayer for the purposes of producing ordinary income
2. To reduce the risk of price or interest-rate changes or currency fluctuations with respect to borrowings made by the taxpayer

Gains or losses from hedging transactions are treated as ordinary income. The timing of the recognition of gains or losses from hedging transactions generally matches the timing of the recognition of income or deduction from the hedged items.

Forward Contracts

Forward contracts are similar to futures contracts in that they are agreements to buy or sell an asset at a certain time in the future for a certain price. However, unlike futures contracts, they are not traded on an exchange. They are private (over-the-counter) agreements between two financial institutions or between a financial institution and one of its corporate clients.

One of the parties to a forward contract assumes a *long position* and agrees to buy the asset at a certain specified date for a certain price. The other party assumes a *short position* and agrees to sell the asset on the same date for the same price. Forward contracts do not have to conform to the standards of a particular exchange. The contract delivery date can be any date mutually convenient to the two parties. Usually, in forward contracts a single delivery date is specified, whereas in futures contracts there is a range of possible delivery dates.

Unlike futures contracts, forward contracts are not marked to market daily. The two parties contract to settle up on the specified delivery date. Whereas most futures contracts are closed out prior to delivery, most forward contracts do lead to delivery of the physical asset or to final settlement in cash. Table 2.6 summarizes the main differences between forward and futures contracts.

TABLE 2.6 Comparison of Forward and Futures Contracts

Forward	*Futures*
Private contract between two parties	Traded on an exchange
Not standardized	Standardized contract
Usually one specified delivery date	Range of delivery dates
Settled at end of contract	Settled daily
Delivery or final cash settlement usually takes place	Contract is usually closed out prior to maturity

DELIVERY PRICE

The specified price in a forward contract is referred to as the *delivery price.* At the time the contract is entered into, the delivery price is chosen so that the value of the contract to both parties is zero. This means that it costs nothing to take a long or a short position. We can think of the delivery price as being determined by supply and demand. However, as we will see in the next chapter, for assets on which forward contracts are normally negotiated, there is a way of calculating the "correct" delivery price from the current spot price of the asset, the delivery date, and other observable variables.

FORWARD PRICE

The *forward price* for a forward contract is similar in general concept to the futures price for a futures contract. A contract's current forward price is the delivery price that would apply if the contract were negotiated today. More formally, we can define the forward price for a certain contract as the delivery price that would make the contract have zero value. The forward price and the delivery price are by definition equal at the time a contract is entered into. As time passes, the delivery price for the contract stays the same. The forward price is liable to change. The two are not therefore equal, except by chance, at any time after the start of a contract. Generally, the forward price at any given time varies with the maturity of the contract being considered. For example, the forward price for a contract to buy or sell in three months will typically be different from that for a contract to buy or sell in six months.

FORWARD CONTRACTS ON FOREIGN EXCHANGE

Forward contracts on foreign exchange are very popular. Most large banks have a "forward desk" within their foreign exchange trading room that is devoted to the trading of forward contracts. Forward foreign exchange rates are frequently quoted alongside spot rates. Consider the following quotes on the sterling–U.S. dollar exchange rate:

Spot	1.8470
30-day forward	1.8442
90-day forward	1.8381
180-day forward	1.8291

The first quote indicates that, ignoring commissions and other transactions costs, sterling can be bought or sold in the spot market (i.e., for virtually immediate delivery) at the rate of $1.8470 per pound; the second quote indicates that the forward price for a contract to buy or sell sterling in 30 days is $1.8442 per pound; the third quote indicates that the forward price for a contract to buy or sell sterling in 90 days is $1.8381 per pound; and so on.

FOREIGN EXCHANGE QUOTES

Futures prices are always quoted as the number of U.S. dollars per unit of the foreign currency or as the number of U.S. cents per unit of the foreign currency. Forward prices are always quoted in the same way as spot prices. This means that for the British pound, the forward quotes show the number of U.S. dollars per unit of the foreign currency and are directly comparable with futures quotes. For most other countries, forward quotes show the number of units of the foreign currency per U.S. dollar. Thus, a futures price of 0.6050 dollars per Swiss franc corresponds to a forward price of 1.6529 francs per dollar (1.6529 = 1/0.6050).

FORWARD-RATE AGREEMENTS

Forward contracts are often arranged on domestic interest-rate-bearing instruments as well as on foreign currencies. For example, two companies might agree that a 7 percent per annum rate of interest will apply to a one-year deposit in six months' time. If the actual rate proves to be different from 7 percent per annum, one company pays and the other receives the present value of the difference between two sets of interest cash flows. This is known as a *forward-rate agreement* (FRA) and will be discussed in chapter 5.

HEDGING

As with futures contracts, forward contracts can be used for hedging. Suppose a U.S. corporation knows that it is due to pay £ 1 million in 90 days and the 90-day forward rate is 1.8381. It can choose at no cost to enter into a long forward contract to buy £1 million in 90 days for $1,838,100. In this way, the corporation hedges its foreign exchange risk by locking in the exchange rate that will apply to the sterling it requires. Similarly, a U.S. corporation that knows it is due to receive £1 million in 90 days can at no cost enter into a short forward contract to sell £1 million in 90 days for $1,838,100. In this way, it hedges its foreign exchange risk by locking in the price that will apply to the sterling it receives.

SPECULATION

Forward contracts can be used for speculation as well as hedging. An investor who thinks that sterling will increase in value relative to the U.S. dollar can speculate by taking a long position in a forward contract on sterling. Similarly, an investor who feels that sterling will fall in value can speculate by taking a short position in a forward contract on sterling. Let us again assume that the sterling 90-day forward rate is 1.8381. Suppose that the actual spot sterling exchange rate in 90 days proves to be 1.8600. An investor who has a long position in a 90-day forward contract will be able to purchase pounds for $1.8381 when they are worth $1.8600. The speculator will realize a gain of $0.0219 per pound. Similarly, an investor with a short position in three-month sterling will realize a loss of $0.0219 per pound.

Speculators may well be required to deposit a margin up front. However, the deposit is generally a relatively small proportion of the value of the assets underlying the forward contract. A forward contract, like a futures contract, therefore provides speculators with a high degree of leverage.

The value at maturity or *terminal value* of a long position in a forward contract on one unit of an asset is

$$S_T - K$$

where K is the delivery price and S_T is the spot price of the asset at maturity of the contract. Similarly, the terminal value of a short position in a forward contract on one unit of an asset is

$$K - S_T$$

In the case of the example just given, $S_T = 1.8600$ and $K = 1.8381$, so that $S_T - K = +0.0219$ and $K - S_T = -0.0219$. Since it costs nothing to enter into a forward contract, the terminal value of the contract is also the speculator's total profit from the contract. The profits from a forward contract are illustrated in Figure 2.2.

PROFITS FROM FORWARD AND FUTURES CONTRACTS

Suppose that the sterling exchange rate for a 90-day forward contract is 1.8381 and that this rate is also the futures price for a contract that will be delivered in exactly 90 days. What is the difference between the gains and losses under the two contracts?

Under the forward contract, the whole gain or loss is realized at the end of the life of the contract. Under the futures contract, the gain or loss is realized day by day because of the daily settlement procedures. Suppose that investor A is long £1 million in a 90-day forward contract and investor B is long £1 million in 90-day futures contracts. (Because each futures contract is for the purchase or sale of £62,500, investor B must purchase a total of 16 contracts.) Assume that the spot exchange rate in 90 days proves to be 1.8600. Investor A makes a gain of $21,900 on the ninetieth day. Investor B makes the same gain—but spread out over the 90-day period. On some days investor B may realize a loss, whereas on other days he or she makes a gain. However, in total, when losses are netted against gains, there is a gain of $21,900 over the 90-day period. This example is shown in Table 2.7.

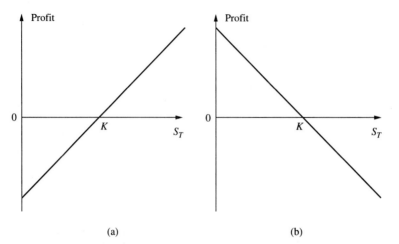

(a)   (b)

FIGURE 2.2 Profit to Speculator from a Forward Contract (a) Long position,
(b) short position; delivery price $= K$, price of asset at maturity $= S_T$.

TABLE 2.7   The Payoffs from Futures and Forward Contracts

From the Trader's Desk

Investor A takes a long position in a 90-day forward contract on £1 million. Forward price is 1.8381.

Investor B takes a long position in 90-day futures contracts on £1 million. Futures price is 1.8381.

At the end of the 90 days, the sterling exchange rate proves to be 1.8600.

Outcome

Investors A and B each make a total gain equal to

$$(1.8600 - 1.8381) \times 1,000,000 = \$21,900$$

Investor A's gain is made entirely on the ninetieth day, whereas investor B's gain is realized day by day over the 90-day period. On some days investor B may realize a loss, whereas on other days he or she will realize a gain.

Summary

In this chapter we have looked at how futures and forward markets operate. In futures markets contracts are traded on an exchange, and it is necessary for the exchange to define carefully the precise nature of what is traded, the procedures that will be followed, and the regulations that will govern the market. Forward contracts are negotiated directly over the telephone by two relatively sophisticated individuals. As a result, there is no need to standardize the product, and an extensive set of rules and procedures is not required.

A very high proportion of the futures contracts that are traded do not lead to the delivery of the underlying asset. They are closed out before the delivery period is reached. However, it is the possibility of final delivery that drives the determination of the futures price. For each futures contract, there is a range of days during which delivery can be made and a well-defined delivery procedure. Some contracts, such as those on stock indices, are settled in cash rather than by delivery of the underlying asset.

The specification of contracts is an important activity for a futures exchange. The two sides to any contract must know what can be delivered, where delivery can take place, and when delivery can take place. They also need to know details on the trading hours, how prices will be quoted, maximum daily price movements, and so on. New contracts must be approved by the Commodity Futures Trading Commission before trading starts.

Margins are an important aspect of futures markets. An investor keeps a margin account with his or her broker. The account is adjusted daily to reflect gains or losses, and from time to time the broker may require the account to be topped up if adverse price movements have taken place. The broker either must be a clearinghouse member or must maintain a margin account with a clearinghouse member. Each clearinghouse member maintains a margin account with the exchange clearinghouse. The balance in the account is adjusted daily to reflect gains and losses on the business for which the clearinghouse member is responsible.

Information on prices in exchange trading is collected in a systematic way and relayed within a matter of seconds to investors throughout the world. Many daily newspapers such as the *Wall Street Journal* carry a summary of the previous day's trading.

To an uninformed observer, the trading pit appears to be a mass of highly excited individuals shouting and signaling to one another. However, the individuals are following well-defined procedures for making and recording trades. There are two main types of traders: locals and commission brokers. Locals are trading on their own account, whereas commission brokers are fulfilling a trade on behalf of someone else.

Forward contracts differ from futures contracts in a number of ways. Forward contracts are private arrangements between two parties, whereas futures contracts are traded on exchanges. There is generally a single delivery date in a forward contract, whereas futures contracts frequently involve a range of such dates. Because they are not traded on exchanges, forward contracts need not be standardized. A forward contract is not usually settled until the end of its life, and most contracts do in fact lead to delivery of the underlying asset or a cash settlement at this time.

In the next few chapters we will look at how forward and futures prices are determined. We will also examine in more detail the ways in which forward and futures contracts can be used for hedging.

Suggestions for Further Reading

Chance, D. *An Introduction to Options and Futures.* Orlando, FL: Dryden Press, 1989.

Chicago Board of Trade. *Commodity Trading Manual.* Chicago, 1989.

Duffie, D. *Futures Markets.* Englewood Cliffs, NJ: Prentice Hall, 1989.

Hicks, J. R. *Value and Capital.* Oxford: Clarendon Press, 1939.

Horn, F. F. *Trading in Commodity Futures.* New York: New York Institute of Finance, 1984.

Keynes, J. M. *A Treatise on Money.* London: Macmillan, 1930.

Kolb, R. *Understanding Futures Markets.* Glenview, IL: Scott, Foresman, 1985.

Schwarz, E. W., J. M. Hill, and T. Schneeweis. *Financial Futures.* Homewood, IL: Richard D. Irwin, 1986.

Teweles, R. J., and F. J. Jones. *The Futures Game.* New York: McGraw-Hill, 1987.

Quiz

1. Distinguish between the terms *open interest* and *trading volume*.
2. What is the difference between a *local* and a *commission broker*?
3. Suppose that you enter into a short futures contract to sell July silver for $5.20 per ounce on the New York Commodity Exchange. The size of the contract is 5,000 ounces. The initial margin is $4,000 and the maintenance margin is $3,000. What change in the futures price will lead to a margin call? What happens if you do not meet the margin call?
4. Suppose that in September 1996 you take a long position in a contract on May 1997 crude oil futures. You close out your position in March 1997. The futures price (per barrel) is $18.30 when you enter into your contract, $20.50 when you close out your position, and $19.10 at the end of December 1996. One contract is for the delivery of 1,000 barrels. What is your total profit? When is it realized? How is it taxed if you are (a) a hedger and (b) a speculator?
5. What does a stop order to sell at $2 mean? When might it be used? What does a limit order to sell at $2 mean? When might it be used?
6. What is the difference between the operation of the margin accounts administered by a clearinghouse and those administered by a broker?
7. What differences exist in the way prices are quoted in the foreign exchange futures market, the foreign exchange spot market, and the foreign exchange forward market?

Questions and Problems

2.1. The party with a short position in a futures contract sometimes has options as to the precise asset that will be delivered, where delivery will take place, when delivery will take place, and so on. Do these options increase or decrease the futures price? Explain your reasoning.

2.2. What are the most important aspects of the design of a new futures contract?

2.3. Explain how margins protect investors against the possibility of default.

2.4. A company enters into a short futures contract to sell 5,000 bushels of wheat for 250 cents per bushel. The initial margin is $3,000 and the maintenance margin is $2,000. What price change would lead to a margin call? Under what circumstances could $1,500 be withdrawn from the margin account?

2.5. An investor enters into two long futures contracts on frozen orange juice. Each contract is for the delivery of 15,000 pounds. The current futures price is 160 cents per pound, the initial margin is $6,000 per contract, and the maintenance margin is $4,500 per contract.

What price change would lead to a margin call? Under what circumstances could $2,000 be withdrawn from the margin account?

2.6. Show that if the futures price of a commodity is greater than the spot price during the delivery period there is an arbitrage opportunity. Does an arbitrage opportunity exist if the futures price is less than the spot price? Explain your answer.

2.7. Explain the difference between a market-if-touched order and a stop order.

2.8. Explain what a stop-limit order to sell at 20.30 with a limit of 20.10 means.

2.9. At the end of one day a clearinghouse member is long 100 contracts, and the settlement price is $50,000 per contract. The original margin is $2,000 per contract. On the following day the member becomes responsible for clearing an additional 20 long contracts, entered into at a price of $51,000 per contract. The settlement price at the end of this day is $50,200. How much does the member have to add to its margin account with the exchange clearinghouse?

2.10. On July 1, 1997 a company enters into a forward contract to buy 10 million Japanese yen on January 1, 1998. On September 1, 1997 it enters into a forward contract to sell 10 million Japanese yen on January 1, 1998. Describe the payoff from this strategy.

2.11. The forward price on the German mark for delivery in 45 days is quoted as 1.8204. The futures price for a contract that will be delivered in 45 days is 0.5479. Explain these two quotes. Which is more favorable for an investor wanting to sell marks?

2.12. Suppose you call your broker and issue instructions to sell one July hogs contract. Describe what happens.

2.13. "Speculation in futures markets is pure gambling. It is not in the public interest to allow speculators to buy seats on a futures exchange." Discuss this viewpoint.

2.14. Identify the contracts with the highest open interest in Table 2.3. Consider each of the following sections separately: grains and oilseeds, livestock and meat, food and fiber, and metals and petroleum.

2.15. What do you think would happen if an exchange started trading a contract in which the quality of the underlying asset was incompletely specified?

2.16. "When a futures contract is traded on the floor of the exchange, it may be the case that the open interest increases by one, stays the same, or decreases by one." Explain this statement.

2.17. "A long forward contract is equivalent to a long position in a call option and a short position in a put option." Explain this statement.

2.18. Suppose that on October 24, 1997 you take a short position in an April 1998 live-cattle futures contract. You close out your position on January 21, 1998. The futures price (per pound) is 61.20 cents when you enter into the contract, 58.30 cents when you close out your position, and 58.80 cents at the end of December 1997. One contract is for the delivery of 40,000 pounds of cattle. What is your total profit? How is it taxed if you are (a) a hedger and (b) a speculator?

CHAPTER **3**

The Determination of Forward and Futures Prices

In this chapter we examine how forward prices and futures prices are related to the price of the underlying asset. Forward contracts are generally easier to analyze than futures contracts because there is no daily settlement—only a single payment at maturity. Consequently, most of the analysis in the first part of the chapter is directed toward determining forward prices rather than futures prices. Key results are provided for forward contracts on

1. Investment assets providing no income
2. Investment assets providing a known cash income
3. Investment assets providing a known dividend yield

It can be shown that the forward price and futures price of an asset are generally very close when the maturities of the two contracts are the same. This means that the key results obtained for forward prices can be assumed to be true for futures prices as well. The second part of the chapter uses the results to calculate futures prices for contracts on stock indices, foreign exchange, gold, and silver.

This chapter draws an important distinction between assets that are held solely for investment by a significant number of investors and those that are held almost exclusively for consumption. Arbitrage arguments enable the forward and futures prices for contracts on investment assets to be determined precisely in terms of spot prices and other observable variables. The same determination is not possible for the forward and futures prices of contracts on consumption assets.

Some Preliminaries

Before we get into the calculation of forward prices, it is useful to review some preliminary material.

CONTINUOUS COMPOUNDING

In this book interest rates will be continuously compounded except where otherwise stated. Readers used to working with interest rates that are compounded annually, semi-annually, or in some other way may find this a little strange at first. However, continuously compounded interest rates are used to such a great extent in pricing options and other complex derivatives that it makes sense to get used to working with them now.

Consider an amount A invested for n years at an interest rate of R per annum. If the rate is compounded once per annum, the terminal value of the investment is

$$A(1 + R)^n$$

If the rate is compounded m times per annum, the terminal value of the investment is

$$A\left(1 + \frac{R}{m}\right)^{mn} \tag{3.1}$$

Suppose $A = \$100$, $R = 10$ percent per annum, and $n = 1$ so that we are considering one year. When we compound once per annum ($m = 1$), this formula shows that the $100 grows to

$$\$100 \times 1.1 = \$110$$

When we compound twice a year ($m = 2$), we earn 5 percent every six months, with the interest being reinvested. As shown by the formula, the $100 grows to

$$\$100 \times 1.05 \times 1.05 = \$110.25$$

When we compound four times a year ($m = 4$), we earn 2.5 percent every three months, with the interest being reinvested. As shown by the formula, the $100 grows to

$$\$100 \times 1.025^4 = \$110.38$$

Table 3.1 shows the effect of increasing the compounding frequency further (i.e., of increasing m). The limit as m tends to infinity is known as *continuous compounding*. With continuous compounding, it can be shown that an amount A invested for n years at rate R grows to

$$Ae^{Rn} \tag{3.2}$$

where $e = 2.71828$. The function e^x is built into most calculators, so the computation of the expression in Equation 3.2 presents no problems. In the example in Table 3.1, $A = 100$, $n = 1$, and $R = 0.1$, so that the value to which A grows with continuous compounding is

$$100e^{0.1} = \$110.52$$

This is (to two decimal places) the same as the value with daily compounding. For most practical purposes, continuous compounding can be thought of as being equivalent to daily compounding. Compounding a sum of money at a continuously compounded rate R for n years involves multiplying it by e^{Rn}. Discounting it at a continuously compounded rate R for n years involves multiplying by e^{-Rn}.

TABLE 3.1	Effect of Compounding Frequency on the Value of $100 at the End of One Year When the Interest Rate is 10 Percent per Annum	
Compounding Frequency		*Value of $100 at End of Year ($)*
Annually ($m = 1$)		110.00
Semiannually ($m = 2$)		110.25
Quarterly ($m = 4$)		110.38
Monthly ($m = 12$)		110.47
Weekly ($m = 52$)		110.51
Daily ($m = 365$)		110.52

Suppose that R_c is a rate of interest with continuous compounding and R_m is the equivalent rate with compounding m times per annum. From the results in Equations 3.1 and 3.2, we must have

$$Ae^{R_c n} = A\left(1 + \frac{R_m}{m}\right)^{mn}$$

or

$$e^{R_c} = \left(1 + \frac{R_m}{m}\right)^{m}$$

This means that

$$R_c = m \ln\left(1 + \frac{R_m}{m}\right) \tag{3.3}$$

and

$$R_m = m(e^{R_c/m} - 1) \tag{3.4}$$

These equations can be used to convert a rate with a compounding frequency of m times per annum to a continuously compounded rate and vice versa. The function ln is the natural logarithm function and is built into most calculators. It is defined so that if $y = \ln x$, then $x = e^y$.

Examples

1. Consider an interest rate that is quoted as 10 percent per annum with semiannual compounding. From Equation 3.3 with $m = 2$ and $R_m = 0.1$, the equivalent rate with continuous compounding is

$$2 \ln\left(1 + \frac{0.1}{2}\right) = 0.09758$$

or 9.758 percent per annum.

2. Suppose that a lender quotes the interest rate on loans as 8 percent per annum with continuous compounding and that interest is actually paid quarterly. From Equation 3.4 with $m = 4$ and $R_c = 0.08$, the equivalent rate with quarterly compounding is

$$4(e^{0.08/4} - 1) = 0.0808$$

or 8.08 percent per annum. This means that on a $1,000 loan, interest payments of $20.20 would be required each quarter.

Finally, we note that a rate expressed with a compounding frequency of m_1 can be converted to a rate with a compounding frequency of m_2. From Equation 3.1

$$A\left(1 + \frac{R_{m_1}}{m_1}\right)^{m_1 n} = A\left(1 + \frac{R_{m_2}}{m_2}\right)^{m_2 n}$$

so that

$$R_{m_2} = \left[\left(1 + \frac{R_{m_1}}{m_1}\right)^{m_1/m_2} - 1\right]m_2$$

SHORT SELLING

Some of the arbitrage strategies presented in this chapter involve short selling. It is appropriate at this stage to explain exactly what is meant by this trading strategy. *Short selling* involves selling securities that are not owned. An investor might contact his or her broker to short 500 IBM shares. The broker will then borrow the shares from another client and sell them in the open market in the usual way. The investor can maintain the short position for as long as desired, provided there are always shares for the broker to borrow. At some stage, however, the investor will close out the position by purchasing 500 IBM shares. These are then replaced in the account of the client from which the shares were borrowed. The investor takes a profit if the stock price has declined and a loss if it has risen. If, at any time while the contract is open, the broker runs out of shares to borrow, the investor is *short-squeezed* and is forced to close out the position immediately even though he or she may not be ready to do so.

Regulators currently allow securities to be sold short only on an *uptick*—that is, when the most recent movement in the price of the security was an increase. A broker requires significant initial margins from clients with short positions. As with futures contracts, if there are adverse movements (i.e., increases) in the price of the security, additional margin may be required. The proceeds of the initial sales of the security belong to the investor and normally form part of the margin account. Some brokers pay interest on margin accounts, and marketable securities such as Treasury bills can be deposited with a broker to meet initial margin requirements. As in the case of futures contracts, the margin does not, therefore, represent a real cost.

An investor with a short position must pay the broker any income such as dividends or interest that would normally be received on the securities that have been shorted. The broker will transfer the payment to the account of the client from whom the securities have been borrowed. Consider the position of an investor who shorts

500 IBM shares in April when the price per share is $50 and closes out his or her position by buying them back in July when the price per share is $30. Suppose that a dividend of $1 per share is paid in May. The investor receives $500 \times \$50 = \$25,000$ in April when the short position is initiated. The dividend leads to a payment of $500 \times \$1 = \$500$ in May. The investor also pays $500 \times \$30 = \$15,000$ when the position is closed out in July. The net gain is therefore

$$\$25,000 - \$500 - \$15,000 = \$9,500$$

This example is summarized in Table 3.2.

ASSUMPTIONS

In this chapter we will assume that the following are all true for some market participants:

1. The market participants are subject to no transactions costs when they trade.
2. The market participants are subject to the same tax rate on all net trading profits.
3. The market participants can borrow money at the same risk-free rate of interest as they can lend money.
4. The market participants take advantage of arbitrage opportunities as they occur.

Note that we do not require these assumptions to be true for all market participants. All that we require is that they be true for a subset of all market participants—for example, large investment banks. The requirement is not unreasonable. As discussed in chapter 1, the fact that certain market participants are prepared to take advantage of arbitrage opportunities as they occur means that in practice arbitrage opportunities disappear almost as soon as they arise. It is reasonable, therefore, to assume for the purposes of our analyses that there are no arbitrage opportunities available to market participants.

THE REPO RATE

The relevant risk-free rate of interest for many arbitrageurs operating in the futures market is known as the *repo rate*. In a *repo* or *repurchase agreement,* the owner of secu-

---

TABLE 3.2   Example of a Short Sale

From the Trader's Desk
   An investor shorts 500 IBM shares in April when the price is $50 and buys them back (to close out the position) in July when the price is $30. A dividend of $1 per share is paid in May.

The Profit
   The investor receives $500 \times \$50$ in April and must pay $500 \times \$1$ in May when the dividend is declared. The cost of closing out the position is $500 \times \$30$. The net gain is therefore

$$(500 \times \$50) - (500 \times \$1) - (500 \times \$30) = \$9,500$$

rities agrees to sell them to a counterparty and buy them back at a slightly higher price later. The counterparty is providing a loan. The difference between the price at which the securities are sold and the price at which they are repurchased is the interest earned by the counterparty. If structured carefully, the loan involves very little credit risk. If the borrowing company does not keep to its side of the agreement, the lender simply keeps the securities. If the lending company does not keep to its side of the agreement, the borrowing company keeps the cash.

The repo rate is only slightly higher than the Treasury bill rate. The most common type of repo is an *overnight repo,* in which the agreement is renegotiated each day. However, longer-term arrangements, known as *term repos,* are sometimes used.

NOTATION

The following notation will be used throughout this chapter:

T: time until delivery date in a forward contract (in years)

S: price of the asset underlying the forward contract today

K: delivery price in the forward contract

f: value of a long position in the forward contract today

F: forward price today

r: risk-free rate of interest per annum today, with continuous compounding, for an investment maturing at the delivery date (i.e., in T years)

It is important to realize that the forward price, F, is quite different from the value of the forward contract, f. As explained in chapter 2, the forward price at any given time is the delivery price that would make the contract have a zero value. When a contract is initiated, the delivery price is set equal to the forward price so that $F = K$ and $f = 0$. As time passes, both f and F change. The analysis and the examples in the next few sections should make clear the distinction between the two variables.

Forward Prices for an Investment Asset That Provides No Income

The easiest forward contract to value is one written on an investment asset that provides the holder with no income. Nondividend-paying stocks and discount bonds (i.e., bonds providing no coupons) are examples of such investment assets.[1]

AN EXAMPLE

Consider a long forward contract to purchase a nondividend-paying stock in three months. Assume the current stock price is $40 and the three-month risk-free interest rate is 5 percent per annum. We consider strategies open to an arbitrageur in two extreme situations.

---

[1]Some of the contracts mentioned in the first half of this chapter (e.g., forward contracts on individual stocks) do not normally arise in practice. However, they form useful examples for developing our ideas.

TABLE 3.3 Arbitrage Opportunity When Forward Price of a Nondividend-paying Stock Is Too High

From the Trader's Desk

The forward price of a stock for a contract with delivery date in three months is $43. The three-month risk-free interest rate is 5 percent per annum, and the current stock price is $40. No dividends are expected.

Opportunity

The forward price is too high relative to the stock price. An arbitrageur can

1. Borrow $40 to buy one share spot
2. Enter into a forward contract to sell one share in three months

At the end of three months, the arbitrageur delivers the share and receives $43. The sum of money required to pay off the loan is $40e^{0.05 \times 3/12} = \$40.50$. The arbitrageur therefore makes a profit at the end of the three-month period of

$$\$43 - \$40.50 = \$2.50$$

Suppose first that the forward price is relatively high at $43. An arbitrageur can borrow $40 at the risk-free interest rate of 5 percent per annum, buy one share, and short a forward contract to sell one share in three months. At the end of the three months, the arbitrageur delivers the share and receives $43. The sum of money required to pay off the loan is

$$40e^{0.05 \times 3/12} = \$40.50$$

By following this strategy, the arbitrageur locks in a profit of $43.00 − $40.50 = $2.50 at the end of the three-month period. The strategy is summarized in Table 3.3.

Suppose next that the forward price is relatively low at $39. An arbitrageur can short one share, invest the proceeds of the short sale at 5 percent per annum for three months, and take a long position in a three-month forward contract. The proceeds of the short sale grow to

$$40e^{0.05 \times 3/12}$$

or $40.50 in three months. At the end of the three months, the arbitrageur pays $39, takes delivery of the share under the terms of the forward contract, and uses it to close out the short position. A net gain of

$$\$40.50 - \$39.00 = \$1.50$$

is therefore made at the end of the three months. This trading strategy is summarized in Table 3.4.

Under what circumstances do arbitrage opportunities such as those in Tables 3.3 and 3.4 not exist? The arbitrage in Table 3.3 works when the forward price is greater than $40.50. The arbitrage in Table 3.4 works when the forward price is less than $40.50. We deduce that for there to be no arbitrage the forward price must be exactly $40.50.

TABLE 3.4   Arbitrage Opportunity When Forward Price of a Nondividend-paying Stock Is Too Low

From the Trader's Desk

The forward price of a stock for a contract with a delivery date in three months is $39. The three-month risk-free interest rate is 5 percent per annum and the current stock price is $40. No dividends are expected.

Opportunity

The forward price is too low relative to the stock price. An arbitrageur can

1. Short one share spot, investing the proceeds of the short sale at 5 percent per annum for three months
2. Take a long position in a three-month forward contract on one share

The proceeds of the short sale (i.e., $40) grow to $40e^{0.05 \times 3/12} = \$40.50$. At the end of the three months, the arbitrageur pays $39 and takes delivery of the share under the terms of the forward contract. The share is used to close out the short position. The arbitrageur therefore makes a net profit at the end of the three-month period of

$$\$40.50 - \$39.00 = \$1.50$$

A GENERALIZATION

To generalize this example, we consider a forward contract on an investment asset with price S that provides no income. Using our notation, T is the time to maturity, r is the risk-free rate, and F is the forward price. We imagine an investor adopting the following strategy:

1. Buy one unit of the asset spot.
2. Short one forward contract.

The forward contract has zero value at the time it is first entered into. The up-front cost of the strategy is therefore S. The forward contract requires the investment asset to be exchanged for the forward price at time T. The asset provides no income. By following the strategy, the investor is simply exchanging a payment of S today for a riskless cash inflow equal to the forward price at time T. It follows that the forward price, F, must be the value to which S would grow if invested at the risk-free interest rate for a time T. This means that

$$F = Se^{rT} \tag{3.5}$$

In the example considered, $S = 40$, $r = 0.05$, and $T = 0.25$ so that

$$F = 40e^{0.05 \times 0.25} = \$40.50$$

which is in agreement with our earlier calculations.

Example

Consider a four-month forward contract to buy a discount bond that will mature one year from today. The current price of the bond is $930. (Since the bond will have eight months to go when the forward contract matures, we can regard the contract as on an eight-month discount bond.) We assume that the four-month risk-free rate of interest (continuously compounded) is 6 percent per annum. Since discount bonds provide no income, we can use Equation 3.5 with $T = 4/12$, $r = 0.06$, and $S = 930$. The forward price, F, is given by

$$F = 930e^{0.06 \times 4/12} = \$948.79$$

This would be the delivery price in a contract negotiated today.

Forward Prices for an Investment Asset That Provides a Known Cash Income

In this section we consider a forward contract on an investment asset that will provide a perfectly predictable cash income to the holder. Examples are stocks paying known dividends and coupon-bearing bonds. We adopt the same approach as in the previous section. We first look at a numerical example and then review the formal arguments.

AN EXAMPLE

Consider a long forward contract to purchase a coupon-bearing bond whose current price is $900. We suppose that the forward contract matures in one year and the bond matures in five years, so that the forward contract is a contract to purchase a four-year bond in one year. We also suppose that coupon payments of $40 are expected after six months and twelve months, with the second coupon payment being immediately prior to the delivery date in the forward contract. We assume the six-month and one-year risk-free interest rates (continuously compounded) are 9 percent per annum and 10 percent per annum, respectively.

Suppose first that the forward price is relatively high at $930. An arbitrageur can borrow $900 to buy the bond and short a forward contract. The first coupon payment has a present value of $40e^{-0.09 \times 0.5} = \$38.24$. Of the $900, $38.24 is therefore borrowed at 9 percent per annum for six months so that it can be repaid with the first coupon payment. The remaining $861.76 is borrowed at 10 percent per annum for one year. The amount owing at the end of the year is $861.76e^{0.1 \times 1} = \$952.39$. The second coupon provides $40 toward this amount, and $930 is received for the bond under the terms of the forward contract. The arbitrageur therefore makes a net profit of

$$\$40 + \$930 - \$952.39 = \$17.61$$

This strategy is summarized in Table 3.5.

Suppose next that the forward price is relatively low at $905. An investor who holds the bond can sell it and enter into a long forward contract.[2] Of the $900 realized

---

[2]The argument here shows that, providing the asset underlying the forward contract is held by individuals solely for investment purposes, we do not need short selling for our no-arbitrage arguments to work. This point will be explored further later in this chapter.

TABLE 3.5	Arbitrage Opportunity When Forward Price of a Coupon-bearing Bond Is Too High

From the Trader's Desk

The forward price of a bond for a contract with a delivery date in one year is $930. The current spot price is $900. Coupon payments of $40 are expected in six months and one year. The six-month and one-year risk-free interest rates are 9 percent per annum and 10 percent per annum, respectively.

Opportunity

The forward price is too high. An arbitrageur can

1. Borrow $900 to buy one bond spot
2. Short a forward contract on one bond

The $900 loan is made up of $38.24 borrowed at 9 percent per annum for six months and $861.76 borrowed at 10 percent per annum for one year. The first coupon payment of $40 is exactly sufficient to repay interest and principal on the $38.24. At the end of one year, the second coupon of $40 is received, $930 is received for the bond under the terms of the forward contract, and $952.39 is required to pay principal and interest on the $861.76. The net profit is therefore

$$\$40.00 + \$930.00 - \$952.39 = \$17.61$$

---

from selling the bond, $38.24 is invested for six months at 9 percent per annum so that it grows into an amount sufficient to equal the coupon that would have been paid on the bond. The remaining $861.76 is invested for twelve months at 10 percent per annum and grows to $952.39. Of this sum, $40 is used to replace the coupon that would have been received on the bond, and $905 is paid under the terms of the forward contract to replace the bond in the investor's portfolio. The investor therefore gains

$$\$952.39 - \$40.00 - \$905.00 = \$7.39$$

relative to the situation the investor would have been in by keeping the bond. This strategy is summarized in Table 3.6.

If F is the forward price, the strategy in Table 3.5 produces a profit when $F > 912.39$, whereas the strategy in Table 3.6 produces a profit when $F < 912.39$. It follows that if there are no arbitrage opportunities, the forward price must be $912.39.

A GENERALIZATION

To generalize from this example, we consider a forward contract on an investment asset that provides income with a present value of I. Consider an investor adopting the following strategy:

1. Buy the asset spot.
2. Enter into a short forward contract.

The forward contract has zero value at the time it is entered into, so that the up-front cost of the strategy is the spot price of the asset, S. The strategy provides the investor

---

TABLE 3.6 Opportunity When the Forward Price of a Coupon-bearing Bond Is Too Low

From the Trader's Desk

The forward price of a bond for a contract with delivery date in one year is $905. The current spot price is $900. Coupon payments of $40 are expected in six months and one year. The six-month and one-year risk-free interest rates are 9 percent per annum and 10 percent per annum, respectively.

Opportunity

The futures price is too low. An investor who holds the bond can

1. Sell one bond

2. Enter into a long forward contract to repurchase the bond in one year

Of the $900 realized from selling the bond, $38.24 is invested for six months at 9 percent per annum and $861.76 is invested for one year at 10 percent per annum. This strategy produces a cash flow of $40 at the six-month point and a cash flow of $952.39 at the one-year point. The $40 replaces the coupon that would have been received on the bond at the six-month point. Of the $952.39, $40 replaces the coupon that would have been received on the bond at the one-year point. Under the terms of the forward contract, the bond is repurchased for $905. The strategy of selling the bond spot and buying it back forward is therefore

$$\$952.39 - \$40.00 - \$905.00 = \$7.39$$

more profitable than simply holding the bond for the year.

---

with income that has a present value of I and a cash flow at T equal to the forward price of the bond, F. Equating the initial outflow with the present value of the cash inflows yields

$$S = I + Fe^{-rT}$$

or

$$\boxed{F = (S - I)e^{rT}}$$ (3.6)

In the example considered, $S = 900.00$, $I = 40e^{-0.09 \times 0.5} + 40e^{-0.10 \times 1} = 74.433$, $r = 0.1$, and $T = 1$ so that

$$F = (900.00 - 74.433)e^{0.1 \times 1} = \$912.39$$

This is in agreement with our earlier calculation.

Example

Consider a 10-month forward contract on a stock with a price of $50. We assume that the risk-free rate of interest (continuously compounded) is 8 percent per annum for all maturities. We also assume that dividends of $0.75 per share are expected after three months, six months, and nine months. The present value of the dividends, I, is given by

$$I = 0.75e^{-0.08 \times 3/12} + 0.75e^{-0.08 \times 6/12} + 0.75e^{-0.08 \times 9/12} = 2.162$$

The variable T is 10 months so that the forward price, F, from Equation 3.6 is given by

$$F = (50 - 2.162)e^{0.08 \times 10/12} = \$51.14$$

If the forward price were less than this, an arbitrageur would short the stock spot and buy forward contracts. If the forward price were greater than this, an arbitrageur would short forward contracts and buy the stock spot.

Forward Prices for an Investment Asset That Provides a Known Dividend Yield

As will be explained in later sections, both currencies and stock indices can be regarded as investment assets that provide known dividend yields. This section provides a general analysis of forward contracts on such investment assets.

A known dividend yield means that the income when expressed as a percentage of the asset price is known. We will assume that the dividend yield is paid continuously at an annual rate q. To illustrate what this means, suppose that $q = 0.05$ so that the dividend yield is 5 percent per annum. When the asset price is $10, dividends in the next small interval of time are paid at the rate of 50 cents per annum; when the asset price is $100, dividends in the next small interval of time are paid at the rate of $5 per annum; and so on. In practice, dividends are not paid continuously. In some situations, however, the continuous dividend yield assumption is a good approximation to reality. Consider an investor adopting the following strategy:

1. Buy spot e^{-qT} of the asset with income from the security being reinvested in the asset.
2. Short a forward contract.

The holding of the asset grows at rate q so that $e^{-qT} \times e^{qT}$, or exactly one unit of the asset, is held at time T.[3] Under the terms of the forward contract, the asset is sold for F at time T. The strategy therefore leads to an initial outflow of Se^{-qT} and a final inflow of F. The present value of the inflow must equal the outflow. Hence

$$Se^{-qT} = Fe^{-rT}$$

or

$$F = Se^{(r-q)T} \tag{3.7}$$

If $F < Se^{(r-q)T}$, an arbitrageur can enter into a long forward contract and short the stock to lock in a riskless profit. If $F > Se^{(r-q)T}$, an arbitrageur can buy the stock and enter into a short forward contract to lock in a riskless profit.

---

[3]These arguments make the unrealistic assumption that one share is divisible. However, we can magnify the holdings in the two portfolios by 100, 10,000, or 1,000,000 and the basic argument is still the same. To illustrate the fact that the holding grows at rate q when dividends are reinvested, suppose that the stock price is $100, the dividend yield, q, is 5 percent per annum, and a short time interval of 0.02 years is considered. If we hold 10,000 shares, the dividend received in the short time interval is $10,000 \times \$100 \times 0.05 \times 0.02 = \$1,000$. As a result, 10 new shares can be purchased, so that the holding grows by 0.1 percent during the time period. This corresponds to the assumed growth rate of 5 percent per annum.

If the dividend yield varies during the life of the forward contract but is a known function of time, it can be shown that Equation 3.7 is still correct, with q equal to the average dividend yield rate during the life of the forward contract.

Example

Consider a six-month forward contract on a security that is expected to provide a continuous dividend yield of 4 percent per annum. The risk-free rate of interest (with continuous compounding) is 10 percent per annum. The stock price is $25. In this case $S = 25, r = 0.10, T = 0.5, q = 0.04$. From Equation 3.7, the forward price F is given by

$$F = 25e^{(0.10 - 0.04) \times 0.5} = \$25.76$$

Valuing Forward Contracts

The value of a forward contract at the time it is first entered into is zero. At a later stage it may prove to have a positive or negative value. There is a general result, applicable to all forward contracts, that gives the value of a long forward contract, f, in terms of the originally negotiated delivery price, K, and the current forward price, F. This is

$$f = (F - K)e^{-rT} \tag{3.8}$$

To see why Equation 3.8 is correct, we compare a long forward contract that has a delivery price of F with an otherwise identical long forward contract that has a delivery price of K. The difference between the two is only in the amount that will be paid for the underlying asset at time T. Under the first contract this amount is F; under the second contract it is K. A cash outflow difference of $F - K$ at time T translates to a difference of $(F - K)e^{-rT}$ today. The contract with a delivery price F is therefore less valuable than the contract with delivery price K by an amount $(F - K)e^{-rT}$. The value of the contract that has a delivery price of F is by definition zero. It follows that the value of the contract with a delivery price of K is $(F - K)e^{-rT}$. This proves Equation 3.8.

Using Equation 3.8 in conjunction with 3.5 gives the following expression for the value of a forward contract on an investment asset that provides no income

$$f = S - Ke^{-rT} \tag{3.9}$$

Similarly, using Equation 3.8 in conjunction with 3.6 gives the following expression for the value of a forward contract on an investment asset that provides a known income with present value I

$$f = S - I - Ke^{-rT} \tag{3.10}$$

Finally, using Equation 3.8 in conjunction with 3.7 gives the following expression for the value of a forward contract on an investment asset that provides a known dividend yield at rate q

$$f = Se^{-qT} - Ke^{-rT} \tag{3.11}$$

Example

Consider a six-month long forward contract on a nondividend-paying stock. The risk-free rate of interest (with continuous compounding) is 10 percent per annum, the stock price is $25, and the delivery price is $24. In this case $S = 25, r = 0.10$, $T = 0.5$, and $K = 24$. From Equation 3.5 the forward price, F, is given by

$$F = 25e^{0.1 \times 0.5} = \$26.28$$

From Equation 3.8, the value of the forward contract is

$$f = (26.28 - 24)e^{-0.1 \times 0.5} = \$2.17$$

Alternatively, Equation 3.9 yields

$$f = 25 - 24e^{-0.1 \times 0.5} = \$2.17$$

Are Forward Prices and Futures Prices Equal?

Appendix 3A provides an arbitrage argument to show that when the risk-free interest rate is constant and the same for all maturities, the forward price for a contract with a certain delivery date is the same as the futures price for a contract with the same delivery date. The argument in Appendix 3A can be extended to cover situations where the interest rate is a known function of time.

When interest rates vary unpredictably (as they do in the real world), forward and futures prices are in theory no longer the same. The proof of the relationship between the two is beyond the scope of this book. However, we can get a sense of the nature of the relationship by considering the situation where the price of the underlying asset, S, is strongly positively correlated with interest rates. When S increases, an investor who holds a long futures position makes an immediate gain because of the daily settlement procedure. The positive correlation indicates that it is likely that interest rates have also increased. The gain will therefore tend to be invested at a higher than average rate of interest. Similarly, when S decreases, the investor will incur an immediate loss. This loss will tend to be financed at a lower than average rate of interest. An investor holding a forward contract rather than a futures contract is not affected in this way by interest-rate movements. It follows that a long futures contract will be more attractive than a similar long forward contract. Hence, when S is strongly positively correlated with interest rates, futures prices will tend to be higher than forward prices. When S is strongly negatively correlated with interest rates, a similar argument shows that forward prices will tend to be higher than futures prices.

The theoretical differences between forward and futures prices for contracts that last only a few months are in most circumstances sufficiently small to be ignored. In practice, there are a number of factors not reflected in theoretical models that may cause forward and futures prices to be different. These include taxes, transactions costs, and the treatment of margins. The risk that the counterparty will default is generally less in the case of a futures contract because of the role of the exchange clearinghouse. Also, in some instances, futures contracts are more liquid and easier to trade than forward contracts. Despite all these points, it is reasonable for most purposes to assume that forward and futures prices are the same. This is the assumption that will be made throughout this book. The symbol F will be used to represent both the futures price and the forward price of an asset.

As the life of a futures contract increases, the differences between forward and futures contracts are liable to become significant. It is then dangerous to assume that forward and futures prices are perfect substitutes for each other. This point is particularly relevant to Eurodollar futures contracts that have maturities as long as 10 years.

EMPIRICAL RESEARCH

Some empirical research that has been carried out comparing forward and futures contracts is listed at the end of this chapter. Cornell and Reinganum studied forward and futures prices on the British pound, Canadian dollar, German mark, Japanese yen, and Swiss franc between 1974 and 1979. They found very few statistically significant differences between the two sets of prices. Their results were confirmed by Park and Chen, who as part of their study looked at the British pound, German mark, Japanese yen, and Swiss franc between 1977 and 1981.

French studied copper and silver during the period 1968 to 1980. The results for silver show that the futures price and the forward price are significantly different (at the 5 percent confidence level), with the futures price generally above the forward price. The results for copper are less clear-cut. Park and Chen looked at gold, silver, silver coin, platinum, copper, and plywood between 1977 and 1981. Their results are similar to those of French for silver. The forward and futures prices are significantly different, with the futures price above the forward price. Rendleman and Carabini studied the Treasury bill market between 1976 and 1978. They also found statistically significant differences between futures and forward prices. In all these studies, it seems likely that the differences observed are due to the factors mentioned in the previous section (taxes, transactions costs, and so on).

Stock Index Futures

A *stock index* tracks the changes in the value of a hypothetical portfolio of stocks. The weight of a stock in the portfolio equals the proportion of the portfolio invested in the stock. The percentage increase in the value of a stock index over a small interval of time is usually defined so that it is equal to the percentage increase in the total value of the stocks comprising the portfolio at that time. A stock index is not usually adjusted for cash dividends. In other words, any cash dividends received on the portfolio are ignored when percentage changes in most indices are being calculated.

It is worth noting that if the hypothetical portfolio of stocks remains fixed, the weights assigned to individual stocks in the portfolio do not remain fixed. If the price of one particular stock in the portfolio rises more sharply than others, more weight is automatically given to that stock. Choosing weights proportional to stock prices is equivalent to keeping the underlying portfolio the same. Choosing weights proportional to market capitalization (stock price × number of shares outstanding) is popular. It leads to automatic adjustments in the underlying portfolio for stock splits, stock dividends, and new equity issues.

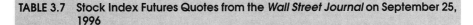

TABLE 3.7 Stock Index Futures Quotes from the *Wall Street Journal* on September 25, 1996

```
                          INDEX
S&P 500 INDEX (CME) $500 times index                              Oct  2087.0 2090.0 2083.0 2091.0 +  14.5 2103.0 2020.0   8,792
                                                    Open          Dec  2098.0 2101.5 2091.5 2102.0 +  14.5 2168.0 1973.0  14,372
      Open High  Low Settle  Chg  High  Low Interest             Mr97 2118.0 2118.0 2117.0 2119.0 +  14.5 2183.5 1921.0   5,045
Dec  692.35 697.50 689.20 692.05 −  .35 697.50 612.70 173,288     Sept  ....   ....  ....  2099.0 +  14.5 2176.0 1980.0   5,420
Mr97 697.40 703.50 695.80 698.40 −  .40 703.50 622.55   3,817     Mr98  ....   ....  ....  2140.5 +  14.5 2221.0 2079.0   2,475
June 702.70 709.80 702.50 704.85 −  .45 709.80 629.05   1,770       Est vol 22,834; vol Mn 16,916; open int 58,343, −420.
Sep    ....   ....  ....  711.35 −  .80   ....  ....      155     FT-SE 100 INDEX (LIFFE)-£25 per index point
  Est vol 71,777; vol Mn 66,734; open int 179,030, −52,042.       Dec  3956.0 3969.0 3939.0 3945.0 +   2.0 4026.0 3452.5 56,465
  Indx prelim High 690.88; Low 683.54; Close 685.61−.87           Mr97   ....   ....  ....  3957.0 +   4.0 4026.0 3452.5    360
S&P MIDCAP 400 (CME) $500 times index                              Est vol 10,748; vol Mn 9,382; open int 56,825, −196.
Dec  240.25 242.45 240.05 242.05 + 1.40 248.35 213.05   9,098     DAX-30 GERMAN STOCK INDEX (DTB)
  Est vol 633; vol Mn 1,005; open int 9,206, −4,390.                DM 100 times index
  The index: High 240.36; Low 238.58; Close 239.78+1.04          Dec  2650.0 2663.0 2648.0 2661.0 +   .72 2667.0 2155.5 71,668
NIKKEI 225 STOCK AVERAGE (CME)-$5 times index                    Mr97 2668.0 2680.0 2668.0 2680.0 +   .85 2682.5 2295.5  3,479
Dec  21200. 21245. 21130.  21190. +    15 22870. 19430.  16,385    Est vol 12,701; vol Mn 12,592; open int 75,226, +638.
  Est vol 860; vol Mn 367; open int 16,395, +119.                  The index: High 2639.31; Low 2633.18; Close 2638.45 +.43
  The  index:  High  21247.75;  Low  21040.03;  Close            ALL ORDINARIES SHARE PRICE INDEX (SFE)
21171.99+59.75                                                      A$25 times index
GSCI (CME)-$250 times nearby index                               Sept 2219.0 2232.0 2212.0 2228.0 +  10.0 2391.0 2086.0 72,268
Oct  201.00 203.00 200.70 203.00 + 2.90 206.50 188.00  15,318    Dec  2233.0 2245.0 2227.0 2243.0 +  11.0 2407.0 2110.0 38,425
  Est vol 276; vol Mn 64; open int 15,349, −16.                   Mr97   ....   ....  2260.0 +  10.0 2385.0  2135.     2,171
  The index: High 203.21; Low 200.03; Close 202.97+2.95          June   ....   ....  2272.0 +  10.0 2365.0 2177.0    2,491
CAC-40 STOCK INDEX (MATIF)-FFr 200 per index pt.                   Est vol 16,035; vol Mn 9,611; open int 115,415, −984.
Sept 2082.5 2087.0 2076.0 2086.0 +  14.5 2146.5 1196.0  22,072    The index: High 2229.3; Low 2213.4; Close 2228.7, +9.5
```

STOCK INDICES

Table 3.7 shows futures prices for contracts on a number of different stock indices as they were reported in the *Wall Street Journal* of September 25, 1996. The prices refer to the close of trading on September 24, 1996. The *Standard & Poor's 500 (S&P 500) Index* is based on a portfolio of 500 different stocks: 400 industrials, 40 utilities, 20 transportation companies, and 40 financial institutions. The weights of the stocks in the portfolio at any given time reflect the stock's total market capitalization. This index accounts for 80 percent of the market capitalization of all the stocks listed on the New York Stock Exchange. One futures contract (traded on the Chicago Mercantile Exchange) is on 500 times the index. The *Standard & Poor's MidCap 400 Index* is similar to the S&P 500, but based on a portfolio of 400 stocks that have somewhat lower market capitalizations.

The *Nikkei 225 Stock Average* is based on a portfolio of 225 of the largest stocks trading on the Tokyo Stock Exchange. Stocks are weighted according to their prices. One futures contract (traded on the Chicago Mercantile Exchange) is on five times the index. The *CAC-40 Index* is based on 40 stocks trading in France. The *DAX-30* is based on 30 stocks trading in Germany. The *FT-SE 100 Index* is based on a portfolio of 100 major UK shares listed on the London Stock Exchange. The *All Ordinaries Share Price Index* is a broadly based index reflecting the value of a portfolio of Australian stocks.

Other stock indices that sometimes underlie derivatives in the United States are the *New York Stock Exchange (NYSE) Composite Index* and the *Major Market Index (MMI)*. The NYSE Composite Index is based on a portfolio of all the stocks listed on the New York Stock Exchange with weights reflecting market capitalizations. The MMI is based on a portfolio of 20 blue-chip stocks listed on the New York Stock Exchange with weights reflecting stock prices. The latter is very closely correlated to the widely quoted *Dow Jones Industrial Average,* which is also based on relatively few stocks.

In the GSCI futures contract shown in Table 3.7, the underlying asset is the *Goldman Sachs Commodity Index.* This is not a stock index. It is a broadly based index of commodity prices. All the major commodity groups, such as energy, livestock, grains and oilseeds, food and fiber, and metals, are represented in the GSCI. Studies by Goldman Sachs have shown that the GSCI is negatively related to the S&P 500 Index, with the correlation being in the range -0.30 to -0.40.

As mentioned in chapter 2, futures contracts on stock indices are settled in cash, not by delivery of the underlying asset. All contracts are marked to market on the last trading day, and the positions are then deemed to be closed. For most contracts the settlement price on the last trading day is set at the closing value of the index on that day. However, as discussed in chapter 2, for the S&P 500 the price is set as the value of the index based on opening prices the next day. For the S&P 500, the last trading day is the Thursday before the third Friday of the delivery month.

FUTURES PRICES OF STOCK INDICES

A stock index can be regarded as the price of an investment asset that pays dividends. The investment asset is the portfolio of stocks underlying the index, and the dividends paid by the investment asset are the dividends that would be received by the holder of this portfolio. To a reasonable approximation, the stocks underlying the index can be assumed to provide a continuous dividend yield. If q is the dividend yield rate, Equation 3.7 gives the futures price, F, as

$$F = Se^{(r-q)T} \tag{3.12}$$

Example

Consider a three-month futures contract on the S&P 500. Suppose that the stocks underlying the index provide a dividend yield of 3 percent per annum, that the current value of the index is 400, and that the continuously compounded risk-free interest rate is 8 percent per annum. In this case, $r = 0.08$, $S = 400$, $T = 0.25$, and $q = 0.03$. Hence, the futures price, F, is given by

$$F = 400e^{(0.08-0.03) \times 0.25} = \$405.03$$

In practice, the dividend yield on the portfolio underlying an index varies week by week throughout the year. For example, a large proportion of the dividends on the NYSE stocks are paid in the first week of February, May, August, and November each year. The chosen value of q should represent the average annualized dividend yield during the life of the contract. The dividends used for estimating q should be those for which the ex-dividend date is during the life of the futures contract. Looking at Table 3.7, we see that the futures prices for the S&P 500 Index appear to be increasing with maturity at about 3.7 percent per annum. This corresponds to the situation where the risk-free interest rate exceeds the dividend yield by about 3.7 percent per annum.

Any analyst who is unhappy working in terms of dividend yields can estimate the dollar amount of dividends that will be paid by the portfolio underlying the index and the timing of those dividends. The index can then be considered to be an investment asset providing known income, and the result in Equation 3.6 can be used to calculate the futures price.

INDEX ARBITRAGE

If $F > Se^{(r-q)T}$, profits can be made by buying spot (i.e., for immediate delivery) the stocks underlying the index and shorting futures contracts. If $F < Se^{(r-q)T}$, profits can be made by doing the reverse—that is, shorting or selling the stocks underlying the index and taking a long position in futures contracts. These strategies are known as *index arbitrage*. When $F < Se^{(r-q)T}$, index arbitrage is often done by a pension fund that owns an indexed portfolio of stocks. When $F > Se^{(r-q)T}$, it is often done by a corporation holding short-term money market investments. For indices involving many stocks, index arbitrage is sometimes accomplished by trading a relatively small representative sample of stocks whose movements closely mirror those of the index. Often index arbitrage is implemented through *program trading,* with a computer system used to generate the trades.

OCTOBER 19, 1987

In normal market conditions, F is very close to $Se^{(r-q)T}$. However, it is interesting to note what happened on October 19, 1987, when the market fell by over 20 percent and the 604 million shares traded on the New York Stock Exchange easily exceeded all previous records. For most of the day, futures prices were at a significant discount to the underlying index. For example, at the close of trading the S&P 500 Index was at 225.06 (down 57.88 on the day), while the futures price for December delivery on the S&P 500 was 201.50 (down 80.75 on the day). This was largely because the delays in processing orders made index arbitraging too risky. On the next day, October 20, 1987, the New York Stock Exchange placed temporary restrictions on the way in which program trading could be done. The result was that the breakdown of the traditional linkage between stock indices and stock index futures continued. At one point the futures price for the December contract was 18 percent less than the S&P 500 Index.

THE NIKKEI FUTURES CONTRACT

Equation 3.12 does not apply to the futures contract on the Nikkei 225. The reason is quite subtle. Define S_F as the value of the Nikkei 225 Index. This is the value of a portfolio measured in yen. The variable underlying the CME futures contract on the Nikkei 225 has a *dollar value* of $5S_F$. In other words, the futures contract takes a variable which is measured in yen and treats it as though it were dollars. We cannot invest in a portfolio whose value will always be $5S_F$ dollars. The best we can do is to invest in one that is always worth $5S_F$ yen or in one that is always worth $5QS_F$ dollars, where Q is the dollar value of one yen. The arbitrage arguments that have been used in this chapter require the spot price underlying the futures price to be the price of something that can be traded by investors. The arguments are not therefore exactly true for the Nikkei 225 contract.

Forward and Futures Contracts on Currencies

We now move on to consider forward and futures contracts on foreign currencies. The variable S is the current spot price in dollars of one unit of the foreign currency. A foreign currency has the property that the holder of the currency can earn interest at the risk-free interest rate prevailing in the foreign country. (For example, the holder can invest the currency in a foreign-denominated bond.) We define r_f as the value of this foreign risk-free interest rate with continuous compounding.

Consider an investor adopting the following strategy:

1. Buy spot $e^{-r_f T}$ of the foreign currency.

2. Short a forward contract on one unit of the foreign currency.

The holding in the foreign currency grows to one unit at time T because of the interest earned. Under the terms of the forward contract, the holding is exchanged for F at time T. The strategy therefore leads to an initial outflow of $Se^{-r_f T}$ and a final inflow of F. The present value of the inflow must equal the outflow. Hence

$$Se^{-r_f T} = Fe^{-rT}$$

or

$$F = Se^{(r - r_f)T} \tag{3.13}$$

This is the well-known interest-rate parity relationship from the field of international finance. From the discussion earlier in this chapter, F is to a reasonable approximation also the futures price.

Note that Equation 3.13 is identical to Equation 3.7 with q replaced by r_f. A foreign currency is in essence an investment asset paying a known dividend yield. The "dividend yield" is the risk-free rate of interest in the foreign currency. To see why this is so, note that interest earned on a foreign currency holding is denominated in the foreign currency. Its value when measured in the domestic currency is therefore proportional to the value of the foreign currency.

Table 3.8 shows futures prices on September 24, 1996 for contracts trading on the Japanese yen, German mark, Canadian dollar, British pound, Swiss franc, Australian dollar, and Mexican peso in the International Monetary Market of the Chicago Mercantile Exchange. In the case of the Japanese yen, prices are expressed as the number of cents per unit of foreign currency. In the case of the other currencies, prices are expressed as the number of U.S. dollars per unit of foreign currency. As mentioned in chapter 2, this can be confusing because spot and forward rates on most currencies are quoted the other way around—that is, as the number of units of the foreign currency per U.S. dollar. A forward quote on the Canadian dollar of 1.2000 would become a futures quote of 0.8333.

When the foreign interest rate is greater than the domestic interest rate ($r_f > r$), Equation 3.13 shows that F is always less than S and that F decreases as the maturity of the contract, T, increases. Similarly, when the domestic interest rate is greater than the foreign interest rate ($r > r_f$), Equation 3.13 shows that F is always greater than S and that F increases as T increases. On September 24, 1996 interest rates in Japan, Ger-

TABLE 3.8 Foreign Exchange Futures Quotes from the *Wall Street Journal* on September 25, 1996

```
                           CURRENCY
                                      Lifetime       Open
           Open  High  Low Settle Change High  Low  Interest
JAPAN YEN (CME)-12.5 million yen; $ per yen (.00)
Dec    .9207 .9270 .9200 .9267 + .0058 1.0500 .9156 69,664
Mr97   .9345 .9392 .9342 .9393 + .0058 1.0045 .9285  1,899
June   ....  ....  .... .9519 + .0058  .9790 .9415    197
   Est vol 18,393; vol Mn 5,381; open Int 71,778, -386.
DEUTSCHEMARK (CME)-125,000 marks; $ per mark
Dec    .6653 .6701 .6640 .6698 + .0047 .7070 .6537 60,644
Mr97   .6690 .6740 .6687 .6743 + .0046 .6937 .6633  1,184
June   ....  ....  .... .6788 + .0044 .6947 .6690  2,112
   Est vol 17,240; vol Mn 11,422; open Int 63,940, +736.
CANADIAN DOLLAR (CME)-100,000 dlrs.; $ per Can $
Dec    .7338 .7353 .7333 .7348 + .0005 .7460 .7130 35,096
Mr97   .7368 .7380 .7364 .7376 + .0005 .7400 .7117    914
June   ....  ....  .... .7396 + .0005 .7405 .7185    608
Sept   ....  ....  .... .7415 + .0005 .7402 .7309    131
   Est vol 3,450; vol Mn 4,507; open Int 36,785, -1,076.
BRITISH POUND (CME)-62,500 pds.; $ per pound
Dec   1.5550 1.5680 1.5550 1.5656 + .0100 1.5712 1.4850 37,566
   Est vol 7,334; vol Mn 3,696; open Int 37,645, +115.
SWISS FRANC (CME)-125,000 francs; $ per franc
Dec    .8166 .8231 .8145 .8227 + .0062 .8999 .7976 47,478
Mr97   .8232 .8315 .8228 .8307 + .0061 .8715 .8050  1,326
   Est vol 11,965; vol Mn 9,995; open int 38,860, -1,177.
AUSTRALIAN DOLLAR (CME) 100,000 dlrs.; $ per A.$
Dec    .7895 .7895 .7825 .7843 - .0059 .7998 .7665  9,545
   Est vol 1,087; vol Mn 415; open int 9,585, -74.
MEXICAN PESO (CME)-500,000 new Mex. peso, $ per MP
Dec    .12600 .12660 .12585 .12632 + .0057 .12660 .09900 12,607
Mr97   .11925 .12000 .11925 .11990 + .0090 .12240 10070  2,320
June   .11350 .11450 .11350 .11410 + .0100 .11550 .10270  1,263
Sep    .10870 .10950 .10870 .10950 + .0130 .10970 .10450    268
   Est vol 8,231; vol Mn 6,261; open Int 16,465, -168.
```

many, Canada, and Switzerland were lower than in the United States. This corresponds to the $r > r_f$ situation and explains why futures prices for these currencies increase with maturity. In Mexico interest rates were higher than in the United States. This corresponds to the $r_f > r$ situation and explains why the futures price for this currency decreases with maturity.

Example

The futures price of the deutschemark in Table 3.8 appears to be increasing at a rate of about 2.7 percent per annum with maturity. The increase suggests that the risk-free interest rate was about 2.7 percent per annum higher in the United States than in Germany on September 24, 1996.

Futures on Commodities

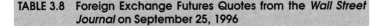

We now move on to consider commodity futures contracts. Here it will prove to be important to distinguish between commodities that are held solely for investment by a significant number of investors (e.g., gold and silver) and those that are held primarily for consumption. Arbitrage arguments can be used to obtain exact futures prices in the case of investment commodities. However, it turns out that such arguments can be used only to give an upper bound to the futures price in the case of consumption commodities.

GOLD AND SILVER

Because gold and silver are held by a significant number of investors solely for investment, these commodities can be considered as investment assets.[4] We adopt the notation introduced earlier, with S as the current spot price of gold or silver. Gold and silver provide no income. Assuming no storage costs, Equation 3.5 shows that the futures price, F, should be given by

$$F = Se^{rT} \tag{3.14}$$

Storage costs can be regarded as negative income. If U is the present value of all the storage costs that will be incurred during the life of a futures contract, it follows from Equation 3.6 that

$$F = (S + U)e^{rT} \tag{3.15}$$

If the storage costs incurred at any time are proportional to the price of the commodity, they can be regarded as providing a negative dividend yield. In this case, from Equation 3.7,

$$F = Se^{(r + u)T} \tag{3.16}$$

where u is the storage costs per annum as a proportion of the spot price.

Example

Consider a one-year futures contract on gold. Suppose that it costs $2 per ounce per year to store gold, with the payment being made at the end of the year. Assume that the spot price is $450 and the risk-free rate is 7 percent per annum for all maturities. This corresponds to $r = 0.07$, $S = 450$, $T = 1$, and

$$U = 2e^{-0.07 \times 1} = 1.865$$

The futures price, F, is given by

$$F = (450 + 1.865)e^{0.07 \times 1} = \$484.63$$

If $F > 484.63$, an arbitrageur can buy gold and short one-year gold futures contracts to lock in a profit. If $F < 484.63$, an investor who already owns gold can improve the return by selling the gold and buying gold futures contracts. Tables 3.9 and 3.10 illustrate these strategies for the situations where $F = 500$ and $F = 470$.

---

[4]Note that, for an asset to be an investment asset, it need not be held solely for investment purposes. What is required is that some individuals hold it for investment purposes and that these individuals be prepared to substitute their spot holdings for futures contracts if the latter look more attractive. This explains why silver, although it has significant industrial uses, is an investment asset.

TABLE 3.9   Arbitrage Opportunity in the Gold Market When Gold Futures Price Is Too High

From the Trader's Desk

The one-year futures price of gold is $500 per ounce. The spot price is $450 per ounce and the risk-free interest rate is 7 percent per annum. The storage costs for gold are $2 per ounce per year payable in arrears.

Opportunity

The futures price of gold is too high. An arbitrageur can

1. Borrow $45,000 at the risk-free interest rate to buy 100 ounces of gold
2. Short one gold futures contract for delivery in one year

At the end of the year $50,000 is received for the gold under the terms of the futures contract, $48,263 is used to pay interest and principal on the loan, and $200 is used to pay storage. The net gain is

$$\$50,000 - \$48,263 - \$200 = \$1,537$$

TABLE 3.10   Arbitrage Opportunity in the Gold Market When Gold Futures Price Is Too Low

From the Trader's Desk

The one-year futures price of gold is $470 per ounce. The spot price is $450 per ounce, and the risk-free interest rate is 7 percent per annum. The storage costs for gold are $2 per ounce per year payable in arrears.

Opportunity

The futures price of gold is too low. An investor who already holds 100 ounces of gold for investment purposes can

1. Sell the gold for $45,000
2. Enter into one long futures contract on gold for delivery in one year

The $45,000 is invested at the risk-free interest rate for one year and grows to $48,263. At the end of the year, under the terms of the futures contract, 100 ounces of gold are purchased for $47,000. The investor therefore ends up with 100 ounces of gold plus

$$\$48,263 - \$47,000 = \$1,263$$

in cash. If the gold is kept throughout the year, the investor ends up with 100 ounces of gold less the $200 paid for storage. The futures strategy therefore improves the investor's position by

$$\$1,263 + \$200 = \$1,463$$

OTHER COMMODITIES

For commodities that are not held primarily for investment purposes (e.g., oil and copper), the arbitrage arguments leading to Equations 3.14, 3.15, and 3.16 need to be reviewed carefully.

Suppose that instead of Equation 3.15, we have

$$F > (S + U)e^{rT} \qquad (3.17)$$

To take advantage of this opportunity, an arbitrageur can implement the following strategy:

1. Borrow an amount $S + U$ at the risk-free rate and use it to purchase one unit of the commodity and to pay storage costs.
2. Short a futures contract on one unit of the commodity.

If we regard the futures contract as a forward contract, this strategy is certain to lead to a profit of $F - (S + U)e^{rT}$ at time T. The strategy is illustrated for gold in Table 3.9. There is no problem in implementing the strategy for any commodity. However, as arbitrageurs do so, there will be a tendency for S to increase and F to decrease until Equation 3.17 is no longer true. We conclude that Equation 3.17 cannot hold for any significant length of time.

Suppose next that

$$F < (S + U)e^{rT} \qquad (3.18)$$

For gold and silver, we can argue that many investors hold the commodity solely for investment. When they observe the inequality in Equation 3.18, they will find it profitable to

1. Sell the commodity, save the storage costs, and invest the proceeds at the risk-free interest rate.
2. Buy the futures contract.

This strategy is illustrated for gold in Table 3.10. The result is a riskless profit at maturity of $(S + U)e^{rT} - F$ relative to the position the investors would have been in if they had held the gold or silver. It follows that Equation 3.18 cannot hold for long. Since neither Equation 3.17 nor Equation 3.18 can hold for long, we must have $F = (S + U)e^{rT}$.

For commodities that are not to any significant extent held for investment, this argument cannot be used. Individuals and companies who keep such a commodity in inventory do so because of its consumption value—not because of its value as an investment. They are reluctant to sell the commodity and buy futures contracts, because futures contracts cannot be consumed. There is therefore nothing to stop Equation 3.18 from holding. Because Equation 3.17 cannot hold, all we can assert for a consumption commodity is

$$F \leq (S + U)e^{rT} \qquad (3.19)$$

If storage costs are expressed as a proportion u of the spot price, the equivalent result is

$$F \leq Se^{(r + u)T} \qquad (3.20)$$

CONVENIENCE YIELDS

We do not necessarily have equality in Equations 3.19 and 3.20, because users of the commodity may feel that ownership of the physical commodity provides benefits that are not obtained by holders of futures contracts. These benefits may include the ability to profit from temporary local shortages or the ability to keep a production process running. The benefits are sometimes referred to as the *convenience yield* provided by the product. If the dollar amount of storage costs is known and has a present value, U, the convenience yield, y, is defined so that

$$Fe^{yT} = (S + U)e^{rT}$$

If the storage costs per unit are a constant proportion, u, of the spot price, y is defined so that

$$Fe^{yT} = Se^{(r+u)T}$$

or

$$F = Se^{(r+u-y)T} \qquad \textbf{(3.21)}$$

The convenience yield simply measures the extent to which the left-hand side is less than the right-hand side in Equation 3.19 or 3.20. For investment assets the convenience yield must be zero; otherwise, there are opportunities such as those in Table 3.10. Table 2.3 of Chapter 2 shows that the futures prices of some commodities (e.g., soybean meal and crude oil) tended to decrease as the maturity of the contract increased on September 24, 1996. This pattern suggests that the convenience yield, y, is greater than $r + u$ for these commodities.

The convenience yield reflects the market's expectations concerning the future availability of the commodity. The greater the possibility that shortages will occur during the life of the futures contract, the higher the convenience yield. If users of the commodity have high inventories, there is very little chance of shortages in the near future and the convenience yield tends to be low. On the other hand, low inventories tend to lead to high convenience yields.

The Cost of Carry

The relationship between futures prices and spot prices can be summarized in terms of the *cost of carry*. This measures the storage cost plus the interest that is paid to finance the asset less the income earned on the asset. For a nondividend-paying stock, the cost of carry is r, because there are no storage costs and no income is earned; for a stock index, it is $r - q$, because income is earned at rate q on the asset. For a currency, it is $r - r_f$; for a commodity with storage costs that are a proportion u of the price, it is $r + u$; and so on.

Define the cost of carry as c. For an investment asset, the futures price is

$$F = Se^{cT} \qquad \textbf{(3.22)}$$

For a consumption asset, it is

$$F = Se^{(c-y)T}$$

(3.23)

where y is the convenience yield.

Delivery Options

Whereas a forward contract normally specifies that delivery is to take place on a particular day, a futures contract often allows the party with the short position to choose to deliver at any time during a certain period. (Typically the party has to give a few days' notice of its intention to deliver.) The choice introduces a complication into the determination of futures prices. Should the maturity of the futures contract be assumed to be the beginning, middle, or end of the delivery period? Even though most futures contracts are closed out prior to maturity, it is important to know when delivery would have taken place in order to calculate the theoretical futures price.

If the futures price is an increasing function of the time to maturity, it can be seen from Equation 3.23 that $c > y$, so that the benefits from holding the asset (including convenience yield and net of storage costs) are less than the risk-free rate. It is usually optimal in such a case for the party with the short position to deliver as early as possible, because the interest earned on the cash received outweighs the benefits of holding the asset. As a rule, futures prices in these circumstances should be calculated on the basis that delivery will take place at the beginning of the delivery period. If futures prices are decreasing as maturity increases ($c < y$), the reverse is true. It is then usually optimal for the party with the short position to deliver as late as possible, and futures prices should, as a rule, be calculated on this assumption.

Futures Prices and the Expected Future Spot Price

One question that is often raised is whether the futures price of an asset is equal to its expected future spot price. If you have to guess what the price of an asset will be in three months, is the futures price an unbiased estimate? Chapter 2 presented the arguments of Keynes and Hicks. These authors contend that speculators will not trade a futures contract unless their expected profit is positive. By contrast, hedgers are prepared to accept a negative profit because of the risk-reduction benefits they get from a futures contract. If more speculators are long than short, the futures price will tend to be less than the expected future spot price. On average, speculators can then expect to make a gain, because the futures price converges to the spot price at maturity. Similarly, if more speculators are short than long, the futures price will tend to be greater than the expected future spot price.

RISK AND RETURN

Another explanation of the relationship between futures prices and expected future spot prices can be obtained by considering the relationship between risk and expected return in the economy. In general, the higher the risk of an investment, the higher the expected return demanded by an investor. Readers familiar with the capital asset pricing model will know that there are two types of risk in the economy: systematic and nonsystematic. Nonsystematic risk should not be important to an investor. It can be almost completely eliminated by holding a well-diversified portfolio. An investor should not therefore require a higher expected return for bearing nonsystematic risk. Systematic risk, by contrast, cannot be diversified away. It arises from a correlation between returns from the investment and returns from the stock market as a whole. An investor generally requires a higher expected return than the risk-free interest rate for bearing positive amounts of systematic risk. Also, an investor is prepared to accept a lower expected return than the risk-free interest rate when the systematic risk in an investment is negative.

THE RISK IN A FUTURES POSITION

Let us consider a speculator who takes a long futures position in the hope that the spot price of the asset will be above the futures price at maturity. We suppose that the speculator puts the present value of the futures price into a risk-free investment while simultaneously taking a long futures position. We assume that the futures contract can be treated as a forward contract. The proceeds of the risk-free investment are used to buy the asset on the delivery date. The asset is then immediately sold for its market price. The cash flows to the speculator are

Time 0: $-Fe^{-rT}$
Time T: $+S_T$

where S_T is the price of the asset at time T.

The present value of this investment is

$$-Fe^{-rT} + E(S_T)e^{-kT}$$

where k is the discount rate appropriate for the investment (i.e., the expected return required by investors on the investment) and E denotes expected value. Assuming that all investment opportunities in securities markets have zero net present value,

$$-Fe^{-rT} + E(S_T)e^{-kT} = 0$$

or

$$F = E(S_T)e^{(r-k)T} \tag{3.24}$$

The value of k depends on the systematic risk of the investment. If S_T is uncorrelated with the level of the stock market, the investment has zero systematic risk. In this case $k = r$ and Equation 3.24 shows that $F = E(S_T)$. If S_T is positively correlated with the stock market as a whole, the investment has positive systematic risk. In this case $k > r$ and Equation 3.24 shows that $F < E(S_T)$. Finally, if S_T is negatively correlated with the stock market, the investment has negative systematic risk. In this case $k < r$ and Equation 3.24 shows that $F > E(S_T)$.

EMPIRICAL EVIDENCE

If $F = E(S_T)$, the futures price will drift up or down only if the market changes its views about the expected future spot price. Over a long period of time, we can reasonably assume that the market revises its expectations about future spot prices upward as often as it does so downward. It follows that when $F = E(S_T)$, the average profit from holding futures contracts over a long period of time should be zero. The $F < E(S_T)$ situation corresponds to the positive systematic risk situation. Since the futures price and the spot price must be equal at maturity of the futures contract, a futures price should on average drift up and a trader should over a long period of time make positive profits from consistently holding long futures positions. Similarly, the $F > E(S_T)$ situation implies that a trader should over a long period of time make positive profits from consistently holding short futures positions.

How do futures prices behave in practice? Some of the empirical work that has been carried out is listed at the end of this chapter. The results are mixed. Houthakker's study looked at futures prices for wheat, cotton, and corn from 1937 to 1957. It showed that significant profits could be earned by taking long futures positions. This suggests that an investment in corn has positive systematic risk and $F < E(S_T)$. Telser's study contradicted the findings of Houthakker. His data covered the period from 1926 to 1950 for cotton and from 1927 to 1954 for wheat and gave rise to no significant profits for traders taking either long or short positions.[5] To quote from Telser: "The futures data offer no evidence to contradict the simple . . . hypothesis that the futures price is an unbiased estimate of the expected future spot price." Gray's study looked at corn futures prices during the period 1921 to 1959 and resulted in similar findings to those of Telser. Dusak's study used data on corn, wheat, and soybeans from 1952 to 1967 and took a different approach. It attempted to estimate the systematic risk of an investment in these commodities by calculating the correlation of movements in the commodity prices with movements in the S&P 500. The results suggest that there is no systematic risk and lend support to the $F = E(S_T)$ hypothesis. However, more recent work by Chang using the same commodities and more advanced statistical techniques supports the $F < E(S_T)$ hypothesis.

Summary

For most purposes, the futures price of a contract with a certain delivery date can be considered to be the same as the forward price for a contract with the same delivery date. It can be shown that in theory the two should be exactly the same when interest rates are perfectly predictable and should be very close to each other when interest rates vary unpredictably.

For the purposes of understanding futures (or forward) prices, it is convenient to divide futures contracts into two categories: those in which the underlying asset is held for investment by a significant number of investors and those in which the underlying asset is held primarily for consumption purposes.

In the case of investment assets, we have considered three different situations:

1. The asset provides no income.
2. The asset provides a known dollar income.
3. The asset provides a known dividend yield.

---

[5]See L. G. Telser, "Futures Trading and the Storage of Cotton and Wheat," *Journal of Political Economy* 66 (June 1958): 233–255.

TABLE 3.11   Summary of Results for a Contract with Maturity *T* on an Investment Asset with Price *S* When the Risk-free Interest Rate for a *T*-Year Period Is *r*

Asset	Forward/Futures Price	Value of Long Forward Contract with Delivery Price K
Provides no income	Se^{rT}	$S - Ke^{-rT}$
Provides known income with present value, I	$(S - I)e^{rT}$	$S - I - Ke^{-rT}$
Provides known dividend yield, q	$Se^{(r-q)T}$	$Se^{-qT} - Ke^{-rT}$

The results are summarized in Table 3.11. They enable futures prices to be obtained for contracts on stock indices, currencies, gold, and silver.

In the case of consumption assets, it is not possible to obtain the futures price as a function of the spot price and other observable variables. Here the parameter known as the asset's convenience yield becomes important. It measures the extent to which users of the commodity feel that ownership of the physical asset provides benefits that are not obtained by the holders of the futures contract. These benefits may include the ability to profit from temporary local shortages or the ability to keep a production process running. It is possible to obtain only an upper bound for the futures price of consumption assets using arbitrage arguments.

The concept of cost of carry is sometimes useful. The cost of carry is the storage cost of the underlying asset plus the cost of financing it minus the income received from it. In the case of investment assets, the futures price is greater than the spot price by an amount reflecting the cost of carry. In the case of consumption assets, the futures price is greater than the spot price by an amount reflecting the cost of carry net of the convenience yield.

If we assume the capital asset pricing model is true, the relationship between the futures price and the expected future spot price depends on whether the spot price is positively or negatively correlated with the level of the stock market. Positive correlation will tend to lead to a futures price lower than the expected future spot price. Negative correlation will tend to lead to a futures price higher than the expected future spot price. Only when the correlation is zero will the theoretical futures price be equal to the expected future spot price.

Suggestions for Further Reading

On empirical research concerning forward and futures prices

Cornell, B., and M. Reinganum. "Forward and Futures Prices: Evidence from Foreign Exchange Markets," *Journal of Finance* 36 (December 1981): 1035–1045.

French, K. "A Comparison of Futures and Forward Prices," *Journal of Financial Economics* 12 (November 1983): 311–342.

Park, H. Y., and A. H. Chen. "Differences between Futures and Forward Prices: A Further Investigation of Marking-to-Market Effects," *Journal of Futures Markets* 5 (February 1985): 77–88.

Rendleman, R., and C. Carabini. "The Efficiency of the Treasury Bill Futures Markets," *Journal of Finance* 34 (September 1979): 895–914.

Viswanath, P. V. "Taxes and the Futures-Forward Price Difference in the 91-Day T-Bill Market," *Journal of Money, Credit, and Banking* 21, no. 2 (May 1989): 190–205.

On empirical research concerning the relationship between futures prices and expected future spot prices

Chang, E. C. "Returns to Speculators and the Theory of Normal Backwardation," *Journal of Finance* 40 (March 1985): 193–208.

Dusak, K. "Futures Trading and Investor Returns: An Investigation of Commodity Risk Premiums," *Journal of Political Economy* 81 (December 1973): 1387–1406.

Gray, R. W. "The Search for a Risk Premium," *Journal of Political Economy* 69 (June 1961): 250–260.

Houthakker, H. S. "Can Speculators Forecast Prices?" *Review of Economics and Statistics* 39 (1957): 143–151.

Telser, L. G. "Futures Trading and the Storage of Cotton and Wheat," *Journal of Political Economy* 66 (June 1958): 233–255.

On the theoretical relationship between forward and futures prices

Cox, J. C., J. E. Ingersoll, and S. A. Ross. "The Relation between Forward Prices and Futures Prices," *Journal of Financial Economics* 9 (December 1981): 321–346.

Jarrow, R. A., and G. S. Oldfield. "Forward Contracts and Futures Contracts," *Journal of Financial Economics* 9 (December 1981): 373–382.

Kane, E. J. "Market Incompleteness and Divergences between Forward and Futures Interest Rates," *Journal of Finance* 35 (May 1980): 221–234.

Margrabe, W. "A Theory of Forward and Futures Prices," Working paper, The Wharton School, University of Pennsylvania, 1976.

Richard, S., and M. Sundaresan. "A Continuous-Time Model of Forward and Futures Prices in a Multigood Economy," *Journal of Financial Economics* 9 (December 1981): 347–372.

Other

Hicks, J. R. *Value and Capital.* Oxford: Oxford University Press, 1939.

Keynes, J. M. *A Treatise on Money.* London: Macmillan, 1930.

Quiz

1. A bank quotes you an interest rate of 14 percent per annum with quarterly compounding. What is the equivalent rate with (a) continuous compounding and (b) annual compounding?

2. Explain what happens when an investor shorts a certain share.

3. Suppose that you enter into a six-month forward contract on a nondividend-paying stock when the stock price is $30 and the risk-free interest rate (with continuous compounding) is 12 percent per annum. What is the forward price?

4. A stock index currently stands at 350. The risk-free interest rate is 8 percent per annum (with continuous compounding), and the dividend yield on the index is 4 percent per annum. What should the futures price for a four-month contract be?

5. Explain carefully why the futures price of gold can be calculated from its spot price and other observable variables whereas the futures price of copper cannot.

6. Explain carefully the meaning of the terms *convenience yield* and *cost of carry*. What is the relationship between futures price, spot price, convenience yield, and cost of carry?

7. Is the futures price of a stock index greater than or less than the expected future value of the index? Explain your answer.

Questions and Problems

3.1. An investor receives $1100 in one year in return for an investment of $1,000 now. Calculate the percentage return per annum with:
   a. Annual compounding
   b. Semiannual compounding
   c. Monthly compounding
   d. Continuous compounding

3.2. What rate of interest with continuous compounding is equivalent to 15 percent per annum with monthly compounding?

3.3. A deposit account pays 12 percent per annum with continuous compounding, but interest is actually paid quarterly. How much interest will be paid each quarter on a $10,000 deposit?

3.4. A one-year long forward contract on a nondividend-paying stock is entered into when the stock price is $40 and the risk-free rate of interest is 10 percent per annum with continuous compounding.
   a. What are the forward price and the initial value of the forward contract?
   b. Six months later, the price of the stock is $45 and the risk-free interest rate is still 10 percent. What are the forward price and the value of the forward contract?

3.5. A stock is expected to pay a dividend of $1 per share in two months and in five months. The stock price is $50 and the risk-free rate of interest is 8 percent per annum with continuous compounding for all maturities. An investor has just taken a short position in a six-month forward contract on the stock.
   a. What are the forward price and the initial value of the forward contract?
   b. Three months later, the price of the stock is $48 and the risk-free rate of interest is still 8 percent per annum. What are the forward price and the value of the short position in the forward contract?

3.6. The risk-free rate of interest is 7 percent per annum with continuous compounding, and the dividend yield on a stock index is 3.2 percent per annum. The current value of an index is 150. What is the six-month futures price?

3.7. Assume that the risk-free interest rate is 9 percent per annum with continuous compounding and that the dividend yield on a stock index varies throughout the year. In February, May, August, and November, it is 5 percent per annum. In other months, it is 2 percent per annum. Suppose that the value of the index on July 31, 1997 is 300. What is the futures price for a contract deliverable on December 31, 1997?

3.8. Suppose that the risk-free interest rate is 10 percent per annum with continuous compounding and that the dividend yield on a stock index is 4 percent per annum. The index is standing at 400, and the futures price for a contract deliverable in four months is 405. What arbitrage opportunities does this create?

3.9. Estimate the difference between risk-free rates of interest in Japan and the United States from the information in Table 3.8.

3.10. The two-month interest rates in Switzerland and the United States are 3 percent and 8 percent per annum, respectively, with continuous compounding. The spot price of the Swiss franc is $0.6500. The futures price for a contract deliverable in two months is $0.6600. What arbitrage opportunities does this create?

3.11. The current price of silver is $9 per ounce. The storage costs are $0.24 per ounce per year payable quarterly in advance. Assuming a flat term structure with a continuously compounded interest rate of 10 percent, calculate the futures price of silver for delivery in nine months.

3.12. A bank offers a corporate client a choice between borrowing cash at 11 percent per annum and borrowing gold at 2 percent per annum. (If gold is borrowed, interest must be repaid in gold. Thus, 100 ounces borrowed today would require 102 ounces to be repaid in one year.) The risk-free interest rate is 9.25 percent per annum and storage costs are 0.5 percent per annum. Discuss whether the rate of interest on the gold loan is too high or too low in relation to the rate of interest on the cash loan. The interest rates on the two loans are expressed with annual compounding. The risk-free interest rate and storage costs are expressed with continuous compounding.

3.13. Suppose that F_1 and F_2 are two futures contracts on the same commodity with maturity dates of t_1 and t_2 and with $t_2 > t_1$. Prove that

$$F_2 \le F_1 e^{r(t_2 - t_1)}$$

where r is the interest rate (assumed constant) and there are no storage costs. For the purposes of this problem, assume that a futures contract is the same as a forward contract.

3.14. When a known future cash outflow in a foreign currency is hedged by a company using a forward contract, there is no foreign exchange risk. When it is hedged using futures contracts, the marking-to-market process does leave the company exposed to some risk. Explain the nature of this risk. In particular, consider whether the company is better off using a futures contract or a forward contract when
a. The value of the foreign currency falls rapidly during the life of the contract
b. The value of the foreign currency rises rapidly during the life of the contract
c. The value of the foreign currency first rises and then falls back to its initial value
d. The value of the foreign currency first falls and then rises back to its initial value

Assume that the forward price equals the futures price.

3.15. It is sometimes argued that a forward exchange rate is an unbiased predictor of future exchange rates. Under what circumstances is this so?

3.16. A company that is uncertain about the exact date when it will pay or receive a foreign currency may try to negotiate with its bank a forward contract that specifies a period during which delivery can be made. The company wants to reserve the right to choose the exact delivery date to fit in with its own cash flows. Put yourself in the position of the bank. How would you price the product that the company wants?

APPENDIX 3A

A Proof That Forward and Futures Prices Are Equal When Interest Rates Are Constant

This appendix demonstrates that forward and futures prices are equal when interest rates are constant. Suppose that a futures contract lasts for n days and that F_i is the futures price at the end of day i $(0 < i < n)$. Define δ as the risk-free rate per day (assumed constant). Consider the following strategy.[6]

1. Take a long futures position of e^{δ} at the end of day 0 (i.e., at the beginning of the contract).

2. Increase long position to $e^{2\delta}$ at the end of day 1.

3. Increase long position to $e^{3\delta}$ at the end of day 2.

And so on.

This strategy is summarized in Table 3.12. By the beginning of day i, the investor has a long position of $e^{\delta i}$. The profit (possibly negative) from the position on day i is

$$(F_i - F_{i-1})e^{\delta i}$$

Assume that the profit is compounded at the risk-free rate until the end of day n. Its value at the end of day n is

$$(F_i - F_{i-1})e^{\delta i}e^{(n-i)\delta} = (F_i - F_{i-1})e^{n\delta}$$

The value at the end of day n of the entire investment strategy is therefore

$$\sum_{i=1}^{n}(F_i - F_{i-1})e^{n\delta}$$

---

[6]This strategy was proposed by J. C. Cox, J. E. Ingersoll, and S. A. Ross, "The Relationship between Forward Prices and Futures Prices," *Journal of Financial Economics* 9 (December 1981): 321–346.

TABLE 3.12 **The Investment Strategy to Show That Futures and Forward Prices Are Equal**

	0	1	2	...	$n-1$	n
			Day			
Futures price	F_0	F_1	F_2	...	F_{n-1}	F_n
Futures position	e^{δ}	$e^{2\delta}$	$e^{3\delta}$	...	$e^{n\delta}$	0
Gain/loss	0	$(F_1 - F_0)e^{\delta}$	$(F_2 - F_1)e^{2\delta}$	...	...	$(F_n - F_{n-1})e^{n\delta}$
Gain/loss compounded to day n	0	$(F_1 - F_0)e^{n\delta}$	$(F_2 - F_1)e^{n\delta}$	...	...	$(F_n - F_{n-1})e^{n\delta}$

This is

$$[(F_n - F_{n-1}) + (F_{n-1} - F_{n-2}) + \cdots + (F_1 - F_0)]e^{n\delta} = (F_n - F_0)e^{n\delta}$$

Since F_n is the same as the terminal asset spot price, S_T, the terminal value of the investment strategy can be written

$$(S_T - F_0)e^{n\delta}$$

An investment of F_0 in a risk-free bond combined with the strategy just given yields

$$F_0 e^{n\delta} + (S_T - F_0)e^{n\delta} = S_T e^{n\delta}$$

at time T. No investment is required for all the long futures positions described. It follows that an amount F_0 can be invested to give an amount $S_T e^{n\delta}$ at time T.

Suppose next that the forward price at the end of day 0 is G_0. Investing G_0 in a riskless bond and taking a long forward position of $e^{n\delta}$ forward contracts also guarantees an amount $S_T e^{n\delta}$ at time T. Thus, there are two investment strategies—one requiring an initial outlay of F_0, and the other requiring an initial outlay of G_0—both of which yield $S_T e^{n\delta}$ at time T. It follows that in the absence of arbitrage opportunities

$$F_0 = G_0$$

In other words, the futures price and the forward price are identical. Note that in this proof there is nothing special about the time period of one day. The futures price based on a contract with weekly settlements is also the same as the forward price when corresponding assumptions are made.

Hedging Strategies Using Futures

Many of the participants in futures markets are hedgers. Their aim is to use futures markets to reduce a particular risk that they face. This risk might relate to the price of oil, a foreign exchange rate, the level of the stock market, or some other variable. A *perfect hedge* is one that completely eliminates the risk. In practice, perfect hedges are rare. To quote one trader: "The only perfect hedge is in a Japanese garden." For the most part, therefore, a study of hedging using futures contracts is a study of the ways in which hedges can be constructed so that they perform as close to perfectly as possible.

In this chapter we consider a number of general issues associated with the way hedges are set up. When is a short futures position appropriate? When is a long futures position appropriate? Which futures contract should be used? What is the optimal size of the futures position for reducing risk? At this stage we restrict our attention to what might be termed *hedge-and-forget strategies*. We assume that no attempt is made to adjust the hedge once it has been put in place. The hedger simply takes a futures position at the beginning of the life of the hedge and closes out the position at the end of the life of the hedge. In chapter 14 we will examine dynamic hedging strategies in which the hedge is monitored closely and frequent adjustments are made.

Basic Principles

When an individual or company chooses to use futures markets to hedge a risk, the objective is usually to take a position that neutralizes the risk as far as possible. Consider a company that knows it will gain $10,000 for each 1 cent increase in the price of a commodity over the next three months and lose $10,000 for each 1 cent decrease in the price during this period. To hedge, the company's treasurer should take a short futures position that is designed to offset this risk. The futures position should lead to a loss of $10,000 for each 1 cent increase in the price of the commodity over the three months and a gain of $10,000 for each 1 cent decrease in the price during this period. If the price of the commodity goes down, the gain on the futures position offsets the loss on the rest of the company's business. If the price of the commodity goes up, the loss on the futures position is offset by the gain on the rest of the company's business.

SHORT HEDGES

A *short hedge* is a hedge, such as the one just described, that involves a short position in futures contracts. A short hedge is appropriate when the hedger already owns an asset and expects to sell it at some time in the future. For example, a short hedge could be used by a farmer who owns some hogs and knows that they will be ready for sale at the local market in two months. A short hedge can also be used when an asset is not owned right now but will be owned at some time in the future. Consider, for example, a U.S. exporter who knows that he or she will receive German marks in three months. The exporter will realize a gain if the mark increases in value relative to the U.S. dollar and will sustain a loss if the mark decreases in value relative to the U.S. dollar. A short futures position leads to a loss if the mark increases in value and a gain if it decreases in value. It has the effect of offsetting the exporter's risk.

To provide a more detailed illustration of the operation of a short hedge in a specific situation, we assume that it is May 15 today and company X has just negotiated a contract to sell 1 million barrels of oil. It has been agreed that the price that will apply in the contract is the market price on August 15. Company X is therefore in the position where it will gain $10,000 for each 1 cent increase in the price of oil over the next three months and lose $10,000 for each 1 cent decrease in the price during this period. Suppose that the spot price on May 15 is $19 per barrel and the August oil futures price on the New York Mercantile Exchange (NYMEX) is $18.75 per barrel. Since each futures contract on NYMEX is for the delivery of 1,000 barrels, the company can hedge its exposure by shorting 1,000 August futures contracts. If company X closes out its position on August 15, the effect of the strategy should be to lock in a price close to $18.75 per barrel.

As an example of what might happen, suppose that the spot price on August 15 proves to be $17.50 per barrel. The company realizes $17.5 million for the oil under its sales contract. Since August is the delivery month for the futures contract, the futures price on August 15 should be very close to the spot price of $17.50 on that date. The company therefore gains approximately

$$\$18.75 - \$17.50 = \$1.25$$

per barrel, or $1.25 million in total from the short futures position. The total amount realized from both the futures position and the sales contract is therefore approximately $18.75 per barrel, or $18.75 million in total.

For an alternative outcome, suppose that the price of oil on August 15 proves to be $19.50 per barrel. The company realizes $19.50 for the oil and loses approximately

$$\$19.50 - \$18.75 = \$0.75$$

per barrel on the short futures position. Again, the total amount realized is approximately $18.75 million. It is easy to see that in all cases the company ends up with approximately $18.75 million. This example is summarized in Table 4.1.

TABLE 4.1 A Short Hedge

From the Trader's Desk—May 15

Company X has negotiated a contract to sell 1 million barrels of oil. The price in the sales contract is the spot price on August 15. Quotes:

Spot price of crude oil: $19.00 per barrel

August oil futures price: $18.75 per barrel

Hedging Strategy

May 15: Short 1,000 August futures contracts on crude oil.

August 15: Close out futures position.

Result

The company ensures that it will receive a price close to $18.75 per barrel.

Example 1:

Price of oil on August 15 is $17.50 per barrel.

Company receives $17.50 per barrel under the sales contract.

Company gains about $1.25 per barrel from the futures contract.

Example 2:

Price of oil on August 15 is $19.50 per barrel.

Company receives $19.50 per barrel from the sales contract.

Company loses about $0.75 per barrel from the futures contract.

LONG HEDGES

Hedges that involve taking a long position in a futures contract are known as *long hedges*. A long hedge is appropriate when a company knows it will have to purchase a certain asset in the future and wants to lock in a price now.

Suppose that it is now January 15. A copper fabricator knows it will require 100,000 pounds of copper on May 15 to meet a certain contract. The spot price of copper is 140 cents per pound and the May futures price is 120 cents per pound. The fabricator can hedge its position by taking a long position in four May futures contracts on COMEX and closing its position on May 15. Each contract is for the delivery of 25,000 pounds of copper. The strategy has the effect of locking in the price of the copper that is required at close to 120 cents per pound.

This example is summarized in Table 4.2. Suppose that the price of copper on May 15 proves to be 125 cents per pound. Since May is the delivery month for the futures contract, this should be very close to the futures price. The fabricator therefore gains approximately

$$100{,}000 \times (\$1.25 - \$1.20) = \$5{,}000$$

on the futures contracts. It pays $100{,}000 \times \$1.25 = \$125{,}000$ for the copper, making the total cost approximately $\$125{,}000 - \$5{,}000 = \$120{,}000$. For an alternative outcome, suppose that the futures price is 105 cents per pound on May 15. The fabricator then loses approximately

$$100{,}000 \times (\$1.20 - \$1.05) = \$15{,}000$$

on the futures contract and pays $100{,}000 \times \$1.05 = \$105{,}000$ for the copper. Again the total cost is approximately $120,000, or 120 cents per pound.

TABLE 4.2 A Long Hedge

From the Trader's Desk—January 15

A copper fabricator knows it will require 100,000 pounds of copper on May 15 to meet a certain contract. The spot price of copper is 140 cents per pound and the May futures price is 120 cents per pound.

Hedging Strategy

January 15: Take a long position in four May futures contracts on copper.

May 15: Close out the position.

Result

The company ensures that its cost will be close to 120 cents per pound.

Example 1:

Cost of copper on May 15 is 125 cents per pound.

The company gains 5 cents per pound from the futures contract.

Example 2:

Cost of copper on May 15 is 105 cents per pound.

The company loses 15 cents per pound from the futures contract.

Note that it is better for the company to use futures contracts than to buy the copper on January 15 in the spot market. If it does the latter, it will pay 140 cents per pound instead of 120 cents per pound and will incur both interest costs and storage costs. For a company using copper on a regular basis, this disadvantage would be offset by the convenience yield associated with having the copper on hand. (See chapter 3 for a discussion of convenience yields.) However, for a company that knows it will not require the copper until May 15, the convenience yield has no value.

Long hedges can also be used to partially offset an existing short position. Consider an investor who has shorted a certain stock. Part of the risk faced by the investor is related to the performance of the stock market as a whole. The investor can neutralize this risk by taking a long position in index futures contracts. This type of hedging strategy is discussed further later in the chapter.

In both the example in Table 4.2 and the example in Table 4.1, we assume that the futures position is closed out in the delivery month. The hedge has the same basic effect if delivery is allowed to happen. However, making or taking delivery can be a costly business. For this reason, delivery is not usually made even when the hedger keeps the futures contract until the delivery month. As will be discussed later, hedgers with long positions usually avoid any possibility of having to take delivery by closing out their positions before the delivery period.

We have also assumed in the two examples that a futures contract is the same as a forward contract. In practice, marking to market does have a small effect on the performance of a hedge. It means that the payoff from the futures contract is realized day by day throughout the life of the hedge rather than all at the end.

Arguments for and against Hedging

The arguments in favor of hedging are so obvious that they hardly need to be stated. Most companies are in the business of manufacturing or retailing or wholesaling or providing a service. They have no particular skills or expertise in predicting variables such as interest rates, exchange rates, and commodity prices. It makes sense to hedge the risks associated with these variables as they arise. The companies can then focus on their main activities—in which presumably they do have particular skills and expertise. By hedging, they avoid unpleasant surprises such as sharp rises in the price of a commodity.

In practice, many risks are left unhedged. In the rest of this section we will explore some of the reasons.

HEDGING AND SHAREHOLDERS

One argument sometimes put forward is that the shareholders can, if they wish, do the hedging themselves. They do not need the company to do it for them. This argument is, however, open to question. It assumes that shareholders have as much information about the risks faced by a company as does the company's management. In most instances this is not the case. The argument also ignores commissions and other transactions costs. These are less expensive per dollar of hedging for large transactions than for small transactions. Hedging is therefore likely to be less expensive when carried out by the company than by individual shareholders. Indeed, the size of futures contracts makes hedging by individual shareholders impossible in many situations.

One thing that shareholders can do far more easily than a corporation is diversify risk. A shareholder with a well-diversified portfolio may be immune to many of the risks faced by a corporation. For example, in addition to holding shares in a company that uses copper, a well-diversified shareholder may hold shares in a copper producer, so that there is very little overall exposure to the price of copper. If companies are acting in the best interests of well-diversified shareholders, it can be argued that hedging is unnecessary in many situations. However, the extent to which managements are in practice influenced by this type of argument is open to question.

HEDGING AND COMPETITORS

If hedging is not the norm in a certain industry, it may not make sense for one particular company to choose to be different from all others. Competitive pressures within the industry may be such that the prices of the goods and services produced by the industry fluctuate to reflect raw material costs, interest rates, exchange rates, and so on. A company that does not hedge can expect its profit margins to be roughly constant. However, a company that does hedge can expect its profit margins to fluctuate!

To illustrate this point, consider two manufacturers of gold jewelry, company A and company B. We assume that most companies in the industry do not hedge against movements in the price of gold and that company B is no exception. However, company A has decided to be different from its competitors and use futures contracts to hedge its purchase of gold over the next 18 months. If the price of gold goes up, economic pressures will tend to lead to a corresponding increase in the wholesale price of the jewelry, so that company B's profit margin is unaffected. By contrast, company A's profit margin will increase after the effects of the hedge have been taken into account. If the price of gold goes down, economic pressures will tend to lead to a corresponding decrease in the wholesale price of the jewelry. Again, company B's profit margin is unaffected. However, company A's profit margin goes down. In extreme conditions,

TABLE 4.3 Danger in Hedging When Competitors Do Not

Change in Gold Price	Effect on Price of Gold Jewelry	Effect on Profits of Nonhedger	Effect on Profits of Hedger
Increase	Increase	None	Increase
Decrease	Decrease	None	Decrease

company A's profit margin could become negative as a result of the "hedging" carried out! This example is summarized in Table 4.3.

OTHER CONSIDERATIONS

It is important to realize that a hedge using futures contracts can result in a decrease or an increase in a company's profits relative to the position it would be in with no hedging. In the example in Table 4.1, if the price of oil goes down, the company loses money on its sale of 1 million barrels of oil, and the futures position leads to an offsetting gain. The treasurer can be congratulated for having had the foresight to put the hedge in place. Clearly, the company is better off than it would be with no hedging. Other executives in the organization, it is hoped, will appreciate the contribution made by the treasurer. If the price of oil goes up, the company gains from its sale of the oil, and the futures position leads to an offsetting loss. The company is in a worse position than it would be with no hedging. Although the hedging decision was perfectly logical, the treasurer may in practice have a difficult time justifying it. Suppose that the price of oil is $21.75 on August 15 in Table 4.1 so that the company loses $3 per barrel on the futures contract. We can imagine a conversation such as the following between the treasurer and the president.

PRESIDENT: This is terrible. We've lost $3 million in the futures market in the space of three months. How could it happen? I want a full explanation.

TREASURER: The purpose of the futures contracts was to hedge our exposure to the price of oil — not to make a profit. Don't forget that we made about $3 million from the favorable effect of the oil price increases on our business.

PRESIDENT: What's that got to do with it? That's like saying that we do not need to worry when our sales are down in California because they are up in New York.

TREASURER: If the price of oil had gone down ...

PRESIDENT: I don't care what would have happened if the price of oil had gone down. The fact is that it went up. I really do not know what you were doing playing the futures markets like this. Our shareholders will expect us to have done particularly well this quarter. I'm going to have to explain to them that your actions reduced profits by $3 million. I'm afraid this is going to mean no bonus for you this year.

TREASURER: That's unfair. I was only ...

PRESIDENT: Unfair! You are lucky not to be fired. You lost $3 million.
TREASURER: It all depends how you look at it . . .

It is easy to see why many treasurers are reluctant to hedge! Hedging reduces risk for the company. However, it may increase risks for the treasurer if others do not fully understand what is being done. The only real solution to this problem involves ensuring that all senior executives within the organization fully understand the nature of hedging before a hedging program is put in place. Ideally, hedging strategies are set by a company's board of directors and are clearly communicated to both the company's management and the shareholders.

Basis Risk

The hedges in the examples considered so far have been almost too good to be true. The hedger was able to identify the precise date in the future when an asset would be bought or sold. The hedger was then able to use futures contracts to remove almost all the risk arising from the price of the asset on that date. In practice, hedging is often not quite as straightforward. Some of the reasons are as follows:

1. The asset whose price is to be hedged may not be exactly the same as the asset underlying the futures contract.

2. The hedger may be uncertain as to the exact date when the asset will be bought or sold.

3. The hedge may require the futures contract to be closed out well before its expiration date.

These problems give rise to what is termed *basis risk*. This concept will now be explained.

THE BASIS

The *basis* in a hedging situation is as follows:[1]

$$\text{Basis} = \text{Spot price of asset to be hedged}$$
$$- \text{Futures price of contract used}$$

If the asset to be hedged and the asset underlying the futures contract are the same, the basis should be zero at the expiration of the futures contract. Prior to expiration, the basis may be positive or negative. From the analysis in chapter 3, when the underlying asset is a low-interest-rate currency or gold or silver, the futures price is greater than the spot price. This means that the basis is negative. For high-interest-rate currencies and many commodities, the reverse is true and the basis is positive.

When the spot price increases by more than the futures price, the basis increases. This is referred to as a *strengthening of the basis*. When the futures price increases by more than the spot price, the basis declines. This is referred to as a *weakening of the*

---

[1] This is the usual definition. However, the alternative definition

$$\text{Basis} = \text{Futures price} - \text{Spot price}$$

is sometimes used, particularly when the futures contract is on a financial asset.

basis. Figure 4.1 illustrates how a basis might change over time. Note that the basis is positive prior to expiration of the futures contract.

To examine the nature of basis risk, we will use the following notation:

S_1: spot price at time t_1

S_2: spot price at time t_2

F_1: futures price at time t_1

F_2: futures price at time t_2

b_1: basis at time t_1

b_2: basis at time t_2

We will assume that a hedge is put in place at time t_1 and closed out at time t_2. As an example, we will consider the case where the spot and futures prices at the time the hedge is initiated are $2.50 and $2.20, respectively, and that at the time the hedge is closed out they are $2.00 and $1.90, respectively. This means that $S_1 = 2.50$, $F_1 = 2.20$, $S_2 = 2.00$, and $F_2 = 1.90$.

From the definition of the basis

$$b_1 = S_1 - F_1$$
$$b_2 = S_2 - F_2$$

and in our example, $b_1 = 0.30$ and $b_2 = 0.10$.

Consider first the situation of a hedger who knows that the asset will be sold at time t_2 and takes a short futures position at time t_1. The price realized for the asset is S_2 and the profit on the futures position is $F_1 - F_2$. The effective price that is obtained for the asset with hedging is therefore

$$S_2 + F_1 - F_2 = F_1 + b_2$$

In our example this is $2.30. The value of F_1 is known at time t_1. If b_2 were also known at this time, a perfect hedge would result. The hedging risk is the uncertainty associated

FIGURE 4.1 Variation of Basis over Time

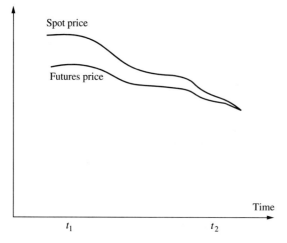

with b_2 and is known as *basis risk*. Consider next a situation where a company knows it will buy the asset at time t_2 and initiates a long hedge at time t_1. The price paid for the asset is S_2 and the loss on the hedge is $F_1 - F_2$. The effective price that is paid with hedging is therefore

$$S_2 + F_1 - F_2 = F_1 + b_2$$

This is the same expression as before and is $2.30 in the example. The value of F_1 is known at time t_1, and the term b_2 represents basis risk.

For investment assets such as currencies, stock indices, gold, and silver, the basis risk tends to be less than for consumption commodities. The reason, as shown in chapter 3, is that arbitrage arguments lead to a well-defined relationship between the futures price and the spot price of an investment asset. The basis risk for an investment asset arises mainly from uncertainty as to the level of the risk-free interest rate in the future. In the case of a consumption commodity, imbalances between supply and demand and the difficulties sometimes associated with storing the commodity can lead to large variations in the convenience yield. The result is an additional source of basis risk.

The asset that gives rise to the hedger's exposure is sometimes different from the asset underlying the hedge.[2] The basis risk is then usually greater. Define S_2^* as the price of the asset underlying the futures contract at time t_2. As before, S_2 is the price of the asset being hedged at time t_2. By hedging, a company ensures that the price that will be paid (or received) for the asset is

$$S_2 + F_1 - F_2$$

This can be written as

$$F_1 + (S_2^* - F_2) + (S_2 - S_2^*)$$

The terms $S_2^* - F_2$ and $S_2 - S_2^*$ represent the two components of the basis. The $S_2^* - F_2$ term is the basis that would exist if the asset being hedged were the same as the asset underlying the futures contract. The $S_2 - S_2^*$ term is the basis arising from the difference between the two assets.

Note that basis risk can lead to an improvement or a worsening of a hedger's position. Consider a short hedge. If the basis strengthens unexpectedly, the hedger's position improves; if the basis weakens unexpectedly, the hedger's position worsens. For a long hedge, the reverse holds. If the basis strengthens unexpectedly, the hedger's position worsens; if the basis weakens unexpectedly, the hedger's position improves.

CHOICE OF CONTRACT

One key factor affecting basis risk is the choice of the futures contract to be used for hedging. This choice has two components:

1. The choice of the asset underlying the futures contract
2. The choice of the delivery month

---

[2]For example, airlines sometimes use the NYMEX heating oil futures contract to hedge their exposure to the price of jet fuel. See the article by Nikkhah referenced at the end of this chapter for a description.

If the asset being hedged exactly matches an asset underlying a futures contract, the first choice is generally fairly easy. In other circumstances, it is necessary to carry out a careful analysis to determine which of the available futures contracts has futures prices that are most closely correlated with the price of the asset being hedged.

The choice of the delivery month is likely to be influenced by several factors. In the examples earlier in this chapter, we assumed that when the expiration of the hedge corresponds to a delivery month, the contract with that delivery month is chosen. In fact, a contract with a later delivery month is usually chosen in these circumstances. The reason is that futures prices are in some instances quite erratic during the delivery month. Also, a long hedger runs the risk of having to take delivery of the physical asset if the contract is held during the delivery month. Taking delivery can be expensive and inconvenient.

In general, basis risk increases as the time difference between the hedge expiration and the delivery month increases. A good rule of thumb is therefore to choose a delivery month that is as close as possible to, but later than, the expiration of the hedge. Suppose delivery months are March, June, September, and December for a particular contract. For hedge expirations in December, January, and February, the March contract will be chosen; for hedge expirations in March, April, and May, the June contract will be chosen; and so on. This rule of thumb assumes that there is sufficient liquidity in all contracts to meet the hedger's requirements. In practice, liquidity tends to be greatest in short maturity futures contracts. The hedger may therefore, in some situations, be inclined to use short maturity contracts and roll them forward. This strategy is discussed at the end of the chapter.

EXAMPLES

We now illustrate some of the points made so far in this section. Suppose it is March 1. A U.S. company expects to receive 50 million Japanese yen at the end of July. Yen futures contracts on the IMM have delivery months of March, June, September, and December. One contract is for the delivery of 12.5 million yen. The criteria mentioned earlier for the choice of a contract suggest that the September contract be chosen for hedging purposes.

The company therefore shorts four September yen futures contracts on March 1. When the yen are received at the end of July, the company closes out its position. The basis risk arises from uncertainty about the difference between the futures price and the spot price at this time. We suppose that the futures price on March 1 in cents per yen is 0.7800 and that the spot and futures prices when the contract is closed out are 0.7200 and 0.7250, respectively. The basis is –0.0050 and the gain from the futures contracts is 0.0550. The effective price obtained in cents per yen is the spot price plus the gain on the futures:

$$0.7200 + 0.0550 = 0.7750$$

This can also be written as the initial futures price plus the basis:

$$0.7800 - 0.0050 = 0.7750$$

The company receives a total of 50×0.00775 million dollars, or $387,500. This example is summarized in Table 4.4.

TABLE 4.4 Basis Risk in a Short Hedge

From the Trader's Desk—March 1
    It is March 1. A U.S. company expects to receive 50 million Japanese yen at the end of July. The September futures price for the yen is currently 0.7800.

Strategy
    The company can

1. Short four September yen futures contracts on March 1
2. Close out the contract when the yen arrive at the end of July

Basis Risk
    The basis risk arises from the hedger's uncertainty as to the difference between the spot price and September futures price of the Japanese yen at the end of July.

The Outcome
    When the yen arrived at the end of July, it turned out that the spot price was 0.7200 and the futures price was 0.7250. It follows that

$$\text{Basis} = 0.7200 - 0.7250 = -0.0050$$
$$\text{Gain on futures} = 0.7800 - 0.7250 = +0.0550$$

The effective price in cents per yen received by the hedger is the end-of-July spot price plus the gain on the futures:

$$0.7200 + 0.0550 = 0.7750$$

This can also be written as the initial September futures price plus the basis:

$$0.7800 - 0.0050 = 0.7750$$

For our next example, we suppose it is June 8 and a company knows that it will need to purchase 20,000 barrels of crude oil at some time in October or November. Oil futures contracts are currently traded for delivery every month on NYMEX and the contract size is 1,000 barrels. Following the criteria indicated, the company decides to use the December contract for hedging. On June 8 it takes a long position in 20 December contracts. At that time, the futures price is $18.00 per barrel. The company finds that it is ready to purchase the crude oil on November 10. It therefore closes out its futures contract on that date. The basis risk arises from uncertainty as to what the basis will be on the day the contract is closed out. We suppose that the spot price and futures price on November 10 are $20.00 per barrel and $19.10 per barrel, respectively. The basis is therefore $0.90 and the effective price paid is $18.90 per barrel, or $378,000 in total. This example is summarized in Table 4.5.

Minimum Variance Hedge Ratio

The *hedge ratio* is the ratio of the size of the position taken in futures contracts to the size of the exposure. Up to now we have always used a hedge ratio of 1.0. In Table 4.5, for example, the hedger's exposure was on 20,000 barrels of oil, and futures contracts

TABLE 4.5 Basis Risk in a Long Hedge

From the Trader's Desk—June 8
    It is June 8. A company knows that it will need to purchase 20,000 barrels of crude oil at some time in October or November. The current December oil futures price is $18.00 per barrel.

Strategy
    The company

1. Takes a long position in 20 NYM December oil futures contracts on June 8.
2. Closes out the contract when it finds it is ready to purchase the oil.

Basis Risk
    The basis risk arises from the hedger's uncertainty as to the difference between the spot price and the December futures price of oil at the time when the oil is required.

The Outcome
    The company was ready to purchase the oil on November 10 and closed out its futures contract on that date. The spot price was $20.00 per barrel and the futures price was $19.10 per barrel. It follows that

$$\text{Basis} = \$20.00 - \$19.10 = \$0.90$$
$$\text{Gain on futures} = \$19.10 - \$18.00 = \$1.10$$

The effective cost of the oil purchased is the November 10 price less the gain on the futures:

$$\$20.00 - \$1.10 = \$18.90 \text{ per barrel}$$

This can also be written as the initial December futures price plus the basis:

$$\$18.00 + \$0.90 = \$18.90 \text{ per barrel}$$

---

were entered into for the delivery of exactly this amount of oil. If the objective of the hedger is to minimize risk, setting the hedge ratio equal to 1.0 is not necessarily optimal.
    We will use the following notation:

ΔS: change in spot price, S, during a period of time equal to the life of the hedge
ΔF: change in futures price, F, during a period of time equal to the life of the hedge
σ_S: standard deviation of ΔS
σ_F: standard deviation of ΔF
ρ: coefficient of correlation between ΔS and ΔF
h^*: hedge ratio that minimizes the variance of the hedger's position

    In Appendix 4A we show that

$$h^* = \rho \frac{\sigma_S}{\sigma_F} \tag{4.1}$$

The optimal hedge ratio is the product of the coefficient of correlation between ΔS and ΔF and the ratio of the standard deviation of ΔS to the standard deviation of ΔF. Figure 4.2 shows how the variance of the value of the hedger's position depends on the hedge ratio chosen.

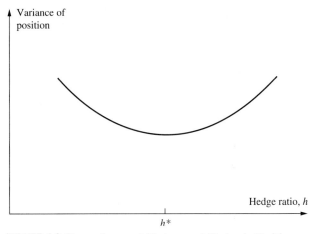

FIGURE 4.2 Dependence of Variance of Hedger's Position on
Hedge Ratio

If $\rho = 1$ and $\sigma_F = \sigma_S$, the hedge ratio, h^*, is 1.0. This is to be expected, because in this case the futures price mirrors the spot price perfectly. If $\rho = 1$ and $\sigma_F = 2\sigma_S$, the hedge ratio h^* is 0.5. This result is also as expected, because in this case the futures price always changes by twice as much as the spot price.

The optimal hedge ratio, h^*, is the slope of the best fit line when ΔS is regressed against ΔF, as indicated in Figure 4.3. This is intuitively reasonable, because we require

FIGURE 4.3 Regression of Change in Spot Price against Change
in Futures Price

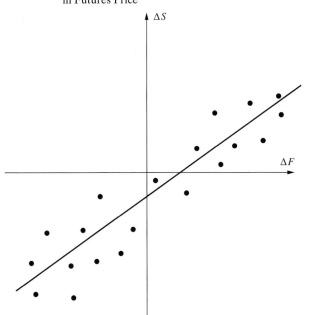

h^* to correspond to the ratio of changes in ΔS to changes in ΔF. The *hedge effectiveness* can be defined as the proportion of the variance that is eliminated by hedging. This is ρ^2, or

$$h^{*2}\frac{\sigma_F^2}{\sigma_S^2}$$

ESTIMATION

The parameters ρ, σ_F, and σ_S in Equation 4.1 are usually estimated from historical data on ΔS and ΔF. (The implicit assumption is that the future will in some sense be like the past.) A number of equal nonoverlapping time intervals are chosen, and the values of ΔS and ΔF for each of the intervals are observed. Ideally, the length of each time interval is the same as the length of the time interval for which the hedge is in effect. In practice, this sometimes severely limits the number of observations that are available, and a shorter time interval is used.

To illustrate how the calculations are carried out, Table 4.6 gives sample data on ΔF and ΔS. We suppose that the duration of the hedge is one month, so that ΔF and ΔS measure the changes in F and S during successive one-month periods. The futures contract observed is the one that would actually be used for hedging an exposure during the month under consideration. We will denote the ith observations on ΔF and ΔS by x_i and y_i, respectively, and suppose that there are n observations in total. It can be shown that

$$\sum x_i = -0.013 \qquad \sum x_i^2 = 0.0138$$

$$\sum y_i = 0.003 \qquad \sum y_i^2 = 0.0097$$

$$\sum x_i y_i = 0.0107$$

TABLE 4.6 Data to Calculate Minimum Variance Hedge Ratio

Month *i*	ΔF for Month $= x_i$	ΔS for Month $= y_i$
1	0.021	0.029
2	0.035	0.020
3	-0.046	-0.044
4	0.001	0.008
5	0.044	0.026
6	-0.029	-0.019
7	-0.026	-0.010
8	-0.029	-0.007
9	0.048	0.043
10	-0.006	0.011
11	-0.036	-0.036
12	-0.011	-0.018
13	0.019	0.009
14	-0.027	-0.032
15	0.029	0.023

Standard formulas from statistics give the estimate of σ_F as

$$\sqrt{\frac{\sum x_i^2}{n-1} - \frac{(\sum x_i)^2}{n(n-1)}} = 0.0313$$

The estimate of σ_S is

$$\sqrt{\frac{\sum y_i^2}{n-1} - \frac{(\sum y_i)^2}{n(n-1)}} = 0.0263$$

The estimate of ρ is

$$\frac{n \sum x_i y_i - \sum x_i \sum y_i}{\sqrt{[n \sum x_i^2 - (\sum x_i)^2][n \sum y_i^2 - (\sum y_i)^2]}} = 0.928$$

The minimum variance hedge ratio, h^*, is therefore

$$0.928 \times \frac{0.0263}{0.0313} = 0.78$$

Thus, the futures contracts bought or sold should have 78 percent of the face value of the asset being hedged. In practice, of course, the number of futures contracts used must be an integer, and the hedger can achieve only an approximation to the optimal hedge.

OPTIMAL NUMBER OF CONTRACTS

We adopt the following notation:

N_A: size of position being hedged (units)

Q_F: size of one futures contract (units)

N^*: optimal number of futures contracts for hedging

The futures contracts used should have a face value of $h^* N_A$. The number of futures contracts required is therefore given by

$$N^* = \frac{h^* N_A}{Q_F} \tag{4.2}$$

Suppose that, for the example in Table 4.5, h^* is calculated as 0.7. Because $N_A = 20{,}000$ and $Q_F = 1{,}000$, the optimal number of contracts, N^*, is given by

$$N^* = \frac{0.7 \times 20{,}000}{1{,}000} = 14$$

A CHANGE OF NOTATION

For the rest of this chapter and the next chapter, it is convenient to redefine S, F, σ_S, and σ_F. From now onward, S will denote the value of the position being hedged (N_A times the old S) and F will denote the futures contract price (Q_F times the old F). The variables σ_S, σ_F, and ρ will denote the standard deviation of the new S, the standard deviation of the new F, and the correlation coefficient between the new S and F, respectively. The new σ_S is N_A times the old σ_S, the new σ_F is Q_F times the old σ_F, and ρ is the same as before. From Equations 4.1 and 4.2, it can be seen that the equation for N^* is the same as our earlier equation for h^*:

$$N^* = \rho\frac{\sigma_S}{\sigma_F} \qquad \textbf{(4.3)}$$

Stock Index Futures

Stock index futures were introduced in chapter 3. They are frequently used to hedge portfolios of stocks in the way described in the previous section. Readers familiar with the capital asset pricing model will know that the relationship between the return on a portfolio of stocks and the return on the market is described by a parameter β. Beta is the slope of the best fit line obtained when the excess return on the portfolio over the risk-free rate is regressed against the excess return on the market over the risk-free rate. When $\beta = 1.0$, the return on the portfolio tends to mirror the return on the market; when $\beta = 2.0$, the excess return on the portfolio tends to be twice as great as the excess return on the market; when $\beta = 0.5$, it tends to be half as great; and so on.

Consistent with our new notation, S is the value of the portfolio and F is the price of a futures contract (futures price times size of contract). It can be shown that as an approximation the optimal number of contracts, N^*, is given by: [3]

$$N^* = \beta\frac{S}{F} \qquad \textbf{(4.4)}$$

An example will demonstrate that this approximation gives reasonable results. Suppose that

Value of S&P 500 index = 200

Value of portfolio = \$2,040,000

Risk-free interest rate = 10 percent per annum

Dividend yield on index = 4 percent per annum

Beta of portfolio = 1.5

We assume that a futures contract on the S&P 500 with four months to maturity is used to hedge the value of the portfolio over the next three months. One futures

---

[3]To prove Equation 4.4, we denote $\Delta S/S$ by R_S, and $\Delta F/F$ by R_F. Also, we denote the standard deviations of R_S and R_F by σ_1 and σ_2, respectively, and the coefficient of correlation between R_S and R_F by ρ^*. R_S is the return on the portfolio, and as an approximation we can assume that R_F is the return on the market. An approximate expression for β is therefore $\beta = \rho^*\sigma_1/\sigma_2$. Approximate expressions for σ_1, σ_2, and ρ^* are $\sigma_1 = \sigma_S/S$, $\sigma_2 = \sigma_F/F$, and $\rho^* = \rho$. It follows that β is approximately given by

$$\beta = \rho\frac{\sigma_S F}{\sigma_F S}$$

When used in conjunction with Equation 4.3, this leads to Equation 4.4.

contract is for delivery of $500 times the index. From Equation 3.12, the current futures price should be

$$200e^{(0.10-0.04) \times 1/3} = 204.04$$

and the price of a futures contract, F, should be $500 \times 204.04 = \$102,020$. From Equation 4.4, the number of futures contracts that should be shorted to hedge the portfolio is

$$1.5 \times \frac{2,040,000}{102,020} = 30$$

Suppose the index turns out to be 180 in three months. The futures price will be

$$180e^{(0.10-0.04) \times 1/12} = 180.90$$

The gain from the short futures position is therefore

$$30 \times (204.04 - 180.90) \times 500 = \$347,100$$

The loss on the index is 10 percent. The index pays a dividend of 4 percent per annum, or 1 percent per three months. When dividends are taken into account, an investor in the index would therefore earn –9 percent in the three-month period. The risk-free interest rate is approximately 2.5 percent per three months.[4] Since the portfolio has a β of 1.5,

Expected return on portfolio − Risk-free interest rate

$$= 1.5 \times (\text{Return on index} - \text{Risk-free interest rate})$$

It follows that the expected return (%) on the portfolio is

$$2.5 + [1.5 \times (-9.0 - 2.5)] = -14.75$$

The expected value of the portfolio (inclusive of dividends) at the end of the three months is therefore

$$\$2,040,000 \times (1 - 0.1475) = \$1,739,100$$

It follows that the expected value of the hedger's position, including the gain on the hedge, is

$$\$1,739,100 + \$347,100 = \$2,086,200$$

Table 4.7 summarizes these calculations together with similar calculations for other values of the index at maturity. It can be seen that the total value of the hedger's position in three months is almost independent of the value of the index.

Table 4.7 assumes that the dividend yield on the index is predictable, the risk-free interest rate remains constant, and the return on the index over the three-month period is perfectly correlated with the return on the portfolio. In practice, these assumptions do not hold perfectly, and the hedge works rather less well than is indicated by Table 4.7.

---

[4]For ease of presentation, the fact that the interest rate and dividend yield are continuously compounded has been ignored. This makes very little difference.

TABLE 4.7 Performance of Stock Index Hedge

Value of index in three months	180.00	190.00	200.00	210.00	220.00
Futures price of index in three months	180.90	190.95	201.00	211.05	221.10
Gain (loss) on futures position ($000)	347.1	195.3	45.6	(105.1)	(255.9)
Value of portfolio (including dividends) in three months ($000)	1739.1	1892.1	2045.1	2198.1	2351.1
Total value of position in three months ($000)	2086.2	2087.4	2090.7	2093.0	2095.2

REASONS FOR HEDGING A PORTFOLIO

Table 4.7 shows that the hedging scheme results in a value for the hedger's position very close to $2,090,000 at the end of three months. This is greater than the $2,040,000 initial value of the position by about 2.5 percent. There is no surprise here. The risk-free interest rate is 10 percent per annum, or about 2.5 percent per quarter. The hedge results in the hedger's position growing at the risk-free interest rate.

It is natural to ask why the hedger should go to the trouble of using futures contracts. To earn the risk-free interest rate, the hedger can simply sell the portfolio and invest the proceeds in Treasury bills.

One answer to this question is that hedging can be justified if the hedger feels that the stocks in the portfolio have been chosen well. In these circumstances, the hedger might be very uncertain about the performance of the market as a whole but confident that the stocks in the portfolio will outperform the market (after appropriate adjustments have been made for the beta of the portfolio). A hedge using index futures removes the risk arising from market moves and leaves the hedger exposed only to the performance of the portfolio relative to the market. Another reason for hedging may be that the hedger is planning to hold a portfolio for a long period of time and requires short-term protection in an uncertain market situation. The alternative strategy of selling the portfolio and buying it back later might involve unacceptably high transaction costs.

CHANGING BETA

In the example in Table 4.7, the beta of the hedger's portfolio is reduced to zero. Sometimes futures contracts are used to change the beta of a portfolio to some value other than zero. In the example, to reduce the beta of the portfolio from 1.5 to 0.75, the number of contracts shorted should be 15 rather than 30; to increase the beta of the portfolio to 2.0, a long position in 10 contracts should be taken; and so on. In general, to change the beta of the portfolio from β to β^* where $\beta > \beta^*$, a short position in

$$(\beta - \beta^*)\frac{S}{F}$$

contracts is required. When $\beta < \beta^*$, a long position in

$$(\beta^* - \beta)\frac{S}{F}$$

is required.

EXPOSURE TO THE PRICE OF AN INDIVIDUAL STOCK

Stock index futures can be used to hedge an exposure to the price of an individual stock. The number of contracts that the hedger should enter into is given by $\beta S/F$, where β is the beta of the stock, S is the total value of the shares being hedged, and F is the total price of one index futures contract. Note that although the number of contracts entered into is calculated in the same way as it is when a portfolio of stocks is being hedged, the performance of the hedge is considerably worse. The hedge provides protection only against the risk arising from market movements, and this risk is a relatively small proportion of the total risk in the price movements of individual stocks. The hedge is appropriate when an investor feels that the stock will outperform the market but is unsure about the performance of the market. It can also be used by an investment bank that has underwritten a new issue of the stock.

Consider an investor who in June holds 20,000 IBM shares, each worth $50. The investor feels that the market will be very volatile over the next month but that IBM has a good chance of outperforming the market. The investor decides to use the CBOT August futures contract on the Major Market Index (MMI) to hedge the position during the one-month period. The β of IBM is estimated at 1.1. The current futures price for the August contract on the MMI is 450, and each contract is for delivery of $500 times the index. This means that the total futures price corresponding to one contract is $500 \times 450 = \$225,000$. The total value of the stocks being hedged is $1 million. The number of contracts that should be shorted is therefore

$$1.1 \times \frac{1,000,000}{225,000} = 4.89$$

Rounding to the nearest integer, the hedger shorts five contracts, closing out the position one month later. Suppose IBM rises to $62.50 during the month, and the futures price of the Major Market Index rises to 540. The investor gains $20,000 \times (\$62.50 - \$50) = \$250,000$ on IBM while losing $5 \times 500 \times (540 - 450) = \$225,000$ on the futures contracts. The example is summarized in Table 4.8.

In this example, the hedge offsets a gain on the underlying asset with a loss on the futures contracts. The offset might seem to be counterproductive. However, it cannot be emphasized often enough that the purpose of a hedge is to reduce risk. A hedge tends to make unfavorable outcomes less unfavorable and favorable outcomes less favorable.

TABLE 4.8 Hedging a Position in an Individual Stock

From the Trader's Desk—June
An investor holds 20,000 IBM shares. The investor is concerned about the volatility of the market during the next month. The current market price of IBM is $50 and the August futures price of the Major Market Index is 450.

Strategy
  The investor

  1. Shorts five August contracts on the Major Market Index

  2. Closes out the position one month later

Outcome
  One month later the price of IBM is $62.50, and the futures price for the August Major Market Index contract is 540. The investor gains

$$20,000 \times (\$62.50 - \$50) = \$250,000$$

on the IBM shares and loses

$$5 \times 500 \times (540 - 450) = \$225,000$$

on the futures contract.

Rolling the Hedge Forward

Sometimes the expiration date of the hedge is later than the delivery dates of all the futures contracts that can be used. The hedger must then roll the hedge forward by closing out one futures contract and taking the same position in a futures contract with a later delivery date. Hedges can be rolled forward many times. Consider a company that wishes to use a short hedge to reduce the risk associated with the price to be received for an asset at time T. If there are futures contracts 1, 2, 3, ..., n (not all necessarily in existence at the present time) with progressively later delivery dates, the company can use the following strategy:

  Time t_1: Short futures contract 1.
  Time t_2: Close out futures contract 1.
          Short futures contract 2.
  Time t_3: Close out futures contract 2.
          Short futures contract 3.
          $\vdots$ $\vdots$
  Time t_n: Close out futures contract $n - 1$.
          Short futures contract n.
  Time T: Close out futures contract n.

  An example of this strategy is shown in Table 4.9. In April 1997 a company realizes that it will have 100,000 barrels of oil to sell in June 1998 and decides to hedge its risk with a hedge ratio of 1.0. The current spot price is $19. Although futures contracts are

TABLE 4.9 Rolling the Hedge Forward

From the Trader's Desk—April 1997

The price of oil is $19 per barrel. A company knows it will have 100,000 barrels of oil to sell in June 1998 and wishes to hedge its position. Contracts are traded on the NYMEX for every delivery month up to one year in the future. However, only the first six delivery months provide sufficient liquidity to meet the company's needs. The contract size is 1,000 barrels.

The Strategy

April 1997:	The company shorts 100 October 1997 contracts.
September 1997:	The company closes out the 100 October contracts. The company shorts 100 March 1998 contracts.
February 1998:	The company closes out the 100 March contracts. The company shorts 100 July 1998 contracts.
June 1998:	The company closes out the 100 July contracts. The company sells 100,000 barrels of oil.

The Outcome

October 1997 futures contract:	Shorted in April 1997 at $18.20 and closed out in September 1997 at $17.40
March 1998 futures contracts:	Shorted in September 1997 at $17.00 and closed out in February 1998 at $16.50
July 1998 futures contracts:	Shorted in February 1998 at $16.30 and closed out in June 1998 at $15.90
Spot oil price in June 1998:	$16 per barrel

The gain from the futures contracts is ($18.20−$17.40)+($17.00−$16.50)+($16.30−$15.90) = $1.70 per barrel. This partly offsets the $3 decline in oil prices between April 1997 and June 1998.

---

traded with maturities stretching several years into the future, we suppose that only the first six delivery months have sufficient liquidity to meet the company's needs. The company therefore shorts 100 October 1997 contracts. In September 1997 it rolls the hedge forward into the March 1998 contract. In February 1998 it rolls the hedge forward again into the July 1998 contract.

As one possible outcome, we suppose that the price of oil drops $3 to $16 per barrel in June 1998. We suppose that the October 1997 futures contract was shorted at $18.20 per barrel and closed out at $17.40 per barrel for a profit of $0.80 per barrel; the March 1998 contract was shorted at $17.00 per barrel and closed out at $16.50 per barrel for a profit of $0.50 per barrel. The July 1998 contract was shorted at $16.30 per barrel and closed out at $15.90 per barrel for a profit of $0.40 per barrel. In this case, the futures contracts provide a total of $1.70 per barrel compensation for the $3 per barrel oil price decline.

Receiving only $1.70 per barrel compensation for a price decline of $3.00 may appear unsatisfactory. However, we cannot expect total compensation for a price decline when futures prices are below spot prices. The best we can hope for is to lock in the futures price that would apply to a June 1998 contract if it were actively traded.

METALLGESELLSCHAFT

Sometimes rolling the hedge forward can lead to cash flow pressures. The problem was illustrated dramatically by the activities of a German company, Metallgesellschaft (MG), in the early 1990s.

MG sold a huge volume of 5- to 10-year heating oil and gasoline fixed-price supply contracts to its customers at 6 to 8 cents above market prices. It hedged its exposure with long positions in short futures contracts that were rolled over. As it turned out, the price of oil fell and there were margin calls on the futures position. Considerable short-term cash flow pressures were placed on MG. The members of MG who devised the hedging strategy argued that these short-term cash outflows were offset by positive cash flows that would ultimately be realized on the long-term fixed-price contracts. However, the company's senior management and its bankers became concerned about the huge cash drain. As a result, the company closed out all the hedge positions and agreed with its customers that the fixed-price contracts would be abandoned. The result was a loss to MG of $1.33 billion.[5]

Summary

This chapter has discussed various ways in which a company can take a position in futures contracts to offset an exposure to the price of an asset. If the exposure is such that the company gains when the price of the asset increases and loses when the price of the asset decreases, a short hedge is appropriate. If the exposure is the other way round (i.e., the company gains when the price of the asset decreases and loses when the price of the asset increases), a long hedge is appropriate.

Hedging is a way of reducing risk. As such, it should be welcomed by most executives. In reality, there are a number of theoretical and practical reasons that companies do not hedge. On a theoretical level, we can argue that shareholders, by holding well-diversified portfolios, can eliminate many of the risks faced by a company. They do not require the company to hedge these risks. On a practical level, a company may find that it is increasing rather than decreasing risk by hedging if none of its competitors does so. Also, a treasurer may fear criticism from other executives if the company makes a gain from movements in the price of the underlying asset and a loss on the hedge.

An important concept in hedging is basis risk. The basis is the difference between the spot price of an asset and its futures price. Basis risk is created by a hedger's uncertainty as to what the basis will be at maturity of the hedge. Basis risk is generally greater for consumption assets than for investment assets.

The hedge ratio is the ratio of the size of the position taken in futures contracts to the size of the exposure. It is not always optimal to use a hedge ratio of 1.0. If the hedger wishes to minimize the variance of a position, a hedge ratio different from 1.0 may be appropriate. The optimal hedge ratio is the slope of the best fit line obtained when changes in the spot price are regressed against changes in the futures price. When a stock index futures contract is used to hedge a position in a portfolio of stocks or a

---

[5] For a discussion of MG, see "MG's Trial by Essay," *RISK* (October 1994): 228–234, and M. Miller and C. Culp, "Risk Management Lessons from Metallgesellschaft," *Journal of Applied Corporate Finance* (Fall 1994).

position in an individual stock, the optimal number of futures contracts is equal to the beta of the position times the ratio of the value of the portfolio to the futures contract price.

When there is no liquid futures contract that matures later than the expiration of the hedge, a strategy known as rolling the hedge forward may be appropriate. This involves entering into a sequence of futures contracts. When the first futures contract is near expiration, it is closed out and the hedger enters into a second contract with a later delivery month. When the second contract is close to expiration, it is closed out and the hedger enters into a third contract with a later delivery month; and so on. Rolling the hedge works well if there is a close correlation between changes in the futures prices and changes in the spot prices.

Suggestions for Further Reading

Chicago Board of Trade. *Introduction to Hedging.* Chicago, 1984.

Ederington, L. H. "The Hedging Performance of the New Futures Market," *Journal of Finance* 34 (March 1979): 157–170.

Franckle, C. T. "The Hedging Performance of the New Futures Market: Comment," *Journal of Finance* 35 (December 1980): 1273–1279.

Johnson, L. L. "The Theory of Hedging and Speculation in Commodity Futures Markets," *Review of Economics Studies* 27 (October 1960): 139–151.

McCabe, G. M., and C. T. Franckle. "The Effectiveness of Rolling the Hedge Forward in the Treasury Bill Futures Market," *Financial Management* 12 (Summer 1983): 21–29.

Miller, M., and C. Culp. "Risk Management Lessons from Metallgesellschaft," *Journal of Applied Corporate Finance* (Fall 1994).

Nikkhah, S. "How End Users Can Hedge Fuel Costs in Energy Markets," *Futures* (October 1987): 66–67.

Stulz, R. M. "Optimal Hedging Policies," *Journal of Financial and Quantitative Analysis* 19 (June 1984): 127–140.

Quiz

1. Under what circumstances are (a) a short hedge and (b) a long hedge appropriate?
2. Explain what is meant by *basis risk* when futures contracts are used for hedging.
3. Explain what is meant by a *perfect hedge.* Does a perfect hedge always lead to a better outcome than an imperfect hedge? Explain your answer.
4. Under what circumstances does a minimum variance hedge portfolio lead to no hedging at all?
5. Give three reasons that the treasurer of a company might not hedge the company's exposure to a particular risk.
6. Suppose that the standard deviation of quarterly changes in the prices of a commodity is \$0.65, the standard deviation of quarterly changes in a futures price on the commodity is \$0.81, and the coefficient of correlation between the two changes is 0.8. What is the optimal hedge ratio for a three-month contract? What does it mean?

7. A company has a $10 million portfolio with a beta of 1.2. It would like to use futures contracts on the Major Market Index to hedge its risk. The index is currently standing at 270, and each contract is for delivery of $500 times the index. What is the hedge that minimizes risk? What should the company do if it wants to reduce the beta of the portfolio to 0.6?

Questions and Problems

4.1. In the Chicago Board of Trade's corn futures contract, the following delivery months are available: March, May, July, September, and December. State the contract that should be used for hedging when the expiration of the hedge is in
a. June
b. July
c. January

4.2. Does a perfect hedge always succeed in locking in the current spot price of an asset for a future transaction? Explain your answer.

4.3. Explain why a short hedger's position improves when the basis strengthens unexpectedly and worsens when the basis weakens unexpectedly.

4.4. Imagine you are the treasurer of a Japanese company exporting electronic equipment to the United States. Discuss how you would design a foreign exchange hedging strategy and the arguments you would use to sell the strategy to your fellow executives.

4.5. Suppose that in Table 4.5 the company decides to use a hedge ratio of 0.8. How does the decision affect the way in which the hedge is implemented and the result?

4.6. "If the minimum variance hedge ratio is calculated as 1.0, the hedge must be perfect." Is this statement true? Explain your answer.

4.7. "If there is no basis risk, the minimum variance hedge ratio is always 1.0." Is this statement true? Explain your answer.

4.8. "When the convenience yield is high, long hedges are likely to be particularly attractive." Explain this statement. Illustrate it with an example.

4.9. The standard deviation of monthly changes in the spot price of live cattle is (in cents per pound) 1.2. The standard deviation of monthly changes in the futures price of live cattle for the closest contract is 1.4. The correlation between the futures price changes and the spot price changes is 0.7. It is now October 15. A beef producer is committed to purchasing 200,000 pounds of live cattle on November 15. The producer wants to use the December live-cattle futures contracts to hedge its risk. Each contract is for the delivery of 40,000 pounds of cattle. What strategy should the beef producer follow?

4.10. A U.S. company is interested in using the futures contracts traded on the CME to hedge its German mark exposure. Define r as the interest rate (all maturities) on the U.S. dollar and r_f as the interest rate (all maturities) on the mark. Assume that r and r_f are constant and that the company uses a contract expiring at time T to hedge an exposure at time t ($T > t$). Using the results in chapter 3, show that the optimal hedge ratio is

$$e^{(r_f - r)(T - t)}$$

4.11. On July 1 an investor holds 50,000 shares of a certain stock. The market price is $30 per share. The investor is interested in hedging against movements in the market over the next two months and decides to use the December NYSE Index futures contract. The futures price is currently 150 and one contract is for delivery of $500 times the index. The beta of the stock is 1.3. What strategy should the investor follow?

4.12. It is July 16. A company has a portfolio of stocks worth $10 million. The beta of the portfolio is 1.0. The company would like to use the CME December futures contract on the S&P 500 to change the beta of the portfolio to 0.5 during the period July 16 to November 16. The contract's futures price is currently 400. What should the company do?

4.13. Suppose that in Problem 4.12 the company would like to change the beta of the portfolio to 1.5. What should it do?

4.14. The following table gives data on monthly changes in the spot price and the futures price for a certain commodity. Use the data to calculate a minimum variance hedge ratio.

Spot price change	+0.50	+0.61	−0.22	−0.35	+0.79
Futures price change	+0.56	+0.63	−0.12	−0.44	+0.60

Spot price change	+0.04	+0.15	+0.70	−0.51	−0.41
Futures price change	−0.06	+0.01	+0.80	−0.56	−0.46

4.15. Suppose that in Table 4.9 the company decides to use a hedge ratio of 1.5. How does the decision affect the way the hedge is implemented and the result?

APPENDIX 4A

A Proof of the Minimum Variance Hedge Ratio Formula

Suppose we expect to sell N_A units of an asset at time t_2 and choose to hedge at time t_1 by shorting futures contracts on N_F units of a similar asset. The hedge ratio, which we will denote by h, is

$$h = \frac{N_F}{N_A} \tag{4A.1}$$

We will denote the total amount realized for the asset when the profit or loss on the hedge is taken into account by Y, so that

$$Y = S_2 N_A - (F_2 - F_1) N_F$$

or

$$Y = S_1 N_A + (S_2 - S_1) N_A - (F_2 - F_1) N_F \tag{4A.2}$$

where S_1 and S_2 are the asset prices at times t_1 and t_2, and F_1 and F_2 are the futures prices at times t_1 and t_2. From Equation 4A.1, the expression for Y in Equation 4A.2 can be written

$$Y = S_1 N_A + N_A(\Delta S - h \Delta F) \tag{4A.3}$$

where

$$\Delta S = S_2 - S_1$$
$$\Delta F = F_2 - F_1$$

Since S_1 and N_A are known at time t_1, the variance of Y in Equation 4A.3 is minimized when the variance of $\Delta S - h \Delta F$ is minimized. The variance of $\Delta S - h \Delta F$ equals

$$\sigma_S^2 + h^2 \sigma_F^2 - 2h \rho \sigma_S \sigma_F$$

This can be written as

$$(h\sigma_F - \rho\sigma_S)^2 + \sigma_S^2 - \rho^2\sigma_S^2$$

The second and third terms do not involve h. The variance is therefore minimized when

$$(h\sigma_F - \rho\sigma_S)^2$$

is zero—that is, when

$$h = \rho\frac{\sigma_S}{\sigma_F}$$

5

Interest-Rate Futures

An interest-rate futures contract is a futures contract on an asset whose price is dependent solely on the level of interest rates. In this chapter we examine the mechanics of how interest rate futures contracts work and how prices are quoted. We also review the way in which futures prices can be related to spot prices and consider the concept of duration along with a number of hedging strategies involving interest-rate futures.

Hedging a company's exposure to interest rates is more complicated than hedging its exposure to, say, the price of copper. A whole term structure is necessary to provide a full description of the level of interest rates, whereas the price of copper can be described by a single number. When wishing to hedge its interest-rate exposure, a company must decide not only the maturity of the hedge it requires but also the maturity of the interest rate to which it is exposed. It must then find a way of using available interest-rate futures contracts so that an appropriate hedge is obtained.

Some Preliminaries

Before we examine the nature of interest-rate futures contracts, it is appropriate to review a few topics concerned with the term structure of interest rates.

SPOT AND FORWARD INTEREST RATES

The n-year spot interest rate or n-year zero-coupon rate is the interest rate on an investment that is made for a period of time starting today and lasting for n years. Thus, the three-year spot rate is the rate of interest on an investment lasting three years; the five-year spot rate is the rate of interest on an investment lasting five years; and so on. The investment considered is a "pure" n-year investment with no intermediate payments. This means that all the interest and the principal are repaid to the investor at the end of year n.

Forward interest rates are the rates of interest implied by current spot rates for periods of time in the future. To illustrate how they are calculated, we suppose that the

TABLE 5.1 Calculation of Forward Rates

Year (n)	Spot Rate for an n-Year Investment (% per annum)	Forward Rate for nth Year (% per annum)
1	10.0	
2	10.5	11.0
3	10.8	11.4
4	11.0	11.6
5	11.1	11.5

spot rates are as shown in the second column of Table 5.1. The rates are assumed to be continuously compounded. Thus, the 10 percent per annum rate for one year means that, in return for an investment of $100 today, the investor receives $100e^{0.1} = \$110.52$ in one year; the 10.5 percent per annum rate for two years means that, in return for an investment of $100 today, the investor receives $100e^{0.105 \times 2} = \$123.37$ in two years; and so on.[1]

The forward interest rate in Table 5.1 for year 2 is 11 percent per annum. This is the rate of interest that is implied by the spot rates for the period of time between the end of the first year and the end of the second year. It can be calculated from the one-year spot interest rate of 10 percent per annum and the two-year spot interest rate of 10.5 percent per annum. It is the rate of interest for year 2 that, when combined with 10 percent per annum for year 1, gives 10.5 percent overall for the two years. To show that the correct answer is 11 percent per annum, suppose that $100 is invested. A rate of 10 percent for the first year and 11 percent for the second year yields

$$100e^{0.1}e^{0.11} = \$123.37$$

at the end of the second year. A rate of 10.5 percent per annum for two years yields

$$100e^{0.105 \times 2}$$

which is also $123.37. This example illustrates the general result that when interest rates are continuously compounded and rates in successive time periods are combined, the overall equivalent rate is simply the arithmetic average of the rates (10.5 percent is the average of 10 percent and 11 percent). The result is only approximately true when the rates are not continuously compounded.

The forward rate for year 3 is the rate of interest that is implied by a 10.5 percent per annum two-year spot rate and a 10.8 percent per annum three-year spot rate. It is 11.4 percent per annum. The reason is that an investment for two years at 10.5 percent per annum combined with an investment for one year at 11.4 percent per annum gives an overall return for the three years of 10.8 percent per annum. The other forward rates can be calculated similarly and are shown in the third column of the table. In general, if R_1 and R_2 are the spot rates for maturities T_1 and T_2, respectively, and R_F is the forward

---

[1]Continuous compounding and the role played by *e* were explained at the beginning of chapter 3.

interest rate for the period of time between T_1 and T_2:

$$R_F = \frac{R_2 T_2 - R_1 T_1}{T_2 - T_1} \qquad (5.1)$$

To illustrate this formula, consider the calculation of the year 4 forward rate from the data in Table 5.1: $T_1 = 3$, $T_2 = 4$, $R_1 = 0.108$, and $R_2 = 0.11$, and the formula gives $R_F = 0.116$.

Assuming that an investor can borrow or invest at the spot rate, the investor can lock in the forward rate for borrowing or investing during a future time period. For example, with the interest rates in Table 5.1, if an investor borrows $100 at 10 percent for one year and then invests the money at 10.5 percent for two years, the result is a cash outflow of $100e^{0.1} = \$110.52$ at the end of year 1 and an inflow of $100e^{0.105 \times 2} = \$123.37$ at the end of year 2. Because $123.37 = 110.52e^{0.11}$, a return equal to the forward rate (11 percent) is earned on $110.52 during the second year. For another example, suppose that the investor borrows $100 for four years at 11 percent and invests it for three years at 10.8 percent. The result is a cash inflow of $100e^{0.108 \times 3} = \$138.26$ at the end of the third year and a cash outflow of $100e^{0.11 \times 4} = \$155.27$ at the end of the fourth year. Because $155.27 = 138.26e^{0.116}$, money is being borrowed for the fourth year at the forward rate of 11.6 percent.

THE ZERO-COUPON YIELD CURVE

A *zero-coupon bond* is a bond that pays no coupons. The holder of the bond receives all interest and principal at the end of the bond's life. Zero-coupon bonds are not often issued in practice. However, they are sometimes created artificially by "stripping" coupons from regular coupon-bearing bonds and selling the coupons separately from the principal. By definition the yield on an *n*-year zero-coupon bond is the *n*-year spot rate.

The *zero-coupon yield curve* is a curve showing the relationship between the yields on zero-coupon bonds and maturity. (Equivalently, it is a curve showing the relationship between spot rates and maturity.) Figure 5.1 shows the zero-coupon yield curve for the data in Table 5.1. It is important to distinguish between the zero-coupon yield curve and

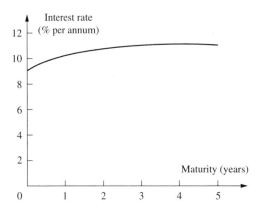

FIGURE 5.1 Zero-Coupon Yield Curve for the Data in Table 5.1

a yield curve for coupon-bearing bonds. In a situation such as that shown in Figure 5.1, where the yield curve is upward sloping, the zero-coupon yield curve will always be above the yield curve for coupon-bearing bonds. The yield on a coupon-bearing bond is affected by the fact that the investor gets some payments before the maturity of the bond, and the discount rates corresponding to these payment dates are lower than the discount rate corresponding to the final payment date. One particular coupon-bearing bond yield that is often considered is a *par bond yield*. This is the yield on a bond whose coupon is chosen so that it sells for exactly its face value of 100.

Analysts sometimes also look at the curve relating forward rates to the maturity of the forward contract. The forward rates can be defined so that they apply to future periods that have a length of three months or six months or any other convenient time period. As illustrated by Table 5.1, when the yield curve is upward sloping, forward rates are higher than zero-coupon yields.

Figure 5.2 shows the zero-coupon yield curve, coupon-bearing yield curve, and forward rate curve when the yield curve is upward sloping. The forward rate curve is above the zero-coupon yield curve, which is in turn above the coupon-bearing yield curve. Figure 5.3 shows the situation when the yield curve is downward sloping. In this

FIGURE 5.2 Situation When Yield Curve Is Upward Sloping

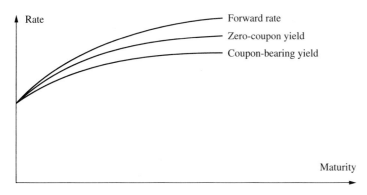

FIGURE 5.3 Situation When Yield Curve Is Downward Sloping

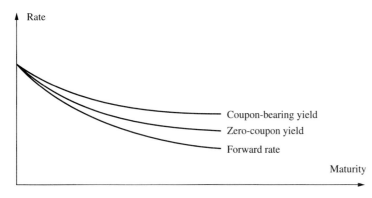

case the coupon-bearing yield curve is above the zero-coupon yield curve, which is in turn above the forward rate curve.

DETERMINATION OF ZERO-COUPON YIELD CURVE

In practice, spot rates (or zero-coupon yields) cannot usually be observed directly. What can be observed are the prices of coupon-bearing bonds. An important issue therefore is how the zero-coupon yield curve can be extracted from the prices of coupon-bearing bonds.

One approach is known as the *bootstrap method*. To illustrate it, consider the data in Table 5.2 on the prices of five bonds. Since the first three bonds pay no coupons, the continuously compounded spot rates corresponding to the maturities of these bonds can easily be calculated using Equation 3.3. The three-month bond provides a return of 2.5 on an initial investment of 97.5 in three months. With quarterly compounding the rate is 2.5/97.5 = 2.56 percent per three months. With continuous compounding, Equation 3.3 shows that it becomes

$$4 \ln\left(1 + \frac{2.5}{97.5}\right) = 0.1013$$

or 10.13 percent per annum. Similarly, the six-month rate with continuous compounding is

$$2 \ln\left(1 + \frac{5.1}{94.9}\right) = 0.1047$$

or 10.47 percent per annum, and the one-year rate with continuous compounding is

$$\ln\left(1 + \frac{10}{90.0}\right) = 0.1054$$

or 10.54 percent per annum.

The fourth bond lasts 1.5 years. The payments are as follows:

6 months: $4
1 year: $4
1.5 years: $104

TABLE 5.2 Data for Bootstrap Method

Bond Principal ($)	Time to Maturity (years)	Annual Coupon ($)*	Bond Price ($)
100	0.25	0	97.5
100	0.50	0	94.9
100	1.00	0	90.0
100	1.50	8	96.0
100	2.00	12	101.6

* Half the stated coupon is assumed to be paid every six months.

From our earlier calculations, we know that the discount rate for the payment at the end of six months is 10.47 percent and the discount rate for the payment at the end of 1 year is 10.54 percent. We also know that the bond's price, $96, must equal the present value of all the payments received by the bondholder. Suppose the 1.5-year spot rate is denoted by R. It follows that

$$4e^{-0.1047 \times 0.5} + 4e^{-0.1054 \times 1.0} + 104e^{-R \times 1.5} = 96$$

This reduces to

$$e^{-1.5R} = 0.85196$$

or

$$R = -\frac{\ln(0.85196)}{1.5} = 0.1068$$

The 1.5-year spot rate is therefore 10.68 percent. This is the only spot rate that is consistent with the six-month and one-year spot rate and consistent with the data in Table 5.2.

The two-year spot rate can be calculated similarly from the six-month, one-year, and 1.5-year spot rates and the information on the fifth bond in Table 5.2. If R is the two-year spot rate,

$$6e^{-0.1047 \times 0.5} + 6e^{-0.1054 \times 1.0} + 6e^{-0.1068 \times 1.5} + 106e^{-R \times 2.0} = 101.6$$

This gives $R = 0.1081$, or 10.81 percent.

By continuing in this way, we can obtain a complete term structure. The points obtained on the zero curve are joined by straight lines, as indicated in Figure 5.4. In the example just considered, the 1.25-year spot rate would be $0.5 \times 10.54 + 0.5 \times 10.68 = 10.61$ percent.

FIGURE 5.4 Zero Rates Given by the Bootstrap Method

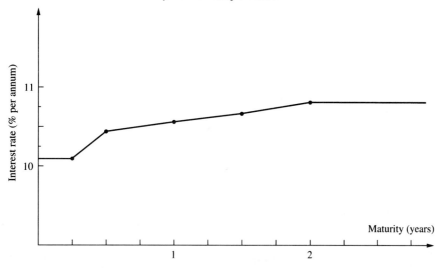

DAY COUNT CONVENTIONS

In chapter 3 we discussed the interpretation of the compounding frequency that is used when an interest rate is quoted. We now examine the day count convention. This is a quite separate issue from compounding frequency. The day count defines the way in which interest accrues over time. Generally, we know the interest earned over some reference period (e.g., the time between coupon payments), and we are interested in calculating the interest earned over some other period.

The day count convention is usually expressed as X/Y. When we are calculating the interest earned between two dates, X defines the way in which the number of days between the two dates is calculated, and Y defines the way in which the total number of days in the reference period is measured. The interest earned between the two dates is

$$\frac{\text{Number of days between dates}}{\text{Number of days in reference period}} \times \text{Interest earned in reference period}$$

Three day count conventions that are commonly used in the United States are:

1. Actual/actual (in period)
2. 30/360
3. Actual/360

Actual/actual (in period) is used for U.S. Treasury bonds; 30/360 is used for U.S. corporate and municipal bonds; and actual/360 is used for U.S. Treasury bills and other money market instruments.

The use of actual/actual (in period) for Treasury bonds indicates that accrued interest is based on the ratio of the actual days elapsed to the actual number of days in the period between coupon payments. Suppose that the bond principal is $100, coupon payment dates are March 1 and September 1, and the coupon rate is 8 percent. We wish to calculate the interest earned between March 1 and July 3. The reference period is from March 1 to September 1. There are 184 (actual) days in this period, and interest of $4 is earned during the period. There are 124 (actual) days between March 1 and July 3. The interest earned between March 1 and July 3 is therefore

$$\frac{124}{184} \times 4 = 2.6957$$

The use of 30/360 for corporate and municipal bonds indicates that we assume 30 days per month and 360 days per year when carrying out calculations. With 30/360, the total number of days between March 1 and September 1 is 180. The total number of days between March 1 and July 3 is $(4 \times 30) + 2 = 122$. In a corporate bond with the same terms as the Treasury bond just considered, the interest earned between March 1 and July 3 would therefore be

$$\frac{122}{180} \times 4 = 2.7111$$

The use of actual/360 for a money market instrument indicates that the reference period is 360 days. The interest earned during part of a year is calculated by dividing the actual number of elapsed days by 360 and multiplying by the rate. The interest earned in 90 days is therefore exactly one-fourth of the quoted rate. Note that the interest earned in a whole year of 365 days is 365/360 times the quoted rate.

THEORIES OF THE TERM STRUCTURE

A number of different theories of the term structure have been proposed. The simplest is *expectations theory,* which conjectures that long-term interest rates should reflect expected future short-term interest rates. More precisely, it argues that a forward interest rate corresponding to a certain period is equal to the expected future spot interest rate for that period. Another approach, *market segmentation theory,* conjectures that there need be no relationship between short-, medium-, and long-term interest rates. Under the theory, different institutions invest in bonds of different maturities and do not switch maturities. The short-term interest rate is determined by supply and demand in the short-term bond market; the medium-term interest rate is determined by supply and demand in the medium-term bond market; and so on.

The theory that is in some ways most appealing is *liquidity preference theory,* which argues that forward rates should always be higher than expected future spot interest rates. The basic assumption underlying the theory is that investors prefer to preserve their liquidity and invest funds for short periods of time. Borrowers, on the other hand, usually prefer to borrow at fixed rates for long periods of time. If the interest rates offered by banks and other financial intermediaries were such that the forward rate equaled the expected future spot rate, long-term interest rates would equal the average of expected future short-term interest rates. In the absence of any incentive to do otherwise, investors would tend to deposit their funds for short time periods and borrowers would tend to choose to borrow for long time periods. Financial intermediaries would then find themselves financing substantial amounts of long-term fixed-rate loans with short-term deposits. Excessive interest-rate risk would result. In practice, in order to match depositors with borrowers and avoid interest-rate risk, financial intermediaries raise long-term interest rates relative to expected future short-term interest rates. This strategy reduces the demand for long-term fixed-rate borrowing and encourages investors to deposit their funds for long terms.

Liquidity preference theory leads to a situation in which forward rates are greater than expected future spot rates. It is also consistent with the empirical result that yield curves tend to be upward sloping more often than they are downward sloping.

Forward-Rate Agreements

A *forward-rate agreement (FRA)* is a forward contract in which the parties agree that a certain interest rate will apply to a certain principal during a specified future period of time. An FRA is generally settled in cash at the beginning of the specified period of time. In this section we examine how forward-rate agreements can be valued in terms of forward rates.

Consider a forward-rate agreement in which it is agreed that an interest rate of R_K will be earned for the period of time between T_1 and T_2 on a principal of 100. The forward-rate agreement is an agreement to the following cash flows:

Time T_1: -100

Time T_2: $+100e^{R_K(T_2-T_1)}$

The value of the agreement, V, can be found by taking the present value of these cash flows:

$$V = 100e^{R_K(T_2-T_1)}e^{-R_2T_2} - 100e^{-R_1T_1} \tag{5.2}$$

As in Equation 5.1, we assume that R_1 and R_2 are the spot rates for maturities of T_1 and T_2, respectively, and R_F is the forward rate for the period of time between T_1 and T_2. As with all other forward contracts, an FRA is worth zero when it is initiated. Setting $V = 0$ in Equation 5.2, we see that

$$R_K(T_2 - T_2) - R_2T_2 = -R_1T_1$$

or

$$R_K = \frac{R_2T_2 - R_1T_1}{T_2 - T_1}$$

Comparing this with Equation (5.1), we see that the agreed rate, R_K, equals the forward interest rate, R_F, when the forward rate is initiated.

Substituting for R_2T_2 from Equation 5.1 into Equation 5.2, we obtain

$$V = 100e^{R_K(T_2-T_1)}e^{-R_F(T_2-T_1)-R_1T_1} - 100e^{-R_1T_1}$$

or

$$V = [100e^{R_K(T_2-T_1)}e^{-R_F(T_2-T_1)} - 100]e^{-R_1T_1} \tag{5.3}$$

If we knew that the rate for the period between times T_1 and T_2 was going to be R_F, the expression

$$100e^{R_K(T_2-T_1)}e^{-R_F(T_2-T_1)}$$

would be the value of the cash flow at time T_2 as seen at time T_1. The right hand side of Equation 5.3 would therefore represent the present value of the FRA's cash flows. It follows that we can always value FRAs on the assumption that the current forward rates are realized. This will prove to be a useful result in the valuation of swaps in chapter 6.

Example

Suppose that the zero-coupon yield curve is as in Table 5.1 and that we have entered into an FRA where we will receive a rate of 12 percent with annual compounding on a principal of $1 million between the end of year 1 and the end of year 2. We can value the FRA on the assumption that the forward rate is realized. In this case, the forward rate is 11 percent with continuous compounding or 11.6278 percent with annual compounding. The value of the forward contract is therefore the present value of the difference between receiving $120,000 (12% of 1 million) and $116,278 (11.6278% of 1 million) at the end of year 2. From Table 5.1 the two-year zero rate is 10.5 percent with continuous compounding. It follows that the value of the FRA is

$$(120,000 - 116,278)e^{-0.105 \times 2} = \$3,017$$

Treasury Bond and Treasury Note Futures

Table 5.3 shows interest-rate futures quotes as they appeared in the *Wall Street Journal* on September 25, 1996. The most popular long-term interest-rate futures contract is the Treasury bond futures contract traded on the Chicago Board of Trade. In this contract, any government bond that has more than 15 years to maturity on the first day of the delivery month and that is not callable within 15 years from that day can be delivered. As will be explained later, the CBOT has developed a procedure for adjusting the price received by the party with the short position according to the particular bond delivered.

The Treasury note and five-year Treasury note futures contract are also actively traded. In the Treasury note futures contract, any government bond (or note) with a maturity between $6\frac{1}{2}$ and 10 years can be delivered. As in the case of the Treasury bond futures contract, there is a way of adjusting the price received by the party with the short position according to the particular note delivered. In the five-year Treasury note futures contract, any of the four most recently auctioned Treasury notes can be delivered.

The remaining discussion in this section focuses on Treasury bond futures. However, many of the points made are applicable to the other contracts on bonds.

QUOTES

Treasury bond prices are quoted in dollars and thirty-seconds of a dollar. The quoted price is for a bond with a face value of $100. Thus, a quote of 90-05 means that the indicated price for a bond with a face value of $100,000 is $90,156.25.

The quoted price is not the same as the cash price that is paid by the purchaser. In general,

Cash price = Quoted price + Accrued interest since last coupon date

To illustrate this formula, suppose that it is March 5, 1998 and the bond under consideration is an 11 percent coupon bond maturing on July 10, 2001 with a quoted price of 95-16, or $95.50. Since coupons are paid semiannually on government bonds, the most recent coupon date is January 10, 1998 and the next coupon date is July 10, 1998. The number of days between January 10, 1998 and March 5, 1998 is 54, whereas the number of days between January 10, 1998 and July 10, 1998 is 181. On a bond with $100 face value, the coupon payment is $5.50 on January 10 and July 10. The accrued interest on March 5, 1998 is the share of the July 10 coupon accruing to the bondholder on March 5, 1998. Since actual/actual is used for Treasury bonds, this is

$$\frac{54}{181} \times \$5.5 = \$1.64$$

The cash price per $100 face value for the July 10, 2001 bond is therefore

$$\$95.5 + \$1.64 = \$97.14$$

Thus, the cash price of a $100,000 bond is $97,140.

TABLE 5.3 Interest Rate Futures Quotes from the *Wall Street Journal* on September 25, 1996

TREASURY BONDS (CBT)-$100,000; pts. 32nds of 100%

	Open	High	Low	Settle	Change	Lifetime High	Lifetime Low	Open Interest
Dec	108-03	109-00	107-25	108-20	+ 17	120-15	92-27	359,672
Mr97	107-20	108-16	107-13	108-05	+ 17	120-00	104-24	20,336
June	107-12	107-22	107-12	107-22	+ 16	118-21	104-09	5,074
Sept	....	....	....	107-10	+ 16	110-08	104-31	117
Dec	....	....	....	106-31	+ 16	109-28	105-28	241

Est vol 275,000; vol Mn 107,347; op int 394,371, −9,461.

TREASURY BONDS (MCE)-$50,000; pts. 32nds of 100%

	Open	High	Low	Settle	Change	Lifetime High	Lifetime Low	Open Interest
Dec	108-05	109-01	107-26	108-19	+ 16	117-29	105-01	9,882

Est vol 4,500; vol Mn 1,573; open int 10,329, −261.

TREASURY NOTES (CBT)-$100,000; pts. 32nds of 100%

	Open	High	Low	Settle	Change	Lifetime High	Lifetime Low	Open Interest
Dec	106-17	107-08	106-11	106-30	+ 13	108-27	104-12	268,061
Mr97	106-09	106-27	106-06	106-21	+ 14	113-09	104-15	3,045
June	....	....	....	106-06	+ 13	107-00	104-19	120

Est vol 50,005; vol Mn 25,796; open int 278,971, +961.

5 YR TREAS NOTES (CBT)-$100,000; pts. 32nds of 100%

	Open	High	Low	Settle	Change	Lifetime High	Lifetime Low	Open Interest
Dec	05025	105-22	104-29	05135	+ 11.5	106-31	103-18	143,307

Est vol 35,000; vol Mn 16,741; open int 147,367, −336.

2 YR TREAS NOTES (CBT)-$200,000; pts. 32nds of 100%

	Open	High	Low	Settle	Change	Lifetime High	Lifetime Low	Open Interest
Dec	102-22	103-00	102-21	03055	+ 5.7	03-065	02-035	16,275

Est vol 2,000; vol Mn 158; open int 17,503, −36.

30-DAY FEDERAL FUNDS (CBT)-$5 million; pts. of 100%

	Open	High	Low	Settle	Change	Lifetime High	Lifetime Low	Open Interest
Sept	94.690	94.715	94.680	94.715	+.025	95.430	94.360	4,490
Oct	94.58	94.72	94.57	94.71	+.13	95.51	94.20	7,707
Nov	94.50	94.62	94.48	94.62	+.12	95.54	94.14	7,437
Dec	94.36	94.49	94.35	94.48	+.12	95.47	94.00	1,658
Ja97	94.25	94.35	94.25	94.35	+.12	95.35	93.90	263
Feb	94.20	94.30	94.20	94.30	+.12	94.44	93.98	146
Mar	94.12	94.23	94.12	94.23	+.12	94.38	93.94	206

Est vol 8,899; vol Mn 6,469; open int 21,908, +2,528.

MUNI BOND INDEX (CBT)-$1,000; times Bond Buyer MBI

	Open	High	Low	Settle	Chg	High	Low	Open Interest
Dec	113-05	113-27	112-28	113-20	+ 17	114-10	107-10	6,885

Est vol 3,000; vol Mn 1,130; open int 6,886, +74.
The index: Close 115-18; Yield 6.07.

TREASURY BILLS (CME)-$1 mil.; pts. of 100%

	Open	High	Low	Settle	Chg	Discount Settle	Chg	Open Interest
Dec	94.62	94.75	94.62	94.74	+.12	5.26	−.12	4,023
Mr97	94.47	94.59	94.46	94.57	+.13	5.43	−.13	1,488

Est vol 696; vol Mon 207; open int 5,526, −69.

LIBOR-1 MO. (CME)-$3,000,000; points of 100%

	Open	High	Low	Settle	Chg	Yield Settle	Chg	Open Interest
Oct	94.41	94.58	94.39	94.55	+.15	5.45	−.15	22,203
Nov	94.29	94.42	94.28	94.42	+.14	5.58	−.14	17,396
Dec	94.06	94.20	94.06	94.18	+.11	5.82	−.11	11,262
Ja97	94.18	94.30	94.18	94.29	+.11	5.71	−.11	2,086
Feb	94.08	94.21	94.08	94.21	+.12	5.79	−.12	459
Mar	94.02	94.13	94.02	94.14	+.13	5.86	−.13	380
Apr	....	....	....	94.07	+.13	5.93	−.13	190
May	....	....	....	94.01	+.13	5.99	−.13	124
June	....	....	....	93.96	+.12	6.04	−.12	389
July	....	....	....	93.90	+.12	6.10	−.12	100
Aug	....	....	....	93.85	+.12	6.15	−.12	186

Est vol 10,731; vol Mon 6,154; open int 54,775, +1,821.

EURODOLLAR (CME)-$1 million; pts of 100%

	Open	High	Low	Settle	Chg	Yield Settle	Chg	Open Interest
Oct	94.23	94.37	94.23	94.36	+.13	5.64	−.13	29,882
Nov	94.11	94.24	94.11	94.23	+.12	5.77	−.12	7,345
Dec	94.06	94.20	94.04	94.18	+.12	5.82	−.12	477,138
Mr97	93.90	94.05	93.89	94.02	+.13	5.98	−.13	346,799
June	93.74	93.90	93.70	93.85	+.12	6.15	−.12	260,760
Sept	93.59	93.75	93.57	93.70	+.12	6.30	−.12	176,971
Dec	93.44	93.58	93.39	93.51	+.10	6.49	−.10	143,642
Mr98	93.36	93.49	93.34	93.44	+.09	6.56	−.09	125,949
June	93.27	93.39	93.25	93.35	+.09	6.65	−.09	98,528
Sept	93.21	93.33	93.20	93.29	+.09	6.71	−.09	82,389
Dec	93.11	93.21	93.10	93.18	+.08	6.82	−.08	69,427
Mr99	93.09	93.18	93.08	93.15	+.07	6.85	−.07	59,057
June	93.02	93.11	93.01	93.08	+.07	6.92	−.07	56,582
Sept	92.97	93.12	92.95	93.03	+.07	6.97	−.07	44,280
Dec	92.88	92.97	92.87	92.94	+.07	7.06	−.07	36,275
Mr00	92.87	92.96	92.86	92.93	+.07	7.07	−.07	39,258
June	92.81	92.90	92.80	92.87	+.07	7.13	−.07	34,393
Sept	92.77	92.86	92.76	92.82	+.06	7.18	−.06	26,751
Dec	92.70	92.77	92.68	92.74	+.06	7.26	−.06	24,138
Mr01	92.70	92.77	92.68	92.74	+.06	7.26	−.06	22,741
June	92.64	92.72	92.63	92.69	+.06	7.31	−.06	17,714
Sept	92.59	92.67	92.57	92.64	+.06	7.36	−.06	8,509
Dec	92.51	92.60	92.50	92.57	+.06	7.43	−.06	8,082
Mr02	92.51	92.60	92.50	92.57	+.06	7.43	−.06	5,580
June	92.46	92.56	92.46	92.53	+.06	7.47	−.06	5,192
Sept	92.45	92.53	92.43	92.49	+.05	7.51	−.05	5,302
Dec	92.37	92.45	92.37	92.42	+.05	7.58	−.05	6,506
Mr03	92.37	92.45	92.37	92.42	+.05	7.58	−.05	5,386
June	92.33	92.41	92.33	92.38	+.05	7.62	−.05	4,908
Sept	92.30	92.38	92.30	92.35	+.05	7.65	−.05	4,135
Dec	....	....	....	92.28	+.05	7.72	−.05	3,159
Mr04	....	....	....	92.28	+.05	7.72	−.05	1,693
June	....	....	....	92.24	+.05	7.76	−.05	3,234
Sept	92.19	92.24	92.19	92.22	+.05	7.78	−.05	2,961
Dec	....	....	....	92.15	+.05	7.85	−.05	3,426
Mr05	....	....	....	92.16	+.05	7.84	−.05	1,638
June	....	....	....	92.12	+.05	7.88	−.05	2,031
Sept	....	....	....	92.10	+.05	7.90	−.05	1,447
Dec	....	....	....	92.03	+.05	7.97	−.05	1,012
Mr06	....	....	....	92.04	+.05	7.96	−.05	1,130
June	....	....	....	92.01	+.05	7.99	−.05	375

Est vol 514,779; vol Mon 146,439; open int 2,255,760, +489.

EUROYEN (CME) -Yen 100,000,000; pts. of 100%

	Open	High	Low	Settle	Change	Lifetime High	Lifetime Low	Open interest
Dec	99.36	99.44	99.35	99.41	+.06	99.44	98.39	8,080
Mr97	99.17	99.27	99.17	99.23	+.06	99.27	98.09	4,583
June	98.99	99.08	98.98	99.04	+.07	99.08	97.80	4,464
Sept	98.77	98.85	98.77	98.85	+.10	98.85	97.50	1,064
Dec	98.57	98.63	98.56	98.63	+.09	98.63	97.30	1,035
Mr98	98.33	98.39	98.33	98.38	+.07	98.39	97.04	894
June	98.12	98.16	98.12	98.16	+.09	98.16	96.81	293
Sept	....	....	....	97.92	+.08	97.90	96.62	212
Dec	....	....	....	97.67	+.06	97.65	96.39	44
Mr99	....	....	....	97.42	+.06	97.37	96.67	207

Est vol 8,564; vol Mon 3,012; open int 20,876, +296.

STERLING (LIFFE)-£500,000; pts of 100%

	Open	High	Low	Settle	Change	Lifetime High	Lifetime Low	Open Interest
Dec	94.04	94.06	93.99	94.00	−.04	94.32	90.30	119,027
Mr97	93.84	93.88	93.80	93.83	−.01	94.13	90.20	78,419
June	93.52	93.55	93.47	93.51	0	93.81	90.05	77,398
Sept	93.17	93.19	93.12	93.15	−.01	93.48	89.92	41,674
Dec	92.86	92.88	92.81	92.82	−.01	93.28	90.10	31,541
Mr98	92.63	92.65	92.61	92.61	−.01	93.06	90.58	23,724
June	92.49	92.49	92.44	92.46	−.01	92.92	90.89	20,340
Sept	92.36	92.38	92.35	92.35	+ 0	92.78	91.30	12,390
Dec	92.27	92.28	92.25	92.25	+ 0	92.66	91.27	12,685
Mr99	92.16	92.17	92.16	92.15	+.01	92.29	91.45	5,913
June	92.04	92.04	92.04	92.04	+.02	92.16	91.53	3,961
Sept	91.96	91.97	91.96	91.94	+ 0	92.02	91.92	498

Est vol 83,603; vol Mon 67,104; open int 427,570, +2,043.

LONG GILT (LIFFE)-£50,000; 32nds of 100%

	Open	High	Low	Settle	Change	Lifetime High	Lifetime Low	Open Interest
Sept	108-05	108-07	108-03	108-05	+ 0-03	108-27	103-15	11,839
Dec	107-13	107-17	107-11	107-15	+ 0-03	108-06	104-31	119,193

Est vol 40,352; vol Mon 35,209; open int 131,036, −3,289.

EUROMARK (LIFFE)-DM 1,000,000; pts of 100%

	Open	High	Low	Settle	Change	Lifetime High	Lifetime Low	Open Interest
Dec	96.79	96.81	96.78	96.80	+.02	96.88	92.42	229,381
Mr97	96.66	96.72	96.68	96.71	+.04	96.75	92.22	212,194
June	96.48	96.52	96.47	96.51	+.04	96.58	92.20	163,487
Sept	96.21	96.24	96.20	96.24	+.04	96.32	92.06	128,244
Dec	95.87	95.91	95.86	95.91	+.04	96.00	91.94	93,608
Mr98	95.53	95.58	95.53	95.57	+.03	95.68	92.00	59,948
June	95.23	95.26	95.23	95.25	+.04	95.33	92.59	44,412
Sept	94.93	94.95	94.92	94.94	+.03	95.02	93.38	32,793
Dec	94.63	94.65	94.63	94.65	+.04	94.71	93.40	24,891
Mr99	94.36	94.38	94.36	94.38	+.05	94.42	93.24	20,940
June	94.11	94.11	94.07	94.11	+.06	94.14	93.29	13,054
Sept	93.84	93.84	93.83	93.85	+.06	93.88	93.80	4,167

Est vol 100,025; vol Mon 59,940; open int 1,027,119, +6,010.

EUROSWISS (LIFFE)-SFr 1,000,000; pts of 100%

	Open	High	Low	Settle	Change	Lifetime High	Lifetime Low	Open Interest
Dec	98.17	98.18	98.14	98.14	−.03	98.25	96.96	42,483
Mr97	98.07	98.08	98.02	98.03	−.02	98.10	96.72	21,743
June	97.82	97.82	97.78	97.79	−.02	97.84	96.47	8,391
Sept	97.52	97.52	97.51	97.51	−.02	97.57	96.28	2,237
Dec	....	....	....	97.26	−.02	97.31	96.02	1,269
Mr98	97.06	97.06	97.06	97.05	−.02	97.15	96.92	447

Est vol 7,069; vol Mon 12,774; open int 76,570, −536.

continues on next page, column 1

TABLE 5.3 (cont.)

3-MONTH EURO LIRA (LIFFE)
ITL 1,000,000,000; pts of 100%

Dec	91.97	92.04	91.93	92.02	− .03	92.46	87.84	58,052
Mr97	92.31	92.42	92.31	92.41	+ .02	92.55	89.41	31,184
June	92.46	92.60	92.46	92.58	+ .03	92.61	90.30	24,791
Sept	92.53	92.62	92.53	92.62	+ .05	92.65	90.49	11,748
Dec	92.52	92.59	92.50	92.59	+ .07	92.60	91.72	6,414
Mr97	92.45	92.49	92.42	92.49	+ .05	92.50	92.26	1,498

Est vol 40,964; vol Mon 20,622; open int 133,687, +1,609.

GERMAN GOVT. BOND (LIFFE)
250,000 marks; pts of 100%

Dec	97.96	98.24	97.85	98.17	+ .29	98.36	93.62	226,429
Mr97	96.94	97.16	96.94	97.19	+ .27	97.24	95.15	1,770

Est vol 129,438; vol Mon 129,567; open int 228,199, −5,900.

ITALIAN GOVT. BOND (LIFFE)
ITL 200,000,000; pts of 100%

Dec	118.23	119.29	118.18	119.17	+ .46	119.29	114.19	76,890
Mr97	....	....	....	118.47	+ .46	117.20	116.30	718

Est vol 56,389; vol Mon 44,440; open int 77,608, −1,449.

CANADIAN BANKERS ACCEPTANCE (ME)-C$1,000,000

Dec	95.52	95.73	95.50	95.67	+ .15	95.73	90.20	36,600
Mr97	95.15	95.35	95.14	95.32	+ .15	95.35	92.08	21,874
June	94.77	94.96	94.75	94.93	+ .15	94.96	92.10	12,393
Sept	94.39	94.54	94.38	94.54	+ .14	94.55	92.40	7,065
Dec	94.05	94.19	94.02	94.18	+ .14	94.19	92.45	5,354
Mr98	....	....	....	93.85	+ .14	93.81	92.35	2,374
June	93.47	93.49	93.47	93.56	+ .14	93.50	92.46	2,389

Est vol 10,838; vol Mn 5,098; open int 88,131, +2,497.

10 YR. CANADIAN GOVT. BONDS (ME)-C$100,000

Dec	110.22	110.80	109.98	110.62	+ .52	110.82	107.70	18,252

Est vol 4,544; vol Mn 913; open int 18,252, +458.

10 YR. FRENCH GOVT. BONDS (MATIF)
FFr 500,000; 100ths of 100%

Dec	123.88	124.14	123.88	124.12	+ 0.28	124.26	117.76	204,902
Mr97	123.72	123.98	123.72	123.98	+ 0.28	124.14	114.90	18,781

Est vol 99,942: vol Mn 72,794; open int 224,077, −3,452.

PIBOR-3 MONTH (MATIF) FF5,000,000

Dec	96.17	96.21	96.15	96.20	....	96.27	95.06	62,279
Mr97	96.14	96.16	96.11	96.15	....	96.22	94.61	39,473
June	96.01	96.04	95.99	96.04	+ .02	96.08	94.52	24,772
Sept	95.82	95.88	95.81	95.87	+ .03	95.90	93.60	16,359
Dec	95.64	95.67	95.64	95.66	+ .02	95.71	93.16	10,122
Mr98	95.42	95.46	95.42	95.46	+ .03	95.50	93.79	8,734
June	95.18	95.21	95.18	95.21	+ .02	95.23	93.39	6,481
Sept	94.92	94.95	94.92	94.95	+ .03	94.98	92.90	5,062
Dec	94.65	94.67	94.65	94.67	+ .01	94.71	93.77	6,472
Mr99	94.39	94.39	94.38	94.40	+ .01	94.44	93.52	8,525
June	94.14	94.16	94.14	94.14	....	94.18	93.37	2,014

Est vol 37,206; vol Mn 31,062; open int 190,407, +2,798.

3 YR. COMMONWEALTH T-BONDS (SFE)-A$100,000

Dec	92.78	92.81	92.78	92.80	+ 0.02	92.86	91.78	127,105

Est vol 22,293; vol Mn 9,936; open int 127,105, +1,926.

EUROYEN (SIMEX)-Yen 100,000,000 pts of 100%

Dec	99.36	99.37	99.35	99.36	....	99.36	94.70	109,960
Mr97	99.17	99.18	99.16	99.18	+ .01	99.20	94.76	75,673
June	98.98	98.99	98.97	98.98	+ .01	99.02	94.55	47,620
Sept	98.76	98.78	98.76	98.77	+ .02	99.08	94.55	25,810
Dec	98.53	98.57	98.53	98.56	+ .02	98.61	94.78	18,440
Mr98	98.34	98.34	98.34	98.33	+ .02	98.37	95.65	13,736
June	98.11	98.13	98.11	98.12	+ .03	98.13	96.60	7,512
Sept	97.89	97.89	97.89	97.89	+ .03	97.88	96.50	4,547
Dec	97.65	97.66	97.65	97.66	+ .03	97.66	96.37	1,960
Mr99	....	....	....	97.43	+ .02	97.44	96.24	1,353
June	....	....	....	97.23	+ .02	97.19	96.65	570
Sept	....	....	....	97.04	+ .02	97.02	96.99	510

Est vol 19,370; vol Mn 6,256; open int 307,691, +3,637.

BOBL-MED.TERM BOND (DTB)-DM 250,000; DM per $

Dec	102.81	102.99	102.73	102.99	+ .24	106.00	97.39	302,719
Mr97	101.87	101.87	101.87	101.87	+ .10	105.10	99.30	11,449

Est vol 56,215: vol Mn 47,467: open int 324.168, +15,303.

Treasury bond futures prices are quoted in the same way as the Treasury bond prices themselves. Table 5.3 shows that the settlement price for the December 1996 contract on September 24, 1996 was 108-20, or $108\frac{5}{8}$. One contract involves the delivery of $100,000 face value of the bond. Thus, a $1 change in the quoted futures price would lead to a $1,000 change in the value of the futures contract. Delivery can take place at any time during the delivery month.

CONVERSION FACTORS

As mentioned, the Treasury bond futures contract provides for the party with the short position to choose to deliver any bond that has a maturity of more than 15 years and that is not callable within 15 years. When a particular bond is delivered, a parameter known as its *conversion factor* defines the price received by the party with the short position. The quoted price applicable to the delivery is the product of the conversion factor and the quoted futures price. Taking accrued interest into account, we have the following relationship for each $100 face value of the bond delivered:

$$\text{Cash received by party with short position} = (\text{Quoted futures price} \times \text{Conversion factor for bond delivered})$$

$$+ \text{ Accrued interest since last coupon date on bond delivered}$$

Each contract is for the delivery of $100,000 face value of bonds. Suppose the quoted futures price is 90-00, the conversion factor for the bond delivered is 1.3800, and the accrued interest on this bond at the time of delivery is $3 per $100 face value. The cash received by the party with the short position (and paid by the party with the long position) is then

$$(1.38 \times 90.00) + 3.00 = \$127.20$$

per \$100 face value. A party with the short position in one contract would deliver bonds with face value of \$100,000 and receive \$127,200.

The conversion factor for a bond is equal to the value of the bond on the first day of the delivery month on the assumption that the interest rate for all maturities equals 8 percent per annum (with semiannual compounding). The bond maturity and the times to the coupon payment dates are rounded down to the nearest three months for the purposes of the calculation. The practice enables the CBOT to produce comprehensive tables. If after rounding, the bond lasts for an exact number of half years, the first coupon is assumed to be paid in six months. If after rounding, the bond does not last for an exact number of six months (i.e., there is an extra three months), the first coupon is assumed to be paid after three months and accrued interest is subtracted.

Examples

1. Consider a 14 percent coupon bond with 20 years and two months to maturity. For the purposes of calculating the conversion factor, the bond is assumed to have exactly 20 years to maturity. The first coupon payment is assumed to be made after six months. Coupon payments are then assumed to be made at six-month intervals until the end of the 20 years when the principal payment is made. We will work in terms of a \$100 face value bond. On the assumption that the discount rate is 8 percent per annum with semiannual compounding (or 4 percent per six months), the value of the bond is

$$\sum_{i=1}^{40} \frac{7}{1.04^i} + \frac{100}{1.04^{40}} = \$159.38$$

Dividing by the face value gives a credit conversion factor of 1.5938.

2. Consider a 14 percent coupon bond with 18 years and four months to maturity. For the purposes of calculating the conversion factor, the bond is assumed to have exactly 18 years and three months to maturity. Discounting all the payments back to a point in time three months from today gives a value of

$$\sum_{i=0}^{36} \frac{7}{1.04^i} + \frac{100}{1.04^{36}} = \$163.72$$

The interest rate for a three-month period is $\sqrt{1.04} - 1$ or 1.9804 percent. Hence, discounting back to the present gives the bond's value as $163.72/1.019804 = \$160.55$. Subtracting the accrued interest of 3.5, this becomes \$157.05. The conversion factor is therefore 1.5705.

CHEAPEST-TO-DELIVER BOND

At any given time, there are about 30 bonds that can be delivered in the CBOT Treasury bond futures contract. These vary widely as far as coupon and maturity are concerned.

The party with the short position can choose which of the available bonds is "cheapest" to deliver. Since the party with the short position receives

(Quoted futures price × Conversion factor) + Accrued interest

and the cost of purchasing a bond is

Quoted price + Accrued interest

the cheapest-to-deliver bond is the one for which

Quoted price − (Quoted futures price × Conversion factor)

is least. This can be found by examining each of the bonds in turn.

Example

The party with the short position has decided to deliver and is trying to choose among the three bonds in Table 5.4. Assume the current quoted futures price is 93-08, or $93.25. The cost of delivering each of the bonds is as follows:

Bond 1: 99.50 − (93.25 × 1.0382) = $2.69
Bond 2: 143.50 − (93.25 × 1.5188) = $1.87
Bond 3: 119.75 − (93.25 × 1.2615) = $2.12

The cheapest-to-deliver bond is bond 2.

A number of factors determine the cheapest-to-deliver bond. When yields are in excess of 8 percent, the conversion factor system tends to favor the delivery of low-coupon, long-maturity bonds. When yields are less than 8 percent, the system tends to favor the delivery of high-coupon, short-maturity bonds. Also, when the yield curve is upward sloping, there is a tendency for bonds with a long time to maturity to be favored, whereas when it is downward sloping, there is a tendency for bonds with a short time to maturity to be delivered. Finally, some bonds tend to sell for more than their theoretical value. Examples are low-coupon bonds and bonds whose coupons can be stripped. These bonds are unlikely to prove to be cheapest to deliver in any circumstances.

THE WILD CARD PLAY

Trading in the CBOT Treasury bond futures contract ceases at 2:00 P.M. Chicago time. However, Treasury bonds themselves continue trading in the spot market until 4:00 P.M. Furthermore, a trader with a short futures position has until 8:00 P.M. to issue to the

TABLE 5.4   Deliverable Bonds in Example

Bond	Quoted Price ($)	Conversion Factor
1	99.50	1.0382
2	143.50	1.5188
3	119.75	1.2615

clearinghouse a notice of intention to deliver. If the notice is issued, the invoice price is calculated on the basis of the settlement price that day. This is the price at which trading was conducted just before the closing bell at 2:00 P.M.

This practice gives rise to an option known as the *wild card play*. If bond prices decline after 2:00 P.M., the party with the short position can issue a notice of intention to deliver and proceed to buy cheapest-to-deliver bonds in preparation for delivery. If the bond price does not decline, the party with the short position keeps the position open and waits until the next day, when the same strategy can be used.

As with the other options open to the party with the short position, the wild card option is not free. Its value is reflected in the futures price, which is lower than it would be without the option.

DETERMINING THE QUOTED FUTURES PRICE

An exact theoretical futures price for the Treasury bond contract is difficult to determine because the short party's options concerned with the timing of delivery and choice of the bond that is delivered cannot easily be valued. However, if we assume that both the cheapest-to-deliver bond and the delivery date are known, the Treasury bond futures contract is a futures contract on a security providing the holder with known income. Equation 3.6 from chapter 3 then shows that the futures price, F, is related to the spot price, S, by

$$F = (S - I)e^{rT} \tag{5.4}$$

where I is the present value of the coupons during the life of the futures contract, T is the time until the futures contract matures, and r is the risk-free interest rate applicable to a time period of length T.

In Equation 5.4, F is the cash futures price and S is the cash bond price. The correct procedure to determine the quoted futures price is as follows:

1. Calculate the cash price of the cheapest-to-deliver bond from the quoted price.
2. Calculate the cash futures price from the cash bond price using Equation 5.4.
3. Calculate the quoted futures price from the cash futures price.
4. Divide the quoted futures price by the conversion factor to allow for the difference between the cheapest-to-deliver bond and the standard 15-year 8 percent bond.

The procedure is best illustrated with an example.

Example

Suppose that, in a Treasury bond futures contract, it is known that the cheapest-to-deliver bond will be a 12 percent coupon bond with a conversion factor of 1.4000. Suppose also that it is known that delivery will take place in 270 days. Coupons are payable semiannually on the bond. As illustrated in Figure 5.5, the last coupon date was 60 days ago, the next coupon date is in 122 days, and the coupon date thereafter is in 305 days. The term structure is flat, and the rate of interest (with continuous compounding) is 10 percent per annum. Assume that the current quoted bond price is $120. The cash price of the bond is obtained by

FIGURE 5.5 Time Chart for Example

adding to this quoted price the proportion of the next coupon payment that accrues to the holder. The cash price is therefore

$$120 + \frac{60}{60 + 122} \times 6 = 121.978$$

A coupon of $6 will be received after 122 days ($= 0.3342$ year). The present value of this is

$$6e^{-0.1 \times 0.3342} = 5.803$$

The futures contract lasts for 270 days (0.7397 year). The cash futures price if the contract were written on the 12 percent bond would therefore be

$$(121.978 - 5.803)e^{0.1 \times 0.7397} = 125.094$$

At delivery there are 148 days of accrued interest. The quoted futures price if the contract were written on the 12 percent bond would therefore be

$$125.094 - 6 \times \frac{148}{305 - 122} = 120.242$$

The contract is in fact written on a standard 8 percent bond, and 1.4000 standard bonds are considered equivalent to each 12 percent bond. The quoted futures price should therefore be

$$\frac{120.242}{1.4000} = 85.887$$

Treasury Bill and Eurodollar Futures

Two of the most popular short-term interest-rate contracts are the Treasury bill and Eurodollar futures contracts traded on the CME.

TREASURY BILL FUTURES

In the Treasury bill futures contract, the underlying asset is a 90-day Treasury bill. Under the terms of the contract, the party with the short position must deliver $1 million of Treasury bills on any of three successive business days. The first delivery day is the first day of the delivery month on which a 13-week Treasury bill is issued, and a one-year Treasury bill has 13 weeks remaining to maturity. In practice, this means that the Treasury bill may have 89 or 90 or 91 days to expiration when it is delivered.

A Treasury bill is what is known as a *discount instrument*. It pays no coupons, and the investor receives the face value at maturity. Prior to maturity of the futures contract, the underlying asset is a Treasury bill with a maturity longer than 90 days. For example, if the futures contract matures in 160 days, the underlying asset is a 250-day Treasury bill.

To provide a general analysis, we suppose that the futures contract matures in T_1 years and the Treasury bill underlying the futures contract matures in T_2 years. (The difference between T_1 and T_2 is 90 days.) We suppose further that R_1 and R_2 are the continuously compounded interest rates for risk-free investments maturing at times T_1 and T_2, respectively. If we assume that the Treasury bill underlying the futures contract has a face value of $100, its current value, V is given by

$$V = 100e^{-R_2 T_2}$$

Since no income is paid on the instrument, we know from Equation 3.5 that the futures price, F, is $e^{R_1 T_1}$ times V, or

$$F = 100e^{-R_2 T_2} e^{R_1 T_1} = 100e^{R_1 T_1 - R_2 T_2}$$

From Equation 5.1, this reduces to

$$F = 100e^{-R_F(T_2 - T_1)}$$

where R_F is the forward rate for the time period between T_1 and T_2. The expression shows that the futures price of a Treasury bill is the price it will have if the 90-day interest rate on the delivery date proves to be equal to the current forward rate. This is analogous to the result produced earlier in the chapter for FRAs.

ARBITRAGE OPPORTUNITIES

If the forward interest rate implied by the Treasury bill futures price is different from that implied by the rates on Treasury bills themselves, there is a potential arbitrage opportunity. Suppose that the 45-day Treasury bill rate is 10 percent, the 135-day Treasury bill rate is 10.5 percent, and the rate corresponding to the Treasury bill futures prices for a contract maturing in 45 days is 10.6 percent (with all rates being continuously compounded on an actual/actual basis). The forward rate for the period between 45 and 135 days implied by the Treasury bill rates is, from Equation 5.1,

$$\frac{135 \times 10.5 - 45 \times 10}{90} = 10.75\%$$

This is greater than the 10.6 percent forward rate implied by the futures price. An arbitrageur should attempt to borrow for the period of time between 45 and 135 days at 10.6 percent and invest at 10.75 percent, using the following strategy:

1. Short the futures contract.
2. Borrow 45-day money at 10 percent per annum.
3. Invest the borrowed money for 135 days at 10.5 percent per annum.

We will refer to this as a *type 1 arbitrage*. The first trade ensures that a Treasury bill yielding 10.6 percent can be sold after 45 days have elapsed. It in effect locks in a rate of interest of 10.6 percent on borrowed funds for this time period. The second and third trades ensure that a rate of interest of 10.75 percent is earned during the time period.

If, instead, the rate of interest corresponding to the Treasury bill futures were greater than 10.75 percent, the opposite strategy would be appropriate:

1. Take a long position in the futures contract.

2. Borrow 135-day money at 10.5 percent per annum.

3. Invest the borrowed money for 45 days at 10 percent per annum.

We will refer to this as a *type 2 arbitrage.*

Both of these arbitrage possibilities involve borrowing at, or close to, the Treasury bill rate. As discussed in chapter 3, repos provide a way for companies that own portfolios of marketable securities to do this for short periods of time. In testing for arbitrage opportunities in the Treasury bill market, traders frequently calculate the *implied repo rate.* This is the rate of interest on a short-term Treasury bill implied by the futures price for a contract maturing at the same time as the short-term Treasury bill and the price of a Treasury bill maturing 90 days later than the short-term Treasury bill. If the implied repo rate is greater than the actual short-term Treasury bill rate, a type 1 arbitrage is in principle possible. If the implied repo rate is less than the short-term Treasury bill rate, a type 2 arbitrage is in principle possible.

Example

The cash price (per $100 face value) of a Treasury bill maturing in 146 days is $95.21, and the cash futures price for a 90-day Treasury bill futures contract maturing in 56 days is $96.95. Since 90 days is 0.2466 year and 146 days is 0.4000 year, $T_1 = 0.2466$ and $T_2 = 0.4000$. The continuously compounded 146-day rate, R_2, is

$$-\frac{1}{0.4000} \ln 0.9521 = 0.1227$$

or 12.27 percent, and the continuously compounded forward rate, R_F, implied by the futures price, is

$$-\frac{1}{0.2466} \ln 0.9695 = 0.1256$$

or 12.56 percent. Rearranging Equation 5.1, we see that the continuously compounded 56-day rate, R_1, implied by R_2 and R_F, is

$$R_1 = \frac{R_2 T_2 - R_F (T_2 - T_1)}{T_1}$$

This is the implied repo rate. In this case, it is

$$\frac{12.27 \times 146 - 12.56 \times 90}{56} = 11.80\%$$

If the actual 56-day rate is less than 11.80% per annum, a type 1 arbitrage is indicated. If it is greater than 11.80%, a type 2 arbitrage is indicated.

QUOTES FOR TREASURY BILLS

As mentioned earlier in this chapter, the actual/360 day count convention is used for Treasury bills in the United States. Price quotes are for a Treasury bill with a face value of $100. There is a difference between the cash price and quoted price for a Treasury bill. If Y is the cash price of a Treasury bill that has a face value of $100 and n days to maturity, the quoted price is

$$\frac{360}{n}(100 - Y)$$

This is referred to as the *discount rate*. It is the annualized dollar return provided by the Treasury bill expressed as a percentage of the face value. If for a 90-day Treasury bill the cash price, Y, were 98, the quoted price would be 8.00.

The discount rate or quoted price is not the same as the rate of return earned on the Treasury bill. The latter is calculated as the dollar return divided by the cost. In the preceding example, where the quoted price is 8.00, the rate of return would be 2/98, or 2.04 percent per 90 days. This amounts to

$$\frac{2}{98} \times \frac{365}{90} = 0.0828$$

or 8.28 percent per annum with compounding every 90 days.[2] When converted to semi-annual compounding, this rate of return is sometimes referred to as the *bond equivalent yield*.

A 90-day Treasury bill futures contract is for delivery of $1 million of Treasury bills. Treasury bill futures prices are not quoted in the same way as the prices of Treasury bills themselves. The following relationship is used:[3]

Treasury bill futures price quote $= 100 -$ Corresponding Treasury bill price quote

A Treasury bill price quote of 8.00 corresponds to a futures quote of 92.00. If Z is the quoted futures price and Y is the corresponding price that would be paid for delivery of $100 of 90-day Treasury bills, then

$$Z = 100 - 4(100 - Y)$$

or, equivalently,

$$Y = 100 - 0.25(100 - Z)$$

Since $1 million face value of Treasury bills underlie one Treasury bill futures contract, the contract price is:

$$10,000[100 - 0.25(100 - Z)] \tag{5.5}$$

Thus, the closing futures price quote of 94.74 for December 1996 Treasury bill futures in Table 5.3 corresponds to a Treasury bill price of $100 - 0.25(100 - 94.74) = 98.685$ and to a contract price of $986,850.

---

[2]It is interesting to note that the compounding frequency convention for a money market instrument such as a Treasury bill is to set the compounding period equal to the life of the instrument. This means that the quoted yields on money market instruments of different maturities are not directly comparable.

[3]The reason for quoting Treasury bill futures prices in this way is to ensure that the bid price is below the ask price.

The amount that is paid or received by each side each day in the marking-to-market process equals the change in the contract price. For example, when the futures price changes by one basis point (i.e., by 0.01), Equation 5.5 shows that the amount paid by one side and received by the other side on one contract is $10,000 \times 0.25 \times 0.01 = \$25$. If 90-day Treasury bills are delivered by the party with the short position, the price received is the contract price in Equation 5.5. If the Treasury bills that are delivered have 89 days to maturity, the price received is calculated by replacing the 0.25 in the preceding formula by 89/360, or 0.2472. If they have 91 days to maturity, the 0.25 in the formula becomes 91/360, or 0.2528.

Example

Suppose that the 140-day interest rate is 8 percent per annum and the 230-day rate is 8.25 percent per annum (with continuous compounding and actual/actual being used for both rates). The forward rate for the time period between day 140 and day 230 is

$$\frac{0.0825 \times 230 - 0.08 \times 140}{90} = 0.0864$$

or 8.64 percent. Since 90 days is 0.2466 year, the futures price for $100 of 90-day Treasury bills deliverable in 140 days is

$$100e^{-0.0864 \times 0.2466} = 97.89$$

This would be quoted as $100 - 4(100 - 97.89) = 91.56$. (The calculation ignores the difference between futures and forward contracts.)

EURODOLLAR FUTURES

The Eurodollar futures contract is the most successful of the short-term interest rate futures contracts. It is traded on the Chicago Mercantile Exchange (CME). A Eurodollar is a dollar deposited in a U.S. or foreign bank outside the United States. The Eurodollar interest rate is the rate of interest earned on Eurodollars deposited by one bank with another bank and is also known as the three-month London Interbank Offer Rate (LIBOR). Eurodollar interest rates are generally higher than the corresponding Treasury bill interest rates. The reason is that the Eurodollar interest rate is a commercial lending rate, whereas the Treasury bill rate is the rate at which governments borrow.

On the surface, a Eurodollar futures contract appears to be structurally the same as the Treasury bill futures contract. Suppose the quoted futures price is Z. The formula for calculating the value of one contract from the quoted futures price is Equation 5.5, the same as that used for Treasury bill futures. The quote of 94.18 for the December 1996 contract in Table 5.3 corresponds to a contract price of

$$10,000[100 - 0.25(100 - 94.18)] = \$985,450$$

and a change of one basis point or 0.01 in a Eurodollar futures quote corresponds to a contract price change of $25.

However, there are some important differences between the Treasury bill and Eurodollar futures contracts. For a Treasury bill, the contract price converges at maturity to the price of a 90-day $1 million face value Treasury bill. If a contract is held until maturity, this is the instrument delivered. A Eurodollar futures contract is settled in cash on the second London business day before the third Wednesday of the month. The final marking to market sets the futures price equal to $100 - R$, where R is the actual rate per 90 days on Eurodollar deposits (with quarterly compounding) at that time. The variable R underlying the Eurodollar futures contract is a true interest rate, not a discount rate. The Eurodollar futures contract is therefore a futures contract on an interest rate. By contrast, the Treasury bill futures contract is a futures contract on the price of a Treasury bill or a discount rate.

If we ignore the difference between futures and forwards, a Eurodollar futures quote of Z implies a forward interest rate of $100 - Z$ for the period covered by the contract. Thus the quote of 94.18 for the December 1996 contract in Table 5.3 corresponds to a forward rate of 5.82 percent for a 90-day period starting in December. (The day count convention is actual/360 and the compounding frequency 90 days.) In fact, as noted in chapter 3, futures prices and forward prices are not exactly equal and the difference is greatest for long-dated contracts. This point is particularly relevant to Eurodollar futures contracts, which have maturities up to 10 years. For contracts lasting only a year or two, it is reasonable to assume that the futures price is the forward price or, equivalently, that the rate calculated from the futures price is a forward interest rate. For longer-dated contracts, this assumption is far less reasonable.

Duration

Duration is an important concept in the use of interest-rate futures for hedging. The *duration* of a bond is a measure of how long on average the holder of the bond has to wait before receiving cash payments. A zero-coupon bond that matures in n years has a duration of n years. However, a coupon-bearing bond maturing in n years has a duration of less than n years, because the holder receives some of the cash payments prior to year n.

Suppose that a bond provides the holder with payments c_i at time t_i ($1 \le i \le n$). The price B and yield y (continuously compounded) are related by

$$B = \sum_{i=1}^{n} c_i e^{-yt_i} \tag{5.6}$$

The duration D of the bond is defined as

$$D = \frac{\sum_{i=1}^{n} t_i c_i e^{-yt_i}}{B} \tag{5.7}$$

This can be written

$$D = \sum_{i=1}^{n} t_i \left[\frac{c_i e^{-yt_i}}{B} \right]$$

The term in square brackets is the ratio of the present value of the payment at time t_i to the bond price. The bond price is the present value of all payments. The duration is therefore a weighted average of the times when payments are made, with the weight applied to time t_i being equal to the proportion of the bond's total present value provided by the payment at time t_i. The sum of the weights is 1.0.

From Equation 5.6, it can be shown that

$$\Delta B = -\Delta y \sum_{i=1}^{n} c_i t_i e^{-yt_i} \tag{5.8}$$

where Δy is a small change in y and ΔB is the corresponding small change in B. (Note that there is a negative relationship between B and y. When bond yields increase, bond prices decrease. When bond yields decrease, bond prices increase.) From Equations 5.7 and 5.8,

$$\Delta B = -BD\,\Delta y \tag{5.9}$$

This is an important equation that underlies most duration-based hedging schemes. It can also be written as

$$\frac{\Delta B}{B} = -D\,\Delta y \tag{5.10}$$

showing that the percentage change in a bond price for a particular small change in the yield is proportional to its duration.

Example

Consider a three-year 10 percent coupon bond with a face value of $100. Suppose that the yield on the bond is 12 percent per annum with continuous compounding. This means that $y = 0.12$. Coupon payments of $5 are made every six months. Table 5.5 shows the calculations necessary to determine the bond's duration. The present values of the payments using the yield as the discount rate are shown in column 3. (For example, the present value of the first payment is $5e^{-0.12 \times 0.5} = 4.709$.) The sum of the numbers in column 3 gives the bond's price as 94.213. The weights are calculated by dividing the numbers in column 3 by 94.213. The sum of the numbers in column 5 gives the duration as 2.654 years. From Equation 5.9,

$$\Delta B = -94.213 \times 2.654\Delta y$$

TABLE 5.5 Calculation of Duration

Time (years)	Payment ($)	Present Value	Weight	Time × Weight
0.5	5	4.709	0.050	0.025
1.0	5	4.435	0.047	0.047
1.5	5	4.176	0.044	0.066
2.0	5	3.933	0.042	0.084
2.5	5	3.704	0.039	0.098
3.0	105	73.256	0.778	2.334
	130	94.213	1.000	2.654

that is,

$$\Delta B = -250.04 \Delta y$$

If $\Delta y = +0.001$, so that y increases to 0.121, the formula indicates that we expect ΔB to be -0.25. In other words, we expect the bond price to go down to $94.213 - 0.250 = 93.963$. By recomputing the bond price for a yield of 12.1 percent, we can verify that this is indeed what happens.

The duration of a bond portfolio can be defined as a weighted average of the durations of the individual bonds in the portfolio, with the weights being proportional to the bond prices. Equation 5.9 then applies to a portfolio of bonds as well as to individual bonds, provided the yields of all bonds in the portfolio are assumed to change by the same amount.

The preceding analysis is based on the assumption that y is expressed with continuous compounding. If y is expressed with annual compounding, it can be shown that Equation 5.9 becomes

$$\Delta B = -\frac{BD \, \Delta y}{1 + y}$$

More generally, if y is expressed with a compounding frequency of m times per year,

$$\Delta B = -\frac{BD \, \Delta y}{1 + y/m}$$

The expression

$$\frac{D}{1 + y/m}$$

is sometimes referred to as *modified duration*.

DURATION MATCHING AND CONVEXITY

A portfolio of fixed-income securities can be described in terms of its average duration. Financial institutions frequently try to match the average duration of their assets with the average duration of their liabilities. (The liabilities can be regarded as short positions in bonds.) This strategy is known as *duration matching* or *portfolio immunization*. It is based on the assumption that the yield curve always exhibits parallel shifts. When the durations of assets and liabilities are matched, a small parallel shift in interest rates should have little effect on the whole portfolio. Equation 5.9 shows that the gain (loss) on the assets should offset the loss (gain) on the liabilities.

When moderate or large changes in interest rates are considered, a factor known as *convexity* is sometimes important. Figure 5.6 shows the relationship between the percentage change in value and change in yield for two portfolios having the same duration. The gradients of the two curves are the same for the current yield. This means that both portfolios change in value by the same percentage for small interest-rate changes and is consistent with Equation 5.10. For large interest-rate changes, the portfolios behave differently. Portfolio X has more convexity (or curvature) than portfolio Y. Its value increases by a greater percentage amount than that of portfolio Y when yields decline, and its value decreases by less than that of portfolio Y when yields increase.

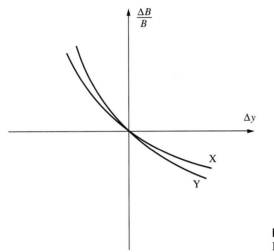

FIGURE 5.6 Bond Portfolios with Different Convexity

The convexity of a bond portfolio tends to be greatest when the portfolio provides payments evenly over a long period of time. It is least when the payments are concentrated around one particular point in time. For long positions in bond portfolios, it is clear from Figure 5.6 that a high-convexity portfolio with a certain duration is always more attractive than a low-convexity bond portfolio with the same duration. Not surprisingly, it is generally also more expensive.

DURATION-BASED HEDGING STRATEGIES

The general approach to hedging described in chapter 4 requires a historical analysis of the relationship between the change in the futures price and the change in the value of the asset being hedged. The optimal number of contracts, N^*, is given in Equation 4.3 by

$$N^* = \rho \frac{\sigma_S}{\sigma_F} \qquad (5.11)$$

where σ_S and σ_F are the standard deviations of changes in the value of the asset position and changes in the futures contract price, respectively, and ρ is the coefficient of correlation between the two changes. This approach can be used when interest-rate futures are used for hedging. However, the duration concept provides a useful alternative.

Consider the situation where a position in an interest-rate-dependent asset such as a bond portfolio or a money market security is being hedged using an interest-rate futures contract. We define

F: contract price for the interest-rate futures contract

D_F: duration of asset underlying futures contract at expiration of the futures contract

S: value of asset being hedged

D_S: duration of asset being hedged at expiration of the hedge

We assume that the change in the yield, Δy, is the same for all maturities—which means that only parallel shifts in the yield curve can occur. From Equation 5.9

$$\Delta S = -SD_S \Delta y \qquad (5.12)$$

To a reasonable approximation, it is also true that

$$\Delta F = -FD_F \Delta y \qquad (5.13)$$

Since the Δy's are assumed to be the same, $\rho = 1$ in Equation 5.11. From Equations 5.12 and 5.13, ΔS is always $(SD_S)/(FD_F)$ times ΔF. It follows that

$$\frac{\sigma_S}{\sigma_F} = \frac{SD_S}{FD_F}$$

and Equation 5.11 gives the optimal number of contracts to use for hedging as

$$N^* = \frac{SD_S}{FD_F} \qquad (5.14)$$

This is the *duration-based hedge ratio.*[4] It is sometimes also called the *price sensitivity hedge ratio.* Using it has the effect of making the duration of the whole position zero.

Equation 5.14 is a useful result. However, the hedge to which it gives rise is by no means perfect. One reason is the assumption that Δy is the same for all yields. In practice, short-term yields are usually more volatile than, and not closely correlated with, long-term yields. (Sometimes it even happens that short- and long-term yields move in opposite directions.) As a result, hedge performance can be disappointing, particularly if there is a big difference between D_S and D_F. Another (less important) potential effect on the performance of the hedge is convexity. If the convexity of the asset underlying the futures contract is markedly different from the convexity of the asset being hedged, and there is a large change in interest rates, hedge performance may be worse than expected. Finally, it is worth noting that in order to calculate D_F, an assumption as to what will be the cheapest-to-deliver bond is necessary when Treasury bond or Treasury note futures contracts are used. If the duration of the cheapest-to-deliver bond changes, the optimal number of contracts also changes.

Examples

This section presents three examples of how the duration-based model can be used for interest-rate hedging. Generally, the hedger tries to choose the futures contract so that the duration of the underlying asset is as close as possible to the duration of the asset being hedged. Treasury bill and Eurodollar futures contracts are therefore used

---

[4]If y is defined with annual compounding, Equation 5.14 becomes

$$h^* = [SD_S(1 + y_F)]/[FD_F(1 + y_S)]$$

where y_S and y_F are the yields on S and F. This is not the same as Equation 5.14 except when $y_S = y_F$. The reason for the difference is that the assumption that $\Delta y_S = \Delta y_F$ when yields are continuously compounded is not quite the same assumption as $\Delta y_S = \Delta y_F$ when yields are compounded once a year.

CHAPTER 5 *Interest-Rate Futures* **131**

for exposures to short-term interest rates, whereas Treasury bond and Treasury note futures contracts are used for exposures to longer-term rates.

When hedges are constructed using interest-rate futures, it is important to bear in mind that interest rates and futures prices move in opposite directions. When interest rates go up, the price of the asset underlying the futures contract goes down. This in turn causes the futures price itself to go down. When interest rates go down, the reverse happens and the futures price goes up. Thus, a company in a position to lose money if interest rates drop should hedge by taking a long futures position. Similarly, a company in a position to lose money if interest rates rise should hedge by taking a short futures position.

HEDGING THE FUTURE PURCHASE OF A SIX-MONTH TREASURY BILL

Suppose that on May 20 a corporate treasurer learns that $3.3 million will be received on August 5. The funds will be needed for a major capital investment the following February. The treasurer therefore plans to invest in six-month Treasury bills as soon as the funds are received. The current yield on six-month Treasury bills, expressed with semiannual compounding, is 11.2 percent. The treasurer is concerned that the yield may decline between May 20 and August 5 and decides to hedge using Treasury bill futures. The quoted price for the September Treasury bill futures contract is 89.44.

In this case, because the company will lose money if interest rates go down, a long hedge is required. If interest rates do go down, the Treasury bill price will go up and a gain will be made on the futures position.

To calculate the number of Treasury bill futures contracts that should be purchased, we note that the asset underlying the futures contract lasts for three months. Since it is a discount instrument, its duration is also three months, or 0.25 years. Similarly, the six-month Treasury bill investment planned by the treasurer has a duration of six months, or 0.50 years. Each Treasury bill futures contract is for the delivery of $1 million of Treasury bills. The contract price is

$$10,000[100 - 0.25(100 - 89.44)] = \$973,600$$

The number of contracts that should be purchased, using Equation 5.14, is

$$\frac{3,300,000}{973,600} \times \frac{0.5}{0.25} = 6.78$$

Rounding to the nearest whole number, the treasurer should purchase seven contracts.

Between May 20 and August 5, the treasurer's worst fears were realized and the yield on six-month Treasury bills (with semiannual compounding) declined by 1.4 percent, from 11.2 percent per annum to 9.8 percent per annum. This cost the treasurer $3,300,000 \times 0.014 \times 0.5 = \$23,100$ in lost interest. The price quote for the September Treasury bill futures contract was 90.56 on August 5. This corresponds to a contract price of $976,400. The gain on the futures contract was therefore $7 \times (\$976,400 - \$973,600) = \$19,600$. When invested for six months at 9.8 percent per annum, the gain grew to $20,560. The company therefore lost only $23,100 - \$20,560 = \$2,540$ relative to the position it would have been in if the interest rate had remained unchanged between May 20 and August 5. The effective rate of interest earned on the six-month

TABLE 5.6 Hedging the Future Purchase of a Six-Month Treasury Bill

From the Trader's Desk—May 20

A corporate treasurer has just learned that $3.3 million will be received on August 5. The treasurer plans to invest the money in six-month Treasury bills and would like to hedge against a reduction in interest rates.

Quotes:

1. The six-month Treasury bill yield, expressed with semiannual compounding, is 11.2 percent per annum.

2. The quoted price for the September Treasury bill futures contract is 89.44. This corresponds to a contract price of $973,600.

The Strategy

1. Take a long position in seven September Treasury bill futures contracts on May 20.

2. Close out the position on August 5.

The Result

The yield on six-month Treasury bills, expressed with semiannual compounding, declined from 11.2 percent per annum to 9.8 percent per annum between May 20 and August 5. This cost the treasurer $3,300,000 × 0.014 × 0.5 = $23,100 in interest.

The price quoted for the September Treasury bill futures contract was 90.56 on August 5. This corresponds to a contract price of $976,400. The gain on the futures contract was therefore 7 × ($976,400 − $973,600) = $19,600.

When invested for six months at 9.8 percent, the gain grew to $20,560. The company was therefore only $23,100 − $20,560 = $2,540 worse off than it would have been if interest rates had remained unchanged between May 20 and August 5.

---

investment was

$$0.098 + \frac{20,560 \times 2}{3,300,000} = 0.1105$$

or 11.05 percent per annum. This example is summarized in Table 5.6.

HEDGING A BOND PORTFOLIO

For our next example, we suppose it is August 2. A fund manager has $10 million invested in government bonds and is concerned that interest rates are expected to be highly volatile over the next three months. The fund manager decides to use the December Treasury bond futures contract to hedge the value of the portfolio. The current futures price is 93-02, or 93.0625. Since each contract is for the delivery of $100,000 face value of bonds, the futures contract price is $93,062.50.

The average duration of the bond portfolio in three months will be 6.8 years. The cheapest-to-deliver bond in the Treasury bond contract is expected to be a 20-year, 12 percent per annum coupon bond. The yield on this bond is currently 8.8 percent per annum, and the duration will be 9.2 years at maturity of the futures contract.

The fund manager requires a short position in Treasury bond futures to hedge the bond portfolio. If interest rates go up, a gain will be made on the short futures position and a loss will be made on the bond portfolio. If interest rates decrease, a loss will be made on the short position, but there will be a gain on the bond portfolio. The number of bond futures contracts that should be shorted can be calculated from Equation 5.14 as

$$\frac{10,000,000}{93,062.50} \times \frac{6.80}{9.20} = 79.42$$

Rounding to the nearest whole number, the portfolio manager should short 79 contracts.

During the period August 2 to November 2, interest rates declined rapidly. The value of the bond portfolio increased from $10 million to $10,450,000. On November 2 the Treasury bond futures price was 98-16. This corresponds to a contract price of $98,500. The total loss on the Treasury bond futures contracts was

$$79 \times (\$98,500.00 - \$93,062.50) = \$429,562.50$$

The net change in the value of the portfolio manager's position was therefore only

$$\$450,000.00 - \$429,562.50 = \$20,437.50$$

This example is summarized in Table 5.7. Since the fund incurs a loss on the futures position, the manager may regret having implemented the hedge. On average, we can expect half our hedges to lead to these sorts of regrets. The problem is that we do not know in advance which half of the hedges it will be!

TABLE 5.7 Hedging a Bond Portfolio

From the Trader's Desk—August 2
    A fund manager responsible for a $10 million bond portfolio is concerned that interest rates are expected to be highly volatile over the next three months. The fund manager decides to use Treasury bond futures to hedge the value of the bond portfolio. The quoted price for the December Treasury bond futures contract is 93-02. This means that the contract price is $93,062.50.

The Strategy

1. Short 79 December Treasury bond futures contracts on August 2.
2. Close out the position on November 2.

The Result
    During the period August 2 to November 2, interest rates declined rapidly. The value of the bond portfolio increased from $10 million to $10,450,000.
    On November 2 the Treasury bond futures price was 98-16. This corresponds to a contract price of $98,500.00. A loss of $79 \times (\$98,500.00 - \$93,062.50) = \$429,562.50$ was therefore made on the Treasury bond futures contracts.
    Overall, the value of the portfolio manager's position changed by only $450,000.00 - $429,562.50 = $20,437.50.

LONDON INTERBANK OFFER RATE

Before we look at the next example, it is appropriate to review the meaning of LIBOR, the London Interbank Offer Rate. LIBOR is widely used in specifying corporate borrowing rates in international markets. It is a floating reference rate of interest similar to prime. LIBOR is determined by the trading of deposits between banks on the Eurocurrency market. The one-month LIBOR at any given time is the rate of interest being offered by one bank to another on one-month deposits at that time. When the interest rate on a loan is equal to one-month LIBOR, the interest rate on the loan is reset equal to one-month LIBOR at monthly intervals. Other LIBOR rates such as three-month LIBOR and six-month LIBOR are defined and used analogously.

HEDGING A FLOATING-RATE LOAN

Interest-rate futures can be used to hedge the rate of interest paid by a borrower on a floating-rate loan. Generally, Eurodollar futures are preferred to Treasury bill futures for this purpose, because the Eurodollar interest rate is more closely related to the rate of interest at which corporations borrow than is the Treasury bill rate. We will consider the use of Eurodollar futures to hedge a three-month loan in which the interest rate is reset every month. This will produce a simple example. The same principles can be used for loans that last far longer than three months. The liquid contracts traded on the CME have maturities of at least five years, and longer-maturity contracts can be created by rolling contracts forward in the way described in chapter 4.

We suppose that it is April 29 and a company has just borrowed $15 million for three months at an interest rate equal to the one-month LIBOR rate plus 1 percent. At the time the loan is negotiated, the one-month LIBOR rate is 8 percent per annum, so that the company must pay 9 percent per annum for the first month. Because the one-month LIBOR rate is quoted with monthly compounding, the interest for the first month is 0.75 percent of $15 million, or $112,500. This is known for certain at the time the loan is negotiated and does not have to be hedged.

The interest paid at the end of the second month is determined by the one-month LIBOR rate at the beginning of the second month. It can be hedged by taking a position in the June Eurodollar futures contract. Suppose that the quoted price for this contract is 91.88. Each contract is for a deposit with a face value of $1 million. The contract price is therefore

$$10,000[100 - 0.25(100 - 91.88)] = \$979,700$$

The company will lose money if interest rates rise and gain if interest rates fall. It therefore requires a short position in the futures contracts. The duration of the asset underlying the futures contract at maturity of the contract is three months, or 0.25 years. The duration of the asset being hedged at maturity of the hedge is one month, or 0.0833 years. From Equation 5.14, the number of contracts that should be used to hedge the interest payment in the second month is

$$\frac{0.08333}{0.25} \times \frac{15,000,000}{979,700} = 5.10$$

Rounding to the nearest whole number, five contracts are required.

For the third month, the September Eurodollar futures contract can be used. Suppose the quoted price for this contract is 91.44, which corresponds to a futures price of $978,600. The number of futures contracts that should be shorted can be calculated as before:

$$\frac{0.08333}{0.25} \times \frac{15,000,000}{978,600} = 5.11$$

Again, we find that, to the nearest whole number, five contracts are required. Thus, five of the June contracts should be shorted to hedge the LIBOR rate applicable to the second month, and five of the September contracts should be shorted to hedge the LIBOR rate applicable to the third month. The June contracts are closed out on May 29 and the September contracts are closed out on June 29.

On May 29 the one-month LIBOR rate was 8.8 percent and the June futures price was 91.12. The latter corresponds to a contract price of $977,800, so that the company made a profit of

$$5 \times (\$979,700 - \$977,800) = \$9,500$$

on the June contracts. This provided compensation for the extra $10,000 interest (one-twelfth of 0.8 percent of $15 million) that had to be paid at the end of the second month as a result of the LIBOR increase from 8 percent to 8.8 percent.

On June 29 the one-month LIBOR rate was 9.4 percent and the September futures price was 90.16. A similar calculation to that just given shows that the company gained $16,000 on the short futures position but incurred extra interest costs of $17,500 as a result of the increase in one-month LIBOR from 8 percent per annum to 9.4 percent per annum. This example is summarized in Table 5.8.

Summary

In this chapter we have discussed four of the most popular interest rate futures contracts: the Treasury bond, Treasury note, Treasury bill, and Eurodollar contracts. We have also considered different ways in which these contracts can be used for hedging. Because bond prices are inversely related to interest rates, a long hedge provides protection against a reduction in interest rates; a short hedge provides protection against an increase in interest rates.

In the Treasury bond and Treasury note futures contracts, the party with the short position has a number of interesting delivery options:

1. Delivery can be made on any day during the delivery month.
2. There are a number of alternative bonds that can be delivered.
3. On any day during the delivery month, the notice of intention to deliver at the 2:00 P.M. settlement price can be made any time up to 8:00 P.M.

These options all tend to reduce the futures price.

The concept of duration is important in hedging interest-rate risk. Duration measures how long on average an investor has to wait before receiving payments. It is a weighted average of the times until payments are received, with the weight for a particular payment time being proportional to the present value of the payment.

TABLE 5.8 Hedging a Floating-Rate Loan

From the Trader's Desk—April 29

A company has just borrowed $15 million for three months at an interest rate equal to one-month LIBOR plus 1 percent and would like to hedge its risk.

Quotes:

1. The one-month LIBOR rate is 8 percent.

2. The June Eurodollar futures price is 91.88.

3. The September Eurodollar futures price is 91.44.

The Strategy

1. Short five June contracts and five September contracts.

2. Close out the June contracts on May 29.

3. Close out the September contracts on June 29.

The Result

On May 29 the one-month LIBOR rate was 8.8 percent and the June futures price was 91.12. The company gained $5 \times (\$979,700 - \$977,800) = \$9,500$ on the five June contracts. This provided compensation for the $10,000 extra interest payment necessary in the second month because of the increase in LIBOR from 8 percent to 8.8 percent.

On June 29 the one-month LIBOR rate was 9.4 percent and the September futures price was 90.16. The company gained $16,000 on the five September contracts. This provided compensation for extra interest costs of $17,500.

A key result underlying the duration-based hedging scheme described in this chapter is

$$\Delta B = -BD\,\Delta y$$

where B is a bond price, D is its duration, Δy is a small change in its yield (continuously compounded), and ΔB is the resultant small change in B. The equation enables a hedger to assess the sensitivity of a bond price to small changes in its yield. It also enables the hedger to assess the sensitivity of an interest-rate futures price to small changes in the yield of the underlying bond. If the hedger is prepared to assume that Δy is the same for all bonds, the result enables the hedger to calculate the number of futures contracts necessary to protect a bond or bond portfolio against small changes in interest rates.

The key assumption underlying the duration-based hedging scheme is that all interest rates change by the same amount. This means that only parallel shifts in the term structure are allowed for. In practice, short-term interest rates are generally more volatile than are long-term interest rates, and hedge performance is liable to be poor if the duration of the bond underlying the futures contract differs markedly from the duration of the asset being hedged.

We have looked at three situations in which the duration-based hedging model can be used. There should be no difficulty applying the same basic principles to other situations. In all cases, the number of contracts used for hedging is chosen using Equation 5.14, so that the duration of the whole position is zero.

Suggestions for Further Reading

Allen, S. L., and A. D. Kleinstein. *Valuing Fixed-Income Investments and Derivative Securities.* New York: New York Institute of Finance, 1991.

Chicago Board of Trade. *Interest Rate Futures for Institutional Investors.* Chicago, 1987.

Fabozzi, F. J. *Fixed-Income Mathematics: Analytical and Statistical Techniques.* Chicago: Probus, 1993.

Figlewski, S. *Hedging with Financial Futures for Institutional Investors.* Cambridge, MA: Ballinger, 1986.

Gay, G. D., R. W. Kolb, and R. Chiang. "Interest Rate Hedging: An Empirical Test of Alternative Strategies," *Journal of Financial Research* 6 (Fall 1983): 187–197.

Klemkosky, R. C., and D. J. Lasser. "An Efficiency Analysis of the T-Bond Futures Market," *Journal of Futures Markets* 5 (1985): 607–620.

Kolb, R. W. *Interest Rate Futures: A Comprehensive Introduction.* Richmond, VA: R. F. Dame, 1982.

Kolb, R. W., and R. Chiang. "Improving Hedging Performance Using Interest Rate Futures," *Financial Management* 10 (Fall 1981): 72–79.

Resnick, B. G. "The Relationship between Futures Prices for U.S. Treasury Bonds," *Review of Research in Futures Markets* 3 (1984): 88–104.

Resnick, B. G., and E. Hennigar. "The Relationship between Futures and Cash Prices for U.S. Treasury Bonds," *Review of Research in Futures Markets* 2 (1983): 282–299.

Senchak, A. J., and J. C. Easterwood. "Cross Hedging CDs with Treasury Bill Futures," *Journal of Futures Markets* 3 (1983): 429–438.

Veit, W. T., and W. W. Reiff. "Commercial Banks and Interest Rate Futures: A Hedging Survey," *Journal of Futures Markets* 3 (1983): 283–293.

Quiz

1. Suppose that spot interest rates with continuous compounding are as follows:

Maturity (years)	Rate (% per annum)
1	8.0
2	7.5
3	7.2
4	7.0
5	6.9

Calculate forward interest rates for the second, third, fourth, and fifth years.

2. The term structure is upward sloping. Put the following in order of magnitude:
   a. The five-year spot rate
   b. The yield on a five-year coupon-bearing bond
   c. The forward rate corresponding to the period between 5 and 5.25 years in the future
   What is the answer to this question when the term structure is downward sloping?

3. The six-month and one-year spot rates are both 10 percent per annum. For a bond that lasts 18 months and pays a coupon of 8 percent per annum (with a coupon payment

having just been made), the yield is 10.4 percent per annum. What is the bond's price? What is the 18-month spot rate? All rates are quoted with semiannual compounding.

4. It is January 9, 1997. The price of a Treasury bond with a 12 percent coupon that matures on October 12, 1999 is quoted as 102-07. What is the cash price?

5. The price of a 90-day Treasury bill is quoted as 10.00. What continuously compounded return does an investor earn on the Treasury bill for the 90-day period?

6. What assumptions does a duration-based hedging scheme make about the way in which the term structure moves?

7. It is January 30. You are managing a bond portfolio worth $6 million. The average duration of the portfolio is 8.2 years. The September Treasury bond futures price is currently 108-15, and the cheapest-to-deliver bond has a duration of 7.6 years. How should you hedge against changes in interest rates over the next seven months?

Questions and Problems

5.1. Suppose that spot interest rates with continuous compounding are as follows:

Maturity (years)	Rate (% per annum)
1	12.0
2	13.0
3	13.7
4	14.2
5	14.5

Calculate forward interest rates for the second, third, fourth, and fifth years.

5.2. Suppose that spot interest rates with continuous compounding are as follows:

Maturity (months)	Rate (% per annum)
3	8.0
6	8.2
9	8.4
12	8.5
15	8.6
18	8.7

Calculate forward interest rates for the second, third, fourth, fifth, and sixth quarters.

5.3. The cash prices of six-month and one-year Treasury bills are 94.0 and 89.0. A 1.5-year bond that will pay coupons of $4 every six months currently sells for $94.84. A two-year bond that will pay coupons of $5 every six months currently sells for $97.12. Calculate the six-month, one-year, 1.5-year, and two-year spot rates.

5.4. A 10-year, 8 percent coupon bond currently sells for $90. A 10-year, 4 percent coupon bond currently sells for $80. What is the 10-year spot rate? (Hint: Consider taking a long position in two of the 4 percent coupon bonds and a short position in one of the 8 percent coupon bonds.)

5.5. Explain carefully why liquidity preference theory is consistent with the observation that the term structure tends to be upward sloping more often than it is downward sloping.

5.6. It is May 5, 1997. The quoted price of a government bond with a 12 percent coupon that matures on July 27, 2001 is 110-17. What is the cash price?

5.7. Suppose that the Treasury bond futures price is 101-12. Which of the following four bonds is cheapest to deliver?

Bond	Price	Conversion Factor
1	125-05	1.2131
2	142-15	1.3792
3	115-31	1.1149
4	144-02	1.4026

5.8. It is July 30, 1997. The cheapest-to-deliver bond in a September 1997 Treasury bond futures contract is a 13 percent coupon bond, and delivery is expected to be made on September 30, 1997. Coupon payments on the bond are made on February 4 and August 4 each year. The term structure is flat, and the rate of interest with semiannual compounding is 12 percent per annum. The conversion factor for the bond is 1.5. The current quoted bond price is $110. Calculate the quoted futures price for the contract.

5.9. An investor is looking for arbitrage opportunities in the Treasury bond futures market. What complications are created by the fact that the party with a short position can choose to deliver any bond with a maturity of over 15 years?

5.10. Suppose that the Treasury bill futures price for a contract maturing in 33 days is quoted as 90.04 and the discount rate for a 123-day Treasury bill is 10.03. What is the implied repo rate? How can it be used?

5.11. Suppose that the nine-month interest rate is 8 percent per annum and the six-month interest rate is 7.5 percent per annum (both with continuous compounding). Estimate the futures price of 90-day Treasury bills with a face value of $1 million for delivery in six months. How would the price be quoted?

5.12. Assume that a bank can borrow or lend money at the same interest rate in Euromarkets. The 90-day rate is 10 percent per annum and the 180-day rate is 10.2 percent per annum, both expressed with continuous compounding. The Eurodollar futures price for a contract maturing in 90 days is quoted as 89.5. What arbitrage opportunities are open to the bank?

5.13. A Canadian company wishes to create a Canadian interest-rate futures contract from a U.S. Treasury bill futures contract and forward contracts on foreign exchange. Using an example, explain how the company should proceed. For the purposes of this problem, assume that a futures contract is the same as a forward contract.

5.14. A five-year bond with a yield of 11 percent (continuously compounded) pays an 8 percent coupon at the end of each year.
a. What is the bond's price?
b. What is the bond's duration?

    c. Use the duration to calculate the effect on the bond's price of a 0.2 percent decrease in its yield.

    d. Recalculate the bond's price on the basis of a 10.8 percent per annum yield and verify that the result is in agreement with your answer to (c).

5.15. Portfolio A consists of a 1-year discount bond with a face value of $2,000 and a 10-year discount bond with a face value of $6,000. Portfolio B consists of a 5.95-year discount bond with a face value of $5,000. The current yield on all bonds is 10 percent per annum.

    a. Show that both portfolios have the same duration.

    b. Show that the percentage changes in the values of the two portfolios for a 0.1 percent per annum increase in yields are the same.

    c. What are the percentage changes in the values of the two portfolios for a 5 percent per annum increase in yields?

    d. Which portfolio has the higher convexity?

5.16. Suppose that a bond portfolio with a duration of 12 years is hedged using a futures contract in which the underlying asset has a duration of 4 years. What is likely to be the impact on the hedge of the fact that the 12-year rate is less volatile than the 4-year rate?

5.17. Suppose that it is February 20 and a treasurer realizes that on July 17 the company will have to issue $5 million of commercial paper with a maturity of 180 days. If the paper were issued today, the company would realize $4,820,000. (In other words, the company would receive $4,820,000 for its paper and have to redeem it at $5,000,000 in 180 days' time.) The September Eurodollar futures price is quoted as 92.00. How should the treasurer hedge the company's exposure?

5.18. On August 1 a portfolio manager has a bond portfolio worth $10 million. The duration of the portfolio is 7.1 years. The December Treasury bond futures price is currently 91-12 and the cheapest-to-deliver bond has a duration of 8.8 years. How should the portfolio manager immunize the portfolio against changes in interest rates over the next two months?

5.19. How can the portfolio manager change the duration of the portfolio to 3.0 years in Problem 5.18?

5.20. Between February 28, 1998 and March 1, 1998 you have a choice between owning a government bond paying a 10 percent coupon and a corporate bond paying a 10 percent coupon. Consider carefully the day count conventions discussed in this chapter and decide which of the two bonds you would prefer to own. Ignore the risk of default.

5.21. Suppose that a Eurodollar futures quote is 88 for a contract maturing in 60 days. What is the LIBOR forward rate for the 60- to 150-day period? Ignore the difference between futures and forwards for the purposes of this question.

5.22. Suppose that a Treasury bill futures quote is 88 for a contract maturing in 60 days. What is the Treasury forward rate for the 60- to 150-day period? Ignore the difference between futures and forwards for the purposes of this question.

C H A P T E R

Swaps

Swaps are private agreements between two companies to exchange cash flows in the future according to a prearranged formula. They can be regarded as portfolios of forward contracts. The study of swaps is therefore a natural extension of the study of forward and futures contracts.

The first swap contracts were negotiated in 1981. Since then the market has grown very rapidly. Hundreds of billions of dollars of contracts are currently negotiated each year. In this chapter we examine how swaps are designed, how they are used, and how they can be valued. We also consider briefly the nature of the credit risk facing financial institutions when they trade swaps and similar financial contracts.

Mechanics of Interest-Rate Swaps

The most common type of swap is a "plain vanilla" interest-rate swap. Party B agrees to pay party A cash flows equal to interest at a predetermined fixed rate on a notional principal for a number of years. At the same time, party A agrees to pay party B cash flows equal to interest at a floating rate on the same notional principal for the same period of time. The currencies of the two sets of interest cash flows are the same. The life of the swap can range from 1 year to over 15 years.

LONDON INTERBANK OFFER RATE

The floating rate in many interest-rate swap agreements is the London Interbank Offer Rate (LIBOR). LIBOR is the rate of interest offered by banks on deposits from other banks in Eurocurrency markets. One-month LIBOR is the rate offered on one-month deposits; three-month LIBOR is the rate offered on three-month deposits; and so on. LIBOR rates are determined by trading between banks and change continuously as economic conditions change. Just as prime is often the reference rate of interest for floating-rate loans in the domestic financial market, LIBOR is frequently a reference rate of interest for loans in international financial markets. To understand how it is used, consider a loan with a rate of interest specified as six-month LIBOR plus 0.5

percent per annum. The life of the loan is divided into six-month periods. For each period the rate of interest is set at 0.5 percent per annum above the six-month LIBOR rate at the beginning of the period. Interest is paid at the end of the period. As mentioned in chapter 5, three-month LIBOR is the rate of interest underlying the very popular Eurodollar futures contract that trades on the Chicago Mercantile Exchange.

AN EXAMPLE

Consider a three-year swap initiated on March 1, 1998 in which company B agrees to pay to company A a rate of 5 percent per annum on a notional principal of $100 million, and in return company A agrees to pay to company B the six-month LIBOR rate on the same notional principal. We assume the agreement specifies that payments are to be exchanged every six months and the 5 percent interest rate is quoted with semiannual compounding. The swap is represented diagrammatically in Figure 6.1.

The first exchange of payments would take place on September 1, 1998, six months after the initiation of the agreement. Company B would pay company A $2.5 million. This is the interest on the $100 million principal for six months at 5 percent. Company A would pay company B interest on the $100 million principal at the six-month LIBOR rate prevailing six months prior to September 1, 1998—that is, on March 1, 1998. Suppose that the six-month LIBOR rate on March 1, 1998 is 4.2 percent. Company A pays company B $0.5 \times 0.042 \times \$100 = \$2.1$ million. Note that there is no uncertainty about this first exchange of payments, because it is determined by the LIBOR rate at the time the contract is entered into.

The second exchange of payments would take place on March 1, 1999, one year after the initiation of the agreement. Company B would pay $2.5 million to company A. Company A would pay interest on the $100 million principal to company B at the six-month LIBOR rate prevailing six months prior to March 1, 1999—that is, on September 1, 1998. Suppose that the six-month LIBOR rate on September 1, 1998 is 4.8 percent. Company A pays $0.5 \times 0.048 \times \$100 = \$2.4$ million to company B.

In total, there are six exchanges of payment on the swap. The fixed payments are always $2.5 million. The floating-rate payments on a payment date are calculated using the six-month LIBOR rate prevailing six months before the payment date. An interest-rate swap is generally structured so that one side remits the difference between the two payments to the other side. In the example given, company B would pay company A $0.4 million (= $2.5 million − $2.1 million) on September 1, 1998 and $0.1 million (= $2.5 million − $2.4 million) on March 1, 1999.

Table 6.1 provides a complete example of the payments to be made under the swap for one particular set of six-month LIBOR rates. The table shows the swap cash flows from the perspective of company B. Note that the $100 million principal is used only for the calculation of interest payments. The principal itself is not exchanged. This is why it is termed the *notional principal.*

FIGURE 6.1 Interest-Rate Swap between Companies A and B

TABLE 6.1 Cash Flows (Millions of Dollars) to Company B in a $100 Million Three-Year Interest-Rate Swap When a Fixed Rate of 5 Percent Is Paid and LIBOR Is Received

Date	LIBOR Rate (%)	Floating Cash Flow Received	Fixed Cash Flow Paid	Net Cash Flow
March 1, 1998	4.20			
September 1, 1998	4.80	+2.10	−2.50	−0.40
March 1, 1999	5.30	+2.40	−2.50	−0.10
September 1, 1999	5.50	+2.65	−2.50	+0.15
March 1, 2000	5.60	+2.75	−2.50	+0.25
September 1, 2000	5.90	+2.80	−2.50	+0.30
March 1, 2001	6.40	+2.95	−2.50	+0.45

If the principal were exchanged at the end of the life of the swap, the nature of the deal would not be changed in any way. The principal is the same for both the fixed and floating payments. Exchanging $100 million for $100 million at the end of the life of the swap is a transaction that would have no financial value to either party. Table 6.2 shows the cash flows in Table 6.1 with a final exchange of principal added in. The cash flows in the third column of this table are the cash flows from a long position in a floating-rate bond. The cash flows in the fourth column of the table are the cash flows from a short position in a fixed-rate bond. The table shows that the swap can be regarded as the exchange of a fixed-rate bond for a floating-rate bond. Company B, whose position is described by Table 6.2, is long a floating-rate bond and short a fixed-rate bond. Company A is long a fixed-rate bond and short a floating-rate bond.

This characterization of the cash flows in the swap helps to explain why the floating rate in the swap is set six months before it is paid. On a floating-rate instrument, interest is generally set at the beginning of the period to which it will apply and is paid at the end

TABLE 6.2 Cash Flows (Millions of Dollars) from Table 6.1 When There Is a Final Exchange of Principal

Date	LIBOR Rate (%)	Floating Cash Flow Received	Fixed Cash Flow Paid	Net Cash Flow
March 1, 1998	4.20			
September 1, 1998	4.80	+2.10	−2.50	−0.40
March 1, 1999	5.30	+2.40	−2.50	−0.10
September 1, 1999	5.50	+2.65	−2.50	+0.15
March 1, 2000	5.60	+2.75	−2.50	+0.25
September 1, 2000	5.90	+2.80	−2.50	+0.30
March 1, 2001	6.40	+102.95	−102.50	+0.45

of the period. The timing of the floating-rate payments in a "plain vanilla" interest-rate swap such as the one in Table 6.2 reflects this characterization.

USING THE SWAP TO TRANSFORM A LIABILITY

For company B the swap could be used to transform a floating-rate loan into a fixed-rate loan. Suppose that company B has arranged to borrow $100 million at LIBOR plus 80 basis points. (One basis point is one-hundredth of 1 percent, so the rate is LIBOR plus 0.8 percent.) After company B has entered into the swap, it has three sets of cash flows:

1. It pays LIBOR plus 0.8 percent to its outside lenders.
2. It receives LIBOR under the terms of the swap.
3. It pays 5 percent under the terms of the swap.

These three sets of cash flows net out to an interest-rate payment of 5.8 percent. Thus, for company B the swap could have the effect of transforming borrowings at a floating rate of LIBOR plus 80 basis points into borrowings at a fixed rate of 5.8 percent.

For company A the swap could have the effect of transforming a fixed-rate loan into a floating-rate loan. Suppose that company A has a three-year $100 million loan outstanding on which it pays 5.2 percent. After it has entered into the swap, it has three sets of cash flows:

1. It pays 5.2 percent to its outside lenders.
2. It pays LIBOR under the terms of the swap.
3. It receives 5 percent under the terms of the swap.

These three sets of cash flows net out to an interest-rate payment of LIBOR plus 0.2 percent (or LIBOR plus 20 basis points). Thus, for company A the swap could have the effect of transforming borrowings at a fixed rate of 5.2 percent into borrowings at a floating rate of LIBOR plus 20 basis points. These potential uses of the swap by companies A and B are illustrated in Figure 6.2.

USING THE SWAP TO TRANSFORM AN ASSET

Swaps can also be used to transform the nature of an asset. Consider company B in our example. The swap could have the effect of transforming an asset earning a fixed rate of interest into an asset earning a floating rate of interest. Suppose that company B owns $100 million in bonds that will provide interest at 4.7 percent per annum over the next three years. After company B has entered into the swap, it has three sets of cash flows:

1. It receives 4.7 percent on the bonds.
2. It receives LIBOR under the terms of the swap.
3. It pays 5 percent under the terms of the swap.

FIGURE 6.2 Companies A and B Use the Swap to Transform a Liability

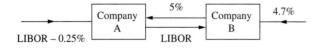

FIGURE 6.3 Companies A and B Use the Swap to Transform an Asset

These three sets of cash flows net out to an interest-rate inflow of LIBOR minus 30 basis points. Thus, one possible use of the swap for company B is to transform an asset earning 4.7 percent into an asset earning LIBOR minus 30 basis points.

Consider next company A. The swap could have the effect of transforming an asset earning a floating rate of interest into an asset earning a fixed rate of interest. Suppose that company A has an investment of $100 million that yields LIBOR minus 25 basis points. After it has entered into the swap, it has three sets of cash flows:

1. It receives LIBOR minus 25 basis points on its investment.
2. It pays LIBOR under the terms of the swap.
3. It receives 5 percent under the terms of the swap.

These three sets of cash flows net out to an interest-rate inflow of 4.75 percent. Thus, one possible use of the swap for company A is to transform an asset earning LIBOR minus 25 basis points into an asset earning 4.75 percent. These potential uses of the swap by companies A and B are illustrated in Figure 6.3.

ROLE OF FINANCIAL INTERMEDIARY

Usually two nonfinancial companies do not get in touch directly to arrange a swap in the way indicated in Figures 6.2 and 6.3. They each deal with a financial intermediary such as a bank or other financial institution. "Plain vanilla" fixed-for-floating swaps on U.S. interest rates are usually structured so that the financial institution earns about 3 or 4 basis points (0.03 percent to 0.04 percent) on a pair of offsetting transactions.

Figure 6.4 shows what the role of the financial institution might be in the situation in Figure 6.2. The financial institution enters into two offsetting swap transactions with companies A and B. Assuming that neither A nor B defaults, the financial institution is certain to make a profit of 0.03 percent (3 basis points) per year on the principal of $100 million. (This amounts to $30,000 per year for the three-year period.) Company B ends up borrowing at 5.815 percent (instead of 5.8 percent, as in Figure 6.2). Company A ends up borrowing at LIBOR plus 21.5 basis points (instead of at LIBOR plus 20 basis points, as in Figure 6.2).

Figure 6.5 illustrates the role of the financial institution in the situation in Figure 6.3. Again, the financial institution is certain to make a profit of 3 basis points if neither company defaults on the swap. Company B ends up earning LIBOR minus 31.5 basis points (instead of LIBOR minus 30 basis points, as in Figure 6.3). Company A ends up earning 4.735 percent (instead of 4.75 percent, as in Figure 6.3).

Note that in each case the financial institution has two separate contracts: one with company A and the other with company B. In most instances, company A will not even

FIGURE 6.4 Interest-Rate Swap from Figure 6.2 When Financial Institution Is Used

FIGURE 6.5 Interest-Rate Swap from Figure 6.3 When Financial Institution Is Used

know that the financial institution has entered into an offsetting swap with company B, and vice versa. If one of the companies defaults, the financial institution still has to honor its agreement with the other company. The 3-basis-point spread earned by the financial institution is partly to compensate it for the default risk it is bearing.

PRICING SCHEDULES

The fixed rate in a "plain vanilla" swap is normally quoted as a certain number of basis points above the Treasury note yield. Table 6.3 shows an *indication pricing schedule* that was used by swap traders working for financial institutions at 4:00 P.M. New York time on October 17, 1996. It indicates the prices quoted to prospective counterparties. For example, it shows that in a five-year swap in which the financial institution will pay fixed and receive six-month LIBOR, the fixed rate should be set 23 basis points above the current five-year Treasury note rate of 6.24 percent. In other words, the financial institution should set the fixed rate at 6.47 percent. When it is negotiating a five-year swap in which it will receive fixed and pay six-month LIBOR for five years, the schedule indicates that the institution should set the fixed rate at 27 basis points above the current five-year Treasury note rate, or at 6.51 percent. The bank's profit, or its bid-ask spread from negotiating two offsetting five-year swaps, would be 4 basis points (0.04 percent) per annum.[1]

At any given time, swap spreads are determined by supply and demand. If more market participants want to receive fixed than receive floating, swap spreads tend to fall.

TABLE 6.3 Indication Pricing for Interest Rate Swaps at 4:00 P.M. New York Time on Thursday October 17, 1996

Maturity (years)	Bank Pays Fixed Rate	Bank Receives Fixed Rate	Current TN* Rate (%)
2	2-yr TN + 17 bps†	2-yr TN + 20 bps	5.86
3	3-yr TN + 19 bps	3-yr TN + 22 bps	6.02
4	4-yr TN + 22 bps	4-yr TN + 26 bps	6.13
5	5-yr TN + 23 bps	5-yr TN + 27 bps	6.24
7	7-yr TN + 30 bps	7-yr TN + 33 bps	6.35
10	10-yr TN + 32 bps	10-yr TN + 36 bps	6.51

*TN = Treasury note.
†bps = basis points.

---

[1] In the early days of swaps, bid-ask spreads as high as 100 basis points were possible. As Table 6.3 indicates, the market is now much more competitive.

If the reverse is true, swap spreads tend to rise. Table 6.3 would be updated regularly as market conditions changed.

The day count conventions discussed in chapter 5 affect payments on a swap. Because it is a money market rate, six-month LIBOR is quoted on an actual/360 basis with semiannual compounding. The Treasury note rate is quoted on an actual/actual (in period) basis with semiannual compounding. This can be confusing. To make a six-month LIBOR rate comparable with a Treasury note rate in a 365-day year, either the six-month LIBOR rate must be multiplied by 365/360 or the Treasury note rate must be multiplied by 360/365. A LIBOR-based floating-rate cash flow on a swap payment date is calculated as $QRn/360$, where Q is the principal, R is the relevant LIBOR rate, and n is the number of days since the last payment date.[2]

WAREHOUSING

In practice, it is unlikely that two companies will contact a financial institution at the same time and want to take opposite positions in exactly the same swap. For this reason, most large financial institutions are prepared to warehouse interest-rate swaps. Typically they enter into a swap with one counterparty, then hedge the interest-rate risk until a counterparty wanting to take an opposite position is found. The interest-rate futures contracts discussed in chapter 5 are one way of carrying out the hedging.

The Comparative-Advantage Argument

An explanation commonly put forward about the popularity of swaps concerns comparative advantages. Consider the use of an interest-rate swap to transform a liability. Some companies, it is argued, have a comparative advantage when borrowing in fixed-rate markets, whereas other companies have a comparative advantage in floating-rate markets. To obtain a new loan, it makes sense for a company to go to the market where it has a comparative advantage. As a result, the company may borrow fixed when it wants floating, or borrow floating when it wants fixed. The swap is used to transform a fixed-rate loan into a floating-rate loan, and vice versa.

AN EXAMPLE

Suppose that two companies, A and B, both wish to borrow $10 million for five years and have been offered the rates shown in Table 6.4. We assume that company B wants to borrow at a fixed rate of interest, whereas company A wants to borrow floating funds at a rate linked to six-month LIBOR. Company B clearly has a lower credit rating than company A, because it pays a higher rate of interest than company A in both fixed and floating markets.

---

[2]Some of the numbers calculated earlier in this chapter do not perfectly reflect the day count convention for LIBOR. For example, in Table 6.1 the first floating-rate cash flow in millions of dollars would be

$$100 \times 0.042 \times \frac{184}{360} = 2.1467$$

The fixed-rate cash flow is exactly $2.5 million on all payment dates. The net cash flow on the first payment date is therefore $0.3533 million.

TABLE 6.4 Borrowing Rates That Provide a Basis for the Comparative-Advantage Argument

	Fixed	Floating
Company A	10.0%	6-month LIBOR + 0.3%
Company B	11.2%	6-month LIBOR + 1.0%

A key feature of the rates offered to companies A and B is that the difference between the two fixed rates is greater than the difference between the two floating rates. Company B pays 1.2 percent more than company A in fixed-rate markets and only 0.7 percent more than company A in floating-rate markets. Company B appears to have a comparative advantage in floating-rate markets, whereas company A appears to have a comparative advantage in fixed-rate markets.[3] It is this apparent anomaly that can lead to a swap being negotiated. Company A borrows fixed-rate funds at 10 percent per annum. Company B borrows floating-rate funds at LIBOR plus 1 percent per annum. They then enter into a swap agreement to ensure that A ends up with floating-rate funds and B ends up with fixed-rate funds.

To understand how the swap might work, we first assume that A and B get in touch with each other directly. The sort of swap they might negotiate is shown in Figure 6.6. Company A agrees to pay company B interest at six-month LIBOR on $10 million. In return, company B agrees to pay company A interest at a fixed rate of 9.95 percent per annum on $10 million.

Company A has three sets of interest-rate cash flows:

1. It pays 10 percent per annum to outside lenders.

2. It receives 9.95 percent per annum from B.

3. It pays LIBOR to B.

The net effect of the three cash flows is that A pays LIBOR plus 0.05 percent per annum. This is 0.25 percent per annum less than it would pay if it went directly to floating-rate markets.

Company B also has three sets of interest-rate cash flows:

1. It pays LIBOR + 1 percent per annum to outside lenders.

2. It receives LIBOR from A.

3. It pays 9.95 percent per annum to A.

FIGURE 6.6 Swap Agreement between A and B When Rates in Table 6.4 Apply

---

[3] Note that B's comparative advantage in floating-rate markets does not imply that B pays less than A in this market. It means that the extra amount that B pays over the amount paid by A is less in this market. One of my students summarized the situation as follows: "A pays more less in fixed-rate markets; B pays less more in floating-rate markets."

The net effect of the three cash flows is that B pays 10.95 percent per annum. This is 0.25 percent per annum less than it would pay if it went directly to fixed-rate markets.

The swap arrangement appears to improve the position of both A and B by 0.25 percent per annum. The total gain is therefore 0.5 percent per annum. The result could have been calculated in advance. The total apparent gain from an interest-rate swap agreement is always $|a - b|$, where a is the difference between the interest rates facing the two companies in fixed-rate markets, and b is the difference between the interest rates facing the two companies in floating-rate markets. In this case, $a = 1.2$ percent and $b = 0.7$ percent.

If A and B did not deal directly with each other and used a financial institution, an arrangement such as that shown in Figure 6.7 might result. In this case, A ends up borrowing at LIBOR + 0.07 percent, B ends up borrowing at 10.97 percent, and the financial institution earns a spread of 4 basis points per year. The gain to company A is 0.23 percent; the gain to company B is 0.23 percent; and the gain to the bank is 0.04 percent. The total gain to all three parties is 0.50 percent as before. Table 6.5 summarizes this example.

CRITICISM OF THE COMPARATIVE-ADVANTAGE ARGUMENT

The comparative-advantage argument for explaining the attractiveness of interest-rate swaps is open to question. Why in Table 6.4 should the spreads between the rates offered to A and B be different in fixed and floating markets? Now that the swap market has been in existence for some time, we might reasonably expect these types of differences to have been arbitraged away.

The reason that spread differentials appear to continue to exist may be due in part to the nature of the contracts available to companies in fixed and floating markets. The 10 percent and 11.2 percent rates available to A and B in fixed-rate markets are likely to be the rates at which the companies can issue five-year fixed-rate bonds. The LIBOR + 0.3 percent and LIBOR + 1 percent rates available to A and B in floating-rate markets are six-month rates. In the floating-rate market, the lender usually has the opportunity to review the floating rates every six months. If the creditworthiness of A or B has declined, the lender has the option of increasing the spread over LIBOR that is charged. In extreme circumstances, the lender can refuse to roll over the loan at all. The providers of fixed-rate financing do not have the option to change the terms of the loan in this way.[4]

The spreads between the rates offered to A and B are a reflection of the extent to which B is more likely to default than A. During the next six months, there is very little

FIGURE 6.7 Swap Agreement between A and B When Rates in Table 6.4 Apply and a Financial Intermediary Is Involved

---

[4] If the floating-rate loans are structured so that the spread over LIBOR is guaranteed in advance regardless of changes in credit rating, the comparative advantage in Table 6.4 generally disappears.

TABLE 6.5 An Interest-Rate Swap Arrangement Based on Apparent Comparative Advantages

From the Trader's Desk

Company A and company B both wish to borrow $10 million for five years. Company A wants to arrange a floating-rate loan in which the rate of interest is linked to six-month LIBOR. Company B wants to arrange a fixed-rate loan. They have been offered the following terms.

	Fixed	*Floating*
Company A	10.0%	6-month LIBOR + 0.3%
Company B	11.2%	6-month LIBOR + 1.0%

The Strategy

1. Company A borrows fixed-rate funds at 10 percent per annum.
2. Company B borrows floating-rate funds at LIBOR + 1 percent per annum.
3. They then enter into a swap agreement.

The Swap with No Intermediary

The arrangement is shown in Figure 6.6. Company A agrees to pay company B the six-month LIBOR rate of interest on $10 million. In return, company B agrees to pay company A 10.95 percent per annum on $10 million. The net result is that A ends up borrowing at LIBOR + 0.05 percent, whereas B ends up borrowing at 10.95 percent. The swap makes both sides 0.25 percent per annum better off.

The Swap with Intermediary

The arrangement is shown in Figure 6.7. Each of A and B enters into a swap agreement with a financial intermediary. Company A ends up borrowing at LIBOR + 0.07 percent per annum, company B ends up borrowing at 10.97 percent per annum, and the intermediary achieves a spread of 0.04 percent per annum. The swap makes each of company A and B 0.23 percent per annum better off.

chance that either A or B will default. As we look further ahead, default statistics show that the probability of a default by a company with a relatively low credit rating (such as B) increases faster than the probability of a default by a company with a relatively high credit rating (such as A). This is why the spread between the five-year rates is greater than the spread between the six-month rates.

After negotiating a floating-rate loan at LIBOR + 1 percent and entering into the swap shown in Figure 6.7, B appears to obtain a fixed-rate loan at 10.97 percent. The arguments presented now show that this is not really the case. In practice, the rate paid is 10.97 percent only if B can continue to borrow floating-rate funds at a spread of 1 percent over LIBOR. (For example, if the credit rating of B declines so that the floating-rate loan is rolled over at LIBOR + 2 percent, the rate paid by B increases to 11.97 percent.) The relatively high five-year borrowing rate offered to B in Table 6.4 suggests that the market considers that B's spread over six-month LIBOR for borrowed funds is more likely to rise than fall. Assuming this is so, B's expected average borrowing rate if it enters into the swap is greater than 10.97 percent.

The swap in Figure 6.7 locks in LIBOR + 0.07 percent for company A for the whole of the next five years, not just for the next six months. Unless there is a strong reason for supposing that company A's credit rating will improve, it appears to be a good deal for company A. The downside of the arrangement to company A is the possibility (perhaps very small) of a default by the financial institution.

Valuation of Interest-Rate Swaps

If we assume no possibility of default, an interest-rate swap can be valued either as a long position in one bond combined with a short position in another bond or as a portfolio of forward-rate agreements.

RELATIONSHIP OF SWAP VALUE TO BOND PRICES

As illustrated in Table 6.2, a swap can be characterized as the difference between two bonds. Consider the swap between the financial institution and company B in Figure 6.4. Although the principal is not exchanged, we can assume without changing the value of the swap that, at the end of the agreement, A pays B the notional principal of $100 million and B pays A the same notional principal. The swap is then the same as an arrangement in which

1. Company B has lent the financial institution $100 million at the six-month LIBOR rate
2. The financial institution has lent company B $100 million at a fixed rate of 5.015 percent per annum

To put it another way, the financial institution has sold a $100 million floating-rate (LIBOR) bond to company B and has purchased a $100 million fixed-rate (5.015 percent per annum) bond from company B. The value of the swap to the financial institution is therefore the difference between the values of two bonds.

Suppose that, under the terms of a swap, a financial institution receives fixed payments of k dollars at times t_i $(1 \leq i \leq n)$ and makes floating LIBOR payments at the same times. We define

V_{swap}: value of swap to the financial institution

B_{fix}: value of fixed-rate bond underlying the swap

B_{fl}: value of floating-rate bond underlying the swap

Q: notional principal in swap agreement

It follows that

$$V_{swap} = B_{fix} - B_{fl} \tag{6.1}$$

It is customary to discount the cash flows in a swap at LIBOR rates. The implicit assumption is that the risk associated with the swap cash flows is the same as the risk associated with the cash flows on a loan in the interbank market.[5] A LIBOR zero-coupon

---

[5]This is an approximation. For example, the cash flows on a swap with the federal government should clearly be discounted at a lower rate than the cash flows on the same swap with a BBB-rated counterparty.

yield curve is usually calculated from Eurodollar futures quotes and swap quotes such as those in Table 6.3. For this purpose, it is assumed that a swap entered into at the average of the bid and ask quotes has a value of zero. The floating-rate bond underlying such a swap is worth par. It follows that the fixed-rate bond is also worth par. An indication schedule such as Table 6.3 therefore defines a number of fixed-rate bonds that are worth par. These are known as *par yield bonds*.

Consider, for example, the five-year swap quotes in Table 6.3. When we average the bid and ask quotes, we obtain a swap in which 6.49 percent is exchanged for LIBOR. The bonds underlying both the fixed and floating sides of this swap are assumed to be worth par. When constructing the zero-coupon LIBOR curve, we therefore assume that a five-year bond paying a coupon of 6.49 percent interest is worth par; we similarly assume that a seven-year bond paying a coupon of 6.665 percent is worth par; and so on. The bootstrap procedure described in chapter 5 is used to determine the zero-coupon yield curve from Eurodollar futures quotes and these par yield bonds. The zero-coupon yield curve defines the appropriate discount rates to use in evaluating Equation 6.1 for an existing swap.

To see how Equation 6.1 is used, we define r_i as the discount rate corresponding to maturity t_i. Since B_{fix} is the value of a bond that pays k at time t_i $(1 \leq i \leq n)$ and the principal amount of Q at time t_n,

$$B_{\text{fix}} = \sum_{i=1}^{n} ke^{-r_i t_i} + Qe^{-r_n t_n}$$

Consider next the floating-rate bond. Immediately after a payment date, B_{fl} is always equal to notional principal Q. Between payment dates, we can use the fact that B_{fl} will equal Q immediately after the next payment date. In our notation, the time until the next payment date is t_1, so that

$$B_{\text{fl}} = Qe^{-r_1 t_1} + k^* e^{-r_1 t_1}$$

where k^* is the floating-rate payment (already known) that will be made at time t_1.

In the situation where the financial institution is paying fixed and receiving floating, B_{fix} and B_{fl} are calculated in the same way and

$$V_{\text{swap}} = B_{\text{fl}} - B_{\text{fix}}$$

The value of the swap is zero when it is first negotiated. During its life it may have a positive or negative value.

Example

Suppose that, under the terms of a swap, a financial institution has agreed to pay six-month LIBOR and receive 8 percent per annum (with semiannual compounding) on a notional principal of $100 million. The swap has a remaining life of 1.25 years. The relevant discount rates with continuous compounding for 3-month, 9-month, and 15-month maturities are 10 percent, 10.5 percent, and 11 percent, respectively. The 6-month LIBOR rate at the last payment date was 10.2 percent (with semiannual compounding). In this case, $k = \$4$ million and $k^* = \$5.1$ million, so that

$$B_{\text{fix}} = 4e^{-0.1 \times 0.25} + 4e^{-0.105 \times 0.75} + 104e^{-0.11 \times 1.25}$$
$$= \$98.24 \text{ million}$$
$$B_{\text{fl}} = 5.1e^{-0.1 \times 0.25} + 100e^{-0.1 \times 0.25}$$
$$= \$102.51 \text{ million}$$

Hence the value of the swap is

$$98.24 - 102.51 = -\$4.27 \text{ million}$$

If the bank had been in the opposite position of paying fixed and receiving floating, the value of the swap would be $+\$4.27$ million. Note that a more precise calculation would take account of the actual/360 day count convention in calculating k^* (see footnote 2). It would also take account of the precise timing of the fixed-rate payments.

RELATIONSHIP OF SWAP VALUE TO FORWARD-RATE AGREEMENTS

Forward-rate agreements were introduced in chapter 5. They are agreements that a certain interest rate will apply for a certain period of time in the future. An interest-rate swap can be decomposed into a series of forward-rate agreements. To illustrate, let us return to the swap agreement between the financial institution and company B in Figure 6.4. Under this agreement, the financial institution has agreed that a rate of 5.015 percent per annum will apply for periods in the future regardless of prevailing market rates. The agreement for each period is a forward-rate agreement (FRA). The entire swap is a portfolio of FRAs.

As shown in chapter 5, an FRA can be valued by assuming that forward interest rates are realized. Since a swap is a portfolio of forward-rate agreements, a swap can also be valued by making the assumption that forward interest rates are realized. The procedure is as follows:[6]

1. Calculate forward rates for each of the LIBOR rates that will determine swap cash flows.
2. Calculate swap cash flows on the assumption that the LIBOR rates will equal the forward rates.
3. Set the swap value equal to the present value of these cash flows.

Example

Consider again the situation in the previous example. The cash flows that will be exchanged in 3 months have already been determined. A rate of 8 percent will be exchanged for 10.2 percent. The value of the exchange to the financial institution is

$$0.5 \times 100 \times (0.08 - 0.102)e^{-0.1 \times 0.25} = -1.07$$

---

[6]Note that this procedure does not always work for nonstandard swaps.

To calculate the value of the exchange in 9 months, we must first calculate the forward rate corresponding to the period between 3 and 9 months. From Equation 5.1, this is

$$\frac{0.105 \times 0.75 - 0.10 \times 0.25}{0.5} = 0.1075$$

or 10.75 percent with continuous compounding. From Equation 3.4, this value becomes 11.044 percent with semiannual compounding. The value of the FRA corresponding to the exchange in 9 months is therefore

$$0.5 \times 100 \times (0.08 - 0.11044)e^{-0.105 \times 0.75} = -1.41$$

To calculate the value of the exchange in 15 months, we must first calculate the forward rate corresponding to the period between 9 and 15 months. From Equation 5.1, this is

$$\frac{0.11 \times 1.25 - 0.105 \times 0.75}{0.5} = 0.1175$$

or 11.75 percent with continuous compounding. From Equation 3.4, this value becomes 12.102 percent with semiannual compounding. The value of the FRA corresponding to the exchange in 15 months is therefore

$$0.5 \times 100 \times (0.08 - 0.12102)e^{-0.11 \times 1.25} = -1.79$$

The total value of the swap is

$$-1.07 - 1.41 - 1.79 = -4.27$$

or −$4.27 million. This is in agreement with the calculation based on bond prices.

At the time the swap is entered into, it is worth approximately zero. This means that the sum of the value of the FRAs underlying the swap is zero, not that the value of each individual FRA is zero. In general, some FRAs will have positive values whereas others have negative values.

Consider again the FRAs underlying the swap between the financial institution and company B in Figure 6.4.

Value of FRA to financial institution < 0 when forward interest rate > 5.015%
Value of FRA to financial institution = 0 when forward interest rate = 5.015%
Value of FRA to financial institution > 0 when forward interest rate < 5.015%

Suppose that the term structure is upward sloping at the time the swap is negotiated. This means that the forward interest rates increase as the maturity of the FRA increases. Since the sum of the values of the FRAs is zero, the forward interest rate must be less than 5.015 percent for the early payment dates and greater than 5.015 percent for the later payment dates. The value to the financial institution of the FRAs corresponding to early payment dates is therefore positive, whereas the value of FRAs corresponding to later payment dates is negative. If the term structure is downward sloping at the time the swap is negotiated, the reverse is true. The impact of the shape of the term structure on the values of the forward contracts underlying a swap is summarized in Figure 6.8.

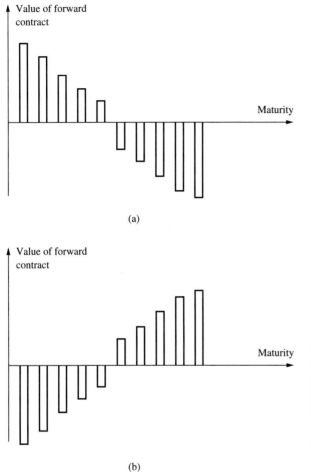

(a)

(b)

FIGURE 6.8 Value of Forward Contracts Underlying a Swap as a Function of Maturity
In (a) the yield curve is upward sloping and we receive fixed or the yield curve is downward sloping and we receive floating; in (b) the yield curve is upward sloping and we receive floating or the yield curve is downward sloping and we receive fixed.

Currency Swaps

Another popular type of swap is known as a *currency swap*. In its simplest form, this involves exchanging principal and fixed-rate interest payments on a loan in one currency for principal and fixed-rate interest payments on an approximately equivalent loan in another currency.

REASONS FOR CURRENCY SWAPS

A currency swap can be used to transform a loan in one currency into a loan in another currency. To illustrate how a currency swap works, we suppose that the costs to company A and to company B of borrowing for five years in U.S. dollars and sterling are as shown in Table 6.6. The data in the table suggest that sterling interest rates are generally higher than U.S. interest rates. Also, company A is probably more creditworthy than company B, because it faces a more favorable rate of interest in both currencies. From the viewpoint of a swap trader, the interesting aspect of Table 6.6 is that the

TABLE 6.6	Borrowing Rates Motivating Currency Swap	
	*Dollars**	*Sterling**
Company A	8.0%	11.6%
Company B	10.0%	12.0%

*Quoted rates have been adjusted to reflect tax advantages and disadvantages.

differences between the rates for A and B in the two markets are not the same. Company B pays 2 percent more than company A in the U.S. dollar market and only 0.4 percent more than company A in the sterling market.

This situation is analogous to that in Table 6.4. Company A has a comparative advantage in the U.S. dollar market, whereas company B has a comparative advantage in the sterling market. Earlier it was argued that comparative advantages are largely illusory when fixed and floating rates are compared. Here we are comparing the rates offered in two different currencies, and it is more likely that the comparative advantages are genuine. The comparative advantage shown in Table 6.6 might arise when company A is an American company that is better known to U.S. investors and company B is a UK company that is better known to British investors. It may also arise from the tax environments in which A and B operate. (We suppose that the rates in Table 6.6 have been adjusted to reflect the differential impact of taxes.)

We assume that A wants to borrow sterling and B wants to borrow dollars. This creates a perfect situation for a currency swap. Company A and company B each borrow in the market where they have a comparative advantage; that is, company A borrows dollars whereas company B borrows sterling. They then use a currency swap to transform A's loan into a sterling loan and B's loan into a dollar loan.

As already mentioned, the difference between the dollar interest rates is 2.0 percent, whereas the difference between the sterling interest rates is 0.4 percent. By analogy with the interest rate swap case, we expect the total gain to all parties to be 2.0 − 0.4 = 1.6 percent per annum.

There are many ways in which the swap can be organized. Figure 6.9 shows one possible arrangement. Company A borrows dollars and company B borrows sterling. The effect of the swap is to transform the U.S. dollar interest rate of 8 percent per annum to a sterling interest rate of 11 percent per annum for company A. As a result, company A is 0.6 percent per annum better off than it would be if it went directly to sterling markets. Similarly company B exchanges a sterling loan at 12 percent for a dollar loan at 9.4 percent and ends up 0.6 percent better off than it would be if it went directly to dollar markets. The financial intermediary gains 1.4 percent per annum on its dollar cash flows and loses 1 percent per annum on its sterling cash flows. If we ignore the

FIGURE 6.9 A Currency Swap

difference between the two currencies, the intermediary makes a net gain of 0.4 percent per annum. As predicted, the total gain to all parties is 1.6 percent per annum.

A currency swap agreement requires the principal to be specified in each of the two currencies. The principal amounts are usually exchanged at the beginning and at the end of the life of the swap. They are chosen so that they are approximately equal at the exchange rate at the beginning of the swap's life. In the example in Figure 6.9, the principal amounts might be $15 million and £ 10 million. Initially, the principal amounts flow in the opposite direction to the arrows in Figure 6.9. The interest payments during the life of the swap and the final principal payment flow in the same direction as the arrows. Thus, at the outset of the swap, company A pays $15 million and receives £ 10 million. Each year during the life of the swap contract, company A receives $1.20 million (= 8 percent of $15 million) and pays £ 1.10 million (= 11 percent of £ 10 million). At the end of the life of the swap, it pays a principal of £ 10 million and receives a principal of $15 million.

Table 6.7 summarizes this example. In Figure 6.9 the financial institution is exposed to foreign exchange risk. Each year it makes a gain of $210,000 (= 1.4 percent of $15 million) and incurs a loss of £ 100,000 (= 1 percent of £ 10 million). The intermediary can avoid this risk by buying £ 100,000 per annum in the forward market for each year of the life of the swap, thus locking in a net gain in U.S. dollars. Redesigning the swap so that the financial institution made a 0.4 percent spread in dollars and a zero spread in sterling might lead to the arrangement in Figure 6.10 or Figure 6.11. In

---

TABLE 6.7 A Currency Swap Arrangement

From the Trader's Desk

Company A wants to borrow £ 10 million at a fixed rate of interest for five years. Company B wants to borrow $15 million at a fixed rate of interest for five years. The companies have been offered the following rates:

	Dollars	*Sterling*
Company A	8.0%	11.6%
Company B	10.0%	12.0%

The Strategy

1. Company A borrows dollars at 8 percent per annum.

2. Company B borrows sterling at 12 percent per annum.

3. They enter into a swap agreement.

The Swap

One possible arrangement is shown in Figure 6.9. Principal payments flow in the opposite direction to the arrows at the start of the swap and in the same direction as the arrows at the end of the life of the swap. Company A ends up borrowing sterling at 11 percent per annum. Company B ends up borrowing dollars at 9.4 percent per annum The financial institution makes a gain of 1.4 percent per annum in dollars and loses 1 percent per annum in sterling. The financial institution can hedge its sterling outflows to lock in a profit in dollars.

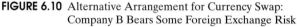

FIGURE 6.10 Alternative Arrangement for Currency Swap:
Company B Bears Some Foreign Exchange Risk

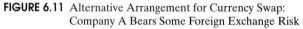

FIGURE 6.11 Alternative Arrangement for Currency Swap:
Company A Bears Some Foreign Exchange Risk

Figure 6.10 company B bears some foreign exchange risk because it pays 1.0 percent per annum in sterling and 8.4 percent in dollars. In Figure 6.11 company A bears some foreign exchange risk because it receives 1 percent per annum in dollars and pays 12 percent in sterling. In general, it makes sense for the financial institution to bear the foreign exchange risk, because it is in the best position to hedge.

As with interest-rate swaps, currency swaps are frequently warehoused by a financial institution. The institution then carefully monitors its exposures to various currencies so that it can hedge its risk.

Valuation of Currency Swaps

In the absence of default risk, a currency swap can be decomposed into a position in two bonds, as is the case with an interest-rate swap. Consider the position of company B in Figure 6.9. It is long a sterling bond that pays interest at 12 percent per annum and short a dollar bond that pays interest at 9.4 percent per annum. In general, if V_{swap} is the value of a swap such as the one in Figure 6.9 to the party paying U.S. dollar interest rates,

$$V_{swap} = SB_F - B_D$$

where B_F is the value, measured in the foreign currency, of the foreign-denominated bond underlying the swap, B_D is the value of the U.S. dollar bond underlying the swap, and S is the spot exchange rate (expressed as number of units of domestic currency per unit of foreign currency). The value of a swap can therefore be determined from the term structure of interest rates in the domestic currency, the term structure of interest rates in the foreign currency, and the spot exchange rate.

Example

Suppose that the term structure of interest rates is flat in both Japan and the United States. The Japanese rate is 4 percent per annum and the U.S. rate is 9 percent per annum (both with continuous compounding). A financial institution has entered into a currency swap in which it receives 5 percent per annum in yen and pays 8 percent per annum in dollars once a year. The principals in the two currencies are $10 million and 1,200 million yen. The swap will last for another three years and the current exchange rate is 110 yen = $1. In this case

$$B_D = 0.8e^{-0.09 \times 1} + 0.8e^{-0.09 \times 2} + 10.8e^{-0.09 \times 3}$$
$$= \$9.64 \text{ million}$$
$$B_F = 60e^{-0.04 \times 1} + 60e^{-0.04 \times 2} + 1{,}260e^{-0.04 \times 3}$$
$$= 1{,}230.55 \text{ million yen}$$

The value of the swap is

$$\frac{1{,}230.55}{110} - 9.64 = \$1.55 \text{ million}$$

If the financial institution had been paying yen and receiving dollars, the value of the swap would have been −$1.55 million.

DECOMPOSITION INTO FORWARD CONTRACTS

An alternative decomposition of the currency swap is into a series of forward contracts. Suppose that in Figure 6.9 there is one payment date per year. On each payment date company B has agreed to exchange an inflow of £ 1.2 million (12 percent of £ 10 million) for an outflow of $1.41 million (9.4 percent of $15 million). In addition, at the final payment date, it has agreed to exchange a £ 10 million inflow for a $15 million outflow. Each of these exchanges represents a forward contract. Suppose that t_i $(1 \leq i \leq n)$ is the time of the ith settlement date, r_i $(1 \leq i \leq n)$ is the continuously compounded U.S. dollar interest rate applicable to a time period of length t_i, and F_i $(1 \leq i \leq n)$ is the forward exchange rate applicable to time t_i. In chapter 3 we saw that the value of a long forward contract is in all circumstances the present value of the amount by which the forward price exceeds the delivery price. The value to company B of the forward contract corresponding to the exchange of interest payments at time t_i is therefore

$$(1.2F_i - 1.41)e^{-r_i t_i}$$

for $1 \leq i \leq n$. The value to company B of the forward contract corresponding to the exchange of principal payments at time t_n is

$$(10F_n - 15)e^{-r_n t_n}$$

Thus, the value of a currency swap can always be calculated from forward exchange rates and the term structure of domestic interest rates.

Example

Consider the situation in the previous example. The current spot rate is 110 yen per dollar, or 0.009091 dollar per yen. Since the difference between the dollar and yen interest rates is 5 percent per annum, Equation 3.13 can be used to give the one-year, two-year, and three-year forward exchange rates as

$$0.009091e^{0.05 \times 1} = 0.0096$$
$$0.009091e^{0.05 \times 2} = 0.0100$$
$$0.009091e^{0.05 \times 3} = 0.0106$$

respectively. The exchange of interest involves receiving 60 million yen and paying $0.8 million. The risk-free interest rate in dollars is 9 percent per annum. From Equation 3.8 the values of the forward contracts corresponding to the exchange of interest are (in millions of dollars)

$$(60 \times 0.0096 - 0.8)e^{-0.09 \times 1} = -0.21$$
$$(60 \times 0.0101 - 0.8)e^{-0.09 \times 2} = -0.16$$
$$(60 \times 0.0106 - 0.8)e^{-0.09 \times 3} = -0.13$$

The final exchange of principal involves receiving 1,200 million yen and paying $10 million. From Equation 3.8, the value of the forward contract corresponding to the exchange is (in millions of dollars)

$$(1,200 \times 0.0106 - 10)e^{-0.09 \times 3} = 2.04$$

The total value of the swap is $2.04 - 0.13 - 0.16 - 0.21 = \$1.54$ million, which (allowing for rounding errors) is in agreement with the result of the calculations in the previous example.

Assume that the principal amounts in the two currencies are exactly equivalent at the start of a currency swap. At this time, the total value of the swap is zero. However, as in the case of interest-rate swaps, this does not mean that each of the individual forward contracts underlying the swap has zero value. It can be shown that when interest rates in two currencies are significantly different, the payer of the low-interest-rate currency is in the position where the forward contracts corresponding to the early exchanges of cash flows have positive values and the forward contract corresponding to final exchange of principals has a negative expected value. The payer of the high-interest-rate currency is likely to be in the opposite position; that is, the early exchanges of cash flows have negative values and the final exchange has a positive expected value.

For the payer of the low-interest-rate currency, the swap will tend to have a negative value during most of its life. The forward contracts corresponding to the early exchanges of payments have positive values, and once these exchanges have taken place, there is a tendency for the remaining forward contracts to have, in total, a negative value. For the payer of the high-interest-rate currency, the reverse is true. The value of the swap will tend to be positive during most of its life. These results are important when the credit risk in the swap is being evaluated.

Other Swaps

A swap in its most general form is a contract that involves the exchange of cash flows according to a formula that depends on the value of one or more underlying variables. There is no limit to the number of different types of swaps that can be invented.

In an interest-rate swap, a number of different floating reference rates can be used. Six-month LIBOR is the most common. Among the others used are the three-month LIBOR, the one-month commercial paper rate, the Treasury bill rate, and the municipal bond tax-exempt rate. Swaps can be constructed to swap one floating rate (say, LIBOR) for another floating rate (say, prime). This flexibility allows a financial institution to hedge an exposure arising from assets that are subject to one floating rate being financed by liabilities that are subject to a different floating rate.

The principal in a swap agreement can be varied throughout the term of the swap to meet the needs of a counterparty. In an *amortizing swap* the principal reduces in a predetermined way. The agreement might be designed to correspond to the amortization schedule on a loan. In a *step-up swap* the principal increases in a predetermined way that might be designed to correspond to the drawdowns on a loan agreement. *Deferred swaps* or *forward swaps* in which parties do not begin to exchange interest payments until some future date can also be arranged.

One popular swap is an agreement to exchange a fixed interest rate in one currency for a floating interest rate in another currency. As such, it is a combination of the "plain vanilla" interest-rate swap and currency swap discussed earlier in this chapter.

Swaps can be extendable or puttable. In an *extendable swap* one party has the option to extend the life of the swap beyond the specified period. In a *puttable swap* one party has the option to terminate the swap early. Options on swaps or *swaptions* are also available. An option on an interest-rate swap is in essence an option to exchange a fixed-rate bond for a floating-rate bond. Since the floating-rate bond is worth its face value at the start of the swap, swaptions can be considered as options on the value of the fixed-rate bond with a strike price equal to the face value. Swaptions are discussed further in chapter 18.

A *constant maturity swap* (CMS swap) is an agreement to exchange a LIBOR rate for a swap rate. (An example is an agreement to exchange six-month LIBOR for the 10-year swap rate every six months for the next 5 years.) A *constant maturity Treasury swap* (CMT swap) is a similar agreement to exchange a LIBOR rate for a particular Treasury rate (e.g., the 10-year Treasury rate). In an *index amortizing rate swap* (sometimes also called an *indexed principal swap*) the principal reduces in a way dependent on the level of interest rates. (The lower the interest rate, the greater the reduction in the principal.) In a *differential swap* or *diff swap* a floating interest rate in the domestic currency is exchanged for a floating interest rate in a foreign currency, with both interest rates being applied to the same domestic principal.

An *equity swap* is an agreement to exchange the dividends and capital gains realized on an equity index for either a fixed or a floating rate of interest. Equity swaps can be used by portfolio managers to switch from an investment in bonds to an investment in equity, or vice versa. *Commodity swaps* are now becoming increasingly popular. A company that consumes 100,000 barrels of oil per year could agree to pay $2 million each year for the next 10 years and to receive in return $100,000S$, where S is the current market price of oil per barrel. The agreement would in effect lock in the company's oil cost at $20 per barrel. An oil producer might agree to the opposite exchange, thereby locking in the price it realized for its oil at $20 per barrel.

Credit Risk

Contracts such as swaps that are private arrangements between two companies entail credit risks. Consider a financial institution that has entered into offsetting contracts with two companies, A and B (see Figures 6.4, 6.5, or 6.7). If neither party defaults, the financial institution remains fully hedged. A decline in the value of one contract will always be offset by an increase in the value of the other contract. However, there is a chance that one party will get into financial difficulties and default. The financial institution then still has to honor the contract it has with the other party.

Suppose that some time after the initiation of the contracts in Figure 6.4, the contract with company B has a positive value to the financial institution whereas the contract with company A has a negative value. If company B defaults, the financial institution is liable to lose the whole of the positive value it has in this contract. To maintain a hedged position, it would have to find a third party willing to take company B's position. To induce the third party to take the position, the financial institution would have to pay the third party an amount roughly equal to the value of its contract with B prior to the default.

A financial institution has credit-risk exposure from a swap only when the value of the swap to the financial institution is positive. What happens when this value is negative and the counterparty gets into financial difficulties? In theory, the financial institution could realize a windfall gain, because a default would lead to it getting rid of a liability. In practice, it is likely that the counterparty would choose to sell the contract to a third party or rearrange its affairs in some way so that its positive value in the contract is not lost. The most realistic assumption for the financial institution is therefore as follows. If the counterparty goes bankrupt, there will be a loss if the value of the swap to the financial institution is positive, and there will be no effect on the financial institution's position if the value of the swap to the financial institution is negative. This situation is summarized in Figure 6.12.

Sometimes a financial institution can predict which of two offsetting contracts is more likely to have a positive value. Consider the currency swap in Figure 6.9. Sterling interest rates are higher than U.S. interest rates. This means that, as time passes, the financial institution is likely to find that its swap with A has a negative value whereas its swap with B has a positive value. The creditworthiness of B is therefore more important than the creditworthiness of A.

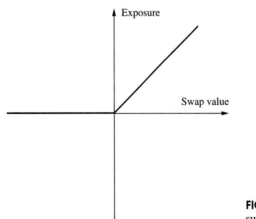

FIGURE 6.12 The Credit Exposure in a Swap

In general, the expected loss from a default on a currency swap is greater than the expected loss from a default on an interest-rate swap. The reason is that, in a currency swap, principal amounts in different currencies are exchanged. In both types of swaps, the expected loss from a default is much less than the expected loss from a default on a regular loan with approximately the same principal as the swap.

It is important to distinguish between the credit risk and market risk to a financial institution in any contract. As discussed earlier, the credit risk arises from the possibility of a default by the counterparty when the value of the contract to the financial institution is positive. The market risk arises from the possibility that market variables such as interest rates and exchange rates will move in such a way that the value of a contract to the financial institution becomes negative. Market risks can be hedged by entering into offsetting contracts; credit risks are less easy to hedge.

Summary

The two most common types of swaps are interest-rate swaps and currency swaps. In an interest-rate swap, one party agrees to pay the other party interest at a fixed rate on a notional principal for a number of years. In return, it receives interest at a floating rate on the same notional principal for the same period of time. In a currency swap, one party agrees to pay interest on a principal amount in one currency. In return, it receives interest on a principal amount in another currency.

Principal amounts are not usually exchanged in an interest-rate swap. In a currency swap, principal amounts are usually exchanged at both the beginning and the end of the life of the swap. For a party paying interest in the foreign currency, the foreign principal is received and the domestic principal is paid at the beginning of the life of the swap. At the end of the life of the swap, the foreign principal is paid and the domestic principal is received.

An interest-rate swap can be used to transform a floating-rate loan into a fixed-rate loan, or vice versa. It can also be used to transform a floating-rate investment to a fixed-rate investment, or vice versa. A currency swap can be used to transform a loan in one currency into a loan in another currency. A swap is a long position in one bond combined with a short position in another bond. Alternatively, it can be considered as a portfolio of forward contracts.

Swaps are usually arranged by financial institutions. To eliminate interest-rate or exchange-rate risk, a financial institution would like to enter into offsetting swap agreements with two parties at the same time. In practice, financial institutions frequently warehouse swaps. This means that they enter into a swap agreement with one party and then hedge their risk on a day-to-day basis while they attempt to find a party wanting to take the opposite position.

When a financial institution enters into a pair of offsetting swaps with different counterparties, it is exposed to credit risk. If one of the counterparties defaults when the financial institution has positive value in its swap with that counterparty, the financial institution loses money, because it still has to honor its swap agreement with the other counterparty.

Suggestions for Further Reading

Bicksler, J., and A. H. Chen. "An Economic Analysis of Interest Rate Swaps," *Journal of Finance* 41, no. 3 (1986): 645–655.

Hull, J. "Assessing Credit Risk in a Financial Institution's Off-Balance Sheet Commitments," *Journal of Financial and Quantitative Analysis* 24 (December 1989), 489–502.

Hull, J., and A. White. "The Impact of Default Risk on the Prices of Options and Other Derivative Securities," *Journal of Banking and Finance* 19 (1995): 299–322.

Hull, J., and A. White. "The Price of Default," *RISK* (September 1992): 101–103.

International Swaps and Derivatives Association. "Code of Standard Working Assumptions and Provisions for Swaps." New York.

Layard-Liesching, R. "Swap Fever," *Euromoney* supplement (January 1986): 108–113.

Litzenberger, R. H. "Swaps: Plain and Fanciful," *Journal of Finance* 47, no. 3 (1992): 831–850.

Marshall, J. F., and K. R. Kapner. *Understanding Swap Finance*. Cincinnati, OH: South-Western, 1990.

Smith, C. W., C. W. Smithson, and L. M. Wakeman. "The Evolving Market for Swaps," *Midland Corporate Finance Journal* 3 (Winter 1986): 20–32.

Turnbull, S. M. "Swaps: A Zero-Sum Game," *Financial Management* 16, no. 1 (Spring 1987): 15–21.

Wall, L. D., and J. J. Pringle. "Alternative Explanations of Interest Rate Swaps: A Theoretical and Empirical Analysis," *Financial Management* 18, no. 2 (Summer 1989): 59–73.

Quiz

1. Companies A and B have been offered the following rates per annum on a $20 million five-year loan:

	Fixed Rate	*Floating Rate*
Company A	12.0%	LIBOR + 0.1%
Company B	13.4%	LIBOR + 0.6%

Company A requires a floating-rate loan; company B requires a fixed-rate loan. Design a swap that will net a bank, acting as intermediary, 0.1 percent per annum and that will appear equally attractive to both companies.

2. Company X wishes to borrow U.S. dollars at a fixed rate of interest. Company Y wishes to borrow Japanese yen at a fixed rate of interest. The amounts required by the two companies are roughly the same at the current exchange rate. The companies have been quoted the following interest rates, which have been adjusted for the impact of taxes:

	Yen	*Dollars*
Company X	5.0%	9.6%
Company Y	6.5%	10.0%

Design a swap that will net a bank, acting as intermediary, 50 basis points per annum. Make the swap equally attractive to the two companies and ensure that all foreign exchange risk is assumed by the bank.

3. A $100 million interest-rate swap has a remaining life of 10 months. Under the terms of the swap, six-month LIBOR is exchanged for 12 percent per annum (compounded semiannually). The average of the bid-ask rate being exchanged for six-month LIBOR in swaps of all maturities is currently 10 percent per annum with continuous compounding. The six-month LIBOR rate was 9.6 percent per annum two months ago. What is the current value of the swap to the party paying floating? What is its value to the party paying fixed?

4. What is meant by warehousing swaps?

5. A currency swap has a remaining life of 15 months. It involves exchanging interest at 14 percent on £ 20 million for interest at 10 percent on $30 million once a year. The term structure of interest rates in both the United Kingdom and the United States is currently flat, and if the swap were negotiated today the interest rates exchanged would be 8 percent in dollars and 11 percent in sterling. All interest rates are quoted with annual compounding. The current exchange rate (dollars per pound sterling) is 1.6500. What is the value of the swap to the party paying sterling? What is the value of the swap to the party paying dollars?

6. Explain the difference between the credit risk and the market risk in a financial contract. Which of the risks can be hedged?

7. Explain why a bank is subject to credit risk when it enters into two offsetting swap contracts.

Questions and Problems

6.1. Companies X and Y have been offered the following rates per annum on a $5 million 10-year investment:

	Fixed Rate	*Floating Rate*
Company X	8.0%	LIBOR
Company Y	8.8%	LIBOR

Company X requires a fixed-rate investment; company Y requires a floating-rate investment. Design a swap that will net a bank, acting as intermediary, 0.2 percent per annum and that will appear equally attractive to X and Y.

6.2. Company A, a British manufacturer, wishes to borrow U.S. dollars at a fixed rate of interest. Company B, a U.S. multinational, wishes to borrow sterling at a fixed rate of interest. They have been quoted the following rates per annum (adjusted for tax effects):

	Sterling	*U.S. Dollars*
Company A	11.0%	7.0%
Company B	10.6%	6.2%

Design a swap that will net a bank, acting as intermediary, 10 basis points per annum and that will produce a gain of 15 basis points per annum for each of the two companies.

6.3. Under the terms of an interest-rate swap, a financial institution has agreed to pay 10 percent per annum and to receive three-month LIBOR in return on a notional principal of $100 million with payments being exchanged every three months. The swap has a remaining life of 14 months. The average of the bid-ask fixed rate currently being swapped for three-month LIBOR is 12 percent per annum for all maturities. The three-month LIBOR rate one month ago was 11.8 percent per annum. All rates are compounded quarterly. What is the value of the swap?

6.4. Suppose that the term structure of interest rates is flat in the United States and Germany. The dollar interest rate is 11 percent per annum, and the mark interest rate is 8 percent per annum. The current exchange rate is 2.1 marks = $1. Under the terms of a swap agreement, a financial institution pays 5 percent per annum in marks and receives 10 percent per annum in dollars. The principals in the two currencies are $10 million and 20 million marks. Payments are exchanged every year, with one exchange having just taken place. The swap will last two more years. What is the value of the swap to the financial institution? Assume all interest rates are continuously compounded.

6.5. A financial institution has entered into an interest-rate swap with company X. Under the terms of the swap, it receives 10 percent per annum and pays six-month LIBOR on a principal of $10 million for five years. Payments are made every six months. Suppose that company X defaults on the sixth payment date (end of year 3), when the interest rate (with semiannual compounding) is 8 percent per annum for all maturities. What is the loss to the financial institution? Assume that six-month LIBOR was 9 percent per annum halfway through year 3.

6.6. A financial institution has entered into a 10-year currency swap with company Y. Under the terms of the swap, it receives interest at 3 percent per annum in Swiss francs and pays interest at 8 percent per annum in U.S. dollars. Interest payments are exchanged once a year. The principal amounts are $7 million and 10 million francs. Suppose that company Y defaults at the end of year 6, when the exchange rate is $0.80 per franc. What is the cost to the financial institution? Assume that, at the end of year 6, the interest rate is 3 percent per annum in Swiss francs and 8 percent per annum in U.S. dollars for all maturities. All interest rates are quoted with annual compounding.

6.7. Companies A and B face the following interest rates:

	A	B
U.S. dollars (floating rate)	LIBOR + 0.5%	LIBOR + 1.0%
German marks (fixed rate)	5.0%	6.5%

Assume that A wants to borrow dollars at a floating rate of interest and B wants to borrow marks at a fixed rate of interest. A financial institution is planning to arrange a swap and requires a 50 basis point spread. If the swap is equally attractive to A and B, what rates of interest will A and B end up paying?

6.8. Company X is based in the United Kingdom and would like to borrow $50 million at a fixed rate of interest for five years in U.S. funds. Because the company is not well known in the United States, this has proved to be impossible. However, the company has been quoted 12 percent per annum on fixed-rate five-year sterling funds. Company Y is based in the United States and would like to borrow the equivalent of $50 million in sterling funds for five years at a fixed rate of interest. It has been unable to get a quote but has been offered U.S. dollar funds at 10.5 percent per annum. Five-year government bonds currently yield 9.5 percent per annum in the United States and 10.5 percent in the United Kingdom. Suggest an appropriate currency swap that will net the financial intermediary 0.5 percent per annum.

6.9. After it hedges its foreign exchange risk using forward contracts, is the financial institution's average spread in Figure 6.9 likely to be greater than or less than 40 basis points? Explain your answer.

6.10. How can a deferred swap be created from two other swaps?

6.11. "Companies with high credit risks are the ones that cannot access fixed-rate markets directly. They are the companies that are most likely to be paying fixed and receiving floating in an interest-rate swap." Assume that this statement is true. Do you think it increases or decreases the risk of a financial institution's swap portfolio? Assume that companies are most likely to default when interest rates are high.

6.12. How can a financial institution that warehouses interest-rate swaps monitor its exposure to interest-rate changes?

6.13. Why is the expected loss from a default on a swap less than the expected loss from the default on a loan with the same principal?

6.14. A bank finds that its assets are not matched with its liabilities. It is taking floating-rate deposits and making fixed-rate loans. How can swaps be used to offset the risk?

6.15. Explain how you would value a swap that is the exchange of a floating rate in one currency for a fixed rate in another currency.

Mechanics of Options Markets

C H A P T E R 7

The rest of this book is concerned with options. This chapter explains how options markets are organized, what terminology is used, how the contracts are traded, how margin requirements are set, and so on. Later chapters will examine such topics as trading strategies involving options, the determination of option prices, and the ways in which portfolios of options can be hedged. This chapter is concerned primarily with stock options. Details on the markets for currency options, index options, and futures options are provided in chapters 12 and 13.

Options are fundamentally different from forward and futures contracts. An option gives the holder of the option the right to do something. The holder does not have to exercise this right. By contrast, in a forward or futures contract, the two parties have committed themselves to some action. Whereas a forward or futures contract costs nothing to enter (except for the margin requirements), the purchase of an option requires an up-front payment.

Types of Options

As mentioned in chapter 1, there are two basic types of options. A *call option* gives the holder the right to buy an asset by a certain date for a certain price. A *put option* gives the holder the right to sell an asset by a certain date for a certain price. The date specified in the contract is known as the *expiration date*, the *exercise date*, the *strike date*, or the *maturity*. The price specified in the contract is known as the *exercise price* or *strike price*.

Options can be either American or European, a distinction that has nothing to do with geographical location. *American options* can be exercised at any time up to the expiration date, whereas *European options* can be exercised only on the expiration date itself. Most of the options that are traded on exchanges are American. However,

169

European options are generally easier to analyze than American options, and some of the properties of an American option are frequently deduced from those of its European counterpart.

EXAMPLE OF A CALL OPTION

Consider the situation of an investor who buys a European call option with a strike price of $100 to purchase 100 IBM shares. Suppose that the current share price is $98, the expiration date of the option is in four months, and the price of an option to purchase one share is $5. The initial investment is $500. Because the option is European, the investor can exercise only on the expiration date. If the share price on this date is less than $100, the investor will clearly choose not to exercise. (There is no point in buying, for $100, a share that has a market value of less than $100.) In these circumstances, the investor loses the whole of the initial investment of $500. If the share price is above $100 on the expiration date, the option will be exercised. Suppose, for example, that the share price is $115. By exercising the option, the investor is able to buy 100 shares for $100 per share. If the shares are sold immediately, the investor makes a gain of $15 per share, or $1,500, ignoring transactions costs. When the initial cost of the option is taken into account, the net profit to the investor is $1,000.

Table 7.1 summarizes this example. Figure 7.1 shows how the investor's net profit or loss on an option to purchase one share varies with the terminal share price in the example. It is important to realize that an investor sometimes exercises an option and makes a loss overall. Suppose that in the example the share price of IBM is $102 at the expiration of the option. The investor would exercise the option for a gain of $100 \times$ ($102 − $100) = $200 and realize a loss overall of $300 when the initial cost of the option is taken into account. It is tempting to argue that the investor should not exercise the option in these circumstances. However, not exercising would lead to an overall loss of $500, which is worse than the $300 loss when the investor exercises. In general, call options should always be exercised at the expiration date if the stock price is above the strike price.

TABLE 7.1 Profit from Call Option

From the Trader's Desk

An investor buys a call option to purchase 100 IBM shares.

Strike price = $100
Current share price = $98
Price of an option to buy one share = $5

The initial investment is $100 \times $5 = $500.

The Outcome

At the expiration of the option, IBM's share price is $115. At this time, the option is exercised for a gain of

$$($55 − $40) \times 100 = $1,500$$

When the initial cost of the option is taken into account, the net gain is

$$$1,500 − $500 = $1,000$$

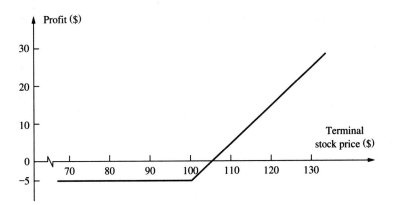

FIGURE 7.1 Profit from Buying a European Call Option on One IBM Share. Option price = $5; strike price = $100.

EXAMPLE OF A PUT OPTION

Whereas the purchaser of a call option is hoping that the stock price will increase, the purchaser of a put option is hoping that it will decrease. Consider an investor who buys a European put option to sell 100 Exxon shares with a strike price of $70. Suppose that the current share price is $65, the expiration date of the option is in three months, and the price of an option to sell one share is $7. The initial investment is $700. Since the option is European, it will be exercised only if the share price is below $70 at the expiration date. Suppose that the share price is $55 on this date. The investor can buy 100 shares for $55 per share and, under the terms of the put option, sell the same shares for $70 to realize a gain of $15 per share, or $1,500. (Again, transactions costs are ignored.) When the $700 initial cost of the option is taken into account, the investor's net profit is $800. There is no guarantee that the investor will make a gain. If the final stock price is above $70, the put option expires worthless and the investor loses $700. Table 7.2 summarizes this example. Figure 7.2 shows the way in which the investor's profit or loss on an option to sell one share varies with the terminal stock price in this example.

EARLY EXERCISE

As already mentioned, stock options are generally American rather than European. That is, the investor in the foregoing examples does not have to wait until the expiration date before exercising the option. We will see later that there are some circumstances under which it is optimal to exercise American options prior to maturity.

Option Positions

There are two sides to every option contract. On one side is the investor who has taken the long position (i.e., has bought the option). On the other side is the investor who has taken a short position (i.e., has sold or *written* the option). The writer of an option receives cash up front but has potential liabilities later. The writer's profit or loss is the

TABLE 7.2 Profit from Put Option

From the Trader's Desk
    An investor buys a put option to purchase 100 Exxon shares.

> Strike price = $70
> Current share price = $65
> Price of an option to buy one share = $7

    The initial investment is 100 × $7 = $700.

The Outcome
    At the expiration of the option, Exxon's share price is $55. At this time, the investor buys 100 Exxon shares and, under the terms of the put option, sells them for $70 per share to realize a gain of $15 per share, or $1,500 in total. When the initial cost of the option is taken into account, the net gain is

$$\$1,500 - \$700 = \$800$$

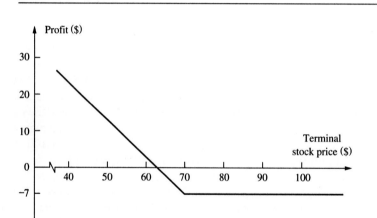

FIGURE 7.2 Profit from Buying a European Put Option on One Exxon Share. Option price = $7; strike price = $70.

reverse of that for the purchaser of the option. Figures 7.3 and 7.4 show the variation of the profit or loss with the final stock price for writers of the options considered in Figures 7.1 and 7.2.
    There are four types of options positions:

1. A long position in a call option
2. A long position in a put option
3. A short position in a call option
4. A short position in a put option

    It is often useful to characterize European option positions in terms of the terminal value or payoff to the investor at maturity. The initial cost of the option is then not included in the calculation. If X is the strike price and S_T is the final price of the

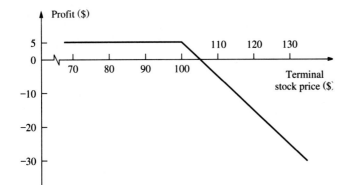

FIGURE 7.3 Profit from Writing a European Call Option on One IBM Share. Option price = $5; strike price = $40.

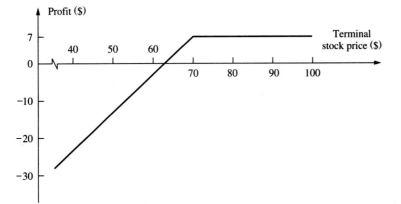

FIGURE 7.4 Profit from Writing a European Put Option on One Exxon Share. Option price = $7; strike price = $70.

underlying asset, the payoff from a long position in a European call option is

$$\max(S_T - X, 0)$$

This reflects the fact that the option will be exercised if $S_T > X$ and will not be exercised if $S_T \leq X$. The payoff to the holder of a short position in the European call option is

$$-\max(S_T - X, 0) = \min(X - S_T, 0)$$

The payoff to the holder of a long position in a European put option is

$$\max(X - S_T, 0)$$

and the payoff from a short position in a European put option is

$$-\max(X - S_T, 0) = \min(S_T - X, 0)$$

Figure 7.5 illustrates these payoffs graphically.

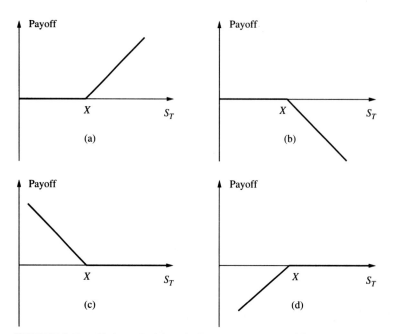

FIGURE 7.5 Payoffs from Positions in European Options. (a) Long call, (b) short call, (c) long put, (d) short put. Strike price $= X$; price of asset at maturity $= S_T$.

The Underlying Assets

Exchange-traded options are currently actively traded on stocks, stock indices, foreign currencies, and futures contracts. Table 7.3 provides a list of U.S. exchanges that trade options. Most of these exchanges trade options on futures contracts as well as the futures contracts themselves.

STOCK OPTIONS

The exchanges trading stock options in the United States are the Chicago Board Options Exchange (CBOE), the Philadelphia Stock Exchange (PHLX), the American Stock Exchange (AMEX), the Pacific Stock Exchange (PSE), and the New York Stock Exchange (NYSE). Options trade on over 500 different stocks. Among the most actively traded options contracts are those on IBM, Kodak, and General Motors. One contract gives the holder the right to buy or sell 100 shares at the specified strike price. The contract size is convenient, because the shares themselves are normally traded in lots of 100.

FOREIGN CURRENCY OPTIONS

The major exchange for trading foreign currency options is the Philadelphia Stock Exchange. It offers both European and American contracts on a variety of different currencies. The size of one contract depends on the currency. For example, in the case of the

TABLE 7.3 U.S. Exchanges That Trade Options

Chicago Board Options Exchange (CBOE) 400 South LaSalle Street Chicago, IL 60605 312-786-7465	American Stock Exchange (AMEX) 86 Trinity Place New York, NY 10006 212-306-1000
Philadelphia Stock Exchange (PHLX) 1900 Market Street Philadelphia, PA 19103 215-496-5000	Pacific Stock Exchange (PSE) 301 Pine Street San Francisco, CA 94104 415-393-4000
New York Stock Exchange (NYSE) 11 Wall Street New York, NY 10005 212-656-3000	

British pound, one contract gives the holder the right to buy or sell £31,250; in the case of the Japanese yen, one contract gives the holder the right to buy or sell 6.25 million yen. Foreign currency options contracts are discussed further in chapter 12.

INDEX OPTIONS

Many different index options currently trade in the United States. The most popular contracts are those on the S&P 500 Index (CBOE) and the S&P 100 Index (CBOE). Index options may be European or American. For example, the contract on the S&P 500 is European, whereas that on the S&P 100 is American. One contract is to buy or sell 100 times the index at the specified strike price. Settlement is always in cash rather than by delivering the portfolio underlying the index. Consider, for example, one call contract on the S&P 100 with a strike price of 280. If it is exercised when the value of the index is 292, the writer of the contract pays the holder $(292 - 280) \times 100 = \$1,200$. This cash payment is based on the index value at the end of the day on which exercise instructions are issued. Not surprisingly, investors usually wait until the end of a day before issuing these instructions. Index options are discussed further in chapter 12.

FUTURES OPTIONS

In a futures option (or options on futures), the underlying asset is a futures contract. The futures contract normally matures shortly after the expiration of the option. Futures options are now available for most of the assets on which futures contracts are traded. When a call option is exercised, the holder acquires from the writer a long position in the underlying futures contract plus a cash amount equal to the excess of the futures price over the strike price. When a put option is exercised, the holder acquires a short position in the underlying futures contract plus a cash amount equal to the excess of the strike price over the futures price. Futures options contracts are discussed further in chapter 13.

Specification of Stock Options

In the rest of this chapter, we will focus on stock options. As already mentioned, an exchange-traded stock option is an American-style option contract to buy or sell 100 shares of the stock. Details of the contract—the expiration date, the strike price, what happens when dividends are declared, how large a position investors can hold, and so on—are specified by the exchange.

EXPIRATION DATES

One of the items used to describe a stock option is the month in which the expiration date occurs. Thus, a January call on IBM is a call option on IBM with an expiration date in January. The precise expiration date is 10:59 P.M. Central Time on the Saturday immediately following the third Friday of the expiration month. The last day on which options trade is the third Friday of the expiration month. An investor with a long position in an option normally has until 4:30 P.M. Central Time on that Friday to instruct a broker to exercise the option. The broker then has until 10:59 P.M. the next day to complete the paperwork notifying the exchange that exercise is to take place.

Stock options are on a January, February, or March cycle. The January cycle consists of the months of January, April, July, and October. The February cycle consists of the months of February, May, August, and November. The March cycle consists of the months of March, June, September, and December. If the expiration date for the current month has not yet been reached, options trade with expiration dates in the current month, the following month, and the next two months in its cycle. If the expiration date of the current month has passed, options trade with expiration dates in the next month, the next-but-one month, and the next two months of the expiration cycle. For example, IBM is on a January cycle. At the beginning of January, options are traded with expiration dates in January, February, April, and July; at the end of January, they are traded with expiration dates in February, March, April, and July; at the beginning of May, they are traded with expiration dates in May, June, July, and October; and so on. When one option reaches expiration, trading in another is started. Longer-term options, known as LEAPS (long-term equity anticipation securities), also trade on some stocks. These have expiration dates up to three years into the future. The expiration dates for LEAPS on stocks are always in January.

STRIKE PRICES

The exchange chooses the strike prices at which options can be written. For stock options, strike prices are normally spaced $2\frac{1}{2}$, $5, or $10 apart. (An exception occurs when there has been a stock split or a stock dividend, as will be described shortly.) The usual rule followed by exchanges is to use a $2\frac{1}{2}$ spacing for strike prices when the stock price is less than $25, a $5 spacing when it is between $25 and $200, and a $10 spacing when it is greater than $200. For example, when the price of a stock is $12, we might expect to see options trading with strike prices of 10, $12\frac{1}{2}$, and 15; when the stock price is $100, we might expect to see strike prices of 90, 95, 100, 105, and 110.

When a new expiration date is introduced, the two strike prices closest to the current stock price are usually selected by the exchange. If one of these is very close to the existing stock price, the third strike price closest to the current stock price may also be selected. If the stock price moves outside the range defined by the highest and lowest strike price, trading is usually introduced in an option with a new strike price. To illustrate these rules, suppose that the stock price is $53 when trading begins in the October options. Call and put options would first be offered with strike prices of 50 and 55. If the stock price rose above $55, a strike price of 60 would be offered; if it fell below $50, a strike price of 45 would be offered; and so on.

TERMINOLOGY

For any given asset at any given time, many different option contracts may be trading. Consider a stock that has four expiration dates and five strike prices. If call and put options trade with every expiration date and every strike price, there are a total of 40 different contracts. All options of the same type (calls or puts) are referred to as an *option class*. For example, IBM calls are one class whereas IBM puts are another class. An *option series* consists of all the options of a given class with the same expiration date and strike price. In other words, an option series refers to a particular contract that is traded. The IBM 50 October calls are an option series.

Options are referred to as *in the money, at the money,* or *out of the money.* An in-the-money option is one that would give the holder a positive cash flow if it were exercised immediately. Similarly, an at-the-money option would lead to zero cash flow if it were exercised immediately, and an out-of-the-money option would lead to a negative cash flow if it were exercised immediately. If S is the stock price and X is the strike price, a call option is in the money when $S > X$, at the money when $S = X$, and out of the money when $S < X$. A put option is in the money when $S < X$, at the money when $S = X$, and out of the money when $S > X$. Clearly, an option will be exercised only when it is in the money. In the absence of transactions costs, an in-the-money option will always be exercised on the expiration date if it has not been exercised previously.

The *intrinsic value* of an option is defined as the maximum of zero and the value the option would have if it were exercised immediately. For a call option, the intrinsic value is therefore $\max(S - X, 0)$. For a put option, it is $\max(X - S, 0)$. An in-the-money American option must be worth at least as much as its intrinsic value, because the holder can realize the intrinsic value by exercising immediately. Often it is optimal for the holder of an in-the-money American option to wait rather than exercise immediately. The option is then said to have *time value*. The total value of an option can be thought of as the sum of its intrinsic value and its time value.

FLEX OPTIONS

Some exchanges now offer *flex options*. These are options for which the traders on the floor of the exchange agree to nonstandard terms. These nonstandard terms might involve a strike price or an expiration date that is different from what is usually offered by the exchange. Flex options are an attempt by option exchanges to regain business from the over-the-counter markets.

DIVIDENDS AND STOCK SPLITS

The early over-the-counter options were dividend protected. If a company declared a cash dividend, the strike price for options on the company's stock was reduced on the ex-dividend day by the amount of the dividend. Exchange-traded options are not generally adjusted for cash dividends. In other words, when a cash dividend is declared there are no adjustments to the terms of the option contract. As we will see in chapter 11, this has significant implications for the way in which options are valued.

Exchange-traded options are adjusted for stock splits. A stock split occurs when the existing shares are "split" into more shares. For example, in a 3-for-1 stock split, three new shares are issued to replace each existing share. Since a stock split does not change the assets or the earning ability of a company, we should not expect it to have any effect on the wealth of the company's shareholders. All else being equal, the 3-for-1 stock split should cause the stock price to go down to one-third of its previous value. In general, an n-for-m stock split should cause the stock price to go down to m/n of its previous value. The terms of option contracts are adjusted to reflect expected changes in a stock price arising from a stock split. After an n-for-m stock split, the strike price is reduced to m/n of its previous value, and the number of shares covered by one contract is increased to n/m of its previous value. If the stock price declines in the way expected, the positions of both the writer and the purchaser of a contract remain unchanged.

Example

Consider a call option to buy 100 shares of a company for $30 per share. Suppose that the company makes a 2-for-1 stock split. The terms of the option contract are then changed so that it gives the holder the right to purchase 200 shares for $15 per share.

Stock options are adjusted for stock dividends. A stock dividend involves a company issuing more shares to its existing shareholders. For example, a 20 percent stock dividend means that investors receive one new share for each five already owned. A stock dividend, like a stock split, has no effect on either the assets or the earning power of a company. The stock price can be expected to go down as a result of a stock dividend. The 20 percent stock dividend referred to is essentially the same as a 6-for-5 stock split. All else being equal, it should cause the stock price to decline to 5/6 of its previous value. The terms of an option are adjusted to reflect the expected price decline arising from a stock dividend in the same way as they are for that arising from a stock split.

Example

Consider a put option to sell 100 shares of a company for $15 per share. Suppose that the company declares a 25 percent stock dividend. This is equivalent to a 5-for-4 stock split. The terms of the option contract are changed so that it gives the holder the right to sell 125 shares for $12.

Adjustments are also made for rights issues. The basic procedure is to calculate the theoretical price of the rights and then to reduce the strike price by this amount. As pointed out by Brown, the procedure leaves the option holder slightly worse off than he or she was before the issue.[1]

POSITION LIMITS AND EXERCISE LIMITS

The exchange specifies a *position limit* for each stock upon which options are traded. This defines the maximum number of option contracts that an investor can hold on one side of the market. For this purpose, long calls and short puts are considered to be on the same side of the market. Also, short calls and long puts are considered to be on the same side of the market. The *exercise limit* equals the position limit. It defines the maximum number of contracts that can be exercised by any individual (or group of individuals acting together) in any period of five consecutive business days. The position/exercise limit is usually 3,000, 5,500, or 8,000 contracts. Options on actively traded stocks with high market capitalizations normally have position/exercise limits of 8,000. Options on smaller-capitalization stocks usually have position/exercise limits of 3,000 or 5,500.

Position limits and exercise limits are designed to prevent the market from being unduly influenced by the activities of an individual investor or group of investors. However, whether such limits are really necessary is a controversial issue.

Newspaper Quotes

Many newspapers carry options quotations. In the *Wall Street Journal,* stock option quotations can currently be found under the heading "Listed Options" in the Money and Investing section. Table 7.4 shows the quotations as they appeared in the *Wall Street Journal* of Wednesday, September 25, 1996. The quotations refer to trading that took place on the previous day (Tuesday, September 24, 1996).

The company on whose stock the option is written together with the closing stock price is listed in the first column. The strike price and maturity month appear in the second and third columns. If a call option traded with a given strike price and maturity month, the next two columns show the volume of trading and the price at last trade for the call option. The final two columns show the same for a put option.

The quoted price is the price of an option to buy or sell one share. As mentioned earlier, one contract is for the purchase or sale of 100 shares. A contract therefore costs 100 times the price shown. Since most options are priced at less than $10 and some are priced at less than $1, investors do not have to be extremely wealthy to trade options.

The *Wall Street Journal* also shows the total call volume, put volume, call open interest, and put open interest for each exchange. The numbers reported in the newspaper on September 25, 1996 are shown in Table 7.5. The volume is the total number of contracts traded on the day. The open interest is the number of contracts outstanding.

---

[1]See R. L. Brown, "Adjusting Option Contracts to Reflect Capitalization Changes," *Journal of Business Finance and Accounting* 16 (1989): 247–254.

TABLE 7.4 Stock Option Quotations from the *Wall Street Journal* on September 25, 1996

Option/Strike		Exp.	–Call– Vol.	–Call– Last	–Put– Vol.	–Put– Last
ADC Tel	50	Nov	250	14	...	...
ADT	20	Oct	55	1 3/16	...	...
AGCO	25	Nov	60	7/8	...	...
A M R	75	Oct	280	8	...	...
80 7/8	80	Oct	350	4	17	2 1/8
80 7/8	85	Oct	78	1 1/8	10	4 1/2
A S A	37 1/2	Oct	60	1 7/8	...	...
39 1/4	40	Oct	272	3/4	...	...
39 1/4	42 1/2	Nov	59	3/8	...	...
AST Rs	5	Nov	80	1/2	...	...
AT&T	45	Oct	143	6 3/4	283	3/16
51 1/2	45	Jan	139	8	37	1/2
51 1/2	45	Apr	67	8 1/2	30	3/4
51 1/2	50	Oct	1115	2 3/4	2372	11/16
51 1/2	50	Jan	495	4	697	1 3/4
51 1/2	50	Apr	59	5	224	2 1/8
51 1/2	55	Oct	7086	3/8	688	3 1/2
51 1/2	55	Nov	1066	15/16	136	3 5/8
51 1/2	55	Jan	1923	1 11/16	510	4 3/8
51 1/2	55	Apr	150	2 3/8	71	4 1/2
51 1/2	60	Oct	1796	1/8	76	8 3/8
51 1/2	60	Jan	500	5/8	57	8 1/2
51 1/2	60	Apr	53	1	11	8 1/2
51 1/2	65	Jan	345	1/4	45	13 1/2
51 1/2	70	Jan	679	1/8	...	...
AamesF	45	Oct	363	4 7/8	41	1 3/16
48 7/8	45	Dec	610	5 1/4	8	3 5/8
48 7/8	50	Oct	28	2 1/8	64	3 3/8
48 7/8	50	Dec	18	3 1/4	250	5
48 7/8	55	Dec	74	2 1/2	...	...
AccuStff	25	Oct	100	1	10	1 3/4
24 3/8	25	Nov	261	2	...	...
Actel	17 1/2	Oct	81	1 1/4	40	1 1/4
AdacLb	20	Oct	60	1 1/8	...	...
Adaptc	55	Oct	51	4	18	2 1/8
56 1/2	60	Oct	287	1 1/2	1	4 1/2
56 1/2	60	Jan	100	4 3/4	...	...
AdobeS	30	Oct	2	8 1/4	65	1/8
36 7/8	35	Oct	75	3 1/2	288	1 5/8
36 7/8	40	Oct	541	1 1/4	25	4 1/4
36 7/8	40	Jan	183	3 1/2	...	...
36 7/8	45	Oct	52	7/16	...	...
Adtran	45	Nov	172	8 1/2	141	3
51	50	Oct	306	4 5/8	94	3 5/8
51	50	Nov	140	6 1/8	36	6
51	55	Oct	281	2 7/16	110	6 3/8
51	60	Oct	494	1 1/16	50	9 3/8
51	60	Nov	65	2 1/8	...	...
51	65	Oct	82	9/16	...	...
A M D	12 1/2	Oct	88	2 5/8	7	3/16
15	12 1/2	Nov	354	2 7/8	22	1/4
15	12 1/2	Jan	534	3 3/8	...	...
15	15	Oct	1103	3/4	63	7/8
15	15	Nov	111	1 1/16	10	1 1/8
15	15	Jan	184	1 3/4	...	...
15	15	Apr	137	2 1/2	8	1 7/8
15	17 1/2	Oct	177	1/8	3	2 7/8
15	17 1/2	Jan	115	3/4	110	3 1/4
15	20	Jan	420	7/16	...	...
AdvSem	7 1/2	Dec	68	2 1/16	...	...
8 7/8	10	Oct	100	5/16	25	1 7/16
8 7/8	10	Nov	50	11/16	...	...
AdvTis	10	Dec	100	7 1/4	...	...
17	15	Oct	10	3	500	5/8
17	15	Dec	73	4	306	2
17	17 1/2	Oct	511	1	11	1 3/4
17	17 1/2	Dec	120	2 5/8	...	...
17	17 1/2	Mar	55	4	...	...
17	20	Dec	318	1 3/4	...	...
Advnta	45	Nov	600	2 1/4	...	...
Aetna	65	Oct	110	3 1/2	...	...
67 3/8	70	Nov	500	1 1/4	...	...
Agnico	15	Nov	50	1 11/16	...	...
Ahman	25	Jan	...	...	500	5/8
Airgas	25	Oct	226	1/2	...	...
Airtch	30	Oct	212	1/2	250	1 5/8
28 1/2	30	Nov	101	13/16	...	...
28 1/2	35	Jan	300	7/16	...	...
Albtsn	40	Oct	...	...	60	9/16
AlgLud	22 1/2	Oct	...	...	190	1/2
22 1/4	25	Apr	28	1 1/16	100	3 3/8
Allergan	40	Oct	188	3/4	...	...
AlnEnt	5	Oct	52	1	...	...
AlianP	20	Nov	88	1	...	...
17 1/4	22 1/2	Nov	50	1/2	...	...

Option/Strike		Exp.	–Call– Vol.	–Call– Last	–Put– Vol.	–Put– Last
BancOne	12 1/2	Feb	106	1 3/4	...	...
40 7/8	40	Oct	112	1 5/8	...	...
40 7/8	40	Nov	57	1 15/16	9	1 3/16
BankNY	25	Apr	...	...	80	3/4
BankAm	80	Oct	104	3	436	1 1/8
80 1/2	80	Jan	82	6 1/2	18	3 1/8
80 1/2	85	Nov	1000	1 5/8	...	...
BkrsTr	65	Oct	288	15 1/2	99	1/16
80	70	Oct	885	10 1/2	10	1/8
80	75	Oct	677	5 1/8	...	...
80	80	Oct	41	1 1/4	85	2
80	80	Jan	45	3 7/8	422	4
80	85	Oct	211	1/4	...	...
80	90	Jan	80	5/8	...	...
BarickG	25	Oct	1126	2 1/8	285	5/16
26 5/8	25	Nov	95	2 3/8	105	9/16
26 5/8	25	Jan	151	3	74	1
26 5/8	30	Oct	264	1/8	54	4 3/8
26 5/8	30	Nov	240	3/8	...	...
26 5/8	30	Jan	1111	3/4	2730	4
BattlM	7 1/2	Nov	114	7/8	...	...
8 1/4	10	Jan	64	3/8	...	...
Baxter	40	Oct	100	5 1/2	...	...
BayNwk	22 1/2	Oct	115	7 7/8	10	1/8
29 1/2	25	Oct	421	4 3/4	736	5/16
29 1/2	27 1/2	Oct	550	2 7/8	358	7/8
29 1/2	27 1/2	Dec	122	4 5/8	185	2 1/8
29 1/2	30	Oct	4789	1 3/4	460	1 7/8
29 1/2	32 1/2	Oct	1164	7/8	5	3
29 1/2	32 1/2	Dec	493	2 5/16	21	4 3/8
29 1/2	37 1/2	Dec	110	1	...	...
29 1/2	40	Dec	52	3/4	11	10 1/2
BecDic	45	Oct	55	1/2	...	...
BellSo	37 1/2	Jan	253	2 1/8	3	2
37 1/2	40	Jan	57	1	...	...
BergBr	30	Dec	54	3	...	...
BestBuy	20	Dec	4	3 5/8	55	3/4
21 7/8	22 1/2	Oct	55	7/8	302	1 1/16
21 7/8	25	Oct	50	1/4	...	...
21 7/8	25	Dec	72	3/4	...	...
21 7/8	30	Dec	...	...	100	7 5/8
Beth S	7 1/2	Apr	50	2 7/8	...	...
9 7/8	10	Oct	77	3/8	130	1/2
Big B	17 1/2	Dec	533	1/2	75	1 11/16
16 3/4	17 1/2	Mar	260	7/8	...	...
Bill Info	17 1/2	Nov	...	...	100	3/8
21	20	Oct	620	1 3/4	...	...
21	20	Feb	...	...	120	1 3/4
21	22 1/2	Feb	100	2	...	...
BioVasc	7 1/2	Oct	55	1 1/8	...	...
BioPhar	40	Jan	50	3 7/8	...	...
Biogen	70	Oct	234	4	38	2
Biomet	17 1/2	Jan	88	1/2	...	...
BioTcG	10	Oct	95	1/16	...	...
Biovail	30	Oct	114	5 3/8	...	...
34 1/4	35	Oct	67	2	...	...
34 1/4	40	Jan	260	3 1/8	...	...
Block	30	Oct	63	7/8	28	1
BocaRs	12 1/2	Oct	72	7/16	...	...
Boeing	80	Nov	280	15 5/8	...	...
94 1/4	80	Feb	15	17 1/8	50	1
94 1/4	90	Oct	50	4 7/8	18	7/8
94 1/4	90	Nov	6	6 5/8	63	1 13/16
94 1/4	95	Oct	446	1 15/16	43	2 1/2
94 1/4	95	Nov	245	3 1/2	20	3 1/2
Borland	7 1/2	Nov	100	1/2	...	...
6 7/8	7 1/2	Jan	55	7/8	50	1 1/4
BostChkn	30	Jan	85	5 7/8	10	1 1/8
34 3/8	35	Oct	244	1	15	1 11/16
34 3/8	40	Jan	132	1 5/16	...	...
BostTc	15	Oct	61	1/4	...	...
13 1/2	15	Jan	75	1 1/8	...	...
BoxEnB	10	Oct	90	1/4	40	1 3/8
8 3/4	10	Jan	90	9/16	20	1 9/16
BoydGm	10	Oct	210	9/16	170	5/16
BrMSq	90	Oct	11	5 3/8	50	3/8
94 7/8	90	Dec	40	6 5/8	120	15/16
94 7/8	95	Oct	396	1 3/4	35	1
94 7/8	95	Nov	3	3 1/2	53	2
94 7/8	95	Dec	176	3 1/4	150	2 3/16
94 7/8	95	Mar	232	5 5/8	...	...
94 7/8	100	Oct	60	1/2	...	...
94 7/8	100	Dec	614	1 7/16	5	4 3/4
Broderbnd	22 1/2	Oct	124	6 1/4	...	...
28 1/2	22 1/2	Dec	...	...	60	1/2

Option/Strike		Exp.	–Call– Vol.	–Call– Last	–Put– Vol.	–Put– Last
ClairSt o	23 3/8	Nov	111	1 1/8	...	...
...	23 3/8	Feb	170	2 3/8	...	...
ClaytH	17 1/2	Nov	...	...	50	5/16
21	22 1/2	Feb	50	1 1/8	...	...
Clorox	95	Jan	250	5 1/2	...	...
Coastl	45	Dec	123	9/16	...	...
Coke	45	Nov	84	7 1/8	210	5/16
51	45	May	...	...	156	1 1/4
51	50	Oct	137	2 5/8	662	11/16
51	50	Nov	188	3	163	1 1/4
51	55	Oct	1324	1/4	146	3 1/8
51	55	Nov	461	3/4	22	4
CocaCE	45	Nov	364	1 1/2	...	...
CoeurM	15	Nov	60	5/8	...	...
ColgPl	85	Nov	120	4 3/8	...	...
87 5/8	90	Nov	110	1 11/16	...	...
ColData	12 1/2	Oct	160	11/16	...	...
ColHsp	55	Nov	...	...	302	3/4
58 3/8	60	Oct	92	13/16	10	2 3/4
ColLb	12 1/2	Mar	...	...	50	2 5/8
CPsy	10	Jan	66	1/2	8	1 1/4
CmpUSA	50	Oct	23	4 5/8	105	1 5/8
53	55	Oct	65	1 3/4	...	...
ChileT	95	Nov	...	...	75	2 1/8
Compaq	50	Oct	330	13 1/4	363	3/16
62 7/8	50	Jan	77	14 5/8	...	...
62 7/8	55	Oct	141	8 5/8	185	9/16
62 7/8	55	Nov	...	...	123	1 1/8
62 7/8	55	Jan	17	12 1/4	105	1 7/8
62 7/8	60	Oct	273	4 1/2	1472	1 5/8
62 7/8	60	Jan	142	7 1/2	40	3 5/8
62 7/8	65	Oct	584	1 7/8	893	3 7/8
62 7/8	65	Nov	268	3 1/8	45	3 7/8
62 7/8	65	Jan	320	4 3/4	24	5 7/8
62 7/8	70	Oct	236	11/16	11	7 3/4
62 7/8	70	Nov	109	1 3/4	...	...
62 7/8	70	Jan	284	3 1/2	...	...
62 7/8	70	Apr	62	4 3/4	50	9 3/8
CmpuSrv	15	Nov	8	1 7/8	80	1 5/16
14 5/8	15	Jan	...	...	70	1 13/16
14 5/8	17 1/2	Oct	53	1/4	...	...
14 5/8	17 1/2	Jan	31	1 3/16	210	3 1/8
Cmpcm	10	Mar	90	1 1/16	...	...
CmpAsoc	50	Oct	200	10 7/8	50	1/4
62 1/8	55	Oct	9	7 5/8	95	1/2
62 1/8	55	Nov	...	...	160	1
62 1/8	60	Oct	45	3 3/8	65	1 3/4
62 1/8	65	Oct	132	1 1/4	5	4 1/2
62 1/8	65	Nov	75	2 5/8	...	...
CmptHz	30	Oct	361	2	71	1 15/16
CmpPr	17 1/2	Oct	100	1 5/16	15	1
CompSc	75	Oct	70	2 5/8	...	...
75 1/4	75	Dec	150	4 1/2	...	...
CmpTsk	25	Oct	103	6 3/4	...	...
Cmptvsn	10	Oct	80	5/16	...	...
8 3/4	10	Jan	70	1 1/16	...	...
Cmpuwr	40	Oct	5	4 1/4	150	1 13/16
42 1/4	50	Nov	71	1 1/4	...	...
Comsat	22 1/2	Jan	50	2 3/4	...	...
CmstRs	12 1/2	Nov	165	1/2	...	...
Comvrs	40	Oct	104	2 1/8	10	2 1/2
ConAgr	50	Mar	1021	1 1/2	...	...
CncEFS	22 1/2	Dec	200	5 1/8	...	...
Cnseco	40	Nov	50	6 1/8	10	3/8
45 7/8	45	Oct	377	2 1/16	...	...
45 7/8	50	Oct	175	1/2	...	...
ConFrt	25	Oct	50	5/16	...	...
ConPap	55	Oct	125	1/8	...	...
Copytl	7 1/2	Nov	65	1/2	...	...
6 5/8	7 1/2	Dec	95	3/4	...	...
Corel	10	Jan	50	1 1/4	...	...
CorpEx	35	Apr	...	...	100	3 5/8
CntwCrd	22 1/2	Oct	63	2 5/8	...	...
CrkrBr	25	Oct	50	13/16	10	9/16
CrTchn	5	Oct	209	1 15/16	20	3/16
6 7/8	5	Jan	121	2 5/16	...	...
6 7/8	7 1/2	Oct	298	1/2	54	1 1/8
6 7/8	7 1/2	Jan	157	1 3/8	...	...
6 7/8	10	Jan	124	1/2	...	...
CredSys	15	Oct	147	1 1/16	...	...
15 3/8	15	Nov	50	1 5/8	...	...
15 3/8	20	Nov	73	3/8	...	...
CreeRsh	15	Nov	100	3/4	...	...
12 3/4	15	Dec	63	7/8	...	...
CrosTmb	25	Oct	100	7/16	...	...

	Call	Call	Put	Put
Exchange	*Volume*	*Open Interest*	*Volume*	*Open Interest*
Chicago Board	416,621	6,757,254	357,350	4,742,077
American	141,035	4,386,239	65,757	2,108,078
Philadelphia	66,193	1,708,700	16,890	741,071
Pacific	102,472	2,364,546	53,419	1,112,426
New York	9,116	913,042	2,613	420,211
Total	735,437	16,129,781	396,029	9,123,863

TABLE 7.5 Volume and Open Interest Reported in the *Wall Street Journal* on September 25, 1996

From Table 7.4 it appears that there were arbitrage opportunities on September 24, 1996. For example, an October put on AT&T with a strike price of 60 was priced at $8\frac{3}{8}$. Since the stock price was $51\frac{1}{2}$, it appears that this put could have been purchased and then exercised immediately for a profit of $\frac{1}{8}$. In fact, these types of arbitrage opportunities almost certainly did not exist. For both options and stocks, Table 7.4 gives the prices at which the last trade took place on September 24, 1996. The last trade for the October AT&T put with a strike price of 60 probably occurred much earlier in the day than the last trade on the stock. If an option trade had been attempted at the time of the last trade on the stock, the put price would have been higher than $8\frac{3}{8}$.

Trading

Options trading is in many respects similar to futures trading (see chapter 2). An exchange has a number of members (individuals and firms) who are referred to as having seats on the exchange. A seat on an exchange entitles the member to go on the floor of the exchange and trade with other members.

MARKET MAKERS

Most options exchanges (including the CBOE) use a market maker system to facilitate trading. A market maker for a certain option is an individual who, when asked to do so, will quote both a bid and an ask price on the option. The bid is the price at which the market maker is prepared to buy, and the ask is the price at which the market maker is prepared to sell. At the time the bid and the ask are quoted, the market maker does not know whether the trader who asked for the quotes wants to buy or sell the option. The ask is always higher than the bid, and the amount by which the ask exceeds the bid is referred to as the bid-ask spread. The exchange sets upper limits for the bid-ask spread. For example, it might specify that the spread be no more than $0.25 for options priced at less than $0.50, $0.50 for options priced between $0.50 and $10, $0.75 for options priced between $10 and $20, and $1 for options priced over $20.

The existence of the market maker ensures that buy and sell orders can always be executed at some price without any delays. Market makers therefore add liquidity to the market. The market makers themselves make their profits from the bid-ask spread. They use some of the schemes discussed later in this book to hedge their risks.

THE FLOOR BROKER

Floor brokers execute trades for the general public. When an investor contacts a broker to buy or sell an option, the broker relays the order to the firm's floor broker in the exchange on which the option trades. If the brokerage house does not have its own floor broker, it generally has an arrangement whereby it uses either an independent floor broker or the floor broker of another firm.

The types of orders that can be placed by the general public are similar to those that can be placed in the futures market (see chapter 2). A market order is to be executed immediately; a discretionary or market-not-held order leaves the timing of the trade to the floor broker's discretion; a limit order specifies the least favorable price at which the order can be executed; and so on.

The floor broker trades either with another floor broker or with the market maker. Floor brokers may be on commission or may be paid a salary by the brokerage houses for which they execute trades.

THE ORDER BOOK OFFICIAL

Many orders that are relayed to floor brokers are limit orders. This means that they can be executed only at the specified price or at a more favorable price. Often when a limit order reaches a floor broker, it cannot be executed immediately. (For example, a limit order to buy a call at $5 cannot be executed immediately when the market maker is quoting a bid of $4\frac{3}{4}$ and an ask of $5\frac{1}{4}$.) In most exchanges, the floor broker will then pass the order to an individual known as the *order book official* (or *board broker*). This official enters the order into a computer along with other public limit orders to ensure that as soon as the limit price is reached, the order is executed. The information on all outstanding limit orders is available to all traders.

The system based on a market maker and order book official can be contrasted with the specialist system, which is used in options exchanges such as AMEX and PHLX and is the most common system for trading stocks. Under the specialist system, an individual known as the *specialist* is responsible for being a market maker and keeping a record of limit orders. Unlike the order book official, the specialist does not make information on limit orders available to other traders.

OFFSETTING ORDERS

An investor who has purchased an option can close out the position by issuing an offsetting order to sell the same option. Similarly, an investor who has written an option can close out the position by issuing an offsetting order to buy the same option. If, when an options contract is traded, neither investor is offsetting an existing position, the open interest increases by one contract. If one investor is offsetting an existing position and the other is not, the open interest stays the same. If both investors are offsetting existing positions, the open interest goes down by one contract.

Commissions

For a retail investor, commissions vary significantly from broker to broker. Discount brokers generally charge lower commissions than full-service brokers. The actual amount charged is usually calculated as a fixed cost plus a proportion of the dollar amount of the trade. Table 7.6 shows the sort of schedule that might be offered by a discount broker. Under this schedule the purchase or sale of one contract always costs $30 (both the maximum and minimum commission is $30 for the first contract). Thus, the purchase of eight contracts when the option price is $3 would cost $20 + (0.02 × $2,400) = $68 in commissions.

If an option position is closed out by entering into an offsetting trade, the commission must be paid again. If the option is exercised, the commission is the same as it would be if the investor placed an order to buy or sell the underlying stock. Typically, this is 1 percent to 2 percent of the stock's value.

Consider an investor who buys one call contract with a strike price of $50 when the stock price is $49. We suppose the option price is $4.50, so that the cost of the contract is $450. Under the schedule in Table 7.6, the commission paid when the option is bought is $30. Suppose that the stock price rises and the option is exercised when the stock reaches $60. Assuming that the investor pays 1.5 percent commission on stock trades, the commission payable when the option is exercised is

$$0.015 \times \$60 \times 100 = \$90$$

The total commission paid is therefore $120, and the net profit to the investor is

$$\$1,000 - \$450 - \$120 = \$430$$

Note that selling the option for $10 instead of exercising it would save the investor $60 in commissions. (The commission payable when an option is sold is only $30 in our example.) In general, the commission system tends to push retail investors in the direction of selling options rather than exercising them.

A hidden cost in option trading (and in stock trading) is the market maker's bid-ask spread. Suppose that, in the example just considered, the bid price was $4.00 and

TABLE 7.6   A Typical Commission Schedule for a Discount Broker

Dollar Amount of Trade	Commission*
<$2,500	$20 + 0.02 of dollar amount
$2,500 to $10,000	$45 + 0.01 of dollar amount
>$10,000	$120 + 0.0025 of dollar amount

*Maximum commission is $30 per contract for the first five contracts plus $20 per contract for each additional contract. Minimum commission is $30 per contract for the first contract plus $2 per contract for each additional contract.

the ask price was $4.50 at the time the option was purchased. We can reasonably assume that a "fair" price for the option is halfway between the bid and the ask price, or $4.25. The cost to the buyer and to the seller of the market maker system is the difference between the fair price and the price paid. This is $0.25 per option, or $25 per contract.

MARGINS

When shares are purchased, an investor can either pay cash or use a margin account. The initial margin is usually 50 percent of the value of the shares, and the maintenance margin is usually 25 percent of the value of the shares. The margin account operates in the same way as it does for an investor entering into a futures contract (see chapter 2). When call and put options are purchased, the option price must be paid in full. Investors are not allowed to buy options on margin, because options already contain substantial leverage. Buying on margin would raise this leverage to an unacceptable level.

An investor who writes options is required to maintain funds in a margin account. Both the investor's broker and the exchange want to be satisfied that the investor will not default if the option is exercised. The size of the margin required depends on the circumstances.

WRITING NAKED OPTIONS

A *naked option* is an option that is not combined with an offsetting position in the underlying stock. The initial margin for a written naked option is the greater of the results of the following two calculations:

1. A total of 100 percent of the proceeds of the sale plus 20 percent of the underlying share price less the amount if any by which the option is out of the money
2. A total of 100 percent of the option proceeds plus 10 percent of the underlying share price

The 20 percent in the preceding calculations is replaced by 15 percent for options on a broadly based index, because the index price is usually less volatile than the price of an individual stock.

Example

An investor writes four naked call option contracts on a stock. The option price is $5, the strike price is $40, and the stock price is $38. Since the option is $2 out of the money, the first calculation gives

$$400[5 + 0.2 \times 38 - 2] = \$4,240$$

The second calculation gives

$$400[5 + 0.1 \times 38] = \$3,520$$

The initial margin requirement is therefore $4,240. Note that if the option had been a put, it would be $2 in the money and the margin requirement would be

$$400[5 + 0.2 \times 38] = \$5,040$$

In both cases the proceeds of the sale, $2,000, can be used to form part of the margin account.

A calculation similar to the initial margin calculation (but with the current market price replacing the proceeds of sale) is repeated every day. Funds can be withdrawn from the margin account when the calculation indicates that the margin required is less than the current balance in the margin account. When the calculation indicates that a significantly greater margin is required, a margin call will be made.

WRITING COVERED CALLS

Writing covered calls involves writing call options when the shares that might have to be delivered are already owned. Covered calls are far less risky than naked calls, because the worst that can happen is that the investor is required to sell shares already owned at below their market value. If covered call options are out of the money, no margin is required. The shares owned can be purchased using a margin account, as described previously, and the price received for the option can be used to partially fulfill this margin requirement. If the options are in the money, no margin is required for the options. However, for the purposes of calculating the investor's equity position, the share price is reduced by the extent if any to which the option is in the money. This may limit the amount which the investor can withdraw from the margin account if the share price increases.

Example

An investor decides to buy 200 shares of a certain stock on margin and to write two call option contracts on the stock. The stock price is $63, the strike price is $60, and the price of the option is $7. The margin account allows the investor to borrow 50 percent of the price of the stock, or $6,300. The investor is also able to use the price received for the option, $7 \times 200 = $1,400, to finance the purchase of the shares. The shares cost $63 \times 200 = $12,600. The minimum cash initially required from the investor for the trades is therefore

$$\$12,600 - \$6,300 - \$1,400 = \$4,900$$

In chapter 9 we will examine more complicated option trading strategies such as spreads, combinations, straddles, and strangles. There are special rules for determining the margin requirements when these trading strategies are used.

The Options Clearing Corporation

The Options Clearing Corporation (OCC) performs much the same function for options markets as the clearinghouse does for futures markets (see chapter 2). It guarantees that options writers will fulfill their obligations under the terms of the options contracts and keeps a record of all long and short positions. The OCC has a number of members, and all options trades must be cleared through a member. If a brokerage house is not itself a member of an exchange's OCC, it must arrange to clear its trades with a member. Members are required to have a certain minimum amount of capital and to contribute to a special fund that can be used if any member defaults on an options obligation.

When purchasing an option, the buyer must pay for it in full by the morning of the next business day. The funds are deposited with the OCC. The writer of the option maintains a margin account with a broker, as described earlier. The broker maintains a margin account with the OCC member that clears its trades. The OCC member in turn maintains a margin account with the OCC. The margin requirements described in the previous section are the margin requirements imposed by the OCC on its members. A brokerage house may require higher margins from its clients. However, it cannot require lower margins.

EXERCISING AN OPTION

When an investor notifies a broker to exercise an option, the broker in turn notifies the OCC member that clears its trades. This member then places an exercise order with the OCC. The OCC randomly selects a member with an outstanding short position in the same option. The member, using a procedure established in advance, selects a particular investor who has written the option. If the option is a call, this investor is required to sell stock at the strike price. If it is a put, the investor is required to buy stock at the strike price. The investor is said to be *assigned*. When an option is exercised, the open interest goes down by one.

At the expiration of the option, all in-the-money options should be exercised unless the transactions costs are so high as to wipe out the payoff from the option. Some brokerage firms will automatically exercise options for their clients at expiration when it is in their clients' interest to do so. Many exchanges also have rules for exercising options that are in the money at expiration.

Regulation

Options markets are regulated in a number of different ways. Both the exchange and its Options Clearing Corporation have rules governing the behavior of traders. In addition, there are both federal and state regulatory authorities. In general, options markets have demonstrated a willingness to regulate themselves. There have been no major scandals or defaults by OCC members. Investors can have a high level of confidence in the way the market is run.

The Securities and Exchange Commission is responsible for regulating options markets in stocks, stock indices, currencies, and bonds at the federal level. The Commodity Futures Trading Commission is responsible for regulating markets for options on futures. The major options markets are in the states of Illinois and New York. These states actively enforce their own laws on unacceptable trading practices.

Taxation

Determining the tax implications of options strategies can be tricky, and an investor who is in doubt about a position should consult a tax specialist. The general rule for all investors is that gains and losses from the trading of stock options are taxed as capital gains and losses. The way in which capital gains and losses are taxed in the United States was discussed in chapter 2. The holder of an option recognizes a gain or loss when (1) the option is allowed to expire unexercised, (2) the option is sold, or (3) the option is exercised. If a call option is exercised, the writer is deemed to have sold stock at the strike price plus the original call price. The party with a long position is deemed to have purchased the stock at the strike price plus the call price. (This is then used as a basis for calculating this party's gain or loss when the stock is eventually sold.) If a put option is exercised, the party with a long position is deemed to have sold stock for the strike price less the original put price. The writer is deemed to have bought stock for the strike price less the original put price. (This is used as a basis for calculating the writer's gain or loss when the stock is eventually sold.) In all cases, brokerage commissions are deductible.

WASH SALE RULE

One tax consideration in option trading in the United States is the wash sale rule. To understand this rule, imagine an investor who buys a stock when the price is $60 and plans to keep it for the long term. If the stock price drops to $40, the investor might be tempted to sell the stock and then immediately repurchase it so that the $20 loss is realized for tax purposes. To prevent this sort of thing, the tax authorities have ruled that when the repurchase is within 30 days of the sale (i.e., between 30 days before the sale and 30 days after the sale) any loss on the sale is not deductible. This rule is relevant to options traders because, for the purposes of the wash sale rule, a call option on a stock is regarded as the same security as the stock itself. Thus, selling a stock at a loss and buying a call option within a 30-day period will lead to the loss being disallowed.

TAX PLANNING USING OPTIONS

Tax practitioners sometimes use options and other derivatives to minimize tax costs or maximize tax benefits. One simple transaction is a cross-border arbitrage. A company buys an option in one tax jurisdiction where the cost of the option can be offset against tax immediately while selling an identical option in another jurisdiction where the income arising from the option sale is taxed only when the option is exercised or expires. Other transactions are more complex. For example, it is sometimes advantageous for a U.S. corporation to sell an in-the-money option on one of its assets to a related entity in a foreign jurisdiction. The U.S. corporation is not taxed on the income until the option is exercised. The result is that the corporation has obtained a loan from the foreign entity without withholding tax being charged on the interest. If carefully structured, options can also be used to create a hybrid instrument that is treated as equity for rating or financial reporting purposes and as debt for tax purposes. As a debt instrument, the option can significantly reduce the corporation's cost of capital, because it obtains the tax benefit on the interest or dividend it pays.

Tax authorities in many jurisdictions have proposed legislation designed to combat the use of derivatives for tax purposes. Before entering into any tax-motivated transaction, a treasurer should explore in detail how the structure could be unwound in the event of legislative change and how costly the process could be.

Warrants and Convertibles

For the exchange-traded options described so far, the writers and purchasers meet on the floor of the exchange. As trading takes place, the number of contracts outstanding fluctuates. A warrant is an option that arises in a quite different way. *Warrants* are issued (i.e., written) by a company or a financial institution. In some cases they are subsequently traded on an exchange. The number of contracts outstanding is determined by the size of the original issue and changes only when options are exercised or expire. Warrants are bought and sold in much the same way as stocks, and there is no need for an Options Clearing Corporation to become involved. When a warrant is exercised, the original issuer settles up with the current holder of the warrant.

Call warrants are frequently issued by companies on their own stock. For example, in a debt issue a company might offer investors a package consisting of bonds plus call warrants on its stock. If the warrants are exercised, the company issues new treasury stock to the warrant holders in return for the strike price specified in the contract. The strike price and exercise date of the warrants do not have to correspond to those of the regular exchange-traded call options. Typically warrants have longer maturities than regular exchange-traded call options.

Put and call warrants are also issued by financial institutions to satisfy a demand in the market. The underlying asset is typically an index, a currency, or a commodity. Once it has written the warrant, the financial institution must hedge its risk. The techniques for doing so are described in chapter 14.

Convertible bonds are debt instruments with embedded options. The holder has the right to exchange a convertible bond for equity in the issuing corporation at certain times in the future according to a certain exchange ratio. Very often the convertible is *callable*. This means that it can be repurchased by the issuer at a certain price at certain times in the future. Once the bonds have been called, the holder can always choose to convert prior to repurchase. Thus, the effect of a call provision is often to give the issuer the right to force conversion of the bonds into equity at an earlier time than the holders would otherwise choose. The company provides the holder with new treasury stock in exchange for the bonds when the convertible is converted. If, as a rough approximation, interest rates are assumed constant and call provisions are ignored, a convertible can be regarded as a regular debt instrument plus call warrants.

Over-the-Counter Markets

The over-the-counter market for options has become increasingly important since the early 1980s. In this market financial institutions, corporate treasurers, and fund managers trade over the phone. There is a wide range of assets underlying the options. Over-the-counter options on foreign exchange and interest rates are particularly popular. The chief potential disadvantage of the over-the-counter market is that both sides to the transaction are subject to some credit risk. In an attempt to overcome this disadvantage, market participants are adopting a number of measures such as requiring counterparties to post collateral.

The instruments traded in the over-the-counter market are often structured by financial institutions to meet the precise needs of their clients. Sometimes this involves choosing exercise dates, strike prices, and contract sizes that are different from those traded by the exchange. In other cases the nature of the option is changed. The option is then referred to as an *exotic option*. Below are examples of exotic options that regularly trade in the over-the-counter market.[2]

Example 1: Barrier Options

The most popular barrier options are knock-out and knock-in options. A knock-out option ceases to exist if the price of the underlying asset reaches a certain prespecified level, referred to as a barrier. A knock-in option comes into existence only if the price of the asset reaches the barrier level. There are four different types of knock-in and knock-out call options. A *down-and-out call* is a knock-out call where the barrier is below the current asset price. A *down-and-in call* is a knock-in call where the barrier is below the current asset price. An *up-and-out call* is a knock-out call where the barrier is above the current asset price. An *up-and-in call* is a knock-in call where the barrier is above the current asset price. Four different types of knock-out and knock-in puts are defined analogously.

Example 2: Asian Options

Asian options provide a payoff based on the average asset price during the life of the option, not the final asset price. An *average-price call* provides a payoff equal to the greater of zero and the amount by which the average price of the asset exceeds the strike price. An *average-price put* provides a payoff equal to the greater of zero and the amount by which the strike price exceeds the average price of the asset.

Example 3: Binary Options

Binary options are options with discontinuous payoffs. One example is a *cash-or-nothing call*. This pays off nothing if the asset price is below the strike price and a fixed amount if it is above. Another example is an *asset-or-nothing call*. This pays off the asset price if the asset price is above the strike price and zero otherwise. *Cash-or-nothing puts* and *asset-or-nothing puts* are defined similarly.

Example 4: Chooser Options

With a chooser option, at some date prior to maturity the holder can choose whether the option is a call or a put.

Example 5: Compound Options

A compound option is an option on an option. There are four types: a call option to enter into a call option, a call option to enter into a put option, a put option to

---

[2]The software included with this book, DerivaGem, allows readers to value the options listed here and investigate their properties.

enter into a call option, and a put option to enter into a put option. In each case there are two strike prices: one for the exercise of the first option, the other for the exercise of the second option.

Example 6: Lookback Options

In a lookback option the payoff depends on the maximum or minimum price of the asset during the life of the option. In a *lookback call* the payoff is the final asset price minus the minimum asset price. In a *lookback put* the payoff is the maximum stock price minus the final stock price.

Summary

There are two types of options: calls and puts. A call option gives the holder the right to buy the underlying asset for a certain price by a certain date. A put option gives the holder the right to sell the underlying asset by a certain date for a certain price. There are four possible positions in options markets: a long position in a call, a short position in a call, a long position in a put, and a short position in a put. Taking a short position in an option is known as writing it. Options are currently traded on stocks, stock indices, foreign currencies, futures contracts, and bonds.

An exchange must specify the terms of the option contracts it trades. In particular, it must specify the size of the contract, the precise expiration time, and the strike price. One stock option contract gives the holder the right to buy or sell 100 shares. The expiration of a stock option contract is 10.59 P.M. Central Time on the Saturday immediately following the third Friday of the expiration month. Options with four different expiration months trade at any given time. Strike prices are at $2\frac{1}{2}$, $5, or $10 intervals, depending on the stock price. The strike price is generally fairly close to the current stock price when trading in an option begins.

The terms of a stock option are not adjusted for cash dividends. However, they are adjusted for stock dividends, stock splits, and rights issues. The aim of the adjustment is to keep the positions of both the writer and the buyer of a contract unchanged.

Most options exchanges use a market maker system. A market maker is an individual who is prepared to quote both a bid (price at which he or she is prepared to buy) and an ask (price at which he or she is prepared to sell). Market makers improve the liquidity of the market and ensure that there is never any delay in executing market orders. They themselves make a profit from the difference between their bid and ask prices (known as their bid-ask spread). The exchange has rules specifying upper limits for the bid-ask spread.

Writers of options have potential liabilities and are required to maintain margins with their brokers. If it is not a member of the Options Clearing Corporation, the broker will maintain a margin account with a firm that is a member. This firm will in turn maintain a margin account with the Options Clearing Corporation. The Options Clearing Corporation is responsible for keeping a record of all outstanding contracts, handling exercise orders, and so on.

Not all options are traded on exchanges. Many options are traded by phone in the over-the-counter market. An advantage of over-the-counter options is that they can be tailored by a financial institution to meet the particular needs of a corporate treasurer or fund manager.

Suggestions for Further Reading

Brown, R. L. "Adjusting Option Contracts to Reflect Capitalization Changes," *Journal of Business Finance and Accounting* 16 (1989): 247–254.

Chance, D. M. *An Introduction to Options and Futures Markets.* Orlando, FL: Dryden Press, 1989.

Chicago Board Options Exchange. *Margin Manual.* Chicago, 1991.

Chicago Board Options Exchange. *Reference Manual.* Chicago, 1982.

Chicago Board Options Exchange. *Understanding Options.* Chicago, 1985.

Clasing, H. K. *The Dow Jones–Irwin Guide to Put and Call Trading.* Homewood, IL: Dow Jones–Irwin, 1978.

Cox, J. C., and M. Rubinstein. *Options Markets.* Englewood Cliffs, NJ: Prentice Hall, 1985.

Gastineau, G. *The Stock Options Manual.* New York: McGraw-Hill, 1979.

McMillan, L. G. *Options as a Strategic Investment.* New York: New York Institute of Finance, 1986.

Phillips, S. M., and C. W. Smith. "Trading Costs for Listed Options: The Implications for Market Efficiency," *Journal of Financial Economics* 8 (1980): 179–201.

Quiz

1. An investor buys a European put on a share for $3. The stock price is $42 and the strike price is $40. Under what circumstances does the investor make a profit? Under what circumstances will the option be exercised? Draw a diagram showing the variation of the investor's profit with the stock price at the maturity of the option.

2. An investor sells a European call on a share for $4. The stock price is $47 and the strike price is $50. Under what circumstances does the investor make a profit? Under what circumstances will the option be exercised? Draw a diagram showing the variation of the investor's profit with the stock price at the maturity of the option.

3. An investor buys a call with strike price X and writes a put with the same strike price. Describe the investor's position.

4. Explain why brokers require margins when clients write options but not when they buy options.

5. A stock option is on a February, May, August, and November cycle. What options trade on (a) April 1 and (b) May 30?

6. A company declares a 3-for-1 stock split. Explain how the terms change for a call option with a strike price of $60.

7. Explain the difference between the specialist system and the market maker/order book official system for the organization of trading at an exchange.

Questions and Problems

7.1. Suppose that a European call option to buy a share for $50.00 costs $2.50 and is held until maturity. Under what circumstances will the holder of the option make a profit?

Under what circumstances will the option be exercised? Draw a diagram illustrating how the profit from a long position in the option depends on the stock price at maturity of the option.

7.2. Suppose that a European put option to sell a share for $60 costs $4 and is held until maturity. Under what circumstances will the seller of the option (the party with the short position) make a profit? Under what circumstances will the option be exercised? Draw a diagram illustrating how the profit from a short position in the option depends on the stock price at maturity of the option.

7.3. Describe the terminal value of the following portfolio: a newly entered-into long forward contract on an asset and a long position in a European put option on the asset with the same maturity as the forward contract and a strike price that is equal to the forward price of the asset at the time the portfolio is set up. Show that the European put option has the same value as a European call option with the same strike price and maturity.

7.4. Draw a diagram showing the variation of an investor's profit or loss with the terminal stock price for a portfolio consisting of
   a. One share and a short position in one call option
   b. Two shares and a short position in one call option
   c. One share and a short position in two call options
   d. One share and a short position in four call options

In each case, assume that the call option has a strike price equal to the current stock price.

7.5. Explain why an American option is always worth at least as much as a European option on the same asset with the same strike price and exercise date.

7.6. Explain why an American option is always worth at least as much as its intrinsic value.

7.7. Explain carefully the difference between writing a call option and buying a put option.

7.8. The treasurer of a corporation is trying to choose between options and forward contracts to hedge the corporation's foreign exchange risk. Discuss the advantages and disadvantages of each.

7.9. Suppose that sterling-U.S. dollar spot and forward exchange rates are as follows:

Spot	1.8470
90-day forward	1.8381
180-day forward	1.8291

What opportunities are open to an investor in the following situations?
   a. A 180-day European call option to buy £1 for $1.80 costs $0.0250.
   b. A 90-day European put option to sell £1 for $1.86 costs $0.0200.

7.10. Consider an exchange-traded call option contract to buy 500 shares with a strike price of $40 and maturity in four months. Explain how the terms of the option contract change when there is
   a. A 10 percent stock dividend
   b. A 10 percent cash dividend
   c. A 4-for-1 stock split

7.11. "If most of the call options on a stock are in the money, it is likely that the stock price has risen rapidly in the last few months." Discuss this statement.

7.12. What is the effect of an unexpected cash dividend on (a) a call option price and (b) a put option price?

7.13. Options on General Motors stock are on a March, June, September, and December cycle. What options trade on (a) March 1, (b) June 30, and (c) August 5?

7.14. Explain why the market maker's bid-ask spread represents a real cost to options investors.

7.15. An investor writes five naked call option contracts. The option price is $3.50, the strike price is $60.00, and the stock price is $57.00. What is the initial margin requirement?

7.16. An investor buys 500 shares of a stock and sells five call option contracts on the stock. The strike price is $30. The price of the option is $3. What is the investor's minimum cash investment if the stock price is $28?

7.17. Describe the payoff from a portfolio consisting of a down-and-out European call and a down-and-in European call on the same asset. Both options have the same strike price, barrier, and time to maturity.

7.18. Describe the payoff from a portfolio consisting of a lookback call and a lookback put on the same asset with the same maturity.

8

Basic Properties of Stock Options

In this chapter we look at the factors affecting stock option prices. We also consider a number of different arbitrage arguments to explore the relationships between European option prices, American option prices, and the underlying stock price. The most important of these relationships is put–call parity, which is a relationship between European call option prices and European put option prices. The chapter also examines whether American options should be exercised early. It shows that it is never optimal to exercise an American call option on a nondividend-paying stock prior to the option's expiration, but that under some circumstances the early exercise of an American put option on such a stock is optimal.

Factors Affecting Option Prices

There are six factors affecting the price of a stock option:

1. The current stock price, S
2. The strike price, X
3. The time to expiration, T
4. The volatility of the stock price, σ
5. The risk-free interest rate, r
6. The dividends expected during the life of the option

In this section we consider what happens to option prices when one of these factors changes with all the others remaining fixed. The results are summarized in Table 8.1.

Figures 8.1 and 8.2 show how the price of a European call and put depends on the first five factors in the situation where $S = 50, X = 50, r = 5$ percent per annum, $\sigma = 30$ percent per annum, $T = 1$ year, and there are no dividends. In this case the call price is 7.116 and the put price is 4.677.

TABLE 8.1 Summary of the Effect on the Price of a Stock Option of Increasing One Variable While Keeping All Others Fixed∗

Variable	European Call	European Put	American Call	American Put
Stock price	+	−	+	−
Strike price	−	+	−	+
Time to expiration	?	?	+	+
Volatility	+	+	+	+
Risk-free rate	+	−	+	−
Dividends	−	+	−	+

∗+ indicates that an increase in the variable causes the option price to increase;
− indicates that an increase in the variable causes the option price to decrease;
? indicates that the relationship is uncertain.

STOCK PRICE AND STRIKE PRICE

If a call option is exercised at some time in the future, the payoff will be the amount by which the stock price exceeds the strike price. Call options therefore become more valuable as the stock price increases and less valuable as the strike price increases. For a put option, the payoff on exercise is the amount by which the strike price exceeds the stock price. Put options therefore behave in the opposite way from call options. They become less valuable as the stock price increases and more valuable as the strike price increases. Figures 8.1a, b, c, and d illustrate the way in which put and call prices depend on the stock price and strike price.

TIME TO EXPIRATION

Consider next the effect of the expiration date. Both put and call American options become more valuable as the time to expiration increases. Consider two options that differ only as far as the expiration date is concerned. The owner of the long-life option has all the exercise opportunities open to the owner of the short-life option—and more. The long-life option must therefore always be worth at least as much as the short-life option. Figures 8.1e and f illustrate the way in which calls and puts depend on the time to expiration.

European put and call options do not necessarily become more valuable as the time to expiration increases. The owner of a long-life European option does not have all the exercise opportunities open to the owner of a short-life European option. The long-life owner can exercise only at the maturity of the European option. Consider two European call options on a stock: one with an expiration date in one month, the other with an expiration date in two months. Suppose that a very large dividend is expected in six weeks. The dividend will cause the stock price to decline, so that the short-life option could be worth more than the long-life option.

VOLATILITY

The precise way in which volatility is defined is discussed in chapter 11. Roughly speaking, the *volatility* of a stock price is a measure of how uncertain we are about future

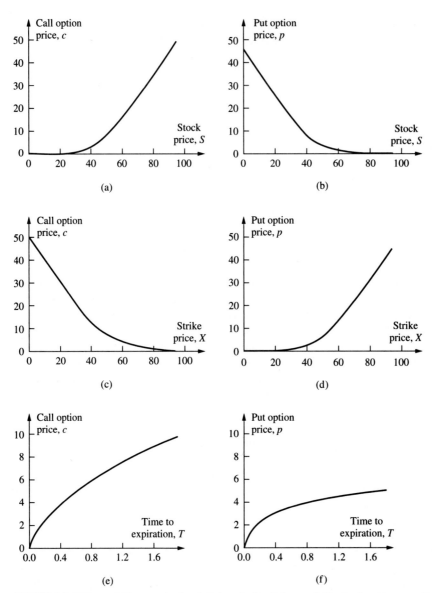

FIGURE 8.1 Effect of Changes in Stock Price, Strike Price, and Expiration Date on Options Prices $S = 50, X = 50, r = 5$ percent, $\sigma = 30$ percent, and $T = 1$.

stock price movements. As volatility increases, the chance that the stock will do very well or very poorly increases. For the owner of a stock, these two outcomes tend to offset each other. However, this is not so for the owner of a call or put. The owner of a call benefits from price increases but has limited downside risk in the event of price decreases, because the most that the owner can lose is the price of the option. Similarly, the owner of a put benefits from price decreases but has limited downside risk in the

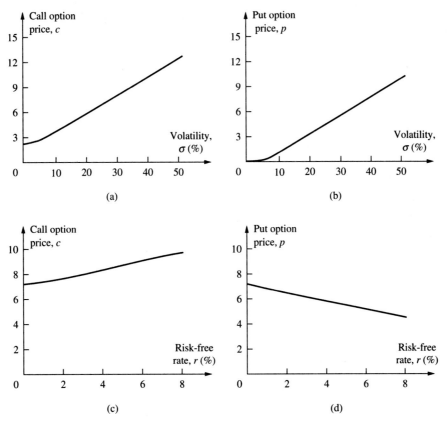

FIGURE 8.2 Effect of Changes in Volatility and Risk-Free Interest Rate on Option Prices
$S = 50, X = 50, r = 5$ percent, $\sigma = 30$ percent, and $T = 1$.

event of price increases. The values of both calls and puts therefore increase as volatility increases (see Figures 8.2a and b).

RISK-FREE INTEREST RATE

The risk-free interest rate affects the price of an option in a less clear-cut way. As interest rates in the economy increase, the expected growth rate of the stock price tends to increase. However, the present value of any future cash flows received by the holder of the option decreases. These two effects both tend to decrease the value of a put option. Hence, put option prices decline as the risk-free interest rate increases (see Figure 8.2d). In the case of calls, the first effect tends to increase the price, whereas the second effect tends to decrease it. It can be shown that the first effect always dominates the second effect; that is, the prices of calls always increase as the risk-free interest rate increases (see Figure 8.2c).

It should be emphasized that these results assume that all other variables remain fixed. In practice, when interest rates rise (fall), stock prices tend to fall (rise). The net effect of an interest-rate change and the accompanying stock price change may be the opposite of that just given.

DIVIDENDS

Dividends have the effect of reducing the stock price on the ex-dividend date. This is bad news for the value of call options and good news for the value of put options. The value of a call option is therefore negatively related to the sizes of any anticipated dividends, and the value of a put option is positively related to the sizes of any anticipated dividends.

Assumptions

In this chapter we will make assumptions similar to those made for deriving forward and futures prices in chapter 3. We assume that there are some market participants, such as large investment banks, for which

1. There are no transactions costs
2. All trading profits (net of trading losses) are subject to the same tax rate
3. Borrowing and lending are possible at the risk-free interest rate

We assume that these market participants are prepared to take advantage of arbitrage opportunities as they arise. As discussed in chapters 1 and 3, this means that any available arbitrage opportunities disappear very quickly. For the purposes of our analyses, it is therefore reasonable to assume that there are no arbitrage opportunities.

Notation

We will use the following notation:

S: current stock price

X: exercise price of option

T: time to expiration of option

S_T: stock price at time T

r: continuously compounded risk-free rate of interest for an investment maturing at time T

C: value of American call option to buy one share

P: value of American put option to sell one share

c: value of European call option to buy one share

p: value of European put option to sell one share

It should be noted that r is the nominal rate of interest, not the real rate of interest. We can assume that $r > 0$. Otherwise, a risk-free investment would provide no advantages over cash. (Indeed, if $r < 0$, cash would be preferable to a risk-free investment.)

Upper and Lower Bounds for Option Prices

In this section we derive upper and lower bounds for option prices. These bounds do not depend on any particular assumptions about the factors mentioned in the previous section (except $r > 0$). If an option price is above the upper bound or below the lower bound, there are profitable opportunities for arbitrageurs.

UPPER BOUNDS

An American or European call option gives the holder the right to buy one share of a stock for a certain price. No matter what happens, the option can never be worth more than the stock. Hence, the stock price is an upper bound to the option price:

$$c \leq S \text{ and } C \leq S$$

If these relationships were not true, an arbitrageur could easily make a riskless profit by buying the stock and selling the call option.

An American or European put option gives the holder the right to sell one share of a stock for X. No matter how low the stock price becomes, the option can never be worth more than X. Hence,

$$p \leq X \text{ and } P \leq X$$

For European options, we know that at time T the option will be worth less than X. It follows that it must now be worth less than the present value of X:

$$p \leq Xe^{-rT}$$

If this were not true, an arbitrageur could make a riskless profit by writing the option and investing the proceeds of the sale at the risk-free interest rate.

LOWER BOUND FOR CALLS
ON NONDIVIDEND-PAYING STOCKS

A lower bound for the price of a European call option on a nondividend-paying stock is

$$S - Xe^{-rT}$$

We first look at a numerical example and then consider a more formal argument.

Suppose that $S = \$20$, $X = \$18$, $r = 10$ percent per annum, and $T = 1$ year. In this case

$$S - Xe^{-rT} = 20 - 18e^{-0.1} = 3.71$$

or $3.71. Consider the situation where the European call price is $3.00, which is less than the theoretical minimum of $3.71. An arbitrageur can buy the call and short the stock to provide a cash inflow of $20.00 - \$3.00 = \$17.00$. If invested for one year at 10 percent per annum, the $17.00 grows to $17e^{0.1} = \$18.79$. At the end of the year, the option expires. If the stock price is greater than $18.00, the arbitrageur exercises the option for $18.00, closes out the short position, and makes a profit of

$$\$18.79 - \$18.00 = \$0.79$$

If the stock price is less than $18.00, the stock is bought in market and the short position is closed out. The arbitrageur then makes an even greater profit. For example, if the stock price is $17.00, the arbitrageur's profit is

$$\$18.79 - \$17.00 = \$1.79$$

This example is illustrated in Table 8.2.

For a more formal argument, we consider the following two portfolios:

Portfolio A: one European call option plus an amount of cash equal to Xe^{-rT}

Portfolio B: one share

In portfolio A, the cash, if it is invested at the risk-free interest rate, will grow to X at time T. If $S_T > X$, the call option is exercised at time T and portfolio A is worth S_T. If $S_T < X$, the call option expires worthless and the portfolio is worth X. Hence, at time T portfolio A is worth

$$\max(S_T, X)$$

TABLE 8.2   Arbitrage Opportunity When European Call Price Is Less Than the Lower Bound

From the Trader's Desk

An investor has just obtained the following quotes for a European call option on a nondividend-paying stock with a strike price of $18 and an expiration date in one year:

      Stock price: $20
      Option price: $3

The risk-free interest rate for a one-year investment is 10 percent per annum.

Opportunity

  1. Buy the option.

  2. Short the stock.

  3. Invest surplus cash at 10 percent per annum.

The Result

This strategy provides an immediate positive cash flow of $20.00 - $3.00 = $17.00. The $17.00 is invested at 10 percent per annum and grows to $17e^{0.1} = \$18.79$ at the end of one year. At this time the option expires. If the price of the stock is greater than $18.00, the investor exercises the option and closes out the short position for a profit of

$$\$18.79 - \$18.00 = \$0.79$$

If the price of the stock is less than $18.00 at the end of one year, the stock is bought in the market and the short position is closed out. The investor then makes a profit equal to

$$18.79 - S_T$$

where S_T is the stock price. Since $S_T < 18$, the profit is at least as great as $0.79.

Portfolio B is worth S_T at time T. Hence, portfolio A is always worth as much as, and is sometimes worth more than, portfolio B at time T. It follows that in the absence of arbitrage opportunities this must also be true today. Hence,

$$c + Xe^{-rT} > S$$

or

$$c > S - Xe^{-rT}$$

Because the worst that can happen to a call option is that it expires worthless, its value must be positive. This means that $c > 0$ and therefore

$$c > \max(S - Xe^{-rT}, 0) \tag{8.1}$$

Example

Consider a European call option on a nondividend-paying stock when the stock price is $51, the exercise price is $50, the time to maturity is six months, and the risk-free rate of interest is 12 percent per annum. In this case, $S = 51$, $X = 50$, $T = 0.5$, and $r = 0.12$. From Equation 8.1, a lower bound for the option price is $S - Xe^{-rT}$, or

$$51 - 50e^{-0.12 \times 0.5} = \$3.91$$

LOWER BOUND FOR EUROPEAN PUTS ON NONDIVIDEND-PAYING STOCKS

For a European put option on a nondividend-paying stock, a lower bound for the price is

$$Xe^{-rT} - S$$

Again, we first consider a numerical example and then look at a more formal argument. Suppose that $S = \$37$, $X = \$40$, $r = 5$ percent per annum, and $T = 0.5$ years. In this case

$$Xe^{-rT} - S = 40e^{-0.05 \times 0.5} - 37 = \$2.01$$

Consider the situation where the European put price is $1.00, which is less than the theoretical minimum of $2.01. An arbitrageur can borrow $38.00 for six months to buy both the put and the stock. At the end of the six months, the arbitrageur will be required to repay $38e^{0.05 \times 0.5} = \$38.96$. If the stock price is below $40.00, the arbitrageur exercises the option to sell the stock for $40.00, repays the loan, and makes a profit of

$$\$40.00 - \$38.96 = \$1.04$$

If the stock price is greater than $40.00, the arbitrageur discards the option, sells the stock, and repays the loan for an even greater profit. For example, if the stock price is $42.00, the arbitrageur's profit is

$$\$42.00 - \$38.96 = \$3.04$$

This example is illustrated in Table 8.3.

For a more formal argument, we consider the following two portfolios:

Portfolio C: one European put option plus one share

Portfolio D: an amount of cash equal to Xe^{-rT}

If $S_T < X$, the option in portfolio C is exercised at time T and the portfolio becomes worth X. If $S_T > X$, the put option expires worthless and the portfolio is worth S_T at time T. Hence, portfolio C is worth

$$\max(S_T, X)$$

at time T. Assuming the cash is invested at the risk-free interest rate, portfolio D is worth X at time T. Hence, portfolio C is always worth as much as, and is sometimes worth more than, portfolio D at time T. It follows that in the absence of arbitrage opportunities portfolio C must be worth more than portfolio D today. Hence,

$$p + S > Xe^{-rT}$$

or

$$p > Xe^{-rT} - S$$

TABLE 8.3   Arbitrage Opportunities When European Put Price Is Less Than the Lower Bound

From the Trader's Desk

An investor has just obtained the following quotes for a European put option on a nondividend-paying stock with a strike price of $40 and an expiration date in six months.

Stock price: $37
Option price: $1

The risk-free interest rate for a six-month investment is 10 percent per annum.

Opportunity

1. Borrow $38 for six months.

2. Buy one option.

3. Buy one share of the stock.

The Result

At the end of the six months, $38e^{0.05 \times 0.5} = \$38.96$ is required to pay off the loan. If the stock price at this time is below $40.00, the investor exercises the option to sell the stock for $40.00 and makes a profit of

$$\$40.00 - \$38.96 = \$1.04$$

If the price of the stock is greater than $40.00, the investor sells the stock and repays the loan for a profit of

$$S_T - 38.96$$

where S_T is the stock price. The profit is at least as great as $1.04.

Since the worst that can happen to a put option is that it expires worthless, its value must be positive. This means that

$$p > \max(Xe^{-rT} - S, 0) \tag{8.2}$$

Example

Consider a European put option on a nondividend-paying stock when the stock price is $38, the exercise price is $40, the time to maturity is three months, and the risk-free rate of interest is 10 percent per annum. In this case $S = 38$, $X = 40$, $T = 0.25$, and $r = 0.10$. From Equation 8.2, a lower bound for the option price is $Xe^{-rT} - S$, or

$$40e^{-0.1 \times 0.25} - 38 = \$1.01$$

Put–call Parity

We now derive an important relationship between p and c. Consider the following two portfolios that were used in the previous section:

Portfolio A: one European call option plus an amount of cash equal to Xe^{-rT}

Portfolio C: one European put option plus one share

Both are worth

$$\max(S_T, X)$$

at expiration of the options. Because the options are European, they cannot be exercised prior to the expiration date. The portfolios must therefore have identical values today. This means that

$$c + Xe^{-rT} = p + S \tag{8.3}$$

This relationship is known as *put–call parity*. It shows that the value of a European call with a certain exercise price and exercise date can be deduced from the value of a European put with the same exercise price and exercise date, and vice versa.

If Equation 8.3 does not hold, there are arbitrage opportunities. Suppose that the stock price is $31, the exercise price is $30, the risk-free interest rate is 10 percent per annum, the price of a three-month European call option is $3, and the price of a three-month European put option is $2.25. In this case

$$c + Xe^{-rT} = 3 + 30e^{-0.1 \times 0.25} = \$32.26$$

$$p + S = 2.25 + 31 = \$33.25$$

Portfolio C is overpriced relative to portfolio A. The correct arbitrage strategy is to buy the securities in portfolio A and short the securities in portfolio C. The strategy involves buying the call and shorting both the put and the stock to generate a positive cash flow of

$$-3 + 2.25 + 31 = \$30.25$$

up front. When invested at the risk-free interest rate, this amount grows to $30.25e^{0.1 \times 0.25} = \$31.02$ in three months.

If the stock price at expiration of the option is greater than $30, the call will be exercised. If it is less than $30, the put will be exercised. In either case, the investor ends up buying one share for $30. This share can be used to close out the short position. The net profit is therefore

$$\$31.02 - \$30.00 = \$1.02$$

This example is illustrated in Table 8.4.

For an alternative situation, suppose that the call price is $3 and the put price is $1. In this case

$$c + Xe^{-rT} = 3 + 30e^{-0.1 \times 0.25} = \$32.26$$

$$p + S = 1 + 31 = \$32.00$$

Portfolio A is overpriced relative to portfolio C. An arbitrageur can short the securities in portfolio A and buy the securities in portfolio C to lock in a profit. The strategy involves shorting the call and buying both the put and the stock, with an initial

---

TABLE 8.4 Arbitrage Opportunity When Put–Call Parity Does Not Hold: Call Price Too Low Relative to Put Price

From the Trader's Desk

An investor has just obtained the following quotes for options on a stock worth $31 when the three-month risk-free interest rate is 10 percent per annum. Both options have a strike price of $30 and an expiration date in three months.

European call: $3
European put: $2\frac{1}{4}$

Strategy

1. Buy the call.

2. Short the put.

3. Short the stock.

The Result

This strategy leads to an initial cash flow of $31.00 − \$3.00 + \$2.25 = \$30.25$. When invested for three months at the risk-free interest rate, this amount grows to $30.25e^{0.1 \times 025} = \$31.02$. At the end of the three months, the possible situations are as follows:

1. Stock price is greater than $30.00. The investor exercises the call. This involves buying one share for $30.00. The short position is closed out and the net profit is $\$31.02 - \$30.00 = \$1.02$.

2. Stock price is less than $30.00. The counterparty exercises the put. This also involves the investor in buying one share for $30.00. The short position is closed out and the net profit is again $\$31.02 - \$30.00 = \$1.02$.

TABLE 8.5 Arbitrage Opportunity When Put–Call Parity Does Not Hold: Put Price Too Low Relative to Call Price

From the Trader's Desk

An investor has just obtained the following quotes for options on a stock worth $31 when the three-month risk-free interest rate is 10 percent per annum. Both options have a strike price of $30 and an expiration date in three months.

> European call: $3
> European put: $1

Strategy

1. Sell the call.
2. Buy the put.
3. Buy the stock.

The Outcome

This strategy involves an investment of $31 + $1 − $3 = $29 at time zero. When the investment is financed at the risk-free interest rate, a repayment of $29e^{0.1 \times 0.25} = \$29.73$ is required at the end of three months. The possible situations are as follows:

1. Stock price is greater than $30.00. The counterparty exercises the call. This means that the investor has to sell the share owned for $30.00. The net profit is $30.00 − $29.73 = $0.27.
2. Stock price is less than $30.00. The investor exercises the put. This also means that the share is sold for $30.00. The net profit is again $30.00 − $29.73 = $0.27.

---

investment of

$$\$31 + \$1 - \$3 = \$29$$

When the investment is financed at the risk-free interest rate, a repayment of $29e^{0.1 \times 0.25} = \$29.73$ is required at the end of the three months. As in the previous case, either the call or the put will be exercised. The short call and long put option position therefore leads to the stock being sold for $30.00. The net profit is

$$\$30.00 - \$29.73 = \$0.27$$

This example is illustrated in Table 8.5.

Early Exercise: Calls on a Nondividend-Paying Stock

This section demonstrates that it is never optimal to exercise an American call option on a nondividend-paying stock before the expiration date.

To illustrate the general nature of the argument, consider an American call option on a nondividend-paying stock with one month to expiration when the stock price is $50 and the strike price is $40. The option is deep in the money and the investor who owns the option might well be tempted to exercise it immediately. However, if the investor plans to hold the stock for more than one month, this is not the best strategy. A better course of action is to keep the option and exercise it at the end of the month. The $40 strike price is then paid out one month later than it would be if the option were exercised immediately, so that interest is earned on the $40 for one month. Because the stock pays no dividend, no income from the stock is sacrificed. A further advantage of waiting rather than exercising immediately is that there is some chance (however remote) that the stock price will fall below $40 in one month. In this case the investor will not exercise and will be glad that the decision to exercise early was not taken!

This argument shows that there are no advantages to exercising early if the investor plans to keep the stock for the remaining life of the option (one month, in this case). What if the investor thinks the stock is currently overpriced and is wondering whether to exercise the option and sell the stock? In this case, the investor is better off selling the option than exercising it.[1] The option will be bought by another investor who does want to hold the stock. Such investors must exist. Otherwise the current stock price would not be $50. The price obtained for the option will be greater than its intrinsic value of $10, for the reasons mentioned earlier. In fact, Equation 8.1 shows that the market price of the option must always be greater than

$$50 - 40e^{-0.1 \times 0.08333} = \$10.33$$

Otherwise there are arbitrage opportunities.

To present a more formal argument, consider the following two portfolios:

Portfolio E: one American call option plus an amount of cash equal to Xe^{-rT}

Portfolio F: one share

The value of the cash in portfolio E at expiration of the option is X. At some earlier time t, it is $Xe^{-r(T-t)}$. If the call option is exercised at time t, the value of portfolio E is

$$S - X + Xe^{-r(T-t)}$$

This is always less than S when $t < T$, because $r > 0$. Portfolio E is therefore always worth less than portfolio F if the call option is exercised prior to maturity. If the call option is held to expiration, the value of portfolio E at time T is

$$\max(S_T, X)$$

The value of portfolio F is S_T. There is always some chance that $S_T < X$. This means that portfolio E is always worth as much as, and is sometimes worth more than, portfolio F.

We have seen that portfolio E is worth less than portfolio F if the option is exercised immediately but is worth at least as much as portfolio F if the holder of the option delays exercising it until the expiration date. It follows that a call option on a nondividend-paying stock should never be exercised prior to the expiration date. An American call option on a nondividend-paying stock is therefore worth the same as the

---

[1] As an alternative strategy, the investor can keep the option and short the stock to lock in a better profit than $10.

corresponding European call option on the same stock:

$$C = c$$

For a quicker proof, we can use Equation 8.1:

$$c > S - Xe^{-rT}$$

Because the owner of an American call has all the exercise opportunities open to the owner of the corresponding European call, we must have

$$C \geq c$$

Hence,

$$C > S - Xe^{-rT}$$

Given $r > 0$, it follows that $C > S - X$. If it were optimal to exercise early, C would equal $S - X$. We deduce that it can never be optimal to exercise early.

Figure 8.3 shows the general way in which the call price varies with S and X. It indicates that the call price is always above its intrinsic value of max$(S - X, 0)$. As r or T or the volatility increases, the call price moves in the direction indicated by the arrows (i.e., farther away from the intrinsic value).

One reason a call option should not be exercised early relates to the insurance that it provides. A call option, when held instead of the stock itself, in effect insures the holder against the stock price falling below the exercise price. Once the option has been exercised and the exercise price has been exchanged for the stock price, this insurance vanishes. Another reason concerns the time value of money. From the perspective of the option holder, the later the strike price is paid out the better.

FIGURE 8.3 Variation of Price of an American or European Call Option on a Nondividend-paying Stock with the Stock Price S

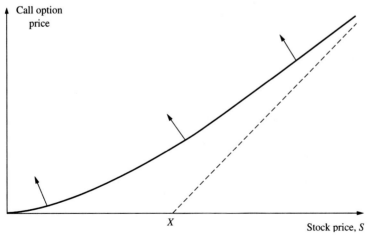

Early Exercise: Puts on a Nondividend-paying Stock

It can be optimal to exercise an American put option on a nondividend-paying stock early. Indeed, at any given time during its life, a put option should always be exercised early if it is sufficiently deeply in the money.

To illustrate, consider an extreme situation. Suppose that the strike price is $10 and the stock price is virtually zero. By exercising immediately, an investor makes an immediate gain of $10. If the investor waits, the gain from exercise might be less than $10 but it cannot be more than $10, because negative stock prices are impossible. Furthermore, receiving $10 now is preferable to receiving $10 in the future. It follows that the option should be exercised immediately.

It is instructive to consider the following two portfolios:

Portfolio G: one American put option plus one share

Portfolio H: an amount of cash equal to Xe^{-rT}

If the option is exercised at time $t < T$, portfolio G becomes worth X, whereas portfolio H is worth $Xe^{-r(T-t)}$. Portfolio G is therefore worth more than portfolio H. If the option is held to expiration, portfolio G becomes worth

$$\max(X, S_T)$$

whereas portfolio H is worth X. Portfolio G is therefore worth at least as much as, and possibly more than, portfolio H. Note the difference between this situation and the one in the previous section. Here we cannot argue that early exercise is undesirable, because portfolio G looks more attractive than portfolio H regardless of the decision on early exercise.

Like a call option, a put option can be viewed as providing insurance. A put option, when held in conjunction with the stock, insures the holder against the stock price falling below a certain level. However, a put option is different from a call option in that it may be optimal for an investor to forgo this insurance and exercise early in order to realize the strike price immediately. In general, the early exercise of a put option becomes more attractive as S decreases, as r increases, and as the volatility decreases.

It will be recalled from Equation 8.2 that

$$p > Xe^{-rT} - S$$

For an American put with price P, the stronger condition

$$P \geq X - S$$

must always hold, because immediate exercise is always possible.

Figure 8.4 shows the general way in which the price of an American put varies with S. Provided that $r > 0$, it is always optimal to exercise an American put immediately when the stock price is sufficiently low. When early exercise is optimal, the value of the option is $X - S$. The curve representing the value of the put therefore merges into the put's intrinsic value, $X - S$, for a sufficiently small value of S. In Figure 8.4 this value

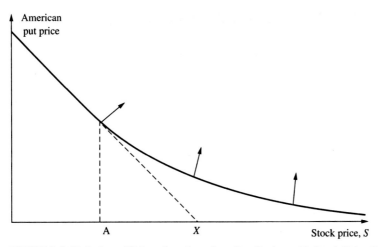

FIGURE 8.4 Variation of Price of an American Put Option with Stock Price S

of S is shown as point A. The value of the put moves in the direction indicated by the arrows when r decreases, when the volatility increases, and when T increases.

Because there are some circumstances when it is desirable to exercise an American put option early, it follows that an American put option is always worth more than the corresponding European put option. Further, because an American put is sometimes worth its intrinsic value (see Figure 8.4), it follows that a European put option must sometimes be worth less than its intrinsic value. Figure 8.5 shows the variation of the European put price with the stock price. Note that point B in Figure 8.5, at which the price of the option is equal to its intrinsic value, must represent a higher value of the stock price than point A in Figure 8.4. Point E in Figure 8.5 is where $S = 0$ and the European put price is Xe^{-rT}.

FIGURE 8.5 Variation of Price of a European Put Option with Stock Price S

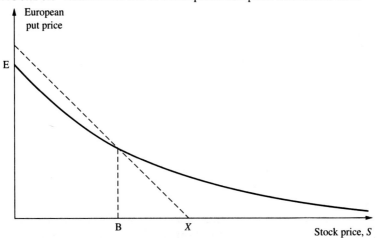

Relationship between American Put and Call Prices

Put–call parity holds only for European options. However, it is possible to derive some relationships for American option prices. From $P > p$ and Equation 8.3 it follows that

$$P > c + Xe^{-rT} - S$$

and from $c = C$,

$$P > C + Xe^{-rT} - S$$

or

$$C - P < S - Xe^{-rT} \tag{8.4}$$

For a further relationship between C and P, consider

Portfolio I: One European call option plus an amount of cash equal to X

Portfolio J: One American put option plus one share

Both options have the same exercise price and expiration date. Assume that the cash in portfolio I is invested at the risk-free interest rate. If the put option is not exercised early, portfolio J is worth

$$\max(S_T, X)$$

at time T. Portfolio I is worth

$$\max(S_T, X) + Xe^{rT} - X$$

at this time. Portfolio I is therefore worth more than portfolio J. Suppose next that the put option in portfolio J is exercised early—say, at time t. Portfolio J is then worth X at time t. However, even if the call option were worthless, portfolio I would be worth Xe^{rt} at time t. It follows that portfolio I is worth more than portfolio J in all circumstances. Hence,

$$c + X > P + S$$

From $c = C$,

$$C + X > P + S$$

or

$$C - P > S - X$$

Combining this with Equation 8.4, we obtain

$$S - X < C - P < S - Xe^{-rT} \tag{8.5}$$

Example

An American call option on a nondividend-paying stock with exercise price $20.00 and maturity in five months is worth $1.50. This must also be the value of a

European call option on the same stock with the same exercise price and maturity. Suppose that the current stock price is $19.00 and the risk-free interest rate is 10 percent per annum. From a rearrangement of Equation 8.3, the price of a European put with exercise price $20 and maturity in five months is

$$1.50 + 20e^{-0.1 \times 5/12} - 19 = \$1.68$$

From Equation 8.5

$$19 - 20 < C - P < 19 - 20e^{-0.1 \times 5/12}$$

or

$$1 > P - C > 0.18$$

showing that $P - C$ lies between $1.00 and $0.18. With C at $1.50, P must lie between $1.68 and $2.50. In other words, upper and lower bounds for the price of an American put with the same strike price and expiration date as the American call are $2.50 and $1.68.

Effect of Dividends

The results produced so far in this chapter have assumed that we are dealing with options on a nondividend-paying stock. In this section we examine the impact of dividends. In the United States exchange-traded stock options generally have less than eight months to maturity. The dividends payable during the life of the option can usually be predicted with reasonable accuracy. We will use D to denote the present value of the dividends during the life of the option. In the calculation of D, a dividend is assumed to occur at the time of its ex-dividend date.

LOWER BOUND FOR CALLS AND PUTS

We can redefine portfolios A and B as follows:

Portfolio A: one European call option plus an amount of cash equal to $D + Xe^{-rT}$

Portfolio B: one share

A similar argument to the one used to derive Equation 8.1 shows that

$$c > S - D - Xe^{-rT} \tag{8.6}$$

We can also redefine portfolios C and D as follows:

Portfolio C: one European put option plus one share

Portfolio D: an amount of cash equal to $D + Xe^{-rT}$

A similar argument to the one used to derive Equation 8.2 shows that

$$p > D + Xe^{-rT} - S \tag{8.7}$$

EARLY EXERCISE

When dividends are expected, we can no longer assert than an American call option will not be exercised early. Sometimes it is optimal to exercise an American call immediately prior to an ex-dividend date. The dividend will cause the stock price to jump down, making the option less attractive. It is never optimal to exercise a call at other times. This point is discussed further in chapter 11.

PUT–CALL PARITY

Comparing the value at time T of the redefined portfolios A and C shows that, with dividends, the put–call parity result in Equation 8.3 becomes

$$c + D + Xe^{-rT} = p + S \tag{8.8}$$

Dividends cause Equation 8.5 to be modified to

$$S - D - X < C - P < S - Xe^{-rT} \tag{8.9}$$

To prove this inequality, we redefine portfolios I and J as

Portfolio I: one European call option plus an amount of cash equal to $D + X$
Portfolio J: one American put option plus a share

Regardless of what happens, it can be shown that portfolio I is worth more than portfolio J. Hence,

$$P + S < c + D + X$$

Because a European call is never worth more than its American counterpart, or $c < C$, it follows that

$$P + S < C + D + X$$

or

$$S - D - X < C - P$$

This proves the first half of the inequality in Equation 8.9. For a nondividend-paying stock, we saw in Equation 8.5 that

$$C - P < S - Xe^{-rT}$$

Since dividends decrease the value of a call and increase the value of a put, this inequality must also be true for options on a dividend-paying stock. This proves the second half of the inequality in Equation 8.9.

Empirical Research

Empirical research to test the results in this chapter might seem to be relatively simple to carry out once the appropriate data have been assembled. In fact, there are a number of complications:

1. It is important to be sure that option prices and stock prices are being observed at exactly the same time. For example, testing for arbitrage opportunities by looking at the price at which the last trade is done each day is inappropriate. This point was made in chapter 7 in connection with the data in Table 7.4.

2. It is important to consider carefully whether a trader could take advantage of any observed arbitrage opportunity. If the opportunity exists only momentarily, there may in practice be no way of exploiting it.

3. Transactions costs must be taken into account when determining whether arbitrage opportunities are possible.

4. Put–call parity holds only for European options. Exchange-traded stock options are American.

5. Dividends to be paid during the life of the option must be estimated.

Some of the empirical research that has been carried out is described in the papers by Bhattacharya, Galai, Gould and Galai, Klemkosky and Resnick, and Stoll, all referenced at the end of this chapter. Galai and Bhattacharya test whether option prices are ever less than their theoretical lower bounds; Stoll, Gould and Galai, and the two papers by Klemkosky and Resnick test whether put–call parity holds. We will consider the results of Bhattacharya and Klemkosky and Resnick.

Bhattacharya's study examined whether the theoretical lower bounds for call options applied in practice. He used data consisting of the transactions prices for options on 58 stocks over a 196-day period between August 1976 and June 1977. The first test examined whether the options satisfied the condition that price be greater than intrinsic value—that is, whether $C > \max(S - X, 0)$. Over 86,000 option prices were examined and about 1.3 percent were found to violate this condition. In 29 percent of the cases, the violation disappeared by the next trade, indicating that in practice traders would not have been able to take advantage of it. When transactions costs were taken into account, the profitable opportunities created by the violation disappeared. Bhattacharya's second test examined whether options sold for more than the lower bound $S - D - Xe^{-rT}$. (See Equation 8.6.) He found that 7.6 percent of his observations did in fact sell for less than this lower bound. However, when transactions costs were taken into account, these did not give rise to profitable opportunities.

Klemkosky and Resnick's tests of put–call parity used data on option prices taken from trades between July 1977 and June 1978. They subjected their data to several tests to determine the likelihood of options being exercised early, and they discarded data for which early exercise was considered probable. In doing so, they felt they were justified in treating American options as European. They identified 540 situations where an arbitrage opportunity similar to that in Table 8.4 existed and 540 situations where an arbitrage opportunity similar to that in Table 8.5 existed. After transactions costs were allowed for, 38 of the Table 8.4 opportunities (call price too low relative to put price) and 147 of the Table 8.5 opportunities (call price too high relative to the put price) were still profitable. The opportunities persisted when either a 5- or a 15-minute delay between the opportunity being noted and trades being executed was assumed. Klemkosky and Resnick's conclusion was that arbitrage opportunities were available to some traders, particularly market makers, during the period they studied.

Summary

There are six factors affecting the value of a stock option: the current stock price, the strike price, the expiration date, the stock price volatility, the risk-free interest rate, and the dividends expected during the life of the option. The value of a call generally increases as the current stock price, the time to expiration, the volatility, and the risk-free interest rate increase. The value of a call decreases as the strike price and expected dividends increase. The value of a put generally increases as the strike price, the time to expiration, the volatility, and the expected dividends increase. The value of a put decreases as the current stock price and the risk-free interest rate increase.

It is possible to reach some conclusions about the value of stock options without making any assumptions about the volatility of stock prices. For example, the price of a call option on a stock must always be worth less than the price of the stock itself. Similarly, the price of a put option on a stock must always be worth less than the option's strike price.

A call option on a nondividend-paying stock must be worth more than

$$\max(S - Xe^{-rT}, 0)$$

where S is the stock price, X is the exercise price, r is the risk-free interest rate, and T is the time to expiration. A put option on a nondividend-paying stock must be worth more than

$$\max(Xe^{-rT} - S, 0)$$

When dividends with present value D will be paid, the lower bound for a call option becomes

$$\max(S - D - Xe^{-rT}, 0)$$

and the lower bound for a put option becomes

$$\max(Xe^{-rT} + D - S, 0)$$

Put–call parity is a relationship between the price, c, of a European call option on a stock and the price, p, of a European put option on a stock. For a nondividend-paying stock, it is

$$c + Xe^{-rT} = p + S$$

For a dividend-paying stock, the put–call parity relationship is

$$c + D + Xe^{-rT} = p + S$$

Put–call parity does not hold for American options. However, it is possible to use arbitrage arguments to obtain upper and lower bounds for the difference between the price of an American call and the price of an American put.

In chapter 11 we will carry the analyses in this chapter further by making specific assumptions about the probabilistic behavior of stock prices. The analysis will enable us to derive exact pricing formulas for European stock options. In chapter 16 we will see how numerical procedures can be used to price American options.

Suggestions for Further Reading

Bhattacharya, M. "Transaction Data Tests of Efficiency of the Chicago Board Options Exchange," *Journal of Financial Economics* 12 (1983): 161–185.

Galai, D. "Empirical Tests of Boundary Conditions for CBOE Options," *Journal of Financial Economics* 6 (1978): 187–211.

Gould, J. P., and D. Galai. "Transactions Costs and the Relationship between Put and Call Prices," *Journal of Financial Economics* 1 (1974): 105–129.

Klemkosky, R. C., and B. G. Resnick. "An Ex-Ante Analysis of Put–Call Parity," *Journal of Financial Economics* 8 (1980): 363–378.

Klemkosky, R. C., and B. G. Resnick. "Put–Call Parity and Market Efficiency," *Journal of Finance* 34 (December 1979): 1141–1155.

Merton, R. C. "The Relationship between Put and Call Prices: Comment," *Journal of Finance* 28 (March 1973): 183–184.

Merton, R. C. "Theory of Rational Option Pricing," *Bell Journal of Economics and Management Science* 4 (Spring 1973): 141–183.

Stoll, H. R. "The Relationship between Put and Call Option Prices," *Journal of Finance* 31 (May 1969): 319–332.

Quiz

1. List the six factors affecting stock option prices.
2. What is a lower bound for the price of a four-month call option on a nondividend-paying stock when the stock price is $28, the strike price is $25, and the risk-free interest rate is 8 percent per annum?
3. What is a lower bound for the price of a one-month European put option on a nondividend-paying stock when the stock price is $12, the strike price is $15, and the risk-free interest rate is 6 percent per annum?
4. Give two reasons that the early exercise of an American call option on a nondividend-paying stock is not optimal. The first reason should involve the time value of money. The second reason should apply even if interest rates are zero.
5. "The early exercise of an American put is a trade-off between the time value of money and the insurance value of a put." Explain this statement.
6. A European call option and put option on a stock both have a strike price of $20 and an expiration date in three months. Both sell for $3. The risk-free interest rate is 10 percent per annum, the current stock price is $19, and a $1 dividend is expected in one month. Identify the arbitrage opportunity open to a trader.
7. Explain why the arguments leading to put–call parity for European options cannot be used to give a similar result for American options.

Questions and Problems

8.1. What is a lower bound for the price of a six-month call option on a nondividend-paying stock when the stock price is $80, the strike price is $75, and the risk-free interest rate is 10 percent per annum?
8.2. What is a lower bound for the price of a two-month European put option on a nondividend-paying stock when the stock price is $58, the strike price is $65, and the risk-free interest rate is 5 percent per annum?

8.3. A four-month European call option on a dividend-paying stock is currently selling for $5. The stock price is $64, the strike price is $60, and a dividend of $0.80 is expected in one month. The risk-free interest rate is 12 percent per annum for all maturities. What opportunities are there for an arbitrageur?

8.4. A one-month European put option on a nondividend-paying stock is currently selling for $2\frac{1}{2}$. The stock price is $47, the strike price is $50, and the risk-free interest rate is 6 percent per annum. What opportunities are there for an arbitrageur?

8.5. Give an intuitive explanation of why the early exercise of an American put becomes more attractive as the risk-free rate increases and volatility decreases.

8.6. The price of a European call which expires in six months and has a strike price of $30 is $2. The underlying stock price is $29, and a dividend of $0.50 is expected in two months and again in five months. The term structure is flat, with all risk-free interest rates being 10 percent. What is the price of a European put option that expires in six months and has a strike price of $30?

8.7. Explain carefully the arbitrage opportunities in Problem 8.6 if the European put price is $3.

8.8. The price of an American call on a nondividend-paying stock is $4. The stock price is $31, the strike price is $30, and the expiration date is in three months. The risk-free interest rate is 8 percent. Derive upper and lower bounds for the price of an American put on the same stock with the same strike price and expiration date.

8.9. Explain carefully the arbitrage opportunities in Problem 8.8 if the American put price is greater than the calculated upper bound.

8.10. Suppose that c_1, c_2, and c_3 are the prices of European call options with strike prices X_1, X_2, and X_3, respectively, where $X_3 > X_2 > X_1$ and $X_3 - X_2 = X_2 - X_1$. All options have the same maturity. Show that

$$c_2 \leq 0.5(c_1 + c_3)$$

(Hint: Consider a portfolio that is long one option with strike price X_1, long one option with strike price X_3, and short two options with strike price X_2.)

8.11. What is the result corresponding to that in Problem 8.10 for European put options?

8.12. Suppose that you are the manager and sole owner of a highly leveraged company. All the debt will mature in one year. If at that time the value of the company is greater than the face value of the debt, you will pay off the debt. If the value of the company is less than the face value of the debt, you will declare bankruptcy and the debt holders will own the company.
   a. Express your position as an option on the value of the company.
   b. Express the position of the debt holders in terms of options on the value of the company.
   c. What can you do to increase the value of your position?

8.13. Use the software DerivaGem to verify that Figures 8.1 and 8.2 are correct. Consider next an up-and-out barrier call option on a stock with the same parameters as the option considered in Figures 8.1 and 8.2 and a barrier at $80. Use the software to value the option and graph the relationship between (a) the option price and the stock price, (b) the option price and the time to maturity, and (c) the option price and the volatility. Explain the reasons for the differences between the results given by the software for the regular option and the up-and-out option.

9

Trading Strategies Involving Options

The profit pattern from an investment in a single stock option is discussed in chapter 7. In this chapter we cover more fully the range of profit patterns obtainable using options. The profit patterns are explained on the assumption that the underlying asset is a stock. However, similar profit patterns can be obtained for other underlying assets such as foreign currencies, stock indices, and futures contracts.

In the first section we consider what happens when a position in a stock option is combined with a position in the stock itself. We then move on to examine the profit patterns obtained when an investment is made in two or more different options on the same stock. One of the attractions of options is that they can be used to create a wide range of different payoff functions. Unless otherwise stated, the options we consider are all European. Toward the end of this chapter, we will see that if European options were available with every single possible strike price, any payoff function could in theory be created.

Strategies Involving a Single Option and a Stock

There are a number of different trading strategies involving a single option on a stock and the stock itself. The profits from these are illustrated in Figure 9.1. In this figure and in other figures throughout this chapter, the dashed line shows the relationship between profit and stock price for the individual securities constituting the portfolio, whereas the solid line shows the relationship between profit and stock price for the whole portfolio.

In Figure 9.1a the portfolio consists of a long position in a stock plus a short position in a call option. The investment strategy represented by this portfolio is known as *writing a covered call*. The long stock position "covers" or protects the investor from the possibility of a sharp rise in the stock price. In Figure 9.1b a short position in a stock is combined with a long position in a call option. This is the reverse of writing a

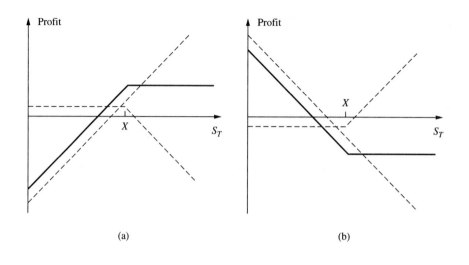

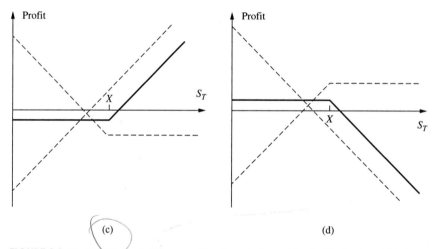

FIGURE 9.1 Profit Patterns. (a) Long position in a stock combined with short position in a call, (b) short position in a stock combined with long position in a call, (c) long position in a put combined with long position in a stock, (d) short position in a put combined with short position in a stock.

covered call. In Figure 9.1c the investment strategy involves buying a put option on a stock and the stock itself. The approach is sometimes referred to as a *protective put strategy*. In Figure 9.1d a short position in a put option is combined with a short position in the stock. This is the reverse of a protective put.

The profit patterns in Figures 9.1a, b, c, and d have the same general shape as the profit patterns discussed in chapter 7 for short put, long put, long call, and short call, respectively. Put–call parity provides a way of understanding why this is so. It will be recalled from chapter 8 that the put–call parity relationship is

$$p + S = c + Xe^{-rT} + D \qquad \textbf{(9.1)}$$

where p is the price of a European put, S is the stock price, c is the price of a European call, X is the strike price of both call and put, r is the risk-free interest rate, T is the time to maturity of both call and put, and D is the present value of the dividends anticipated during the life of the option.

Equation 9.1 shows that a long position in a put combined with a long position in the stock is equivalent to a long call position plus a certain amount ($= Xe^{-rT} + D$) of cash. This explains why the profit pattern in Figure 9.1c is similar to the profit pattern from a long call position. The position in Figure 9.1d is the reverse of that in Figure 9.1c and therefore leads to a profit pattern similar to that from a short call position.

Equation 9.1 can be rearranged to become

$$S - c = Xe^{-rT} + D - p$$

In other words, a long position in a stock combined with a short position in a call is equivalent to a short put position plus a certain amount ($= Xe^{-rT} + D$) of cash. This equality explains why the profit pattern in Figure 9.1a is similar to the profit pattern from a short put position. The position in Figure 9.1b is the reverse of that in Figure 9.1a and therefore leads to a profit pattern similar to that from a long put position.

Spreads

A spread trading strategy involves taking a position in two or more options of the same type (i.e., two or more calls or two or more puts).

BULL SPREADS

One of the most popular types of spreads is a *bull spread*. It can be created by buying a call option on a stock with a certain strike price and selling a call option on the same stock with a higher strike price. Both options have the same expiration date. The strategy is illustrated in Figure 9.2. The profits from the two option positions taken

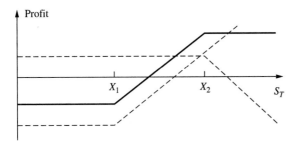

FIGURE 9.2 Bull Spread Created Using Call Options

TABLE 9.1 Payoff from a Bull Spread

Stock Price Range	Payoff from Long Call Option	Payoff from Short Call Option	Total Payoff
$S_T \geq X_2$	$S_T - X_1$	$X_2 - S_T$	$X_2 - X_1$
$X_1 < S_T < X_2$	$S_T - X_1$	0	$S_T - X_1$
$S_T \leq X_1$	0	0	0

separately are shown by the dashed lines. The profit from the whole strategy is the sum of the profits given by the dashed lines and is indicated by the solid line. Since a call price always decreases as the strike price increases, the value of the option sold is always less than the value of the option bought. A bull spread, when created from calls, therefore requires an initial investment.

Suppose that X_1 is the strike price of the call option bought, X_2 is the strike price of the call option sold, and S_T is the stock price on the expiration date of the options. Table 9.1 shows the total payoff that will be realized from a bull spread in different circumstances. If the stock price does well and is greater than the higher strike price, the payoff is the difference between the two strike prices, or $X_2 - X_1$. If the stock price on the expiration date lies between the two strike prices, the payoff is $S_T - X_1$. If the stock price on the expiration date is below the lower strike price, the payoff is zero. The profit in Figure 9.2 is calculated by subtracting the initial investment from the payoff.

A bull spread strategy limits the investor's upside potential as well as downside risk. The strategy can be described by saying that the investor has a call option with a strike price equal to X_1 and has chosen to give up some upside potential by selling a call option with strike price X_2 ($X_2 > X_1$). In return for giving up the upside potential, the investor gets the price of the option with strike price X_2. Three types of bull spreads can be distinguished:

1. Both calls are initially out of the money.
2. One call is initially in the money, the other call is initially out of the money.
3. Both calls are initially in the money.

The most aggressive bull spreads are those of type 1. They cost very little to set up and have a small probability of giving a relatively high payoff ($= X_2 - X_1$). As we move from type 1 to type 2 and from type 2 to type 3, the spreads become more conservative.

Example

An investor buys for $3 a call with a strike price of $30 and sells for $1 a call with a strike price of $35. The payoff from this bull spread strategy is $5 if the stock price is above $35 and zero if it is below $30. If the stock price is between $30 and $35, the payoff is the amount by which the stock price exceeds $30. The cost of

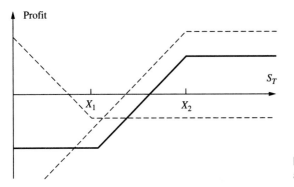

FIGURE 9.3 Bull Spread Created Using Put Options

the strategy is $3 - $1 = 2. The profit is therefore as follows:

Stock Price Range	Profit
$S_T \leq 30$	-2
$30 < S_T < 35$	$S_T - 32$
$S_T \geq 35$	3

Bull spreads can also be created by buying a put with a low strike price and selling a put with a high strike price, as illustrated in Figure 9.3. Unlike the bull spread created from calls, bull spreads created from puts involve a positive cash flow to the investor up front (ignoring margin requirements) and a payoff that is either negative or zero.

BEAR SPREADS

An investor who enters into a bull spread is hoping that the stock price will increase. By contrast, an investor who enters into a *bear spread* is hoping that the stock price will decline. As with a bull spread, a bear spread can be created by buying a call with one strike price and selling a call with another strike price. However, in the case of a bear spread, the strike price of the option purchased is greater than the strike price of the option sold. In Figure 9.4 the profit from the spread is shown by the solid line.

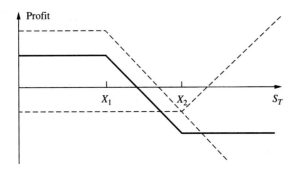

FIGURE 9.4 Bear Spread Created Using Call Options

TABLE 9.2 **Payoff from a Bear Spread**

Stock Price Range	Payoff from Long Call Option	Payoff from Short Call Option	Total Payoff
$S_T \geq X_2$	$S_T - X_2$	$X_1 - S_T$	$-(X_2 - X_1)$
$X_1 < S_T < X_2$	0	$X_1 - S_T$	$-(S_T - X_1)$
$S_T \leq X_1$	0	0	0

A bear spread created from calls involves an initial cash inflow (when margin requirements are ignored), because the price of the call sold is greater than the price of the call purchased.

Assume that the strike prices are X_1 and X_2, with $X_1 < X_2$. Table 9.2 shows the payoff that will be realized from a bear spread in different circumstances. If the stock price is greater than X_2, the payoff is negative at $-(X_2 - X_1)$. If the stock price is less than X_1, the payoff is zero. If the stock price is between X_1 and X_2, the payoff is $-(S_T - X_1)$. The profit is calculated by adding the initial cash inflow to the payoff.

Example

An investor buys for $1 a call with a strike price of $35 and sells for $3 a call with a strike price of $30. The payoff from this bear spread strategy is $-\$5$ if the stock price is above $35 and zero if it is below $30. If the stock price is between $30 and $35, the payoff is $-(S_T - 30)$. The investment generates $3 - \$1 = \$2$ up front. The profit is therefore as follows:

Stock Price Range	Profit
$S_T \leq 30$	$+2$
$30 < S_T < 35$	$32 - S_T$
$S_T \geq 35$	-3

Like bull spreads, bear spreads limit both the upside profit potential and the downside risk. Bear spreads can be created using puts instead of calls. The investor buys a put with a high strike price and sells a put with a low strike price, as illustrated in Figure 9.5. Bear spreads created with puts require an initial investment. In essence, the investor has bought a put with a certain strike price and chosen to give up some of the profit potential by selling a put with a lower strike price. In return for the profit given up, the investor gets the price of the option sold.

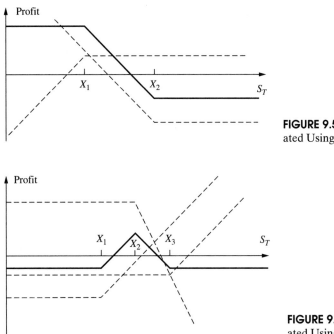

FIGURE 9.5 Bear Spread Created Using Put Options

FIGURE 9.6 Butterfly Spread Created Using Call Options

BUTTERFLY SPREADS

A *butterfly spread* involves positions in options with three different strike prices. It can be created by buying a call option with a relatively low strike price, X_1; buying a call option with a relatively high strike price, X_3; and selling two call options with a strike price, X_2, halfway between X_1 and X_3. Generally X_2 is close to the current stock price. The pattern of profits from the strategy is shown in Figure 9.6. A butterfly spread leads to a profit if the stock price stays close to X_2 but gives rise to a small loss if there is a significant stock price move in either direction. It is therefore an appropriate strategy for an investor who feels that large stock price moves are unlikely. The strategy requires a small investment initially. The payoff from a butterfly spread is shown in Table 9.3.

Suppose that a certain stock is currently worth $61. Consider an investor who feels that a significant price move is unlikely in the next six months. Suppose that the market prices of six-month calls are as follows:

Strike Price ($)	Call Price ($)
55	10
60	7
65	5

The investor could create a butterfly spread by buying one call with a $55 strike price, buying one call with a $65 strike price, and selling two calls with a $60 strike price.

TABLE 9.3 Payoff from a Butterfly Spread

Stock Price Range	Payoff from First Long Call	Payoff from Second Long Call	Payoff from Short Calls	Total Payoff*
$S_T < X_1$	0	0	0	0
$X_1 < S_T < X_2$	$S_T - X_1$	0	0	$S_T - X_1$
$X_2 < S_T < X_3$	$S_T - X_1$	0	$-2(S_T - X_2)$	$X_3 - S_T$
$S_T > X_3$	$S_T - X_1$	$S_T - X_3$	$-2(S_T - X_2)$	0

*These payoffs are calculated using the relationship $X_2 = 0.5(X_1 + X_3)$.

It costs $10 + \$5 - (2 \times \$7) = \$1$ to create the spread. If the stock price in six months is greater than $65 or less than $55, there is no payoff and the investor incurs a net loss of $1. If the stock price is between $56 and $64, a profit is made. The maximum profit, $4, occurs when the stock price in six months is $60. The example is summarized in Table 9.4.

Butterfly spreads can be created using put options. The investor buys a put with a low strike price, buys a put with a high strike price, and sells two puts with an intermediate strike price, as illustrated in Figure 9.7. The butterfly spread in the example just considered would be created by buying a put with a strike price of $55, buying a put with a strike price of $65, and selling two puts with a strike price of $60. If all options are European, the use of put options results in exactly the same spread as the use of

TABLE 9.4 Use of Butterfly Spread

From the Trader's Desk

A stock is currently selling for $61. The prices of call options expiring in six months are quoted as follows:

> Strike price = $55, call price = $10
> Strike price = $60, call price = $7
> Strike price = $65, call price = $5

An investor feels it is unlikely that the stock price will move significantly in the next six months.

Strategy

The investor sets up a butterfly spread:

1. Buy one call with a $55 strike.
2. Buy one call with a $65 strike.
3. Sell two calls with a $60 strike.

The cost is $10 + \$5 - (2 \times \$7) = \$1$. The strategy leads to a net loss (maximum $1) if the stock price moves outside the $56-to-$64 range but leads to a profit if it stays within this range. The maximum profit of $4 is realized if the stock price is $60 on the expiration date.

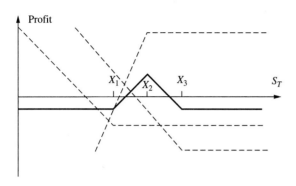

FIGURE 9.7 Butterfly Spread Created Using Put Options

call options. Put–call parity can be used to show that the initial investment is the same in both cases.

A butterfly spread can be sold or shorted by following the reverse strategy. Options are sold with strike prices of X_1 and X_3, and two options with the middle strike price X_2 are purchased. This strategy produces a modest profit if there is a significant movement in the stock price.

CALENDAR SPREADS

Up to now we have assumed that the options used to create a spread all expire at the same time. We now move on to *calendar spreads,* in which the options have the same strike price and different expiration dates.

A calendar spread can be created by selling a call option with a certain strike price and buying a longer-maturity call option with the same strike price. The longer the maturity of an option, the more expensive it is. A calendar spread therefore requires an initial investment. Assuming that the long-maturity option is sold when the short-maturity option expires, the profit pattern given by a calendar spread is as shown in Figure 9.8. The pattern is similar to the profit from the butterfly spread in Figure 9.6. The

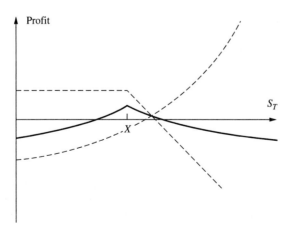

FIGURE 9.8 Calendar Spread Created Using Two Calls

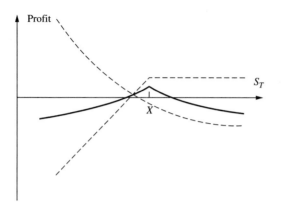

FIGURE 9.9 Calendar Spread
Created Using Two Puts

investor makes a profit if the stock price at the expiration of the short-maturity option is close to the strike price of the short-maturity option. However, a loss is incurred when the stock price is significantly above or significantly below this strike price.

To understand the profit pattern from a calendar spread, first consider what happens if the stock price is very low when the short-maturity option expires. The short-maturity option is worthless and the value of the long-maturity option is close to zero. The investor therefore incurs a loss that is only a little less than the cost of setting up the spread initially. Consider next what happens if the stock price, S_T, is very high when the short-maturity option expires. The short-maturity option costs the investor $S_T - X$, and the long-maturity option (assuming early exercise is not optimal) is worth a little more than $S_T - X$, where X is the strike price of the options. Again, the investor makes a net loss that is a little less than the cost of setting up the spread initially. If S_T is close to X, the short-maturity option costs the investor either a small amount or nothing at all. However, the long-maturity option is still quite valuable. In this case a significant net profit is made.

In a *neutral calendar spread* a strike price close to the current stock price is chosen. A *bullish calendar spread* involves a higher strike price, whereas a *bearish calendar spread* involves a lower strike price.

Calendar spreads can be created with put options as well as call options. The investor buys a long-maturity put option and sells a short-maturity put option. As shown in Figure 9.9, the profit pattern is similar to that obtained from using calls.

A *reverse calendar spread* is the opposite to that in Figures 9.8 and 9.9. The investor buys a short-maturity option and sells a long-maturity option. A small profit arises if the stock price at the expiration of the short-maturity option is well above or well below the strike price of the short-maturity option. However, a significant loss results if it is close to the strike price.

DIAGONAL SPREADS

Bull, bear, and calendar spreads can all be created from a long position in one call and a short position in another call. In the case of bull and bear spreads, the calls have different strike prices and the same expiration date. In the case of calendar spreads,

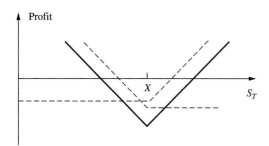

FIGURE 9.10 A Straddle

the calls have the same strike price and different expiration dates. In a *diagonal spread* both the expiration date and the strike price of the calls are different. There are several different types of diagonal spreads. Their profit patterns are generally variations on the profit patterns from the corresponding bull or bear spreads.

Combinations

A *combination* is an option trading strategy that involves taking a position in both calls and puts on the same stock. We will consider straddles, strips, straps, and strangles.

STRADDLE

One popular combination is a *straddle,* which involves buying a call and put with the same strike price and expiration date. The profit pattern is shown in Figure 9.10. The strike price is denoted by X. If the stock price is close to this strike price at expiration of the options, the straddle leads to a loss. However, if there is a sufficiently large move in either direction, a significant profit will result. The payoff from a straddle is calculated in Table 9.5.

A straddle is appropriate when an investor is expecting a large move in a stock price but does not know in which direction the move will be. Consider an investor who feels that the price of a certain stock, currently valued at $69 by the market, will move significantly in the next three months. The investor could create a straddle by buying both a put and a call with a strike price of $70 and an expiration date in three months. Suppose that the call costs $4 and the put costs $3. If the stock price stays at $69, it is easy to see that the strategy costs the investor $6. (An up-front investment of $7 is required, the call expires worthless, and the put expires worth $1.) If the stock price moves

TABLE 9.5 Payoff from a Straddle

Range of Stock Price	Payoff from Call	Payoff from Put	Total Payoff
$S_T \leq X$	0	$X - S_T$	$X - S_T$
$S_T > X$	$S_T - X$	0	$S_T - X$

TABLE 9.6   Use of a Straddle

From the Trader's Desk
A stock is currently trading at $69. A three-month call with a strike price of $70 costs $4, whereas a three-month put with the same strike price costs $3. An investor feels that the stock price is likely to experience a significant jump (either up or down) in the next three months.

The Strategy
The trader buys both the put and the call. The worst that can happen is that the stock price is $70 in three months. In this case the strategy costs $7. The farther away from $70 the stock price is, the more profitable the strategy becomes. For example, if the stock price is $90, the strategy leads to a profit of $13. If the stock price is $55, the strategy leads to a profit of $8.

---

to $70, a loss of $7 is experienced. (This is the worst that can happen.) However, if the stock price jumps up to $90, a profit of $13 is made; if the stock moves down to $55, a profit of $8 is made; and so on. The example is summarized in Table 9.6.

For a straddle to be an effective strategy, the investor's beliefs about the stock must be different from those of most other market participants. If the general view of the market is that there will be a large jump in the stock price, that view will be reflected in the prices of options. The investor will find options on the stock to be significantly more expensive than those on a similar stock for which no jump is expected. (The point is explored further in chapter 17.)

The straddle in Figure 9.10 is sometimes referred to as a *bottom straddle* or *straddle purchase*. A *top straddle* or *straddle write* is the reverse position. It is created by selling a call and a put with the same exercise price and expiration date. It is a highly risky strategy. If the stock price on the expiration date is close to the strike price, a significant profit results. However, the loss arising from a large move in either direction is unlimited.

STRIPS AND STRAPS

A *strip* consists of a long position in one call and two puts with the same strike price and expiration date. A *strap* consists of a long position in two calls and one put with the same strike price and expiration date. The profit patterns from strips and straps are shown in Figure 9.11. In a strip the investor is betting that there will be a big stock price move and considers a decrease in the stock price to be more likely than an increase. In a strap the investor is also betting that there will be a big stock price move. However, in this case, an increase in the stock price is considered to be more likely than a decrease.

STRANGLES

In a *strangle,* sometimes called a *bottom vertical combination,* an investor buys a put and a call with the same expiration date and different strike prices. The profit pattern that is obtained is shown in Figure 9.12. The call strike price, X_2, is higher than the put strike price, X_1. The payoff function for a strangle is calculated in Table 9.7.

A strangle is a similar strategy to a straddle. The investor is betting that there will be a large price move but is uncertain whether it will be an increase or a decrease. Comparing Figures 9.12 and 9.10, we see that the stock price has to move farther in a strangle than in a straddle for the investor to make a profit. However, the downside risk if the stock price ends up at a central value is less with a strangle.

The profit pattern obtained with a strangle depends on how close together the strike prices are. The farther they are apart, the less the downside risk and the farther the stock price has to move for a profit to be realized.

The sale of a strangle is sometimes referred to as a *top vertical combination*. It can be appropriate for an investor who feels that large stock price moves are unlikely. However, as with the sale of a straddle, it is a risky strategy involving unlimited potential loss to the investor.

FIGURE 9.11 Profit Patterns
(a) Strip; (b) strap.

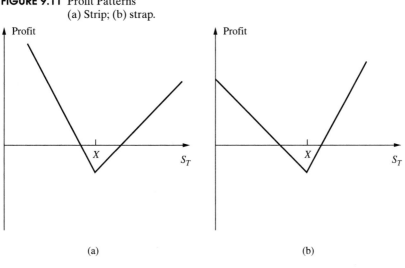

(a)   (b)

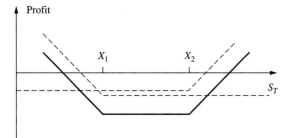

FIGURE 9.12 A Strangle

TABLE 9.7	Payoff from a Strangle		
Range of Stock Price	*Payoff from Call*	*Payoff from Put*	*Total Payoff*
$S_T \leq X_1$	0	$X_1 - S_T$	$X_1 - S_T$
$X_1 < S_T < X_2$	0	0	0
$S_T \geq X_2$	$S_T - X_2$	0	$S_T - X_2$

Other Payoffs

This chapter has demonstrated just a few of the ways in which options can be used to produce an interesting relationship between profit and stock price. If European options expiring at time T were available with every single possible strike price, any payoff function at time T could in theory be obtained. The easiest illustration of this involves a series of butterfly spreads. Recall that a butterfly spread is created by buying options with strike prices X_1 and X_3 and selling two options with strike price X_2 where $X_1 < X_2 < X_3$ and $X_3 - X_2 = X_2 - X_1$. Figure 9.13 shows the payoff from a butterfly spread. The pattern could be described as a spike. As X_1 and X_3 move closer together, the spike becomes smaller. Through the judicious combination of a large number of very small spikes, any payoff function can be approximated.

Summary

A number of common trading strategies involve a single option and the underlying stock. For example, writing a covered call involves buying the stock and selling a call option on the stock; a protective put involves buying a put option and buying the stock. The former is similar to selling a put option; the latter is similar to buying a call option.

Spreads involve either taking a position in two or more calls or taking a position in two or more puts. A bull spread can be created by buying a call (put) with a low strike price and selling a call (put) with a high strike price. A bear spread can be created by buying a call (put) with a high strike price and selling a call (put) with a low strike price. A butterfly spread involves buying calls (puts) with a low and high strike price and selling two calls (puts) with some intermediate strike price. A calendar spread involves selling a call (put) with a short time to expiration and buying a call (put) with a longer

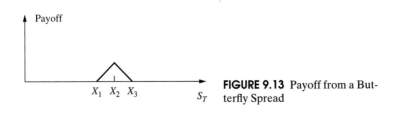

FIGURE 9.13 Payoff from a Butterfly Spread

time to expiration. A diagonal spread involves a long position in one option and a short position in another option such that both the strike price and the expiration date are different.

Combinations involve taking a position in both calls and puts on the same stock. A straddle combination involves taking a long position in a call and a long position in a put with the same strike price and expiration date. A strip consists of a long position in one call and two puts with the same strike price and expiration date. A strap consists of a long position in two calls and one put with the same strike price and expiration date. A strangle consists of a long position in a call and a put with different strike prices and the same expiration date. There are many other ways in which options can be used to produce interesting payoffs. It is not surprising that option trading has steadily increased in popularity and continues to fascinate investors.

Suggestions for Further Reading

Bookstaber, R. M. *Option Pricing and Strategies in Investing.* Reading, MA: Addison-Wesley, 1981.

Chance, D. M. *An Introduction to Options and Futures.* Orlando, FL: Dryden Press, 1989.

Degler, W. H., and H. P. Becker. "19 Option Strategies and When to Use Them," *Futures* (June 1984).

Gastineau, G. *The Stock Options Manual.* 2d ed. New York: McGraw-Hill, 1979.

McMillan, L. G. *Options as a Strategic Investment.* 2d ed. New York: New York Institute of Finance, 1986.

Slivka, R. "Call Option Spreading," *Journal of Portfolio Management* 7 (Spring 1981): 71–76.

Welch, W. W. *Strategies for Put and Call Option Trading.* Cambridge, MA: Winthrop, 1982.

Yates, J. W., and R. W. Kopprasch. "Writing Covered Call Options: Profits and Risks," *Journal of Portfolio Management* 6 (Fall 1980): 74–80.

Quiz

1. What is meant by a protective put? What position in call options is equivalent to a protective put?
2. Explain two ways in which a bear spread can be created.
3. When is it appropriate for an investor to purchase a butterfly spread?
4. Call options on a stock are available with strike prices of $15, $17\frac{1}{2}$, and $20 and expiration dates in three months. Their prices are $4, $2, and $\frac{1}{2}$, respectively. Explain how the options can be used to create a butterfly spread. Construct a table showing how profit varies with stock price for the butterfly spread.
5. What trading strategy creates a reverse calendar spread?
6. What is the difference between a strangle and a straddle?
7. A call option with a strike price of $50 costs $2. A put option with a strike price of $45 costs $3. Explain how a strangle can be created from these two options. What is the pattern of profits from the strangle?

Questions and Problems

9.1. Use put–call parity to relate the initial investment for a bull spread using calls to the initial investment for a bull spread using puts.

9.2. Explain how an aggressive bear spread can be created using put options.

9.3. Suppose that put options on a stock with strike prices $30 and $35 cost $4 and $7, respectively. How can the options be used to create (a) a bull spread and (b) a bear spread? Construct a table that shows the profit and payoff for both spreads.

9.4. Three put options on a stock have the same expiration date and strike prices of $55, $60, and $65. The market prices are $3, $5, and $8, respectively. Explain how a butterfly spread can be created. Construct a table showing the profit from the strategy. For what range of stock prices would the butterfly spread lead to a loss?

9.5. Use put–call parity to show that the cost of a butterfly spread created from European puts is identical to the cost of a butterfly spread created from European calls.

9.6. A diagonal spread is created by buying a call with strike price X_2 and exercise date T_2 and selling a call with strike price X_1 and exercise date T_1 ($T_2 > T_1$). Draw a diagram showing the profit when (a) $X_2 > X_1$ and (b) $X_2 < X_1$.

9.7. A call with a strike price of $60 costs $6. A put with the same strike price and expiration date costs $4. Construct a table that shows the profit from a straddle. For what range of stock prices would the straddle lead to a loss?

9.8. Construct a table showing the payoff from a bull spread when puts with strike prices X_1 and X_2 are used ($X_2 > X_1$).

9.9. An investor believes that there will be a big jump in a stock price but is uncertain as to the direction. Identify six different strategies the investor can follow and explain the differences among them.

9.10. How can a forward contract on a stock with a certain delivery price and delivery date be created from options?

9.11. A box spread is a combination of a bull call spread with strike prices X_1 and X_2 and a bear put spread with the same strike prices. The expiration dates of all options are the same. What are the characteristics of a box spread?

9.12. What is the result if the strike price of the put is higher than the strike price of the call in a strangle?

9.13. Draw a diagram showing the variation of an investor's profit and loss with the terminal stock price for a portfolio consisting of:
   a. One share and a short position in one call option
   b. Two shares and a short position in one call option
   c. One share and a short position in two call options
   d. One share and a short position in four call options

   In each case, assume that the call option has an exercise price equal to the current stock price.

9.14. One deutschemark is currently worth $0.64. A one-year butterfly spread is set up using European call options with strike prices of $0.60, $0.65, and $0.70. The risk-free interest rates in the United States and Germany are 5 percent and 4 percent, respectively, and the volatility of the exchange rate is 15 percent. Use the DerivaGem software to calculate the cost of setting up the butterfly spread position. Show that the cost is the same if European put options are used instead of European call options.

CHAPTER 10

An Introduction to Binomial Trees

A useful and very popular technique for pricing a stock option involves constructing a *binomial tree*. This is a diagram which represents different possible paths that might be followed by the stock price over the life of the option. In this chapter we will take a first look at binomial trees and their relationship to an important principle known as risk-neutral valuation. The general approach adopted here is similar to that in an important paper published by Cox, Ross, and Rubinstein in 1979.

The material in this chapter is intended to be introductory. More details on how numerical procedures involving binomial trees can be implemented are in chapter 16.

A One-Step Binomial Model

We start by considering a very simple situation: A stock price is currently $20, and it is known that at the end of three months the stock price will be either $22 or $18. We are interested in valuing a European call option to buy the stock for $21 in three months. This option will have one of two values at the end of the three months. If the stock price turns out to be $22, the value of the option will be $1; if the stock price turns out to be $18, the value of the option will be zero. The situation is illustrated in Figure 10.1.

It turns out that a relatively simple argument can be used to price the option in this example. The only assumption needed is that no arbitrage opportunities exist. We set up a portfolio of the stock and the option in such a way that there is no uncertainty about the value of the portfolio at the end of the three months. We then argue that, because the portfolio has no risk, the return earned on it must equal the risk-free interest rate. We can then work out the cost of setting up the portfolio and therefore the option's price. Since there are two securities (the stock and the stock option) and only two possible outcomes, it is always possible to set up the riskless portfolio.

233

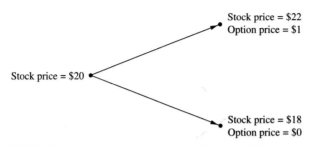

FIGURE 10.1 Stock Price Movements in Numerical Example

Consider a portfolio consisting of a long position in Δ shares of the stock and a short position in one call option. We will calculate the value of Δ that makes the portfolio riskless. If the stock price moves up from $20 to $22, the value of the shares is 22Δ and the value of the option is 1, so that the total value of the portfolio is 22Δ − 1. If the stock price moves down from $20 to $18, the value of the shares is 18Δ and the value of the option is zero, so that the total value of the portfolio is 18Δ. The portfolio is riskless if the value of Δ is chosen so that the final value of the portfolio is the same for both alternatives. This means

$$22\Delta - 1 = 18\Delta$$

or

$$\Delta = 0.25$$

A riskless portfolio is therefore

Long: 0.25 shares

Short: 1 option

If the stock price moves up to $22, the value of the portfolio is

$$22 \times 0.25 - 1 = 4.5$$

If the stock price moves down to $18, the value of the portfolio is

$$18 \times 0.25 = 4.5$$

Regardless of whether the stock price moves up or down, the value of the portfolio is always 4.5 at the end of the life of the option.

Riskless portfolios must, in the absence of arbitrage opportunities, earn the risk-free rate of interest. Suppose that in this case the risk-free rate is 12 percent per annum. It follows that the value of the portfolio today must be the present value of 4.5, or

$$4.5e^{-0.12 \times 0.25} = 4.367$$

The value of the stock price today is known to be $20. Suppose the option price is denoted by f. The value of the portfolio today is therefore

$$20 \times 0.25 - f = 5 - f$$

It follows that

$$5 - f = 4.367$$

or

$$f = 0.633$$

This shows that, in the absence of arbitrage opportunities, the current value of the option must be 0.633. If the value of the option were more than 0.633, the portfolio would cost less than 4.367 to set up and would earn more than the risk-free rate. If the value of the option were less than 0.633, shorting the portfolio would provide a way of borrowing money at less than the risk-free rate.

A GENERALIZATION

We can generalize the argument just presented by considering a stock whose price is S and an option on the stock whose current price is f. We suppose that the option lasts for time T and that during the life of the option the stock price can either move up from S to a new level, Su, or down from S to a new level, Sd $(u > 1; d < 1)$. The proportional increase in the stock price when there is an up movement is $u - 1$; the proportional decrease when there is a down movement is $1 - d$. If the stock price moves up to Su, we suppose that the payoff from the option is f_u; if the stock price moves down to Sd, we suppose the payoff from the option is f_d. The situation is illustrated in Figure 10.2.

As before, we imagine a portfolio consisting of a long position in Δ shares and a short position in one option. We calculate the value of Δ that makes the portfolio riskless. If there is an up movement in the stock price, the value of the portfolio at the end of the life of the option is

$$Su\Delta - f_u$$

If there is a down movement in the stock price, the value becomes

$$Sd\,\Delta - f_d$$

The two are equal when

$$Su\Delta - f_u = Sd\,\Delta - f_d$$

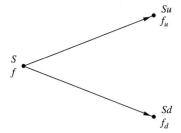

FIGURE 10.2 Stock and Options Prices in a General One-Step Tree

or

$$\Delta = \frac{f_u - f_d}{Su - Sd}$$ (10.1)

In this case the portfolio is riskless and must earn the risk-free interest rate. Equation 10.1 shows that Δ is the ratio of the change in the option price to the change in the stock price as we move between the nodes.

If we denote the risk-free interest rate by r, the present value of the portfolio is

$$[Su\Delta - f_u]e^{-rT}$$

The cost of setting up the portfolio is

$$S\Delta - f$$

It follows that

$$S\Delta - f = [Su\Delta - f_u]e^{-rT}$$

Substituting from Equation 10.1 for Δ and simplifying, we can reduce this equation to

$$f = e^{-rT}[pf_u + (1 - p)f_d]$$ (10.2)

where

$$p = \frac{e^{rT} - d}{u - d}$$ (10.3)

Equations 10.2 and 10.3 enable an option to be priced using a one-step binomial model.

In the numerical example considered previously (see Figure 10.1), $u = 1.1, d = 0.9, r = 0.12, T = 0.25, f_u = 1$, and $f_d = 0$. From Equation 10.3,

$$p = \frac{e^{0.12 \times 0.25} - 0.9}{1.1 - 0.9} = 0.6523$$

and from Equation 10.2,

$$f = e^{-0.12 \times 0.25}[0.6523 \times 1 + 0.3477 \times 0] = 0.633$$

The result agrees with the answer obtained earlier in this section.

IRRELEVANCE OF THE STOCK'S EXPECTED RETURN

The option pricing formula in Equation 10.2 does not involve the probabilities of the stock price moving up or down. For example, we get the same option price when the probability of an upward movement is 0.5 as we do when it is 0.9. This is surprising and seems counterintuitive. It is natural to assume that, as the probability of an upward movement in the stock price increases, the value of a call option on the stock increases and the value of a put option on the stock decreases. Such is not the case.

The key reason is that we are not valuing the option in absolute terms. We are calculating its value in terms of the price of the underlying stock. The probabilities of future up or down movements are already incorporated into the price of the stock. It turns out that we do not need to take them into account again when valuing the option in terms of the stock price.

Risk-Neutral Valuation

Although we do not need to make any assumptions about the probabilities of up and down movements in order to derive Equation 10.2, it is natural to interpret the variable p in Equation 10.2 as the probability of an up movement in the stock price. The variable $1 - p$ is then the probability of a down movement, and the expression

$$pf_u + (1 - p)f_d$$

is the expected payoff from the option. With this interpretation of p, Equation 10.2 then states that the value of the option today is its expected future value discounted at the risk-free rate.

We now investigate the expected return from the stock when the probability of an up movement is assumed to be p. The expected stock price at time T, $E(S_T)$, is given by

$$E(S_T) = pSu + (1 - p)Sd$$

or

$$E(S_T) = pS(u - d) + Sd$$

Substituting from Equation 10.3 for p, we obtain

$$E(S_T) = Se^{rT} \tag{10.4}$$

showing that the stock price grows on average at the risk-free rate. Setting the probability of the up movement equal to p is therefore equivalent to assuming that the return on the stock equals the risk-free rate.

In a *risk-neutral world* all individuals are indifferent to risk. In such a world investors require no compensation for risk, and the expected return on all securities is the risk-free interest rate. Equation 10.4 shows that we are assuming a risk-neutral world when we set the probability of an up movement to p. Equation 10.2 shows that the value of the option is its expected payoff in a risk-neutral world discounted at the risk-free rate.

This result is an example of an important general principle in option pricing known as *risk-neutral valuation*. The principle states that we can with complete impunity assume the world is risk neutral when pricing options. The resulting prices are correct not just in a risk-neutral world, but in other worlds as well.

THE ONE-STEP BINOMIAL EXAMPLE REVISITED

To illustrate the principle of risk-neutral valuation, consider again the example in Figure 10.1. The stock price is currently $20 and will move either up to $22 or down to $18 at the end of three months. The option considered is a European call option with a strike price of $21 and an expiration date in three months. The risk-free interest rate is 12 percent per annum.

We define p as the probability of an upward movement in the stock price in a risk-neutral world. We can calculate p from Equation 10.3. Alternatively we can argue that the expected return on the stock in a risk-neutral world must be the risk-free rate of 12 percent. This means that p must satisfy

$$22p + 18(1 - p) = 20e^{0.12 \times 0.25}$$

or

$$4p = 20e^{0.12 \times 0.25} - 18$$

That is, p must be 0.6523.

At the end of the three months, the call option has a 0.6523 probability of being worth 1 and a 0.3477 probability of being worth zero. Its expected value is therefore

$$0.6523 \times 1 + 0.3477 \times 0 = 0.6523$$

Discounted at the risk-free rate, the value of the option today is

$$0.6523e^{-0.12 \times 0.25}$$

or $0.633. This is the same as the value obtained earlier, demonstrating that no-arbitrage arguments and risk-neutral valuation give the same answer.

Two-Step Binomial Trees

We can extend the analysis to a two-step binomial tree such as that shown in Figure 10.3. Here the stock price starts at $20 and in each of two time steps may go up by 10 percent

FIGURE 10.3 Stock Prices in a Two-Step Tree

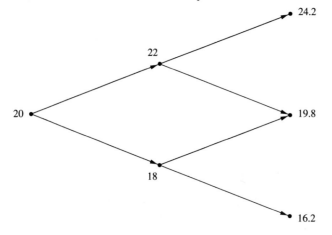

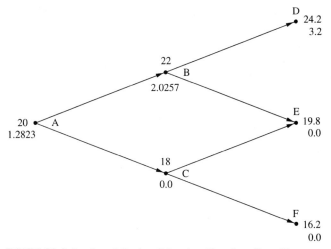

FIGURE 10.4 Stock and Option Prices in a Two-Step Tree. The upper number at each node is the stock price; the lower number is the option price.

or down by 10 percent. We suppose that each time step is three months long and the risk-free interest rate is 12 percent per annum. As before, we consider an option with a strike price of $21.

   The objective of the analysis is to calculate the option price at the initial node of the tree. This can be done by repeatedly applying the principles established earlier in the chapter. Figure 10.4 shows the same tree as Figure 10.3, but with both the stock price and the option price at each node. (The stock price is the upper number and the option price is the lower number.) The option prices at the final nodes of the tree are easily calculated. They are the payoffs from the option. At node D the stock price is 24.2 and the option price is $24.2 - 21 = 3.2$; at nodes E and F the option is out of the money and its value is zero.

   At node C the option price is zero, because node C leads to either node E or node F and at both nodes the option price is zero. We calculate the option price at node B by focusing our attention on the part of the tree shown in Figure 10.5. The notation

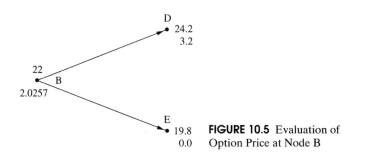

FIGURE 10.5 Evaluation of Option Price at Node B

introduced earlier in the chapter ($u = 1.1$, $d = 0.9$, $r = 0.12$, and $T = 0.25$, so that $p = 0.6523$) and Equation 10.2 give the value of the option at node B as

$$e^{-0.12 \times 0.25}[0.6523 \times 3.2 + 0.3477 \times 0] = 2.0257$$

It remains for us to calculate to option price at the initial node A. We do so by focusing on the first step of the tree. We know that the value of the option at node B is 2.0257 and that at node C it is zero. Equation 10.2 therefore gives the value at node A as

$$e^{-0.12 \times 0.25}[0.6523 \times 2.0257 + 0.3477 \times 0] = 1.2823$$

The value of the option is $1.2823.

Note that this example was constructed so that u and d (the proportional up and down movements) were the same at each node of the tree and so that the time steps were of the same length. As a result, the risk-neutral probability, p, as calculated by Equation 10.3, is the same at each node.

A GENERALIZATION

We can generalize the case of two time steps by considering the situation in Figure 10.6. The stock price is initially S. During each time step, it either moves up to u times its initial value or moves down to d times its initial value. The notation for the value of the option is shown on the tree. (For example, after two up movements the value of the option is f_{uu}.) We suppose that the risk-free interest rate is r and the length of the time step is ΔT years.

Repeated application of Equation 10.2 gives

$$f_u = e^{-r\Delta T}[pf_{uu} + (1 - p)f_{ud}] \tag{10.5}$$

FIGURE 10.6 Stock and Options Prices in a General Two-Step Tree

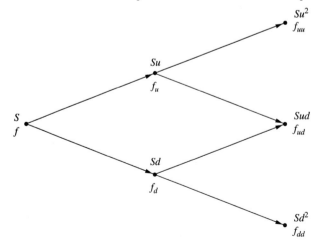

$$f_d = e^{-r\Delta T}[pf_{ud} + (1-p)f_{dd}] \qquad \textbf{(10.6)}$$

$$f = e^{-r\Delta T}[pf_u + (1-p)f_d] \qquad \textbf{(10.7)}$$

Substituting from Equations 10.5 and 10.6 in 10.7, we get

$$f = e^{-2r\Delta T}[p^2 f_{uu} + 2p(1-p)f_{ud} + (1-p)^2 f_{dd}] \qquad \textbf{(10.8)}$$

This is consistent with the principle of risk-neutral valuation mentioned earlier. The variables p^2, $2p(1-p)$, and $(1-p)^2$ are the probabilities that the upper, middle, and lower final nodes will be reached. The option price is equal to its expected payoff in a risk-neutral world discounted at the risk-free interest rate.

If we generalize the use of binomial trees still further by adding more steps, we find that the risk-neutral valuation principle continues to hold. The option price is always equal to its expected payoff in a risk-neutral world, discounted at the risk-free interest rate.

A Put Example

The procedures described in this chapter can be used to price any derivative dependent on a stock whose price changes are binomial. Consider a two-year European put with a strike price of $52 on a stock whose current price is $50. We suppose that there are two time steps of one year, and in each time step the stock price either moves up by a proportional amount of 20 percent or moves down by a proportional amount of 20 percent. We also suppose that the risk-free interest rate is 5 percent.

The tree is shown in Figure 10.7. The value of the risk-neutral probability, p, is given by

$$p = \frac{e^{0.05 \times 1} - 0.8}{1.2 - 0.8} = 0.6282$$

The possible final stock prices are $72, $48, and $32. In this case $f_{uu} = 0$, $f_{ud} = 4$, and $f_{dd} = 20$. From Equation 10.8,

$$f = e^{-2 \times 0.05 \times 1}[0.6282^2 \times 0 + 2 \times 0.6282 \times 0.3718 \times 4 + 0.3718^2 \times 20] = 4.1923$$

The value of the put is $4.1923. This result can also be obtained using Equation 10.2 and working back through the tree one step at a time. Figure 10.7 shows the intermediate option prices that are calculated.

American Options

Up to now all the options we have considered have been European. We now move on to consider how American options can be valued using a binomial tree such as that in Figures 10.4 or 10.7. The procedure is to work back through the tree from the end to the beginning, testing at each node to see whether early exercise is optimal. The value

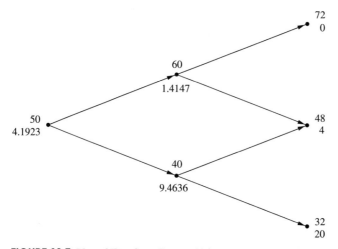

FIGURE 10.7 Use of Two-Step Tree to Value European Put Option. At each node the upper number is the stock price; the lower number is the option price.

of the option at the final nodes is the same as for the European option. At earlier nodes the value of the option is the greater of

1. The value given by Equation 10.2
2. The payoff from early exercise

As an illustration, we consider how Figure 10.7 is affected if the option under consideration is American rather than European. The stock prices and their probabilities are unchanged. The values for the option at the final nodes are also unchanged. At node B, Equation 10.2 gives the value of the option as 1.4147, whereas the payoff from early exercise is negative ($= -8$). Clearly early exercise is not optimal at node B and the value of the option at this node is 1.4147. At node C, Equation 10.2 gives the value of the option as 9.4636, whereas the payoff from early exercise is 12. In this case early exercise is optimal and the value of the option at the node is 12. At the initial node A, the value given by Equation 10.2 is

$$e^{-0.05 \times 1}[0.6282 \times 1.4147 + 0.3718 \times 12.0] = 5.0894$$

and the payoff from early exercise is 2. In this case early exercise is not optimal. The value of the option is therefore $5.0894. Figure 10.8 shows the new tree values.

More details on the use of binomial trees to value American options are given in chapter 16.

Delta

At this stage it is appropriate to discuss *delta*, an important parameter in the pricing and hedging of options.

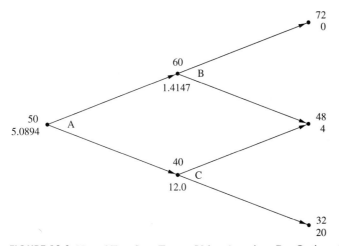

FIGURE 10.8 Use of Two-Step Tree to Value American Put Option. At each node the upper number is the stock price; the lower number is the option price.

The delta of a stock option is the ratio of the change in the price of the stock option to the change in the price of the underlying stock. It is the number of units of the stock we should hold for each option shorted in order to create a riskless hedge. It is the same as the Δ introduced earlier in this chapter. The construction of a riskless hedge is sometimes referred to as *delta hedging*. The delta of a call option is positive, whereas the delta of a put option is negative.

From Figure 10.1 we can calculate the value of the delta of the call option being considered as

$$\frac{1 - 0}{22 - 18} = 0.25$$

This is because when the stock price changes from $18 to $22, the option price changes from $0 to $1.

In Figure 10.4 the delta corresponding to stock price movements over the first time step is

$$\frac{2.0257 - 0}{22 - 18} = 0.5064$$

The delta for stock price movements over the second time step is

$$\frac{3.2 - 0}{24.2 - 19.8} = 0.7273$$

if there is an upward movement over the first time step and

$$\frac{0 - 0}{19.8 - 16} = 0$$

if there is a downward movement over the first time step.

From Figure 10.7 delta is

$$\frac{1.4147 - 9.4636}{60 - 40} = -0.4024$$

at the end of the first time step and either

$$\frac{0 - 4}{72 - 48} = -0.1667$$

or

$$\frac{4 - 20}{48 - 32} = -1.0000$$

at the end of the second time step.

The two-step examples show that delta changes over time. (In Figure 10.4 delta changes from 0.5064 to either 0.7273 or 0; in Figure 10.7 it changes from −0.4024 to either −0.1667 or −1.0000.) Thus, in order to maintain a riskless hedge using an option and the underlying stock, we need to adjust our holdings in the stock periodically. This is a feature of options that we will return to in chapters 11 and 14.

Binomial Trees in Practice

The binomial models presented so far have been unrealistically simple. Clearly an analyst can expect to obtain only a very rough approximation to an option price by assuming that stock price movements during the life of the option consist of one or two binomial steps.

When binomial trees are put in practice, the life of the option is typically divided into 30 or more time steps. In each time step there is a binomial stock price movement. With 30 time steps this means that 31 terminal stock prices and 2^{30}, or about 1 billion, possible stock price paths are considered.

The values of u and d are determined from the stock price volatility, σ. There are a number of different ways to make the determination. If we define Δt as the length of one time step, one possibility is to set

$$u = e^{\sigma \sqrt{\Delta t}}$$

and

$$d = \frac{1}{u}$$

The complete set of equations defining the tree is then

$$u = e^{\sigma \sqrt{\Delta t}}; \qquad d = e^{-\sigma \sqrt{\Delta t}}$$

$$p = \frac{e^{r \Delta t} - d}{u - d}$$

Chapter 16 provides a further discussion of these formulas and practical issues involved in the construction and use of binomial trees.

Summary

This chapter has provided a first look at the valuation of stock options. If stock price movements during the life of an option are governed by a one-step binomial tree, it is possible to set up a portfolio consisting of a stock option and the stock that is riskless. In a world with no arbitrage opportunities, riskless portfolios must earn the risk-free interest. This enables the stock option to be priced in terms of the stock. It is interesting to note that no assumptions are required about the probabilities of up and down movements in the stock price at each node of the tree.

When stock price movements are governed by a multistep binomial tree, we can treat each binomial step separately and work back from the end of the life of the option to the beginning to obtain the current value of the option. Again only no-arbitrage arguments are used, and no assumptions are required about the probabilities of up and down movements in the stock price at each node.

Another approach to valuing stock options involves risk-neutral valuation. This very important principle states that it is permissible to assume the world is risk neutral when valuing an option in terms of the underlying stock. This chapter has shown, through both numerical examples and algebra, that no-arbitrage arguments and risk-neutral valuation always lead to the same option prices.

The delta of a stock option, Δ, considers the effect of a small change in the underlying stock price on the change in the option price. It is the ratio of the change in the option price to the change in the stock price. For a riskless position an investor should buy Δ shares for each option sold. An inspection of a typical binomial tree shows that delta is liable to change during the life of an option. This means that riskless positions do not automatically remain riskless. They must be adjusted periodically.

In the next chapter we examine the Black–Scholes analytic approach to pricing stock options. In chapters 12 and 13 we review other types of options. In chapter 14 we move on to consider hedge statistics such as delta. In chapter 16 we then return to binomial trees and give a more complete discussion of how they are implemented.

Suggestions for Further Reading

Cox, J., S. Ross, and M. Rubinstein. "Option Pricing: A Simplified Approach," *Journal of Financial Economics* 7 (October 1979): 229–264.

Rendleman, R., and B. Bartter. "Two-State Option Pricing," *Journal of Finance* 34 (1979): 1092–1110.

Quiz

1. A stock price is currently $40. It is known that at the end of one month it will be either $42 or $38. The risk-free interest rate is 8 percent per annum with continuous

compounding. What is the value of a one-month European call option with a strike price of $39?

2. Explain the no-arbitrage and risk-neutral valuation approaches to valuing a European option using a one-step binomial tree.

3. What is meant by the delta of a stock option?

4. A stock price is currently $50. It is known that at the end of six months it will be either $45 or $55. The risk-free interest rate is 10 percent per annum with continuous compounding. What is the the value of a six-month European put option with a strike price of $50?

5. A stock price is currently $100. Over each of the next two six-month periods it is expected to go up by 10 percent or down by 10 percent. The risk-free interest rate is 8 percent per annum with continuous compounding. What is the value of a one-year European call option with a strike price of $100?

6. For the situation considered in Quiz no. 5, what is the value of a one-year European put option with a strike price of $100? Verify that the European call and European put prices satisfy put–call parity.

7. Consider the situation in which stock price movements during the life of a European option are governed by a two-step binomial tree. Explain why it is not possible to set up a position in the stock and the option that remains riskless for the whole of the life of the option.

Questions and Problems

10.1. A stock price is currently $50. It is known that at the end of two months it will be either $53 or $48. The risk-free interest rate is 10 percent per annum with continuous compounding. What is the value of a two-month European call option with a strike price of $49? Use no-arbitrage arguments.

10.2. A stock price is currently $80. It is known that at the end of four months it will be either $75 or $85. The risk-free interest rate is 5 percent per annum with continuous compounding. What is the value of a four-month European put option with a strike price of $80? Use no-arbitrage arguments.

10.3. A stock price is currently $50. It is known that at the end of six months it will be either $60 or $42. The risk-free rate of interest with continuous compounding is 12 percent per annum. Calculate the value of a six-month European call option on the stock with an exercise price of $48. Verify that no-arbitrage arguments and risk-neutral valuation arguments give the same answers.

10.4. A stock price is currently $40. It is known that at the end of three months it will be either $45 or $35. The risk-free rate of interest with quarterly compounding is 8 percent per annum. Calculate the value of a three-month European put option on the stock with an exercise price of $40. Verify that no-arbitrage arguments and risk-neutral valuation arguments give the same answers.

10.5. A stock price is currently $50. Over each of the next two three-month periods it is expected to go up by 6 percent or down by 5 percent. The risk-free interest rate is 5 percent per annum with continuous compounding. What is the value of a six-month European call option with a strike price of $51?

10.6. For the situation considered in Problem 10.5, what is the value of a six-month European put option with a strike price of $51? Verify that the European call and European put prices satisfy put–call parity. If the put option were American, would it ever be optimal to exercise it early at any of the nodes on the tree?

10.7. A stock price is currently $40. Over each of the next two three-month periods it is expected to go up by 10 percent or down by 10 percent. The risk-free interest rate is 12 percent per annum with continuous compounding.

a. What is the value of a six-month European put option with a strike price of $42?

b. What is the value of a six-month American put option with a strike price of $42?

10.8. Using "trial and error," estimate how high the strike price has to be in Problem 10.7 for it to be optimal to exercise the option immediately.

10.9. A stock price is currently $25. It is known that at the end of two months it will be either $23 or $27. The risk-free interest rate is 10 percent per annum with continuous compounding. Suppose S_T is the stock price at the end of two months. What is the value of a derivative that pays off S_T^2 at this time?

CHAPTER 11

The Pricing of Stock Options Using Black–Scholes

In the early 1970s Fischer Black, Myron Scholes, and Robert Merton made a major breakthrough in the pricing of stock options.[1] Their work has had a huge influence on the way in which market participants price and hedge options. In this chapter we examine the Black–Scholes results and the assumptions upon which they are based. We also consider more fully than in previous chapters the meaning of volatility and show how volatility can be either estimated from historical data or implied from option prices. Toward the end of the chapter we review how the Black–Scholes results can be extended to deal with European call options on dividend-paying stocks.

The Assumption about How Stock Prices Evolve

A stock option pricing model must make some assumptions about how stock prices evolve over time. If a stock price is $100 today, what is the probability distribution for the price in one day or in one week or in one year?

The assumption underlying the Black–Scholes model is that stock prices follow a *random walk*. This means that proportional changes in the stock price in a short period of time are normally distributed. We define

μ: the expected return on the stock

σ: the volatility of the stock price

---

[1]See F. Black and M. Scholes, "The Pricing of Options and Corporate Liabilities," *Journal of Political Economy* 81 (May–June 1973): 637–659; and R. C. Merton, "Theory of Rational Option Pricing," *Bell Journal of Economics and Management Science* 4 (Spring 1973): 141–183.

The mean of the proportional change in time Δt is $\mu\Delta t$. The standard deviation of the proportional change is $\sigma\sqrt{\Delta t}$. The assumption underlying Black–Scholes is therefore

$$\frac{\Delta S}{S} \sim \phi(\mu\Delta t, \sigma\sqrt{\Delta t}) \qquad\qquad\text{(11.1)}$$

where ΔS is the change in S in time Δt and $\phi(m, s)$ denotes a normal distribution with mean m and standard deviation s.

THE LOGNORMAL DISTRIBUTION

The random-walk assumption implies that the stock price at any future time has a *lognormal* distribution. The general shape of a lognormal distribution is shown in Figure 11.1. It can be contrasted with the more familiar normal distribution in Figure 11.2. Whereas a variable with a normal distribution can take any positive or negative value, a lognormally distributed variable is restricted to being positive. A normal distribution is symmetrical; a lognormal distribution is skewed with the mean, median, and mode all different.

FIGURE 11.1 A Lognormal Distribution

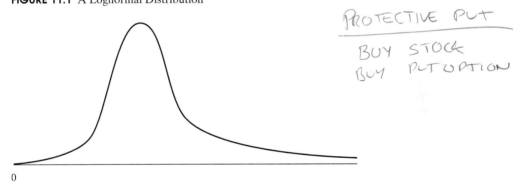

0

FIGURE 11.2 A Normal Distribution

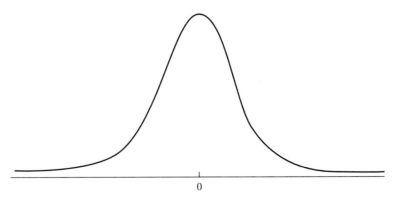

0

A variable with a lognormal distribution has the property that its natural logarithm is normally distributed. The Black–Scholes assumption for stock prices therefore implies that $\ln S_T$ is normal, where S_T is the stock price at a future time T. The mean and standard deviation of $\ln S_T$ can be shown to be

$$\ln S + \left(\mu - \frac{\sigma^2}{2} \right) T$$

and

$$\sigma \sqrt{T}$$

where S is the current stock price. We can write this result as

$$\ln S_T \sim \phi \left[\ln S + \left(\mu - \frac{\sigma^2}{2} \right) T, \sigma \sqrt{T} \right] \tag{11.2}$$

The expected value or mean value of S_T, $E(S_T)$, is given by

$$E(S_T) = Se^{\mu T} \tag{11.3}$$

This fits in with the definition of μ as the expected rate of return. The variance of S_T, $\text{var}(S_T)$, can be shown to be given by

$$\text{var}(S_T) = S^2 e^{2\mu T} (e^{\sigma^2 T} - 1)$$

Example

Consider a stock with an initial price of $40, an expected return of 16 percent per annum, and a volatility of 20 percent per annum. From Equation 11.2, the probability distribution of the stock price, S_T, in six months is given by

$$\ln S_T \sim \phi \left[\ln 40 + \left(0.16 - \frac{0.2^2}{2} \right) 0.5, 0.2 \sqrt{0.5} \right]$$

or

$$\ln S_T \sim \phi(3.759, 0.141)$$

There is a 95 percent probability that a normally distributed variable has a value within two standard deviations of its mean. Hence, with 95 percent confidence,

$$3.477 < \ln S_T < 4.041$$

This implies

$$e^{3.477} < S_T < e^{4.041}$$

or

$$32.36 < S_T < 56.88$$

Thus, there is a 95 percent probability that the stock price in six months will lie between 32.36 and 56.88. The mean and variance of S_T are

$$40e^{0.16 \times 0.5} = 43.33$$

and

$$40^2 e^{2 \times 0.16 \times 0.5} (e^{0.2 \times 0.2 \times 0.5} - 1) = 37.93$$

From Equation 11.2 it can be shown that

$$\ln \frac{S_T}{S} \sim \phi \left[\left(\mu - \frac{\sigma^2}{2} \right) T, \sigma \sqrt{T} \right] \qquad (11.4)$$

When $T = 1$, the expression $\ln(S_T/S)$ is the continuously compounded return provided by the stock in one year.[2] The mean and standard deviation of the continuously compounded return in one year are therefore $\mu - \sigma^2/2$ and σ, respectively.

Example

Consider a stock with an expected return of 17 percent per annum and a volatility of 20 percent per annum. The probability distribution for the rate of return (continuously compounded) realized over one year is normal, with mean

$$0.17 - \frac{0.2^2}{2} = 0.15$$

or 15 percent and standard deviation 20 percent. Because there is a 95 percent chance that a normally distributed variable will lie within two standard deviations of its mean, we can be 95 percent confident that the return realized over one year will be between -25 percent and $+55$ percent.

We now consider in more detail the nature of the expected return and volatility parameter in the lognormal stock price model.

The Expected Return

The expected return, μ, required by investors from a stock depends on the riskiness of the stock. The higher the risk, the higher the return. It also depends on the level of interest rates in the economy. The higher the risk-free interest rate, the higher the expected return required on any given stock. Fortunately, we do not have to concern ourselves with the determinants of μ in any detail. It turns out that the value of a stock option, when expressed in terms of the value of the underlying stock, does not depend on μ at all. Nevertheless, there is one aspect of the expected return from a stock that frequently causes confusion and is worth explaining.

---

[2] As discussed in chapter 3, it is important to distinguish between the continuously compounded return and the return with no compounding. The former is $\ln(S_T/S)$. The latter is $(S_T - S)/S$.

Equation 11.1 shows that $\mu \Delta t$ is the expected proportional change in S in a very short period of time, Δt. This means that μ is the (annualized) expected return in time Δt expressed with a compounding frequency of Δt. Because Δt is very small, it is natural to assume that μ is also the expected continuously compounded return. However, this is not the case. Equation 11.4 shows that the expected continuously compounded return per year is $\mu - \sigma^2/2$.

To understand what is going on here, it is useful to consider a simple example. Suppose that the following is a sequence of returns per annum on a stock, measured using annual compounding:

$$15\%, \quad 20\%, \quad 30\%, \quad -20\%, \quad 25\%$$

The arithmetic mean of the returns, calculated by taking the sum of the returns and dividing by 5, is 14 percent. However, an investor would actually earn less than 14 percent per annum by leaving the money in the stock for five years. The dollar value of $100 at the end of the five years would be

$$100 \times 1.15 \times 1.20 \times 1.30 \times 0.80 \times 1.25 = \$179.40$$

By contrast, a 14 percent return with annual compounding would give

$$100 \times 1.14^5 = \$192.54$$

The actual average return earned by the investor, with annual compounding, is

$$(1.7940)^{1/5} - 1 = 0.124$$

or 12.4 percent per annum.

This example illustrates the general result that the mean of the returns earned in different years is not necessarily the same as the mean return per annum over several years with annual compounding. It can be shown that, unless the returns happen to be the same in each year, the former is always greater than the latter.[3]

There is nothing magical about the time period of one year in this result. Suppose that the time period over which returns are measured is made progressively shorter and the number of observations is increased. We obtain the following two estimates:

1. The average of the returns earned in very short periods of time of length Δt, expressed with a compounding frequency of Δt

2. The expected rate of return over a longer period of time, expressed with a compounding frequency of Δt

Analogously to the foregoing, we would expect estimate 1 to be greater than estimate 2. This is in fact the case. In the limit as Δt approaches zero, the first estimate is μ whereas the second estimate is $\mu - \sigma^2/2$.

The arguments in this section show that the term *expected return* is ambiguous. It can refer either to μ or to $\mu - \sigma^2/2$. Unless otherwise stated, it will be used to refer to μ throughout this book.

---

[3]Some readers may recognize the result as equivalent to the statement that the arithmetic mean of a set of numbers is always greater than the geometric mean if the numbers are not identical.

Volatility

The volatility of a stock, σ, is a measure of our uncertainty about the returns provided by the stock. Typical values of the volatility of a stock are in the range 0.2 to 0.4 per annum. Often volatilities are expressed as percentages. Thus, we might refer to the volatility of IBM as being 25 percent per annum. Assuming time is measured in years, this means that $\sigma = 0.25$.

Equation 11.4 suggests the following as a precise definition of volatility:

> The volatility of a stock price is the standard deviation of the return provided by the stock in one year when the return is expressed using continuous compounding.

As a rough approximation, $\sigma \sqrt{T}$ is the standard deviation of the proportional change in the stock price in time T. Consider the situation where $\sigma = 0.3$, or 30 percent per annum. The standard deviation of the proportional change in one year is approximately 30 percent; the standard deviation of the proportional change in six months is approximately $30 \sqrt{0.5} = 21.2$ percent; the standard deviation of the proportional change in three months is approximately $30 \sqrt{0.25} = 15$ percent; and so on. More precisely, we can say that the standard deviation of the change in $\ln S$ in time T is $\sigma \sqrt{T}$.

Notice that our uncertainty about a future stock price, as measured by its standard deviation, increases with the square root of how far ahead we are looking. It does not increase linearly.

Estimating Volatility from Historical Data

A record of stock price movements can be used to estimate volatility. The stock price is usually observed at fixed intervals of time (e.g., every day, every week, or every month). We define

$n + 1$: number of observations

S_i: stock price at end of ith interval ($i = 0, 1, \ldots, n$)

τ: length of time interval in years

and let

$$u_i = \ln\left(\frac{S_i}{S_{i-1}}\right)$$

An estimate, s, of the standard deviation of the u_i's is given by

$$s = \sqrt{\frac{1}{n-1} \sum_{i=1}^{n} (u_i - \bar{u})^2}$$

or

$$s = \sqrt{\frac{1}{n-1} \sum_{i=1}^{n} u_i^2 - \frac{1}{n(n-1)} \left(\sum_{i=1}^{n} u_i \right)^2}$$

where $\bar{u}$ is the mean of the u_i's.

From Equation 11.4 the standard deviation of the u_i's is $\sigma \sqrt{\tau}$. The variable s is therefore an estimate of $\sigma \sqrt{\tau}$. It follows that σ itself can be estimated as $\hat{\sigma}$, where

$$\hat{\sigma} = \frac{s}{\sqrt{\tau}}$$

The standard error of this estimate can be shown to be approximately $\hat{\sigma}/\sqrt{2n}$.

Choosing an appropriate value for n is not easy. More data generally lead to more accuracy, but σ does change over time and data that are too old may not be relevant for predicting the future. A compromise which seems to work reasonably well is to use closing prices from daily data over the most recent 90 to 180 days. There is an important issue concerned with whether time should be measured in calendar days or trading days when volatility parameters are being estimated and used. This question will be discussed more fully later in this chapter.

Example

Table 11.1 shows a possible sequence of stock prices during 21 consecutive trading days. In this case

$$\sum u_i = 0.09531 \text{ and } \sum u_i^2 = 0.00333$$

TABLE 11.1 Computation of Volatility

Day	Closing Stock Price ($)	Price Relative S_i/S_{i-1}	Daily Return $u_i = \ln(S_i/S_{i-1})$
0	20		
1	$20\frac{1}{8}$	1.00625	0.00623
2	$19\frac{7}{8}$	0.98758	−0.01250
3	20	1.00629	0.00627
4	$20\frac{1}{2}$	1.02500	0.02469
5	$20\frac{1}{4}$	0.98781	−0.01227
6	$20\frac{7}{8}$	1.03086	0.03040
7	$20\frac{7}{8}$	1.00000	0.00000
8	$20\frac{7}{8}$	1.00000	0.00000
9	$20\frac{3}{4}$	0.99401	−0.00601
10	$20\frac{3}{4}$	1.00000	0.00000
11	21	1.01205	0.01198
12	$21\frac{1}{8}$	1.00595	0.00593
13	$20\frac{7}{8}$	0.98817	−0.01190
14	$20\frac{7}{8}$	1.00000	0.00000
15	$21\frac{1}{4}$	1.01796	0.01780
16	$21\frac{3}{8}$	1.00588	0.00587
17	$21\frac{3}{8}$	1.00000	0.00000
18	$21\frac{1}{4}$	0.99415	−0.00587
19	$21\frac{3}{4}$	1.02353	0.02326
20	22	1.01149	0.01143

and the estimate of the standard deviation of the daily return is

$$\sqrt{\frac{0.00333}{19} - \frac{0.09531^2}{380}} = 0.0123$$

Assuming that there are 252 trading days per year, $\tau = 1/252$ and the data give an estimate for the volatility per annum of $0.0123 \sqrt{252} = 0.195$. The estimated volatility is 19.5 percent per annum. The standard error of this estimate is

$$\frac{0.195}{\sqrt{2 \times 20}} = 0.031$$

or 3.1 percent per annum.

The foregoing analysis assumes that the stock pays no dividends. It can be adapted to accommodate dividend-paying stocks. The return, u_i, during a time interval that includes an ex-dividend day is given by

$$u_i = \ln \frac{S_i + D}{S_{i-1}}$$

where D is the amount of the dividend. The return in other time intervals is still

$$u_i = \ln \frac{S_i}{S_{i-1}}$$

Because tax factors play a part in determining returns around an ex-dividend date, it is probably best to discard altogether data for intervals that include an ex-dividend date.

Assumptions Underlying Black–Scholes

The assumptions made by Black and Scholes when they derived their option pricing formula were as follows:

1. Stock price behavior corresponds to the lognormal model developed earlier in this chapter with μ and σ constant.
2. There are no transactions costs or taxes. All securities are perfectly divisible.
3. There are no dividends on the stock during the life of the option.
4. There are no riskless arbitrage opportunities.
5. Security trading is continuous.
6. Investors can borrow or lend at the same risk-free rate of interest.
7. The short-term risk-free rate of interest, r, is constant.

Some of these assumptions have been relaxed by other researchers. For example, variations on the Black–Scholes formula can be used when r and σ are functions of time, and as we will see later in this chapter, the formula can be adjusted to take dividends into account.

The Black–Scholes/Merton Analysis

The Black–Scholes/Merton analysis is analogous to the no-arbitrage analysis used in chapter 10 to value options when stock price changes are binomial. A riskless portfolio consisting of a position in the option and a position in the underlying stock is set up. In the absence of arbitrage opportunities, the return from the portfolio must be the risk-free interest rate, r. This results in a differential equation that must be satisfied by the option.

The reason a riskless portfolio can be set up is that the stock price and the option price are both affected by the same underlying source of uncertainty: stock price movements. In any short period of time, the price of a call option is perfectly positively correlated with the price of the underlying stock; the price of a put option is perfectly negatively correlated with the price of the underlying stock. In both cases, when an appropriate portfolio of the stock and the option is set up, the gain or loss from the stock position always offsets the gain or loss from the option position so that the overall value of the portfolio at the end of the short period of time is known with certainty.

Suppose, for example, that at a particular point in time the relationship between a small change in the stock price, ΔS, and the resultant small change in the price of a European call option, Δc, is given by

$$\Delta c = 0.4 \Delta S$$

This means that the slope of the line representing the relationship between c and S is 0.4, as indicated in Figure 11.3. The riskless portfolio would consist of

1. A long position in 0.4 share
2. A short position in 1 call option

There is one important difference between the Black–Scholes/Merton analysis and the analysis using a binomial model in chapter 10. In Black–Scholes/Merton the position that is set up is riskless for only a very short period of time. (Theoretically, it remains riskless only for an instantaneously short period of time.) To remain riskless, it

FIGURE 11.3 Relationship between c and S

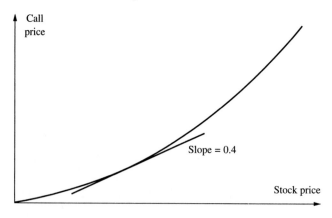

must be frequently adjusted or *rebalanced.*[4] For example, the relationship between Δc and ΔS might change from $\Delta c = 0.4\,\Delta S$ today to $\Delta c = 0.5\,\Delta S$ in two weeks. If so, 0.5 rather than 0.4 shares must then be owned for each call option sold. It is nevertheless true that the return from the riskless portfolio in any short period of time must be the risk-free interest rate. This is the key element in the Black–Scholes/Merton arguments and leads to their pricing formulas.

THE PRICING FORMULAS

The Black–Scholes formulas for the prices of European calls and puts on nondividend-paying stocks are[5]

$$c = SN(d_1) - Xe^{-rT}N(d_2) \tag{11.5}$$

$$p = Xe^{-rT}N(-d_2) - SN(-d_1) \tag{11.6}$$

where

$$d_1 = \frac{\ln(S/X) + (r + \sigma^2/2)T}{\sigma\sqrt{T}}$$

$$d_2 = \frac{\ln(S/X) + (r - \sigma^2/2)T}{\sigma\sqrt{T}} = d_1 - \sigma\sqrt{T}$$

The function $N(x)$ is the cumulative probability function for a standardized normal variable. In other words, it is the probability that a variable with a standard normal distribution, $\phi(0, 1)$, will be less than x. It is illustrated in Figure 11.4. The remaining notation in Equations 11.5 and 11.6 should be familiar. The variables c and p are the European call and put prices, S is the stock price, X is the strike price, r is the risk-free interest rate, T is the time to expiration, and σ is the volatility of the stock price. Because the American call price, C, equals the European call price, c, for a nondividend-paying stock, Equation 11.5 also gives the price of an American call. Unfortunately, no

FIGURE 11.4 Shaded Area Represents $N(x)$

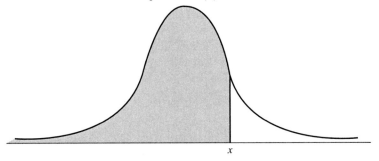

x

---

exact analytic formula for the value of an American put on a nondividend-paying stock has been produced. We will look at numerical procedures in chapter 16.

In theory, the Black–Scholes formula is correct only if the short-term interest rate, r, is constant. In practice, the formula is usually used with the interest rate, r, being set equal to the risk-free interest rate on an investment that lasts for time T.

PROPERTIES OF THE BLACK–SCHOLES FORMULAS

A full proof of the Black–Scholes formulas is beyond the scope of this book. At this stage we show that the formulas have the right general properties by considering what happens when some of the parameters take extreme values.

When the stock price, S, becomes very large, a call option is almost certain to be exercised. It then becomes very similar to a forward contract with delivery price X. From Equation 3.9 we therefore expect the call price to be

$$S - Xe^{-rT}$$

This is in fact the call price given by Equation 11.5 because, when S becomes very large, both d_1 and d_2 become very large, and $N(d_1)$ and $N(d_2)$ are both close to 1.0.

When the stock price becomes very large, the price of a European put option, p, approaches zero. This result is consistent with Equation 11.6, because $N(-d_1)$ and $N(-d_2)$ are both close to zero.

When the stock price becomes very small, both d_1 and d_2 become very large and negative. $N(d_1)$ and $N(d_2)$ are then both very close to zero, and Equation 11.5 gives a price close to zero for the call option. This is as expected. Also, $N(-d_1)$ and $N(-d_2)$ become close to 1, so that the price of the put option given by Equation 11.6 is close to $Xe^{-rT} - S$. This is also as expected.

THE CUMULATIVE NORMAL DISTRIBUTION FUNCTION

The only problem in applying Equations 11.5 and 11.6 is the computation of the cumulative normal distribution function, N. Tables for N are provided at the end of this book. The function can also be evaluated using a polynomial approximation. One such approximation that can easily be obtained using a hand calculator is given by the equations

$$N(x) = 1 - (a_1 k + a_2 k^2 + a_3 k^3) N'(x) \quad \text{when } x \geq 0$$

$$N(x) = 1 - N(-x) \qquad\qquad\qquad\quad \text{when } x < 0$$

where

$$k = \frac{1}{1 + \alpha x}$$

$$\alpha = 0.33267$$

$$a_1 = 0.4361836$$

$$a_2 = -0.1201676$$

$$a_3 = 0.9372980$$

and

$$N'(x) = \frac{1}{\sqrt{2\pi}} e^{-x^2/2}$$

This provides values for $N(x)$ that are always accurate to 0.0002.

Example

The stock price six months from the expiration of an option is \$42, the exercise price of the option is \$40, the risk-free interest rate is 10 percent per annum, and the volatility is 20 percent per annum. This means that $S = 42, X = 40, r = 0.1$, $\sigma = 0.2, T = 0.5$,

$$d_1 = \frac{\ln(42/40) + (0.1 + 0.2^2/2) \times 0.5}{0.2\sqrt{0.5}} = 0.7693$$

$$d_2 = \frac{\ln(42/40) + (0.1 - 0.2^2/2) \times 0.5}{0.2\sqrt{0.5}} = 0.6278$$

and

$$Xe^{-rT} = 40e^{-0.1 \times 0.5} = 38.049$$

Hence, if the option is a European call, its value, c, is given by

$$c = 42N(0.7693) - 38.049N(0.6278)$$

If the option is a European put, its value, p, is given by

$$p = 38.049N(-0.6278) - 42N(-0.7693)$$

Using the polynomial approximation just given or the tables at the end of the book, we get

$$N(0.7693) = 0.7791, \qquad N(-0.7693) = 0.2209$$

$$N(0.6278) = 0.7349, \qquad N(-0.6278) = 0.2651$$

so that

$$c = 4.76, \qquad p = 0.81$$

The stock price has to rise by \$2.76 for the purchaser of the call to break even. Similarly, the stock price has to fall by \$2.81 for the purchaser of the put to break even.

Risk-Neutral Valuation

An important result in the pricing of derivatives is known as risk-neutral valuation. The principle was introduced in chapter 10 and can be stated as follows:

Any security dependent on other traded securities can be valued on the assumption that investors are risk neutral.

Note that risk-neutral valuation does not state that investors are risk neutral. What it does state is that derivatives such as options can be valued on the assumption that investors are risk neutral. It means that investors' risk preferences have no effect on the value of a stock option when it is expressed as a function of the price of the underlying stock. It explains why Equations 11.5 and 11.6 do not involve μ.

Risk-neutral valuation is a very powerful tool, because in a risk-neutral world two particularly simple results hold:

1. The expected return from all securities is the risk-free interest rate.
2. The risk-free interest rate is the appropriate discount rate to apply to any expected future cash flow.

Options and other derivatives that provide a payoff at one particular time can be valued using risk-neutral valuation. The procedure is as follows:

1. Assume that the expected return from the underlying asset is the risk-free interest rate r (i.e., assume $\mu = r$).
2. Calculate the expected payoff from the option at its maturity.
3. Discount the expected payoff at the risk-free interest rate.

Application to Forward Contract

This procedure can be used to derive the Black–Scholes formulas, but the mathematics is fairly complicated and will not be presented here. Instead, as an illustration, the procedure will be used to value a forward contract on a nondividend-paying stock. (This contract has already been valued in chapter 3 using a different approach.) We will make the assumption that interest rates are constant and equal to r.

Consider a long forward contract that matures at time T with delivery price K. The value of the contract at maturity is

$$S_T - K$$

The expected value of S_T was shown earlier in this chapter to be $Se^{\mu T}$. In a risk-neutral world it becomes Se^{rT}. The expected payoff from the contract at maturity in a risk-neutral world is therefore

$$Se^{rT} - K$$

Discounting at the risk-free rate r for time T gives the value f of the forward contract today as

$$f = e^{-rT}(Se^{rT} - K) = S - Ke^{-rT}$$

This is in agreement with the result in Equation 3.9.

Implied Volatilities

The one parameter in the Black–Scholes pricing formulas that cannot be observed directly is the volatility of the stock price. Earlier in this chapter we saw how volatility can be estimated from a history of the stock price. At this stage it is appropriate to introduce the notion of *implied volatility*. This is the volatility implied by an option price observed in the market.[6]

To illustrate the basic idea, suppose that the value of a call on a nondividend-paying stock is $1\frac{7}{8}$ ($= 1.875$) when $S = 21$, $X = 20$, $r = 0.1$, and $T = 0.25$. The implied volatility is the value of σ, which when substituted into Equation 11.5 gives $c = 1.875$. It is not possible to invert Equation 11.5 so that σ is expressed as a function of S, X, r, T, and c, but an iterative search procedure can be used to find the implied σ. We could start by trying $\sigma = 0.20$. This gives a value of c equal to 1.76, which is too low. Since c is an increasing function of σ, a higher value of σ is required. We could next try a value of 0.30 for σ. This gives a value of c equal to 2.10, which is too high, and means that σ must lie between 0.20 and 0.30. Next we try a value of 0.25 for σ. This also proves to be too high, showing that σ lies between 0.20 and 0.25. Proceeding in this way, we can halve the range for σ at each iteration and thereby calculate the correct value of σ to any required accuracy.[7] In this example the implied volatility is 0.235, or 23.5 percent per annum.

Implied volatilities can be used to monitor the market's opinion about the volatility of a particular stock. Traders often calculate an implied volatility from an actively traded option and use it to calculate the price of a less actively traded option on the same stock. Very often, several implied volatilities are obtained simultaneously from different options on the same stock, and a composite implied volatility for the stock is then calculated by taking a suitable weighted average of the individual implied volatilities. The amount of weight given to each implied volatility in this calculation should reflect the sensitivity of the option price to the volatility. To illustrate, suppose that two implied volatility estimates are available. The first is 21 percent per annum and is based on an at-the-money option; the second is 26 percent per annum and is based on a deep-out-of-the-money option with the same maturity. The price of the at-the-money option is far more sensitive to volatility than the price of the deep-out-of-the-money option. It is therefore providing more information about the "true" implied volatility. We might then choose a weight of 0.9 for the at-the-money implied volatility and a weight of 0.1 for the deep-out-of-the-money option. The weighted-average implied volatility would then be

$$0.9 \times 0.21 + 0.1 \times 0.26 = 0.215$$

or 21.5 percent per annum. Different weighting schemes are discussed by Beckers, Chiras and Manaster, Latane and Rendleman, and Whaley (see the end-of-chapter references). The sensitivity of an option price to volatility is the rate of change of the

---

[6]Implied volatilities for European and American options on stocks, stock indices, foreign currencies, and futures can be calculated using the software supplied with this book.

[7]This method is presented for illustration. Other, more powerful procedures are usually used in practice.

price with respect to volatility.[8] Beckers, after examining various weighting schemes, concluded that best results are obtained by using only the option whose price is most sensitive to σ. Thus, the Beckers approach would estimate 21 percent for the volatility in our example.

The Causes of Volatility

We now move on to consider the causes of volatility. Some analysts claim that the volatility of a stock price is caused solely by the random arrival of new information about the future returns from the stock. Others maintain that volatility is caused largely by trading. An interesting question therefore is whether volatility is the same when the exchange is open as when it is closed.

Fama and French (see the end-of-chapter references) have tested this question empirically. They collected data on the stock price at the close of each trading day over a long period of time and then calculated

1. The variance of stock price returns between the close of trading on one day and the close of trading on the next trading day when there are no intervening nontrading days

2. The variance of the stock price returns between the close of trading on Friday and the close of trading on Monday

If trading and nontrading days are equivalent, the variance in situation 2 should be three times as great as the variance in situation 1. Fama found that it was only 22 percent higher. French's results were similar. He found that it was 19 percent higher.

These results suggest that volatility is far larger when the exchange is open than when it is closed. Proponents of the traditional view that volatility is caused only by new information might be tempted to argue that most new information on stocks arrives during trading hours.[9] However, studies of futures prices of agricultural commodities, which depend largely on the weather, have shown that they exhibit much the same behavior as stock prices; that is, they are much more volatile during trading hours. Presumably, news about the weather is equally likely to arise on any day. The only reasonable conclusion seems to be that volatility is to a large extent caused by trading itself.[10]

What are the implications of all this for the measurement of volatility and the Black-Scholes model? The results suggest that days when the exchange is closed should be ignored when volatilities are calculated from historical data and when volatilities are used to value options. For example, the volatility per annum should be calculated from the volatility per trading day using the formula

$$\text{Volatility per annum} = \text{Volatility per trading day} \times \sqrt{\text{Number of trading days per annum}}$$

This is the approach that was used earlier in this chapter in connection with the data in Table 11.1. The number of trading days in a year is usually assumed to be 252 for stocks.

---

[8]The calculation of the rate of change of the price with respect to volatility is discussed in chapters 14 and 16.

[9]In fact, this argument is questionable. Often important announcements (e.g., those concerned with sales and earnings) are made when exchanges are closed.

[10]For a discussion, see the article by French and Roll referred to at the end of the chapter. We will consider one way in which trading can generate volatility when we look at portfolio insurance schemes in chapter 14.

Dividends

Up to now we have assumed that the stock upon which the option is written pays no dividends. In practice, this is not always the case. We now extend our results by assuming that the dividends paid on the stock during the life of an option can be predicted with certainty. Because traded options usually last for less than eight months, the assumption is not unreasonable.

The critical date for the valuation of options is the ex-dividend date. On this date the stock price declines by the amount of the dividend.[11] The effect is to reduce the value of calls and increase the value of puts.

EUROPEAN OPTIONS

European options can be analyzed by assuming that the stock price is the sum of two components: a riskless component that will be used to pay the known dividends during the life of the option and a risky component. The riskless component at any given time is the present value of all the dividends during the life of the option discounted from the ex-dividend dates to the present at the risk-free rate. The Black–Scholes formula is then correct if S is set equal to the risky component. Operationally this means that the Black–Scholes formula can be used provided the stock price is reduced by the present value of all the dividends during the life of the option, the discounting being done from the ex-dividend dates at the risk-free rate. A dividend is included in the calculations only if its ex-dividend date occurs during the life of the option.

Example

Consider a European call option on a stock with ex-dividend dates in two months and five months. The dividend on each ex-dividend date is expected to be $0.50. The current share price is $40, the exercise price is $40, the stock price volatility is 30 percent per annum, the risk-free rate of interest is 9 percent per annum, and the time to maturity is six months. The present value of the dividends is

$$0.5e^{-0.09 \times 2/12} + 0.5e^{-0.09 \times 5/12} = 0.9741$$

The option price can therefore be calculated from the Black–Scholes formula with $S = 39.0259$, $X = 40$, $r = 0.09$, $\sigma = 0.3$, and $T = 0.5$.

$$d_1 = \frac{\ln(39.0259/40) + (0.09 + 0.3^2/2) \times 0.5}{0.3\sqrt{0.5}} = 0.2017$$

$$d_2 = \frac{\ln(39.0259/40) + (0.09 + 0.3^2/2)}{0.3\sqrt{0.5}} = -0.0104$$

---

[11] For tax reasons the stock price may go down by somewhat less than the cash amount of the dividend. To take account of this phenomenon, we need to interpret the word *dividend* in the context of option pricing as the reduction in the stock price on the ex-dividend date caused by the dividend. Thus, if a dividend of $1 per share is anticipated and the share price normally goes down by 80 percent of the dividend on the ex-dividend date, the dividend should be assumed to be $0.80 for the purposes of the analysis.

Using the polynomial approximation gives

$$N(d_1) = 0.5800 \quad \text{and} \quad N(d_2) = 0.4959$$

and from Equation 11.5 the call price is

$$39.0259 \times 0.5800 - 40e^{-0.09 \times 0.5} \times 0.4959 = 3.67$$

or $3.67.

With this procedure, σ in the Black–Scholes formula should be the volatility of the risky component of the stock price—not the volatility of the stock price itself. In practice, the two are often assumed to be the same. In theory, the volatility of the risky component is approximately $S/(S - D)$ times the volatility of the stock price, where D is the present value of the dividends and S is the stock price.

AMERICAN CALL OPTIONS

In chapter 8 we saw that American call options should never be exercised early when the underlying stock pays no dividends. When dividends are paid, it is sometimes optimal to exercise at a time immediately before the stock goes ex-dividend. The reason is easy to understand. The dividend will make both the stock and the call option less valuable. If the dividend is sufficiently large and the call option is sufficiently in the money, it may be worth forgoing the remaining time value of the option in order to avoid the adverse effects of the dividend on the stock price.

In practice, call options are most likely to be exercised early immediately before the final ex-dividend date. The analysis in appendix 11A indicates why this is so and derives the conditions under which early exercise can be optimal. Here we will describe an approximate procedure suggested by Fischer Black for valuing American calls on dividend-paying stocks.

BLACK'S APPROXIMATION

Black's approximation involves calculating the prices of two European options:

1. An option that matures at the same time as the American option
2. An option maturing just before the latest ex-dividend date that occurs during the life of the option

The strike price, initial stock price, risk-free interest rate, and volatility are the same as for the option under consideration. The American option price is set equal to the higher of these two European option prices.

Example

Return to the previous example but suppose that the option is American rather than European. The present value of the first dividend is given by

$$0.5e^{-0.1667 \times 0.09} = 0.4926$$

The value of the option on the assumption that it expires just before the final ex-dividend date can be calculated using the Black–Scholes formula, with

$S = 39.5074$, $X = 40$, $r = 0.09$, $\sigma = 0.30$, and $T = 0.4167$. It is \$3.52. Black's approximation involves taking the greater of this value and the value of the option when it can be exercised only at the end of six months. From the previous example, we know that the latter is \$3.67. Black's approximation therefore gives the value of the American call as \$3.67.

Summary

The usual assumption in stock option pricing is that the price of a stock at some future time given its price today is lognormal. This in turn implies that the continuously compounded return from the stock in a period of time is normally distributed. Our uncertainty about future stock prices increases as we look further ahead. As a rough approximation, we can say that the standard deviation of the stock price is proportional to the square root of how far ahead we are looking.

To estimate the volatility, σ, of a stock price empirically, we need to observe the stock price at fixed intervals of time (e.g., every day, every week, or every month). For each time period the natural logarithm of the ratio of the stock price at the end of the time period to the stock price at the beginning of the time period is calculated. The volatility is estimated as the standard deviation of these numbers divided by the square root of the length of the time period in years. Usually days when the exchanges are closed are ignored in measuring time for the purposes of volatility calculations.

Stock option valuation involves setting up a riskless position in the option and the stock. Because the stock price and the option price both depend on the same underlying source of uncertainty, such a position can always be achieved. The position remains riskless for only a very short period of time. However, the return on a riskless position must always be the risk-free interest rate if there are to be no arbitrage opportunities. It is this fact that enables the option price to be valued in terms of the stock price. The original Black–Scholes equation gives the value of a European call or put option on a nondividend-paying stock in terms of five variables: the stock price, the strike price, the risk-free interest rate, the volatility, and the time to expiration.

Surprisingly the expected return on the stock does not enter into the Black–Scholes equation. There is a general principle known as risk-neutral valuation, which states that any security dependent on other traded securities can be valued on the assumption that the world is risk neutral. The result proves to be very useful in practice. In a risk-neutral world the expected return from all securities is the risk-free interest rate, and the correct discount rate for expected cash flows is also the risk-free interest rate.

An implied volatility is the volatility which, when substituted into the Black–Scholes equation or its extensions, gives the market price of the option. Traders monitor implied volatilities and sometimes use the implied volatility from one stock option price to calculate the price of another option on the same stock. Empirical results show that the volatility of a stock is much higher when the exchange is open than when it is closed. This suggests that to some extent trading itself causes stock price volatility.

The Black–Scholes results can easily be extended to cover European call and put options on dividend-paying stocks. One procedure is to use the Black–Scholes formula with the stock price reduced by the present value of the dividends anticipated during the life of the option, and the volatility equal to the volatility of the stock price net of the present value of these dividends. Fischer Black has suggested an approximate way of valuing American call options on a dividend-paying stock. His approach involves setting the price equal to the greater of two European option prices. The first European option expires at the same time as the American option; the second expires immediately prior to the final ex-dividend date.

Suggestions for Further Reading

On the Black–Scholes formula and its extensions

Black, F. "Fact and Fantasy in the Use of Options and Corporate Liabilities," *Financial Analysts Journal* 31 (July–August 1975): 36–41, 61–72.

Black, F., and M. Scholes. "The Pricing of Options and Corporate Liabilities," *Journal of Political Economy* 81 (May–June 1973): 637–659.

Hull, J. *Options, Futures, and Other Derivatives.* 3d ed. Englewood Cliffs, NJ: Prentice Hall, 1997.

Merton, R. C. "Theory of Rational Option Pricing," *Bell Journal of Economics and Management Science* 4 (Spring 1973): 141–183.

Smith, C. W. "Option Pricing: A Review," *Journal of Financial Economics* 3 (March 1976), 3–51.

On weighting schemes for implied volatilities

Beckers, S. "Standard Deviations in Option Prices as Predictors of Future Stock Price Variability," *Journal of Banking and Finance* 5 (September 1981): 363–382.

Chiras, D. P. and S. Manaster. "The Information Content of Option Prices and a Test of Market Efficiency," *Journal of Financial Economics* 6 (1978): 213–234.

Latane, H., and R. J. Rendleman. "Standard Deviation of Stock Price Ratios Implied by Option Premia," *Journal of Finance* 31 (May 1976): 369–382.

Whaley, R. E. "Valuation of American Call Options on Dividend-paying Stocks: Empirical Tests," *Journal of Financial Economics* 10 (March 1982): 29–58.

On the causes of volatility

Fama, E. E. "The Behavior of Stock Market Prices," *Journal of Business* 38 (January 1965): 34–105.

French, K. R. "Stock Returns and the Weekend Effect," *Journal of Financial Economics* 8 (March 1980): 55–69.

French, K., and R. Roll. "Stock Return Variances: The Arrival of Information and the Reaction of Traders," *Journal of Financial Economics* 17 (September 1986): 5–26.

On analytic solutions to the pricing of American calls

Geske, R. "Comments on Whaley's Note," *Journal of Financial Economics* 9 (June 1981): 213–215.

Geske, R. "A Note on an Analytic Valuation Formula for Unprotected American Call Options on Stocks with Known Dividends," *Journal of Financial Economics* 7 (1979): 375–380.

Roll, R. "An Analytical Formula for Unprotected American Call Options on Stocks with Known Dividends," *Journal of Financial Economics* 5 (1977); 251–258.

Whaley, R. "On the Valuation of American Call Options on Stocks with Known Dividends," *Journal of Financial Economics* 9 (1981): 207–211.

Quiz

1. What does the Black–Scholes stock option pricing model assume about the probability distribution of the stock price in one year? What does it assume about the continuously compounded rate of return on the stock during the year?
2. The volatility of a stock price is 30 percent per annum. What is the standard deviation of the proportional price change in one trading day?
3. Explain how risk-neutral valuation could be used to derive the Black-Scholes formulas.
4. Calculate the price of a three-month European put option on a nondividend-paying stock with a strike price of $50 when the current stock price is $50, the risk-free interest rate is 10 percent per annum, and the volatility is 30 percent per annum.
5. What difference does it make to your calculations in the previous question if a dividend of $1.50 is expected in two months?
6. What is meant by implied volatility? How would you calculate the volatility implied by a European put option price?
7. What is Black's approximation for valuing an American call option on a dividend-paying stock?

Questions and Problems

11.1. A stock price is currently $50. Assume that the expected return from the stock is 18 percent per annum and its volatility is 30 percent per annum. What is the probability distribution for the stock price in two years? Calculate the mean and standard deviation of the distribution. Determine 95 percent confidence intervals.

11.2. A stock price is currently $40. Assume that the expected return from the stock is 15 percent and its volatility is 25 percent. What is the probability distribution for the rate of return (with continuous compounding) earned over a one-year period?

11.3. A stock price has an expected return of 16 percent and a volatility of 35 percent. The current price is $38.
    a. What is the probability that a European call option on the stock with an exercise price of $40 and a maturity date in six months will be exercised?
    b. What is the probability that a European put option on the stock with the same exercise price and maturity will be exercised?

11.4. Prove that, with the notation in the chapter, a 95 percent confidence interval for S_T is between

$$Se^{(\mu-\sigma^2/2)T-2\sigma\sqrt{T}} \quad \text{and} \quad Se^{(\mu-\sigma^2/2)T+2\sigma\sqrt{T}}$$

11.5. A portfolio manager announces that the average of the returns realized in each of the last 10 years is 20 percent per annum. In what respect is this statement misleading?

11.6. Suppose that observations on a stock price (in dollars) at the end of each of 15 consecutive weeks are as follows:

$$30\tfrac{1}{4}, \quad 32, \quad 31\tfrac{1}{8}, \quad 30\tfrac{1}{8}, \quad 30\tfrac{1}{4}, \quad 30\tfrac{3}{8}, \quad 30\tfrac{5}{8}, \quad 33,$$

$$32\tfrac{7}{8}, \quad 33, \quad 33\tfrac{1}{2}, \quad 33\tfrac{1}{2}, \quad 33\tfrac{3}{4}, \quad 33\tfrac{1}{2}, \quad 33\tfrac{1}{4}$$

Estimate the stock price volatility. What is the standard error of your estimate?

11.7. Assume that a nondividend-paying stock has an expected return of μ and a volatility of σ. An innovative financial institution has just announced that it will trade a derivative which pays off a dollar amount equal to

$$\frac{1}{T} \ln\left(\frac{S_T}{S_0}\right)$$

at time T. The variables S_0 and S_T denote the values of the stock price at time zero and time T.
a. Describe the payoff from this derivative.
b. Use risk-neutral valuation to calculate the price of the derivative at time zero.
c. Use risk-neutral valuation to calculate the price of the derivative at time t in terms of the stock price S at time t when $0 \leq t \leq T$.

11.8. If the derivative in Problem 11.7 is a success, the financial institution plans to offer another derivative which pays off a dollar amount equal to S_T^2 at time T. Use risk-neutral valuation to calculate the price of the derivative at time t in terms of the stock price S at time t when $0 \leq t \leq T$. (*Hint:* The expected value of S_T^2 can be calculated from the mean and variance of S_T given in this chapter.)

11.9. What is the price of a European call option on a nondividend-paying stock when the stock price is $52, the strike price is $50, the risk-free interest rate is 12 percent per annum, the volatility is 30 percent per annum, and the time to maturity is three months?

11.10. What is the price of a European put option on a nondividend-paying stock when the stock price is $69, the strike price is $70, the risk-free interest rate is 5 percent per annum, the volatility is 35 percent per annum, and the time to maturity is six months?

11.11. Consider an option on a nondividend-paying stock when the stock price is $30, the exercise price is $29, the risk-free interest rate is 5 percent per annum, the volatility is 25 percent per annum, and the time to maturity is four months.
a. What is the price of the option if it is a European call?
b. What is the price of the option if it is an American call?
c. What is the price of the option if it is a European put?
d. Verify that put–call parity holds.

11.12. Assume that the stock in Problem 11.11 is due to go ex-dividend in 1.5 months. The expected dividend is 50 cents.
a. What is the price of the option if it is a European call?
b. What is the price of the option if it is a European put?

11.13. A call option on a nondividend-paying stock has a market price of $2\tfrac{1}{2}$. The stock price is $15, the exercise price is $13, the time to maturity is three months, and the risk-free interest rate is 5 percent per annum. What is the implied volatility?

11.14. Show that the Black–Scholes formula for a call option gives a price which tends to $\max(S - X, 0)$ as $T \to 0$.

11.15. Consider an American call option when the stock price is $18, the exercise price is $20, the time to maturity is six months, the volatility is 30 percent per annum, and the risk-free interest rate is 10 percent per annum. Two equal dividends of 40 cents are expected during the life of the option, with ex-dividend dates at the end of two months and five months. Use Black's approximation and the DerivaGem software to value the option.

11.16. Explain carefully why Black's approach to evaluating an American call option on a dividend-paying stock may give an approximate answer even when only one dividend is anticipated. Does the answer given by Black's approach understate or overstate the true option value? Explain your answer.

11.17. Consider an American call option on a stock. The stock price is $70, the time to maturity is eight months, the risk-free rate of interest is 10 percent per annum, the exercise price is $65, and the volatility is 32 percent. A dividend of $1 is expected after three months and again after six months. Use the results in the appendix to show that it can never be optimal to exercise the option on either of the two dividend dates. Use DerivaGem to calculate the price of the option.

11.18. A stock price is currently $50 and the risk-free interest rate is 5 percent. Use the DerivaGem software to translate the following table of European call options on the stock into a table of implied volatilities, assuming no dividends. Are the option prices consistent with Black–Scholes?

	Maturity (months)		
Strike Price ($)	*3*	*6*	*12*
45	7.0	8.3	10.5
50	3.5	5.0	7.5
55	1.6	3.0	5.8

APPENDIX 11A

The Early Exercise of American Call Options on Dividend-paying Stocks

In chapter 8 we saw that it is never optimal to exercise an American call option on a nondividend-paying stock before the expiration date. A similar argument shows that the only times when a call option on a dividend-paying stock should be exercised are immediately before an ex-dividend date and on the expiration date. We assume that n ex-dividend dates are anticipated and that $t_1, t_2, \ldots, t_n$ are the moments in time immediately prior to the stock going ex-dividend, with $t_1 < t_2 < \cdots < t_n$. The dividends at these times will be denoted by $D_1, D_2, \ldots, D_n$, respectively.

We start by considering the possibility of early exercise immediately prior to the final ex-dividend date (i.e., at time t_n). If the option is exercised at time t_n, the investor receives

$$S(t_n) - X$$

If the option is not exercised, the stock price drops to $S(t_n) - D_n$. As shown in chapter 8, a lower bound for the price of the option is then

$$S(t_n) - D_n - Xe^{-r(T - t_n)}$$

It follows that if

$$S(t_n) - D_n - Xe^{-r(T - t_n)} \geq S(t_n) - X$$

that is,

$$D_n \leq X(1 - e^{-r(T - t_n)}) \tag{11A.1}$$

it cannot be optimal to exercise at time t_n. On the other hand, if

$$D_n > X(1 - e^{-r(T - t_n)}) \tag{11A.2}$$

it can be shown that it is always optimal to exercise at time t_n for a sufficiently high value of $S(t_n)$. The inequality in Equation 11A.2 is most likely to be satisfied when the final ex-dividend date is fairly close to the maturity of the option (i.e., when $T - t_n$ is small) and the dividend is large.

Consider next, time t_{n-1}, the penultimate ex-dividend date. If the option is exercised at time t_{n-1}, the investor receives

$$S(t_{n-1}) - X$$

If the option is not exercised at time t_{n-1}, the stock price drops to $S(t_{n-1}) - D_{n-1}$, and the earliest subsequent time at which exercise could take place is t_n. A lower bound to the option price if it is not exercised at time t_{n-1} is

$$S(t_{n-1}) - D_{n-1} - Xe^{-r(t_n - t_{n-1})}$$

It follows that if

$$S(t_{n-1}) - D_{n-1} - Xe^{-r(t_n - t_{n-1})} \geq S(t_{n-1}) - X$$

or

$$D_{n-1} \leq X(1 - e^{-r(t_n - t_{n-1})})$$

it is not optimal to exercise at time t_{n-1}. Similarly, for any $i < n$, if

$$D_i \leq X(1 - e^{-r(t_{i+1} - t_i)}) \tag{11A.3}$$

it is not optimal to exercise at time t_i.

The inequality in Equation 11A.3 is approximately equivalent to

$$D_i \leq Xr(t_{i+1} - t_i)$$

Assuming that X is fairly close to the current stock price, the dividend yield on the stock would have to be either close to or above the risk-free rate of interest for the inequality not to be satisfied. This is not usually the case.

We can conclude from this analysis that, in most circumstances, the only time that needs to be considered for the early exercise of an American call is the final ex-dividend date, t_n. Furthermore, if the inequality in Equation 11A.3 holds for $i = 1, 2, \ldots, n - 1$ and the inequality in Equation 11A.1 also holds, we can be certain that early exercise is never optimal.

Example

Consider the example that was used in this chapter to value European options on dividend-paying stocks: $S = 40$, $X = 40$, $r = 0.09$, $\sigma = 0.30$, $t_1 = 0.1667$, $t_2 = 0.4167$, $T = 0.5$, and $D_1 = D_2 = 0.5$. We suppose that the option is American rather than European. In this case

$$X(1 - e^{-r(T_2 - t_1)}) = 40(1 - e^{-0.09 \times 0.25}) = 0.89$$

Because this is greater than 0.5, it follows from Equation 11A.3 that the option should never be exercised on the first ex-dividend date. Also

$$X(1 - e^{-r(T - t_2)}) = 40(1 - e^{-0.09 \times 0.08333}) = 0.30$$

Because this is less than 0.5, it follows from Equation 11A.1 that when the option is sufficiently deeply in the money, it should be exercised on the second ex-dividend date.

12 Options on Stock Indices and Currencies

In this chapter we tackle the problem of valuing options on stock indices and currencies. As a first step, some of the results in chapters 8, 10, and 11 are extended to cover European options on a stock paying a continuous dividend yield. It is then argued that both stock indices and currencies are analogous to stocks paying continuous dividend yields. The basic results for options on a stock paying a continuous dividend yield can therefore be used for these types of options as well.

A Simple Rule

In this section we consider a simple rule that enables results produced for European options on a nondividend-paying stock to be extended so that they apply to European options on stocks paying a known dividend yield.

Consider the difference between a stock that pays a continuous dividend yield at a rate q per annum and a similar stock that pays no dividends. As explained in chapter 11, the payment of a dividend causes a stock price to drop by an amount equal to the dividend. The payment of a continuous dividend yield at rate q therefore causes the growth rate in the stock price to be less than it would otherwise be by an amount q. If, with a continuous dividend yield of q, the stock price grows from S today to S_T at time T, then in the absence of dividends it would grow from S today to $S_T e^{qT}$ at time T. Alternatively, in the absence of dividends it would grow from Se^{-qT} today to S_T at time T.

This argument shows that we get the same probability distribution for the stock price at time T in each of the following two cases:

1. The stock starts at price S and pays a continuous dividend yield at rate q.
2. The stock starts at price Se^{-qT} and pays no dividend yield.

This leads to a simple rule:

> When valuing a European option lasting for time T on a stock paying a known dividend yield at rate q, we reduce the current stock price from S to Se^{-qT} and then value the option as though the stock pays no dividends.

LOWER BOUNDS FOR OPTIONS PRICES

As a first application of this rule, consider the problem of determining bounds for the price of a European option on a stock paying a dividend yield at rate q. Substituting Se^{-qT} for S in Equation 8.1, we see that a lower bound for the European call option price, c, is given by

$$c > Se^{-qT} - Xe^{-rT} \qquad \textbf{(12.1)}$$

We can also prove this directly by considering the following two portfolios:

Portfolio A: one European call option plus an amount of cash equal to Xe^{-rT}

Portfolio B: e^{-qT} shares with dividends being reinvested in additional shares

In portfolio A the cash, if it is invested at the risk-free interest rate, will grow to X at time T. If $S_T > X$, the call option is exercised at time T and portfolio A is worth S_T. If $S_T < X,$ the call option expires worthless and the portfolio is worth X. Hence, at time T portfolio A is worth

$$\max(S_T, X)$$

Because of the reinvestment of dividends, portfolio B becomes one share at time T. It is therefore worth S_T at this time. It follows that portfolio A is always worth as much as, and is sometimes worth more than, portfolio B at time T. In the absence of arbitrage opportunities, this must also be true today. Hence,

$$c + Xe^{-rT} > Se^{-qT}$$

or

$$c > Se^{-qT} - Xe^{-rT}$$

To obtain a lower bound for a European put option, we can similarly replace S by Se^{-qT} in Equation 8.2 to get

$$p > Xe^{-rT} - Se^{-qT} \qquad \textbf{(12.2)}$$

This result can also be proved directly by considering

Portfolio C: one European put option plus e^{-qT} shares with dividends on the shares being reinvested in additional shares

Portfolio D: an amount of cash equal to Xe^{-rT}

PUT–CALL PARITY

Replacing S by Se^{-qT} in Equation 8.3, we obtain put–call parity for an option on a stock paying a continuous dividend yield at rate q:

$$c + Xe^{-rT} = p + Se^{-qT} \qquad \textbf{(12.3)}$$

This result can also be proved directly by considering the following two portfolios:

Portfolio A: one European call option plus an amount of cash equal to Xe^{-rT}

Portfolio C: one European put option plus e^{-qT} shares with dividends on the shares being reinvested in additional shares

The portfolios are both worth $\max(S_T, X)$ at time T. They must therefore be worth the same today, and the put–call parity result in Equation 12.3 follows.

Pricing Formulas

By replacing S by Se^{-qT} in the Black–Scholes formulas, Equations 11.5 and 11.6, we obtain the price, c, of a European call and the price, p, of a European put on a stock paying a continuous dividend yield at rate q as:

$$c = Se^{-qT} N(d_1) - Xe^{-rT} N(d_2) \tag{12.4}$$

$$p = Xe^{-rT} N(-d_2) - Se^{-qT} N(-d_1) \tag{12.5}$$

Because

$$\ln \frac{Se^{-qT}}{X} = \ln \frac{S}{X} - qT$$

d_1 and d_2 are given by

$$d_1 = \frac{\ln(S/X) + (r - q + \sigma^2/2)T}{\sigma\sqrt{T}}$$

and

$$d_2 = \frac{\ln(S/X) + (r - q - \sigma^2/2)T}{\sigma\sqrt{T}} = d_1 - \sigma\sqrt{T}$$

These results were first derived by Merton.[1] As discussed in chapter 11, the word *dividend* should, for the purposes of option valuation, be defined as the reduction in the stock price on the ex-dividend date arising from any dividends declared. If the dividend yield rate is known but not constant during the life of the option, Equations 12.4 and 12.5 are still true, with q equal to the average annualized dividend yield.

Binomial Trees

We now move on to examine the effect of a dividend yield equal to q on the results for the binomial model in chapter 10.

Consider the situation in Figure 12.1, in which a stock price starts at S and moves either up to Su or down to Sd. As in chapter 10, we define p as the probability of an

---

[1] See R. C. Merton, "Theory of Rational Option Pricing," *Bell Journal of Economics and Management Science* 4 (Spring 1973): 141–183.

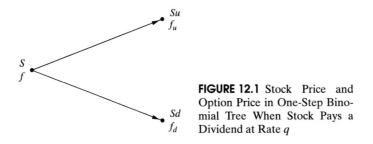

FIGURE 12.1 Stock Price and Option Price in One-Step Binomial Tree When Stock Pays a Dividend at Rate q

up movement in a risk-neutral world. The total return provided by the stock in a risk-neutral world must be the risk-free interest rate, r. The dividends provide a return equal to q. The return in the form of capital gains must be $r - q$. This means that p must satisfy

$$pSu + (1 - p)Sd = Se^{(r-q)T} \tag{12.6}$$

or

$$p = \frac{e^{(r-q)T} - d}{u - d} \tag{12.7}$$

As noted in chapter 10, the value of the derivative at time zero is the expected payoff in a risk-neutral world discounted at the risk-free rate:

$$f = e^{-rT}[pf_u + (1 - p)f_d] \tag{12.8}$$

Example

Suppose that the initial stock price is $30 and the stock price will either move up to $36 or down to $24 during a six-month period. The six-month risk-free interest rate is 5 percent and the stock is expected to provide a dividend yield of 3 percent during the six-month period. In this case $u = 1.2$, $d = 0.8$, and

$$p = \frac{e^{(0.05-0.03)\times 0.5} - 0.8}{1.2 - 0.8} = 0.5251$$

Consider a six-month put option on the stock with a strike price of $28. If the stock price moves up, the payoff is zero; if it moves down, the payoff is 4. The value of the option is therefore

$$e^{-0.05 \times 0.5}[0.5251 \times 0 + 0.4749 \times 4] = 1.85$$

Options on Stock Indices

As discussed in chapter 7, several exchanges trade options on stock indices. Some of the indices track the movement of the market as a whole. Others are based on the performance of a particular sector (e.g., computer technology, oil and gas, transportation, or telephone).

TABLE 12.1 Quotes for Stock Index Options from the *Wall Street Journal*, September 25, 1996

INDEX OPTIONS TRADING

S & P 100 INDEX(OEX)

Oct	555p	856	1/4	...	3,451
Oct	560p	301	5/16	− 1/16	1,547
Nov	560p	306	1	− 3/16	832
Oct	565p	1	3/8	...	1,773
Nov	565p	6	1 1/8	− 1/8	81
Oct	570p	57	1/2	...	3,725
Nov	570p	12	1 3/8	+ 1/4	1,277
Oct	575p	51	1/2	− 1/16	767
Nov	575p	20	1 1/2	− 1/8	50
Oct	580p	184	1/2	− 1/16	1,875
Nov	580p	339	1 7/16	− 3/16	668
Oct	585p	67	5/8	− 1/16	1,305
Oct	590c	60	74	+ 1	239
Oct	590p	44	9/16	− 5/16	2,933
Nov	590p	45	2	− 1/4	869
Oct	595c	3,766	3/4	− 1/4	3,045
Oct	595p	5	3/4	− 1/16	1,950
Nov	595p	50	2 1/4	...	405
Oct	600p	588	7/8	− 1/16	7,007
Nov	600p	144	2 3/4	+ 1/8	2,167
Dec	600c	1	72	+ 1	4
Dec	600p	601	4 3/4	− 5/8	3,669
Oct	605p	311	1	− 1/16	2,346
Nov	605p	58	3	+ 1/16	2,214
Oct	610c	1	54 1/2	+ 1 7/8	407
Oct	610p	563	1 1/8	− 1/8	8,410
Nov	610p	30	3 3/8	− 1/8	1,481
Dec	610p	10	5 3/4	...	945
Oct	615p	309	1 7/16	− 1/16	2,970
Nov	615p	599	3 7/8	− 1/8	726
Dec	615p	1,455	6 7/8	+ 1/8	1
Oct	620c	9	45 1/2	− 1 1/2	1,107
Oct	620p	1,663	1 5/8	− 1/8	8,947
Nov	620p	296	4 1/2	+ 1/4	13,400
Dec	620c	150	54	+ 2 1/2	555
Dec	620p	64	7 1/2	+ 1/2	4,184
Jan	620c	150	57 1/2	...	...
Jan	620p	10	9	− 3/4	34
Oct	625c	110	43 3/8	+ 1/8	979
Oct	625p	1,840	2	...	9,464
Nov	625p	524	5	+ 1/8	2,813
Dec	625p	11	8	− 1	172
Oct	630c	191	36	+ 3/4	7,732
Oct	630p	4,573	2 3/8	− 1/16	14,545
Nov	630c	200	41 1/2	+ 3 1/2	649
Nov	630p	1,507	5 3/4	+ 1/4	1,420
Dec	630c	6	51 1/8	+ 5 5/8	459
Dec	630p	58	9	− 1/4	3,237
Jan	630p	5	11 1/4	...	11
Oct	635c	4	36	+ 5	4,951
Oct	635p	2,347	2 7/8	− 1/8	9,192
Nov	635p	17	6 1/2	+ 1/8	12,487
Dec	635p	65	10 1/4	+ 1/2	561
Oct	640c	151	30 1/2	+ 1/2	26,335
Oct	640p	3,886	3 5/8	...	22,903
Nov	640p	574	8	+ 1	3,300
Dec	640p	147	11	+ 1/2	4,343
Jan	640c	9	40 7/8	...	...
Jan	640p	5	14	− 1/8	10
Oct	645c	1,073	23 5/8	− 1 1/2	10,606
Oct	645p	3,871	4 3/8	...	8,899
Nov	645c	10	31 1/2	+ 4 1/2	3,459
Nov	645p	856	8 5/8	+ 3/8	3,934
Dec	645p	374	12 1/4	− 1 1/4	50
Oct	650c	65	19	− 2 3/8	7,568
Oct	650p	10,172	5 1/2	...	14,634
Nov	650c	28	28 1/2	+ 4 5/8	1,626
Nov	650p	267	10	+ 3/8	1,308
Dec	650c	4	31 3/4	− 1/4	1,645
Dec	650p	224	14	+ 1/2	2,656
Jan	650c	2	33 3/4	...	...
Jan	650p	1	16 1/4	...	...
Oct	655c	534	15 1/4	− 2 3/8	11,471
Oct	655p	8,278	6 3/4	+ 1/8	11,055
Nov	655c	10	20 5/8	− 2 3/4	1,074
Nov	655p	129	11 1/4	+ 1/4	1,396
Dec	655c	4	27 1/8	...	...
Dec	655p	6	15 1/4	− 1 1/2	15
Oct	660c	7,291	12 1/4	− 2	10,028
Oct	660p	16,051	8 1/2	+ 1/4	10,731
Nov	660c	453	17 3/4	− 1 1/2	3,053
Nov	660p	527	13 1/2	+ 1 3/8	734
Dec	660c	405	24	− 1 3/4	3,843
Dec	660p	457	16 3/4	+ 1/4	2,243
Jan	660c	3	29 1/2	...	...
Jan	660p	4	19	...	2
Oct	665c	7,823	9 1/8	− 2	6,470
Oct	665p	7,069	10 3/4	+ 1/2	3,210
Nov	665c	22	17 3/4	+ 1 1/2	1,005
Nov	665p	92	15 1/4	+ 1	86
Dec	665c	3	20 1/4	+ 3/4	1
Dec	665p	111	19 1/2	− 3/8	52
Oct	670c	9,647	6 5/8	− 1 5/8	8,961
Oct	670p	429	13 1/2	+ 1 1/4	612
Nov	670c	84	12	− 1 1/2	1,639
Nov	670p	22	19	− 5/8	56
Dec	670c	10	20	+ 2	3,254
Dec	670p	1	18 3/4	− 2 7/8	40
Jan	670c	10	22 1/2	...	52
Oct	675c	9,347	4 3/4	− 1 1/8	7,156
Oct	675p	136	17	+ 1	138
Nov	675c	169	9 1/4	− 3/8	2,421
Nov	675p	5	20	+ 3/4	7
Oct	680c	9,688	3 1/8	− 7/8	8,003
Oct	680p	32	20 1/2	+ 1 1/4	53
Nov	680c	126	7 1/2	− 1	1,446
Dec	680c	301	13	− 1/2	1,873
Dec	680p	2	27 3/8	+ 1/8	45
Jan	680c	9	17 1/2	...	...
Oct	685c	5,523	2	− 11/16	3,691
Nov	685c	23	5 3/4	− 1	2,115
Dec	685c	55	11 3/4	+ 1 3/8	6
Oct	690c	3,808	1 3/16	− 7/16	7,165
Oct	690p	21	28	+ 3/8	37
Nov	690c	192	5 1/8	...	363
Nov	690p	5	28 1/4	− 5 3/4	...
Dec	690c	36	9 3/4	+ 1	197
Dec	690p	1	31 1/2	− 1/2	5
Jan	690p	2	34 3/8	...	...
Dec	695c	10	7 1/4	...	...
Oct	700c	1,917	7/16	− 1/8	600
Nov	700c	237	2 3/8	+ 1/8	45
Dec	700c	10	6 3/4	+ 1	10
Call Vol.		**63,765**	**Open Int.**		**168,088**
Put Vol.		**73,754**	**Open Int.**		**229,970**

S & P 500 INDEX-AM(SPX)

Dec	450p	90	1/4	...	11,555
Dec	500p	15	1/2	...	9,360
Oct	525p	150	1/16	...	922
Dec	525p	10	11/16	...	10,714
Oct	550p	50	1/8	− 1/16	1,772
Dec	575p	412	1 15/16	− 1/8	24,415
Oct	600c	3	90 1/8	+ 2 1/4	1,414
Oct	600p	172	9/16	...	9,533
Nov	600p	9	1 5/8	− 1/8	2,422
Dec	600c	10,450	94	+ 1 1/2	37,623
Dec	600p	12,261	3	...	81,129
Oct	610p	400	5/8	...	3,293
Dec	610p	4	3 1/4	− 5/8	8,738
Oct	615p	100	3/4	− 3/16	4,838
Oct	620c	15	71	+ 5 7/8	4,745
Oct	620p	2,310	7/8	+ 1/8	10,474
Nov	620p	10	2 1/4	− 1/8	2,252

continues on next page, column 1

Source: Reprinted by permission from the *Wall Street Journal*, September 25, 1996.

TABLE 12.1 (cont.)

Dec	620p	45	4⅜	− ¾	1,502
Oct	625p	30	⅞	− 1/16	6,367
Dec	625p	510	4½	− ¼	39,064
Oct	630p	167	1 11/16	− 1/16	6,021
Nov	630p	514	3⅛	− ⅜	1,585
Dec	630c	10	68	+ 1	20
Dec	630p	12	5¼	− ⅛	4,396
Oct	635p	80	1 3/16	− 3/16	8,929
Nov	635p	500	3¼	...	...
Oct	640c	526	48	+ ¼	603
Oct	640p	1,758	1⅝	+ ⅛	12,204
Nov	640p	43	4	+ ⅛	4,262
Dec	640c	15	59½	+ 4¾	11,392
Dec	640p	9	6⅞	− ⅛	16,533
Oct	645c	150	45⅝	+ 1⅜	267
Oct	645p	576	1⅝	− ⅜	2,393
Nov	645c	10	48¼	...	...
Dec	645c	10	57⅝	+ 7⅝	1,097
Dec	645p	10	7⅝	− ¾	10,405
Oct	650c	160	37½	− 1¾	4,795
Oct	650p	2,050	2⅛	− ⅛	23,179
Nov	650p	189	5⅛	+ ⅛	3,469

Strike		Vol.	Last	Net Chg.	Open Int.
Dec	650p	1,559	8⅛	+ ¼	41,929
Oct	655p	2,289	2¼	− ⅛	16,484
Dec	655p	16	8⅜	− ¼	1,811
Oct	660c	501	31¼	+ ⅛	9,013
Oct	660p	1,693	3	− ⅛	18,067
Nov	660p	281	6⅝	+ ⅛	2,981
Dec	660c	7	44	+ 6	4,493
Dec	660p	88	9⅝	− ⅜	16,252
Oct	665c	511	28½	+ 1½	5,586
Oct	665p	2,360	3½	− ¼	10,463
Nov	665c	10	36	...	...
Nov	665p	3,013	7½	...	...
Dec	665p	225	11⅛	+ ⅜	6,931
Oct	670c	525	22⅞	...	5,448
Oct	670p	1,415	4½	− ¼	20,567
Nov	670p	1,062	8¾	+ ⅜	4,913
Dec	670c	2	35¼	+ 4	4,518
Dec	670p	74	12½	+ ½	3,143
Oct	675c	500	19	...	13,382
Oct	675p	2,191	5⅝	− ¼	12,391
Nov	675c	1	24½	+ 13½	2
Nov	675p	61	8⅝	− 1⅜	3,338
Dec	675p	138	12¾	− 2⅜	19,014
Oct	680c	1,989	14⅜	− 1⅛	12,571
Oct	680p	2,931	6⅞	− ⅜	6,695
Nov	680c	1	19¾	− 1	5,688
Nov	680p	127	11½	− 1⅜	2,345
Dec	680c	2	27⅝	+ 2	792
Dec	680p	319	15¼	+ ⅛	2,390
Oct	685c	1,330	11⅛	− 1⅛	8,609
Oct	685p	9,792	8⅝	...	6,352
Dec	685c	203	23½	− ½	5,799
Dec	685p	523	17⅛	+ ⅜	800
Oct	690c	4,065	8⅜	− 1	14,520
Oct	690p	2,822	9⅝	− 1¼	1,742
Nov	690c	2	16¼	+ 2¼	2,213
Nov	690p	466	15¼	− ¾	173
Dec	690c	206	20	− ⅝	4,403
Dec	690p	222	19½	+ 1½	6,668
Oct	695c	2,349	6⅛	− ⅝	7,914
Oct	695p	187	13½	...	273
Dec	695c	801	17⅜	− ¼	2,774
Oct	700c	8,689	4	− ⅞	15,212
Oct	700p	400	16¼	− ⅞	910
Nov	700c	2,923	10⅜	+ 1	5,944
Nov	700p	6	19¾	− ½	454
Dec	700c	10,676	14⅞	− ½	27,120
Dec	700p	11,474	20¼	− 3	11,471
Oct	705c	5,602	2¾	− ⅜	5,260
Oct	705p	440	16	− 9	2
Nov	705c	1,700	7¾	− ¼	66
Nov	705p	6	21⅝	...	...
Oct	710c	1,895	1¾	− ½	9,986
Oct	710p	351	22⅝	− 1⅛	261
Nov	710c	1	6⅛	+ ⅜	2,605
Nov	710p	78	25⅞	− ⅜	11
Dec	710c	250	11⅛	+ ¾	2,200
Dec	710p	1,134	26¾	− 3½	27
Oct	715c	796	1	− ⅜	814
Oct	715p	152	26⅝	− 1⅜	255
Nov	715c	15	4½	+ 1	562
Nov	715p	1	28	− 4¼	...
Oct	720c	1,171	⅝	− 3/16	2,440
Oct	720p	1	29¾	− 2¼	2,001
Nov	720c	1	3¼	− ⅛	5,357
Oct	725c	117	⅜	− 1/16	8,285
Nov	725c	40	2½	+ ¼	6,375
Dec	725c	390	6⅛	+ ⅛	15,515
Dec	725p	90	37½	− 3⅛	1,844
Dec	750c	120	1⅞	+ ¾	2,719
Call Vol.		59,567	Open Int.		988,266
Put Vol.		78,239	Open Int.		851,793

LEAPS-LONG TERM

S & P 100 INDEX – CB

Dec 97	40p	15	¼	...	8899
Dec 97	42½p	5	⅜	+ ⅛	2536
Dec 97	45p	3	7/16	+ 1/16	4020
Dec 97	55p	40	1⅛	...	9308
Dec 97	60p	76	1⅞	...	17208
Dec 96	62½p	72	13/16	− 1/16	8460
Dec 97	62½p	33	2 7/16	− 1/16	4045
Dec 96	65p	85	1⅜	− 1/16	3201
Dec 97	65c	250	6⅞	...	385
Dec 97	65p	30	3⅜	...	3365
Dec 98	65p	110	4	...	287
Dec 96	67½p	30	2⅜	− ⅛	138
Dec 97	67½p	10	4⅜	...	3982
Dec 96	70p	3	4⅜	+ ⅜	2986

Call vol.............250 Open Int......36,516
Put vol. ....512 Open Int. ...266,790

S & P 500 INDEX – CB

Dec 97	40p	14	¼	+ ⅛	22493
Dec 96	55p	5	⅛	...	11766
Dec 97	57½p	100	1	− 1/16	3465
Dec 96	60p	20	5/16	...	25046
Dec 97	60p	203	1 7/16	...	21093
Dec 98	60p	22	2	...	3744
Dec 97	62½c	64	10½	+ 3⅜	163
Dec 96	65p	370	¾	− 1/16	5403
Dec 97	65p	37	2 7/16	+ 1/16	9219
Dec 98	65c	16	11⅝	+ ⅛	30
Dec 98	65p	3	2⅞	...	45634
Dec 96	67½c	10	3	+ 3/16	38
Dec 97	67½p	90	3⅛	+ ⅛	1437
Dec 98	67½p	7	3½	...	5838
Dec 96	70c	7	1⅝	+ ⅜	184
Dec 97	70p	151	3⅞	...	3514
Dec 98	70p	209	4¼	+ ¼	14576

Call vol.............97 Open Int......15,505
Put vol..........1,231 Open Int. ...374,611

QUOTES

Table 12.1 shows quotes for options on the S&P 100 and S&P 500 index options as they appeared in the Money and Investing section of the *Wall Street Journal* on Wednesday, September 25, 1996. These are the two most popular index options and both trade on the CBOE. The quotes refer to the price at which the last trade was made on Tuesday, September 24, 1996. The closing prices of the S&P 100 and S&P 500 indices were 661.60 and 685.61 on September 24, 1996.

The options on the S&P 500 are European, whereas those on the S&P 100 are American. All are settled in cash rather than by delivering the securities underlying the index. This means that, upon exercise of the option, the holder of a call option receives $S - X$ in cash and the writer of the option pays this amount in cash, where S is the value of the index and X is the strike price. Similarly, the holder of a put option receives $X - S$ in cash and the writer of the option pays this amount in cash. The cash payment is based on the index value at the end of the day on which the exercise instructions are issued. Each contract is for $100 times the value of the index.

Example

In Table 12.1 one October call option contract on the S&P 100 with strike price of 635 cost $36 \times 100 = \$3,600$ on September 24, 1996. The value of the index at the close of trading on that day was 661.60, so that the option was in the money. If the option contract was exercised on September 24, 1996, the holder would receive $(661.60 - 635.00) \times 100 = \$2,660$ in cash.

Table 12.1 shows that in addition to relatively short-dated options, the exchanges trade longer-maturity contracts known as LEAPS. The acronym LEAPS stands for Long-term Equity AnticiPation Securities and was originated by the CBOE. LEAPS are exchange-traded options that last up to three years. The index is divided by 10 for the purposes of quoting the strike price and the option price. One contract is an option on 100 times one-tenth of the index (or 10 times the index). LEAPS on indices have expiration dates in December. LEAPS on the S&P 100 are American, whereas those on the S&P 500 are European. As mentioned in chapter 7, the CBOE and several other exchanges also trade LEAPS on many individual stocks. These have expirations in January.

Another innovation of the CBOE is *caps*, which trade on the S&P 100 and S&P 500. These are options for which the payout is capped so that it cannot exceed $30. The options are European except for the following: A call cap is automatically exercised on a day when the index closes more than $30 above the strike price; a put cap is automatically exercised on a day when the index closes more than $30 below the cap level.

The CBOE also trades *flex options* on indices. As mentioned in chapter 7, these are options where the trader can choose the expiration date, the strike price, whether the option is American or European, and the settlement basis.

PORTFOLIO INSURANCE

Portfolio managers can use index options to limit their downside risk. Suppose that the value of an index is S. Consider a manager in charge of a well-diversified portfolio whose beta is 1.0. A beta of 1.0 implies that the returns from the portfolio mirror those from the index. If the dividend yield from the portfolio is the same as the dividend yield from the index, the percentage changes in the value of the portfolio can be expected to be approximately the same as the percentage changes in the value of the index. Each contract on the S&P 500 is for 100 times the index. It follows that the value of the portfolio is protected against the possibility of the index falling below X if, for each

TABLE 12.2   Using Options to Protect the Value of a Portfolio That Mirrors the S&P 100

From the Trader's Desk

A manager in charge of a portfolio worth $500,000 is concerned that the market might decline rapidly during the next three months and would like to use index options as a hedge. The portfolio is expected to mirror closely the S&P 100, which is currently standing at 250. A three-month put option on the S&P 100 with a strike price of 240 is available.

The Strategy

The manager buys 20 put option contracts with a strike price of 240. This strategy is designed to ensure that the value of the manager's position does not decline below $480,000.

The Outcome

The index dropped to 225 in the three months. The portfolio was worth $450,000. The payoff from the options was $20 \times (240 - 225) \times 100 = \$30,000$, bringing the total value of the position up to $450,000 + \$30,000 = \$480,000$.

$100S$ dollars in the portfolio, the manager buys one put option contract with strike price X. Suppose that the manager's portfolio is worth $500,000 and the value of the index is 250. The portfolio is worth 2,000 times the index. The manager can obtain insurance against the value of the portfolio dropping below $480,000 in the next three months by buying 20 put option contracts with a strike price of 240. To illustrate how this works, consider the situation where the index drops to 225 in three months. The portfolio will be worth about $450,000. However, the payoff from the options will be $20 \times (240 - 225) \times 100 = \$30,000$, bringing the total value of the portfolio up to the insured value of $480,000. This example is summarized in Table 12.2.

WHEN THE PORTFOLIO'S BETA IS NOT 1.0

If the portfolio's returns are not expected to equal those of an index, the capital asset pricing model can be used. This model asserts that the expected excess return of a portfolio over the risk-free interest rate equals β times the excess return of a market index over the risk-free interest rate. Consider a portfolio with $\beta = 2.0$. Suppose that it is currently worth $1 million. Suppose further that the current risk-free interest rate is 12 percent per annum, the dividend yield on both the portfolio and the index is expected to be 4 percent per annum, and the current value of the index is 250. Table 12.3 shows

TABLE 12.3   Relation between Value of Index and Value of Portfolio for $\beta = 2.0$

Value of Index in Three Months	Value of Portfolio in Three Months ($ millions)
270	1.14
260	1.06
250	0.98
240	0.90
230	0.82

the expected relationship between the level of the index and the value of the portfolio in three months. To illustrate the sequence of calculations necessary to derive Table 12.3, consider what happens when the value of the index in three months proves to be 260:

Value of index in three months	260
Return from change in index	10/250, or 4 percent per three months
Dividends from index	$0.25 \times 4 = 1$ percent per three months
Total return from index	$4 + 1 = 5$ percent per three months
Risk-free interest rate	$0.25 \times 12 = 3$ percent per three months
Excess return from index over risk-free interest rate	$5 - 3 = 2$ percent per three months
Excess return from portfolio over risk-free interest rate	$2 \times 2 = 4$ percent per three months
Return from portfolio	$3 + 4 = 7$ percent per three months
Dividends from portfolio	$0.25 \times 4 = 1$ percent per three months
Increase in value of portfolio	$7 - 1 = 6$ percent per three months
Value of portfolio	$1 \times 1.06 = \$1.06$ million

Suppose that S is the value of the index. It can be shown that for each $100S$ dollars in the portfolio, a total of β put contracts should be purchased. The strike price should be the value that the index is expected to have when the value of the portfolio reaches the insured value. Suppose that the insured value is $0.90 million in our example. Table 12.3 shows that the appropriate strike price for the put options purchased is 240. In this case $100S = \$25,000$ and the value of the portfolio is $1 million. Because $1,000,000/25,000 = 40$ and $\beta = 2.0$, the correct strategy is to buy 80 put contracts with a strike price of 240.

TABLE 12.4   Using Options to Protect the Value of a Portfolio That Has a Beta of 2.0

From the Trader's Desk
     A manager in charge of a portfolio worth $1 million is concerned that the market might decline rapidly during the next three months and would like to use index options as a hedge. The portfolio has a beta of 2.0, the S&P 100 is standing at 250, and a three-month put option on the S&P 500 with a strike price of 240 is available. The dividend yield on both the index and the portfolio is expected to be 4 percent per annum, and the risk-free interest rate is 12 percent per annum.

The Strategy
     The manager buys 80 put option contracts with a strike price of 240. The strategy is designed to ensure that the value of the manager's position does not decline below $0.90 million.

The Outcome
     The portfolio's value declined to $0.82 million during the three-month period. The value of the index declined to 230. The options provided a payoff of $80 \times (240 - 230) \times 100 = \$80,000$, bringing the value of the portfolio up to the required $0.90 million.

To illustrate that the required result is obtained, consider what happens if the value of the index falls to 230. As shown in Table 12.3, the value of the portfolio is $0.82 million. The put options pay off $(240 - 230) \times 80 \times 100 = \$80,000$, and this is exactly what is necessary to move the total value of the portfolio manager's position up from $0.82 million to the required level of $0.90 million. This example is summarized in Table 12.4.

VALUATION

In valuing index futures in chapter 3, we assumed that the index could be treated as a security paying a known dividend yield. In valuing index options, we make similar assumptions. This means that Equations 12.1 and 12.2 provide a lower bound for European index options; Equation 12.3 is the put–call parity result for European index options; and Equations 12.4 and 12.5 can be used to value European options on an index. In all cases S is equal to the value of the index, σ is equal to the volatility of the index, and q is equal to the average annualized yield on the index during the life of the option. The calculation of q should include only dividends whose ex-dividend date occurs during the life of the option.

In the United States ex-dividend dates tend to occur during the first week of February, May, August, and November. At any given time the correct value of q is therefore likely to depend on the life of the option. This is even more true for some foreign indices. For example, in Japan all companies tend to use the same ex-dividend dates.

Example

Consider a European call option on the S&P 500 that is two months from maturity. The current value of the index is 310, the exercise price is 300, the risk-free interest rate is 8 percent per annum, and the volatility of the index is 20 percent per annum. Dividend yields of 0.2 percent and 0.3 percent are expected in the first month and the second month, respectively. In this case $S = 310$, $X = 300$, $r = 0.08$, $\sigma = 0.2$, and $T = 2/12$. The total dividend yield during the option's life is $0.2 + 0.3 = 0.5$ percent. This is 3 percent per annum. Hence, $q = 0.03$ and

$$d_1 = \frac{\ln(310/300) + (0.08 - 0.03 + 0.2^2/2) \times 2/12}{0.2 \sqrt{2/12}} = 0.5444$$

$$d_2 = \frac{\ln(310/300) + (0.08 - 0.03 - 0.2^2/2) \times 2/12}{0.2 \sqrt{2/12}} = 0.4628$$

$$N(d_1) = 0.7069, \qquad N(d_2) = 0.6782$$

so that the call price, c, is given by Equation 12.4 as

$$c = 310 \times 0.7069 e^{-0.03 \times 2/12} - 300 \times 0.6782 e^{-0.08 \times 2/12} = 17.28$$

One contract would cost $1,728.

If the absolute amounts of the dividend that will be paid on the stocks underlying the index (rather than the dividend yield) is assumed to be known, the basic Black–

Scholes formula can be used with the initial stock price being reduced by the present value of the dividends. This is the approach recommended in chapter 11 for a stock paying known dividends. The approach may to be difficult to implement for a broadly based stock index, because it requires a knowledge of the dividends expected on every stock underlying the index.

In some circumstances it is optimal to exercise American put options on an index prior to the exercise date. To a lesser extent, this is also true of American call options on an index. American stock index option prices are therefore always worth slightly more than the corresponding European stock index option prices. We will look at numerical procedures for valuing American index options in chapter 16.

Currency Options

The Philadelphia Stock Exchange commenced trading in currency options in 1982. Since then the size of the market has grown very rapidly. The currencies traded include the Australian dollar, British pound, Canadian dollar, German mark, Japanese yen, French franc, and Swiss franc. For most of these currencies, the Philadelphia Stock Exchange trades European as well as American options. A significant amount of trading in foreign currency options is also done outside organized exchanges. Many banks and other financial institutions are prepared to sell or buy foreign currency options that have strike prices, exercise dates, and other features tailored to meet the needs of their corporate clients.

For a corporate client wishing to hedge a foreign exchange exposure, foreign currency options are an interesting alternative to forward contracts. A company due to receive sterling at a known time in the future can hedge its risk by buying put options on sterling which mature at that time. The strategy guarantees that the value of the sterling will not be less than the exercise price while allowing the company to benefit from any favorable exchange-rate movements. Similarly, a company due to pay sterling at a known time in the future can hedge by buying calls on sterling which mature at that time. The approach guarantees that the cost of the sterling will not be greater than a certain amount while allowing the company to benefit from favorable exchange-rate movements. Whereas a forward contract locks in the exchange rate for a future transaction, an option provides a type of insurance. This insurance is not free. It costs nothing to enter into a forward transaction, whereas options require a premium to be paid up front.

QUOTES

Table 12.5 shows the closing prices of some of the currency options traded on the Philadelphia Stock Exchange on Tuesday, September 25, 1996, as reported in the *Wall Street Journal* of Wednesday, September 25, 1996. The precise expiration date of a foreign currency option is the Saturday preceding the third Wednesday of the maturity month. The sizes of contracts are indicated at the beginning of each section of the table. The option prices are for the purchase or sale of one unit of a foreign currency with U.S. dollars. For the Japanese yen, the prices are in hundredths of a cent. For the other

TABLE 12.5   Currency Option Prices on the Philadelphia Exchange, September 24, 1996

OPTIONS — PHILADELPHIA EXCHANGE

	Calls Vol.	Last	Puts Vol.	Last
JYen				**91.16**
6,250,000 Japanese Yen-100ths of a cent per unit.				
93 Nov	50	0.58	...	...
98 Dec	2	0.07	...	...
DMark				**66.28**
62,500 German Mark EOM-European style.				
66 Sep	...	...	50	0.08
62,500 German Marks EOM-European style.				
66½ Sep	25	0.12	...	...
SFranc				**80.96**
62,500 Swiss Franc EOM-European style.				
77½ Oct	465	3.60	...	...
81½ Oct	465	0.63	...	...
62,500 Swiss Francs-European style.				
78 Sep	465	2.93	...	...
83 Sep	465	0.03	...	...
Australian Dollar				**78.75**
50,000 Australian Dollars-cents per unit.				
78 Dec	...	...	10	0.65
British Pound				**156.09**
31,250 British Pound EOM-cents per unit.				
5 Sep	8	0.83	...	...
31,250 British Pounds-cents per unit.				
156 Oct	...	...	80	0.75
156 Dec	...	...	12	1.73

	Calls Vol.	Last	Puts Vol.	Last
British Pound-GMark				**235.52**
31,250 British Pound-German mark EOM.				
236 Sep	256	0.34	...	...
Canadian Dollar				**73.22**
50,000 Canadian Dollars-cents per unit.				
72½ Dec	...	...	14	0.10
73 Nov	4	0.49	...	...
73 Dec	...	...	650	0.27
76 Nov	...	...	18	2.80
ECU				**125.98**
62,500 European Currency Units-cents per unit.				
128 Dec	2	0.82	...	...
German Mark				**66.28**
62,500 German Marks EOM-cents per unit.				
65½ Sep	...	...	100	0.03
65½ Oct	...	...	1	0.25
66½ Sep	300	0.10	...	...
67 Oct	1	0.25	...	...
62,500 German Marks-cents per unit.				
65½ Nov	...	...	50	0.38
66½ Oct	25	0.29	...	...

	Calls Vol.	Last	Puts Vol.	Last
66½ Nov	50	0.63	...	...
67 Oct	...	...	293	1.01
Swiss Franc				**80.96**
62,500 Swiss Francs-European Style.				
78 Oct	10	3.00	...	...
79 Oct	5	2.08	...	...
79 Dec	19	2.95	...	...
80 Oct	45	1.24	...	...
80 Nov	40	2.00	40	0.52
80 Dec	5	2.23	...	...
81 Oct	...	...	15	0.55
82 Oct	...	...	10	1.27
82 Nov	10	0.76	...	...
82 Dec	...	...	10	1.63
83 Oct	...	...	5	1.90
83 Nov	...	...	4	2.05
83 Dec	160	.81	10	2.24
84 Oct	...	...	5	3.03
62,500 Swiss Francs-cents per unit.				
79 Dec	...	...	30	0.52
80 Dec	...	...	5	0.76
82 Nov	50	0.79	...	...
Call Vol 3,256			**Open Int ... 36,553**	
Put Vol 1,670			**Open Int ... 108,553**	

Source: Reprinted by permission from the *Wall Street Journal,* September 25, 1996. Copyright ©1996, Dow Jones & Company, Inc. All rights reserved.

currencies, they are in cents. Thus, one put option contract on the British pound with exercise price 156 cents and exercise month October would give the holder the right to sell £31,250 for U.S. $44,750 ($= 1.56 \times 31{,}250$). The indicated price of the contract is $31{,}250 \times 0.0075 = \$234.37$. The spot exchange rate is shown as 156.09 cents per pound sterling.

VALUATION

To value currency options, we define S as the spot exchange rate. To be precise, S is the value of one unit of the foreign currency in U.S. dollars. As noted in chapter 3, a foreign currency is analogous to a stock paying a known dividend yield. The owner of foreign currency receives a "dividend yield" equal to the risk-free interest rate, r_f, in the foreign currency. Equations 12.1 and 12.2, with q replaced by r_f, provide bounds for the European call price, c, and the European put price, p:

$$c > Se^{-r_f T} - Xe^{-rT}$$

$$p > Xe^{-rT} - Se^{-r_f T}$$

Equation 12.3, with q replaced by r_f, provides the put–call parity result for currency options:

$$c + Xe^{-rT} = p + Se^{-r_f T}$$

Finally, Equations 12.4 and 12.5 provide the pricing formulas for currency options when q is replaced by r_f:

$$c = Se^{-r_f T} N(d_1) - Xe^{-rT} N(d_2) \tag{12.9}$$

$$p = Xe^{-rT} N(-d_2) - Se^{-r_f T} N(-d_1) \tag{12.10}$$

where

$$d_1 = \frac{\ln(S/X) + (r - r_f + \sigma^2/2)T}{\sigma\sqrt{T}}$$

and

$$d_2 = \frac{\ln(S/X) + (r - r_f - \sigma^2/2)T}{\sigma\sqrt{T}} = d_1 - \sigma\sqrt{T}$$

Both the domestic interest rate, r, and the foreign interest rate, r_f, are assumed to be constant and the same for all maturities. Put and call options on a currency are symmetrical in that a put option to sell currency A for currency B at an exercise price X is the same as a call option to buy B with A at $1/X$.

Example

Consider a four-month European call option on the British pound. Suppose that the current exchange rate is 1.6000, the exercise price is 1.6000, the risk-free interest rate in the United States is 8 percent per annum, the risk-free interest rate in Britain is 11 percent per annum, and the option price is 4.3 cents. In this case $S = 1.6, X = 1.6, r = 0.08, r_f = 0.11, T = 0.3333$, and $c = 0.043$. The implied volatility can be calculated by trial and error. A volatility of 20 percent gives an option price of 0.0639; a volatility of 10 percent gives an option price of 0.0285; and so on. The implied volatility is 14.1 percent.

From Equation 3.13, the forward rate, F, for a maturity T is given by

$$F = Se^{(r - r_f)T}$$

Thus, Equations 12.9 and 12.10 can be simplified to

$$c = e^{-rT}[FN(d_1) - XN(d_2)] \tag{12.11}$$

$$p = e^{-rT}[XN(-d_2) - FN(-d_1)] \tag{12.12}$$

where

$$d_1 = \frac{\ln(F/X) + \sigma^2 T/2}{\sigma\sqrt{T}}$$

$$d_2 = \frac{\ln(F/X) - \sigma^2 T/2}{\sigma\sqrt{T}} = d_1 - \sigma\sqrt{T}$$

Note that, for Equations 12.11 and 12.12 to apply, the maturities of the forward contract and the option must be the same.

In some circumstances it is optimal to exercise American currency options prior to maturity. Thus, American currency options are worth more than their European counterparts. In general, call options on high-interest currencies and put options on low-interest currencies are the most likely to be exercised prior to maturity. The reason is that a high-interest currency is expected to depreciate relative to the U.S. dollar, and a low-interest currency is expected to appreciate relative to the U.S. dollar. Unfortunately, analytic formulas do not exist for the evaluation of American currency options. We will look at numerical procedures in chapter 16.

Summary

The Black–Scholes formula for valuing European options on a nondividend-paying stock can be extended to cover European options on a stock paying a continuous known dividend yield. In practice, stocks do not pay continuous dividend yields. However, a number of other assets upon which options are written can be considered to be analogous to a stock paying a continuous dividend yield. This chapter has used the following results:

1. A stock index is analogous to a stock paying a continuous dividend yield. The dividend yield is the dividend yield on the stocks comprising the index.
2. A foreign currency is analogous to a stock paying a continuous dividend yield. The dividend yield is the foreign risk-free interest rate.

The extension to Black–Scholes can therefore be used to value European options on stock indices and foreign currencies. As we will see in chapter 16, these analogies are also useful in numerically valuing American options on these assets.

Index options are settled in cash. Upon exercise of an index call option, the holder receives the amount by which the index exceeds the strike price at the close of trading. Similarly, upon exercise of an index put option, the holder receives the amount by which the strike price exceeds the index at the close of trading. Index options can be used for portfolio insurance. If the value of the portfolio mirrors the index, it is appropriate to buy one put option for each $100S$ dollars in the portfolio, where S is the value of the index. If the portfolio does not mirror the index, β put options should be purchased for each $100S$ dollars in the portfolio, where β is the beta of the portfolio calculated using the capital asset pricing model. The strike price of the put options purchased should reflect the level of insurance required.

Currency options are traded both on organized exchanges and over the counter. They can be used by corporate treasurers to hedge foreign exchange exposure. For example, a U.S. corporate treasurer who knows that the company will receive sterling at a certain time in the future can hedge by buying put options that mature at that time. Similarly, a U.S. corporate treasurer who knows sterling will be paid at a certain time in the future can hedge by buying call options that mature at that time.

Suggestions for Further Reading

General

Merton, R. C. "Theory of Rational Option Pricing," *Bell Journal of Economics and Management Science* 4 (Spring 1973): 141–183.

Stoll, H. R., and R. E. Whaley. "New Option Instruments: Arbitrageable Linkages and Valuation," *Advances in Futures and Options Research* 1, pt. A (1986): 25–62.

On options on stock indices

Chance, D. M. "Empirical Tests of the Pricing of Index Call Options," *Advances in Futures and Options Research* 1, pt. A (1986): 141–166.

On options on currencies

Amin, K., and R. A. Jarrow. "Pricing Foreign Currency Options under Stochastic Interest Rates," *Journal of International Money and Finance* 10 (1991): 310–329.

Biger, N., and J. Hull. "The Valuation of Currency Options," *Financial Management* 12 (Spring 1983): 24–28.

Bodurtha, J. N., and G. R. Courtadon. "Tests of an American Option Pricing Model on the Foreign Currency Options Market," *Journal of Financial and Quantitative Analysis* 22 (June 1987): 153–167.

Garman, M. B., and S. W. Kohlhagen. "Foreign Currency Option Values," *Journal of International Money and Finance* 2 (December 1983): 231–237.

Grabbe, J. O. "The Pricing of Call and Put Options on Foreign Exchange," *Journal of International Money and Finance* 2 (December 1983): 239–253.

Quiz

1. A portfolio is currently worth $10 million and has a beta of 1.0. The S&P 100 is currently standing at 250. Explain how a put option on the S&P 100 with a strike price of 240 can be used to provide portfolio insurance.

2. "Once we know how to value options on a stock paying a continuous dividend yield, we know how to value options on stock indices and currencies." Explain this statement.

3. A stock index is currently 300, the dividend yield on the index is 3 percent per annum, and the risk-free interest rate is 8 percent per annum. What is a lower bound for the price of a six-month European call option on the index when the strike price is 290?

4. A currency is currently worth $0.80. Over each of the next two months it is expected to increase or decrease in value by 2 percent. The domestic and foreign risk-free interest rates are 6 percent and 8 percent, respectively. What is the value of a two-month European call option with a strike price of $0.80?

5. Explain how corporations can use currency options to hedge their foreign exchange risk.

6. Calculate the value of a three-month at-the-money European call option on a stock index when the index is at 250, the risk-free interest rate is 10 percent per annum, the volatility of the index is 18 percent per annum, and the dividend yield on the index is 3 percent per annum.

7. Calculate the value of an eight-month European put option on a currency with a strike price of 0.50. The current exchange rate is 0.52, the volatility of the exchange rate is 12 percent, the domestic risk-free interest rate is 4 percent per annum, and the foreign risk-free interest rate is 8 percent per annum.

Questions and Problems

12.1. Suppose that an exchange constructs a stock index which tracks the return, including dividends, on a certain portfolio. Explain how you would value (a) futures contracts and (b) European options on the index.

12.2. A foreign currency is currently worth $1.50. The domestic and foreign risk-free interest rates are 5 percent and 9 percent, respectively. Calculate a lower bound for the value of a six-month call option on the currency with a strike price of $1.40 if it is (a) European and (b) American.

12.3. Consider a stock index currently standing at 250. The dividend yield on the index is 4 percent per annum and the risk-free rate is 6 percent per annum. A three-month European call option on the index with a strike price of 245 is currently worth $10. What is the value of a three-month put option on the index with a strike price of 245?

12.4. The S&P index currently stands at 348 and has a volatility of 30 percent per annum. The risk-free rate of interest is 7 percent per annum and the index provides a dividend yield of 4 percent per annum. Calculate the value of a three-month European put with an exercise price of 350.

12.5. Suppose that the spot price of the Canadian dollar is U.S. $0.75 and that the Canadian dollar/U.S. dollar exchange rate has a volatility of 4 percent per annum. The risk-free rates of interest in Canada and the United States are 9 percent and 7 percent per annum, respectively. Calculate the value of a European call option with an exercise price of $0.75 and an exercise date in nine months.

12.6. Show that if C is the price of an American call with exercise price X and maturity T on a stock paying a dividend yield of q, and P is the price of an American put on the same stock with the same strike price and exercise date,

$$Se^{-qT} - X < C - P < S - Xe^{-rT}$$

where S is the stock price, r is the risk-free rate, and $r > 0$. (Hint: To obtain the first half of the inequality, consider possible values of:

Portfolio A: a European call option plus an amount X invested at the risk-free rate
Portfolio B: an American put option plus e^{-qT} of stock with dividends being reinvested in the stock

To obtain the second half of the inequality, consider possible values of:

Portfolio C: an American call option plus an amount Xe^{-rT} invested at the risk-free rate
Portfolio D: a European put option plus one stock with dividends being reinvested in the stock)

12.7. Show that a call option on a currency has the same price as the corresponding put option on the currency when the forward price equals the strike price.

12.8. A stock index currently stands at 300. It is expected to increase or decrease by 10 percent over each of the next two time periods of three months. The risk-free interest rate is 8 percent and the dividend yield on the index is 3 percent. What is the value of a six-month put option on the index with a strike price of 300 if it is (a) European and (b) American?

12.9. Would you expect the volatility of a stock index to be greater or less than the volatility of a typical stock? Explain your answer.

12.10. A mutual fund announces that the salaries of its fund managers will depend on the performance of the fund. If the fund loses money, the salaries will be zero. If the fund makes a profit, the salaries will be proportional to the profit. Describe the salary of a fund manager as an option. How is a fund manager motivated to behave with this type of remuneration package?

12.11. Does the cost of portfolio insurance increase or decrease as the beta of a portfolio increases? Explain your answer.

12.12. Suppose that a portfolio is worth $60 million and the S&P 500 is at 300. If the value of the portfolio mirrors the value of the index, what options should be purchased to provide protection against the value of the portfolio falling below $54 million in one year's time?

12.13. Consider again the situation in Problem 12.12. Suppose that the portfolio has a beta of 2.0, the risk-free interest rate is 5 percent per annum, and the dividend yield on both the portfolio and the index is 3 percent per annum. What options should be purchased to provide protection against the value of the portfolio falling below $54 million?

12.14. Use the DerivaGem software to calculate implied volatilities for the December 690 call and December 690 put on the S&P 500 in Table 12.1. The value of the S&P 500 index on September 24, 1996 was 685.61. Assume the risk-free rate was 5%, the dividend yield was 2%, and the options expire half way through the maturity month. Are the quotes for the two options consistent with put–call parity?

12.15. Use the DerivaGem software to calculate implied volatilities for the November options on the Swiss franc with a strike price of 80 and the December options on the Swiss franc with a strike price of 83 in Table 12.2. Assume that risk-free rates in the U.S. and Switzerland were 5% and 2% respectively. Assume also that November options have a maturity of 7 weeks and the December options have a maturity of 11 weeks.

13

Options on Futures

The options we have considered so far provide the holder with the right to buy or sell a certain asset by a certain date. They can be termed *options on spot* or *spot options,* because, when the options are exercised, the sale or purchase of the asset at the agreed price takes place immediately. In this chapter we move on to consider *options on futures,* also known as *futures options.* In these contracts an exercise of the option gives the holder the right to buy or sell the asset at the agreed price at a future date.

The Commodity Futures Trading Commission authorized the trading of options on futures on an experimental basis in 1982. Permanent trading was approved in 1987, and since then the popularity of the contract with investors has grown very fast.

In this chapter we consider how futures options work and the differences between futures options and spot options. We examine how European futures options can be priced using either binomial trees or formulas similar to the ones produced by Black and Scholes for stock options. We also explore the relative pricing of futures options and spot options.

Nature of Futures Options

An option on a futures is the right, but not the obligation, to enter into a futures contract at a certain futures price by a certain date. Specifically, a call option on a futures is the right to enter into a long futures contract at a certain price; a put option on a futures is the right to enter into a short futures position at a certain price. Most options on futures are American; that is, they can be exercised any time during the life of the contract. The expiration date of an option on a futures contract is generally on or a few days before the earliest delivery date of the underlying futures contract.

To illustrate the operation of futures options contracts, consider the position of an investor who has bought a July call futures option with a strike price of $500 per ounce. The asset underlying one contract is 100 ounces of gold. As with other exchange-traded option contracts, the investor is required to pay for the option when the contract is entered into. If the call futures option is exercised, the investor obtains a long futures contract and there is a cash settlement to reflect the investor entering into the contract at the strike price. Suppose that the July futures price at the time the option is exercised is 540 and the most recent settlement price for the July futures contract is 538. The investor receives a cash amount equal to the excess of the most recent settlement price over the strike price. This amount, $(538 - 500) \times 100$ or \$3,800 in our example, is added to the investor's margin account.

If the investor closes out the July futures contract immediately, the gain on the futures contract is $(540 - 538) \times 100 = \$200$. The total payoff from exercising the futures option contract is therefore \$4,000. This equals the July futures price at the time of exercise less the strike price. If the investor keeps the futures contract he or she may be required to contribute additional margin. The example is summarized in Table 13.1.

The investor who sells (or writes) a call futures option receives the option premium but takes the risk that the contract will be exercised. When the contract is exercised, this investor assumes a short futures position. An amount equal to $F - X$ is deducted from the investor's margin account, where F is the most recent settlement price. The exchange clearinghouse arranges for this sum to be transferred to the investor on the other side of the transaction who chose to exercise the option.

Put futures options work analogously to call options. Consider an investor who buys a September put futures option on corn with a strike price of 200 cents per bushel. Each contract is on 5,000 bushels of corn. If the put futures option is exercised, the investor obtains a short futures contract plus a cash settlement. Suppose the contract is exercised when the September futures price is 180 cents and the most recent settlement price is 179 cents. The investor receives a cash amount equal to the excess of the strike price over the most recent settlement price. The cash amount received, which is $(2.00 - 1.79) \times 5,000 = \$1,050$ in our example, is added to the investor's margin account. If the investor closes out the July futures contract immediately, the loss on the short futures contract is $(1.80 - 1.79) \times 5,000 = \$50$. The total payoff from exercising the futures option contract is therefore \$1,000. This equals the strike price minus the July futures price at the time of exercise. As in the case of call futures, additional margin may be required if the investor decides to keep the futures position. The example is summarized in Table 13.2.

TABLE 13.1 Call Futures Options

From the Trader's Desk

An investor buys a July call futures option contract on gold. The contract size is 100 ounces. The strike price is 500.

The Exercise Decision

The investor exercises when the July gold futures price is 540 and the most recent settlement price is 538.

The Outcome

The investor receives a long futures contract plus a cash amount equal to $(538 - 500) \times 100 = \$3,800$. The investor decides to close out the long futures position immediately for a gain of $(540 - 538) \times 100 = \$200$. The total payoff from the decision to exercise is therefore \$4,000.

TABLE 13.2   Put Futures Options

From the Trader's Desk
   An investor buys a September call futures option contract on corn. The contract size is 5,000 bushels. The strike price is 200 cents.

The Exercise Decision
   The investor exercises when the September put futures price is 180 and the most recent settlement price is 179.

The Outcome
   The investor receives a short futures contract plus a cash amount of $(2.00 - 1.79) \times 5,000 = \$1,050$. The investor decides to close out the short futures position immediately for a loss of $(1.80 - 1.79) \times 5,000 = \$50$. The total payoff from the decision to exercise is therefore $1,000.

The investor on the other side of the transaction (i.e., the investor who sold the put futures option) obtains a long futures position when the option is exercised, and the excess of the strike price over the most recent settlement price is deducted from the investor's margin account.

Quotes

As mentioned earlier, most futures options are American and are referred to by the month in which the underlying futures contract matures—not by the expiration month of the option. The maturity date of the options contract is generally on, or a few days before, the earliest delivery date of the underlying futures contract. For example, the NYSE index futures option and the S&P index futures options both expire on the same day as the underlying futures contract; the CME currency futures options expire two business days prior to the expiration of the futures contract; the CBOT Treasury bond futures option expires on the first Friday preceding by at least five business days the end of the month, just prior to the futures contract expiration month.
   Table 13.3 shows quotes for futures options as they appeared in the *Wall Street Journal* on September 25, 1996. The most popular contracts are on Treasury bonds (CBOT) and Eurodollars (CME). The total of the put and call open interest for Treasury bonds is almost 500,000, whereas that for Eurodollars is over 1.5 million. Other popular contracts include corn (CBOT), soybeans (CBOT), sugar (CSCE), crude oil (NYMEX), heating oil (NYMEX), gold (COMEX), yen (CME), deutsche-marks (CME), Treasury notes (CBOT), five-year Treasury notes (CBOT), Euromarks (LIFFE), German government bonds (LIFFE), and the S&P 500 (CME).

Reasons for the Popularity of Futures Options

It is natural to ask why people choose to trade options on futures rather than options on the underlying asset. The main reason appears to be that a futures contract is, in many circumstances, more liquid and easier to trade than the underlying asset. Furthermore,

TABLE 13.3   Closing Prices of Commodity Futures Options on September 24, 1996

FUTURES OPTIONS PRICES

Tuesday, September 24, 1996.

AGRICULTURAL

CORN (CBT)
5,000 bu.; cents per bu.

Strike	Calls-Settle			Puts-Settle		
Price	Dec	Mar	May	Dec	Mar	May
290	22¾	30¾	36¾	2¼	4¼	4½
300	16	24¼	30¼	5¼	7¾	7¾
310	10⅛	18½	24½	9¾	11⅞	11½
320	6¼	14¼	19⅝	15½	17¼	16¼
330	4¼	10¾	16	23¼	24	22½
340	2⅜	8¼	12½	32⅛	31	28¾

Est vol 19,000 Mn 14,233 calls 7,547 puts
Op int Mon 231,656 calls 207,956 puts

SOYBEANS (CBT)
5,000 bu.; cents per bu.

Strike	Calls-Settle			Puts-Settle		
Price	Nov	Jan	Mar	Nov	Jan	Mar
750	44¼	56½	64¾	3⅜	8⅜	12
775	26¼	40¾	49⅝	10	17⅞	21½
800	14½	28½	38	23¼	30½	34½
825	7½	19¾	28	41	46½	49½
850	3¾	13½	21¾	62¼	65	....
875	2	10	16¾	85¾	....	87

Est vol 15,000 Mn 9,678 calls 4,092 puts
Op int Mon 173,491 calls 105,243 puts

SOYBEAN MEAL (CBT)
100 tons; $ per ton

Strike	Calls-Settle			Puts-Settle		
Price	Dec	Jan	Mar	Dec	Jan	Mar
240	17.50	17.50	17.75	1.80	3.00	6.00
250	10.35	11.90	12.75	4.40	7.40	11.00
260	5.75	8.25	9.00	10.00	13.40	....
270	3.00	5.40	6.40	....	....	....
280	2.00	3.65	4.75	26.10	....	....
290	1.25	2.75	3.50	35.25	....	....

Est vol 500 Mn 1,152 calls 803 puts
Op int Mon 19,447 calls 13,595 puts

SOYBEAN OIL (CBT)
60,000 lbs.; cents per lb.

Strike	Calls-Settle			Puts-Settle		
Price	Dec	Jan	Mar	Dec	Jan	Mar
2400	1.470	....	....	.150	.190	....
2450	1.100	....	....	.280	.340	....
2500	.800	....	1.400	.470	.510	.500
2550	.550	.840	....	.720	.760	....
2600	.400	.650	....	1.080	1.080	1.060
2650	.320	.490	....	1.490	1.420	....

Est vol 1,400 Mn 808 calls 405 puts
Op int Mon 20,216 calls 13,172 puts

WHEAT (CBT)
5,000 bu.; cents per bu.

Strike	Calls-Settle			Puts-Settle		
Price	Dec	Mar	May	Dec	Mar	May
410	25	27¼	24¼	5¾	17	....
420	19	22½	20½	9½	22	....
430	14	18½	17¼	14½	27¾	....
440	10	15¼	14½	20¼	34¼	....
450	7¾	12½	12¼	28	41¼	....
460	5¾	10¼	....	36	49	....

Est vol 4,000 Mn 1,611 calls 1,672 puts
Op int Mon 64,923 calls 31,308 puts

COTTON (CTN)
50,000 lbs.; cents per lb.

Strike	Calls-Settle			Puts-Settle		
Price	Dec	Mar	May	Dec	Mar	May
73	5.11	7.14	8.00	.92	2.05	2.35
74	4.40	6.50	7.40	1.21	2.40	2.76
75	3.74	5.91	6.80	1.56	2.77	3.07
76	3.18	5.36	6.24	1.97	3.18	3.47
77	2.65	4.83	5.72	2.43	3.64	3.91
78	2.19	4.35	5.22	2.97	4.12	4.38

Est vol 3,000 Mn 353 calls 68 puts
Op int Mon 48,959 calls 37,725 puts

ORANGE JUICE (CTN)
15,000 lbs.; cents per lb.

Strike	Calls-Settle			Puts-Settle		
Price	Nov	Dec	Jan	Nov	Dec	Jan
95	....	....	....	.20	....	2.60
100	6.15	....	9.50	.65	3.35	4.35
105	2.40	....	6.55	1.90	5.55	6.35
110	.75	....	4.85	5.00	....	9.35
115	.25	2.35	3.10	9.55	....	12.60
120	.10	....	2.20	14.45	....	16.60

Est vol 500 Mn 308 calls 921 puts
Op int Mon 28,917 calls 24,475 puts

COFFEE (CSCE)
37,500 lbs.; cents per lb.

Strike	Calls-Settle			Puts-Settle		
Price	Nov	Dec	Mar	Nov	Dec	Mar
97.5	8.80	10.00	10.45	.30	1.50	5.23
100	6.43	8.25	8.95	.43	2.25	6.25
105	2.95	5.20	6.70	2.00	4.20	9.00
110	1.10	3.20	5.75	4.35	7.25	13.05
115	.35	2.00	4.30	9.12	11.00	16.60
120	.12	1.10	3.50	14.08	15.10	20.80

Est vol 1,149 Mn 880 calls 992 puts
Op int Mon 22,702 calls 13,250 puts

SUGAR-WORLD (CSCE)
112,000 lbs.; cents per lb.

Strike	Calls-Settle			Puts-Settle		
Price	Nov	Dec	Jan	Nov	Dec	Jan
1000	1.06	1.11	1.09	.02	.07	.05
1050	.60	.65	.67	.06	.11	.13
1100	.19	.22	.32	.15	.22	.30
1150	.03	.09	.15	.52	.55	.61
1200	.01	.03	.05	.97	.99	1.01
1250	.01	.02	.02	1.47	1.48	1.48

Est vol 10,663 Mn 1,597 calls 2,119 puts
Op int Mon 65,898 calls 39,894 puts

COCOA (CSCE)
10 metric tons; $ per ton

Strike	Calls-Settle			Puts-Settle		
Price	Nov	Dec	Mar	Nov	Dec	Mar
1250	117	118	163	1	2	13
1300	67	73	123	1	7	23
1350	26	39	90	10	25	40
1400	7	20	60	41	54	66
1450	1	9	43	85	93	93
1500	1	4	33	135	138	133

Est vol 654 Mn 776 calls 634 puts
Op int Mon 20,405 calls 8,704 puts

OIL

CRUDE OIL (NYM)
1,000 bbls.; $ per bbl.

Strike	Calls-Settle			Puts-Settle		
Price	Nov	Dec	Jan	Nov	Dec	Jan
2300	1.42	1.60	1.45	.35	1.07	1.53
2350	1.11	1.36	....	.54	1.33	....
2400	.82	1.13	1.07	.75	1.60	....
2450	.63	....	....	1.06	....	....
2500	.46	.82	.80	1.39	2.28	....

Est vol na Mn na calls na puts
Op int Mon na calls na puts

HEATING OIL No.2 (NYM)
42,000 gal.; $ per gal.

Strike	Calls-Settle			Puts-Settle		
Price	Nov	Dec	Jan	Nov	Dec	Jan
67	.0431	.0469	....	.0185	.0283	....
68	.0372	.0429	.0448	.0225	.0342	....
69	.0322	.0370	.0415	.0275	....	....
70	.0280	.0335	.0380	.0333	.0448	....
71	.0245	....	....	....	....	....
72	.0215	.0275	.0331	....	....	....

Est vol na Mn na calls na puts
Op int Mon na calls na puts

GASOLINE-Unlead (NYM)
42,000 gal.; $ per gal.

Strike	Calls-Settle			Puts-Settle		
Price	Nov	Dec	Jan	Nov	Dec	Jan
61	.0322	.0358	....	.0163	.0248	....
62	.0268	.0310	.0325	.0208	.0300	....
63	.0220	....	....	.0260	....	....
64	.0180	.0230	....	.0320	....	....
65	.0147	.0198	....	.0386	....	....
66	.0120	.0111	....	....	....	.0559

Est vol na Mon na calls na puts
Op int Mon na calls na puts

NATURAL GAS (NYM)
10,000 MMBtu.; $ per MMBtu.

Strike	Calls-Settle			Puts-Settle		
Price	Nov	Dec	Jan	Nov	Dec	Jan
195	.171	.358	....	.066	.048	.061
200	.142	.321	.383	.087	.061	.074
205	.118	.287	.350	.113	.076	.090
210	.094	.254	.317	.139	.093	.107
215	.076	.224	.287	.171	.113	.126
220	.061	.197	.258	.205	.135	.147

Est vol na Mn na calls na puts
Op int Mon na calls na puts

BRENT CRUDE (IPE)
1,000 net bbls.; $ per bbl.

Strike	Calls-Settle			Puts-Settle		
Price	Nov	Dec	Jan	Nov	Dec	Jan
21.50	2.11	1.96	1.59	.15	.57	.83
22.00	1.69	1.68	1.35	.23	.79	1.09
22.50	1.35	1.37	1.15	.39	.98	1.39
23.00	1.05	1.15	.98	.59	1.26	1.72
23.50	.75	.96	.83	.79	1.57	2.07
24.00	.54	.80	.71	1.08	1.91	2.45

Est vol 970 Mn 15 calls 0 puts
Op int Mon 6,979 calls 19,455 puts

GAS OIL (IPE)
100 metric tons; $ per ton

Strike	Calls-Settle			Puts-Settle		
Price	Oct	Nov	Dec	Oct	Nov	Dec
215	10.80	9.60	8.85	2.55	9.60	15.60
220	7.70	7.45	7.25	4.45	12.45	19.00
225	5.50	5.65	5.95	7.25	15.65	22.70
230	3.00	4.45	4.85	9.75	19.45	26.60
235	1.30	3.50	4.35	13.05	23.50	31.10
240	.68	2.60	4.00	17.40	27.60	35.75

Est vol 220 Mn 50 calls 200 puts
Op int Mon 6,174 calls 3,470 puts

LIVESTOCK

CATTLE-FEEDER (CME)
50,000 lbs.; cents per lb.

Strike	Calls-Settle			Puts-Settle		
Price	Sep	Oct	Nov	Sep	Oct	Nov
62	1.60	2.02	2.82	0.00	0.42	0.50

continues on next page, column 1

TABLE 13.3   (cont.)

	Calls-Settle			Puts-Settle		
63	0.60	....	....	0.00	....	....
64	0.02	0.85	1.50	0.40	1.20	1.15
65	0.00	....	....	....	....	....
66	0.00	0.25	0.65	....	2.65	2.27
67	0.00	....	....	....	....	....

Est vol 452 Mn 92 calls 86 puts
Op int Mon 5,839 calls 8,010 puts

CATTLE-LIVE (CME)
40,000 lbs.; cents per lb.

Strike	Calls-Settle			Puts-Settle		
Price	Oct	Nov	Dec	Oct	Nov	Dec
71	1.92	....	0.35	0.20	....	....
72	1.07	....	0.20	0.35	....	....
73	0.50	....	0.10	0.77	....	....
74	0.15	....	0.05	1.42	....	....
75	0.02	....	....	....	....	....

Est vol 3,107 Mn 1,000 calls 720 puts
Op int Mon 21,346 calls 27,176 puts

HOGS-LIVE (CME)
40,000 lbs.; cents per lb.

Strike	Calls-Settle			Puts-Settle		
Price	Oct	Dec	Feb	Oct	Dec	Feb
55	2.40	3.45	....	0.17	1.32	....
56	1.62	2.82	....	0.40	1.67	....
57	1.02	2.25	....	0.80	2.12	....
58	0.55	1.82	....	1.32	2.67	....
59	0.27	1.45	....	....	....	....
60	0.12	1.10	....	....	....	0.12

Est vol 1,494 Mn 133 calls 278 puts
Op int Mon 8,494 calls 11,436 puts

METALS

COPPER (CMX)
25,000 lbs.; cents per lb.

Strike	Calls-Settle			Puts-Settle		
Price	Oct	Nov	Dec	Oct	Nov	Dec
86	3.25	5.00	5.85	.10	1.80	2.70
88	1.50	3.80	4.75	.35	2.60	3.60
90	.40	2.70	3.70	1.25	3.60	4.80
92	.10	.190	2.90	2.95	4.80	5.75
94	.05	1.45	2.30	4.90	6.20	7.15
96	.05	1.00	1.70	6.90	7.80	8.65

Est vol 425 Mn 233 calls 78 puts
Op int Mon 15,074 calls 2,916 puts

GOLD (CMX)
100 troy ounces; $ per troy ounce

Strike	Calls-Settle			Puts-Settle		
Price	Nov	Dec	Feb	Nov	Dec	Feb
360	25.70	25.70	28.10	.10	.10	.30
370	15.70	15.80	18.40	.10	.30	.60
380	6.10	6.80	9.60	.40	1.10	1.90
390	.50	1.50	4.10	4.80	5.80	6.10
400	.20	.40	1.60	14.50	14.70	13.30
410	.10	.20	.70	24.30	2-.40	22.20

Est vol 5,200 Mn 1,658 calls 378 puts
Op int Mon 228,321 calls 73,511 puts

SILVER (CMX)
5,000 troy ounces; cts per troy ounce

Strike	Calls-Settle			Puts-Settle		
Price	Nov	Dec	Mar	Nov	Dec	Mar
450	43.5	44.0	54.7	.7	1.8	5.0
475	20.5	23.0	36.0	2.2	5.2	11.0
500	5.0	9.2	22.8	11.5	15.7	21.7
525	1.3	3.5	13.5	32.7	35.0	37.5
550	.4	1.5	8.0	57.0	58.4	56.5
575	.2	.8	5.4	82.0	82.5	78.0

Est vol 4,000 Mn 6,265 calls 910 puts
Op int Mon 55,541 calls 20,762 puts

INTEREST RATE

T-BONDS (CBT)
$100,000; points and 64ths of 100%

Strike	Calls-Settle			Puts-Settle		
Price	Nov	Dec	Mar	Nov	Dec	Mar
107	2-10	....	....	0-34	....	....
108	1-31	2-00	2-48	0-55	1-24	2-38
109	0-60	....	....	1-20	....	....
110	0-35	1-03	1-55	1-59	2-27	3-43
111	0-20	....	....	2-44	....	....
112	0-09	0-30	1-13	....	3-53	4-62

Est. vol. 275,000;
Mn vol. 13,701 calls; 28,548 puts
Op. int. Mon 278,973 calls; 208,727 puts

T-NOTES (CBT)
$100,000; points and 64ths of 100%

Strike	Calls-Settle			Puts-Settle		
Price	Nov	Dec	Mar	Nov	Dec	Mar
105	....	2-24	2-50	0-12	0-29	1-10
106	1-22	1-42	2-12	0-27	0-47	1-34
107	0-48	1-06	1-43	0-52	1-10	2-00
108	0-23	0-43	1-16	....	1-47	2-37
109	0-09	0-24	0-58	....	2-27	....
110	0-03	0-12	0-41	....	3-15	....

Est vol 50,005 Mn 3,909 calls 6,704 puts
Op int Mon 133,163 calls 117,877 puts

5 YR TREAS NOTES (CBT)
$100,000; points and 64ths of 100%

Strike	Calls-Settle			Puts-Settle		
Price	Nov	Dec	Mar	Nov	Dec	Mar
10400	....	1-45	....	....	0-10	....
10450	1-10	1-21	....	1-39	0-35	....
10500	0-52	1-00	....	....	0-25	1-17
10550	0-34	0-47	....	....	0-39	....
10600	0-21	0-33	....	....	....	....
10650	0-12	0-22	....	....	....	....

Est vol 35,000 Mn 4,387 calls 4,166 puts
Op int Mon 42,505 calls 42,863 puts

EURODOLLAR (CME)
$ million; pts. of 100%

Strike	Calls-Settle			Puts-Settle		
Price	Oct	Nov	Dec	Oct	Nov	Dec
9375	0.43	....	0.45	0.00	0.01	0.03
9400	0.19	0.22	0.24	0.02	0.04	0.06
9425	0.04	0.07	0.09	0.11	0.14	0.16
9450	0.00	0.02	0.02	0.32	....	0.34
9475	0.00	....	0.00	....	....	0.57
9500	0.00	....	0.00	....	....	0.82

Est. vol. 131,200;
Mn. vol. 31,476 calls; 38,782 puts
Op. int. Mon 803,933 calls; 894,431 puts

2 YR. MID-CURVE EURODLR (CME)
$1,000,000 contract units; pts. of 100%

Strike	Calls-Settle			Puts-Settle		
Price	Dec	Mar	....	Dec	Mar	....
9275	....	....	....	0.25	....	....
9300	0.81	0.82	....	0.32	0.40	....
9325	0.65	0.67	....	0.40	0.49	....
9350	0.51	0.54	....	0.50	0.60	....
9375	0.39	0.43	....	0.62	....	....
9400	0.29	0.34	....	0.76	0.87	....

Est vol 1,000 Mn 0 calls 150 puts
Op int Mon 15,845 calls 17,635 puts

EUROMARK (LIFFE)
$1 million; pts. of 100%

Strike	Calls-Settle			Puts-Settle		
Price	Oct	Nov	Dec	Oct	Nov	Dec
9625	0.55	0.55	0.56	....	....	0.01
9650	0.31	0.32	0.32	0.01	0.02	0.02
9675	0.07	0.10	0.12	0.02	0.05	0.07
9700	0.01	0.02	0.03	0.21	0.22	0.23
9725	....	....	....	0.45	0.45	0.45
9750	....	....	....	0.70	0.70	0.70

Vol Tu 3,531 calls 678 puts
Op int Mon 325,873 calls 244,972 puts

LONG GILT (LIFFE)
£50,000; 64ths of 100%

Strike	Calls-Settle			Puts-Settle		
Price	Nov	Dec	Jan	Nov	Dec	Jan
106	1-47	2-02	1-52	0-17	0-36	1-06
107	1-02	1-24	1-19	0-36	0-58	1-37
108	0-33	0-55	0-57	1-03	1-25	2-11
109	0-13	0-32	0-37	1-47	2-02	2-55
110	0-04	0-16	0-23	2-38	2-50	3-41
111	0-01	0-08	0-14	3-35	3-42	4-32

Vol Tu 724 calls 327 puts
Op int Mon 16,323 calls 15,056 puts

GERMAN GOVT BOND (LIFFE)
$250,000 marks; pts. of 100%

Strike	Calls-Settle			Puts-Settle		
Price	Nov	Dec	Jan	Nov	Dec	Jan
9700	1.34	1.54	1.02	0.17	0.37	0.83
9750	0.94	1.18	0.77	0.27	0.51	1.08
9800	0.62	0.87	0.57	0.45	0.70	1.38
9850	0.37	0.61	0.39	0.70	0.94	1.70
9900	0.20	0.41	0.27	1.03	1.24	2.08
9950	0.10	0.26	0.17	1.43	1.59	2.48

Vol Tu 15,500 calls 11,581 puts
Op int Mon 123,144 calls 120,637 puts

CURRENCY

JAPANESE YEN (CME)
12,500,000 yen; cents per 100 yen

Strike	Calls-Settle			Puts-Settle		
Price	Oct	Nov	Dec	Oct	Nov	Dec
9150	1.28	....	1.02	0.11	0.47	0.76
9200	0.89	1.32	1.62	0.22	0.65	0.96
9250	0.55	1.05	1.36	0.38	0.88	1.19
9300	0.34	0.83	1.13	0.67	1.16	1.46
9350	0.22	0.65	0.94	1.05	1.47	....
9400	0.14	0.51	0.78	1.47	1.83	2.09

Est vol 2,533 Mn 1,004 calls 1,126 puts
Op int Mon 51,904 calls 34,615 puts

DEUTSCHEMARK (CME)
125,000 marks; cents per mark

Strike	Calls-Settle			Puts-Settle		
Price	Oct	Nov	Dec	Oct	Nov	Dec
6600	1.05	1.28	1.47	0.07	0.31	0.50
6650	0.63	0.94	1.16	0.15	0.46	0.68
6700	0.33	0.66	0.88	0.35	0.68	0.90
6750	0.15	0.47	0.68	0.67	0.99	1.19
6800	0.07	0.31	0.50	1.09	1.32	1.52
6850	0.04	0.21	0.37	1.56	1.72	....

Est vol 5,346 Mn 2,807 calls 2,528 puts
Op int Mon 64,013 calls 51,895 puts

CANADIAN DOLLAR (CME)
100,000 Can.$, cents per Can.$

Strike	Calls-Settle			Puts-Settle		
Price	Oct	Nov	Dec	Oct	Nov	Dec
7250	....	....	1.07	0.01	....	0.10
7300	0.51	....	0.68	0.03	0.11	0.20
7350	0.14	0.27	0.38	0.16	....	0.40
7400	0.02	0.09	0.20	....	....	0.71
7450	....	....	0.09	....	....	1.10
7500	....	....	0.06	....	....	1.57

Est vol 1,154 Mn 217 calls 128 puts
Op int Mon 3,594 calls 3,386 puts

BRITISH POUND (CME)
62,500 pounds; cents per pound

Strike	Calls-Settle			Puts-Settle		
Price	Oct	Nov	Dec	Oct	Nov	Dec
15500	1.66	2.04	2.38	0.10	0.50	0.84
15600	0.86	1.38	1.80	0.30	0.82	1.24
15700	0.32	0.90	1.30	0.76	....	....
15800	0.14	0.56	0.92	1.58	2.00	2.34

continues on next page, column 1

TABLE 13.3 (cont.)

Price	0.06	0.32	0.62			
15900	0.06	0.32	0.62	....	....	....
16000	0.04	....	0.42	3.48	....	3.82

Est vol 942 Mn 181 calls 201 puts
Op int Mon 27,097 calls 26,716 puts

SWISS FRANC (CME)
125,000 francs; cents per franc

Strike	Calls-Settle			Puts-Settle		
Price	Oct	Nov	Dec	Oct	Nov	Dec
8100	1.40	1.80	2.05	0.13	0.54	0.78
8150	0.98	1.47	12.73	0.21	0.71	0.97
8200	0.64	1.18	1.47	0.37	0.91	1.20
8250	0.40	0.93	1.24	0.63	1.16	....
8300	0.24	0.72	1.03	0.97	1.44	1.75
8350	0.15	0.56	0.85	1.38	1.78	....

Est vol 2,254 Mn 1,167 calls 1,144 puts
Op int Mon 31,515 calls 22,366 puts

BRAZILIAN REAL (CME)
100,000 Braz. reais; $ per reais

Est vol 100 Mn 0 calls 200 puts
Op int Mon 0 calls 20,616 puts

INDEX

S&P 500 STOCK INDEX (CME)
$500 times premium

Strike	Calls-Settle			Puts-Settle		
Price	Oct	Nov	Dec	Oct	Nov	Dec
680	17.60	22.25	26.70	5.60	10.30	14.80
685	14.00	18.90	23.45	7.00	11.90	16.50
690	10.80	15.80	20.40	8.75	13.75	18.40
695	8.00	12.95	17.65	10.95	....	20.55
700	5.75	10.45	15.00	13.65	18.35	22.85
705	3.90	8.25	12.65	....	....	....

Est vol 8,420 Mn 26,842 calls 6,981 puts
Op int Mon 74,512 calls 126,465 puts

OTHER OPTIONS

Final or settlement prices of selected contracts. Volume and open interest are totals in all contract months.

LUMBER (CME)
80,000 bd. ft., $ per 1,000 bd.ft.
New contract prices begin with May96

Strike	Calls-Settle			Puts-Settle		
Price	Nov	Jan	Mar	Nov	Jan	Mar
340	....	30.30	....	....	16.00	....

Est vol 33 Mn 55 calls 63 puts
Op int Mon 879 calls 774 puts

NASDAQ 100 (CME)
$100 times NASDAQ 100 Index

Strike	Calls-Settle			Puts-Settle		
Price	Oct	Nov	Dec	Oct	Nov	Dec
750	15.25	....	....	....	....	....

Est vol 16 Mn 192 calls 14 puts
Op int Mon 58 calls 400 puts

NYSE COMPOSITE (NYSE)
$500 times premium

Strike	Calls-Settle			Puts-Settle		
Price	Oct	Nov	Dec	Oct	Nov	Dec
368	4.90	7.60	9.95	5.00	7.70	10.05

Est vol 51 Mn 37 calls 18 puts
Op int Mon 370 calls 1,274 puts

OATS (CBT)
5,000 bu.; cents per bu.

Strike	Calls-Settle			Puts-Settle		
Price	Dec	Mar	May	Dec	Mar	May
170	6¼	....	....	8½	....	....

Est vol 100 Mn 11 calls 12 puts
Op int Mon 3,319 calls 1,255 puts

PLATINUM (NYM)
50 troy oz.; $ per troy oz.

Strike	Calls-Settle			Puts-Settle		
Price	Oct	Nov	Dec	Oct	Nov	Dec
390	7.80	....	....	5.80	....	....

Est vol na Mn na calls na puts
Op int Mon na calls na puts

RICE-ROUGH (CBT)
2000 cwt.; $ per cwt.

Strike	Calls-Settle			Puts-Settle		
Price	Nov	Jan	Mar	Nov	Jan	Mar
10000	.230	.500	....	.200	.320	.420

Est vol 50 Mn 16 calls 6 puts
Op int Mon 925 calls 599 puts

SOYBEANS (MCE)
1,000 bu.; cents per bu.

Strike	Calls-Settle			Puts-Settle		
Price	Nov	Jan	Mar	Nov	Jan	Mar
800	14½	28½	38	23¼	30½	34½

Est vol 25 Mn 47 calls 13 puts
Op int Mon 1,000 calls 854 puts

WHEAT (KC)
5,000 bu.; cents per bu.

Strike	Calls-Settle			Puts-Settle		
Price	Dec	Mar	May	Dec	Mar	May
440	15	20	....	18	33	....

Est vol 182 Mn 21 calls 328 puts
Op int Mon 5,330 calls 1,811 puts

U.S. DOLLAR INDEX (FINEX)
100 times USDX

Strike	Calls-Settle			Puts-Settle		
Price	Oct	Nov	Dec	Oct	Nov	Dec
87	17	51	79	55	90	116

Est vol 100 Mn 45 calls 61 puts
Op int Mon 1,889 calls 1,828 puts

a futures price is known immediately from trading on the futures exchange, whereas the spot price of the underlying asset may not be so readily available.

Consider Treasury bonds. The market for Treasury bond futures is much more active than the market for any particular Treasury bond. Also, the price of Treasury bond futures contracts is known immediately from trading on the CBOT. By contrast, the current market price of a bond can be obtained only by contacting one or more dealers. It is not surprising that investors would rather take delivery of a Treasury bond futures contract than Treasury bonds.

Other examples of assets whose futures are easier to trade than the underlying asset are commodities. It is much easier and more convenient to make or take delivery of a live-hogs futures contract than it is to make or take delivery of the hogs themselves.

An important point about a futures option is that exercising it does not usually lead to delivery of the underlying asset, since in most circumstances the underlying futures contract is closed out prior to delivery. Futures options are therefore normally settled in cash. This is appealing to many investors, particularly those with limited capital who may find it difficult to come up with the funds to buy the underlying asset when an option is exercised.

Another advantage sometimes cited is that futures and futures options are traded in pits side by side in the same exchange. This facilitates hedging, arbitrage, and speculation. It also tends to make the markets more efficient.

A final point is that futures options tend to entail lower transactions costs than spot options in many situations.

Put–Call Parity

In chapter 8 we derived a put–call parity relationship for European stock options. We now consider a similar argument to derive a put–call parity relationship for European futures options.

Consider European call and put futures options, both with strike price X and time to expiration T. We can form two portfolios:

Portfolio A: a European call futures option plus an amount of cash equal to Xe^{-rT}

Portfolio B: a European put futures option plus a long futures contract plus an amount of cash equal to Fe^{-rT}

In portfolio A the cash can be invested at the risk-free rate, r, and grows to X at time T. Let F_T be the futures price at maturity of the option. If $F_T > X$, the call option in portfolio A is exercised and portfolio A is worth F_T. If $F_T \le X$, the call is not exercised and portfolio A is worth X. The value of portfolio A at time T is therefore

$$\max(F_T, X)$$

In portfolio B the cash can be invested at the risk-free rate to grow to F at time T. The put option provides a payoff of $\max(X - F_T, 0)$. The futures contract provides a payoff of $F_T - F$.[1] The value of portfolio B at time T is therefore

$$F + (F_T - F) + \max(X - F_T, 0) = \max(F_T, X)$$

Since the two portfolios have the same value at time T and there are no early exercise opportunities, it follows that they are worth the same today. The value of portfolio A today is

$$c + Xe^{-rT}$$

where c is the price of the call futures option. The marking-to-market process ensures that the futures contract in portfolio B is worth zero today. Portfolio B is therefore worth

$$p + Fe^{-rT}$$

where p is the price of the put futures option. Hence

$$c + Xe^{-rT} = p + Fe^{-rT} \tag{13.1}$$

Example

Suppose that the price of a European call option on silver futures for delivery in six months is $0.56 per ounce when the exercise price is $8.50. Assume that the silver futures price for delivery in six months is currently $8.00 and the risk-free interest

---

[1] This analysis assumes no difference between the payoffs from futures contracts and forward contracts when they are both entered into at the same time.

rate for an investment which matures in six months is 10 percent per annum. From a rearrangement of Equation 13.1, the price of a European put option on silver futures with the same maturity and exercise date as the call option is

$$0.56 + 8.50e^{-0.1 \times 0.5} - 8.00e^{-0.1 \times 0.5} = 1.04$$

Consider next an American call futures option with price C and an American put futures with price P. Both have the same strike price, X, and time to maturity, T. The no-arbitrage relationship between C and P is

$$Fe^{-rT} - X < C - P < F - Xe^{-rT} \qquad \textbf{(13.2)}$$

To prove this we can consider

Portfolio C: one European call futures option plus an amount of cash equal to X

Portfolio D: an American put futures option plus a long futures contract plus an amount of cash equal to Fe^{-rT}

Portfolio E: an American call futures plus an amount Xe^{-rT} invested at the risk-free rate

Portfolio F: a European put futures plus an amount of cash F plus a long position in a futures contract

Regardless of the decision made on the early exercise of the American option in portfolio D, portfolio D is always worth less than portfolio C at the time of the exercise of the American option. Hence, portfolio D is worth less than portfolio C today and

$$P + Fe^{-rT} < c + X$$

Because a European call is always worth less than its American counterpart,

$$c \leq C$$

so that

$$P + Fe^{-rT} < C + X$$

or

$$Fe^{-rT} - X < C - P$$

This proves half the relationship in Equation 13.2.

Regardless of the decision on early exercise of the American option in portfolio E, portfolio F is always worth more than portfolio E at the time of the exercise of the American option. Portfolio F must therefore be worth more than portfolio E today. Hence,

$$C + Xe^{-rT} < p + F$$

With $p \leq P$,

$$C + Xe^{-rT} < P + F$$

or

$$C - P < F - Xe^{-rT}$$

This proves the second half of the relationship in Equation 13.2.

Bounds for Futures Options

The put–call parity relationship in Equation 13.1 provides bounds for European call and put options. Because the price of a put, p, must always be greater than zero, it follows from Equation 13.1 that

$$c + Xe^{-rT} > Fe^{-rT}$$

or

$$c > (F - X)e^{-rT} \tag{13.3}$$

Similarly, because the price of a call option must be greater than zero, it follows from Equation 13.1 that

$$Xe^{-rT} < Fe^{-rT} + p$$

or

$$p > (X - F)e^{-rT} \tag{13.4}$$

These bounds are similar to the ones derived for European stock options in chapter 8. The prices of European call and put options are very close to their lower bounds when the options are deep in the money. To see why this is so, we return to the put–call parity relationship in Equation 13.1. When a call option is deep in the money, the corresponding put option is deep out of the money. This means that p is very close to zero. The difference between c and its lower bound equals p, so that the price of the call option must be very close to its lower bound. A similar argument applies to put options.

Because American futures options can be exercised at any time, we must have

$$C > F - X$$

and

$$P > X - F$$

Thus, if interest rates are positive, the lower bound for an American option price is always higher than the lower bound for a European option. This is consistent with the fact that there is always some chance that an American futures option will be exercised early.

Valuation of Futures Options Using Binomial Trees

This section uses a binomial tree approach similar to that developed in chapter 10 to price futures options. The key difference between the argument presented here and the argument in chapter 10 is that there are no up-front costs when a futures contract is entered into.

Suppose that the current futures price is 30 and that it is expected to move either up to 33 or down to 28 over the next month. Consider a one-month call option on the futures with a strike price of 29. The situation is as indicated in Figure 13.1. If the futures price proves to be 33, the payoff from the option is 4 and the value of the futures contract

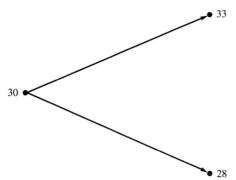

FIGURE 13.1 Futures Price Movements in Numerical Example

is 3. If the futures price proves to be 28, the payoff from the option is zero and the value of the futures contract is -2.

To set up a riskless hedge, we consider a portfolio consisting of a short position in one options contract and a long position in Δ futures contracts. If the futures price moves up to 33, the value of the portfolio is $3\Delta - 4$; if it moves down to 28, the value of the portfolio is -2Δ. The portfolio is riskless when these are the same—that is, when

$$3\Delta - 4 = -2\Delta$$

or $\Delta = 0.8$.

For this value of Δ, we know the portfolio will be worth $3 \times 0.8 - 4 = -1.6$ in one month. Assume a risk-free interest rate of 6 percent. The value of the portfolio today must be

$$-1.6e^{-0.06 \times 0.08333} = -1.592$$

The portfolio consists of one short option and Δ futures contracts. Because the value of the futures contract today is zero, the value of the option today must be 1.592.

A GENERALIZATION

We can generalize this analysis by considering a futures price that starts at F and is anticipated to rise to Fu or move down to Fd over the time period T. We consider an option maturing at time T and suppose that its payoff is f_u if the futures price moves up and f_d if it moves down. The situation is summarized in Figure 13.2.

The riskless portfolio in this case consists of a short position in one option combined with a long position in Δ futures contracts where

$$\Delta = \frac{f_u - f_d}{Fu - Fd}$$

The value of the portfolio at time T is then always

$$(Fu - F)\Delta - f_u$$

Denoting the risk-free interest rate by r, we obtain the value of the portfolio today:

$$[(Fu - F)\Delta - f_u]e^{-rT}$$

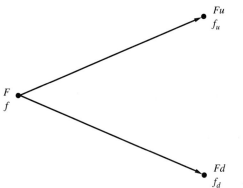

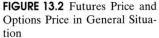

FIGURE 13.2 Futures Price and Options Price in General Situation

Another expression for the present value of the portfolio is $-f$, where f is the value of the option today. It follows that

$$-f = [(Fu - F)\Delta - f_u]e^{-rT}$$

Substituting for Δ and simplifying reduces this equation to

$$f = e^{-rT}[pf_u + (1 - p)f_d] \qquad \text{(13.5)}$$

where

$$p = \frac{1 - d}{u - d} \qquad \text{(13.6)}$$

In the numerical example considered previously (see Figure 13.1), $u = 1.1$, $d = 0.9333$, $r = 0.06$, $T = 0.08333$, $f_u = 4$, and $f_d = 0$. From Equation 13.6,

$$p = \frac{1 - 0.9333}{1.1 - 0.9333} = 0.4$$

and from Equation 13.5

$$f = e^{-0.06 \times 0.08333}[0.4 \times 4 + 0.6 \times 0] = 1.592$$

This result agrees with the answer obtained for this example earlier.

A Futures Price as a Stock Paying a Continuous Dividend Yield

There is a general result that makes the analysis of futures options analogous to the analysis of options on a stock paying a continuous dividend yield. This result is that futures prices behave in the same way as a stock paying a continuous dividend yield at the domestic risk-free rate r.

One clue that this might be so is given by comparing Equations 13.5 and 13.6 with Equations 12.7 and 12.8. The two sets of equations are identical when we set

$q = r$. Another clue is that the lower bounds for futures options prices and the put–call parity relationship for futures options prices are the same as those for options on a stock paying a continuous dividend yield at rate q when the stock price is replaced by the futures price and $q = r$.

We can understand the result by noting that a futures contract requires zero investment. In a risk-neutral world the expected profit from holding a position in an investment that costs zero to set up must be zero. The expected payoff from a futures contract in a risk-neutral world must therefore be zero. The expected growth rate of the futures price in a risk-neutral world must therefore be zero. As pointed out in chapter 12, a stock paying a dividend at rate q grows at an expected rate of $r - q$ in a risk-neutral world. If we set $q = r$, the expected growth rate of the stock price is zero, making it analogous to a futures price.

Black's Model for Valuing Futures Options

European futures options can be valued using Equations 12.4 and 12.5 with $q = r$. Fischer Black was the first to show this in a paper published in 1976. The underlying assumption is that futures prices have the same lognormal property that we assumed for stock prices in chapter 11. The European call price, c, and the European put price, p, for a futures option are given by Equations 12.4 and 12.5 with S replaced by F and $q = r$:

$$c = e^{-rT}[FN(d_1) - XN(d_2)] \tag{13.7}$$

$$p = e^{-rT}[XN(-d_2) - FN(-d_1)] \tag{13.8}$$

where

$$d_1 = \frac{\ln(F/X) + \sigma^2 T/2}{\sigma\sqrt{T}}$$

$$d_2 = \frac{\ln(F/X) - \sigma^2 T/2}{\sigma\sqrt{T}} = d_1 - \sigma\sqrt{T}$$

and σ is the volatility of the futures price. When the cost of carry and the convenience yield are functions only of time, it can be shown that the volatility of the futures price is the same as the volatility of the underlying asset. Note that Black's formula does not require the options contract and the futures contract to mature at the same time.

Example

Consider a European put futures option on crude oil. The time to maturity is four months, the current futures price is $20, the exercise price is $20, the risk-free interest rate is 9 percent per annum, and the volatility of the futures price is 25 percent per annum. In this case $F = 20$, $X = 20$, $r = 0.09$, $T = 4/12$, $\sigma = 0.25$, and

$\ln(F/X) = 0$, so that

$$d_1 = \frac{\sigma \sqrt{T}}{2} = 0.07216$$

$$d_2 = -\frac{\sigma \sqrt{T}}{2} = -0.07216$$

$$N(-d_1) = 0.4712, \qquad N(-d_2) = 0.5288$$

and the put price p is given by

$$p = e^{-0.09 \times 4/12}(20 \times 0.5288 - 20 \times 0.4712) = 1.12$$

or $1.12.

Comparison of Futures Option and Spot Option Prices

The payoffs from a European spot call option with strike price X is

$$\max(S_T - X, 0)$$

where S_T is the spot price at the option's maturity. The payoff from a European futures call option with the same strike price is

$$\max(F_T - X, 0)$$

where F_T is the futures price at the option's maturity. If the European futures option matures at the same time as the futures contract, $F_T = S_T$ and the two options are in theory equivalent. If the European call futures option matures before the futures contract, it is worth more than the corresponding spot option in a normal market (where futures prices are higher than spot prices) and less than the corresponding spot option in an inverted market (where futures prices are lower than spot prices).[2]

Similarly, a European futures put option is worth the same as its spot option counterpart when the futures option matures at the same time as the futures contract. If the European put futures option matures before the futures contract, it is worth less than the corresponding spot option in a normal market and more than the corresponding spot option in an inverted market.

RESULTS FOR AMERICAN OPTIONS

Traded futures options are in practice usually American. Assuming that the risk-free rate of interest, r, is positive, there is always some chance that it will be optimal to exercise an American futures option early. American futures options are therefore worth

---

[2]The spot option "corresponding" to a futures option is defined here as one with the same strike price and the same expiration date.

more than their European counterparts. We will look at numerical procedures for valuing American futures options in chapter 16.

It is not generally true that an American futures option is worth the same as the corresponding American option on the underlying asset when the futures and options contracts have the same maturity. Suppose, for example, that there is a normal market with futures prices consistently higher than spot prices prior to maturity. This is the case with most stock indices, gold, silver, low-interest currencies, and some commodities. An American call futures option must be worth more than the corresponding American call option on the underlying asset. The reason is that in some situations the futures option will be exercised early, in which case it will provide a greater profit to the holder. Similarly, an American put futures option must be worth less than the corresponding American put option on the underlying asset. If there is an inverted market with futures prices consistently lower than spot prices, as is the case with high-interest currencies and some commodities, the reverse must be true. American call futures options are worth less than the corresponding American call option on the underlying asset, whereas American put futures options are worth more than the corresponding American put option on the underlying asset.

The differences just described between American futures options and American asset options hold true when the futures contract expires later than the options contract as well as when the two expire at the same time. In fact, the differences tend to be greater, the later the futures contract expires.

Summary

Futures options require delivery of the underlying futures contract upon exercise. When a call is exercised, the holder acquires a long futures position plus a cash amount equal to the excess of the futures price over the strike price. Similarly, when a put is exercised the holder acquires a short position plus a cash amount equal to the excess of the strike price over the futures price. The futures contract that is delivered typically expires slightly later than the option.

A futures price behaves in the same way as a stock that provides a continuous dividend yield equal to the risk-free rate r. This means that the results produced in chapter 12 for options on stock paying a continuous dividend yield apply to futures options if we replace the stock price by the futures price and set the dividend yield equal to the risk-free interest rate.

Pricing formulas for European futures options were first produced by Fischer Black in 1976. They assume that the futures price has a constant volatility, so that the futures price is lognormally distributed at the expiration of the option.

If we assume that the two expiration dates are the same, a European futures option is worth exactly the same as the corresponding European option on the underlying asset. This is not true of American options. If the futures market is normal, an American call futures is worth more than the American call on the underlying asset, whereas an American put futures is worth less than the American put on the underlying asset. If the futures market is inverted, the reverse is true.

Suggestions for Further Reading

Black, F. "The Pricing of Commodity Contracts," *Journal of Financial Economics* 3 (1976): 167–179.

Brenner, M., G. Courtadon, and M. Subrahmanyam. "Options on Spot and Options on Futures," *Journal of Finance* 40 (December 1985): 1303–1317.

Ramaswamy, K., and S. M. Sundaresan. "The Valuation of Options on Futures Contracts," *Journal of Finance* 40 (December 1985): 1319–1340.

Wolf, A. "Fundamentals of Commodity Options on Futures," *Journal of Futures Markets* 2 (1982): 391–408.

Quiz

1. Explain the difference between a call option on yen and a call option on yen futures.
2. Why are options on bond futures more actively traded than options on bonds?
3. "A futures price is like a stock paying a continuous dividend yield." What is the continuous dividend yield?
4. A futures price is currently 50. At the end of six months it will be either 56 or 46. The risk-free interest rate is 6 percent per annum. What is the value of a six-month European call option with a strike price of 50?
5. How does the put–call parity formula for a futures option differ from put–call parity for an option on a nondividend-paying stock?
6. Consider an American futures call option where the futures contract and the option contract expire at the same time. Under what circumstances is the futures option worth more than the corresponding American option on the underlying asset?
7. Calculate the value of a five-month European put futures option when the futures price is $19, the strike price is $20, the risk-free interest rate is 12 percent per annum, and the volatility of the futures price is 20 percent per annum.

Questions and Problems

13.1. Suppose you buy a put option contract on October gold futures with a strike price of $400 per ounce. Each contract is for the delivery of 100 ounces. What happens if you exercise when the October futures price is $380?

13.2. Suppose you sell a call option contract on April live-cattle futures with a strike price of 70 cents per pound. Each contract is for the delivery of 40,000 pounds. What happens if the contract is exercised when the futures price is 75 cents?

13.3. Consider a two-month call futures option with a strike price of 40 when the risk-free interest rate is 10 percent per annum. The current futures price is 47. What is a lower bound for the value of the futures option if it is (a) European and (b) American?

13.4. Consider a four-month put futures option with a strike price of 50 when the risk-free interest rate is 10 percent per annum. The current futures price is 47. What is a lower bound for the value of the futures option if it is (a) European and (b) American?

13.5. A futures price is currently 40. It is known that at the end of three months the price will be either 35 or 45. What is the value of a three-month European call option on the futures with a strike price of 42 if the risk-free interest rate is 7 percent per annum?

13.6. A futures price is currently 60. It is known that over each of the next two three-month periods it will either rise by 10 percent or fall by 10 percent. The risk-free interest rate is 8 percent per annum. What is the value of a six-month European call option on the futures with a strike price of 60? If the call were American, would it ever be worth exercising it early?

13.7. In Problem 13.6 what is the value of a six-month European put option on futures with a strike price of 60? If the put were American, would it ever be worth exercising it early? Verify that the call prices calculated in Problem 13.6 and the put prices calculated here satisfy put–call parity relationships.

13.8. A futures price is currently 25, its volatility is 30 percent per annum, and the risk-free interest rate is 10 percent per annum. What is the value of a nine-month European call on the futures with a strike price of 26?

13.9. A futures price is currently 70, its volatility is 20 percent per annum, and the risk-free interest rate is 6 percent per annum. What is the value of a five-month European put on the futures with a strike price of 65?

13.10. Calculate the implied volatility of soybean futures prices from the following information concerning a European put on soybean futures:

Current futures price	525
Exercise price	525
Risk-free rate	6 percent per annum
Time to maturity	5 months
Put price	20

13.11. Suppose that a futures price is currently 35. A European call option and a European put option on the futures with a strike price of 34 are both priced at 2 in the market. The risk-free interest rate is 10 percent per annum. Identify an arbitrage opportunity.

13.12. "The price of an at-the-money European call futures option always equals the price of a similar at-the-money European put futures option." Explain why this statement is true.

13.13. Suppose that a futures price is currently 30. The risk-free interest rate is 5 percent per annum. A three-month American call futures option with a strike price of 28 is worth 4. Calculate bounds for the price of a three-month American put futures option with a strike price of 28.

13.14. Use the DerivaGem software to calculate implied volatilities for the options on corn futures in Table 13.3. Assume the futures prices in Table 2.3 apply and that the risk-free rate is 5 percent per annum. Treat the options as American and use 30 time steps. Assume that the December, March, and May options mature in 10, 23, and 36 weeks, respectively. Discuss the pattern of implied volatilities you obtain.

CHAPTER 14

Hedging Positions in Options and the Creation of Options Synthetically

As has been mentioned in earlier chapters, the over-the-counter market now accounts for huge amounts of option trading. In this market trades are agreed over the phone. On one side of the trade is a financial institution. On the other side is a fund manager, a corporate treasurer, or another financial institution. This chapter focuses on the risks that a financial institution bears when it trades in the over-the-counter market and how the risks can be managed. Much of the analysis presented is also applicable to market makers in options on an exchange, and to corporate treasurers and fund managers when they regularly trade options.

In theory, a financial institution can hedge its exposure from an option contract by entering into an opposite position in exactly the same contract. In practice, over-the-counter option contracts are often designed to meet the needs of a particular counterparty so that it is impossible, or prohibitively expensive, to enter into an offsetting trade with another counterparty. Alternative hedging strategies are therefore required. This chapter discusses these alternatives.

The chapter considers delta, gamma, theta, vega, and rho, which are measures of the different dimensions to the risk in a portfolio of options. It also examines how options can be created synthetically. The process turns out to be very closely related to the hedging of options, because creating an option position synthetically is essentially the same task as hedging the opposite option position.

An Example

The next few sections use as an example the position of a financial institution that has sold for $300,000 a European call option on 100,000 shares of a nondividend-paying stock. We assume that the stock price is $49, the strike price is $50, the risk-free interest rate is 5 percent per annum, the stock price volatility is 20 percent per annum, the time to maturity is 20 weeks (0.3846 years), and the expected return from the stock is 13 percent per annum.[1] With our usual notation, this means that

$$S \;=\; 49, \; X \;=\; 50, \; r \;=\; 0.05, \; \sigma \;=\; 0.20, \; T \;=\; 0.3846, \; \mu \;=\; 0.13$$

Financial institutions do not normally write call options on individual stocks. However, a call option on a stock is a convenient example with which to develop our ideas. The points that will be made apply to other types of options and to other derivatives.

The Black–Scholes price of the option is about $240,000. The financial institution has therefore sold the option for $60,000 more than its theoretical value and is faced with the problem of hedging its exposure.

Naked and Covered Positions

One strategy open to the financial institution is to do nothing—to adopt a *naked position*. If the call is exercised, the financial institution will have to buy 100,000 shares at the current market price to cover the call. The cost to the financial institution will be 100,000 times the amount by which the stock price exceeds the strike price. Thus, if after 20 weeks the stock price is $60, the option costs the financial institution $1 million, which is considerably greater than the $300,000 price it received for the option. A naked position works well if the stock price is below $50 at the end of 20 weeks. The option then costs the financial institution nothing, and a profit of $300,000 is realized.

As an alternative to a naked position, the financial institution can adopt a *covered position*. This involves buying 100,000 shares as soon as the option has been sold. If the option is exercised, the strategy works well, but in other circumstances it could lead to a significant loss. If the option is not exercised, the covered position is liable to be expensive. For example, if the stock price drops to $40, the financial institution loses $900,000 on its stock position. Again, this is considerably greater than the $300,000 charged for the option. Put–call parity shows that the exposure from writing a covered call is the same as that from writing a naked put.

Neither a naked position nor a covered position provides a satisfactory hedge. If the assumptions underlying the Black–Scholes formula hold, the cost to the financial institution of writing the option should always be $240,000 on average for both approaches.[2] On any one occasion, however, the cost is liable to range from zero to over

---

[1] As shown in chapters 10 and 11, the expected return is irrelevant to the pricing of an option. It is given here because it can have some bearing on the effectiveness of a hedging scheme.

[2] More precisely, the present value of the expected cost is $240,000 for both approaches, assuming that appropriate risk-adjusted discount rates are used. The value of any security must in equilibrium equal the present value of the expected cash flows that the security provides for the holder.

$1 million. A perfect hedge would ensure that the cost is always $240,000; that is, the standard deviation of the cost of writing the option and hedging it is zero.

A Stop-loss Strategy

One interesting hedging scheme that is sometimes proposed involves a *stop-loss strategy*. To illustrate the basic idea, consider an institution that has written a call option with strike price X to buy one unit of a stock. The hedging scheme involves buying one unit of the stock as soon as its price rises above X and selling it as soon as its price falls below X. The objective is to hold a naked position whenever the stock price is less than X and a covered position whenever the stock price is greater than X. The scheme is designed to ensure that at time T the institution owns the stock if the option closes in the money and does not own it if the option closes out of the money. The strategy appears to produce payoffs that are the same as the payoffs on the option. In the situation illustrated in Figure 14.1, it involves buying the stock at time t_1, selling it at time t_2, buying it at time t_3, selling it at time t_4, buying it at time t_5, and delivering it at time T.

As usual, the initial stock price as denoted by S. The cost of setting up the hedge initially is S if $S > X$ and zero otherwise. At first blush the total cost, Q, of writing and hedging the option would appear to be given by

$$Q = \max(S - X, 0) \tag{14.1}$$

because all purchases and sales subsequent to time zero are made at price X. If this were correct, the hedging scheme would work perfectly in the absence of transactions costs.

FIGURE 14.1 A Stop-loss Strategy

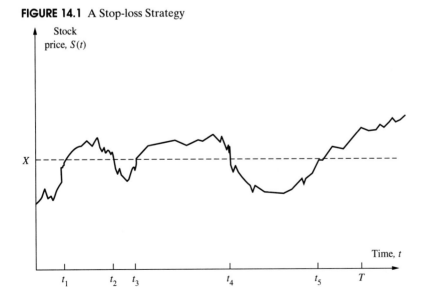

Furthermore, the cost of hedging the option would always be less than its Black-Scholes price. Thus, an investor could earn riskless profits by writing options and hedging them.

There are two basic reasons that Equation 14.1 is incorrect. The first is that the cash flows to the hedger occur at different times and must be discounted. The second is that purchases and sales cannot be made at exactly the same price X. This second point is critical. If we assume a risk-neutral world with zero interest rates, we can justify ignoring the time value of money. But we cannot legitimately assume that both purchases and sales are made at the same price. If markets are efficient, the hedger cannot know whether, when the stock price equals X, it will continue above or below X.

As a practical matter, purchases must be made at a price $X + \delta$ and sales must be made at a price $X - \delta$, for some small positive number, δ. Thus, every purchase and subsequent sale involves a cost (apart from transactions costs) of 2δ. A natural response on the part of the hedger is to monitor price movements more closely so that δ is reduced. Assuming that stock prices change continuously, δ can be made arbitrarily small by monitoring the stock prices closely. But as δ is made smaller, trades tend to occur more frequently. Thus, even though the cost per trade is reduced, it is offset by the increasing frequency of trading. As $\delta \rightarrow 0$, the expected number of trades tends to infinity.

A stop-loss strategy, although superficially attractive, does not work particularly well as a hedging scheme. Consider its use for an out-of-the-money option. If the stock price never reaches the strike price X, the hedging scheme costs nothing. If the path of the stock price crosses the strike price many times, the scheme is liable to be quite expensive. Monte Carlo simulation can be used to assess the overall performance of the scheme. This involves randomly sampling paths for the stock price and observing the results of using the scheme. Table 14.1 shows the results for the option considered earlier. It assumes that the stock price is observed at the end of time intervals of length Δt.[3] The hedge performance measure is the ratio of the standard deviation of the cost of hedging the option to the Black–Scholes price of the option. Each result is based on 1,000 sample paths for the stock price and has a standard error of about 2 percent. It

---

TABLE 14.1   Performance of Stop-loss Strategy

The performance measure is the ratio of the standard deviation of the cost of writing the option and hedging it to the theoretical price of the option.

Δt *(weeks)*	5	4	2	1	0.5	0.25
Hedge performance	1.02	0.93	0.82	0.77	0.76	0.76

---

[3]The precise hedging rule used was as follows. If the stock price moves from below X to above X in a time interval of length Δt, it is bought at the end of the interval. If it moves from above X to below X in the time interval, it is sold at the end of the interval. Otherwise, no action is taken.

appears to be impossible to produce a value for the hedge performance measure below 0.70 regardless of how small Δt is made.

More Sophisticated Hedging Schemes

Most option traders use more sophisticated hedging schemes than those described so far. As a first step they attempt to make their portfolio immune to small changes in the price of the underlying asset in the next small interval of time. This is known as *delta hedging*. They then look at what are known as *gamma* and *vega*. Gamma is the rate of change of delta with respect to the underlying asset's price; vega is the rate of change of the portfolio with respect to the asset's volatility. When gamma is kept close to zero, a portfolio is insensitive to fairly large changes in the price of the asset; when vega is kept close to zero, the portfolio is insensitive to small changes in volatility. Option traders may also look at *theta* and *rho*. Theta is the rate of change of the option portfolio with the passage of time, and rho is its rate of change with respect to the risk-free interest rate. Traders are also likely to carry out scenario analyses. In the next few sections we will examine these approaches in more detail.

Delta Hedging

The *delta* of an option, Δ, was introduced in chapter 10. It is defined as the rate of change of the option price with respect to the price of the underlying asset. It is the slope of the curve that relates the option price to the underlying asset price. Suppose that the delta of a call option on a stock is 0.6. This means that when the stock price changes by a small amount, the option price changes by about 60 percent of that amount. Figure 14.2 shows the relationship between a call price and the underlying stock price. When the stock price corresponds to point A, the option price corresponds to point B, and Δ is the gradient indicated. As an approximation,

$$\Delta = \frac{\Delta c}{\Delta S} \tag{14.2}$$

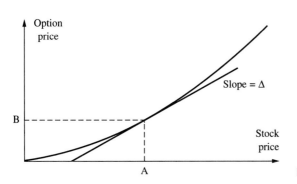

FIGURE 14.2 Calculation of Delta

where ΔS is a small change in the stock price and Δc is the corresponding change in the call price.

Consider a call option whose delta is 0.6. Suppose that the option price is $10 and the stock price is $100. Imagine an investor who has sold 20 option contracts—that is, options to buy 2,000 shares. The investor's position could be hedged by buying $0.6 \times 2,000 = 1,200$ shares. The gain (loss) on the option position would then tend to be offset by the loss (gain) on the stock position. For example, if the stock price goes up by $1 (producing a gain of $1,200 on the shares purchased), the option price will tend to go up by $0.6 \times \$1 = \$0.60$ (producing a loss of $1,200 on the options written); if the stock price goes down by $1 (producing a loss of $1,200 on the shares purchased), the option price will tend to go down by $0.60 (producing a gain of $1,200 on the options written).

In this example the delta of the investor's option position is $0.6 \times (-2,000) = -1,200$. In other words, the investor loses $1,200\Delta S$ on the short option position when the stock price increases by ΔS. The delta of the stock is by definition 1.0, and the long position in 1,200 shares has a delta of +1,200. The delta of the investor's overall position is therefore zero. The delta of the asset position offsets the delta of the option position. A position with a delta of zero is referred to as being *delta neutral*.

It is important to realize that, because delta changes, the investor's position remains delta hedged (or delta neutral) for only a relatively short period of time. In practice, when delta hedging is implemented, the hedge has to be adjusted periodically. This is known as *rebalancing*. In our example, at the end of three days the stock price might increase to $110. As indicated by Figure 14.2, an increase in the stock price leads to an increase in delta. Suppose that delta rises from 0.60 to 0.65. An extra $0.05 \times 2,000 = 100$ shares would then have to be purchased to maintain the hedge. The example is summarized in Table 14.2.

The delta-hedging scheme just described is an example of a *dynamic hedging scheme*. This scheme requires the hedge position to be adjusted periodically. Dynamic hedging can be contrasted with *static hedging,* in which the hedge is set up initially and never adjusted. Static hedging schemes are sometimes also referred to as *hedge-*

TABLE 14.2 Use of Delta Hedging

From the Trader's Desk

An investor has sold 20 option contracts (2,000 options) on a certain stock. The option price is $10, the stock price is $100, and the option's delta is 0.6. The investor wishes to hedge the position.

Strategy

The investor immediately buys $0.6 \times 2,000 = 1,200$ shares. Over the next short period of time, the call price will tend to change by 60 percent of the stock price and the gain (loss) on the call will be offset by the loss (gain) on the stock. As time passes, delta will change and the position in the stock will have to be adjusted. For example, if after three days the delta increases to 0.65, a further $0.05 \times 2,000 = 100$ shares will have to be bought.

and-forget schemes. A number of examples of static hedging schemes are given in chapter 3.

Delta is closely related to the Black–Scholes analysis. As explained in chapter 11, Black and Scholes showed that it is possible to set up a riskless portfolio consisting of a position in an option on a stock and a position in the stock. Expressed in terms of Δ, the Black and Scholes portfolio is

-1:   option
$+\Delta$:   shares of the stock

Using our new terminology, we can say that Black and Scholes valued options by setting up a delta-neutral position and arguing that the return on the position should be the risk-free interest rate.

FORWARD CONTRACTS

The concept of delta can be applied to other derivatives besides options. It is instructive to consider forward contracts on nondividend-paying stocks.

Equation 3.9 shows that when the price of a nondividend-paying stock changes by ΔS, with all else remaining the same, the value of a forward contract on the stock also changes by ΔS. The delta of a forward contract on one share of a nondividend-paying stock is therefore always 1.0. Thus, a short forward contract on one share can be hedged by purchasing one share, whereas a long forward contract on one share can be hedged by shorting one share. These are hedge-and-forget schemes. Since delta is always 1.0, no changes need to be made to the position in the stock during the life of the contract.

DELTA OF EUROPEAN CALLS AND PUTS

For a European call option on a nondividend-paying stock, it can be shown that

$$\Delta = N(d_1)$$

where d_1 is defined as in Equation 11.5. Using delta hedging for a short position in a European call option therefore involves keeping a long position of $N(d_1)$ shares at any given time. Similarly, using delta hedging for a long position in a European call option involves maintaining a short position of $N(d_1)$ shares at any given time.

For a European put option on a nondividend-paying stock, delta is given by

$$\Delta = N(d_1) - 1$$

where d_1 is defined as in Equation 11.5. Delta is negative, which means that a long position in a put option should be hedged with a long position in the underlying stock, and a short position in a put option should be hedged with a short position in the underlying stock. The variation of the delta of a call option and a put option with the stock price is shown in Figure 14.3. Figure 14.4 shows the variation of delta with the time to maturity for in-the-money, at-the-money, and out-of-the-money call options.

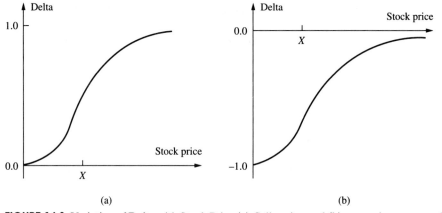

FIGURE 14.3 Variation of Delta with Stock Price (a) Call option and (b) put option on a nondividend-paying stock.

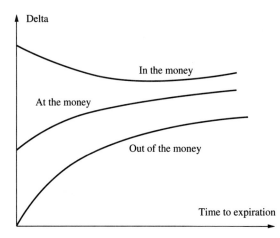

FIGURE 14.4 Variation of Delta with Time to Maturity for a Call Option

SIMULATIONS

Tables 14.3 and 14.4 provide two simulations of the operation of delta hedging for the example considered earlier, in which a financial institution sells an option worth $240,000. The hedge is assumed to be adjusted or rebalanced weekly. In both tables delta is initially calculated as 0.522. As soon as the option is written, $2,557,800 must therefore be borrowed to buy 52,200 shares at a price of $49. An interest cost of $2,500 is incurred in the first week.

In Table 14.3 the stock price falls by the end of the first week to $48\frac{1}{8}$. The delta declines to 0.458, and 6,400 of shares are sold to maintain the hedge. The strategy realizes $308,000 in cash, and the cumulative borrowings at the end of week 1 are reduced to $2,252,300. During the second week the stock price reduces to $47\frac{3}{8}$, delta declines

TABLE 14.3 Simulation of Delta Hedging

Option closes in the money. Cost of hedging is $263,400.

Week	Stock Price	Delta	Shares Purchased	Cost of Shares Purchased ($000)	Cumulative Cost Including Interest ($000)	Interest Cost ($000)
0	49	0.522	52,200	2,557.8	2,557.8	2.5
1	$48\frac{1}{8}$	0.458	(6,400)	(308.0)	2,252.3	2.2
2	$47\frac{3}{8}$	0.400	(5,800)	(274.8)	1,979.7	1.9
3	$50\frac{1}{4}$	0.595	19,600	984.9	2,996.5	2.9
4	$51\frac{3}{4}$	0.693	9,700	502.0	3,471.3	3.3
5	$53\frac{1}{8}$	0.774	8,100	430.3	3,904.9	3.8
6	53	0.771	(300)	(15.9)	3,892.8	3.7
7	$51\frac{7}{8}$	0.706	(6,500)	(337.2)	3,559.3	3.4
8	$51\frac{3}{8}$	0.674	(3,200)	(164.4)	3,398.4	3.3
9	53	0.787	11,300	598.9	4,000.5	3.8
10	$49\frac{7}{8}$	0.550	(23,700)	(1,182.0)	2,822.3	2.7
11	$48\frac{1}{2}$	0.413	(13,700)	(664.4)	2,160.6	2.1
12	$49\frac{7}{8}$	0.542	12,900	643.4	2,806.1	2.7
13	$50\frac{3}{8}$	0.591	4,900	246.8	3,055.6	2.9
14	$52\frac{1}{8}$	0.768	17,700	922.6	3,981.2	3.8
15	$51\frac{7}{8}$	0.759	(900)	(46.7)	3,938.3	3.8
16	$52\frac{7}{8}$	0.865	10,600	560.5	4,502.6	4.3
17	$54\frac{7}{8}$	0.978	11,300	620.1	5,127.0	4.9
18	$54\frac{5}{8}$	0.990	1,200	65.6	5,197.5	5.0
19	$55\frac{7}{8}$	1.000	1,000	55.9	5,258.3	5.1
20	$57\frac{1}{4}$	1.000	0	0.0	5,263.4	

again, and so on. Toward the end of the life of the option, it becomes apparent that the option will be exercised and delta approaches 1.0. By week 20 therefore the hedger has a fully covered position. The hedger receives $5 million for the stock held, so that the total cost of writing the option and hedging it is $263,400.

Table 14.4 illustrates an alternative sequence of events such that the option closes out of the money. As it becomes clear that the option will not be exercised, delta approaches zero. By week 20 the hedger has a naked position and has incurred costs totaling $256,600.

In Tables 14.3 and 14.4 the costs of hedging the option, when discounted to the beginning of the period, are close to but not exactly the same as the Black–Scholes price of $240,000. If the hedging scheme worked perfectly, the cost of hedging would, after discounting, be exactly equal to the Black–Scholes price for every simulated stock price path. The reason for the variation in the cost of delta hedging is that the hedge is

TABLE 14.4 **Simulation of Delta Hedging**

Option closes out of the money. Cost of hedging is $256,600.

Week	Stock Price	Delta	Shares Purchased	Cost of Shares Purchased ($000)	Cumulative Cost Including Interest ($000)	Interest Cost ($000)
0	49	0.522	52,200	2,557.8	2,557.8	2.5
1	$49\frac{3}{4}$	0.568	4,600	228.9	2,789.1	2.7
2	52	0.705	13,700	712.4	3,504.2	3.4
3	50	0.579	(12,600)	(630.0)	2,877.6	2.8
4	$48\frac{3}{8}$	0.459	(12,000)	(580.5)	2,299.8	2.2
5	$48\frac{1}{4}$	0.443	(1,600)	(77.2)	2,224.8	2.1
6	$48\frac{3}{4}$	0.475	3,200	156.0	2,383.0	2.3
7	$49\frac{5}{8}$	0.540	6,500	322.6	2,707.8	2.6
8	$48\frac{1}{4}$	0.420	(12,000)	(579.0)	2,131.4	2.0
9	$48\frac{1}{4}$	0.410	(1,000)	(48.2)	2,085.2	2.0
10	$51\frac{1}{8}$	0.658	24,800	1,267.9	3,355.1	3.2
11	$51\frac{1}{2}$	0.692	3,400	175.1	3,533.5	3.4
12	$49\frac{7}{8}$	0.542	(15,000)	(748.1)	2,788.7	2.7
13	$49\frac{7}{8}$	0.538	(400)	(20.0)	2,771.5	2.7
14	$48\frac{3}{4}$	0.400	(13,800)	(672.7)	2,101.4	2.0
15	$47\frac{1}{2}$	0.236	(16,400)	(779.0)	1,324.4	1.3
16	48	0.261	2,500	120.0	1,445.7	1.4
17	$46\frac{1}{4}$	0.062	(19,900)	(920.4)	526.7	0.5
18	$48\frac{1}{8}$	0.183	12,100	582.3	1,109.5	1.1
19	$46\frac{5}{8}$	0.007	(17,600)	(820.6)	290.0	0.3
20	$48\frac{1}{8}$	0.000	(700)	(33.7)	256.6	

rebalanced only once a week. As rebalancing takes place more frequently, the variation in the cost of hedging is reduced.

Table 14.5 shows statistics on the performance of delta hedging from 1,000 simulations of stock price movements for our example. As in Table 14.1, the performance measure is the ratio of the standard deviation of the cost of hedging the option to the Black–Scholes price of the option. It is clear that delta hedging is a great improvement over a stop-loss strategy. Unlike a stop-loss strategy, a delta-hedging strategy has a performance that gets steadily better as the hedge is monitored more frequently.

Delta hedging aims to keep the total wealth of the financial institution as close to unchanged as possible. Initially, the value of the written option is $240,000. In the situation depicted in Table 14.3, the value of the option can be calculated as $414,500 in week 9. Thus, the financial institution has lost $174,500 on its option position. Its cash position, as measured by the cumulative cost, is $1,442,700 worse in week 9 than in week 0. The value of the shares held has increased from $2,557,800 to $4,171,100.

TABLE 14.5 Performance of Delta Hedging

The performance measure is the ratio of the standard deviation of the cost of writing the option and hedging it to the theoretical price of the option.

Time Between Hedge Rebalancing (weeks)	*5*	*4*	*2*	*1*	*0.5*	*0.25*
Performance Measure	0.43	0.39	0.26	0.19	0.14	0.09

The net effect is that the overall wealth of the financial institution has changed by only $3,900.

WHERE THE COST COMES FROM

The delta-hedging scheme in Tables 14.3 and 14.4 in effect creates a long position in the option synthetically. This neutralizes the short position arising from the option that has been written. The scheme generally involves selling stock just after the price has gone down and buying stock just after the price has gone up. It might be termed a buy-high, sell-low scheme! The cost of $240,000 comes from the average difference between the price paid for the stock and the price realized for it. It should be noted that the simulations in Tables 14.3 and 14.4 are idealized in that they assume that the volatility is constant and there are no transaction costs.

DELTA OF OTHER EUROPEAN OPTIONS

For European call options on a stock index paying a dividend yield q,

$$\Delta = e^{-qT} N(d_1)$$

where d_1 is defined as in Equation 12.4. For European put options on the stock index,

$$\Delta = e^{-qT} [N(d_1) - 1]$$

For European call options on a currency,

$$\Delta = e^{-r_f T} N(d_1)$$

where r_f is the foreign risk-free interest rate and d_1 is defined as in Equation 12.9. For European put options on a currency,

$$\Delta = e^{-r_f T} [N(d_1) - 1]$$

For European call futures options,

$$\Delta = e^{-rT} N(d_1)$$

where d_1 is defined as in Equation 13.7. For European put futures options,

$$\Delta = e^{-rT} [N(d_1) - 1]$$

Example

A bank has written a six-month European option to sell £1 million at an exchange rate of 1.6000. Suppose that the current exchange rate is 1.6200, the risk-free interest rate in the United Kingdom is 13 percent per annum, the risk-free interest rate in the United States is 10 percent per annum, and the volatility of sterling is 15 percent. In this case $S = 1.6200$, $X = 1.6000$, $r = 0.10$, $r_f = 0.13$, $\sigma = 0.15$, and $T = 0.5$. The delta of a put option on a currency is

$$[N(d_1) - 1]e^{-r_f T}$$

where d_1 is given by Equation 12.9. It can be shown that

$$d_1 = 0.0287$$
$$N(d_1) = 0.5115$$

so that the delta of the put option is -0.458. This is the delta of a long position in one put option. (It means that the price of the put goes down by 45.8 percent of the increase in the value of the currency.) The delta of the bank's total short option position is $+458,000$. Delta hedging therefore requires that a short sterling position of £458,000 be set up initially. This short sterling position has a delta of $-458,000$ and neutralizes the delta of the option position. As time passes, the short position must be changed.

USING FUTURES

The delta of the underlying asset is by definition 1.0. In practice, delta hedging is often carried out using a position in a futures contract rather than a position in the underlying asset. The contract that is used does not have to mature at the same time as the option. We define

T^*:   maturity of futures contract

H_A: required position in asset at time t for delta hedging

H_F: alternative required position in futures contracts at time t for delta hedging

If the underlying asset is a nondividend-paying stock, the futures price, F, from Equation 3.5 is given by

$$F = Se^{rT^*}$$

When the stock price increases by ΔS, the gain from the futures contract is $e^{rT^*}\Delta S$. Thus, $e^{rT^*}\Delta S$ futures contracts have the same sensitivity to stock price movements as one share. Hence,

$$H_F = e^{-rT^*}H_A$$

When the underlying asset is a stock or an index paying a dividend yield q, a similar argument shows that

$$H_F = e^{-(r-q)T^*}H_A \tag{14.3}$$

When it is a currency,

$$H_F = e^{-(r-r_f)T^*} H_A$$

Example

Consider the option in the previous example. Suppose that the bank decides to hedge using nine-month currency futures contracts. In this case $T^* = 0.75$ and

$$e^{-(r-r_f)T^*} = 1.0228$$

so that the short position in currency futures required for delta hedging is $1.0228 \times 458,000 = £468,442$. Because each futures contract is for the purchase or sale of £62,500, seven contracts should be shorted. (Seven is the nearest whole number to 468,422/62,500.)

It is interesting to note that the delta of a futures contract is different from the delta of the corresponding forward. This is true even when interest rates are constant and the forward price equals the futures price. Consider the situation where the underlying asset is a nondividend-paying stock. The delta of a futures contract on one unit of the asset is e^{rT^*}, whereas the delta of a forward contract on one unit of the asset is, as discussed earlier, 1.0.

DELTA OF A PORTFOLIO

When a portfolio of options on an asset is held, the delta of the portfolio is simply the sum of the deltas of the individual options in the portfolio. If a portfolio consists of an amount w_i of option i $(1 \leq i \leq n)$, the delta of the portfolio is given by

$$\Delta = \sum_{i=1}^{n} w_i \Delta_i$$

where Δ_i is the delta of ith option. The formula can be used to calculate the position in the underlying asset, or in a futures contract on the underlying asset, necessary to carry out delta hedging. When this position has been taken, the delta of the portfolio is zero and the portfolio is referred to as being delta neutral.

Consider a financial institution that has the following three positions in options to buy or sell German marks:

1. A long position in 100,000 call options with strike price 0.55 and expiration date in three months. The delta of each option is 0.533.

2. A short position in 200,000 call options with strike price 0.56 and expiration date in five months. The delta of each option is 0.468.

3. A short position in 50,000 put options with strike price 0.56 and expiration date in two months. The delta of each option is -0.508.

The delta of the whole portfolio is

$$0.533 \times 100,000 - 200,000 \times 0.468 - 50,000 \times (-0.508) = -14,900$$

TABLE 14.6 Making a Portfolio Delta Neutral

From the Trader's Desk

A financial institution has the following three positions in the German mark:

1. A long position in 100,000 call options with strike price 0.55 and expiration date in three months. The option's delta is 0.553.

2. A short position in 200,000 call options with strike price 0.56 and expiration date in five months. The option's delta is 0.468.

3. A short position in 50,000 put options with strike price 0.56 and expiration date in two months. The option's delta is -0.508.

The financial institution would like to make the portfolio delta neutral. The risk-free interest rates in the United States and Germany are 8 percent per annum and 4 percent per annum, respectively.

Calculation of Delta

The delta of the portfolio is

$$0.533 \times 100,000 - 0.468 \times 200,000 + 0.508 \times 50,000 = -14,900$$

Strategy 1

Take a long position in 14,900 marks.

Strategy 2

Take a long position in six-month futures contracts on

$$14,900e^{-(0.08-0.04) \times 0.5} = 14,605 \text{ marks}$$

This means that the portfolio can be made delta neutral with a long position of 14,900 marks.

A six-month futures contract could also be used to achieve delta neutrality in this example. Suppose that the risk-free rate of interest is 8 percent per annum in the United States and 4 percent per annum in Germany. The long position in mark futures for delta neutrality is

$$14,900e^{-(0.08-0.04) \times 0.5} = 14,605$$

This example is summarized is Table 14.6.

Maintaining a delta-neutral position in a single option and the underlying asset, in the way indicated in Tables 14.3 and 14.4, may be prohibitively expensive because of the transactions costs incurred on trades. For a large portfolio of options, delta neutrality is a much more feasible goal. Only one trade in the underlying asset is necessary to zero out delta for the whole portfolio. The transactions costs of hedging are in effect spread out over many option contracts.

Theta

The *theta* of a portfolio of options, Θ, is the rate of change of the value of the portfolio as time passes (i.e., as T decreases) with all else remaining the same. It is sometimes referred to as the *time decay* of the portfolio. For a European call option on a nondividend-paying stock,

$$\Theta = -\frac{SN'(d_1)\sigma}{2\sqrt{T}} - rXe^{-rT}N(d_2)$$

where d_1 and d_2 are defined as in Equation 11.5 and

$$N'(x) = \frac{1}{\sqrt{2\pi}}e^{-x^2/2} \tag{14.4}$$

For a European put option on the stock,

$$\Theta = -\frac{SN'(d_1)\sigma}{2\sqrt{T}} + rXe^{-rT}N(-d_2)$$

For a European call option on a stock index paying a dividend at rate q,

$$\Theta = -\frac{SN'(d_1)\sigma e^{-qT}}{2\sqrt{T}} + qSN(d_1)e^{-qT} - rXe^{-rT}N(d_2)$$

where d_1 and d_2 are defined as in Equation 12.4. For a European put option on the stock index,

$$\Theta = -\frac{SN'(d_1)\sigma e^{-qT}}{2\sqrt{T}} - qSN(-d_1)e^{-qT} + rXe^{-rT}N(-d_2)$$

With $q = r_f$, these last two equations give thetas for European call and put options on currencies. With $q = r$ and $S = F$, they give thetas for European futures options.

Example

Consider a four-month put option on a stock index. The current value of the index is 305, the strike price is 300, the dividend yield is 3 percent per annum, the risk-free interest rate is 8 percent per annum, and the volatility of the index is 25 percent per annum. In this case $S = 305$, $X = 300$, $q = 0.03$, $r = 0.08$, $\sigma = 0.25$, and $T = 0.3333$. The option's theta is

$$-\frac{SN'(d_1)\sigma e^{-qT}}{2\sqrt{T}} - qSN(-d_1)e^{-qT} + rXe^{-rT}N(-d_2) = -18.15$$

This means that, if 0.01 year (2.5 trading days) passes with no changes to the value of the index or its volatility, the value of the option declines by 0.1815.

Theta is usually negative for an option.[4] The reason is that as the time to maturity decreases with all else remaining the same, the option tends to become less valuable.

---

[4]Examples of options with nonnegative theta are an in-the-money European put option on a nondividend-paying stock and an in-the-money European call option on a currency with a very high interest rate.

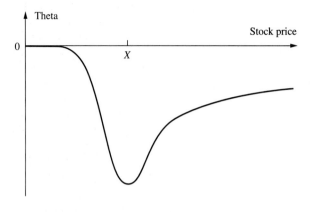

FIGURE 14.5 Variation of Theta of a European Call Option with Stock Price

The variation of Θ with stock price for a call option on a stock is shown in Figure 14.5. When the stock price is very low, theta is close to zero. For an at-the-money call option, theta is large and negative. As the stock price becomes larger, theta tends to $-rXe^{-rT}$. Figure 14.6 shows typical patterns for the variation of Θ with the time to maturity for in-the-money, at-the-money, and out-of-the-money call options.

Theta is not the same type of hedge parameter as delta. There is uncertainty about changes in the underlying asset price over a short period of time, but there is no uncertainty about the passage of time itself. It makes sense to hedge against asset price changes, but it makes very little sense to hedge the effect of the passage of time. In spite of this, many traders regard theta as a useful descriptive statistic for a portfolio. As we will see later, in a delta-neutral portfolio theta is a proxy for gamma.

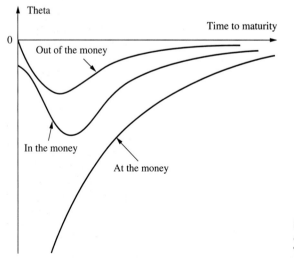

FIGURE 14.6 Variation of Theta of a European Call Option with Time to Maturity

Gamma

The *gamma,* Γ, of a portfolio of options on an underlying asset is the rate of change of the portfolio's delta with respect to the price of the underlying asset. If gamma is small, delta changes slowly, and adjustments to keep a portfolio delta neutral need be made only relatively infrequently. However, if gamma is large in absolute terms, delta is highly sensitive to the price of the underlying asset. It is then quite risky to leave a delta-neutral portfolio unchanged for any length of time. Figure 14.7 illustrates this point. When the stock price moves from S to S', delta hedging assumes that the option price moves from C to C' when in fact it moves from C to C''. The difference between C' and C'' leads to a hedging error. This error depends on the curvature of the relationship between the option price and the stock price. Gamma measures this curvature.[5]

Suppose that ΔS is the change in the price of an underlying asset in a small interval of time, Δt, and $\Delta \Pi$ is the corresponding change in the price of the portfolio. If terms such as Δt^2 are ignored, it can be shown that for a delta-neutral portfolio

$$\Delta \Pi = \Theta \Delta t + \frac{\Gamma \Delta S^2}{2}$$

where Θ is the theta of the portfolio. Figure 14.8 shows the nature of this relationship between $\Delta \Pi$ and ΔS. It can be seen that when gamma is positive, the portfolio declines in value if there is no change in S but increases in value if there is a large positive or negative change in S. When gamma is negative, the reverse is true: The portfolio increases in value if there is no change in S but decreases in value if there is a large positive or negative change in S. As the absolute value of gamma increases, the sensitivity of the value of the portfolio to S increases.

Example

Suppose that the gamma of a delta-neutral portfolio of options on an asset is $-10,000$. The above equation shows that if a change of $+2$ or -2 in the price

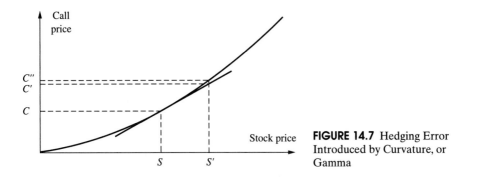

FIGURE 14.7 Hedging Error Introduced by Curvature, or Gamma

---

[5]Indeed, the gamma of an option is sometimes referred to as its *curvature* by practitioners.

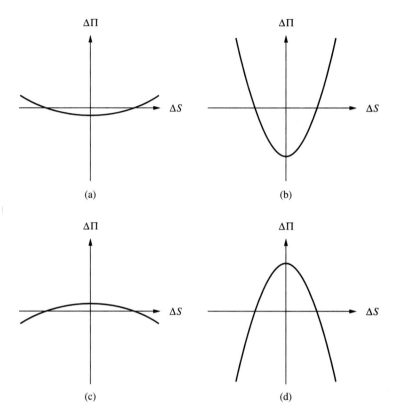

FIGURE 14.8 Alternative Relationships between $\Delta\Pi$ and ΔS for a Delta-Neutral Portfolio (a) Slightly positive gamma, (b) large positive gamma, (c) slightly negative gamma, and (d) large negative gamma.

of the asset occurs over a short period of time, there is an unexpected decrease in the value of the portfolio of approximately $0.5 \times 10,000 \times 2^2 = \$20,000$.

MAKING A PORTFOLIO GAMMA NEUTRAL

A *linear derivative* is one whose value is linearly dependent on the price of the underlying asset. A *nonlinear derivative* is one whose value is a nonlinear function of the price of the underlying asset. Because linear derivatives have zero gamma, it is necessary to introduce a nonlinear derivative into a portfolio in order to change its gamma. A position in the underlying asset itself or a forward contract on the underlying asset both have zero gamma and cannot be used to change the gamma of a portfolio. What is required is a position in an option or similar derivative.

Suppose that a delta-neutral portfolio has a gamma equal to Γ and a traded option has a gamma equal to Γ_T. If the number of traded options added to the portfolio is w_T, the gamma of the portfolio is

$$w_T\Gamma_T + \Gamma$$

Hence, the position in the traded option necessary to make the portfolio gamma neutral is $-\Gamma/\Gamma_T$. Including the traded option is likely to change the delta of the portfolio, so the position in the underlying asset then has to be changed to maintain delta neutrality. Note that the portfolio is gamma neutral only for a short period of time. As time passes, gamma neutrality can be maintained only if the position in the traded option is adjusted so that it is always equal to $-\Gamma/\Gamma_T$.

Making a delta-neutral portfolio gamma neutral can be regarded as a first correction for the fact that the position in the underlying asset cannot be changed continuously when delta hedging is used. Delta neutrality provides protection against relatively small stock price moves between rebalancing. Gamma neutrality provides protection against larger movements in this stock price between hedge rebalancing. Suppose that a portfolio is delta neutral and has a gamma of $-3,000$. The delta and gamma of a particular traded call option are 0.62 and 1.50, respectively. The portfolio can be made gamma neutral by including a long position of

$$\frac{3,000}{1.5} = 2,000$$

traded call options in the portfolio. However, the delta of the portfolio will then change from zero to $2,000 \times 0.62 = 1,240$. A quantity, 1,240, of the underlying asset must therefore be sold from the portfolio to keep it delta neutral. This example is summarized in Table 14.7.

CALCULATION OF GAMMA

For a European call or put option on a nondividend-paying stock, the gamma is given by

$$\Gamma = \frac{N'(d_1)}{S\sigma\sqrt{T}}$$

where d_1 is defined as in Equation 11.5 and $N'(x)$ is as given by Equation 14.4. The gamma is always positive and varies with S in the way indicated in Figure 14.9. The variation of gamma with time to maturity for out-of-the-money, at-the-money, and in-the-money options is shown in Figure 14.10. For an at-the-money option, gamma increases

---

TABLE 14.7 Making a Portfolio Gamma and Delta Neutral

From the Trader's Desk
    An investor's portfolio is delta neutral and has a gamma of $-3,000$. The delta and gamma of a particular traded call option are 0.62 and 1.50, respectively. The investor would like to make the portfolio gamma neutral as well as delta neutral.

Strategy
    The portfolio can be made gamma neutral by buying 2,000 options (20 contracts). However, the purchase creates a delta of 1,240. A quantity, 1,240, of the underlying asset must therefore be sold at the same time as the traded options are purchased.

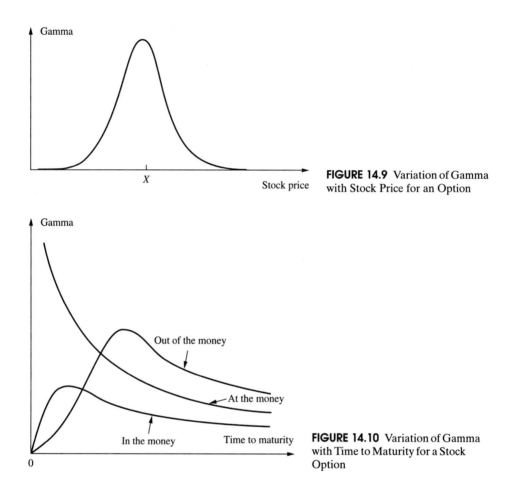

FIGURE 14.9 Variation of Gamma with Stock Price for an Option

FIGURE 14.10 Variation of Gamma with Time to Maturity for a Stock Option

as the time to maturity decreases. Short-life at-the-money options have very high gammas, which means that the value of the option holder's position is highly sensitive to jumps in the stock price.

For a European call or put option on a stock index paying a continuous dividend at rate q,

$$\Gamma = \frac{N'(d_1)e^{-qT}}{S\sigma\sqrt{T}}$$

where d_1 is defined as in Equation 12.4. This formula gives the gamma for a European option on a currency when q is put equal to the foreign risk-free rate and gives the gamma for a European futures option with $q = r$ and $S = F$.

Example

Consider a four-month put option on a stock index. The current value of the index is 305, the strike price is 300, the dividend yield is 3 percent per annum, the risk-free interest rate is 8 percent per annum, and volatility of the index is 25 percent per annum. In this case $S = 305$, $X = 300$, $q = 0.03$, $r = 0.08$, $\sigma = 0.25$, and $T = 4/12$. The gamma of the index option is given by

$$\frac{N'(d_1)e^{-qT}}{S\sigma\sqrt{T}} = 0.00857$$

Thus, an increase of 1 in the index (from 305 to 306) increases the delta of the option by approximately 0.00857.

The Relationship of Delta, Theta, and Gamma

Suppose that f is the value of a call option or a put option or any other derivative whose underlying asset is the price of a stock paying a continuous dividend at rate q. It can be shown that

$$\Theta + (r - q)S\Delta + \frac{1}{2}\sigma^2 S^2\Gamma = rf \tag{14.5}$$

This is true when f is the value of a portfolio of derivatives on the stock as well as for individual derivatives. An analogous result holds when the underlying asset is a currency ($q = r_f$) and when it is a futures price ($q = r$).

For a delta-neutral portfolio, $\Delta = 0$ and

$$\Theta + \frac{1}{2}\sigma^2 S^2\Gamma = rf$$

This equation is consistent with Figure 14.8. It shows that when Θ is large and positive, gamma tends to be large and negative, and vice versa. In other words, theta is a proxy for gamma when a portfolio is delta neutral.

Note that, when both delta and gamma are zero, $\Theta = rf$, showing that the value of the portfolio grows at the risk-free rate.[6]

Vega

Up to now we have implicitly assumed that the volatility of the asset underlying a derivative is constant. In practice, volatilities change over time. Thus, the value of a derivative may change because of movements in volatility as well as because of changes in the asset price and the passage of time.

The *vega* of a portfolio of derivatives, $\mathcal{V}$, is the rate of change of the value of the portfolio with respect to the volatility of the underlying asset.[7] If vega is high in absolute

---

[6]The results in this section are based on the assumption that the volatility of the underlying asset is zero.

[7]Vega is also sometimes referred to as lambda, kappa, or sigma.

terms, the portfolio's value is very sensitive to small changes in volatility. If vega is low in absolute terms, volatility changes have relatively little impact on the value of the portfolio.

A position in the underlying asset has zero vega. The vega of a portfolio can be changed by adding a position in an option. If $\mathcal{V}$ is the vega of the portfolio and $\mathcal{V}_T$ is the vega of a traded option, a position of $-\mathcal{V}/\mathcal{V}_T$ in the traded option makes the portfolio instantaneously vega neutral. Unfortunately, a portfolio that is gamma neutral will not in general be vega neutral, and vice versa. If a hedger requires a portfolio to be both gamma and vega neutral, at least two traded derivatives dependent on the underlying asset must usually be used.

Example

Consider a portfolio that is delta neutral, with a gamma of $-5,000$ and a vega of $-8,000$. A traded option has a gamma of 0.5, a vega of 2.0, and a delta of 0.6. The portfolio can be made vega neutral by including a long position in 4,000 traded options. This would increase delta to 2,400 and require that 2,400 units of the asset be sold to maintain delta neutrality. The gamma of the portfolio would change from $-5,000$ to $-3,000$.

To make the portfolio gamma and vega neutral, we suppose that there is a second traded option with a gamma of 0.8, a vega of 1.2, and a delta of 0.5. If w_1 and w_2 are the amounts of the two traded options included in the portfolio, we require that

$$-5,000 + 0.5w_1 + 0.8w_2 = 0$$

$$-8,000 + 2.0w_1 + 1.2w_2 = 0$$

The solution to these equations is $w_1 = 400$, $w_2 = 6,000$. The portfolio can therefore be made gamma and vega neutral by including 400 of the first traded option and 6,000 of the second traded option. The delta of the portfolio after the addition of the positions in the two traded options is $400 \times 0.6 + 6,000 \times 0.5 = 3,240$. Hence, 3,240 units of the asset would have to be sold to maintain delta neutrality.

For a European call or put option on a nondividend-paying stock, vega is given by

$$\mathcal{V} = S\sqrt{T}\, N'(d_1)$$

where d_1 is defined as in Equation 11.5. The formula for $N'(x)$ is given in Equation 14.4. For a European call or put option on a stock or stock index paying a continuous dividend yield at rate q,

$$\mathcal{V} = S\sqrt{T}\, N'(d_1)e^{-qT}$$

where d_1 is defined as in Equation 12.4. This equation gives the vega for a European currency option with q replaced by r_f. It also gives the vega for a European futures option with q replaced by r, and S replaced by F. The vega of an option is always positive. The general way in which it varies with S is shown in Figure 14.11.

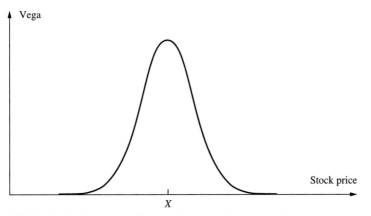

FIGURE 14.11 Variation of Vega with Stock Price for an Option

Gamma neutrality corrects for the fact that time elapses between hedge rebalancing. Vega neutrality corrects for a nonconstant σ. As might be expected, whether it is best to use an available traded option for vega or gamma hedging depends on the time between hedge rebalancing and the volatility of the volatility.[8]

Example

Consider a four-month put option on a stock index. The current value of the index is 305, the strike price is 300, the dividend yield is 3 percent per annum, the risk-free interest rate is 8 percent per annum, and the volatility of the index is 25 percent per annum. In this case $S = 305$, $X = 300$, $q = 0.03$, $r = 0.08$, $\sigma = 0.25$, and $T = 4/12$. The option's vega is given by

$$S \sqrt{T} \, N'(d_1) e^{-qT} = 66.44$$

Thus a 1 percent (0.01) increase in volatility (from 25 percent to 26 percent) increases the value of the option by approximately 0.6644 ($= 0.01 \times 66.44$).

Rho

The *rho* of a portfolio of options is the rate of change of the value of the portfolio with respect to the interest rate. It measures the sensitivity of the value of a portfolio to interest rates. For a European call option on a nondividend-paying stock,

$$\text{rho} = XTe^{-rT} N(d_2)$$

---

[8]For a discussion of this issue, see J. Hull and A. White, "Hedging the Risks from Writing Foreign Currency Options," *Journal of International Money and Finance* 6 (June 1987): 131–152.

where d_2 is defined as in Equation 11.5. For a European put option,

$$\text{rho} = -XTe^{-rT}N(-d_2)$$

These same formulas apply to European call and put options on stocks and stock indices paying a dividend yield at rate q when appropriate changes are made to the definition of d_2.

Example

Consider a four-month put option on a stock index. The current value of the index is 305, the strike price is 300, the dividend yield is 3 percent per annum, the risk-free interest rate is 8 percent per annum, and the volatility of the index is 25 percent per annum. In this case $S = 305$, $X = 300$, $q = 0.03$, $r = 0.08$, $\sigma = 0.25$, and $T = 4/12$. The option's rho is

$$-XTe^{-rT}N(-d_2) = -42.57$$

This means that for a 1 percent (0.01) change in the risk-free interest rate (from 8 percent to 9 percent), the value of the option decreases by $0.4257(= 0.01 \times 42.57)$.

In the case of currency options, there are two rhos corresponding to the two interest rates. The rho corresponding to the domestic interest rate is given by the formulas already presented. The rho corresponding to the foreign interest rate for a European call on a currency is given by

$$\text{rho} = -Te^{-r_f T}SN(d_1)$$

For a European put it is

$$\text{rho} = Te^{-r_f T}SN(-d_1)$$

Hedging in Practice

It is wrong to give the impression that option traders working for financial institutions are continually rebalancing their portfolios to maintain delta neutrality, gamma neutrality, vega neutrality, and so on. For a large portfolio dependent on a single underlying asset, it is usually feasible to maintain delta neutrality by rebalancing the position in the underlying asset daily. Maintaining gamma neutrality and vega neutrality is often not feasible, because it is difficult to find options or other nonlinear derivatives that can be traded in the volume required at competitive prices. In most cases gamma and vega are monitored. When they get too large in either a positive or negative direction, corrective action is taken.

In many markets financial institutions find that the majority of their trades are sales of call and put options to their clients. Short calls and short puts have negative gammas and negative vegas. As time goes by, therefore, both the gamma and vega of a financial institution's portfolio tend to become progressively more negative. In these circumstances traders working for the financial institution are always looking for ways to buy options (i.e., acquire positive gamma and vega) at competitive prices.

Scenario Analysis

In addition to monitoring risks such as delta, gamma, and vega, option traders often also carry out a scenario analysis. The analysis involves calculating the gain or loss on their portfolio over a specified period under a variety of different scenarios. The time period chosen is likely to depend on the liquidity of the instruments. The scenarios can be either chosen by management or generated by a model.

Consider a bank with a portfolio of options on a foreign currency. There are two main variables upon which the value of the portfolio depends. These are the exchange rate and the exchange rate volatility. Suppose that the exchange rate is currently 1.0000 and its volatility is 10 percent per annum. The bank could calculate a table such as Table 14.8 showing the profit or loss experienced during a two-week period under different scenarios. This table considers seven different exchange rates and three different volatilities. Because a one-standard-deviation move in the exchange rate during a two-week period is about 0.02, the exchange rate moves considered are approximately one, two, and three standard deviations.

In Table 14.8 the greatest loss is in the lower right corner of the table. The loss corresponds to the volatility increasing to 12 percent and the exchange rate moving up to 1.06. It should be noted that the nature of an options portfolio is such that the greatest losses do not always correspond to one of the four corners of the table. Suppose, for example, that a bank's portfolio consists of a reverse butterfly spread (see chapter 9). The greatest loss will be experienced if the exchange rate stays where it is.

Portfolio Insurance

A portfolio manager holding a well-diversified stock portfolio is sometimes interested in insuring against the value of the portfolio dropping below a certain level. One way of doing so is by holding, in conjunction with the stock portfolio, put options on a stock index. This strategy was discussed in chapter 12.

Consider a fund manager holding a $30 million portfolio whose value mirrors the value of the S&P 500. Suppose that the S&P 500 is standing at 300 and the manager wishes to insure against the value of the portfolio dropping below $29 million in the next six months. The manager can buy 1,000 six-month put option contracts on the S&P 500 with an exercise price of 290 and a maturity in six months. If the index drops below 290,

TABLE 14.8 Profit or Loss Realized in Two Weeks under Different Scenarios (millions of dollars)

	Exchange Rate						
Volatility	*0.94*	*0.96*	*0.98*	*1.00*	*1.02*	*1.04*	*1.06*
8%	+102	+55	+25	+6	−10	−34	−80
10%	+80	+40	+17	+2	−14	−38	−85
12%	+60	+25	+9	−2	−18	−42	−90

the put options will become in the money and provide the manager with compensation for the decline in the value of the portfolio. Consider the case where the index drops to 270 at the end of six months. The value of the manager's stock portfolio is likely to be about $27 million. Because each option contract is on 100 times the index, the total value of the put options is $2 million. This brings the value of the entire holding back up to $29 million.

CREATING OPTIONS SYNTHETICALLY

An alternative approach open to the portfolio manager is to create the put options synthetically. This strategy involves taking a position in the underlying asset (or futures on the underlying asset) so that the delta of the position is maintained equal to the delta of the required option. If more accuracy is required, the next step is to use traded options to match the gamma and vega of the required option. The position necessary to create an option synthetically is the reverse of that necessary to hedge it. This is simply a reflection of the fact that a procedure for hedging an option involves the creation of an equal and opposite option synthetically.

There are two reasons it may be more attractive for the portfolio manager to create the required put option synthetically than to buy it in the market. The first is that options markets do not always have the liquidity to absorb the trades that managers of large funds would like to carry out. The second is that fund managers often require strike prices and exercise dates that are different from those available in traded options markets.

The synthetic option can be created from trades in stocks themselves or from trades in index futures contracts. We will first examine the creation of a put option by trades in the stocks themselves. Consider again the fund manager with a well-diversified portfolio worth $30 million who wishes to buy a European put on the portfolio with a strike price of $29 million and an exercise date in six months. Recall that the delta of a European put on an index is given by

$$\Delta = e^{-qT}[N(d_1) - 1] \tag{14.6}$$

where, with the usual notation,

$$d_1 = \frac{\ln(S/X) + (r - q + \sigma^2/2)T}{\sigma\sqrt{T}}$$

Because the fund manager's portfolio mirrors the index, this is also the delta of a put on the portfolio when it is regarded as a single security. The delta is negative. Accordingly, in order to create the put option synthetically, the fund manager should ensure that at any given time a proportion

$$e^{-qT}[1 - N(d_1)]$$

of the stocks in the original $30 million portfolio have been sold and the proceeds invested in riskless assets. As the value of the original portfolio declines, the delta of the put becomes more negative and the proportion of the portfolio sold must be increased. As the value of the original portfolio increases, the delta of the put becomes less negative and the proportion of the portfolio sold must be decreased (i.e., some of the original portfolio must be repurchased).

Using this strategy to create portfolio insurance means that at any given time funds are divided between the stock portfolio on which insurance is required and riskless assets. As the value of the stock portfolio increases, riskless assets are sold and the position in the stock portfolio is increased. As the value of the stock portfolio declines, the position in the stock portfolio is decreased and riskless assets are purchased. The cost of the insurance arises from the fact that the portfolio manager is always selling in a declining market and buying after a rise.

USE OF INDEX FUTURES

Using index futures to create portfolio insurance can be preferable to using the underlying stocks, because the transactions costs associated with trades in index futures are generally lower than those associated with the corresponding trades in the underlying stocks. The portfolio manager considered earlier would keep the $30 million stock portfolio intact and short index futures contracts. The dollar amount of the futures contracts shorted as a proportion of the value of the portfolio should from Equations 14.3 and 14.6 be

$$e^{-qT}e^{-(r-q)T^*}[1 - N(d_1)] = e^{q(T^*-T)}e^{-rT^*}[1 - N(d_1)]$$

where T^* is the maturity time of the futures contract. If the portfolio is worth K_1 times the index and each index futures contract is on K_2 times the index, the number of futures contracts shorted at any given time should be

$$e^{q(T^*-T)}e^{-rT^*}[1 - N(d_1)]\frac{K_1}{K_2}$$

Example

In the example given at the beginning of this section, suppose that the volatility of the market is 25 percent per annum, the risk-free interest rate is 9 percent per annum, and the dividend yield on the market is 3 percent per annum. In this case $S = 300, X = 290, r = 0.09, q = 0.03, \sigma = 0.25$, and $T = 0.5$. The delta of the option required is

$$e^{-qT}[N(d_1) - 1] = -0.322$$

Hence, if trades in the portfolio are used to create the option, 32.2 percent of the portfolio should be sold initially. If nine-month futures contracts on the S&P 500 are used, $T^* - T = 0.25, T^* = 0.75, K_1 = 100{,}000, K_2 = 500$, so that the number of futures contracts shorted should be

$$e^{q(T^*-T)}e^{-rT^*}[1 - N(d_1)]\frac{K_1}{K_2} = 61.6$$

Up to now we have assumed that the portfolio mirrors the index. As discussed in chapter 12, the hedging scheme can be adjusted to deal with other situations. The strike price for the options used should be the expected level of the market index when the portfolio's value reaches its insured value. The number of index options used should be β times the number of options that would be required if the portfolio had a beta of 1.0.

FREQUENCY OF REBALANCING AND OCTOBER 19, 1987

An important issue when put options are created synthetically for portfolio insurance is the frequency with which the portfolio manager's position should be adjusted or rebalanced. With no transactions costs, continuous rebalancing is optimal. However, as transactions costs increase, the optimal frequency of rebalancing declines.

Creating put options on the index synthetically does not work well if the volatility of the index changes rapidly or if the index exhibits large jumps. On Monday, October 19, 1987, the Dow Jones Industrial Average dropped by over 500 points. Portfolio managers who had insured themselves by buying traded put options survived this crash well. Those who had chosen to create put options synthetically found that they were unable to sell either stocks or index futures fast enough to protect their position.

Stock Market Volatility

We have already considered the issue of whether volatility is caused solely by the arrival of new information or whether trading itself generates volatility. Portfolio insurance schemes such as those just described have the potential to increase volatility. When the market declines, they cause portfolio managers either to sell stock or to sell index futures contracts. Either action may accentuate the decline. The sale of stock is liable to drive down the market index further in a direct way. The sale of index futures contracts is liable to drive down futures prices. This creates selling pressure on stocks via the mechanism of index arbitrage (see chapter 3), so that the market index is liable to be driven down in this case as well. Similarly, when the market rises, the portfolio insurance schemes cause portfolio managers either to buy stock or to buy futures contracts. This may accentuate the rise.

In addition to formal portfolio insurance schemes, we can speculate that many investors consciously or subconsciously follow portfolio insurance schemes of their own. For example, an investor may be inclined to enter the market when it is rising but will sell when it is falling to limit the downside risk.

Whether portfolio insurance schemes (formal or informal) affect volatility depends on how easily the market can absorb the trades that are generated by portfolio insurance. If portfolio insurance trades are a very small fraction of all trades, there is likely to be no effect. As portfolio insurance becomes more popular, it is liable to have a destabilizing effect on the market.

BRADY COMMISSION REPORT

The report of the Brady Commission on the October 19, 1987 crash provides interesting insights into the effect of portfolio insurance on the market at that time.[9] The Brady

---

[9]See "Report of the Presidential Task Force on Market Mechanisms," January 1988.

Commission estimated that $60 billion to $90 billion of equity assets were under portfolio insurance administration in October 1987. During the period Wednesday, October 14, 1987 to Friday, October 16, 1987, the market declined by about 10 percent with much of this decline taking place on the Friday afternoon. The decline should have generated at least $12 billion of equity or index futures sales as a result of portfolio insurance schemes.[10] In fact, less than $4 billion were sold, which means that portfolio insurers approached the following week with huge amounts of selling already dictated by their models. The Brady Commission estimated that on Monday, October 19 sell programs by three portfolio insurers accounted for almost 10 percent of the sales on the New York Stock Exchange, and that portfolio insurance sales amounted to 21.3 percent of all sales in index futures markets. It seems likely that portfolio insurance caused some downward pressure on the market. It is significant that, in aggregate, portfolio insurers executed only a relatively small proportion of the total trades generated by their models. Needless to say, the popularity of portfolio insurance schemes based on dynamic trading in stocks and futures has declined considerably since October 1987.

Summary

Financial institutions offer a variety of option products to their clients. Often the options do not correspond to the standardized products traded by exchanges. The financial institutions are then faced with the problem of hedging their exposure. Naked and covered positions leave them subject to an unacceptable level of risk. One course of action that is sometimes proposed is a stop-loss strategy. This involves holding a naked position when an option is out of the money and converting it to a covered position as soon as the option moves in the money. Although superficially attractive, the strategy does not work at all well.

The delta, Δ, of an option is the rate of change of its price with respect to the price of the underlying asset. Delta hedging involves creating a position with zero delta (sometimes referred to as a delta-neutral position). Because the delta of the underlying asset is 1.0, one way of hedging is to take a position of $-\Delta$ in the underlying asset for each long option being hedged. The delta of an option changes over time. This means that the position in the underlying asset has to be frequently adjusted.

Once an option position has been made delta neutral, the next stage is often to look at its gamma. The gamma of an option is the rate of change of its delta with respect to the price of the underlying asset. It is a measure of the curvature of the relationship between the option price and the asset price. The impact of this curvature on the performance of delta hedging can be reduced by making an option position gamma neutral. If Γ is the gamma of the position being hedged, the reduction is usually achieved by taking a position in a traded option that has a gamma of $-\Gamma$.

Delta and gamma hedging are both based on the assumption that the volatility of the underlying asset is constant. In practice, volatilities do change over time. The vega of an option or an option portfolio measures the rate of change of its value with

---

[10]To put this in perspective, on Monday, October 19 all previous records were broken when 604 million shares worth $21 billion were traded on the New York Stock Exchange. Approximately $20 billion of S&P 500 futures contracts were traded on that day.

respect to volatility. A trader who wishes to hedge an option position against volatility changes can make the position vega neutral. As with the procedure for creating gamma neutrality, this usually involves taking an offsetting position in a traded option. If the trader wishes to achieve both gamma and vega neutrality, two traded options are usually required.

Two other measures of the risk of an option position are theta and rho. Theta measures the rate of change of the value of the position with respect to the passage of time, with all else remaining constant. Rho measures the rate of change of the value of the position with respect to the short-term interest rate, with all else remaining constant.

Portfolio managers are sometimes interested in creating put options synthetically for the purposes of insuring an equity portfolio. They can do so either by trading the portfolio or by trading index futures on the portfolio. Trading the portfolio involves splitting the portfolio between equities and risk-free securities. As the market declines, more is invested in risk-free securities. As the market increases, more is invested in equities. Trading index futures involves keeping the equity portfolio intact and selling index futures. As the market declines, more index futures are sold; as it rises, fewer are sold. The strategy works well in normal market conditions. On Monday, October 19, 1987, when the Dow Jones Industrial Average dropped by over 500 points, it worked badly. Portfolio insurers were unable to sell either stocks or index futures fast enough to protect their positions.

Suggestions for Further Reading

On hedging option positions

Boyle, P. P., and D. Emanuel. "Discretely Adjusted Option Hedges," *Journal of Financial Economics* 8 (1980): 259–282.

Dillman, S., and J. Harding. "Life after Delta: The Gamma Factor," *Euromoney* supplement (February 1985): 14–17.

Figlewski, S. "Options Arbitrage in Imperfect Markets," *Journal of Finance* 44 (December 1989): 1289–1311.

Galai, D. "The Components of the Return from Hedging Options against Stocks," *Journal of Business* 56 (January 1983): 45–54.

Hull, J., and A. White. "Hedging the Risks from Writing Foreign Currency Options," *Journal of International Money and Finance* 6 (June 1987): 131–152.

On portfolio insurance

Asay, M., and C. Edelberg. "Can a Dynamic Strategy Replicate the Returns on an Option?" *Journal of Futures Markets* 6 (Spring 1986): 63–70.

Bookstaber, R., and J. A. Langsam. "Portfolio Insurance Trading Rules," *Journal of Futures Markets* 8 (February 1988): 15–31.

Etzioni, E. S. "Rebalance Disciplines for Portfolio Insurance," *Journal of Portfolio Insurance* 13 (Fall 1986): 59–62.

Leland, H. E. "Option Pricing and Replication with Transactions Costs," *Journal of Finance* 40 (December 1985): 1283–1301.

Leland, H. E. "Who Should Buy Portfolio Insurance?" *Journal of Finance* 35 (May 1980): 581–594.

Rubinstein, M. "Alternative Paths for Portfolio Insurance," *Financial Analysts Journal* 41 (July–August 1985): 42–52.

Rubinstein, M., and H. E. Leland. "Replicating Options with Positions in Stock and Cash," *Financial Analysts Journal* 37 (July–August 1981): 63–72.

Tilley, J. A., and G. O. Latainer. "A Synthetic Option Framework for Asset Allocation," *Financial Analysts Journal* 41 (May–June 1985): 32–41.

Quiz

1. Explain how a stop-loss hedging scheme can be implemented for the writer of an out-of-the-money call option. Why does it provide a relatively poor hedge?
2. What does it mean to assert that the delta of a call option is 0.7? How can a short position in 1,000 options be made delta neutral when the delta of each option is 0.7?
3. Calculate the delta of an at-the-money six-month European call option on a nondividend-paying stock when the risk-free interest rate is 10 percent per annum and the stock price volatility is 25 percent per annum.
4. What does it mean to assert that the theta of an option position is –0.1 when time is measured in years? If a trader feels that neither a stock price nor its implied volatility will change, what type of option position is appropriate?
5. What is meant by the gamma of an option position? What are the risks in the situation where the gamma of a position is large and negative and the delta is zero?
6. "The procedure for creating an option position synthetically is the reverse of the procedure for hedging the option position." Explain this statement.
7. Why did portfolio insurance not work well on October 19, 1987?

Questions and Problems

14.1. A deposit instrument offered by a bank guarantees that investors will receive a return during a six-month period that is the greater of (a) zero and (b) 40 percent of the return provided by a market index. An investor is planning to put $100,000 in the instrument. Describe the payoff as an option on the index. Assuming that the risk-free rate of interest is 8 percent per annum, the dividend yield on the index is 3 percent per annum, and the volatility of the index is 25 percent per annum, is the product a good deal for the investor?

14.2. The Black–Scholes price of an out-of-the-money call option with an exercise price of $40 is $4. A trader who has written the option plans to use a stop-loss strategy. The trader's plan is to buy at 40\frac{1}{8}$ and to sell at 39\frac{7}{8}$. Estimate the expected number of times the stock will be bought or sold.

14.3. Suppose that a stock price is currently $20 and that a call option with an exercise price of $25 is created synthetically using a continually changing position in the stock. Consider the following two scenarios:
   a. Stock price increases steadily from $20 to $35 during the life of the option.
   b. Stock price oscillates wildly, ending up at $35.

Which scenario would make the synthetically created option more expensive? Explain your answer.

14.4. What is the delta of a short position in 1,000 European call options on silver futures? The options mature in eight months, and the futures contract underlying the option matures in nine months. The current nine-month futures price is $8 per ounce, the exercise price of the options is $8, the risk-free interest rate is 12 percent per annum, and the volatility of silver is 18 percent per annum.

14.5. In Problem 14.4, what initial position in nine-month silver futures is necessary for delta hedging? If silver itself is used, what is the initial position? If one-year silver futures are used, what is the initial position? Assume no storage costs for silver.

14.6. A company uses delta hedging to hedge a portfolio of long positions in put and call options on a currency. Which of the following would give the most favorable result?
   a. A virtually constant spot rate
   b. Wild movements in the spot rate
   Explain your answer.

14.7. Repeat Problem 14.6 for a financial institution with a portfolio of short positions in put and call options for a currency.

14.8. A financial institution has just sold 1,000 seven-month European call options on the Japanese yen. Suppose that the spot exchange rate is 0.80 cent per yen, the exercise price is 0.81 cent per yen, the risk-free interest rate in the United States is 8 percent per annum, the risk-free interest rate in Japan is 5 percent per annum, and the volatility of the yen is 15 percent per annum. Calculate the delta, gamma, vega, theta, and rho of the financial institution's position. Interpret each number.

14.9. A financial institution has the following portfolio of over-the-counter options on sterling:

Type	Position	Delta of Option	Gamma of Option	Vega of Option
Call	−1,000	0.50	2.2	1.8
Call	−500	0.80	0.6	0.2
Put	−2,000	−0.40	1.3	0.7
Call	−500	0.70	1.8	1.4

A traded option is available with a delta of 0.6, a gamma of 1.5, and a vega of 0.8.
   a. What position in the traded option and in sterling would make the portfolio both gamma neutral and delta neutral?
   b. What position in the traded option and in sterling would make the portfolio both vega neutral and delta neutral?

14.10. Consider again the situation in Problem 14.9. Suppose that a second traded option with a delta of 0.1, a gamma of 0.5, and a vega of 0.6 is available. How could the portfolio be made delta, gamma, and vega neutral?

14.11. Under what circumstances is it possible to make a position in an over-the-counter European option on a stock index both gamma neutral and vega neutral by introducing a single traded European option into the portfolio?

14.12. A fund manager has a well-diversified portfolio that mirrors the performance of the S&P 500 and is worth $90 million. The value of the S&P 500 is 300, and the portfolio manager would like to buy insurance against a reduction of more than 5 percent in the value of the portfolio over the next six months. The risk-free interest rate is 6 percent per annum. The dividend yield on both the portfolio and the S&P 500 is 3 percent, and the volatility of the index is 30 percent per annum.
   a. If the fund manager buys traded European put options, how much would the insurance cost?
   b. Explain carefully alternative strategies open to the fund manager involving traded European call options, and show that they lead to the same result.
   c. If the fund manager decides to provide insurance by keeping part of the portfolio in risk-free securities, what should the initial position be?
   d. If the fund manager decides to provide insurance by using nine-month index futures, what should the initial position be?

14.13. Repeat Problem 14.12 on the assumption that the portfolio has a beta of 1.5. Assume that the dividend yield on the portfolio is 4 percent per annum.

14.14. Show by substituting for the various terms in Equation 14.5 that the equation is true for:
   a. A single European call option on a nondividend-paying stock
   b. A single European put option on a nondividend-paying stock
   c. Any portfolio of European put and call options on a nondividend-paying stock

14.15. Suppose that $70 billion of equity assets are the subject of portfolio insurance schemes. Assume that the schemes were designed to ensure that the value of the assets does not decline by more than 5 percent within one year. Making whatever estimates you find necessary, use the DerivaGem software to calculate the value of the stock or futures contracts that the administrators of the portfolio insurance schemes will attempt to sell if the market falls by 23 percent in a single day.

14.16. Does a forward contract have the same delta as the corresponding futures contract? Explain your answer.

14.17. Consider a one-year European call option on a stock when the stock price is $30, the strike price is $30, the risk free rate is 5 percent per annum, and the volatility is 25 percent per annum. Use the DerivaGem software to calculate the price, delta, gamma, vega, theta, and rho of the option. Verify that delta is correct by changing the stock price to $30.1 and recomputing delta. Verify that gamma is correct by recomputing the delta for the situation where the stock price is $30.1. Carry out similar calculations to verify that vega, theta, and rho are correct.

14.18. Use the DerivaGem software to plot the option price, delta, gamma, vega, theta, and rho against the stock price for the stock option in Problem 14.17.

14.19. A bank's position in options on a certain exchange rate has a delta of 30,000 and a gamma of 4,000. Explain how these numbers can be interpreted. The exchange rate (number of units of domestic currency per unit of foreign currency) is 1.35. What position would you take to make the position delta neutral? After a short period of time, the exchange rate moves to 1.37. Estimate the new delta. What additional trade is necessary to keep the position delta neutral? Assuming the bank did set up a delta-neutral position originally, has it gained or lost money from the exchange-rate movement?

15

CHAPTER

Value at Risk

In chapter 14 we looked at measures such as delta, gamma, and vega for describing the different aspects of the risk in a portfolio consisting of options and other financial assets. A financial institution usually calculates each of these measures each day for each of the market variables that it is exposed to. Often there are hundreds, or even thousands, of these market variables. A delta-gamma-vega analysis therefore leads to a huge number of different risk measures being produced each day. These risk measures provide valuable information for the traders who are responsible for managing the various components of the financial institution's portfolio, but they are of limited use to senior management.

Dennis Weatherstone, former chairman of J. P. Morgan, is an example of a senior manager who felt that a single measure of the overall risk should be calculated. He demanded that a one-page report be delivered to him after the close of business each day, summarizing the company's global exposure and providing an estimate of potential losses over the next 24 hours. The result was J. P. Morgan's famous "4.15 Report" (so-called because it was delivered to Weatherstone at 4:15 P.M. each day) and the beginning of an amazingly successful risk management tool known as *value at risk*.

Value at risk (VaR) is an attempt to provide a single number summarizing the total risk in a portfolio of financial assets. It has become widely used by corporate treasurers and fund managers as well as by financial institutions. The calculation of VaR was made easier in October 1994 when J. P. Morgan made its RiskMetrics database of volatilities and correlations freely available to all market participants. Some of the impetus for the use of VaR has also come from the actions of regulators. For example, regulators now require all banks to calculate VaR, and they use VaR in determining the capital a bank is required to keep to reflect the market risks it is bearing.[1]

A VaR calculation is aimed at making a statement of the following form: "We are X percent certain that we will not lose more than V dollars in the next N days." One attractive feature of VaR is that it is easy to understand. In essence, it asks the

---

[1]See P. Jackson, D. J. Maude, and W. Perraudin. "Bank Capital and Value at Risk," *Journal of Derivatives* 4, 3 (Spring 1997): 73–90.

simple question "How bad can things get?" The variable V is the VaR of the portfolio. It is a function of two parameters: N, the time horizon, and X, the confidence level. In calculating a bank's capital, regulators use $N = 10$ and $X = 99$. They are therefore considering losses over a 10-day period that are expected to happen only 1 percent of the time.

Volatilities and Correlations

Volatilities play a key role in the determination of VaR. To remind ourselves of the definition of volatility used in option pricing, we return to Equation 11.4. This shows that the standard deviation of the continuously compounded return on an asset in time T is $\sigma \sqrt{T}$, where σ is the volatility of the asset. In option pricing T is measured in years. Setting $T = 1$, we see that the asset's volatility, σ, is the standard deviation of the continuously compounded return earned by the asset in one year.

In VaR calculations T is measured in days, so that σ is a "volatility per day" rather than a "volatility per year." The volatility of an asset per day can be defined as the standard deviation of the continuously compounded return earned by the asset in one day. What is the relationship between the volatility per year used in option pricing and the volatility per day used in VaR calculations? Let us define σ_{yr} as the volatility per year of a certain asset and σ_{day} as the equivalent volatility per day of the asset. Assuming 252 trading days in a year, we can use Equation 11.4 to write the standard deviation of the continuously compounded return on the asset in one year as either σ_{yr} or $\sigma_{day} \sqrt{252}$. It follows that

$$\sigma_{day} = \frac{\sigma_{yr}}{\sqrt{252}}$$

so that daily volatility is about 6 percent of annual volatility.

In chapter 11 we saw that σ_{yr} is approximately equal to the standard deviation of the proportional change in an asset price in one year. Similarly, σ_{day} is approximately equal to the standard deviation of the proportional change in an asset price in one day. In the case of σ_{day} the approximation is very good, and for the purposes of calculating VaR we assume that the daily volatility of an asset price, or any other market variable, is exactly equal to the standard deviation of the proportional daily changes.

It is worth noting that the J. P. Morgan RiskMetrics database uses a different definition of volatility from the standard one presented here. Its definition of volatility is 1.65 times the standard definition; that is, the RiskMetrics volatility is $1.65\sigma_{day}$. From the tables at the end of this book, $N(-1.65) = 0.05$. If we assume a normal distribution, the RiskMetrics volatility can therefore be interpreted as the decline in a market variable that is expected to be exceeded on only 5 percent of days.

ESTIMATING VOLATILITY

In this section we define σ_n as the volatility per day for a market variable, as calculated on day n. The square of the volatility, σ_n^2, is the *variance rate* of the market variable on day n.

The standard approach to estimating σ_n from historical data is discussed in chapter 11. Suppose that the values of the market variable on days $0, 1, \ldots, n$ are $S_0, S_1, \ldots, S_n$, respectively. We define

$$u_i = \ln \frac{S_i}{S_{i-1}}$$

for $1 \leq i \leq n$ and estimate the variance rate as

$$\sigma_n^2 = \frac{1}{n-1} \sum_{i=1}^{n} (u_i - \bar{u})^2$$

where $\bar{u}$ is the mean of the u_i's:

$$\bar{u} = \frac{1}{n} u_i$$

Without too much loss of accuracy, we can assume that $\bar{u} = 0$. Also, when n is reasonably large, we can replace $n - 1$ by n so that the above formula for σ_n^2 is simplified to

$$\sigma_n^2 = \frac{1}{n} \sum_{i=1}^{n} u_i^2 \tag{15.1}$$

Equation 15.1 gives equal weight to all the u_i^2's. An alternative is to use an *exponentially weighted moving average* (EWMA) in which the weights given to the u_i^2's decrease as we move back through time. This approach leads to a simple formula for calculating the estimate of the volatility on day n from the estimate calculated on day $n - 1$ and the proportional change in the market variable observed between day $n - 1$ and day n. The formula is

$$\sigma_n^2 = \lambda \sigma_{n-1}^2 + (1 - \lambda) u_n^2 \tag{15.2}$$

for some constant λ $(0 < \lambda < 1)$.

To understand what is going on here, we substitute for σ_{n-1}^2 in Equation 15.2 to get

$$\sigma_n^2 = \lambda [\lambda \sigma_{n-2}^2 + (1 - \lambda) u_{n-1}^2] + (1 - \lambda) u_n^2$$

or

$$\sigma_n^2 = (1 - \lambda)(u_n^2 + \lambda u_{n-1}^2) + \lambda^2 \sigma_{n-2}^2$$

Substituting in a similar way for σ_{n-2} gives

$$\sigma_n^2 = (1 - \lambda)(u_n^2 + \lambda u_{n-1}^2 + \lambda^2 u_{n-2}^2) + \lambda^3 \sigma_{n-3}^2$$

Continuing in this way, we see that

$$\sigma_n^2 = (1 - \lambda) \sum_{j=0}^{n-1} \lambda^j u_{n-j}^2 + \lambda^n \sigma_0^2$$

This shows that the weights given to the u_i^2's decline exponentially as we move back through time. Each weight is λ times the previous weight. For a large n the term $\lambda^n \sigma_0^2$ is sufficiently small to be ignored, so that σ_n^2 is determined entirely by a weighted average of the u_i^2.

Example

Suppose that λ is 0.90, the volatility calculated on day $n - 1$ is 1 percent, and the proportional change in the market variable between day $n - 1$ and day n is 2 percent. In this case $\sigma_{n-1}^2 = 0.01^2 = 0.0001$ and $u_n^2 = 0.02^2 = 0.0004$. Equation 15.2 gives

$$\sigma_n^2 = 0.9 \times 0.0001 + 0.1 \times 0.0004 = 0.00013$$

The estimate of the volatility on day n, σ_n, is therefore $\sqrt{0.00013}$, or 1.14 percent. Note that the expected value of u_n^2 is σ_{n-1}^2, or 0.0001. In this example the realized value of u_n^2 is greater than the expected value, and as a result our volatility estimate increases. If the realized value of u_n^2 had been less than its expected value, our estimate of the volatility would have decreased.

The EWMA approach has the attractive feature that relatively little data need to be stored. At any given time we need to remember only the current estimate of the variance rate and the most recent observation on the value of the market variable. When we get a new observation on the value of the market variable, we calculate a new u_n^2 and use Equation 15.2 to update our estimate of the variance rate. The old estimate of the variance rate and the old value of the market variable can then be discarded.

The EWMA approach is designed to track changes in the volatility. For example, if the volatility of a market variable increases, the values calculated for the u_i^2's also tend to increase. From Equation 15.2 this causes our estimates of the daily volatility to move upward. The value of λ governs how responsive the estimate of the daily volatility is to recent observations on the u_i^2's. A low value of λ leads to a great deal of weight being given to the most recent value of u_i^2, and the estimates produced for the volatility on successive days are themselves highly volatile. A high value of λ (i.e., a value close to 1) produces estimates of the daily volatility that respond relatively slowly to new information provided by the u_i^2.

The RiskMetrics database uses the EWMA approach for calculating daily volatilities. After some experimentation, J. P. Morgan found that a value of λ equal to 0.94 produced the best daily volatility forecasts.

ESTIMATING CORRELATIONS

The correlation between two variables X and Y can be defined as

$$\frac{\text{cov}(X, Y)}{\sigma_X \sigma_Y}$$

where σ_X and σ_Y are the standard deviation of X and Y and $\text{cov}(X, Y)$ is the covariance between X and Y. The covariance between X and Y is defined as

$$E\left[(X - \mu_X)(Y - \mu_Y)\right]$$

where μ_X and μ_Y are the means of X and Y, and E denotes expected value.

Consider two different market variables, U and V. We define u_i and v_i as the proportional changes in U and V on day i. We also define

$\sigma_{u,n}$: daily volatility of variable U, calculated on day n

$\sigma_{v,n}$: daily volatility of variable V, calculated on day n

cov_n: covariance between daily changes in U and V, calculated on day n

Our estimate of the correlation between U and V on day n is therefore

$$\frac{cov_n}{\sigma_{u,n}\sigma_{v,n}}$$

Using an equal-weighting scheme and assuming that the means of u_i and v_i are zero, Equation 15.1 shows that we can estimate the variance rates of U and V as

$$\sigma_{u,n}^2 = \frac{1}{n}\sum_{i=1}^{n} u_i^2$$

$$\sigma_{v,n}^2 = \frac{1}{n}\sum_{i=1}^{n} v_i^2$$

A similar estimate for the covariance between U and V is[2]

$$cov_n = \frac{1}{n}\sum_{i=1}^{n} u_i v_i \qquad\qquad \textbf{(15.3)}$$

Equation 15.3 gives equal weight to all the $u_i v_i$'s. An alternative is to use an EWMA model similar to Equation 15.2. The formula for updating the covariance estimate is then

$$cov_n = \lambda cov_{n-1} + (1-\lambda)u_n v_n$$

A similar analysis to that presented for the EWMA volatility model shows that the weights given to observations on the $u_i v_i$'s decline as we move back through time. The lower the value of λ, the greater the weight that is given to recent observations.

Example

Suppose that $\lambda = 0.95$ and that the correlation between two variables U and V calculated on day $n-1$ is 0.6. Suppose further that the volatilities calculated for the U and V on day $n-1$ are 1 percent and 2 percent, respectively. From the relationship between correlation and covariance, the covariance between the U and V on day $n-1$ is

$$0.6 \times 0.01 \times 0.02 = 0.00012$$

Suppose that, between day $n-1$ and day n the proportional changes in U and V

---

[2]Like Equation 15.1, this formula assumes that expected changes in the market variables are zero.

are 0.5 percent and 2.5 percent, respectively. The variance rates and covariance are updated as follows:

$$\sigma_{u,n}^2 = 0.95 \times 0.01^2 + 0.05 \times 0.005^2 = 0.00009625$$

$$\sigma_{v,n}^2 = 0.95 \times 0.02^2 + 0.05 \times 0.025^2 = 0.00041125$$

$$\text{cov}_n^2 = 0.95 \times 0.00012 + 0.05 \times 0.005 \times 0.025 = 0.00012025$$

The new volatility of U is $\sqrt{0.00009625} = 0.981$ percent, and the new volatility of V is $\sqrt{0.00041125} = 2.028$ percent. The new coefficient of correlation between U and V is

$$\frac{0.00012025}{0.00981 \times 0.02028} = 0.6044$$

For technical reasons it is important to be consistent in the way variances and covariances are calculated. If variances are calculated by giving equal weight to the last n data items, the same should be done for covariances; if variances are updated using an EWMA model with $\lambda = 0.94$, the same should be done for covariances; and so on.

Calculation of VaR in Simple Situations

We now move on to see how VaR can be calculated in simple situations. Consider first a portfolio consisting of a position worth $10 million in shares of IBM. We suppose that $N = 10$ and $X = 99$, so that we are interested in a 99 percent confidence level for losses over 10 days.

We assume that the volatility of IBM is 2 percent per day (corresponding to about 32 percent per year). Since the size of the position is $10 million, the standard deviation of daily changes in the value of the position is 2 percent of $10 million, or $200,000. Assuming that the changes on successive days are independent, we expect the standard deviation of the change over a 10-day period to be $\sqrt{10}$ times the change over a one-day period. The standard deviation of the change in the value of the IBM portfolio over a 10-day period is therefore $200,000\sqrt{10}$ or $632,456.

It is customary in VaR calculations to assume that the expected change in the price of a market variable over the time period considered is zero.[3] This is not exactly true but it is a reasonable assumption. The expected change in the price of a market variable over a short time period is generally small when compared with the standard deviation of the change. Suppose, for example, that IBM has an expected return of 18 percent. Over a one-day period, the expected price change is 18/252, or about 0.07 percent, whereas the standard deviation of the price change is 2 percent. Over a 10-day period, the expected price change is 18/25.2, or about 0.7 percent, whereas the standard deviation of the price change is $2\sqrt{10}$, or about 6.3 percent.

---

[3] As noted earlier, this assumption is often also made when volatilities and correlations are calculated for risk management purposes.

So far we have established that the change in the value of the portfolio of IBM shares over a 10-day period has a standard deviation of $632,456 and (at least approximately) a mean of zero. We assume that the change is normally distributed.[4] From the tables at the end of this book, $N(0.01) = -2.33$. This means that there is a 1 percent probability that a normally distributed variable will decrease in value by more than 2.33 standard deviations. Equivalently, it means that we are 99 percent certain that a normally distributed variable will not decrease in value by more than 2.33 standard deviations. The 99 percent/10-day VaR for our portfolio consisting of a $10 million position in IBM is therefore

$$2.33 \times 632,456 = \$1,473,621$$

Consider next a portfolio consisting of a $5 million position in AT&T, and suppose the daily volatility of AT&T is 1 percent (approximately 16 percent per year). A similar calculation to that for IBM shows that the standard deviation of the change in the value of the portfolio per 10 days is

$$5,000,000 \times 0.01 \times \sqrt{10} = 158,144$$

The 99 percent/10-day VaR is therefore

$$158,114 \times 2.33 = \$368,405$$

Now consider a portfolio consisting of both $10 million of IBM shares and $5 million of AT&T shares. We suppose that the correlation between the returns on the two shares over a short time period is 0.7. A standard result in statistics tells us that, if two variables X and Y have standard deviations equal to σ_X and σ_Y with the coefficient of correlation between them being equal to ρ, the standard deviation of $X + Y$ is given by

$$\sigma_{X+Y} = \sqrt{\sigma_X^2 + \sigma_Y^2 + 2\rho\sigma_X\sigma_Y}$$

To apply this result, we set X equal to the change in the value of the position in IBM over a 10-day period and Y equal to the change in the value of the position in AT&T over a 10-day period, so that

$$\sigma_X = 632,456 \qquad \sigma_Y = 158,114$$

The standard deviation of the change in the value of the portfolio consisting of both stocks over a 10-day period is therefore

$$\sqrt{632,456^2 + 158,114^2 + 2 \times 0.7 \times 632,456 \times 158,114} = 751,665$$

This means that the 99 percent/10-day VaR for the portfolio is

$$751,665 \times 2.33 = \$1,751,379$$

This example is summarized in Table 15.1.

---

[4]The assumption that the proportional change in the price of asset over a short period is normal is consistent with the assumption, usually made in option pricing, that the probability distribution of the asset's price at the end of a relatively long period of time is lognormal.

TABLE 15.1   Calculation of VaR in a Simple Situation

From the Trader's Desk

A company has a portfolio consisting of $10 million invested in IBM and $5 million invested in AT&T. The daily volatility of IBM is 2 percent, the daily volatility of AT&T is 1 percent, and the coefficient of correlation between returns from IBM and AT&T is 0.7.

Calculation of Value at Risk

The standard deviation of the change in value of the IBM position per 10 days is $10,000,000 \times 0.02 \times \sqrt{10} = \$632,456$. The standard deviation of the change in value of the AT&T position per 10 days is $5,000,000 \times 0.01 \times \sqrt{10} = \$158,144$. The standard deviation of the change in value of the portfolio per 10 days is therefore

$$\sqrt{632,456^2 + 158,114^2 + 2 \times 0.7 \times 632,456 \times 158,114} = \$751,665$$

The VaR for 10 days with a 99 percent confidence level is

$$751,665 \times 2.33 = \$1,751,379$$

THE BENEFITS OF DIVERSIFICATION

In the example we have just considered:

1. The VaR for the portfolio of IBM shares is $1,473,621
2. The VaR for the portfolio of AT&T shares is $368,405
3. The VaR for the portfolio of both IBM and AT&T shares is $1,751,379

The amount

$$(1,473,621 + 368,405) - 1,751,379 = \$90,647$$

represents the benefits of diversification. If IBM and AT&T were perfectly correlated, the VaR for the portfolio of both IBM and AT&T would equal the VaR for the IBM portfolio plus the VaR for the AT&T portfolio. Less than perfect correlation leads to some of the risk being "diversified away."

A Linear Model

The example we have just considered illustrates that VaR calculations are straightforward when

1. We assume that the change in the value of the portfolio is linearly related to the changes in the values of the underlying market variables
2. The changes in the values of the underlying market variables are normally distributed

To generalize the example, we suppose that there are n underlying market variables and

$$\Delta P = \sum_{i=1}^{n} \alpha_i \Delta x_i \tag{15.4}$$

where ΔP is the dollar change in the portfolio value in one day, the Δx_i's $(1 \leq i \leq n)$ are the proportional changes in the underlying market variables during the day, and the α_i's $(1 \leq i \leq n)$ are constants.

We define σ_i as the daily volatility of the ith market variable and ρ_{ij} as the coefficient of correlation between daily changes in market variable i and market variable j. This means that σ_i is the standard deviation of Δx_i, and ρ_{ij} is the coefficient of correlation between Δx_i and Δx_j. From the properties of the multivariate normal distribution, the standard deviation of ΔP, σ_P, is given by

$$\sigma_P^2 = \sum_{i=1}^{n} \sum_{j=1}^{n} \alpha_i \alpha_j \sigma_i \sigma_j \rho_{ij}$$

This equation can also be written

$$\sigma_P^2 = \sum_{i=1}^{n} \alpha_i^2 \sigma_i^2 + 2 \sum_{i<j} \rho_{ij} \alpha_i \alpha_j \sigma_i \sigma_j \tag{15.5}$$

where the second summation is taken over all values of i and j for which $i < j$.

To illustrate the application of Equation 15.5, we consider the example in the previous section. In that case $n = 2$, and Δx_1 and Δx_2 are the proportional changes in the prices of IBM and AT&T in one day. Measuring values in millions of dollars

$$\Delta P = 10\Delta x_1 + 5\Delta x_2$$

so that $\alpha_1 = 10$ and $\alpha_2 = 5$. Other parameters are $\sigma_1 = 0.02$, $\sigma_2 = 0.01$, and $\rho_{12} = 0.7$. Equation 15.5 gives

$$\sigma_P^2 = 10^2 \times 0.02^2 + 5^2 \times 0.01^2 + 2 \times 10 \times 5 \times 0.7 \times 0.02 \times 0.01 = 0.0565$$

so that $\sigma_P = 0.238$. This is the standard deviation of the change in the portfolio value per day (in millions of dollars). The standard deviation of the change per 10 days is $0.238\sqrt{10} = 0.752$, so that the 99 percent/10-day VaR is $0.752 \times 2.33 = \$1.751$ million. This is the same as the answer obtained in the previous section.

HOW BONDS ARE HANDLED

At this stage it is appropriate to mention how bonds are handled by Equation 15.4. Consider a portfolio of U.S. Treasury bonds. It would be cumbersome to define every single bond in the portfolio as a separate market variable. We therefore use as our market variables zero-coupon bonds with standard maturities of one month, three months, one year, two years, five years, seven years, and so on. The Δx_i's are defined as the proportional changes in the prices of these zero-coupon bonds.

Each Treasury bond in the portfolio must be represented as a portfolio of the standard-maturity zero-coupon bonds. The first stage is to regard a Treasury bond as a portfolio of its constituent zero-coupon bonds. The position in each of the zero-coupon bonds is then mapped into an equivalent position in the adjacent standard-maturity zero-coupon bonds.[5]

---

[5]For a description of how the mapping can be done, see J. P. Morgan, *RiskMetrics Monitor* (Fourth Quarter 1995). The mapping is designed to keep both the value and the volatility of the position unchanged.

As an example, consider a $1 million position in a Treasury bond lasting 1.2 years that pays a coupon of 6 percent semiannually. This bond is in the first instance regarded as a $300,000 position in 0.2-year zero-coupon bond plus a $300,000 position in a 0.7-year zero-coupon bond plus a $1.3 million position in a 1.2-year zero-coupon bond. The position in the 0.2-year bond is then replaced by an equivalent position in one-month and three-month zero-coupon bonds; the position in the 0.7-year bond is replaced by an equivalent position in 3-month and 1-year zero-coupon bonds; and the position in the 1.2-year bond is replaced by an equivalent position in 1-year and 2-year zero-coupon bonds. The result is that the position in the 1.2-year coupon-bearing bond is for VaR purposes regarded as a position in zero-coupon bonds having maturities of one month, three months, one year, and two years.

WHEN THE LINEAR MODEL CAN BE USED

The simplest example of the use of the linear model is for a portfolio with no derivatives consisting of positions in stocks, bonds, foreign exchange, and commodities. In this case the change in the value of the portfolio is linearly dependent on the change in the value of the underlying market variables (stock prices, zero-coupon bond prices, exchange rates, and commodity prices), and the use of Equation 15.5 is an extension of the example in Table 15.1.

An example of a derivative that can be handled by the linear model is a forward contract to buy a foreign currency. Suppose the contract matures at time T. It can be regarded as the exchange of a foreign zero-coupon bond maturing at time T for a domestic zero-coupon bond maturing at time T. For the purposes of calculating VaR, the forward contract is therefore treated as a long position in the foreign bond combined with a short position in the domestic bond.

Consider next an interest-rate swap. As explained in chapter 6, this can be regarded as the exchange of a floating-rate bond for a fixed-rate bond. The fixed-rate bond is a regular coupon-bearing bond that can be handled as a portfolio of zero-coupon bonds in the way already described. The floating-rate bond is worth par just after the next payment date. It can therefore be regarded as a zero-coupon bond with a principal equal to the principal underlying the swap and a maturity date equal to the next reset date. The interest-rate swap therefore reduces to a portfolio of long and short positions in zero-coupon bonds.

THE LINEAR MODEL AND OPTIONS

The linear model is only approximately true when the portfolio contains options. Consider, for example, a portfolio consisting of options on a single stock. Suppose that the delta of the position (calculated in the way described in chapter 14) is δ. Because δ is the rate of change of the value of the portfolio with S, it is approximately true that

$$\delta = \frac{\Delta P}{\Delta S}$$

or

$$\Delta P = \delta \Delta S \tag{15.6}$$

where ΔS is the dollar change in the stock price in one day. We define Δx as the proportional change in the stock price in one day:

$$\Delta x = \frac{\Delta S}{S}$$

It follows that an approximate relationship between ΔP and Δx is

$$\Delta P = S\delta\Delta x$$

When we have a position in several underlying market variables that includes options, we can derive an approximately linear relationship between ΔP and the Δx_i's similarly. This relationship is

$$\Delta P = \sum_i S_i \delta_i \Delta x_i$$

where S_i is the price of the ith market variable and δ_i is the delta of the portfolio with respect to the ith market variable. This corresponds to Equation 15.4

$$\Delta P = \sum_{i=1}^{n} \alpha_i x_i$$

with $\alpha_i = S_i \delta_i$. Equation 15.5 can therefore be used to calculate the standard deviation of ΔP.

Example

Consider an investment in options on IBM and AT&T. The options on IBM have a delta of 1,000 and the options on AT&T have a delta of 20,000. The IBM share price is $120 and the AT&T share price is $30. As an approximation we can write

$$\Delta P = 120 \times 1,000\,\Delta x_1 + 30 \times 20,000\,\Delta x_2$$

or

$$\Delta P = 120,000\,\Delta x_1 + 600,000\,\Delta x_2$$

where Δx_1 and Δx_2 are the proportional changes in the prices of IBM and AT&T in one day and ΔP is the resultant change in the value of the portfolio. Assuming that the daily volatility of IBM is 2 percent and the daily volatility of AT&T is 1 percent, the standard deviation of ΔP (in thousands of dollars) is

$$\sqrt{(120 \times 0.02)^2 + (600 \times 0.01)^2 + 2 \times 120 \times 0.02 \times 600 \times 0.01 \times 0.7} = 7.869$$

The 95 percent/5-day value at risk is therefore

$$1.65 \times \sqrt{5} \times 7,869 = \$29,033$$

A Quadratic Model

When a portfolio includes options, the model discussed in the previous section is at best an approximation. It does not take account of gamma. As discussed in chapter 14, delta

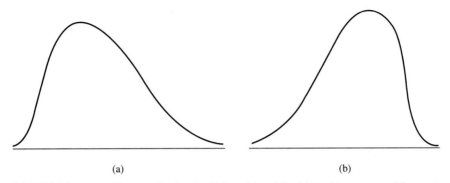

FIGURE 15.1 Probability Distribution for Value of Portfolio (a) Positive gamma, (b) negative gamma.

is defined as the rate of change of the portfolio value with respect to an underlying market variable and gamma is defined as the rate of change of the delta with respect to the market variable. Gamma measures the curvature of the relationship between the portfolio value and an underlying market variable.

Figure 15.1 shows the impact of a nonzero gamma on the probability distribution of ΔP. When gamma is positive, the probability distribution of ΔP tends to be positively skewed; when gamma is negative, it tends to be negatively skewed. Figures 15.2 and 15.3 illustrate the reason for this result. Figure 15.2 shows the relationship between the value of a long call option and the price of the underlying asset. A long call is an example of an option position with positive gamma. The figure shows that, when the probability

FIGURE 15.2 Translation of Normal Probability Distribution for Market Variable into Probability Distribution for Value of a Long Call

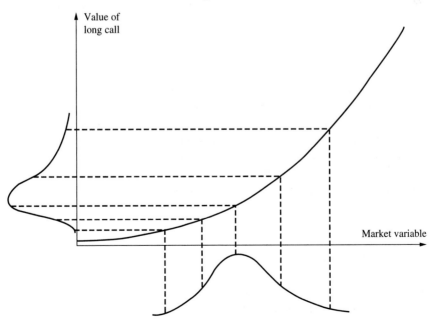

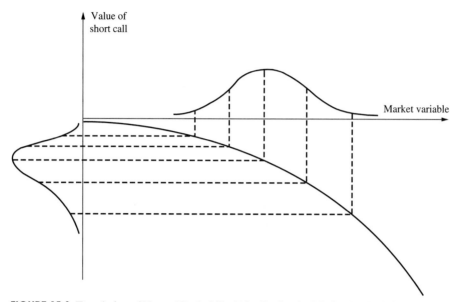

FIGURE 15.3 Translation of Normal Probability Distribution for Market Variable into Probability Distribution for Value of a Short Call

distribution for the price of the underlying asset is normal, the probability distribution for the option price is positively skewed. Figure 15.3 shows the relationship between the value of a short call position and the price of the underlying asset. A short call position has negative gamma. In this case we see that a normal distribution for the price of the underlying asset gets mapped into a negatively skewed distribution for the value of the option position.

The VaR for a portfolio is critically dependent on the left tail of the probability distribution of ΔP. For example, when the confidence level used is 99 percent, the VaR is the value in the left tail below which there is only 1 percent of the distribution. As indicated in Figures 15.1a and 15.2, a positive gamma portfolio tends to have a thin left tail and fat right tail. If we assume the distribution is normal, we will tend to calculate a VaR that is too high. Similarly, as indicated in Figures 15.1b and 15.3, a negative gamma portfolio tends to have a fat left tail and thin right tail. If we assume the distribution is normal, we will tend to calculate a VaR that is too low.

For a more accurate estimate of VaR than that given by the linear model, we can use both delta and gamma measures to relate ΔP to the Δx_i's. Consider a portfolio dependent on a single asset whose price is S. Suppose that the delta of a portfolio is δ and its gamma is γ. An improvement over the approximation in Equation 15.6 is[6]

$$\Delta P = \delta \Delta S + \frac{1}{2}\gamma \Delta S^2$$

---

[6]This approximation arises from a Taylor series expansion of ΔP. As is usual in VaR calculations, we ignore the expected change in ΔP arising from the passage of time.

Setting

$$\Delta x = \frac{\Delta S}{S}$$

reduces this to

$$\Delta P = S\delta\Delta x + \frac{1}{2}S^2\gamma\Delta x^2$$

For a portfolio with n underlying market variables, the equation becomes

$$\Delta P = \sum_{i=1}^{n} S_i\,\delta_i\,\Delta x_i + \sum_{i=1}^{n} \frac{1}{2}S_i^2\gamma_i\,\Delta x_i^2$$

where S_i is the value of the ith market variable, and δ_i and γ_i are the delta and gamma with respect to the ith market variable. This can be written as

$$\Delta P = \sum_{i=1}^{n} \alpha_i\,\Delta x_i + \sum_{i=1}^{n} \beta_i\,\Delta x_i^2 \tag{15.7}$$

where $\alpha_i = S_i\,\delta_i$ and $\beta_i = S_i^2\gamma_i/2$.[7] Unfortunately, this equation is not as easy to work with as Equation 15.4. As we will see later in the chapter, it can be used in conjunction with a simulation approach.

Equation 15.7 can be used to calculate moments for ΔP. The first two moments are

$$E(\Delta P) = \sum_{i=1}^{n} \beta_i\,\sigma_i^2$$

$$E(\Delta P^2) = \sum_{i=1}^{n}\sum_{j=1}^{n} [\alpha_i\,\alpha_j\,\sigma_i\,\sigma_j\,\rho_{ij} + \beta_i\,\beta_j\,\sigma_i^2\sigma_j^2(1 + 2\rho^2)]$$

where E denotes the expectation operator. These can be fitted to a normal distribution, but as already pointed out the assumption that ΔP is normal is less than ideal. An alternative is to calculate higher moments of ΔP. These higher moments can then be used in conjunction with the Cornish-Fisher expansion to estimate the fractiles of the probability distribution of ΔP that correspond to the required VaR.[8] Appendix 15A gives the formula for the third moment of the probability distribution and shows how it can be used to calculate an improved VaR.

---

[7]Equation 15.7 makes the simplifying assumption that each option in the portfolio depends on only one market variable. When this assumption is not made, the equation takes the more general form

$$\Delta P = \sum_{i=1}^{n} \alpha_i\,\Delta x_i + \sum_{i=1}^{n} \beta_{ij}\,\Delta x_i\,\Delta x_j$$

[8]The Cornish-Fisher expansion provides a relationship between the moments of a distribution and its fractiles. For a description, see N. L. Johnson and S. Kotz, *Distributions in Statistics: Continuous Univariate Distributions 1*. New York: John Wiley and Sons, 1972.

Monte Carlo Simulation

As an alternative to the approaches described so far we can use Monte Carlo simulation to generate the probability distribution for ΔP. Suppose we wish to calculate a one-day VaR for a portfolio. The procedure is as follows:

1. Value the portfolio today in the usual way using the current values of market variables.
2. Sample once from the multivariate normal probability distribution of the Δx_i's.[9]
3. Use the values of the Δx_i's that are sampled to determine the value of each market variable at the end of one day.
4. Revalue the portfolio at the end of the day in the usual way.
5. Subtract the value calculated in step 1 from the value in step 4 to determine a sample ΔP.
6. Repeat steps 2 to 5 many times to build up a probability distribution for ΔP.

The VaR is calculated as the appropriate fractile of the probability distribution of ΔP. Suppose, for example, that we calculate 5,000 different sample values of ΔP in the way just described. The 99 percent/1-day VaR is the value of ΔP for the 50th worst outcome; the 95 percent/1-day VaR is the value of ΔP for the 250th worst outcome; and so on. The N-day VaR is calculated as the 1-day VaR multiplied by $\sqrt{N}$.

The drawback of Monte Carlo simulation is that it is very slow, because a company's complete portfolio (which might consist of hundreds of thousands of different instruments) has to be revalued many times. One way of speeding things up is to assume that Equation 15.7 describes the relationship between ΔP and the Δx_i's. We can then jump straight from step 2 to step 5 in the Monte Carlo simulation and avoid the need for a complete revaluation of the portfolio.

Use of Historical Data

Some companies choose not to assume that the probability distributions of market variables are normal. Instead, they calculate VaR from a simulation based on historical movements in the market variables. The first step is to create a database consisting of the daily movements in all market variables over a few years. The first simulation trial assumes that the percentage changes in each market variable are the same as those on the first day covered by the database; the second simulation trial assumes that the percentage changes are the same as those on the second day; and so on. The change in the portfolio value, ΔP, is calculated for each simulation trial and the VaR is calculated as the appropriate fractile of the probability distribution of ΔP. The change in the portfolio value can be obtained either by revaluing the portfolio or by using Equation 15.7.

The advantage of the historical data approach is that it accurately reflects the historical probability distribution of the market variables. Its disadvantage is that the number of simulation trials is limited to the number of days of data that are available.

---

[9]One way of doing so is described in J. C. Hull, *Options, Futures, and Other Derivatives.* 3d ed. Englewood Cliffs, NJ: Prentice Hall, 1997.

Also, sensitivity analyses are difficult, and variables for which there are no market data cannot easily be included in the analysis.

For many market variables, particularly exchange rates, the probability distribution of daily changes calculated from historical data exhibits "fat tails," so that extreme outcomes are more likely than the normal distribution would predict. This phenomenon is known as *positive kurtosis*. A number of authors have suggested that positive kurtosis in a market variable can be modeled by assuming that the probability distribution of the variable's daily changes is a mixture of two normal distributions.[10] Such an approach overcomes the drawbacks of using historical data while providing a good representation of the actual behavior of many market variables.

Stress Testing

In addition to calculating a VaR, many companies carry out a stress test of their portfolio. Stress testing involves estimating how the portfolio would have performed under some of the most extreme market moves seen in the last 10 to 20 years.

For example, to test the impact of an extreme movement in U.S. equity prices, a company might set the proportional change in all market variables equal to those on October 19, 1987 (when the S&P 500 moved by 22.3 standard deviations). If this is considered to be too extreme, the company might choose January 8, 1988 (when the S&P 500 moved by 6.8 standard deviations). To test the effect of extreme movements in UK interest rates, the company might set the proportional change in all market variables equal to those on April 10, 1992 (when 10-year bond yields moved by 7.7 standard deviations).

Stress testing can be considered a way of taking account of extreme events that do occur from time to time but that are virtually impossible according to the probability distributions assumed for market variables. A five-standard-deviation daily move in a market variable is one such extreme event. Under the assumption of a normal distribution, it happens about once every 7,000 years. In practice, it is not uncommon to see a five-standard-deviation daily move once or twice every 10 years.

Summary

A value-at-risk (VaR) calculation is aimed at making a statement of the form "We are X percent certain that we will not lose more than V dollars in the next N days." The variable V is the VaR, X is the confidence level, and N is the time horizon.

The calculation of VaR is greatly simplified if two assumptions can be made:

1. The change in the value of the portfolio (ΔP) is linearly dependent on the proportional changes in the market variables (the Δx_i's).

2. The Δx_i's are normally distributed.

---

[10]See, for example, J. C. Hull and A. White, "Taking Account of the Kurtosis in Market Variables When Calculating Value at Risk." Working paper, University of Toronto, 1997.

The probability distribution of ΔP is then normal, and there are analytic formulas for relating the standard deviation of ΔP to the volatilities and correlations of the underlying market variables. The VaR can be calculated from well-known properties of the normal distribution.

When a portfolio includes options, ΔP is not linearly related to the Δx_i's. From a knowledge of the gamma of the portfolio, we can derive an approximate quadratic relationship between ΔP and the Δx_i's. This enables us to calculate moments of the probability distribution of ΔP and use the Cornish-Fisher expansion to calculate VaR.

Another approach to calculating VaR for a portfolio that includes options is Monte Carlo simulation. It involves repeatedly sampling from the probability distributions of the Δx_i's to calculate a probability distribution for ΔP. The value of ΔP corresponding to a particular set of Δx_i's can be obtained by either revaluing the portfolio or using the approximate quadratic relationship.

An alternative to assuming that the Δx_i's are normal is to base the VaR estimate on a simulation that uses historical data. This approach involves creating a database consisting of the daily movements in all market variables over a period of time. The first simulation trial assumes that the percentage changes in each market variable are the same as those on the first day covered by the database; the second simulation trial assumes that the percentage changes are the same as those on the second day; and so on. The change in the portfolio value, ΔP, is calculated for each simulation trial and the VaR is calculated as the appropriate fractile of the probability distribution of ΔP.

Suggestions for Further Reading

Duffie, D., and J. Pan. "An Overview of Value at Risk," *Journal of Derivatives* 4, 3 (Spring 1997): 7–49.

Hendricks, D. "Evaluation of Value-at-Risk Models Using Historical Data," *Economic Policy Review,* Federal Reserve Bank of New York, vol. 2. (April 1996): 39–69.

Hopper, G. "Value at Risk: A New Methodology for Measuring Portfolio Risk," *Business Review,* Federal Reserve Bank of Philadelphia (July–August 1996): 19–29.

Hull, J. C., and A. White. "Taking Account of the Kurtosis in Market Variables When Calculating Value at Risk." Working paper, University of Toronto, 1997.

Jackson, P., D. J. Maude, and W. Perraudin. "Bank Capital and Value at Risk," *Journal of Derivatives* 4, 3 (Spring 1997): 73–90.

Jamshidian, F., and Y. Zhu. "Scenario Simulation Model: Theory and Methodology." *Finance and Stochastics* 1 (1997): 43–67.

Jorion, P. *Value at Risk: The New Benchmark for Controlling Market Risk.* Chicago: Irwin, 1997.

J. P. Morgan. *RiskMetrics Technical Manual.* New York: J. P. Morgan Bank, 1995.

Risk Publications. "Value at Risk," *RISK* supplement (June 1996).

Quiz

1. Explain the exponentially weighted moving average (EWMA) model for estimating volatility from historical data.

2. The current estimate of the daily volatility of an asset is 1.5 percent and the price of the asset at the close of trading yesterday was $30.00. The parameter λ in the EWMA model is 0.94. Suppose that the price of the asset at the close of trading today is $30.50. How will this cause the volatility to be updated by the EWMA model?

3. Consider a position consisting of a $300,000 investment in asset A and a $500,000 investment in asset B. Assume that the daily volatilities of the assets are 1.8 percent and 1.2 percent, respectively, and that the coefficient of correlation between their returns is 0.3. What is the 95 percent/5-day value at risk for the portfolio?

4. A company uses an EWMA model for forecasting volatility. It decides to change the parameter λ from 0.95 to 0.85. Explain the likely impact on the forecasts.

5. A financial institution owns a portfolio of options on the U.S. dollar/sterling exchange rate. The delta of the portfolio is 56.0. The current exchange rate is 1.5000. Derive an approximate linear relationship between the change in the portfolio value and the proportional change in the exchange rate. If the daily volatility of the exchange rate is 0.7 percent, estimate the 99 percent/10-day VaR.

6. Suppose you know that the gamma of the portfolio in the previous quiz question is 16.0. How does this change your estimate of the relationship between the change in the portfolio value and the proportional change in the exchange rate?

7. Suppose a company has a portfolio consisting of positions in stocks, bonds, foreign exchange, and commodities. Assume there are no derivatives. Explain the assumptions underlying (a) the linear model and (b) the historical data model for calculating VaR.

Questions and Problems

15.1. The volatility of a certain market variable is 30 percent per annum. Calculate a 99 percent confidence interval for the size of the proportional daily change in the variable.

15.2. Explain how an interest-rate swap is mapped into a portfolio of zero-coupon bonds with standard maturities for the purposes of a VaR calculation.

15.3. Explain why the linear model can provide only approximate estimates of VaR for a portfolio containing options.

15.4. The current estimate of the daily volatility of the U.S dollar/sterling exchange rate is 0.6 percent and the exchange rate at 4:00 P.M. yesterday was 1.5000. The parameter λ in the EWMA model is 0.9. Suppose that the exchange rate at 4:00 P.M. today proves to be 1.4950. How would the estimate of daily volatility be updated?

15.5. Suppose that the current daily volatilities of asset A and asset B are 1.6 percent and 2.5 percent, respectively. The current estimate of the coefficient of correlation between the returns on the two assets is 0.25. The prices of the assets at close of trading yesterday were $20 and $40. The parameter λ used in the EWMA model is 0.95.
a. Calculate the current estimate of the covariance between the assets.
b. On the assumption that the prices of the assets at close of trading today are $20.5 and $40.5, update the correlation estimate.

15.6. Suppose that the daily volatility of the FT-SE 100 stock index (measured in pounds sterling) is 1.8 percent and the daily volatility of the dollar/sterling exchange rate is 0.9 percent. Suppose further that the correlation between the FT-SE 100 and the dollar/sterling exchange rate is 0.4. What is the volatility of the FT-SE 100 when it is translated to U.S. dollars? Assume that the dollar/sterling exchange rate is expressed as the number of

U.S. dollars per pound sterling. (Hint: When $Z = XY$, the proportional daily change in Z equals the proportional daily change in X plus the proportional daily change in Y.)

15.7. Suppose that in Problem 15.6 the correlation between the S&P 500 Index (measured in dollars) and the FT-SE 100 Index (measured in sterling) is 0.7, the correlation between the S&P 500 Index (measured in dollars) and the dollar-sterling exchange rate is 0.3, and the daily volatility of the S&P 500 Index is 1.6 percent. What is the correlation between the S&P 500 Index (measured in dollars) and the FT-SE 100 Index when it is translated to dollars? (Hint: For three variables X, Y, and Z, the covariance between $X + Y$ and Z equals the covariance between X and Z plus the covariance between Y and Z.)

15.8. Consider a position consisting of a $300,000 investment in gold and a $500,000 investment in silver. Suppose that the daily volatilities of these two assets are 1.8 percent and 1.2 percent, respectively, and that the coefficient of correlation between their returns is 0.6. What is the 97.5 percent/10-day value at risk for the portfolio? By how much does diversification reduce the VaR?

15.9. Consider a portfolio of options on a single asset. Suppose that the delta of the portfolio is 12, the value of the asset is $10, and the daily volatility of the asset is 2 percent. Estimate the 95 percent/1-day VaR for the portfolio.

15.10. Suppose that the gamma of the portfolio in Problem 15.9 is -2.6. Derive a quadratic relationship between the change in the portfolio value and the proportional change in the underlying asset price in one day.
    a. Calculate the first three moments of the change in the portfolio value.
    b. Using the first two moments and assuming that the change in the portfolio is normally distributed, calculate the 95 percent/1-day VaR for the portfolio.
    c. Use the third moment and the Cornish-Fisher expansion to revise your answer to (b).

15.11. A company has entered into a six-month forward contract to buy £1 million for $1.5 million. The daily volatility of a six-month zero-coupon sterling LIBOR bond (when its price is translated to dollars) is 0.06 percent, and the daily volatility of a six-month zero-coupon dollar LIBOR bond is 0.05 percent. The correlation between returns from the two bonds is 0.8. The current exchange rate is 1.53. Calculate the standard deviation of the change in the dollar value of the forward contract in one day. What is the 99 percent/10-day VaR? Assume that the six-month interest rate in both sterling and dollars is 5 percent per annum with continuous compounding.

APPENDIX 15A

Use of the Cornish-Fisher Expansion to Estimate VaR

As shown in Equation 15.7, we can approximate ΔP for a portfolio containing options as

$$\Delta P = \sum_{i=1}^{n} \alpha_i \Delta x_i + \sum_{i=1}^{n} \beta_i \Delta x_i^2 \tag{15A.1}$$

It can be shown that this implies

$$E(\Delta P) = \sum_i \beta_i \sigma_i^2$$

$$E(\Delta P^2) = \sum_{i,j} [\alpha_i \alpha_j \sigma_i \sigma_j \rho_{ij} + \beta_i \beta_j \sigma_i^2 \sigma_j^2 (1 + 2\rho^2)]$$

$$E(\Delta P^3) = 3 \sum_{i,j,k} \alpha_i \alpha_j \beta_k \sigma_k^2 \sigma_i \sigma_j (\rho_{ij} + 2\rho_{ki} \rho_{kj})$$

$$+ \sum_{i,j,k} \beta_i \beta_j \beta_k \sigma_i^2 \sigma_j^2 \sigma_k^2 (1 + 2\rho_{jk}^2 + 2\rho_{ik}^2 + 2\rho_{ij}^2 + 8\rho_{ij} \rho_{jk} \rho_{ki})$$

Define μ_P and σ_P as the mean and standard deviation of ΔP. The skewness of the probability distribution of ΔP, ξ_P, is defined as

$$\xi_P = \frac{1}{\sigma_P^3} E[(\Delta P - \mu_P)^3] = \frac{1}{\sigma_P^3} [E(\Delta P^3) - 3E(\Delta P^2)\mu_P + 2\mu_P^3]$$

On the basis of the third moment of ΔP, the Cornish-Fisher expansion estimates the q-percentile of the distribution of ΔP as [11]

---

[11] For more precision we can use higher moments.

$$\mu_P + w_q \sigma_P$$

where

$$w_q = z_q + \frac{1}{6}(z_q^2 - 1)\xi_P$$

and z_q is q-percentile of the standard normal distribution $\phi(0, 1)$.

Example

Suppose that for a certain portfolio we calculate $\mu_P = -0.2$, $\sigma_P = 2.2$, and $\xi_P = -0.4$. If we assume that the probability distribution of ΔP is normal, the 1 percent fractile of the probability distribution of ΔP is

$$-0.2 - 2.33 \times 2.2 = -5.326$$

In other words, we are 99 percent certain that

$$\Delta P > -5.326$$

When we use the Cornish-Fisher expansion to adjust for skewness and set $q = 0.01$, we obtain

$$w_q = -2.33 - \frac{1}{6}(2.33^2 - 1) \times 0.4 = -2.625$$

so that the 1 percent fractile of the distribution is

$$-0.2 - 2.625 \times 2.2 = -5.976$$

Taking account of skewness therefore changes the VaR from 5.326 to 5.976.

Valuing Options Numerically Using Binomial Trees

CHAPTER

16

As we have seen in chapters 11, 12, and 13, the Black–Scholes model and its extensions can be used to value European call and put options on stocks, stock indices, currencies, and futures contracts. In this chapter we cover a popular numerical procedure that can be used to value either European or American options. The procedure is an extension of the analysis in chapter 10. In addition to valuing options, it can be used to calculate the measures delta, gamma, theta, vega, and rho that were introduced in chapter 14.

The Binomial Model for a Nondividend-paying Stock

Chapter 10 introduced one- and two-step binomial trees for nondividend-paying stocks and showed how they can be used to value European and American options. These binomial trees were presented for illustrative purposes and are not a close approximation to actual stock price behavior. A more realistic assumption is that stock price movements are composed of a large number of small binomial movements. This is the assumption that underlies a widely used numerical procedure first proposed by Cox, Ross, and Rubinstein.[1]

Consider the evaluation of an option on a nondividend-paying stock. We start by dividing the life of the option into a large number of small time intervals of length Δt. We assume that in each time interval the stock price moves from its initial value of S to one of two new values, Su or Sd. This model is illustrated in Figure 16.1. In general, $u > 1$ and $d < 1$. The movement from S to Su is therefore an "up" movement, and the

---

[1]See J. Cox, S. Ross, and M. Rubinstein. "Option Pricing: A Simplified Approach," *Journal of Financial Economics* 7 (October 1979): 229–264.

359

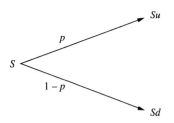

FIGURE 16.1 Stock Price Movements in Time Δt under the Binomial Model

movement from S to Sd is a "down" movement. The probability of an up movement is assumed to be p, and the probability of a down movement is assumed to be $1 - p$.

RISK-NEUTRAL VALUATION

The risk-neutral valuation principle, discussed in chapters 10 and 11, states that any security dependent on a stock price can be valued on the assumption that the world is risk neutral. It means that for the purposes of valuing an option (or any other derivative) we can assume the following:

1. The expected return from all traded securities is the risk-free interest rate.
2. Future cash flows can be valued by discounting their expected values at the risk-free interest rate.

When using the binomial model, we will make use of the risk-neutral valuation principle.

DETERMINATION OF *p, u,* AND *d*

The parameters p, u, and d must give correct values for the mean and variance of the stock price during a time interval Δt. Because we are working in a risk-neutral world, the expected return from a stock is the risk-free interest rate, r. Hence, the expected value of the stock price at the end of a time interval Δt is $Se^{r\Delta t}$, where S is the stock price at the beginning of the time interval. It follows that

$$Se^{r\Delta t} = pSu + (1 - p)Sd \tag{16.1}$$

or

$$e^{r\Delta t} = pu + (1 - p)d \tag{16.2}$$

Recall from the stock price model assumed in chapter 11 that the standard deviation of the proportional change in the stock price in a small time interval Δt is $\sigma \sqrt{\Delta t}$. This means that the variance of the actual change in the stock price in time Δt is $S^2\sigma^2\Delta t$. The variance of a variable Q is defined as $E(Q^2) - E(Q)^2$, where E denotes expected value. It follows that

$$S^2\sigma^2\Delta t = pS^2u^2 + (1 - p)S^2d^2 - S^2[pu + (1 - p)d]^2$$

or

$$\sigma^2\Delta t = pu^2 + (1 - p)d^2 - [pu + (1 - p)d]^2 \tag{16.3}$$

Equations 16.2 and 16.3 impose two conditions on p, u, and d. A third condition commonly used is

$$u = \frac{1}{d}$$

It can be shown that provided Δt is small, the three conditions imply

$$p = \frac{a - d}{u - d} \qquad (16.4)$$

$$u = e^{\sigma \sqrt{\Delta t}} \qquad (16.5)$$

$$d = e^{-\sigma \sqrt{\Delta t}} \qquad (16.6)$$

where

$$a = e^{r \Delta t} \qquad (16.7)$$

Equations 16.4 and 16.7 correspond to Equation 10.3, which was shown to be correct using no-arbitrage arguments as well as risk-neutral valuation arguments.

THE TREE OF STOCK PRICES

The complete tree of stock prices that is considered with the binomial model is illustrated in Figure 16.2. At time zero the stock price S is known. At time Δt there are two possible stock prices, Su and Sd; at time $2\Delta t$ there are three possible stock prices, Su^2, S, and Sd^2; and so on. In general at time $i\,\Delta t$, $i + 1$ stock prices are considered. These are

$$Su^j d^{i-j} \qquad j = 0, 1, \ldots, i$$

Note that the relationship $u = 1/d$ is used in computing the stock price at each node of the tree in Figure 16.2. For example, $Su^2 d = Su$. Note also that the tree recombines in the sense that an up movement followed by a down movement leads to the same stock price as a down movement followed by an up movement. This considerably reduces the number of nodes on the tree.

WORKING BACKWARD THROUGH THE TREE

Options are evaluated by starting at the end of the tree (time T) and working backward. The value of the option is known at time T. For example, a put option is worth $\max(X - S_T, 0)$ and a call option is worth $\max(S_T - X, 0)$, where S_T is the stock price at time T and X is the strike price. Because a risk-neutral world is assumed, the value at each node at time $T - \Delta t$ can be calculated as the expected value at time T discounted at rate r for a time period Δt. Similarly, the value at each node at time $T - 2\Delta t$ can be calculated as the expected value at time $T - \Delta t$ discounted for a time period Δt at rate r, and so on. If the option is American, it is necessary to check at each node to see whether early exercise is preferable to holding the option for a further time period Δt. Eventually, by working back through all the nodes, we obtain the value of the option at time zero.

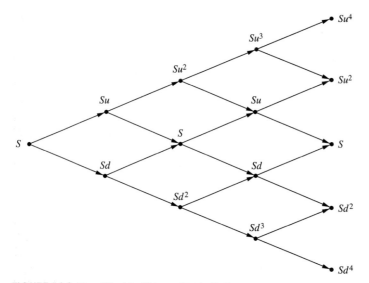

FIGURE 16.2 Tree Used to Value a Stock Option

AN EXAMPLE

An example will make the procedure clear.[2] Consider a five-month American put option on a nondividend-paying stock when the stock price is $50, the strike price is $50, the risk-free interest rate is 10 percent per annum, and the volatility is 40 percent per annum. With our usual notation, this means that $S = 50, X = 50, r = 0.10, \sigma = 0.40$, and $T = 5/12$. Suppose that we divide the life of the option into five intervals of length 1 month (1/12 year) for the purposes of constructing a binomial tree. Then $\Delta t = 1/12$. Using Equations 16.4 to 16.7,

$$u = e^{\sigma\sqrt{\Delta t}} = 1.1224, \qquad d = e^{-\sigma\sqrt{\Delta t}} = 0.8909$$

$$a = e^{r\Delta t} = 1.0084, \qquad p = \frac{a - d}{u - d} = 0.5076$$

$$1 - p = 0.4924$$

Figure 16.3 shows the binomial tree. At each node there are two numbers. The top one shows the stock price at the node; the lower one shows the value of the option at the node. The probability of an up movement is always 0.5076; the probability of a down movement is always 0.4924.

The stock price at the jth node ($j = 0, 1, \ldots, i$) at time $i\Delta t$ is calculated as $Su^j d^{i-j}$. For example, the stock price at node A ($i = 4, j = 1$) is $50 \times 1.1224 \times 0.8909^3 = \$39.69$. The option prices at the final nodes are calculated as $\max(X - S_T, 0)$. For example, the option price at node G is $50 - 35.36 = \$14.64$.

The option prices at the penultimate nodes are calculated from the option prices at the final nodes. First, we assume no exercise of the option at the nodes. This means

---

[2]The DerivaGem software included with this book displays the binomial trees used to calculate an option price.

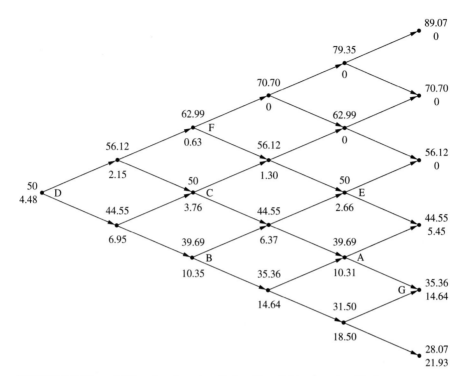

FIGURE 16.3 Binomial Tree for American Put on Nondividend-paying Stock

that the option price is calculated as the present value of the expected option price in time Δt. For example, at node E the option price is calculated as

$$(0.5076 \times 0 + 0.4924 \times 5.45)e^{-0.10 \times 1/12} = \$2.66$$

At node A it is calculated as

$$(0.5076 \times 5.45 + 0.4924 \times 14.64)e^{-0.10 \times 1/12} = \$9.90$$

We then check to see if early exercise is preferable to waiting. At node E early exercise would give a value for the option of zero, because both the stock price and strike price are $50. Clearly it is best to wait. The correct value for the option at node E is therefore $2.66. At node A it is a different story. If the option is exercised, it is worth $50.00 − $39.69 = $10.31. This is more than $9.90. If node A is reached, the option should therefore be exercised, and the correct value of the option at node A is $10.31.

Option prices at earlier nodes are calculated in a similar way. Note that it is not always best to exercise an option early when it is in the money. Consider node B. If the option is exercised, it is worth $50.00 − $39.69 = $10.31. However, if it is held, it is worth

$$(0.5076 \times 6.37 + 0.4924 \times 14.64)e^{-0.10 \times 1/12} = \$10.35$$

The option should therefore not be exercised at this node, and the correct option value at the node is $10.35.

Working back through the tree, we find the value of the option at the initial node to be \$4.48. This is our numerical estimate for the option's current value. In practice, a smaller value of Δt and many more nodes would be used. The true value of the option obtained using many time steps is \$4.29.

EXPRESSING THE APPROACH ALGEBRAICALLY

Suppose that the life of an American put option on a nondividend-paying stock is divided into N subintervals of length Δt. We define f_{ij} as the value of the option at time $i \Delta t$ when the stock price is $Su^j d^{i-j}$ for $0 \le i \le N$, $0 \le j \le i$. This is the value of the option at the (i, j) node. Because the value of an American put at its expiration date is $\max (X - S_T, 0)$, we know that

$$f_{Nj} = \max[X - Su^j d^{N-j}, 0] \qquad j = 0, 1, \ldots, N$$

There is a probability p of moving from the (i, j) node at time $i \Delta t$ to the $(i + 1, j + 1)$ node at time $(i + 1)\Delta t$ and a probability $1 - p$ of moving from the (i, j) node at time $i \Delta t$ to the $(i + 1, j)$ node at time $(i + 1)\Delta t$. If we assume no early exercise, risk-neutral valuation gives

$$f_{ij} = e^{-r\Delta t}[pf_{i+1,j+1} + (1 - p)f_{i+1,j}]$$

for $0 \le i \le N - 1$ and $0 \le j \le i$. When early exercise is taken into account, this value for f_{ij} must be compared with the option's intrinsic value, and we obtain

$$f_{ij} = \max\{X - Su^j d^{i-j}, e^{-r\Delta t}[pf_{i+1,j+1} + (1 - p)f_{i+1,j}]\}$$

Note that because the calculations start at time T and work backward, the value at time $i \Delta t$ captures not only the effect of early exercise possibilities at time $i \Delta t$ but also the effect of early exercise at subsequent times. In the limit, as Δt tends to zero an exact value for the American put is obtained. In practice, $N = 30$ usually gives reasonable results.

ESTIMATING DELTA AND OTHER HEDGE PARAMETERS

It will be recalled that the delta, Δ, of an option is the rate of change of its price with respect to the underlying stock price. In other words,

$$\Delta = \frac{\Delta f}{\Delta S}$$

where ΔS is a small change in the stock price and Δf is the corresponding small change in the option price. At time Δt we have an estimate f_{11} for the option price when the stock price is Su and an estimate f_{10} for the option price when the stock price is Sd. In other words, when $\Delta S = Su - Sd$, $\Delta f = f_{11} - f_{10}$. An estimate of Δ at time Δt is therefore

$$\Delta = \frac{f_{11} - f_{10}}{Su - Sd} \qquad \textbf{(16.8)}$$

To determine gamma, Γ, we note that there are two estimates of Δ at time $2\Delta t$. When $S = (Su^2 + S)/2$ (halfway between the second and third node at time $2\Delta t$), delta is $(f_{22} - f_{21})/(Su^2 - S)$; when $S = (S + Sd^2)/2$ (halfway between the first and second node at time $2\Delta t$), delta is $(f_{21} - f_{20})/(S - Sd^2)$. The difference between the two values of S is h, where

$$h = 0.5(Su^2 - Sd^2)$$

Gamma is the change in delta divided by the change in S, or[3]

$$\Gamma = \frac{[(f_{22} - f_{21})/(Su^2 - S)] - [(f_{21} - f_{20})/(S - Sd^2)]}{h} \qquad \textbf{(16.9)}$$

A further hedge parameter that can be obtained directly from the tree is theta, Θ. This is the rate of change of the option price with time when all else is kept constant. An estimate of theta is therefore

$$\Theta = \frac{f_{21} - f_{00}}{2\Delta t} \qquad \textbf{(16.10)}$$

Vega can be calculated by making a small change, $\Delta\sigma$, in the volatility and constructing a new tree to obtain a new value of the option (Δt should be kept the same). The estimate of vega is

$$\mathcal{V} = \frac{f^* - f}{\Delta\sigma}$$

where f and f^* are the estimates of the option price from the original and the new tree, respectively. Rho can be calculated similarly.

Example

Consider again the tree in Figure 16.3. In this case $f_{1,0} = 6.95$ and $f_{1,1} = 2.15$. Equation 16.8 gives an estimate of delta as

$$\frac{2.15 - 6.95}{56.12 - 44.55} = -0.41$$

From Equation 16.9, an estimate of the gamma of the option can be obtained from the values at nodes B, C, and F as

$$\frac{[(0.63 - 3.76)/(62.99 - 50.00)] - [(3.76 - 10.35)/(50.00 - 39.69)]}{11.65} = 0.034$$

---

[3]These procedures provide estimates of delta at time Δt and of gamma at time $2\Delta t$. In practice, they are often used as estimates of delta and gamma at time zero as well. If slightly more accuracy is required, it makes sense to start the binomial tree at time $-2\Delta t$ and assume that the stock price is S at this time. The required estimate of the price of the option is then f_{21} (rather than f_{00}). More nodes have to be evaluated, but three different values of S are considered at time zero: Sd^2, S, and Su^2. These can be used to provide estimates of delta and gamma.

From Equation 16.10, an estimate of the theta of the option can be obtained from the values at nodes D and C as

$$\frac{3.76 - 4.48}{0.1667} = -4.3$$

These are only rough estimates. They become more precise as the number of time steps on the tree is increased.

Using the Binomial Tree for Options on Indices, Currencies, and Futures Contracts

As shown in chapter 12, the binomial tree approach to valuing options on nondividend-paying stocks can easily be adapted to valuing American calls and puts on a stock paying a continuous dividend yield at rate q.

Since the dividends provide a return of q, the stock price itself must on average in a risk-neutral world provide a return of $r - q$. As shown in Equation 12.7, the risk-neutral probability p is given by

$$p = \frac{e^{(r-q)\Delta t} - d}{u - d}$$

Equations 16.4, 16.5, and 16.6 are therefore still correct but with

$$a = e^{(r-q)\Delta t} \qquad \textbf{(16.11)}$$

The binomial tree numerical procedure can therefore be used exactly as before with this new value of a.

Recall from chapters 12 and 13 that stock indices, currencies, and futures contracts can for the purposes of option evaluation be considered as stocks paying continuous dividend yields. In the case of a stock index, the relevant dividend yield is the dividend yield on the stock portfolio underlying the index; in the case of a currency, it is the foreign risk-free interest rate; in the case of a futures contract, it is the domestic risk-free interest rate. The binomial tree approach can therefore be used to value options on stock indices, currencies, and futures contracts.

Example 1

Consider a four-month American call option on index futures. The current futures price is 300, the exercise price is 300, the risk-free interest rate is 8 percent per annum, and the volatility of the index is 40 percent per annum. We divide the life of the option into four one-month periods for the purposes of constructing the tree. In this case $F = 300$, $X = 300$, $r = 0.08$, $\sigma = 0.4$, $T = 4/12$, and $\Delta t = 1/12$. Because a futures contract is analogous to a stock paying dividends at a continuous rate r, q should be set equal to r in Equation 16.11. This gives $a = 1$. The other parameters necessary to construct the tree are

$$u = e^{\sigma\sqrt{\Delta t}} = 1.1224, \qquad d = \frac{1}{u} = 0.8909$$

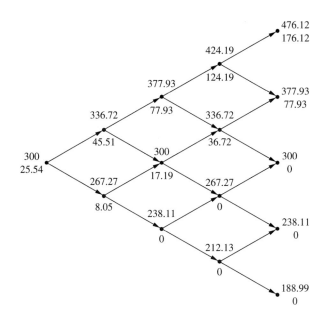

FIGURE 16.4 Binomial Tree for American Call Option on an Index Futures Contract

$$p = \frac{a - d}{u - d} = 0.4713, \qquad 1 - p = 0.5287$$

The tree is shown in Figure 16.4. (The upper number is the futures price; the lower number is the option price.) The estimated value of the option is $25.54.

Example 2

Consider a one-year American put option on the British pound. The current exchange rate is 1.6100, the strike price is 1.6000, the U.S. risk-free interest rate is 8 percent per annum, the sterling risk-free interest rate is 10 percent per annum, and the volatility of the sterling exchange rate is 12 percent per annum. In this case $S = 1.61$, $X = 1.60$, $r = 0.08$, $r_f = 0.10$, $\sigma = 0.12$, and $T = 1.0$. We divide the life of the option into four three-month periods for the purposes of constructing the tree so that $\Delta t = 0.25$. In the case $q = r_f$ and Equation 16.11 gives

$$a = e^{(0.08 - 0.10) \times 0.25} = 0.9950$$

The other parameters necessary to construct the tree are

$$u = e^{\sigma \sqrt{\Delta t}} = 1.0618, \qquad d = \frac{1}{u} = 0.9418$$

$$p = \frac{a - d}{u - d} = 0.4433, \qquad 1 - p = 0.5567$$

The tree is shown in Figure 16.5. (The upper number is the exchange rate; the lower number is the option price.) The estimated value of the option is $0.0782.

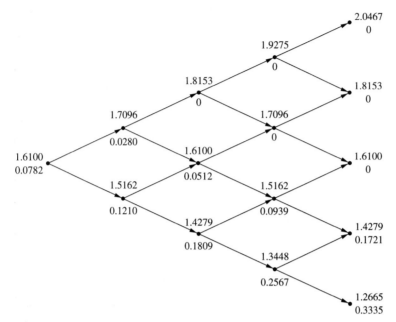

FIGURE 16.5 Binomial Model for American Put Option on a Currency

The Binomial Model for a Dividend-paying Stock

We now move on to the more tricky issue of how the binomial model can be used for a dividend-paying stock. As in chapter 11, the word *dividend* will for the purposes of our discussion be used to refer to the reduction in the stock price on the ex-dividend date as a result of the dividend.

If it is assumed that a single dividend will be paid at a certain time and that it will be a proportion, δ, of the stock price at that time, the tree takes the form shown in Figure 16.6 and can be analyzed in a way that is analogous to that just described. If the time $i \, \Delta t$ is prior to the stock going ex-dividend, the nodes on the tree correspond to stock prices

$$Su^j d^{i-j} \qquad j = 0, 1, \ldots, i$$

where u and d are defined as in Equations 16.5 and 16.6. If the time $i \, \Delta t$ is after the stock goes ex-dividend, the nodes correspond to stock prices

$$S(1 - \delta)u^j d^{i-j} \qquad j = 0, 1, \ldots, i$$

Several known dividends during the life of an option can be dealt with similarly. If δ_i is the total dividend yield associated with all ex-dividend dates between time zero and time $i \, \Delta t$, the nodes at time $i \, \Delta t$ correspond to stock prices

$$S(1 - \delta_i)u^j d^{i-j}$$

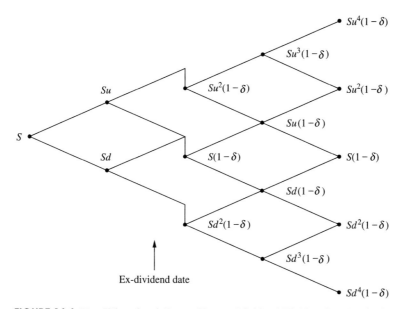

FIGURE 16.6 Tree When Stock Pays a Known Dividend Yield at One Particular Time

A more realistic assumption is that the dollar amount of the dividend is known in advance. If the volatility of the stock, σ, is assumed constant, the tree takes the form shown in Figure 16.7. It does not recombine, which means that the number of nodes that have to be evaluated, particularly if there are several dividends, is likely to become very large. Suppose that there is only one dividend, that the ex-dividend date, τ, is between $k\,\Delta t$ and $(k+1)\Delta t$, and that the dollar amount of the dividend is D. When $i \le k$, the nodes on the tree at time $i\,\Delta t$ correspond to stock prices

$$Su^j d^{i-j} \qquad j = 0, 1, 2, \ldots, i$$

as before. When $i = k+1$, the nodes on the tree correspond to stock prices

$$Su^j d^{i-j} - D \qquad j = 0, 1, 2, \ldots, i$$

When $i = k+2$, the nodes on the tree correspond to stock prices

$$(Su^j d^{i-1-j} - D)u \qquad \text{and} \qquad (Su^j d^{i-1-j} - D)d$$

for $j = 0, 1, 2, \ldots, i-1$, so that there are $2i$ rather than $i+1$ nodes. At time $(k+m)\Delta t$, there are $m(k+1)$ rather than $k+m+1$ nodes.

The problem can be simplified by assuming, as in the analysis of European options in chapter 11, that the stock price has two components: a part that is uncertain and a part that is the present value of all future dividends during the life of the option. Suppose, as before, that there is only one ex-dividend date, τ, during the life of the option

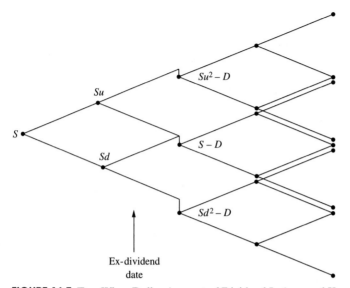

FIGURE 16.7 Tree When Dollar Amount of Dividend Is Assumed Known and Volatility Is Assumed Constant

and that $k\Delta t \leq \tau \leq (k+1)\Delta t$. The value of the uncertain component, S^*, at time x is given by

$$S^*(x) = S(x)$$

when $x > \tau$ and

$$S^*(x) = S(x) - De^{-r(\tau - x)}$$

when $x \leq \tau$, where D is the dividend. We define σ^* as the volatility of S^* and assume that σ^* rather than σ is constant. The parameters p, u, and d can be calculated from Equations 16.4, 16.5, 16.6, and 16.7, with σ replaced by σ^* and a tree can be constructed in the usual way to model S^*. If the present value of future dividends (if any) is added to the stock price at each node, the tree can be converted into another tree that models S. At time $i\Delta t$ the nodes on this tree correspond to the stock prices

$$S^*(t)u^j d^{i-j} + De^{-r(\tau - i\Delta t)} \qquad j = 0, 1, \ldots, i$$

when $i\Delta t < \tau$ and

$$S^*(t)u^j d^{i-j} \qquad j = 0, 1, \ldots, i$$

when $i\Delta t > \tau$. This approach, which involves a perfectly reasonable assumption about the stock price volatility, succeeds in achieving a situation where the tree recombines so that there are $i+1$ nodes at time $i\Delta t$. The approach can be generalized in a straightforward way to deal with the situation where there are several dividends.

AN EXAMPLE

To illustrate the use of the binomial model when there are dividends, consider a five-month put option on a stock that is expected to pay a single dividend of $2.06 during the life of the option. The initial stock price is $52, the strike price is $50, the risk-free interest rate is 10 percent per annum, the volatility is 40 percent per annum, and the ex-dividend date is in 3.5 months.

We first construct a tree to model S^*, the stock price less the present value of future dividends during the life of the option. Initially, the present value of the dividend is

$$2.06e^{-0.1 \times 3.5/12} = 2.00$$

The initial value of S^* is therefore 50. Assuming that the 40 percent per annum volatility refers to S^*, Figure 16.3 provides a binomial tree for S^*. (S^* has the same initial value and volatility as the stock price on which Figure 16.3 was based.) Adding the present value of the dividend at each node leads to Figure 16.8, which is a binomial model for S. The probabilities at each node are, as in Figure 16.3, 0.5076 for an up movement and 0.4924 for a down movement. Working back through the tree in the usual way gives the option price as $4.43.

FIGURE 16.8 Tree for Example Where Stock Pays a Known Dividend at a Certain Time

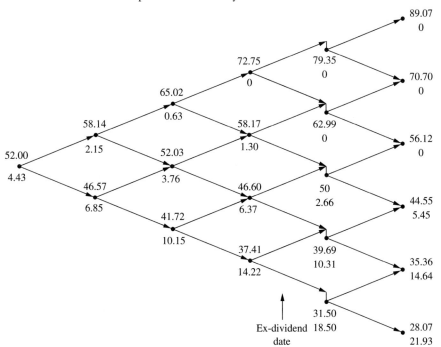

The Control Variate Technique

In most circumstances the binomial tree approach for valuing American options can be improved with the *control variate technique.* This technique involves using the same tree to value both the American option that is of interest and the corresponding European option. The approach may seem wasteful, because the European option price is known from the Black–Scholes formula and its extensions. However, because errors in the calculated price of the American option are generally closely correlated with errors in the calculated price of the European option, it leads to a way of improving the estimate of the price of the American option.

We define

f_A: price of American option calculated from tree

f_E: price of European option calculated from tree

f_{BS}:   Black–Scholes price of European option

An improved estimate of the price of the American option is

$$f_A + f_{BS} - f_E$$

Example

Consider again the American put option being valued in Figure 16.3 ($S = 50$, $X = 50$, $r = 0.10$, $\sigma = 0.40$, and $T = 5/12$). Figure 16.9 uses the same tree as Figure 16.3 to value the corresponding European option. The resulting price is

FIGURE 16.9 Tree for European Version of Option in Figure 16.3. At each node the upper number is the stock price; the lower number is the option price.

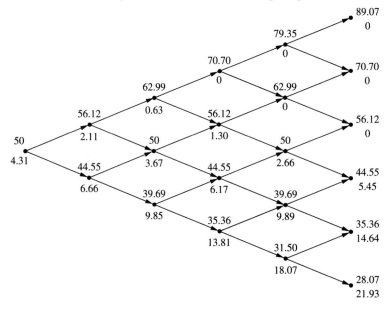

$4.31 (compared with $4.48 for the American option in Figure 16.3). From the Black–Scholes formula, the true European price is $4.08. The control variate estimate of the American price is therefore

$$4.48 + 4.08 - 4.31 = 4.25$$

The true American price is $4.29. Thus, the control variate approach does produce a considerable improvement over the original estimate in this particular case.

Alternative Procedure for Constructing Trees

The original Cox, Ross, and Rubinstein approach is not the only way of building a binomial tree. Instead of imposing the assumption $u = 1/d$ on Equations 16.2 and 16.3, we can set $p = 0.5$. A solution to the equations when terms of higher order than Δt are ignored is then

$$u = e^{(r - \sigma^2/2)\Delta t + \sigma \sqrt{\Delta t}}$$

$$d = e^{(r - \sigma^2/2)\Delta t - \sigma \sqrt{\Delta t}}$$

When the stock provides a continuous dividend yield at rate q, the variable r becomes $r - q$ in these formulas. Trees with $p = 0.5$ can then be built for options on indices, foreign exchange, and futures.

This alternative tree-building procedure has the attractive property that probabilities are always 0.5 regardless of the value of σ or the number of time steps.[4] A disadvantage of the procedure is that it is not quite as easy to calculate accurate values for delta, gamma, and theta as it is when the Cox, Ross, and Rubinstein tree is used.

Example

Consider a nine-month American call option on the Canadian dollar. The current exchange rate is 0.7900, the strike price is 0.8000, the U.S. risk-free interest rate is 6 percent per annum, the Canadian risk-free interest rate is 10 percent per annum, and the volatility of the exchange rate is 4 percent per annum. In this case $S = 0.79$, $X = 0.80$, $r = 0.06$, $r_f = 0.10$, $\sigma = 0.04$, and $T = 0.75$. We divide the life of the option into three-month periods for the purposes of constructing the tree so that $\Delta t = 0.25$. We set the probabilities on each branch to 0.5 and

$$u = e^{(0.06 - 0.10 - 0.0016/2)0.25 + 0.04 \sqrt{0.25}} = 1.0098$$

$$d = e^{(0.06 - 0.10 - 0.0016/2)0.25 - 0.04 \sqrt{0.25}} = 0.9703$$

The tree for the exchange rate is shown in Figure 16.10. The tree gives the value of the option as 0.0016.

---

[4]Very occasionally (when the condition $\sigma < |(r - q)| \sqrt{\Delta t}$ is satisfied) the Cox, Ross, and Rubinstein tree leads to negative probabilities. The alternative procedure described here does not have this drawback.

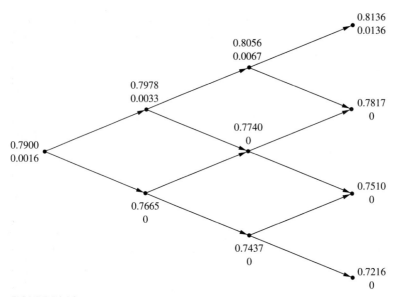

FIGURE 16.10 Binomial Tree for American Call Option on the Canadian Dollar. At each node the uppermost number is the spot exchange rate, and the lower number is the option price. All probabilities are 0.5.

Monte Carlo Simulation

Binomial trees can be used in conjunction with *Monte Carlo simulation* for valuing derivatives. (The use of Monte Carlo simulation for risk management was mentioned in chapters 14 and 15.) Once the tree has been constructed we randomly sample paths through it. Instead of working backward from the end of the tree to the beginning, we work forward through the tree. The basic procedure is as follows. At the first node we sample a random number between 0 and 1. If the number lies between 0 and p, we take the upper branch; if it lies between p and 1, we take the lower branch. We repeat this procedure at the node that is then reached and at all subsequent nodes that are reached until we get to the end of the tree. We then calculate the payoff on the option for the particular path sampled. This completes the first trial. We carry out many additional trials by repeating the whole procedure. Our estimate of the value of the option is the arithmetic average of the payoffs from all the trials discounted at the risk-free interest rate.

Monte Carlo simulation, as just described, cannot be used for American options, because we have no way of knowing whether early exercise is optimal when a certain node is reached. It can be used to value European options so that a check is provided on the pricing formulas for these options. It can also be used to price some of the exotic options mentioned in chapter 7—for example, Asian options and lookback options.

Summary

This chapter has described how options can be valued using the binomial tree approach. This approach, when used for stock options, involves dividing the life of the option into a number of small intervals of length Δt and assuming that a stock price at the beginning of an interval can lead to only one of two alternative stock prices at the end of the interval. One of these alternative stock prices involves an up movement; the other involves a down movement.

The sizes of the up movements and down movements, and their associated probabilities, are chosen so that the change in the stock price has the correct mean and standard deviation for a risk-neutral world. Option prices are calculated by starting at the end of the tree and working backward. At the end of the tree, the price of an option is its intrinsic value. At earlier nodes on the tree, the value of an option, if it is American, must be calculated as the greater of

1. The value it has if exercised immediately
2. The value it has if held for a further period of time of length Δt

If it is exercised at a node, the value of the option is its intrinsic value. If it is held for a further period of length Δt, the value of the option is its expected value at the end of the time period Δt discounted at the risk-free rate.

Delta, gamma, and theta can be estimated directly from the values of the option at the various nodes of the tree. Vega can be estimated by making a small change to the volatility and recomputing the value of the option using a similar tree. Rho can be estimated by making a small change to the interest rate and recomputing the tree.

The binomial tree approach can easily be extended to accommodate options on stocks paying continuous dividend yields. Since stock indices, currencies, and most futures contracts can be regarded as analogous to stocks paying continuous yields, the binomial model can be used to value options on these assets as well.

When the binomial tree approach is used to value options on a stock paying known dollar dividends, it is convenient to use the tree to model the stock price less the present value of all future dividends during the life of the option. This keeps the number of nodes on the tree from becoming unmanageable.

The computational efficiency of the binomial model can be improved by using the control variate technique. This approach involves valuing both the American option that is of interest and the corresponding European option using the same tree. The error in the price of the European option is used as an estimate of the error in the price of the American option.

Binomial trees can be used in conjunction with Monte Carlo simulation, a technique that is particularly useful for valuing some options that provide nonstandard payoffs.

Suggestions for Further Reading

On binomial trees

Boyle, P. P. "A Lattice Framework for Option Pricing with Two-State Variables," *Journal of Financial and Quantitative Analysis* 23 (March 1988): 1–12.

Cox, J., S. Ross, and M. Rubinstein. "Option Pricing: A Simplified Approach," *Journal of Financial Economics* 7 (October 1979): 229–264.

Hull, J. C., and A. White. "The Use of the Control Variate Technique in Option Pricing," *Journal of Financial and Quantitative Analysis* 23 (September 1988): 237–251.

Rendleman, R., and B. Bartter. "Two-State Option Pricing," *Journal of Finance* 34 (1979): 1092–1110.

On other approaches

Barone-Adesi, G., and R. E. Whaley. "Efficient Analytic Approximation of American Option Values," *Journal of Finance* 42 (June 1987): 301–320.

Boyle, P. P. "Options: a Monte Carlo Approach," *Journal of Financial Economics* 4 (1977): 323–338.

Brennan, M. J., and E. S. Schwartz. "Finite Difference Methods and Jump Processes Arising in the Pricing of Contingent Claims: A Synthesis," *Journal of Financial and Quantitative Analysis* 13 (September 1978): 462–474.

Brennan, M. J., and E. S. Schwartz. "The Valuation of American Put Options," *Journal of Finance* 32 (May 1977): 449–462.

Courtadon, G. "A More Accurate Finite Difference Approximation for the Valuation of Options," *Journal of Financial and Quantitative Analysis* 17 (December 1982): 697–705.

Geske, R., and H. E. Johnson. "The American Put Valued Analytically," *Journal of Finance* 39 (December 1984): 1511–1524.

Hull, J. C. *Options, Futures, and Other Derivatives.* 3d ed. Englewood Cliffs, NJ: Prentice Hall, 1997.

Hull, J. C., and A. White. "Valuing Derivative Securities Using the Explicit Finite Difference Method," *Journal of Financial and Quantitative Analysis* 25 (March 1990): 87–100.

Johnson, H. E. "An Analytic Approximation to the American Put Price," *Journal of Financial and Quantitative Analysis* 18 (March 1983): 141–148.

Macmillan, L. W. "Analytic Approximation for the American Put Option," *Advances in Futures and Options Research* 1 (1986): 119–139.

Schwartz, E. S. "The Valuation of Warrants: Implementing a New Approach," *Journal of Financial Economics* 4 (1977): 79–94.

Quiz

1. Which of the following can be estimated for an American option by constructing a single binomial tree: delta, gamma, vega, theta, rho?

2. Calculate the price of a three-month American put option on a nondividend-paying stock when the stock price is $60, the strike price is $60, the risk-free interest rate is 10 percent per annum, and the volatility is 45 percent per annum. Use a binomial tree with a time interval of one month.

3. Explain how the control variate technique is implemented.

4. Calculate the price of a nine-month American call option on corn futures when the current futures price is 198 cents, the strike price is 200 cents, the risk-free interest rate is 8 percent per annum, and the volatility is 30 percent per annum. Use a binomial tree with a time interval of three months.

5. Consider an option that pays off the amount by which the final stock price exceeds the average stock price achieved during the life of the option. Can this be valued by working backward through a binomial tree such as that in Figure 16.3?

6. "For a dividend-paying stock the tree for the stock price does not recombine, but the tree for the stock price less the present value of future dividends does recombine." Explain this statement.

7. Explain why Monte Carlo simulation cannot be used to value American options.

Questions and Problems

16.1. A nine-month American put option on a nondividend-paying stock has a strike price of $49. The stock price is $50, the risk-free rate is 5 percent per annum, and the volatility is 30 percent per annum. Use a three-step binomial tree to calculate the option price.

16.2. Use a three-time-step tree to value a nine-month American call option on wheat futures. The current futures price is 400 cents, the strike price is 420 cents, the risk-free rate is 6 percent, and the volatility is 30 percent per annum. Estimate the delta of the option from your tree.

16.3. An American put option to sell a Swiss franc for dollars has a strike price of $0.80 and a time to maturity of one year. The volatility of the Swiss franc is 10 percent, the dollar interest rate is 6 percent, the Swiss franc interest rate is 3 percent, and the current exchange rate is 0.81. Use a three-time-step tree to value the option. Estimate the delta of the option from your tree.

16.4. A three-month American call option on a stock has a strike price of $20. The stock price is $20, the risk-free rate is 3 percent per annum, and the volatility is 25 percent per annum. A dividend of $2 is expected in 1.5 months. Use a three-step binomial tree to calculate the option price.

16.5. A one-year American put option on a nondividend-paying stock has an exercise price of $18. The current stock price is $20, the risk-free interest rate is 15 percent per annum, and the volatility of the stock is 40 percent per annum. Use the DerivaGem software with four three-month time steps to estimate the value of the option. Display the tree and verify that the option prices at the final and penultimate nodes are correct. Use DerivaGem to value the European version of the option. Use the control variate technique to improve your estimate of the price of the American option.

16.6. A one-year American call option on silver futures has an exercise price of $9.00. The current futures price is $8.50, the risk-free rate of interest is 12 percent per annum, and the volatility of the futures price is 25 percent per annum. Use the DerivaGem software with four three-month time steps to estimate the value of the option. Display the tree and verify that the option prices at the final and penultimate nodes are correct. Use DerivaGem to value the European version of the option. Use the control variate technique to improve your estimate of the price of the American option.

16.7. A two-month American put option on the Major Market Index has an exercise price of 480. The current level of the index is 484, the risk-free interest rate is 10 percent per annum, the dividend yield on the index is 3 percent per annum, and the volatility of the index is 25 percent per annum. Divide the life of the option into four half-month periods and use the binomial tree approach to estimate the value of the option.

16.8. A six-month American call option on a stock is expected to pay dividends of $1 per share at the end of the second month and the fifth month. The current stock price is $30, the exercise price is $34, the risk-free interest rate is 10 percent per annum, and the volatility of the part of the stock price that will not be used to pay the dividends is

30 percent per annum. Use the DerivaGem software with the life of the option divided into six time steps to estimate the value of the option. Compare your answer with that given by Black's method (see chapter 11).

16.9. How would you use the control variate approach to improve the estimate of the delta of an American option when the binomial tree approach is used?

16.10. How would you use the binomial tree approach to value an American option on a stock index when the dividend yield on the index is a function of time?

CHAPTER 17

Biases in the Black–Scholes Model

Since Black and Scholes published their pathbreaking paper in 1973, there has been a great deal of interest in refining their model and identifying differences between the prices calculated from the model and the prices observed in the market. Several alternatives to Black–Scholes have been suggested and a great deal of empirical research has been carried out. In this chapter we review these developments. We identify four different ways in which Black–Scholes can be incorrect and examine the nature of the pricing errors in each case. We consider the ways in which the real world tends to differ from the world assumed by Black–Scholes for currencies and equities. We also examine the ways in which practitioners make adjustments for the imperfections in the Black–Scholes model.

Departures from Lognormality

As explained in chapter 11, the Black–Scholes model assumes that the distribution of the asset price at some future time, conditional on its value today, is lognormal. Equivalently, it assumes that the continuously compounded rate of return on the asset in any given time interval is normally distributed. Tests of option pricing frequently show that in-the-money and out-of-the-money options appear to be mispriced relative to at-the-money options. That is, the volatility for which the Black–Scholes equation correctly prices at-the-money options causes it to misprice in-the-money and out-of-the-money options. These pricing errors can be explained by differences between the lognormal distribution assumed by Black–Scholes and the true distribution.

Figure 17.1 shows four ways in which the true asset price distribution can be different from the lognormal distribution, yet still give the same mean and standard deviation for the asset price return. The characteristics of the distributions are summarized in Table 17.1. In Figure 17.1a both tails of the true distribution are thinner than those of the

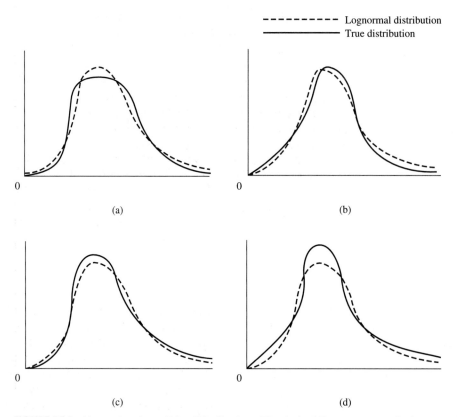

FIGURE 17.1 Alternative Asset Price Distributions. The dashed line represents the lognormal distribution; the solid line, the true distribution. All distributions have the same mean and standard deviation.

lognormal distribution. In Figure 17.1b the right tail is thinner and the left tail is fatter. In Figure 17.1c the right tail is fatter and the left tail is thinner. In Figure 17.1d both tails are fatter.

The true distributions in Figure 17.1 are created from the lognormal distribution by removing probability mass from some regions and adding it to other regions in such a way that the overall mean and standard deviation of asset returns are preserved. For example, in Figure 17.1d probability mass has been added to both tails of the distribution and the central part of the distribution. The addition has been balanced by the removal of probability mass from the parts of the distribution that are between roughly one and two standard deviations from the mean.

EFFECT ON OPTION PRICES

We now consider the difference between the correct option price and the Black–Scholes price that would be observed in the four situations. This difference is sometimes referred to as a *bias*. We consider first a call option that is significantly out of the money.

TABLE 17.1 **Biases Corresponding to Alternative Stock Price Distributions in Figure 17.1**

Distribution	Characteristics	Biases
Figure 17.1a	Both tails thinner	Black–Scholes overprices both out-of-the-money and in-the-money calls and puts.
Figure 17.1b	Left tail fatter, right tail thinner	Black–Scholes overprices out-of-the money calls and in-the-money puts. It underprices out-of-the-money puts and in-the-money calls.
Figure 17.1c	Left tail thinner, right tail fatter	Black–Scholes overprices out-of-the-money puts and in-the-money calls. It underprices in-the-money puts and out-of-the-money calls.
Figure 17.1d	Both tails fatter	Black–Scholes underprices both out-of-the-money and in-the-money calls and puts.

It has a positive value only if there is a large increase in the asset price. Its value therefore depends only on the right tail of the terminal asset price distribution. The fatter this tail, the more valuable the option. Consequently, Black–Scholes will tend to underprice out-of-the-money calls when the asset price distribution is as illustrated in Figures 17.1c and 17.1d, and it will overprice out-of-the-money calls in the cases shown in Figures 17.1a and 17.1b.

We look next at a put option that is significantly out of the money. It has a positive value only if there is a large decrease in the asset price. Its value therefore depends only on the left tail of the terminal asset price distribution. The fatter this tail, the more valuable the option. Black–Scholes will therefore tend to underprice out-of-the-money puts in Figures 17.1b and 17.1d, and it will overprice out-of-the-money puts in Figures 17.1a and 17.1c.

To obtain the biases for in-the-money European options, we can use put–call parity. If S is the asset price, X is the exercise price, r is the risk-free interest rate, T is the time to maturity, c is the price of a European call, p is the price of a European put, and q is the dividend yield,

$$p + Se^{-qT} = c + Xe^{-rT}$$

This relationship is independent of the terminal stock price distribution. If the European call with price c is out of the money, the corresponding European put with price p is in the money, and vice versa. Consequently, an in-the-money European put must exhibit the same pricing biases as the corresponding out-of-the-money European call. Similarly, an in-the-money European call must exhibit the same pricing biases as the corresponding out-of-the-money European put. The biases are therefore as indicated in Table 17.1.

Equities

Because of the impact of leverage on the volatility of a company's equity, equities tend to show the pattern in Figure 17.1b. As leverage increases, the equity becomes more risky and its volatility increases. As leverage decreases, the equity becomes less risky and its volatility decreases.

Suppose that the total market value of the equity of a company is E. As E decreases, a greater proportion of the company is financed by debt, with the result that the volatility of E increases. As E increases, a smaller proportion of the company is financed by debt, with the result that the volatility of E declines.

Black–Scholes assumes a constant volatility. The argument just given shows that volatility of a stock price can be expected to be negatively correlated to the price. When the stock price increases, volatility tends to decrease, making it less likely that very high stock prices will be achieved. When the stock price decreases, volatility tends to increase, making it more likely that very low stock prices will be achieved. The result is the situation in Figure 17.1b.

From the discussion in the previous section, we expect Black–Scholes to overprice out-of-the-money equity calls and in-the-money equity puts. We also expect it to underprice out-of-the-money puts and in-the-money calls. These biases should apply to both individual stocks and stock indices.

Exchange Rates

Exchange rates tend to show the pattern in Figure 17.1d. Extreme movements in the exchange rate are more likely than the Black–Scholes lognormal model would predict. One reason is that the volatility of an exchange rate is itself highly volatile and the correlation between the exchange rate and its volatility is close to zero. (The latter is in marked contrast to the situation for equities discussed above.) The result is that both the left and right tails of the probability distribution are fattened as in Figure 17.1d.

Another reason for Figure 17.1d concerns the tendency of exchange rates to exhibit jumps. The lognormal model for exchange rates is based on the assumption that the exchange-rate variable changes continuously. The effect of jumps is that extreme outcomes become more likely.

The impact of the distribution in Figure 17.1d is that Black–Scholes tends to underprice call and put options that are both significantly out of the money and significantly in the money.

The Time-to-Maturity Effect

An important question is whether pricing biases increase or decrease as the maturity of the option increases. As a rule, pricing errors caused by a nonconstant volatility increase as the time to maturity of the option increases. A nonconstant volatility has relatively little effect when the time to maturity is small, but its effect increases as the maturity of the option increases. The reason is easy to understand. Just as the standard deviation of the stock price distribution increases as we look farther ahead, so the distortions to that distribution caused by uncertainties in the volatility become greater as we look farther ahead.

Jumps are different in that they produce proportionately greater effects when the time to maturity of the option is small. When we look sufficiently far into the future, jumps tend to get "averaged out" so that the stock price distribution arising from jumps is almost indistinguishable from that arising from continuous changes.

When a Single Large Jump Is Anticipated

We now consider the situation where a single large jump in an asset price is anticipated in the near future. The anticipated jump may be the result of some important announcement. In the case of a stock price, the announcement could concern the outcome of a takeover attempt or the verdict in an important lawsuit.

Suppose that a stock price is currently $50 and an important announcement in one month is expected to either increase the stock price by $8 or reduce it by $8. The probability distribution of the stock price in, say, two months might then consist of two lognormal distributions superimposed upon each other, the first corresponding to favorable news in one month, the second to unfavorable news in one month. The situation is illustrated in Figure 17.2. The solid line shows the true stock price distribution in two months; the dashed line shows a lognormal distribution with the same standard deviation as the true distribution.

The true probability distribution in Figure 17.2 is bimodal. One easy way to investigate the general effect of a bimodal stock price distribution is to consider the extreme case where the distribution is binomial. This is the approach we will now take.

Suppose that a stock price is currently $50 and that it is known that in one month it will be either $42 or $58. Suppose further that the risk-free interest rate is 12 percent per annum. The situation is illustrated in Figure 17.3. We can use an approach similar to that developed in chapter 10. The stock price must on average grow from $50 to

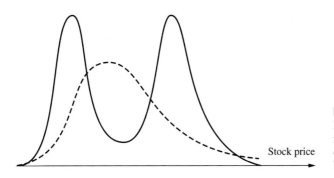

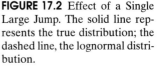
Stock price

FIGURE 17.2 Effect of a Single Large Jump. The solid line represents the true distribution; the dashed line, the lognormal distribution.

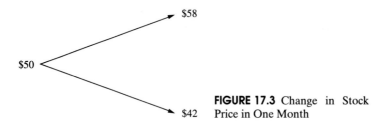

FIGURE 17.3 Change in Stock Price in One Month

$50e^{0.12 \times 0.0833} = \$50.50$ in a risk-neutral world. The probability p of an up movement in a risk-neutral world must therefore satisfy

$$58p + 42(1 - p) = 50.50$$

which means that p is 0.53. The standard deviation of the change in the stock price in one month is 8.0. Its volatility per month is therefore approximately $8/50 = 16$ percent, and its volatility per year is approximately $16\sqrt{12} = 55$ percent.

Table 17.2 shows call and put prices calculated on the basis of the one-step binomial model. Table 17.3 shows the volatilities implied by the prices in Table 17.2 when the Black–Scholes model is used. (From put–call parity, it can be shown that the volatilities implied by the call prices must be the same as the volatilities implied by the put prices.) If the same volatility were used for the whole range of strike prices, it is clear that Black–Scholes would significantly overprice very deep-in-the-money and very deep-out-of-the-money options while underpricing options that are relatively close to the money.

The Black–Scholes Model in Practice

It should be clear from the discussion so far in this chapter that Black–Scholes provides a less-than-perfect description of the real world. Stock prices and other asset prices

TABLE 17.2   Option Prices Using the One-Step Binomial Model

Strike Price ($)	Call Price ($)	Put Price ($)
42	8.42	0.00
44	7.37	0.93
46	6.31	1.86
48	5.26	2.78
50	4.21	3.71
52	3.16	4.64
54	2.10	5.57
56	1.05	6.50
58	0.00	7.42

TABLE 17.3   Implied Volatilities When Black–Scholes Is Used and
the True Distribution of Stock Prices Is Binomial

Strike Price ($)	Implied Volatility (% per annum)
42	0.0
44	58.8
46	66.6
48	69.5
50	69.2
52	66.1
54	60.0
56	49.0
58	0.0

exhibit more complicated behavior than geometric Brownian motion. Why, then, do practitioners continue to use Black–Scholes?

One reason is that the model is easy to use. There is only one parameter that is not directly observable in the market. This is the volatility. Practitioners can infer volatilities from option prices and option prices from volatilities in an unambiguous way. More complicated models generally involve several unobservable parameters and are much less easy to use.

Another reason for the popularity of Black–Scholes is that practitioners have developed "tricks of the trade" to finesse its imperfections. The rest of this section provides a brief review of these tricks.

VOLATILITY SMILE

Practitioners frequently calculate a *volatility smile*. This is a plot of the implied volatility of an option as a function of its strike price. A typical volatility smile for options on a foreign exchange is shown in Figure 17.4. Out-of-the-money and in-the-money options both tend to have higher implied volatilities than at-the-money options.[1] Higher implied volatilities correspond to higher prices. Figure 17.4 is therefore consistent with Figure 17.1d and our earlier discussion concerning exchange rates.

Figure 17.5 shows the implied volatilities for options on the S&P 500 on May 5, 1993 as a function of strike price. This is more a "grimace" than a smile and is typical of the pattern observed for equities. It is consistent with Figure 17.1b and our earlier discussion of equities. Implied volatilities are greater for low-strike-price options than for high-strike-price options.

VOLATILITY TERM STRUCTURE

Practitioners also like to calculate the *volatility term structure*. This is a plot of the variation of the implied volatility with the time to maturity of the option. Figure 17.6 shows

---

[1]For this purpose it is appropriate to define an at-the-money option as an option whose strike price equals the forward price of the asset.

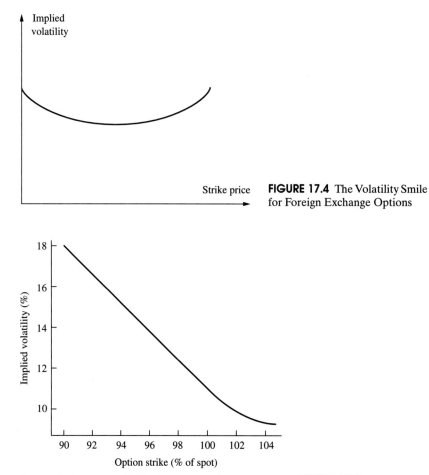

FIGURE 17.4 The Volatility Smile for Foreign Exchange Options

Source: E. Derman and I. Kani, "The Volatility Smile and Its Implied Tree," Quantitative Strategies Publications, Goldman Sachs, January 1994.

FIGURE 17.5 Volatility Smile for Options on the S&P 500 on May 5, 1993

the volatility term structure for options on the S&P 500 on May 5, 1993. It can be seen that the implied volatility was an increasing function of option maturity at this time.

VOLATILITY MATRICES

A common approach to coping with the imperfections in Black–Scholes is to construct a matrix of implied volatilities. An example is shown in Table 17.4.[2] One dimension of the matrix is strike price; the other is time to maturity. The main body of the matrix shows implied volatilities calculated from the Black–Scholes model. At any given time, some of the entries in the matrix are likely to correspond to options for which reliable

---

[2]At-the-money could be defined as the forward price of the underlying asset for the purposes of Table 17.4.

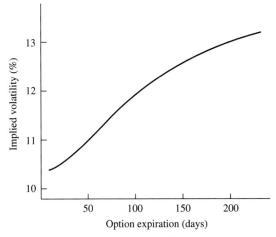

Source: E. Derman and I. Kani, "The Volatility Smile and Its Implied Tree," Quantitative Strategies Publications, Goldman Sachs, January 1994.

FIGURE 17.6 Volatility Term Structure for Options on the S&P 500 on May 5, 1993

market data are available. The volatilities for these options are calculated directly from their market prices and entered into the table. The rest of the matrix is determined using linear interpolation.

When a new option has to be valued, practitioners look up the appropriate volatility in the table. For example, when valuing a nine-month option with a strike price one standard deviation below the at-the-money (ATM) strike price, practitioners would interpolate between 13.5 and 14.8 to obtain a volatility of 14.15 percent. This is the volatility that would be used in the Black–Scholes formula or in the construction of a binomial tree.

THE ROLE OF THE MODEL

How important is the pricing model if practitioners are prepared to use a different volatility for every deal? In practice, an option pricing model is often no more than

TABLE 17.4   Volatility Matrix

	ATM Less 2 SDs*	ATM Less 1 SD	ATM	ATM Plus 1 SD	ATM Plus 2 SDs
1-month	14.2	13.0	12.0	12.8	13.6
3-month	14.2	13.0	12.0	12.8	13.6
6-month	14.7	13.5	12.5	13.3	14.1
1-year	15.9	14.8	13.5	14.5	15.5
2-year	16.6	15.3	14.0	15.0	16.0
5-year	16.6	15.5	14.4	15.2	16.0

*ATM = at the money; SD = standard deviation.

a tool for understanding the volatility environment and for pricing illiquid securities consistently with the market prices of actively traded securities. If practitioners stopped using Black–Scholes and switched to another plausible model, the matrix of volatilities would change and the shape of the smile would change. But arguably the prices quoted in the market would not change appreciably.

Empirical Research

A number of problems arise in carrying out empirical research to test the Black–Scholes and other option pricing models.[3] The first problem is that any statistical hypothesis about how options are priced has to be a joint hypothesis to the effect that (1) the option pricing formula is correct and (2) markets are efficient. If the hypothesis is rejected, it may be the case that (1) is untrue, (2) is untrue, or both (1) and (2) are untrue. A second problem is that the stock price volatility is an unobservable variable. One approach is to estimate the volatility from historical stock price data. Alternatively, implied volatilities can be used in some way. A third problem for the researcher is to make sure that data on the stock price and option price are synchronous. For example, if the option is thinly traded, it is not likely to be acceptable to compare closing option prices with closing stock prices. The closing option price might correspond to a trade at 1:00 P.M., whereas the closing stock price corresponds to a trade at 4:00 P.M.

Black and Scholes and Galai have tested whether it is possible to make excess returns above the risk-free rate of interest by buying options that are undervalued by the market (relative to the theoretical price) and selling options that are overvalued by the market (relative to the theoretical price). A riskless delta-neutral portfolio is assumed to be maintained at all times by trading the underlying stocks on a regular basis, as described in chapter 14. Black and Scholes used data from the over-the-counter options market, in which options are dividend protected. Galai used data from the Chicago Board Options Exchange (CBOE), in which options are not protected against the effects of cash dividends. Galai used Black's procedure as described in chapter 11 to incorporate the effect of anticipated dividends into the option price. Both studies showed that, in the absence of transactions costs, significant excess returns over the risk-free rate can be obtained by buying undervalued options and selling overvalued options. But it is possible that these excess returns are available only to market makers and that when transactions costs are considered, they vanish.

A number of researchers have chosen to make no assumptions about the behavior of stock prices and have tested whether arbitrage strategies can be used to make a riskless profit in options markets. Garman provides a very efficient computational procedure for finding any arbitrage possibilities that exist in a given situation. One study by Klemkosky and Resnick which is frequently cited tests whether the relationship in Equation 8.9 is ever violated. It concludes that some small arbitrage profits are possible from using the relationship. These are due mainly to the overpricing of American calls.

Chiras and Manaster carried out a study using CBOE data to compare the weighted implied standard deviation from options on a stock at a point in time with

---

[3]See the end-of-chapter references for citations to the studies reviewed in this section.

the standard deviation calculated from historical data. They found that the former provide a much better forecast of the volatility of the stock price during the life of the option. We can conclude that option traders are using more than just historical data when determining future volatilities. Chiras and Manaster also tested to see whether it was possible to make above-average returns by buying options with low implied standard deviations and selling options with high implied standard deviations. This strategy showed a profit of 10 percent per month. The Chiras and Manaster study can be interpreted as providing good support for the Black–Scholes model while showing that the CBOE was inefficient in some respects.

MacBeth and Merville tested the Black–Scholes model using a different approach. They looked at different call options on the same stock at the same time and compared the volatilities implied by the option prices. The stocks chosen were AT&T, Avon, Kodak, Exxon, IBM, and Xerox, and the time period considered was the year 1976. They found that implied volatilities tended to be relatively high for in-the-money options and relatively low for out-of-the-money options. A relatively high implied volatility is indicative of a relatively high option price, and a relatively low implied volatility is indicative of a relatively low option price. Therefore, if it is assumed that Black–Scholes prices at-the-money options correctly, it can be concluded that out-of-the-money call options are overpriced by Black–Scholes and in-the-money call options are underpriced by Black–Scholes. These effects become more pronounced as the time to maturity increases and the degree to which the option is in or out of the money increases. MacBeth and Merville's results are consistent with Figure 17.1b, Figure 17.5, and the arguments presented earlier regarding leverage. The results were confirmed by Lauterbach and Schultz in a later study concerned with the pricing of warrants.

Rubinstein has done a great deal of research similar to that of MacBeth and Merville. No clear-cut pattern emerged from his early research, but his more recent research is clearly consistent with Figure 17.1b and Figure 17.5. To quote from his 1994 paper: "Out-of-the-money puts (and hence in-the-money calls perforce by put–call parity) became valued much more highly, eventually leading to the 1990–92 (as well as current) situation where low striking price options had significantly higher implied volatilities than high striking price options." As mentioned earlier in the chapter, leverage and the resultant negative correlation between volatility and stock price may account for the finding. Rubinstein speculates that another reason may be investors' fear of a repeat of the crash of 1987.

A number of authors have researched the pricing of options on assets other than stocks. For example, Shastri and Tandon, and Bodurtha and Courtadon have examined the market prices of currency options; Shastri and Tandon in another paper have examined the market prices of futures options; Chance has examined the market prices of index options.

In most cases the mispricing by Black–Scholes is not sufficient to present profitable opportunities to investors when transactions costs and bid-ask spreads are taken into account. When profitable opportunities are searched for, it is important to bear in mind that, even for a market maker, some time must elapse between a profitable opportunity being identified and action being taken. This delay, even if it is only to the next trade, can be sufficient to eliminate the profitable opportunity.

Summary

The Black–Scholes model and its extensions assume that the probability distribution of the stock price at any given future time is lognormal. If this assumption is incorrect, biases are likely to exist in the prices produced by the model. If the right tail of the true distribution is fatter than the right tail of the lognormal distribution, the Black–Scholes model will tend to underprice out-of-the-money calls and in-the-money puts. If the left tail of the true distribution is fatter than the left tail of the lognormal distribution, the Black–Scholes model will tend to underprice out-of-the-money puts and in-the-money calls. When either tail is too thin relative to the lognormal distribution, the opposite biases are observed.

Because of the impact of leverage, equities tend to exhibit fat left tails and thin right tails relative to the lognormal distribution. Because of the impact of uncertain volatility and jumps in the exchange rate, foreign exchange rates tend to exhibit fat left tails and fat right tails.

The imperfections in Black–Scholes are evidenced by the fact that practitioners need to change the volatility parameter on a regular basis to reflect the latest market information. The biases are also evidenced by the fact that both practitioners and researchers find that implied volatilities depend on strike price (the volatility smile effect) and on time to maturity (the volatility term structure effect). Despite its imperfections, the Black–Scholes model and its extensions are still widely used for valuing options. The model imperfections are handled by using volatility matrices. These matrices are constructed from the latest implied volatility data and incorporate both the volatility smile and the volatility term structure.

Suggestions for Further Reading

On alternative models

Black, F. "How to Use the Holes in Black–Scholes," *RISK* 1 no. 4 (March 1988).

Black, F., and M. Scholes. "The Pricing of Options and Corporate Liabilities," *Journal of Political Economy* 81 (May–June 1973): 637–659.

Cox, J. C., and S. A. Ross. "The Valuation of Options for Alternative Stochastic Processes," *Journal of Financial Economics* 3 (March 1976): 145–160.

Cox, J. C., S. A. Ross, and M. Rubinstein. "Option Pricing: A Simplified Approach," *Journal of Financial Economics* 7 (September 1979): 229–263.

Geske, R. "The Valuation of Compound Options," *Journal of Financial Economics* 7 (1979): 63–81.

Hull, J. C. *Options, Futures, and Other Derivatives*. 3d ed. Englewood Cliffs, NJ: Prentice Hall, 1997.

Hull, J. C., and A. White. "The Pricing of Options on Assets with Stochastic Volatilities," *Journal of Finance* 42 (June 1987): 281–300.

Merton, R. C. "Option Pricing When Underlying Stock Returns Are Discontinuous," *Journal of Financial Economics* 3 (March 1976): 125–144.

Merton, R. C. "Theory of Rational Option Pricing," *Bell Journal of Economics and Management Science* 4 (Spring 1973): 141–183.

Rubinstein, M. "Displaced Diffusion Option Pricing," *Journal of Finance* 38 (March 1983): 213–217.

On empirical research

Black, F., and M. Scholes. "The Valuation of Option Contracts and a Test of Market Efficiency," *Journal of Finance* 27 (May 1972): 399–418.

Bodurtha, J. N., and G. R. Courtadon. "Tests of an American Option Pricing Model on the Foreign Currency Options Market," *Journal of Financial and Quantitative Analysis* 22 (June 1987): 153–168.

Chance, D. M. "Empirical Tests of the Pricing of Index Call Options," *Advances in Futures and Options Research* 1, pt. A (1986): 141–166.

Chiras D., and S. Manaster. "The Information Content of Option Prices and a Test of Market Efficiency," *Journal of Financial Economics* 6 (September 1978): 213–234.

Cumby, R., S. Figlewski, and J. Hasbrouck. "Forecasting Volatilities and Correlations with EGARCH Models," *Journal of Derivatives* 1, no. 2 (Winter 1993): 51–63.

Galai, D. "Tests of Market Efficiency and the Chicago Board Options Exchange," *Journal of Business* 50 (April 1977): 167–197.

Garman, M. B. "An Algebra for Evaluating Hedge Portfolios," *Journal of Financial Economics* 3 (October 1976): 403–427.

Harvey, C. R., and R. E. Whaley. "Dividends and S&P 100 Index Option Valuations," *Journal of Futures Markets* 12 (1992): 123–137.

Harvey, C. R., and R. E. Whaley. "Market Volatility Prediction and the Efficiency of the S&P 100 Index Option Market," *Journal of Financial Economics* 31 (1992): 43–73.

Harvey, C. R., and R. E. Whaley. "S&P 100 Index Option Volatility," *Journal of Finance* 46 (1991): 1551–1561.

Jackwerth, J. C., and M. Rubinstein. "Recovering Probability Distributions from Option Prices," *Journal of Finance* 51 (December 1996): 1611–1631.

Klemkosky, R. C., and B. G. Resnick. "Put-Call Parity and Market Efficiency," *Journal of Finance* 34 (December 1979): 1141–1155.

Lauterbach, B., and P. Schultz. "Pricing Warrants: An Empirical Study of the Black–Scholes Model and Its Alternatives," *Journal of Finance* 4, no. 4 (September 1990): 1181–1210.

MacBeth, J. D., and L. J. Merville. "An Empirical Examination of the Black–Scholes Call Option Pricing Model," *Journal of Finance* 34 (December 1979): 1172–1186.

Noh, J., R. F. Engle, and A. Kane. "A Test of Efficiency for the S&P 500 Index Options Market Using Variance Forecasts," *Journal of Derivatives* 2 (1994): 17–30.

Rubinstein, M. "Implied Binomial Trees," *Journal of Finance* 49, no. 3. (July 1994): 771–818.

Rubinstein, M. "Nonparametric Tests of Alternative Option Pricing Models Using All Reported Trades and Quotes on the 30 Most Active CBOE Option Classes from August 23, 1976 through August 31, 1978," *Journal of Finance* 40 (June 1985): 455–480.

Shastri, K., and K. Tandon. "An Empirical Test of a Valuation Model for American Options on Futures Contracts," *Journal of Financial and Quantitative Analysis* 21 (December 1986): 377–392.

Shastri, K., and K. Tandon. "Valuation of Foreign Currency Options: Some Empirical Tests," *Journal of Financial and Quantitative Analysis* 21 (June 1986): 145–160.

Stutzer, M. "A Simple Nonparametric Approach to Derivative Security Valuation," *Journal of Finance* 51 (December 1996): 1633–1652.

Xu, X., and S. J. Taylor. "The Term Structure of Volatility Implied by Foreign Exchange Options," *Journal of Financial and Quantitative Analysis* 29 (1994): 57–74.

Quiz

1. Determine the option pricing biases likely to be observed when
   a. Both tails of the stock price distribution are thinner than those of the lognormal distribution
   b. The right tail is thinner and the left tail is fatter than for a lognormal distribution
2. What biases would be caused by an uncertain volatility if the stock price were positively correlated with volatility?
3. What biases are caused by jumps in the movements of a stock price? Are these biases likely to be more pronounced for a six-month option than for a three-month option?
4. Explain carefully why Figure 17.5 is consistent with Figure 17.1b.
5. Why are the biases (relative to Black–Scholes) for the market prices of in-the-money call options usually the same as the biases for the market prices of out-of-the-money put options?
6. A stock price is currently $20. Tomorrow news is expected to be announced that will either increase the price by $5 or decrease the price by $5. What are the problems in using Black–Scholes to value options on the stock?
7. What are the major problems in testing a stock option pricing model empirically?

Questions and Problems

17.1. Suppose that a stock price exhibits jumps. Explain carefully why Black–Scholes will give misleading prices for short-life options but will give reasonable answers for longer-life options.
17.2. Suppose that a foreign currency exchange rate follows a jump process and has an uncertain volatility that is uncorrelated with the exchange rate. What sort of time-to-maturity biases would you expect in the option prices observed in the market relative to those given by the Black–Scholes formulas? Assume that implied volatilities are calculated on the basis of at-the-money options.
17.3. Option traders sometimes refer to deep-out-of-the-money options as being options on volatility. Why do you think they do so?
17.4. Explain carefully why the implied volatilities are the same for both put and call options in Table 17.3.
17.5. Explain why the implied volatilities of options with strike prices of $42 and $58 are zero in Table 17.3.
17.6. The risk-free interest rate is 15 percent per annum and the current price of a stock is $30. It is known that the price will be either $20 or $35 in three months. Calculate the prices of call options with strike prices of $21, $25, and $34. What are the volatilities implied by the Black–Scholes model in each of these cases?

17.7. A certain stock is selling for $4. Analysts consider the break-up value of the company to be such that the stock price cannot fall below $3 per share. What are the likely differences between the option prices produced by Black–Scholes and option prices in the market? Consider out-of-the-money and in-the-money calls and puts.

17.8. A European call option on a certain stock has a strike price of $30, a time to maturity of one year, and an implied volatility of 30 percent. A European put option on the same stock has a strike price of $30, a time to maturity of one year, and an implied volatility of 33 percent. What is the arbitrage opportunity open to a trader? Does the arbitrage work only when the lognormal assumption underlying Black–Scholes holds? Explain the reasons for your answer carefully.

18 Interest-rate Options

CHAPTER

Interest-rate options are options whose payoffs are dependent in some way on the level of interest rates. In recent years they have become increasingly popular. Many different types of interest-rate options are now actively traded over the counter and on exchanges. The chapter discusses some of the products and how they are used. It also describes the standard market models that are used to value European bond options, interest-rate caps and floors, and European swap options. These models are in the spirit of the original Black–Scholes model for European stock options. In the case of European bond options, the underlying bond price is assumed to be lognormal. In the case of caps and floors, an interest rate is assumed to be lognormal. In the case of European swap options, the underlying swap rate is assumed to be lognormal.

Exchange-traded Interest-rate Options

The most popular exchange-traded interest-rate options are those on Treasury bond futures, Treasury note futures, and Eurodollar futures. Table 13.3 in chapter 13 shows the closing prices for these instruments on September 24, 1996.

A Treasury bond futures option is an option to enter a Treasury bond futures contract. As mentioned in chapter 5, one Treasury bond futures contract is for the delivery of $100,000 of Treasury bonds. The price of a Treasury bond futures option is quoted as a percentage of the face value of the underlying Treasury bonds to the nearest sixty-fourth of 1 percent. Table 13.3 gives the price of the November call futures option on Treasury bonds as 2-10, or $2\frac{10}{64}$ percent of the debt principal when the strike price is 107 (implying that one contract would cost $2,156.25). The quotes for options on Treasury notes are similar.

An option on Eurodollar futures is an option to enter into a Eurodollar futures contract. As explained in chapter 5, the asset underlying a Eurodollar futures contract is a $1 million three-month deposit. When the Eurodollar quote changes by one basis point, or 0.01, there is a gain or loss on the contract of $25. Similarly, in the pricing of options on Eurodollar futures, one basis point represents \$25. Table 13.3 gives the price of the CME October call futures option on Eurodollars as 0.43 percent when the strike price is 93.75. This implies that one contract costs 43 × \$25 = \$1,075.

Interest-rate futures contracts work in the same way as the other futures contracts discussed in chapter 13. For example, the payoff from a call is max$(F - X, 0)$, where F is the futures price at the time of exercise and X is the strike price. In addition to the cash payoff, the option holder obtains a long position in the futures contract when the option is exercised, and the option writer obtains a corresponding short position.

Interest-rate futures prices increase when bond prices increase (i.e., when interest rates fall). They decrease when bond prices decrease (i.e., when interest rates rise). An investor who thinks that short-term interest rates will rise can speculate by buying put options on Eurodollar futures, whereas an investor who thinks the rates will fall can speculate by buying call options on Eurodollar futures. An investor who thinks that long-term interest rates will rise can speculate by buying put options on Treasury note futures or Treasury bond futures, whereas an investor who thinks the rates will fall can speculate by buying call options on these instruments.

Example 1

Suppose that it is February and the futures price for the June Eurodollar contract is 93.82. (This corresponds to a three-month Eurodollar interest rate of 6.18 percent per annum.) The price of a call option on the contract with a strike price of 94.00 is quoted as 0.20. This option could be attractive to an investor who feels that interest rates are likely to come down. Suppose that short-term interest rates do drop by about 100 basis points over the next three months and the investor exercises the call when the Eurodollar futures price is 94.78. (This corresponds to a three-month Eurodollar interest rate of 5.22 percent per annum.) The payoff is $25 \times 78 = \$1,950$. The cost of the contract is $20 \times 25 = \$500$. The investor's profit is therefore \$1,450.

Example 2

Suppose that it is August and the futures price for the December Treasury bond contract traded on the CBOT is 96-09 (or $96\frac{9}{32} = 96.28125$). The yield on long-term government bonds is about 8.4 percent per annum. An investor who feels that this yield will fall by December might choose to buy December calls with a strike price of 98. Assume that the price of these calls is 1-04 (or $1\frac{4}{64} = 1.0625$ percent of the principal). If long-term rates fall to 8 percent per annum and the Treasury bond futures price rises to 100-00, the investor will make a net profit per \$100 of bond futures of

$$100.00 - 98.00 - 1.0625 = 0.9375$$

Since one option contract is for the purchase or sale of instruments with a face value of \$100,000, the investor would make a profit of \$937.50 per option contract bought.

Embedded Bond Options

Some bonds contain embedded call and put options. For example, a *callable bond* contains provisions that allow the issuing firm to buy back the bond at a predetermined price at certain times in the future. The holder of such a bond has sold a call option to the issuer. The strike price or call price in the option is the predetermined price that must be paid by the issuer to the holder to buy back the bond. Callable bonds usually cannot be called for the first few years of their life. After that the call price is usually a decreasing function of time. For example, a 10-year callable bond might have no call privileges for the first two years. After that the issuer might have the right to buy the bond back at a price of $110.00 in years 3 and 4 of its life, at a price of $107.50 in years 5 and 6, at a price of $106.00 in years 7 and 8, and at a price of $103.00 in years 9 and 10. The value of the call option is reflected in the quoted yields on bonds. Bonds with call features generally offer higher yields than bonds with no call features.

A *puttable bond* contains provisions that allow the holder to demand early redemption at a predetermined price at certain times in the future. The holder of such a bond has purchased a put option on the bond as well as the bond itself. Since the put option increases the value of the bond to the holder, bonds with put features provide lower yields than bonds with no put features. A simple example of a puttable bond is a 10-year retractable bond for which the holder has the right to be repaid at the end of five years.

A number of interest-rate instruments have embedded bond options. For example, early-redemption privileges on fixed-rate deposits are analogous to the put features of a bond. Prepayment privileges on fixed-rate loans are analogous to the call features of a bond. Also, loan commitments made by a bank or other financial institution are put options. Suppose, for example, that a bank quotes a five-year interest rate of 12 percent per annum to a potential borrower and states that the rate is good for the next two months. The client has in effect obtained the right to sell a five-year bond with a 12 percent coupon to the financial institution for its face value any time within the next two months.

Mortgage-backed Securities

A type of interest-rate option is embedded in a *mortgage-backed security (MBS)*. An MBS is created when a financial institution decides to sell part of its residential mortgage portfolio to investors. The mortgages are put into a pool and investors acquire a stake in the pool by buying units. The units are known as mortgage-backed securities. A secondary market is usually created for the units so that investors can sell them to other investors as desired. An investor who owns units representing X percent of a certain pool is entitled to X percent of the principal and interest cash flows received from the mortgages in the pool.

The mortgages in a pool are generally guaranteed by a government-related agency such as the Government National Mortgage Association (GNMA) or the Federal

National Mortgage Association (FNMA) so that investors are protected against defaults. This makes an MBS sound like a regular fixed-income security issued by the government. However, there is a critical difference between an MBS and a regular fixed-income investment. The mortgages in an MBS pool have prepayment privileges, which can be quite valuable to the householder. For example, in the United States mortgages typically last for 25 years and can be prepaid at any time. In other words, the householder has a 25-year American-style option to put the mortgage back to the lender at its face value.

In practice, prepayments on mortgages occur for a variety of reasons. Sometimes interest rates have fallen and the owner of the house decides to refinance at a lower rate of interest. On other occasions a mortgage is prepaid simply because the house is being sold. A critical element in valuing an MBS is the determination of the *prepayment function*. This function describes expected prepayments on the underlying pool of mortgages at a time *t* in terms of the yield curve at time *t* and other relevant variables.

A prepayment function is very unreliable as a predictor of actual prepayment experience for an individual mortgage. When many similar mortgage loans are combined in the same pool, there is a "law of large numbers" effect at work, and prepayments can be predicted from an analysis of historical data more accurately. As already mentioned, prepayments are not always motivated by pure interest-rate considerations. Nevertheless, prepayments tend to be more likely when interest rates are low than when they are high. This means that investors require a higher rate of interest on an MBS than on other fixed-income securities to compensate for the prepayment options they have written.

COLLATERALIZED MORTGAGE OBLIGATIONS

The MBSs described so far are sometimes referred to as *pass-throughs*. All investors receive the same return and bear the same prepayment risk. Not all mortgage-backed securities work in this way. In a *collateralized mortgage obligation (CMO)* the investors are divided into a number of classes, and rules are developed for determining how principal repayments are channeled to different classes.

As an example of a CMO consider an MBS with investors divided into three classes: class A, class B, and class C. All the principal repayments (both those that are scheduled and those that are prepayments) are channeled to class A investors until investors in this class have been completely paid off. Principal repayments are then channeled to class B investors until these investors have been completely paid off. Finally, principal repayments are channeled to class C investors. In this situation class A investors bear the most prepayment risk. The class A securities can be expected to last less long than the class B securities, which in turn can be expected to last less long than the class C securities.

The objective of this type of structure is to create classes of securities that are more attractive to institutional investors than those created by the simpler pass-through MBS. The prepayment risks assumed by the different classes depend on the par value in each class. For example, class C bears very little prepayment risk if the par values in classes A, B, and C are 400, 300, and 100, respectively. It bears rather more prepayment risk if the par values in the classes are 100, 200, and 500.

IOs AND POs

In a *stripped MBS,* principal payments are separated from interest payments. All principal payments are channeled to one class of security, known as a *principal only (PO).* All interest payments are channeled to another class of security, known as an *interest only (IO).* Both IOs and POs are risky investments. As prepayment rates increase, a PO becomes more valuable and an IO becomes less valuable. As prepayment rates decrease, the reverse happens. In a PO a fixed amount of principal is returned to the investor, but the timing is uncertain. A high rate of prepayments on the underlying pool leads to the principal being received early (which is, of course, good news for the holder of the PO). A low rate of prepayments on the underlying pool delays the return of the principal and reduces the yield provided by the PO. In an IO the total of the cash flows received by the investor is not certain. The higher the rate of prepayments, the lower the total cash flows received by the investor, and vice versa.

Black's Model

Since the Black–Scholes model was first published in 1973, it has become a very popular tool. As explained in chapters 12 and 13, the model has been extended so that it can be used to value options on foreign exchange, indices, and futures contracts. Traders have become very comfortable with both the lognormal assumption that underlies the model and the volatility measure that describes uncertainty. It is not surprising therefore that the model has been extended so that it covers interest-rate derivatives.

The extension of the Black–Scholes model that is most widely used in the interest-rate area is known as Black's model.[1] It was originally developed for valuing options on commodity futures, as discussed in chapter 13. In this chapter we examine how it is used to value European bond options, caps and floors, and European swap options.

USING BLACK'S MODEL TO PRICE EUROPEAN OPTIONS

Consider a European call option on a variable V. We define

T: maturity date of the option

F: futures price of V for a contract with maturity T

X: strike price of the option

r: zero-coupon yield for maturity T

σ: volatility of F

V_T: value of V at time T

F_T: value of F at time T

The option pays off $\max(V_T - X, 0)$ at time T. Since $F_T = V_T$, we can also regard the option as paying off $\max(F_T - X, 0)$ at time T. As shown in chapter 13, Black's model

---

[1] See F. Black, "The Pricing of Commodity Contracts," *Journal of Financial Economics* 3 (March 1976): 167–179.

gives the value, c, of the option at time zero as

$$c = e^{-rT}[FN(d_1) - XN(d_2)]$$ **(18.1)**

where

$$d_1 = \frac{\ln(F/X) + \sigma^2 T/2}{\sigma \sqrt{T}}$$

$$d_2 = \frac{\ln(F/X) - \sigma^2 T/2}{\sigma \sqrt{T}} = d_1 - \sigma \sqrt{T}$$

The value, p, of the corresponding put option is given by

$$p = e^{-rT}[XN(-d_2) - FN(-d_1)]$$ **(18.2)**

EXTENSIONS OF BLACK'S MODEL

Black's model assumes that the volatility of F is constant. We can relax this assumption somewhat. Because we are valuing a European option, we do not care about the values of V or F prior to time T. We require only that V have a lognormal probability dis tribution at time T with the standard deviation of $\ln V_T$ equal to $\sigma \sqrt{T}$. To emphasize this point, σ will from now on be referred to as the *volatility measure* of V_T, with the understanding that this means that $\sigma \sqrt{T}$ is the standard deviation of $\ln V_T$.

As a further extension of Black's model, we can allow the time when the payoff is made to be different from T. Assume that the payoff on the option is calculated from the value of the variable V at time T, but that the payoff is delayed until time T^*, where $T^* \geq T$. In this case it is necessary to discount the payoff from time T^* instead of from time T. We define r^* as the zero-coupon yield for maturity T^*, and Equations 18.1 and 18.2 become

$$c = e^{-r^* T^*}[FN(d_1) - XN(d_2)]$$ **(18.3)**

$$p = e^{-r^* T^*}[XN(-d_2) - FN(-d_1)]$$ **(18.4)**

where

$$d_1 = \frac{\ln(F/X) + \sigma^2 T/2}{\sigma \sqrt{T}}$$

$$d_2 = \frac{\ln(F/X) - \sigma^2 T/2}{\sigma \sqrt{T}} = d_1 - \sigma \sqrt{T}$$

HOW THE MODEL IS USED

When Black's model formulas are used to value an interest-rate cap, V is set equal to an interest rate; when they are used to value a bond option, V is set equal to the underlying bond price; when they are used to value a swap option, V is set equal to the underlying swap rate. In all cases the variable F is set equal to the forward price of V rather than its futures price. Recall from chapter 3 that futures prices and forward prices are exactly equal only when interest rates are constant. Because we are dealing with an option on an interest-rate-dependent variable, the assumption that F is a forward price appears questionable. It turns out that this assumption exactly offsets another assumption made by Black's model that interest rates are constant for the purposes of discounting.[2] When used to value interest-rate options, Black's model therefore has a stronger theoretical basis than is sometimes supposed.[3]

European Bond Options

A European bond option is an option to buy or sell a bond for a certain price on a certain date. Equations 18.1 and 18.2 can be used to price the option, with F equal to the forward bond price. The variable σ is the volatility measure for the forward bond price. In other words, we are assuming that the bond price is lognormal at the maturity of the option (time T) and that $\sigma\sqrt{T}$ is the standard deviation of the logarithm of the bond price at this time.

As explained in chapter 5, F can be calculated from the spot bond price, B, using the formula

$$F = (B - I)e^{rT} \tag{18.5}$$

where I is the present value of the coupons that will be paid during the life of the option. In this formula both the spot bond price and the forward bond price are cash prices rather than quoted prices. The relationship between cash and quoted bond prices is explained in chapter 5.

The strike price, X, in Equations 18.1 and 18.2 should be the cash strike price. In the choice of a correct value for X, the precise terms of the option are therefore important. If the strike price is defined as the cash amount that is exchanged for the bond when the option is exercised, X should be put equal to this strike price. If the strike price is the quoted price applicable when the option is exercised (as it is in most exchange-traded bond options), X should be set equal to the strike price plus accrued interest at the expiration date of the option. (Traders refer to the quoted price of a bond as the "clean price" and the cash price as the "dirty price.")

Example

Consider a 10-month European call option on a 9.75-year bond with a face value of $1,000. (When the option matures, the bond will have 8 years and 11 months remaining.) Suppose that the current cash bond price is $960, the strike price is $1,000, the 10-month risk-free interest rate is 10 percent per annum, and the relevant volatility measure for the bond is 9 percent per annum. The bond pays a semiannual coupon of 10 percent, and coupon payments of $50 are expected in 3 months and 9 months. (This means that the accrued interest is $25 and the quoted bond price is $935.) We suppose that the 3-month and 9-month risk-free

[2] See, for example, F. Jamshidian, "Options and Futures Evaluation with Deterministic Volatilities," *Mathematical Finance* 3, no. 2 (1993): 149–159.

[3] Some applications of Black's model to interest-rate derivatives (but not those considered in this chapter) require that a convexity adjustment be made to F. For a discussion, see J. C. Hull, *Options, Futures, and Other Derivatives.* 3d ed. Englewood Cliffs, NJ: Prentice Hall, 1997.

interest rates are 9.0 percent and 9.5 percent per annum, respectively. The present value of the coupon payments is therefore

$$50e^{-0.09 \times 0.25} + 50e^{-0.095 \times 0.75} = 95.45$$

or $95.45. The bond forward price, from Equation 18.5, is given by

$$F = (960 - 95.45)e^{0.1 \times 10/12} = 939.68$$

(a) If the strike price is the cash price that would be paid for the bond on exercise, the parameters for Equation 18.1 are $F = 939.68$, $X = 1,000$, $r = 0.1$, $\sigma = 0.09$, and $T = 0.8333$. The price of the call option is $9.49.

(b) If the strike price is the quoted price that would be paid for the bond on exercise, one month's accrued interest must be added to X, because the maturity of the option is one month after a coupon date. This produces a value for X of

$$1,000 + 50 \times 0.16667 = 1,008.33$$

The values for the other parameters in Equation 18.1 are unchanged ($F = 939.68$, $r = 0.1$, $\sigma = 0.09$, and $T = 0.8333$). The price of the option is $7.97.

The volatility measure used in Black's model to value a bond option depends on both the life of the option and the life of the underlying bond. Figure 18.1 shows how the standard deviation of the logarithm of a bond's price changes with time. The standard deviation is zero today, because there is no uncertainty about the bond's price today. It is also zero at the bond's maturity, because we know that the bond's price will equal its face value at maturity. Between today and the maturity of the bond, the standard deviation first increases and then decreases. The volatility measure, σ, used in Black's model is

$$\frac{\text{Standard deviation of logarithm of bond price at maturity of option}}{\sqrt{\text{Time to maturity of option}}}$$

Figure 18.2 shows a typical pattern for σ as a function of the life of the option. In general σ declines as the life of the option increases. It also tends to be an increasing function of the life of the underlying bond when the life of the option is held fixed.

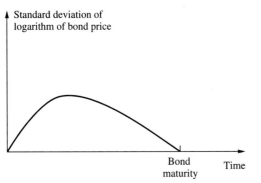

FIGURE 18.1 Standard Deviation of Logarithm of Bond Price as a Function of Time

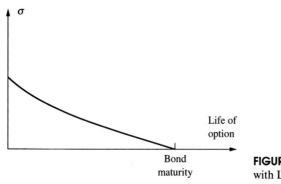

FIGURE 18.2 Variation of σ, with Life of Bond Option

YIELD VOLATILITIES

The volatilities that are quoted for bond options are often yield volatility measures rather than price volatility measures. The duration concept, introduced in chapter 5, is used by the market to convert a quoted yield volatility into a price volatility. Suppose that D is the modified duration of the forward bond underlying the option, as defined in chapter 5. The relationship between the change in the bond's price, B, and its yield, y, at the maturity of the option is

$$\frac{\Delta B}{B} \approx -D\,\Delta y$$

or

$$\frac{\Delta B}{B} \approx -Dy\,\frac{\Delta y}{y}$$

This suggests that the volatility measure, σ, used in Black's model can be approximately related to a yield volatility measure, σ_y, using

$$\sigma = Dy\sigma_y \qquad\qquad\qquad \textbf{(18.6)}$$

When a yield volatility is quoted for a bond option, the implicit assumption is usually that it will be converted to a price volatility using Equation 18.6 and that this measure will then be used in conjunction with Equation 18.1 or 18.2 to obtain a price.

Interest-rate Caps

A popular interest-rate option offered by financial institutions in the over-the-counter market is an *interest-rate cap*. Interest-rate caps are designed to provide insurance against the rate of interest on a floating-rate loan rising above a certain level. This level is known as the *cap rate*. When a cap on a loan and the loan itself are provided by the same financial institution, the cost of the options underlying the cap is often incorporated into the interest rate charged. When they are provided by different financial institutions, an up-front payment for the cap is likely to be required.

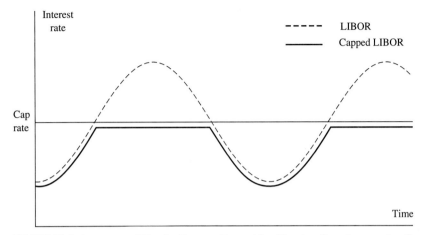

FIGURE 18.3 Borrower's Effective Interest Rate with a Floating-Rate Loan and an Interest-Rate Cap

A CAP AS A PORTFOLIO OF INTEREST-RATE OPTIONS

The operation of a cap is illustrated in Figure 18.3. A cap guarantees that the rate charged on a loan at any given time will be the lesser of the prevailing rate and the cap rate. Suppose that the rate on a loan, where the principal amount is $10 million, is reset every three months equal to three-month LIBOR, and that a financial institution has capped the rate at 10 percent per annum. (Since the payments are made quarterly, the cap rate is also expressed with quarterly compounding.)

To fulfill its obligations under the cap agreement, the financial institution must pay to the borrower at the end of each quarter (in millions of dollars)

$$0.25 \times 10 \times \max{(R - 0.1, 0)}$$

where R is the three-month LIBOR rate (expressed with quarterly compounding) at the beginning of the quarter. For example, when the three-month LIBOR rate at the beginning of the quarter is 11 percent per annum, the financial institution must pay $0.25 \times 10,000,000 \times 0.01 = \$25,000$ at the end of the quarter. When it is 9 percent per annum, the financial institution is not required to pay anything. This example is summarized in Table 18.1. The expression $\max(R - 0.1, 0)$ is the payoff from a call option on R. The cap can therefore be viewed as a portfolio of call options on R with the payoffs from the options occurring three months in arrears. The individual options comprising a cap are sometimes referred to as *caplets*.

In general, if the cap rate is R_X, the principal is L, and interest-reset dates are at times $\tau, 2\tau, \ldots, n\tau$ from the beginning of the life of the cap, the writer of the cap is required to make a payment at time $(k + 1)\tau$ given by

$$\tau L \max{(R_k - R_X, 0)} \qquad \textbf{(18.7)}$$

where R_k is the value at time $k\tau$ of the rate being capped. This is a call option on the rate observed at time $k\tau$ with the payoff occurring at time $(k + 1)\tau$. Caps are normally structured so that there is no payoff at time τ based on the rate at time zero. There are therefore potential payoffs from a cap at times $2\tau, 3\tau, \ldots, n\tau$.

TABLE 18.1 Use of an Interest-rate Cap

From the Trader's Desk
    A company entering into a five-year floating-rate loan agreement is concerned about possible increases in interest rates. The rate on the loan is three-month LIBOR and is currently set at 8 percent per annum. The company would like to buy protection against the rate rising above 10 percent per annum.

The Strategy
    The company buys from a financial institution a five-year interest-rate cap with a cap rate of 10 percent per annum. The financial institution guarantees that whenever the floating rate proves to be greater than 10 percent per annum, it will pay the difference between the floating rate and 10 percent per annum. The cap can be viewed as a portfolio of call options on the three-month rate.

FLOORS AND COLLARS

Interest-rate floors and interest-rate collars (which are sometimes called floor–ceiling agreements) are defined analogously to caps. A *floor* places a lower limit on the interest rate that will be charged. *Collars* specify both the upper and lower limits for the rate that will be charged. Analogously to an interest-rate cap, an interest-rate floor is a portfolio of put options on interest rates. It is often written by the borrower of floating-rate funds. The individual options comprising a floor are sometimes called *floorlets*. A collar is a combination of a long position in a cap and a short position in a floor. It is usually constructed so that the price of the cap equals the price of the floor. The net cost of the collar is then zero.
    There is a put–call parity relationship between the prices of caps and floors. This is

$$\text{Cap price} = \text{Floor price} + \text{Swap price}$$

In this relationship the cap and floor have the same strike price, R_X. The swap is an agreement to receive floating-rate funds and pay a fixed rate of R_X with no exchange of payments on the first reset date.[4] All three instruments have the same life and the same frequency of payments. This result can easily be seen to be true by noting that a long position in the cap combined with a short position in the floor provides the same cash flows as the swap.

VALUATION OF CAPS AND FLOORS

As shown in Equation 18.7, the caplet corresponding to the rate observed at time $k\tau$ provides a payoff at time $(k + 1)\tau$ of

$$\tau L \max (R_k - R_X, 0)$$

---

[4]Note that swaps are usually structured so that the τ-period rate at time zero determines an exchange of payments at time τ. As mentioned earlier, caps and floors are usually structured so that there is no payoff at time τ. This difference explains why we have to exclude the first exchange of payments on the swap.

If the standard deviation of $\ln R_k$ is $\sigma_k \sqrt{k\tau}$ so that σ_k is the volatility measure for the caplet, Equation 18.3 gives the value of this caplet as

$$\tau L e^{-r^*(k+1)\tau}[F_k N(d_1) - R_X N(d_2)] \qquad (18.8)$$

where

$$d_1 = \frac{\ln(F_k/R_X) + \sigma_k^2 k\tau/2}{\sigma_k \sqrt{k\tau}}$$

$$d_2 = \frac{\ln(F_k/R_X) - \sigma_k^2 k\tau/2}{\sigma_k \sqrt{k\tau}} = d_1 - \sigma_k \sqrt{k\tau}$$

and F_k is the forward rate for the period between time $k\tau$ and $(k+1)\tau$. The value of the corresponding floorlet is, from Equation 18.4,

$$\tau L e^{-r^*(k+1)\tau}[R_X N(-d_2) - F_k N(-d_1)] \qquad (18.9)$$

In these equations r^* is the continuously compounded zero rate for a maturity of $(k+1)\tau$. Both R_X and F_k are expressed with a compounding frequency of τ.

Example

Consider a contract that caps the interest rate on a $10,000 loan at 8 percent per annum (with quarterly compounding) for three months starting in one year. This is a caplet and could be one element of a cap. Suppose that the forward interest rate for a three-month period starting in one year is 7 percent per annum (with quarterly compounding), the current 15-month interest rate is 6.5 percent per annum (with continuous compounding), and the volatility measure for the three-month rate underlying the caplet is 20 percent per annum. In Equation 18.8 $F_k = 0.07$, $\tau = 0.25$, $L = 10,000$, $R_X = 0.08$, $r^* = 0.065$, $\sigma_k = 0.20$, and $k\tau = 1.0$. Also

$$d_1 = \frac{\ln 0.875 + 0.02}{0.20} = -0.5677$$

$$d_2 = d_1 - 0.20 = -0.7677$$

so that the caplet price is

$$0.25 \times 10,000 e^{-0.065 \times 1.25}[0.07 N(-0.5677) - 0.08 N(-0.7677)] = 5.19$$

or $5.19.

Each caplet must be valued separately using Equation 18.8. One approach is to use a different volatility for each caplet. The volatilities are then referred to as *forward forward volatilities*. An alternative approach is to use the same volatility for all the caplets comprising any particular cap but to vary this volatility according to the life of the cap. The volatilities used are then referred to as *flat volatilities*. The volatilities quoted by brokers are usually flat volatilities. However, many traders like to work with forward forward volatilities, because they allow them to identify underpriced and overpriced caplets. Options on Eurodollar futures are very similar to caplets, and the

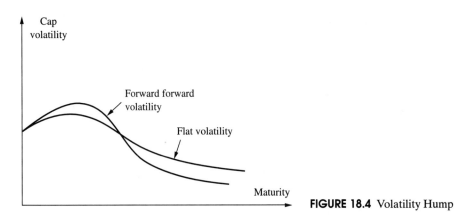

FIGURE 18.4 Volatility Hump

implied forward forward volatilities for caplets on three-month LIBOR are frequently compared with those calculated from the prices of Eurodollar futures options.

Figure 18.4 shows a typical pattern for a forward forward volatility and flat volatility as a function of maturity. (In the case of forward forward volatility, the maturity is the maturity of a caplet; in the case of flat volatility, it is the maturity of a cap.) The flat volatilities are akin to cumulative averages of the forward forward volatilities and therefore exhibit less variability. As indicated by Figure 18.4, a "hump" is usually observed in the volatilities at about the one- to two-year point. This hump is observed both when the volatilities are implied from option prices and when they are calculated from historical data. No really convincing explanation for its existence has been put forward.

European Swap Options

Swap options, or *swaptions,* are options on interest-rate swaps and are an increasingly popular type of interest-rate option. They give the holder the right to enter into a specified interest-rate swap at a certain time in the future. (The holder does not have to exercise this right.) Many large financial institutions that offer interest-rate swap contracts to their corporate clients are also prepared to sell them swaptions or buy swaptions from them.

As an example of how a swaption might be used, consider a company that knows that in six months it will enter into a five-year floating-rate loan agreement and that it will wish to swap the floating-interest payments for fixed-interest payments to convert the loan into a fixed-rate loan. (See chapter 6 for a discussion of how swaps can be used in this way.) At a cost the company could enter into a swaption giving it the right to receive six-month LIBOR and pay a certain fixed rate of interest (say, 12 percent per annum) for a five-year period starting in six months. If the fixed rate on a regular five-year swap in six months turns out to be less than 12 percent per annum, the company will choose not to exercise the swaption and will enter into a swap agreement in the usual way. However, if the fixed rate turns out to be greater than 12 percent per annum, the company will choose to exercise the swaption and will obtain a swap at more favorable terms than those available in the market. This example is summarized in Table 18.2.

TABLE 18.2   Use of a Swaption

From the Trader's Desk

A company knows that it will be entering into a five-year floating-rate loan agreement in six months and plans to swap the floating-interest payments for fixed-interest payments. It would like to ensure that the fixed-interest payments are no more than 12 percent per annum.

The Strategy

The company buys a swaption. The swaption gives it the right (but not the obligation) to exchange the floating-interest payments for fixed-interest payments of 12 percent per annum for a five-year period starting in six months. If the fixed rate on a regular five-year swap in six months' time turns out to be greater than 12 percent per annum, the company will exercise the swaption; under other circumstances, it will choose to negotiate a swap reflecting market rates of interest.

When used in the way just described, swaptions provide companies with a guarantee that the fixed rate of interest they will pay on a loan at some future time will not exceed some level. Swaptions are an alternative to forward swaps (sometimes called *deferred swaps*). Forward swaps involve no up-front cost but have the disadvantage that they obligate the company to enter into a swap agreement. With a swaption, the company is able to benefit from favorable interest-rate movements while acquiring protection from unfavorable interest-rate movements. The difference between a swaption and a forward swap is analogous to the difference between an option on foreign exchange and a forward contract on foreign exchange.

RELATION TO BOND OPTIONS

Recall from chapter 6 that an interest-rate swap can be regarded as an agreement to exchange a fixed-rate bond for a floating-rate bond. At the start of a swap, the value of the floating-rate bond always equals the principal amount of the swap. A swaption can therefore be regarded as an option to exchange a fixed-rate bond for the principal amount of the swap. If a swaption gives the holder the right to pay fixed and receive floating, it is a put option on the fixed-rate bond with strike price equal to the principal. If a swaption gives the holder the right to pay floating and receive fixed, it is a call option on the fixed-rate bond with a strike price equal to the principal.

VALUATION OF EUROPEAN SWAPTIONS

European swaptions are frequently valued by assuming that the swap rate at the maturity of the option is lognormal. Consider a swaption that gives the holder the right to pay a rate R_X and receive floating on a swap that will last n years starting in T years. We suppose that there are m payments per year under the swap and that the principal is L.

Assume that the swap rate at the maturity of the swap option is R. (Both R and R_X are expressed with a compounding frequency of m times per year.) By comparing the cash flows on a swap whose fixed rate is R with the cash flows on a swap whose fixed rate is R_X, we see that the payoff from the swaption consists of a series of cash flows equal to

$$\frac{L}{m} \max(R - R_X, 0)$$

The cash flows are received m times per year for the n years of the life of the swap; that is, they are received at times $T + \frac{1}{m}, T + \frac{2}{m}, \ldots, T + \frac{mn}{m}$, measured in years from today. Each cash flow is the payoff from a call option on R with strike price R_X.

Suppose that $t_i = T + \frac{i}{m}$. From Equation 18.3 the value of the cash flow received at time t_i is

$$\frac{L}{m} e^{-r_i t_i} [FN(d_1) - R_X N(d_2)]$$

where

$$d_1 = \frac{\ln(F/R_X) + \sigma^2 T/2}{\sigma \sqrt{T}}$$

$$d_2 = \frac{\ln(F/R_X) - \sigma^2 T/2}{\sigma \sqrt{T}} = d_1 - \sigma \sqrt{T}$$

F is the forward swap rate, and r_i is the continuously compounded zero-coupon interest-rate for a maturity of t_i.

The total value of the swaption is

$$\sum_{i=1}^{mn} \frac{L}{m} e^{-r_i t_i} [FN(d_1) - R_X N(d_2)]$$

If we define A as the value of a contract that pays \$1 at times t_i ($1 \le i \le mn$), the value of the swaption becomes

$$\frac{LA}{m} [FN(d_1) - R_X N(d_2)] \tag{18.10}$$

where

$$A = \sum_{i=1}^{mn} e^{-r_i t_i}$$

If the swaption gives the holder the right to receive a fixed rate of R_X instead of paying it, the payoff from the swaption is

$$\frac{L}{m} \max(R_X - R, 0)$$

This is a put option on R. As before, the payoffs are received at times t_i ($1 \le i \le mn$). Equation 18.4 gives the value of the swaption as

$$\frac{LA}{m} [R_X N(-d_2) - FN(-d_1)] \tag{18.11}$$

Example

Suppose that the LIBOR yield curve is flat at 6 percent per annum with continuous compounding. Consider a swaption that gives the holder the right to pay 6.2 percent in a three-year swap starting in five years. The volatility measure for the swap rate is 20 percent. Payments are made semiannually and the principal is $100. In this case

$$A = e^{-0.06 \times 5.5} + e^{-0.06 \times 6} + e^{-0.06 \times 6.5} + e^{-0.06 \times 7} + e^{-0.06 \times 7.5} + e^{-0.06 \times 8}$$
$$= 4.0071$$

A rate of 6 percent per annum with continuous compounding translates into 6.09 percent with semiannual compounding. It follows that in this example $F = 0.0609$, $R_X = 0.062$, $T = 5$, and $\sigma = 0.2$, so that

$$d_1 = \frac{\ln(0.0609/0.062) + 0.2^2 \times 5/2}{0.2\sqrt{5}} = 0.1836$$

$$d_2 = d_1 - 0.2\sqrt{5} = -0.2636$$

From Equation 18.10 the value of the swaption is

$$\frac{100 \times 4.0071}{2}[0.0609 \times N(0.1836) - 0.062 \times N(-0.2636)] = 2.07$$

or $2.07.

Term Structure Models

Most traders would like to value all interest-rate derivatives on a consistent basis. They could then assess the extent to which the risks in a cap portfolio can be offset by bond options or swaptions. The standard market models that have been presented for bond options, caps, and swap options are inconsistent. The European bond option model assumes that a bond price at some future time is lognormally distributed. The cap model assumes that an interest rate at some future time is lognormally distributed. The European swap option assumes that a swap rate at some future time is lognormally distributed. These cannot all be so at the same time.

Another problem with the standard market models is that it is difficult to extend them so they can be used to value other securities. For example, Black's model for valuing a European bond option cannot easily be extended to value American bond options. The valuation of American bond options requires the specification of the probability distribution of the underlying bond price at all times during the life of the option, not just at the end. As shown by Figure 18.2, it does not make sense to assume that bond prices are similar to stock prices and have constant volatilities.

A more sophisticated approach to valuing interest-rate derivative securities involves constructing a *term structure model*. This is a model that describes the probabilistic behavior of the term structure over time. Term structure models are more complicated than the models used to describe the movements of a stock price or currency.

This is because they are concerned with movements in a whole term structure—not with changes to a single variable. As time passes, the individual interest rates in the term structure change. In addition, the shape of the curve itself is likely to change.

It is beyond the scope of this book to provide a complete description of how yield curve models are constructed. In the rest of this section we will examine some of the key issues.

THE SHORT-TERM RATE

The short-term interest rate, r, is of central importance in the construction of yield curve models. It can be shown that if we specify a model describing the probabilistic behavior of the short-term interest rate and some information on individual risk preferences, then we have completely specified both the current term structure of interest rates and the yield curve model. (In other words, we have completely specified a probabilistic model for how the term structure changes over time.)

MEAN REVERSION

What sort of model is appropriate for r? We can think of r as having an average *drift,* or expected change, with volatility superimposed upon the drift. In practice, the drift in r seems to incorporate *mean reversion.* That is, the drift tends to pull interest rates back to some long-run average level. When the short-term interest rate is very high, r tends to have a negative drift; when the short-term interest rate is very low, r tends to have a positive drift. This is illustrated in Figure 18.5.

The effect of mean reversion is to make us more certain about long-term interest rates than short-term interest rates. The volatility of a spot interest rate therefore tends to be a decreasing function of its maturity. The ten-year spot interest rate tends to have a lower volatility than the five-year spot interest rate; the five-year spot interest rate tends to have a lower volatility than the one-year spot interest rate; and so on.

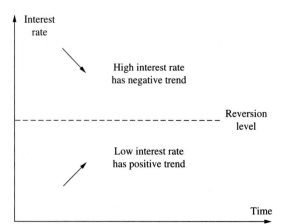

FIGURE 18.5 Mean Reversion

FITTING THE TERM STRUCTURE

Pioneering work in the development of yield curve models has been done by Vasicek, by Cox, Ingersoll, and Ross, and by Brennan and Schwartz. These authors propose models for the short-term interest rate that incorporate mean reversion and involve a number of parameters describing the degree of mean reversion, the reversion level, volatilities, and risk preferences. Typically the parameters are not functions of time and are estimated from data on the current term structure of interest rates and volatilities.

More recently researchers have developed ways of constructing models for *r* that are automatically consistent with the current term structure of interest rates. The first such model, proposed by Ho and Lee in 1986, had a flat volatility term structure. (In other words, all interest rates had the same variability.) More sophisticated models have been developed by Heath, Jarrow, and Morton, by Black, Derman, and Toy, by Black and Karasinski, by Hull and White, and by Jamshidian. Given the increasing popularity of over-the-counter interest-rate options, this area is likely to see a great deal of research in the future.

Summary

Interest-rate options arise in practice in many different ways. For example, options on Treasury bond futures, Treasury note futures, and Eurodollar futures are actively traded by exchanges. Many traded bonds include features that are options. The loans and deposit instruments offered by financial institutions often contain hidden options. Mortgage-backed securities contain embedded interest-rate options.

Black's model is the standard market model for valuing bond options, caps and floors, and swap options. In the case of bond options, the probability distribution of the underlying bond is assumed to be lognormal. In the case of caps and floors, the underlying interest rates are assumed to be lognormal. In the case of swap options, the underlying swap rate is assumed to be lognormal.

Term structure models provide a way of valuing more complicated interest-rate derivatives than those covered by Black's model. It can be shown that if there are no arbitrage opportunities open to investors, term structure models are defined by the behavior of the short-term interest rate together with some information on risk preferences. A number of models of the short-term interest rate have been proposed. For applied work the most useful are those that are designed to be automatically consistent with the current term structure of interest rates.

Suggestions for Further Reading

Amin, K., and A. Morton. "Implied Volatility Functions in Arbitrage-Free Term Structure Models," *Journal of Financial Economics* 35 (1994): 141–180.

Black, F. "Interest Rates as Options," *Journal of Finance* 50, no. 5 (1995): 1371–1376.

Black, F. "The Pricing of Commodity Contracts," *Journal of Financial Economics* 3 (1976): 167–179.

Black, F., E. Derman, and W. Toy. "A One-Factor Model of Interest Rates and Its Application to Treasury Bond Options," *Financial Analysts Journal* (January–February 1990): 33–39.

Black, F., and P. Karasinski. "Bond and Option Pricing When Short Rates Are Lognormal," *Financial Analysts Journal* (July–August 1991): 52–59.

Black, F., and M. Scholes. "The Pricing of Options and Corporate Liabilities," *Journal of Political Economy* 81 (May–June 1973): 637–659.

Brennan, M. J., and E. S. Schwartz. "An Equilibrium Model of Bond Pricing and a Test of Market Efficiency," *Journal of Financial and Quantitative Analysis* 17, no. 3 (September 1982): 301–329.

Burghardt, G., and B. Hoskins. "A Question of Bias," *RISK* (March 1995).

Carverhill, A. "When Is the Short Rate Markovian?" *Mathematical Finance* 4 (1994): 305–312.

Cheyette, O. "Term Structure Dynamics and Mortgage Valuation," *Journal of Fixed Income* (March 1992): 28–41.

Courtadon, G. "The Pricing of Options on Default-Free Bonds," *Journal of Financial and Quantitative Analysis* 17 (March 1982): 75–100.

Cox, J. C., J. E. Ingersoll, and S. A. Ross. "A Theory of the Term Structure of Interest Rates," *Econometrica* 53 (1985): 385–407.

Heath, D., R. Jarrow, and A. Morton. "Bond Pricing and the Term Structure of Interest Rates: A Discrete Time Approximation," *Journal of Financial and Quantitative Analysis* 25, no. 4 (December 1990): 419–440.

Heath, D., R. Jarrow, and A. Morton. "Bond Pricing and the Term Structure of the Interest Rates: A New Methodology," *Econometrica* 60 (1992): 77–105.

Heath, D., R. Jarrow, A. Morton, and M. Spindel. "Easier Done Than Said," *RISK* (May 1993): 77–80.

Ho, T. S. Y., and S.-B. Lee. "Term Structure Movements and Pricing Interest Rate Contingent Claims," *Journal of Finance* 41 (December 1986): 1011–1029.

Hull, J. C. *Options, Futures, and Other Derivatives.* 3d ed. Englewood Cliffs, NJ: Prentice Hall, 1997.

Hull, J. C., and A. White. "Bond Option Pricing Based on a Model for the Evolution of Bond Prices," *Advances in Futures and Options Research* 6 (1993): 1–13.

Hull, J. C., and A. White. "Branching Out," *RISK* (January 1994): 34–37.

Hull, J. C., and A. White. "In the Common Interest," *RISK* (March 1992): 64–68.

Hull, J. C., and A. White. "Numerical Procedures for Implementing Term Structure Models I: Single-Factor Models,"*Journal of Derivatives* 2, no. 1 (Fall 1994): 7–16.

Hull, J. C., and A. White. "Numerical Procedures for Implementing Term Structure Models II: Two-Factor Models,"*Journal of Derivatives* 2, no. 2 (Winter 1994): 37–48.

Hull, J. C., and A. White. "One-Factor Interest Rate Models and the Valuation of Interest Rate Derivative Securities," *Journal of Financial and Quantitative Analysis* 28 (June 1993): 235–254.

Hull, J. C., and A. White. "Pricing Interest Rate Derivative Securities," *Review of Financial Studies* 3, no. 4 (1990): 573–592.

Hull, J. C., and A. White. "Using Hull–White Interest Rate Trees," *Journal of Derivatives* (Spring 1996): 26–36.

Hull, J. C., and A. White. "Valuing Derivative Securities Using the Explicit Finite Difference Method," *Journal of Financial and Quantitative Analysis* 25 (March 1990): 87–100.

Jamshidian, F. "An Exact Bond Option Pricing Formula," *Journal of Finance* 44 (March 1989): 205–209.

Jarrow, R. A. *Modeling Fixed Income Securities and Interest Rate Options.* New York: McGraw-Hill, 1995.

Jeffrey, A. "Single Factor Heath-Jarrow-Morton Term Structure Models Based on Markov Spot Interest Rate Dynamics," *Journal of Financial and Quantitative Analysis* 30 (1995): 619–642.

Li, A., P. Ritchken, and L. Sankarasubramanian. "Lattice Models for Pricing American Interest Rate Claims," *Journal of Finance* 50, no. 2 (June 1995): 719–737.

Longstaff, F. A., and E. S. Schwartz. "Interest Rate Volatility and the Term Structure: A Two-Factor General Equilibrium Model," *Journal of Finance* 47, no. 4 (September 1992): 1259–1282.

Rendleman, R., and B. Bartter. "The Pricing of Options on Debt Securities," *Journal of Financial and Quantitative Analysis* 15 (March 1980): 11–24.

Riccardo, R., *Interest Rate Option Models.* New York: John Wiley & Sons, 1996.

Ritchken, P., and L. Sankarasubramanian. "Volatility Structures of Forward Rates and the Dynamics of the Term Structure," *Mathematical Finance* 5 (1995): 55–72.

Schaefer, S. M., and E. S. Schwartz. "Time-Dependent Variance and the Pricing of Bond Options," *Journal of Finance* 42 (December 1987): 1113–1128.

Vasicek, O. A. "An Equilibrium Characterization of the Term Structure," *Journal of Financial Economics* 5 (1977): 177–188.

Quiz

1. A company caps three-month LIBOR at 10 percent per annum. The principal amount is $20 million. On a reset date three-month LIBOR is 12 percent per annum. What payment would this lead to under the cap? When would the payment be made?

2. Explain what mortgage-backed securities are. Explain why mortgage-backed securities are more risky than regular fixed-income instruments such as government bonds.

3. Explain why a swaption can be regarded as a type of bond option.

4. Use Black's model to value a one-year European put option on a 10-year bond. Assume that the current value of the bond is $125, the strike price is $110, the one-year interest rate is 10 percent per annum, the bond's price volatility measure is 8 percent per annum, and the present value of the coupons that will be paid during the life of the option is $10.

5. Suppose that the LIBOR yield curve is flat at 8 percent with annual compounding. A swaption gives the holder the right to receive 7.6 percent in a five-year swap starting in four years. Payments are made annually. The volatility measure for the swap rate is 25 percent per annum and the principal is $1 million. Use Black's model to price the swaption.

6. Calculate the price of an option that caps the three-month rate starting in 18 months' time at 13 percent (quoted with quarterly compounding) on a principal amount of $1,000. The relevant forward interest rate for the period in question is 12 percent per annum (quoted with quarterly compounding), the 18-month risk-free interest rate (continuously compounded) is 11.5 percent per annum, and the volatility of the forward rate is 12 percent per annum.

7. What are the advantages of yield curve models over the Black and Black–Scholes models for valuing caps, bond options, and other derivatives?

Questions and Problems

18.1. Assume that the volatility of a forward rate increases with the passage of time. Suppose that an implied volatility for a nine-month Eurodollar futures option is calculated using Black's model and that this volatility is then used to value an 18-month Eurodollar futures option. Would you expect the resultant price to be too high or too low? Explain.

18.2. Consider an eight-month European put option on a Treasury bond that currently has 14.25 years to maturity. The bond principal is $1,000. The current cash bond price is $910, the exercise price is $900, and the volatility of the forward bond price is 10 percent per annum. A coupon of $35 will be paid by the bond in three months. The risk-free interest rate is 8 percent for all maturities up to one year. Use Black's model to determine the price of the option. Consider both the case where the strike price corresponds to the cash price of the bond and the case where it corresponds to the quoted price. Confirm that the DerivaGem software gives the same answers as those you calculate.

18.3. Calculate the price of a cap on the three-month LIBOR rate in nine months' time for a principal amount of $1,000. Use Black's model and the following information:

> Quoted nine-month Eurodollar futures price = 92
>
> Interest-rate volatility implied by a nine-month Eurodollar option = 15 percent per annum
>
> Current 12-month interest rate with continuous compounding = 7.5 percent per annum
>
> Cap rate = 8 percent per annum

18.4. Calculate the value of a four-year European call option on a five-year bond using Black's model. The five-year bond price is $105, the price of a four-year bond with the same coupon is $102, the strike price is $100, the four-year risk-free interest rate is 10 percent per annum (continuously compounded), and the volatility of the forward price of the one-year bond whose life starts in four years is 2 percent per annum.

18.5. Does a European option on a 90-day Treasury bill always increase in value as the time to maturity increases, with all else being held constant? Explain your answer.

18.6. A corporation knows that it will have $5 million to invest for 90 days in three months and wishes to guarantee that a certain interest rate will be obtained. What position in exchange-traded interest-rate options provides a hedge against interest-rate moves?

18.7. Explain carefully how you would use (a) forward forward volatilities and (b) flat volatilities to value a five-year cap.

18.8. What other instrument is the same as a five-year zero-cost collar in which the strike price of the cap equals the strike price of the floor? What does the common strike price equal?

18.9. Derive a put–call parity relationship for European bond options.

18.10. Derive a put–call parity relationship for European swap options.

18.11. Explain why there is an arbitrage opportunity if the implied Black (flat) volatility for a cap is different from that for a floor.

18.12. Does the lognormal bond price model permit bond yields to become negative? Explain your answer.

18.13. Use the DerivaGem software to value a five-year collar in which the maximum and minimum interest rates on a LIBOR-based loan (with quarterly resets) are 5 percent and 7 percent, respectively. The LIBOR zero curve (continuously compounded) is currently flat at 6 percent. Use a flat volatility of 20 percent. Assume that the principal is $100.

18.14. Use the DerivaGem software to value a European swap option that gives you the right in two years to enter into a five-year swap in which you pay a fixed rate of 6 percent and receive floating. Cash flows are exchanged semiannually on the swap. The one-year, two-year, five-year, and ten-year zero-coupon interest rates (continuously compounded) are 5 percent, 6 percent, 6.5 percent, and 7 percent, respectively. Assume a principal of $100 and a volatility of 15 percent per annum.

Answers to Quiz Questions

Chapter 1

1. A trader who enters into a long futures position is agreeing to *buy* the underlying asset for a certain price at a certain time in the future. A trader who enters into a short futures position is agreeing to *sell* the underlying asset for a certain price at a certain time in the future.

2. A company is *hedging* when it has an exposure to the price of an asset and takes a position in futures or options markets to offset the exposure. In a *speculation* the company has no exposure to offset. It is betting on the future movements in the price of the asset. *Arbitrage* involves taking a position in two or more different markets to lock in a profit.

3. In (a) the investor is obligated to buy the asset for $50. (The investor does not have a choice.) In (b) the investor has the option to buy the asset for $50. (The investor does not have to exercise the option.)

4. a. The investor is obligated to sell for 50 cents per pound something that is worth 48.20 cents per pound. The gain is ($0.5000 − $0.4820) × 50,000 = $900.
   b. The investor is obligated to sell for 50 cents per pound something that is worth 51.30 cents per pound. The loss is ($0.5130 − $0.5000) × 50,000 = $650.

5. You have sold a put option. You have agreed to buy 100 IBM shares for $40 per share if the party on the other side of the contract chooses to exercise the right to sell for this price. The option will be exercised only when the price of IBM is below $40. Suppose, for example, that the counterparty exercises when the price is $30. You have to buy at $40 shares that are worth $30; you lose $10 per share, or $1,000 in total. If the counterparty exercises when the price is $20, you lose $20 per share, or $2,000 in total. The worst that can happen is that the price of IBM declines to zero during the three-month period. This highly unlikely event would cost you $4,000. In return for the possible future losses, you receive the price of the option from the purchaser.

6. One strategy is to buy 200 shares. Another is to buy 2,000 options (20 contracts). If the share price does well, the second strategy will give rise to greater gains. For example, if the share price goes up to $40, you gain [2,000 × ($40 − $30)] − $5,800 = $14,200 from the second strategy and only 200 × ($40 − $29) = $2,200 from the first strategy. However, if the share price does badly, the second strategy yields greater losses. For example, if the share price goes down to $25, the first strategy leads to a loss of 200 × ($29 − $25) = $800, whereas the second strategy leads to a loss of the whole $5,800 investment.

7. You should buy 50 put option contracts with a strike price of $25 and an expiration date in four months. If at the end of four months the stock price proves to be worth less than $25, you can exercise the options and sell the shares for $25 each.

417

Chapter 2

1. The *open interest* of a futures contract at a particular time is the total number of long positions outstanding. (Equivalently, it is the total number of short positions outstanding.) The *trading volume* during a certain period of time is the number of contracts traded during this period.

2. A *commission broker* trades on behalf of a client and charges a commission. A *local* trades on his or her own behalf.

3. There will be a margin call when $1,000 has been lost from the margin account. This will occur when the price of silver increases by 1,000/5,000 = $0.20. The price of silver must therefore rise to $5.40 per ounce for there to be a margin call. If the margin call is not met, your broker closes out your position.

4. The total profit is ($20.50 − $18.30) × 1,000 = $2,200. Of this ($19.10 − $18.30) × 1,000 = $800 is realized on a day-by-day basis between September 1996 and December 31, 1996. A further ($20.50 − $19.10) × 1,000 = $1,400 is realized on a day-by-day basis between January 1, 1997 and March 1997. A hedger would be taxed on the whole profit of $2,200 in 1997. A speculator would be taxed on $800 in 1996 and $1,400 in 1997.

5. A *stop order* to sell at $2 is an order to sell at the best available price once a price of $2 or less is reached. It could be used to limit the losses from an existing long position. A *limit order* to sell at $2 is an order to sell at a price of $2 or more. It could be used to instruct a broker that a short position should be taken, providing it can be done at a price more favorable than $2.

6. The margin account administered by the clearinghouse is marked to market daily, and the clearinghouse member is required to bring the account back up to the prescribed level daily. The margin account administered by the broker is also marked to market daily. However, the account does not have to be brought up to the initial margin level on a daily basis. It has to be brought up to the initial margin level when the balance in the account falls below the maintenance margin level. The maintenance margin is about 75 percent of the initial margin.

7. In futures markets prices are quoted as the number of U.S. dollars per unit of foreign currency. Spot and forward rates are quoted in this way for British currency. For most other currencies, spot and forward rates are quoted as the number of units of foreign currency per U.S. dollar.

Chapter 3

1. a. The rate with continuous compounding is

$$4 \ln \left(1 + \frac{0.14}{4}\right) = 0.1376$$

   or 13.76 percent per annum.

   b. The rate with annual compounding is

$$\left(1 + \frac{0.14}{4}\right)^4 - 1 = 0.1475$$

   or 14.75 percent per annum.

2. The investor's broker borrows the shares from another client's account and sells them in the usual way. To close out the position, the investor must purchase the shares. The broker then replaces them in the account of the client from whom they were borrowed. The party with the short position must remit to the broker dividends and other income paid on the shares. The broker transfers these funds to the account of the client from whom the shares were borrowed. Occasionally the broker runs out of places from which to borrow the shares. The investor is then short-squeezed and has to close out the position immediately.

3. The forward price is

$$30e^{0.12 \times 0.5} = \$31.86$$

4. The futures price is

$$350e^{(0.08 - 0.04) \times 0.3333} = \$354.7$$

5. Gold is an investment asset. If the futures price is too high, investors will find it profitable to increase their holdings of gold and short futures contracts. If the futures price is too low, they will find it profitable to decrease their holdings of gold and go long in the futures market. Copper is a consumption asset. If the futures price is too high, a strategy of buy copper and short futures works. However, because investors do not in general hold the asset, the strategy of sell copper and buy futures is not available. There is therefore an upper bound but no lower bound to the futures price.

6. *Convenience yield* measures the extent to which there are benefits obtained from ownership of the physical asset that are not obtained by owners of long futures contracts. The *cost of carry* is the interest cost plus storage cost less the income earned. The futures price, F, and spot price, S, are related by

$$F = Se^{(c - y)T}$$

where c is the cost of carry, y is the convenience yield, and T is the time to maturity of the futures contract.

7. The futures price of a stock index is always less than the expected future value of the index. This follows from the fact that the index has positive systematic risk. For an alternative argument, let μ be the expected return required by investors on the index so that $E(S_T) = Se^{(\mu - q)T}$. Because $\mu > r$ and $F = Se^{(r - q)T}$, it follows that $E(S_T) > F$.

Chapter 4

1. A *short hedge* is appropriate when a company owns an asset and expects to sell that asset in the future. It can also be used when the company does not currently own the asset but expects to do so at some time in the future. A *long hedge* is appropriate when a company knows it will have to purchase an asset in the future. It can also be used to offset the risk from an existing short position.

2. *Basis risk* arises from the hedger's uncertainty as to the difference between the spot price and futures price at the expiration of the hedge.

3. A *perfect hedge* is one that completely eliminates the hedger's risk. A perfect hedge does not always lead to a better outcome than an imperfect hedge. It just leads to a more

certain outcome. Consider a company that hedges its exposure to the price of an asset. Suppose the asset's price movements prove to be favorable to the company. A perfect hedge totally neutralizes the company's gain from these favorable price movements. An imperfect hedge, which only partially neutralizes the gains, might well work out better.

4. A minimum variance hedge leads to no hedging at all when the coefficient of correlation between the futures price and the price of the asset being hedged is zero.

5. a. If the company's competitors are not hedging, the treasurer might feel that the company will experience less risk if it does not hedge.
   b. The treasurer might feel that the company's shareholders have diversified the risk away.
   c. If there is a loss on the hedge and a gain from the company's exposure to the underlying asset, the treasurer might feel that he or she will have difficulty justifying the hedging to other executives within the organization.

6. The optimal hedge ratio is

$$0.8 \times \frac{0.65}{0.81} = 0.642$$

This means that the size of the futures position should be 64.2 percent of the size of the company's exposure in a three-month hedge.

7. The formula for the number of contracts that should be shorted gives

$$1.2 \times \frac{10,000,000}{270 \times 500} = 88.9$$

Rounding to the nearest whole number, 89 contracts should be shorted. To reduce the beta to 0.6, half of this position, or a short position in 45 contracts, is required.

Chapter 5

1. Forward rates (percent per annum with continuous compounding) are

   Year 2:   7.0
   Year 3:   6.6
   Year 4:   6.4
   Year 5:   6.5

2. When the term structure is upward sloping, $c > a > b$. When it is downward sloping, $b > a > c$.

3. Suppose the bond has a face value of $100. Its price is obtained by discounting the cash flows at 10.4 percent. The price is

$$\frac{4}{1.052} + \frac{4}{10.52^2} + \frac{104}{1.052^3} = 96.74$$

If the 18-month spot rate is R, we must have

$$\frac{4}{1.05} + \frac{4}{1.05^2} + \frac{104}{(1 + R/2)^3} = 96.74$$

which gives $R = 10.42$ percent.

4. There are 89 days between October 12 and January 9. The cash price of the bond is obtained by adding the accrued interest to the quoted price. It is

$$102.21875 + \frac{89}{182} \times 6 = \$105.15$$

5. The cash price of the Treasury bill is

$$100 - \frac{1}{4} \times 10 = \$97.50$$

The annualized continuously compounded return is

$$\frac{365}{90} \ln \frac{100}{97.5} = 10.27\%$$

6. A duration-based hedging scheme assumes that term structure movements are always parallel. In other words, it assumes that interest rates of all maturities always change by the same amount in a given period of time.

7. The value of a contract is $108.46875 \times 1,000 = \$108,468.75$. The number of contracts that should be shorted is

$$\frac{6,000,000}{108,468.75} \times \frac{8.2}{7.6} = 59.7$$

Rounding to the nearest whole number, 60 contracts should be shorted.

Chapter 6

1. A has an apparent comparative advantage in fixed-rate markets but wants to borrow floating. B has an apparent comparative advantage in floating-rate markets but wants to borrow fixed. This provides the basis for the swap. There is a 1.4 percent per annum differential between the fixed rates offered to the two companies and a 0.5 percent per annum differential between the floating rates offered to the two companies. The total gain to all parties from the swap is therefore $1.4 - 0.5 = 0.9$ percent per annum. Because the bank gets 0.1 percent per annum of this gain, the swap should make each of A and B 0.4 percent per annum better off. This means that it should lead to A borrowing at LIBOR − 0.3 percent and to B borrowing at 13 percent. The appropriate arrangement is therefore as shown in the following diagram.

Swap for Quiz 1 in Chapter 6

2. X has a comparative advantage in yen markets but wants to borrow dollars. Y has a comparative advantage in dollar markets but wants to borrow yen. This provides the basis for the swap. There is a 1.5 percent per annum differential between the yen rates and a 0.4 percent per annum differential between the dollar rates. The total gain to all

parties from the swap is therefore $1.5 - 0.4 = 1.1$ percent per annum. The bank requires 0.5 percent per annum, leaving 0.3 percent per annum for each of X and Y. The swap should lead to X borrowing dollars at $9.6 - 0.3 = 9.3$ percent per annum and to Y borrowing yen at $6.5 - 0.3 = 6.2$ percent per annum. The appropriate arrangement is therefore as shown in the following diagram. All foreign exchange risk is borne by the bank.

Swap for Quiz 2 in Chapter 6

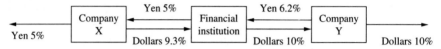

3. In four months $6 million will be received and $4.8 million will be paid. (We ignore the 360-versus-365-day year issue.) In ten months $6 million will be received and the LIBOR rate prevailing in four months' time will be paid. The value of the fixed-rate bond underlying the swap is

$$6e^{-0.3333 \times 0.1} + 106e^{-0.8333 \times 0.1} = \$103.33 \text{ million}$$

The value of the floating-rate bond underlying the swap is

$$(100 + 4.8)e^{-0.3333 \times 0.1} = \$101.36 \text{ million}$$

The value of the swap to the party paying floating is $103.33 - \$101.36 = \$1.97$ million. The value of the swap to the party paying fixed is $-\$1.97$ million. These results can also be derived by decomposing the swap into forward contracts. Consider the party paying floating. The first forward contract involves paying $4.8 million and receiving $6 million in four months. It has a value of $1.2e^{-0.3333 \times 0.1} = \$1.16$ million. To value the second forward contract, we note that the forward interest rate is 10 percent per annum with continuous compounding, or 10.254 percent per annum with semiannual compounding. The value of the forward contract is

$$100 \times (0.12 \times 0.5 - 0.10254 \times 0.5)e^{-0.833 \times 0.1} = \$0.80 \text{ million}$$

The total value of the forward contract is therefore $1.16 + \$0.80 = \$1.96$ million.

4. The term *warehousing swaps* refers to the situation where a financial institution does not enter into two offsetting swaps simultaneously. It enters into one of the swaps and hedges its risk until it can enter into a roughly offsetting swap.

5. The swap involves exchanging the sterling interest of $20 \times 0.14 = 2.8$ million for the dollar interest of $30 \times 0.1 = \$3$ million. The principal amounts are also exchanged at the end of the life of the swap. The value of the sterling bond underlying the swap is

$$\frac{2.8}{(1.11)^{1/4}} + \frac{22.8}{(1.11)^{5/4}} = 22.74 \text{ million}$$

The value of the dollar bond underlying the swap is

$$\frac{3}{(1.08)^{1/4}} + \frac{33}{(1.08)^{5/4}} = \$32.92 \text{ million}$$

The value of the swap to the party paying sterling is therefore

$$32.92 - (22.74 \times 1.65) = -\$4.60 \text{ million}$$

The value of the swap to the party paying dollars is $+\$4.60$ million. The results can also be obtained by viewing the swap as a portfolio of forward contracts. The continuously compounded interest rates in sterling and dollars are 10.43 percent per annum and 7.70 percent per annum. The 3-month and 15-month forward exchange rates are $1.65e^{-0.25 \times 0.0273} = 1.6388$ and $1.65e^{-1.25 \times 0.0273} = 1.5946$. The values of the two forward contracts corresponding to the exchange of interest for the party paying sterling are therefore

$$(3 - 2.8 \times 1.6388)e^{-0.077 \times 0.25} = -\$1.56 \text{ million}$$
$$(3 - 2.8 \times 1.5946)e^{-0.077 \times 1.25} = -\$1.33 \text{ million}$$

The value of the forward contract corresponding to the exchange of principals is

$$(30 - 20 \times 1.5946)e^{-0.077 \times 1.25} = -\$1.72 \text{ million}$$

The total value of the swap is $-\$1.56 - \$1.33 - \$1.72 = -\$4.61$ million.

6. Credit risk arises from the possibility of a default by the counterparty. Market risk arises from movements in market variables such as interest rates and exchange rates. Market risks can be hedged; credit risks cannot easily be hedged.

7. At the start of the swap, both contracts have a value of approximately zero. As time passes it is likely that the swap values will change, so that one swap has a positive value to the bank and the other has a negative value to the bank. If the counterparty on the other side of the positive-value swap defaults, the bank still has to honor its contract with the other counterparty. It loses an amount equal to the positive value of the swap.

Chapter 7

1. The investor makes a profit if the price of the stock on the expiration date is less than $37. In these circumstances the gain from exercising the option is greater than $3. The option will be exercised if the stock price is less than $40 at the maturity of the option. The variation of the investor's profit with the stock price is as shown in the following diagram.

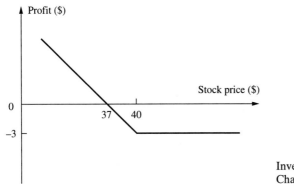

Investor's Profit in Quiz 1 in Chapter 7

2. The investor makes a profit if the price of the stock is below $54 on the expiration date. If the stock price is below $50, the option will not be exercised and the investor makes a profit of $4. If the stock price is between $50 and $54, the option is exercised and the investor makes a profit between $0 and $4. The variation of the investor's profit with the stock price is as shown in the following diagram.

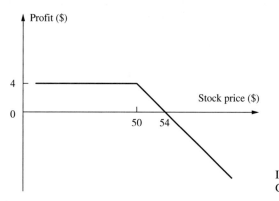

Investor's Profit in Quiz 2 in Chapter 7

3. The payoff to the investor is

$$\max(S_T - X, 0) - \max(X - S_T, 0)$$

This is $S_T - X$ in all circumstances. The investor's position is a forward contract with delivery price X.

4. When an investor buys an option, cash must be paid up front. There is no possibility of future liabilities and therefore no need for a margin account. When an investor sells an option, there are potential future liabilities. To protect against the risk of a default, margins are required.

5. On April 1 options trade with expiration months of April, May, August, and November. On May 30 options trade with expiration months of June, July, August, and November.

6. The strike price is reduced to $20 and the option gives the holder the right to purchase three times as many shares.

7. In the market maker/order book official system, an individual separate from the market maker keeps a record of limit orders and makes information on these orders available to traders. In the specialist system, a single individual acts as market maker and keeps a record of limit orders. Information on limit orders is not made available to other traders.

Chapter 8

1. The six factors affecting stock option prices are the stock price, strike price, risk-free interest rate, volatility, time to maturity, and dividends.

2. The lower bound is

$$28 - 25e^{-0.08 \times 0.3333} = \$3.66$$

3. The lower bound is

$$15e^{-0.06 \times 0.08333} - 12 = \$2.93$$

4. Delaying exercise delays the payment of the strike price. This means that the option holder is able to earn interest on the strike price for a longer period of time. Delaying exercise also provides insurance against the stock price falling below the strike price by the expiration date. Assume that the option holder has an amount of cash X and that interest rates are zero. Exercising early means that the option holder's position will be worth S_T at expiration. Delaying exercise means that it will be worth $\max(X, S_T)$ at expiration.

5. An American put when held in conjunction with the underlying stock provides insurance. It guarantees that the stock can be sold for the strike price, X. If the put is exercised early, the insurance ceases. However, the option holder receives the strike price immediately and is able to earn interest on it between the time of the early exercise and the expiration date.

6. If the call is worth $3, put–call parity shows that the put should be worth

$$3 + 20e^{-0.1 \times 0.25} + e^{-0.1 \times 0.08333} - 19 = \$4.50$$

This is greater than $3. The put is therefore undervalued relative to the call. The correct arbitrage strategy is to buy the put, buy the stock, and short the call.

7. When early exercise is not possible, we can argue that two portfolios that are worth the same at time T must be worth the same at earlier times. When early exercise is possible, the argument falls down. Suppose that $P + S > C + Xe^{-rT}$. This situation does not lead to an arbitrage opportunity. If we buy the call, short the put, and short the stock, we cannot be sure of the result, because we do not know when the put will be exercised.

Chapter 9

1. A protective put consists of a long position in a put option combined with a long position in the underlying shares. It is equivalent to a long position in a call option plus a certain amount of cash. This follows from put–call parity:

$$p + S = c + Xe^{-rT} + D$$

2. A bear spread can be created using two call options with the same maturity and different strike prices. The investor shorts the call option with the lower strike price and buys the call option with the higher strike price. A bear spread can also be created using two put options with the same maturity and different strike prices. In this case the investor sells the put option with the lower strike price and buys the put option with the higher strike price.

3. A butterfly spread involves a position in options with three different strike prices (X_1, X_2, and X_3). A butterfly spread should be purchased when the investor considers that the price of the underlying stock is likely to stay close to the central strike price, X_2.

4. An investor can create a butterfly spread by buying call options with strike prices of $15 and $20, and selling two call options with strike prices of $17\frac{1}{2}$. The initial investment is $4 + \frac{1}{2} - 2 \times 2 = \$\frac{1}{2}$. The following table shows the variation of profit with the final

stock price:

Stock Price (S_T)	Profit
$S_T < 15$	$-\frac{1}{2}$
$15 < S_T < 17\frac{1}{2}$	$(S_T - 15) - \frac{1}{2}$
$17\frac{1}{2} < S_T < 20$	$20 - S_T - \frac{1}{2}$
$S_T > 20$	$-\frac{1}{2}$

5. A reverse calendar spread is created by buying a short-maturity option and selling a long-maturity option, both with the same strike price.

6. Both a straddle and a strangle are created by combining a call and a put. In a straddle the two have the same strike price and expiration date. In a strangle they have different strike prices and the same expiration date.

7. A strangle is created by buying both options. The pattern of profits is as follows:

Stock Price (S_T)	Profit
$S_T < 45$	$(45 - S_T) - 5$
$45 < S_T < 50$	-5
$S_T > 50$	$(S_T - 50) - 5$

Chapter 10

1. Consider a portfolio consisting of

-1:   call option
$+\Delta$:   shares

If the stock price rises to $42, the portfolio is worth $42\Delta - 3$. If the stock price falls to $38, it is worth 38Δ. These are the same when

$$42\Delta - 3 = 38\Delta$$

or $\Delta = 0.75$. The value of the portfolio in one month is 28.5 for both stock prices. Its value today must be the present value of 28.5, or $28.5e^{-0.08 \times 0.08333} = 28.31$. This means that

$$-f + 40\Delta = 28.31$$

where f is the call price. Since $\Delta = 0.75$, the call price is $40 \times 0.75 - 28.31 = \$1.69$. As an alternative approach, we can calculate the probability, p, of an up movement in a risk-neutral world. This must satisfy:

$$42p + 38(1 - p) = 40e^{0.08 \times 0.08333}$$

so that

$$4p = 40e^{0.08 \times 0.08333} - 38$$

or $p = 0.5669$. The value of the option is then its expected payoff discounted at the risk-free rate:

$$[3 \times 0.5669 + 0 \times 0.4331]e^{-0.08 \times 0.08333} = 1.69$$

or $1.69. This agrees with the previous calculation.

2. In the no-arbitrage approach, we set up a riskless portfolio consisting of a position in the option and a position in the stock. By setting the return on the portfolio equal to the risk-free interest rate, we are able to value the option. When we use risk-neutral valuation, we first choose probabilities for the branches of the tree so that the expected return on the stock equals the risk-free interest rate. We then value the option by calculating its expected payoff and discounting this expected payoff at the risk-free interest rate.

3. The delta of a stock option measures the sensitivity of the option price to the price of the stock when small changes are considered. Specifically, it is the ratio of the change in the price of the stock option to the change in the price of the underlying stock.

4. Consider a portfolio consisting of

$$-1: \quad \text{put option}$$
$$+\Delta: \quad \text{shares}$$

If the stock price rises to $55, the portfolio is worth 55Δ. If the stock price falls to $45, it is worth $45\Delta - 5$. These are the same when

$$45\Delta - 5 = 55\Delta$$

or $\Delta = -0.50$. The value of the portfolio in one month is -27.5 for both stock prices. Its value today must be the present value of -27.5, or $-27.5e^{-0.1 \times 0.5} = -26.16$. This means that

$$-p + 50\Delta = -26.16$$

where p is the put price. Since $\Delta = -0.50$, the put price is $1.16. As an alternative approach we can calculate the probability, π, of an up movement in a risk-neutral world. This must satisfy:

$$55\pi + 45(1 - \pi) = 50e^{0.1 \times 0.5}$$

so that

$$10\pi = 50e^{0.1 \times 0.5} - 45$$

or $\pi = 0.7564$. The value of the option is then its expected payoff discounted at the risk-free rate:

$$[0 \times 0.7564 + 5 \times 0.2436]e^{-0.1 \times 0.5} = 1.16$$

or $1.16. This agrees with the previous calculation.

5. In this case $u = 1.10$, $d = 0.90$, and $r = 0.08$, so that

$$p = \frac{e^{0.08 \times 0.5} - 0.90}{1.10 - 0.90} = 0.7041$$

The tree for stock price movements is shown in the following diagram. We can work back from the end of the tree to the beginning, as indicated in the diagram, to give the value of the option as $9.61. The option value can also be calculated directly from Equation 10.8:

$$[0.7041^2 \times 21 + 2 \times 0.7041 \times 0.2959 \times 0 + 0.2959^2 \times 0]e^{-0.08} = 9.61$$

or $9.61.

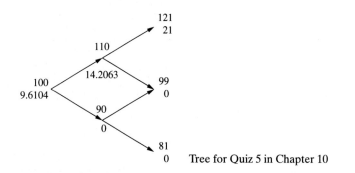

Tree for Quiz 5 in Chapter 10

6. The following diagram shows how we can value the put option using the same tree as in Quiz 5. The value of the option is $1.92. The option value can also be calculated directly from Equation 10.8:

$$e^{-2 \times 0.5 \times 0.08}[0.7041^2 \times 0 + 2 \times 0.7041 \times 0.2959 \times 1 + 0.2959^2 \times 19] = 1.92$$

or $1.92. The stock price plus the put price is $100 + 1.92 = \$101.92$. The present value of the strike price plus the call price is $100e^{-0.08} + 9.61 = \$101.92$. These are the same, verifying that put–call parity holds.

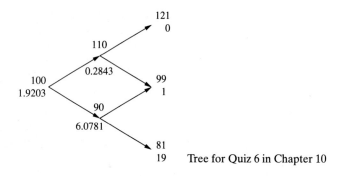

Tree for Quiz 6 in Chapter 10

7. The riskless portfolio consists of a short position in the option and a long position in Δ shares. Since Δ changes during the life of the option, this riskless portfolio must also change.

Chapter 11

1. The Black–Scholes option pricing model assumes that the probability distribution of the stock price in one year (or at any other future time) is lognormal. It also assumes that the continuously compounded rate of return on the stock is normally distributed.
2. The standard deviation of the proportional price change in time Δt is $\sigma \sqrt{\Delta t}$, where σ is the volatility. In this problem $\sigma = 0.3$ and, assuming 250 trading days in one year, $\Delta t = 1/250 = 0.004$, so that $\sigma \sqrt{\Delta t} = 0.3 \sqrt{0.004} = 0.019$ or 1.9 percent.
3. Assuming that the expected return from the stock is the risk-free rate, we calculate the expected payoff from the option. We then discount this payoff from the end of the life of the option to the beginning at the risk-free interest rate.
4. In this case $S = 50$, $X = 50$, $r = 0.1$, $\sigma = 0.3$, $T = 0.25$, and

$$d_1 = \frac{\ln(50/50) + (0.1 + 0.09/2)0.25}{0.3 \sqrt{0.25}} = 0.2417$$

$$d_2 = d_1 - 0.3 \sqrt{0.25} = 0.0917$$

The European put price is

$$50N(-0.0917)e^{-0.1 \times 0.25} - 50N(-0.2417)$$

$$= 50 \times 0.4634e^{-0.1 \times 0.25} - 50 \times 0.4045 = 2.37$$

or $2.37.
5. In this case we must subtract the present value of the dividend from the stock price before using Black–Scholes. Hence, the appropriate value of S is

$$S = 50 - 1.50e^{-0.1667 \times 0.1} = 48.52$$

As before $X = 50$, $r = 0.1$, $\sigma = 0.3$, and $T = 0.25$. In this case

$$d_1 = \frac{\ln(48.52/50) + (0.1 + 0.09/2)0.25}{0.3 \sqrt{0.25}} = 0.0414$$

$$d_2 = d_1 - 0.3 \sqrt{0.25} = -0.1086$$

The European put price is

$$50N(0.1086)e^{-0.1 \times 0.25} - 48.52N(-0.0414)$$

$$= 50 \times 0.5432e^{-0.1 \times 0.25} - 48.52 \times 0.4835 = 3.03$$

or $3.03.
6. The implied volatility is the volatility that makes the Black–Scholes price of an option equal to its market price. It is calculated by trial and error. We keep testing different volatilities until we find the one that gives the European put option price when it is substituted into the Black–Scholes formula.
7. In Black's approximation we calculate the price of a European option expiring at the same time as the American option and the price of a European option expiring just before the final ex-dividend date. We set the American option price equal to the greater of the two.

Chapter 12

1. When the S&P 500 goes down to 240, the value of the portfolio can be expected to be $10 \times (240/250) = \$9.6$ million. (This assumes that the dividend yield on the portfolio equals the dividend yield on the index.) Buying put options on $10,000,000/250 = 40,000$ times the index with a strike of 240 therefore provides protection against a drop in the value of the portfolio below \$9.6 million. Since each contract is on 100 times the index, a total of 400 contracts would be required.

2. A stock index is analogous to a stock paying a continuous dividend yield, the dividend yield being the dividend yield on the index. A currency is analogous to a stock paying a continuous dividend yield, the dividend yield being the foreign risk-free interest rate.

3. The lower bound is given by Equation 12.1 as

$$300e^{-0.03 \times 0.5} - 290e^{-0.08 \times 0.5} = 16.90$$

4. The tree of exchange-rate movements is shown in the following diagram. In this case $u = 1.02$ and $d = 0.98$. The probability of an up movement is

$$p = \frac{e^{(0.06 - 0.08) \times 0.08333} - 0.98}{1.02 - 0.98} = 0.4584$$

The tree shows that the value of an option to purchase one unit of the currency is \$0.0067.

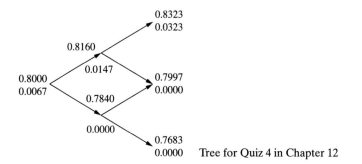

Tree for Quiz 4 in Chapter 12

5. A company that knows it is due to receive a foreign currency at a certain time in the future can buy a put option. This guarantees that the price at which the currency will be sold will be at or above a certain level. A company that knows it is due to pay a foreign currency at a certain time in the future can buy a call option. This guarantees that the price at which the currency will be purchased will be at or below a certain level.

6. In this case $S = 250$, $X = 250$, $r = 0.10$, $\sigma = 0.18$, $T = 0.25$, $q = 0.03$, and

$$d_1 = \frac{\ln(250/250) + (0.10 - 0.03 + 0.18^2/2)0.25}{0.18\sqrt{0.25}} = 0.2394$$

$$d_2 = d_1 - 0.18\sqrt{0.25} = 0.1494$$

and the call price is

$$250N(0.2394)e^{-0.03 \times 0.25} - 250N(0.1494)e^{-0.10 \times 0.25}$$

$$= 250 \times 0.5946e^{-0.03 \times 0.25} - 250 \times 0.5594e^{-0.10 \times 0.25}$$

$$= 11.14$$

7. In this case $S = 0.52$, $X = 0.50$, $r = 0.04$, $r_f = 0.08$, $\sigma = 0.12$, $T = 0.6667$, and

$$d_1 = \frac{\ln(0.52/0.50) + (0.04 - 0.08 + 0.12^2/2)0.6667}{0.12\sqrt{0.6667}} = 0.1771$$

$$d_2 = d_1 - 0.12\sqrt{0.6667} = 0.0791$$

and the put price is

$$0.50N(-0.0791)e^{-0.04 \times 0.6667} - 0.52N(-0.1771)e^{-0.08 \times 0.6667}$$

$$= 0.50 \times 0.4685e^{-0.04 \times 0.6667} - 0.52 \times 0.4297e^{-0.08 \times 0.6667}$$

$$= 0.0162$$

Chapter 13

1. A call option on yen gives the holder the right to buy yen in the spot market at an exchange rate equal to the strike price. A call option on yen futures gives the holder the right to receive the amount by which the futures price exceeds the strike price. If the yen futures option is exercised, the holder also obtains a long position in the yen futures contract.

2. The main reason is that a bond futures contract is a more liquid instrument than a bond. The price of a Treasury bond futures contract is known immediately from trading on CBOT. The price of a bond can be obtained only by contacting dealers.

3. A futures price behaves like a stock paying a continuous dividend yield at the risk-free interest rate.

4. In this case $u = 1.12$ and $d = 0.92$. The probability of an up movement in a risk-neutral world is

$$\frac{1 - 0.92}{1.12 - 0.92} = 0.4$$

From risk-neutral valuation, the value of the call is

$$e^{-0.06 \times 0.5}(0.4 \times 6 + 0.6 \times 0) = 2.33$$

5. The put–call parity formula for futures options is the same as the put–call parity formula for stock options except that the stock price is replaced by Fe^{-rT}, where F is the current futures price, r is the risk-free interest rate, and T is the life of the option.

6. The American futures call option is worth more than the corresponding American option on the underlying asset when the futures price is greater than the spot price prior to the maturity of the futures contract.

7. In this case $F = 19$, $X = 20$, $r = 0.12$, $\sigma = 0.20$, and $T = 0.4167$. The value of the European put futures option is

$$20N(-d_2)e^{-0.12 \times 0.4167} - 19N(-d_1)e^{-0.12 \times 0.4167}$$

where

$$d_1 = \frac{\ln(19/20) + (0.04/2)0.4167}{0.2\sqrt{0.4167}} = -0.3327$$

$$d_2 = d_1 - 0.2\sqrt{0.4167} = -0.4618$$

This is

$$e^{-0.12 \times 0.4167}[20N(0.4618) - 19N(0.3327)]$$

$$= e^{-0.12 \times 0.4167}(20 \times 0.6778 - 19 \times 0.6303)$$

$$= 1.50$$

or $1.50.

Chapter 14

1. A stop-loss scheme can be implemented by arranging to have a covered position when the option is in the money and a naked position when it is out of the money. When using the scheme, the writer of an out-of-the-money call would buy the underlying asset as soon as the price moved above the strike price, X, and sell the underlying asset as soon as the price moved below X. In practice, when the price of the underlying asset equals X, there is no way of knowing whether it will subsequently move above or below X. The asset will therefore be bought at $X + \delta$ and sold at $X - \delta$ for some small δ. The cost of hedging depends on the number of times the asset price equals X. The hedge is therefore relatively poor. It will cost nothing if the asset price never reaches X; on the other hand, it will be quite expensive if the asset price equals X many times. In a good hedge the cost of hedging is known in advance to a reasonable level of accuracy.

2. A delta of 0.7 means that when the price of the stock increases by a small amount, the price of the option increases by 70 percent of this amount. Similarly, when the price of the stock decreases by a small amount, the price of the option decreases by 70 percent of this amount. A short position in 1,000 options has a delta of -700 and can be made delta neutral with the purchase of 700 shares.

3. In this case $S = X$, $r = 0.1$, $\sigma = 0.25$, and $T = 0.5$. Also,

$$d_1 = \frac{\ln(S/X) + [(0.1 + 0.25^2)/2]0.5}{0.25\sqrt{0.5}} = 0.3712$$

The delta of the option is $N(d_1)$, or 0.64.

4. A theta of -0.1 means that if Δt years pass with no change in either the stock price or its volatility, the value of the option declines by $0.1\Delta t$. A trader who feels that neither the stock price nor its implied volatility will change should write an option with as high a negative theta as possible. Relatively short-life at-the-money options have the most negative thetas.

5. The gamma of an option position is the rate of change of the delta of the position with respect to the asset price. For example, a gamma of 0.1 indicates that when the asset price increases by a certain small amount, delta increases by 0.1 of this amount. When the gamma of an option writer's position is large and negative and the delta is zero, the option writer will lose significant amounts of money if there is a large movement (either an increase or a decrease) in the asset price.

6. To hedge an option position, it is necessary to create the opposite option position synthetically. For example, to hedge a long position in a put, it is necessary to create a short position in a put synthetically. It follows that the procedure for creating an option position synthetically is the reverse of the procedure for hedging the option position.

7. Portfolio insurance involves creating a put option synthetically. It assumes that as soon as a portfolio's value declines by a small amount the portfolio manager's position is re-balanced by either (a) selling part of the portfolio or (b) selling some index futures. On October 19, 1987 the market declined so quickly that the sort of rebalancing anticipated in portfolio insurance schemes could not be accomplished.

Chapter 15

1. Define u_i as $\ln(S_i/S_{i-1})$, where S_i is value of a market variable on day i. In the EWMA model, the variance rate of the market variable (i.e., the square of its volatility) is a weighted average of the u_i^2's. For some constant λ $(0 < \lambda < 1)$ the weight given to u_{i-1}^2 (which is calculated on day $i - 1$) is λ times the weight given to u_i^2 (which is calculated on day i). The volatility estimated on day n, σ_n, is related to the volatility estimated on day $n - 1$, σ_{n-1}, by

$$\sigma_n^2 = \lambda\sigma_{n-1}^2 + (1 - \lambda)u_n^2$$

This formula shows that the EWMA model has one very attractive property. To calculate the volatility estimate on day n, it is sufficient to know the volatility estimate on day $n - 1$ and u_n^2.

2. In this case $\sigma_{n-1} = 0.015$ and $u_n = \ln(30.5/30) = 0.01653$, so that Equation 15.2 gives

$$\sigma_n^2 = 0.94 \times 0.015^2 + 0.06 \times 0.01653^2 = 0.0002279$$

The volatility estimate on day n is therefore 1.5096 percent.

3. Measured in thousands of dollars, the variance of daily changes in the portfolio value is

$$300^2 \times 0.018^2 + 500^2 \times 0.012^2 + 2 \times 300 \times 500 \times 0.018 \times 0.012 \times 0.3 = 78.44$$

The standard deviation of daily changes in the portfolio is $\sqrt{78.44} = 8.86$. The standard deviation of changes over five days is $8.86\sqrt{5} = 19.80$. The 95 percent/5-day VaR for the portfolio is therefore $1.65 \times 19.80 = 32.68$, or \$32,680.

4. Reducing λ from 0.95 to 0.85 means that more weight is put on recent observations of u_i^2 and less weight is given to older observations. Volatilities calculated with $\lambda = 0.85$ will react more quickly to new information and will "bounce around" much more than volatilities calculated with $\lambda = 0.95$.

5. The approximate relationship beween the daily change in the portfolio value, ΔP, and the daily change in the exchange rate, ΔS, is

$$\Delta P = 56\Delta S$$

The proportional daily change in the exchange rate, Δx, equals $\Delta S/1.5$. It follows that

$$\Delta P = 56 \times 1.5\Delta x$$

or

$$\Delta P = 84\Delta x$$

The standard deviation of Δx equals the daily volatility of the exchange rate, or 0.7 percent. The standard deviation of ΔP is therefore $84 \times 0.007 = 0.588$. It follows that the 99 percent/10-day VaR for the portfolio is

$$0.588 \times 2.33 \times \sqrt{10} = 4.33$$

6. The relationship is

$$\Delta P = 56 \times 1.5\Delta x + \frac{1}{2} \times 1.5^2 \times 16.2 \times \Delta x^2$$

or

$$\Delta P = 84\Delta x + 18\Delta x^2$$

7. The linear model assumes that the proportional daily change in each market variable has a normal probability distribution. The historical data model assumes that the probability distribution observed for the proportional daily changes in the market variables in the past is the probability distribution that will apply in the future.

Chapter 16

1. Delta, gamma, and theta can be determined from a single binomial tree. Vega is determined by making a small change to the volatility and recomputing the option price using a new tree. Rho is calculated by making a small change to the interest rate and recomputing the option price using a new tree.
2. In this case $S = 60$, $X = 60$, $r = 0.1$, $\sigma = 0.45$, $T = 0.25$, and $\Delta t = 0.0833$. Also

$$u = e^{\sigma\sqrt{\Delta t}} = e^{0.45\sqrt{0.0833}} = 1.1387$$

$$d = \frac{1}{u} = 0.8782$$

$$a = e^{r\Delta t} = e^{0.1 \times 0.0833} = 1.0084$$

$$p = \frac{a - d}{u - d} = 0.4998$$

$$1 - p = 0.5002$$

The tree is shown in the following diagram. The calculated price of the option is $5.16.

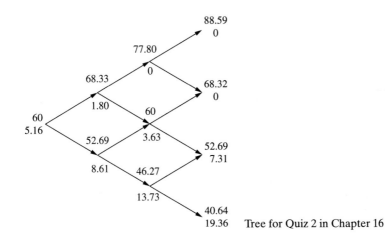

Tree for Quiz 2 in Chapter 16

3. The control variate technique is implemented by
   a. Valuing an American option using a binomial tree in the usual way (to get f_A)
   b. Valuing the European option with the same parameters as the American option using the same tree (to get f_E)
   c. Valuing the European option using Black–Scholes (to get f_{BS})
   The price of the American option is estimated as $f_A + f_{BS} - f_E$.

4. In this case $F = 198$, $X = 200$, $r = 0.08$, $\sigma = 0.3$, $T = 0.75$, and $\Delta t = 0.25$. Also

$$u = e^{0.3\sqrt{0.25}} = 1.1618; \qquad d = \frac{1}{u} = 0.8607$$

$$a = 1; \qquad p = \frac{a - d}{u - d} = 0.4626$$

$$1 - p = 0.5373$$

The tree is as shown in the following diagram. The calculated price of the option is 20.3 cents.

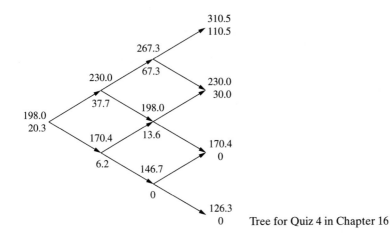

Tree for Quiz 4 in Chapter 16

5. No! This is an example of a *history-dependent option*. The payoff depends on the path followed by the stock price as well as on its final value. The option cannot be valued by starting at the end of the tree and working backward, because the payoff at a final branch depends on the path used to reach it. European options for which the payoff depends on the average stock price can be valued using Monte Carlo simulation.

6. Suppose a dividend equal to D is paid during a certain time interval. If S is the stock price at the beginning of the time interval, it will be either $Su - D$ or $Sd - D$ at the end of the time interval. At the end of the next time interval, it will be one of $(Su - D)u$, $(Su - D)d$, $(Sd - D)u$, and $(Sd - D)d$. Because $(Su - D)d$ does not equal $(Sd - D)u$, the tree does not recombine. If S is equal to the stock price less the present value of future dividends, this problem is avoided.

7. In Monte Carlo simulation we sample paths through the tree, working from the beginning to the end. When a node is reached we have no way of knowing whether early exercise is optimal.

Chapter 17

1. When both tails of the stock price distribution are thinner than those of the lognormal distribution, Black–Scholes will tend to overprice options when they are either significantly out of the money or significantly in the money. When the right tail is thinner and the left tail is fatter, Black–Scholes will tend to overprice out-of-the-money calls and in-the-money puts. It will tend to underprice out-of-the-money puts and in-the-money calls.

2. When the asset price is positively correlated with volatility, the volatility tends to increase as the asset price increases, producing thin left tails and fat right tails. Black–Scholes will tend to underprice out-of-the-money calls and in-the-money puts. It will tend to overprice out-of-the-money puts and in-the-money calls.

3. Jumps tend to make both tails of the stock price distribution fatter than those of the lognormal distribution. This means that Black–Scholes will tend to underprice options that are either significantly in the money or significantly out of the money. These biases are likely to be less pronounced for long options than for short options.

4. Figure 17.5 indicates that practitioners use high volatilities for low strike prices and low volatilities for high strike prices. Out-of-the-money puts and in-the-money calls have low strike prices. Out-of-the-money calls and in-the-money puts have high strike prices. It follows that Figure 17.5 indicates that practitioners increase the prices of out-of-the-money puts and in-the-money calls while decreasing the prices of out-of-the-money calls and in-the-money puts. The strategy makes their prices consistent with the solid line in Figure 17.1b.

5. These biases are the same because of put–call parity. Suppose that p and c are the Black–Scholes prices of a European put and call and that p^* and c^* are the put and call prices based on another model. Put–call parity is true for all models. Hence, with the usual notation,

$$c + Xe^{-rT} = p + S$$

$$c^* + Xe^{-rT} = p^* + S$$

so that

$$c - c^* = p - p^*$$

showing that the bias for the call price is the same as the bias for the put price. When the call is in the money, the put is out of the money, and vice versa. This explains why the biases for in-the-money call options are usually the same as the biases for out-of-the-money put options.

6. The probability distribution of the stock price at some future time (say, in one month) is not lognormal. Possibly it consists of two lognormal distributions superimposed upon each other and is bimodal. Black–Scholes is clearly inappropriate, because it assumes that the stock price at any future time is lognormal.

7. There are a number of problems in testing an option pricing model empirically. These include the problem of obtaining synchronous data on stock prices and option prices, the problem of estimating the dividends that will be paid on the stock during the option's life, the problem of distinguishing between situations where the market is inefficient and situations where the option pricing model is incorrect, and the problems of estimating stock price volatility.

Chapter 18

1. An amount

$$\$20,000,000 \times 0.02 \times 0.25 = \$100,000$$

would be paid out three months later.

2. An investor in a mortgage-backed security has a stake in a portfolio of residential mortgages. The mortgages are insured so that the investor is protected against defaults. The investor receives his or her share of the cash flows (both interest and principal) paid on the mortgages in the portfolio. A mortgage-backed security is more risky than a government bond because the investor's return depends on the extent to which the prepayment options embedded in the mortgages are exercised.

3. A swaption is an option to enter into an interest-rate swap at a certain time in the future with a certain fixed rate being exchanged for floating. An interest-rate swap can be regarded as the exchange of a fixed-rate bond for a floating-rate bond. Thus, a swaption is the option to exchange a fixed-rate bond for a floating-rate bond. The floating-rate bond will be worth its face value at the beginning of the life of the swap. The swaption is therefore an option on a fixed-rate bond with the strike price equal to the face value of the bond.

4. In this case $F = (125-10)e^{0.1 \times 1} = 127.09, X = 110, r = 0.1, \sigma = 0.08,$ and $T = 1.0.$

$$d_1 = \frac{\ln(127.09/110) + (0.08^2/2)}{0.08} = 1.8456$$

$$d_2 = d_1 - 0.08 = 1.7656$$

The value of the put option is

$$110e^{-0.1}N(-1.7656) - 115N(-1.8456) = 0.12$$

or $0.12.

5. The payoff from the swaption is a series of five cash flows equal to $\max(0.076 - R, 0)$ in millions of dollars, where R is the five-year swap rate in four years. The value of an annuity that provides $1 per year at the end of years $5, 6, 7, 8,$ and 9 is

$$\sum_{i=5}^{9} \frac{1}{1.08^i} = 2.9348$$

The value of the swaption in millions of dollars is therefore

$$2.9348[0.076N(-d_2) - 0.08N(-d_1)]$$

where

$$d_1 = \frac{\ln(0.08/0.076) + 0.25^2 \times 4/2}{0.25\sqrt{4}} = 0.3526$$

and

$$d_2 = \frac{\ln(0.08/0.076) - 0.25^2 \times 4/2}{0.25\sqrt{4}} = -0.1474$$

The value of the swaption is

$$2.9348[0.076N(0.1474) - 0.08N(-0.3526) = 0.0396$$

or $39,600.

6. In this case $L = 1,000$, $\tau = 0.25$, $F = 0.12$, $R_X = 0.13$, $r = 0.115$, $\sigma = 0.12$, and $T = 1.5$.

$$\frac{\tau L}{1 + F\tau} = 242.72$$

$$d_1 = \frac{\ln(0.12/0.13) + 0.12^2 \times 1.5/2}{0.12\sqrt{1.5}} = -0.4711$$

$$d_2 = -0.4711 - 0.12\sqrt{1.5} = -0.6181$$

The value of the option is

$$242.7e^{-0.115 \times 1.5}[0.12N(-0.4711) - 0.13N(-0.6181)] = 242.7 \times 0.0028 = 0.69$$

or $0.69.

7. There are two main advantages of yield curve models. First, they enable all interest-rate derivative securities to be valued on a consistent basis. Second, they enable securities that cannot be handled using Black's model to be valued. An example of a security that cannot be valued using Black's model but can be valued using yield curve models is a long-dated American bond option.

Computer Software

The software included with this text, DerivaGem, is a Windows-based program that can be used to value and produce hedge statistics for:

1. European and American call and put options on stocks, currencies, stock indices, and futures contracts
2. The following exotic options (if they are written on nondividend-paying stocks, currencies, stock indices, or futures options): Asian options, barrier options, binary options, chooser options, compound options, and lookback options
3. The following interest-rate options: caps and floors, European bond options, and European swap options

The software can also be used to calculate implied volatilities from European or American call and put prices.

DerivaGem can be run under either Windows 3.1 or Windows 95. The *File* menu can be used to save or retrieve data and to print the results. Multiple deals can be handled within the same application.

Updates to the software can be downloaded from the author's Web site:

http : //www.mgmt.utoronto.ca/ ~ hull

Special Features

DerivaGem has two special features to facilitate learning:

1. It displays the binomial tree used to value an option.
2. It displays plots of any one of option price, delta, gamma, vega, theta, and rho *against* any one of asset price, strike price, interest rate, volatility, and time to maturity.

Installation

To run DerivaGem from your C-drive, it is necessary to create a directory and copy both the files GRID.VBX and DERIVGEM.EXE into the directory. The installation program can be used to do this automatically. The installation program uses the name DERIVGEM for the directory. To run the installation program, load the floppy disk into drive A and run INSTALL.BAT. (You can do the latter by typing

INSTALL.BAT after the A\ > prompt in DOS; alternatively you can double-click on the INSTALL.BAT file name when in Windows.)

The software can be run from the Windows file manager or Windows Explorer by double clicking on DERIVGEM.EXE. In Windows 3.1 an icon can be created by entering the program manager and doing the following:

1. Click on FILE
2. Select NEW
3. Select PROGRAM ITEM
4. Click on BROWSE
5. Choose derivgem\derivgem.exe
6. Click OK

Under Windows 95 an icon is created by choosing DERIVGEM.EXE from the Windows Explorer and clicking on *Shortcut*. The shortcut file that is created is then dragged to the required icon location.

Operation of the Software

REGULAR OPTIONS

To value a regular option, you must first click on the *Regular Option* radio button in the first "control center" screen. You must then choose the underlying asset (stock, currency, index, or futures). You must also specify whether the option is American or European and whether an implied volatility is to be calculated. If the implied volatility box is checked, you must also specify the option type (call or put).

Once all the information has been entered on the first screen, you should click on the *Edit* button and proceed to input the parameters of the option under consideration in the *Security Editor* screen. The *Tab* key is a convenient way of moving between fields. Note that all interest rates input are continuously compounded.

In the case of stock options, you may wish to input dividend information. You can do so by clicking on the *Dividend Edit* button within the *Security Editor*. This causes a *Dividend Table* to appear. (If the *Dividend Table* fails to appear, it is likely because GRID.VBX has not been loaded.) The times input on the table should be the times of the ex-dividend dates, measured in years from today. The dividends should be entered in chronological order. Do not enter dividends that occur later than the maturity of the option. Again, the *Tab* key is a convenient way of moving between fields. Once all the dividend information has been entered, you should click on the *OK* button.

Once all the option data have been entered, click on the *OK* button to return to the control center. To value the option click on *Compute*. The *Valuation Results* screen is then displayed. Note the following definitions:

Delta: change in option price per dollar change in underlying

Gamma: change in delta per dollar change in underlying

Vega: change in option price per 1 percent change in volatility

Rho: change in option price per 1 percent change in interest rate

Theta: change in option price when one day passes

By clicking on *Close,* you return to the control center. From there you can click on *View Tree* to display the tree used in computations. (If more than seven time steps are specified in the *Security Editor,* only the first seven steps of the tree will be displayed. Otherwise all the steps are displayed.) By clicking on *Graph* from the *Valuation Results* screen, you can plot any one of option price, delta, gamma, vega, theta, and rho against any one of asset price, strike price, interest rate, volatility, and time to maturity. Results for either the call or the put, or both, can be displayed.

The graphs can also be accessed from the control center by clicking on *Plot Results.*

EXOTIC OPTIONS

To value an exotic option, you must first click on the *Exotic Option* button in the control center screen. You must then choose the underlying asset (stock, currency, index, or futures) and choose one of the following exotic instruments: Asian option, barrier option, binary option, compound option, chooser, and lookback option.

Once all the information has been entered on the control center screen, you should click the *Edit* button and proceed to input the parameters of the option under consideration, as in the case of regular options. Once all the option data have been entered, click on the *OK* button to return to the control center. To value the option, click on *Compute.* The *Valuation Results* screen is then displayed. The definitions of delta, gamma, vega, rho, and theta are as for regular options.

By clicking on *Close,* you return to the control center screen. By clicking on *Graph,* you can see plots of any one of option price, delta, gamma, vega, theta, and rho against any one of asset price, strike price, interest rate, volatility, and time to maturity. Either the call or the put, or both, can be displayed. The graphs can also be accessed from the control center screen by clicking on *Plot Results.*

INTEREST-RATE OPTIONS

To value an interest-rate option, you must first click on the *Interest-Rate Option* button in the control center screen. You must then choose one of the following interest-rate options: bond option, cap or floor, and swap option.

Once all the information has been entered on the control center screen, you should click on the *Edit* button and proceed to input the parameters of the option under consideration. The *Tab* key is a convenient way of moving between fields.

Note that for a cap or floor, you enter the maturity of the cap or floor (years from today) and the starting point (years from today). The software starts at the maturity and works backward, calculating the values of caplets or floorlets. It stops when the next step would take it beyond the starting point. The cap rate is expressed with a compounding frequency corresponding to the reset frequency. The volatility is a flat "Black volatility" applied to all forward rates, as described in chapter 18.

For a swap option you enter the maturity of swap start (years from today) and the end of the life of the swap (years from today). The option is assumed to end at the beginning of the swap life. The swap rate is expressed with a compounding frequency corresponding to the reset frequency. The volatility is a "Black volatility" applied to the forward swap rate, as described in chapter 18.

For a bond option the bond price can be either input by the user or calculated from the zero curve. The bond price is input as a cash (dirty) price rather than a quoted (clean) price. The strike price can be input as a cash price or a quoted price. The volatility is a "Black volatility" applied to the forward bond price, as described in chapter 18.

It is necessary to input a zero-coupon yield curve. You do this by clicking on *Zero Rates* within the *Security Editor*. A table of times and rates will then appear. (If this table does not appear, it is likely because GRID.VBX is not loaded.) You should use it to input points on the zero curve in chronological order. The software assumes that the zero curve is flat out to the first time specified. It then linearly interpolates between the points specified and assumes that the curve is flat from the final point onward. The *Tab* key is a convenient way of moving around the table. When all zero-rate data have been input, click on the *OK* button.

Once all the *Security Editor* data have been entered, click on the *OK* button to return to the control center. To value the option, click on *Compute*. The *Valuation Results* screen is then displayed. Note the following definitions:

DV01:   change in option price for a one-basis-point increase in all rates

Gamma01:   change in DV01 multiplied by 10,000 for a one-basis-point increase in all rates

Vega: change in option price per 1 percent change in volatility

By clicking on *Close,* you return to the control center. By clicking on *Graph,* you can see approximate plots of the zero curve and forward curve.

Table for $N(x)$ When $x \leq 0$

This table shows values of $N(x)$ for $x \leq 0$. The table should be used with interpolation. For example,

$$N(-0.1234) = N(-0.12) - 0.34[N(-0.12) - N(-0.13)]$$
$$= 0.4522 - 0.34 \times (0.4522 - 0.4483)$$
$$= 0.4509$$

x	.00	.01	.02	.03	.04	.05	.06	.07	.08	.09
−0.0	0.5000	0.4960	0.4920	0.4880	0.4840	0.4801	0.4761	0.4721	0.4681	0.4641
−0.1	0.4602	0.4562	0.4522	0.4483	0.4443	0.4404	0.4364	0.4325	0.4286	0.4247
−0.2	0.4207	0.4168	0.4129	0.4090	0.4052	0.4013	0.3974	0.3936	0.3897	0.3859
−0.3	0.3821	0.3783	0.3745	0.3707	0.3669	0.3632	0.3594	0.3557	0.3520	0.3483
−0.4	0.3446	0.3409	0.3372	0.3336	0.3300	0.3264	0.3228	0.3192	0.3156	0.3121
−0.5	0.3085	0.3050	0.3015	0.2981	0.2946	0.2912	0.2877	0.2843	0.2810	0.2776
−0.6	0.2743	0.2709	0.2676	0.2643	0.2611	0.2578	0.2546	0.2514	0.2483	0.2451
−0.7	0.2420	0.2389	0.2358	0.2327	0.2296	0.2266	0.2236	0.2206	0.2177	0.2148
−0.8	0.2119	0.2090	0.2061	0.2033	0.2005	0.1977	0.1949	0.1922	0.1894	0.1867
−0.9	0.1841	0.1814	0.1788	0.1762	0.1736	0.1711	0.1685	0.1660	0.1635	0.1611
−1.0	0.1587	0.1562	0.1539	0.1515	0.1492	0.1469	0.1446	0.1423	0.1401	0.1379
−1.1	0.1357	0.1335	0.1314	0.1292	0.1271	0.1251	0.1230	0.1210	0.1190	0.1170
−1.2	0.1151	0.1131	0.1112	0.1093	0.1075	0.1056	0.1038	0.1020	0.1003	0.0985
−1.3	0.0968	0.0951	0.0934	0.0918	0.0901	0.0885	0.0869	0.0853	0.0838	0.0823
−1.4	0.0808	0.0793	0.0778	0.0764	0.0749	0.0735	0.0721	0.0708	0.0694	0.0681
−1.5	0.0668	0.0655	0.0643	0.0630	0.0618	0.0606	0.0594	0.0582	0.0571	0.0559
−1.6	0.0548	0.0537	0.0526	0.0516	0.0505	0.0495	0.0485	0.0475	0.0465	0.0455
−1.7	0.0446	0.0436	0.0427	0.0418	0.0409	0.0401	0.0392	0.0384	0.0375	0.0367
−1.8	0.0359	0.0351	0.0344	0.0336	0.0329	0.0322	0.0314	0.0307	0.0301	0.0294
−1.9	0.0287	0.0281	0.0274	0.0268	0.0262	0.0256	0.0250	0.0244	0.0239	0.0233
−2.0	0.0228	0.0222	0.0217	0.0212	0.0207	0.0202	0.0197	0.0192	0.0188	0.0183
−2.1	0.0179	0.0174	0.0170	0.0166	0.0162	0.0158	0.0154	0.0150	0.0146	0.0143
−2.2	0.0139	0.0136	0.0132	0.0129	0.0125	0.0122	0.0119	0.0116	0.0113	0.0110
−2.3	0.0107	0.0104	0.0102	0.0099	0.0096	0.0094	0.0091	0.0089	0.0087	0.0084
−2.4	0.0082	0.0080	0.0078	0.0075	0.0073	0.0071	0.0069	0.0068	0.0066	0.0064

(continued)

(cont.)

x	.00	.01	.02	.03	.04	.05	.06	.07	.08	.09
−2.5	0.0062	0.0060	0.0059	0.0057	0.0055	0.0054	0.0052	0.0051	0.0049	0.0048
−2.6	0.0047	0.0045	0.0044	0.0043	0.0041	0.0040	0.0039	0.0038	0.0037	0.0036
−2.7	0.0035	0.0034	0.0033	0.0032	0.0031	0.0030	0.0029	0.0028	0.0027	0.0026
−2.8	0.0026	0.0025	0.0024	0.0023	0.0023	0.0022	0.0021	0.0021	0.0020	0.0019
−2.9	0.0019	0.0018	0.0018	0.0017	0.0016	0.0016	0.0015	0.0015	0.0014	0.0014
−3.0	0.0014	0.0013	0.0013	0.0012	0.0012	0.0011	0.0011	0.0011	0.0010	0.0010
−3.1	0.0010	0.0009	0.0009	0.0009	0.0008	0.0008	0.0008	0.0008	0.0007	0.0007
−3.2	0.0007	0.0007	0.0006	0.0006	0.0006	0.0006	0.0006	0.0005	0.0005	0.0005
−3.3	0.0005	0.0005	0.0005	0.0004	0.0004	0.0004	0.0004	0.0004	0.0004	0.0003
−3.4	0.0003	0.0003	0.0003	0.0003	0.0003	0.0003	0.0003	0.0003	0.0003	0.0002
−3.5	0.0002	0.0002	0.0002	0.0002	0.0002	0.0002	0.0002	0.0002	0.0002	0.0002
−3.6	0.0002	0.0002	0.0001	0.0001	0.0001	0.0001	0.0001	0.0001	0.0001	0.0001
−3.7	0.0001	0.0001	0.0001	0.0001	0.0001	0.0001	0.0001	0.0001	0.0001	0.0001
−3.8	0.0001	0.0001	0.0001	0.0001	0.0001	0.0001	0.0001	0.0001	0.0001	0.0001
−3.9	0.0000	0.0000	0.0000	0.0000	0.0000	0.0000	0.0000	0.0000	0.0000	0.0000
−4.0	0.0000	0.0000	0.0000	0.0000	0.0000	0.0000	0.0000	0.0000	0.0000	0.0000

Table for N(x) When x ≥ 0

This table shows values of $N(x)$ for $x \geq 0$. The table should be used with interpolation. For example,

$$N(0.6278) = N(0.62) + 0.78[N(0.63) - N(0.62)]$$
$$= 0.7324 + 0.78 \times (0.7357 - 0.7324)$$
$$= 0.7350$$

x	.00	.01	.02	.03	.04	.05	.06	.07	.08	.09
0.0	0.5000	0.5040	0.5080	0.5120	0.5160	0.5199	0.5239	0.5279	0.5319	0.5359
0.1	0.5398	0.5438	0.5478	0.5517	0.5557	0.5596	0.5636	0.5675	0.5714	0.5753
0.2	0.5793	0.5832	0.5871	0.5910	0.5948	0.5987	0.6026	0.6064	0.6103	0.6141
0.3	0.6179	0.6217	0.6255	0.6293	0.6331	0.6368	0.6406	0.6443	0.6480	0.6517
0.4	0.6554	0.6591	0.6628	0.6664	0.6700	0.6736	0.6772	0.6808	0.6844	0.6879
0.5	0.6915	0.6950	0.6985	0.7019	0.7054	0.7088	0.7123	0.7157	0.7190	0.7224
0.6	0.7257	0.7291	0.7324	0.7357	0.7389	0.7422	0.7454	0.7486	0.7517	0.7549
0.7	0.7580	0.7611	0.7642	0.7673	0.7704	0.7734	0.7764	0.7794	0.7823	0.7852
0.8	0.7881	0.7910	0.7939	0.7967	0.7995	0.8023	0.8051	0.8078	0.8106	0.8133
0.9	0.8159	0.8186	0.8212	0.8238	0.8264	0.8289	0.8315	0.8340	0.8365	0.8389
1.0	0.8413	0.8438	0.8461	0.8485	0.8508	0.8531	0.8554	0.8577	0.8599	0.8621
1.1	0.8643	0.8665	0.8686	0.8708	0.8729	0.8749	0.8770	0.8790	0.8810	0.8830
1.2	0.8849	0.8869	0.8888	0.8907	0.8925	0.8944	0.8962	0.8980	0.8997	0.9015
1.3	0.9032	0.9049	0.9066	0.9082	0.9099	0.9115	0.9131	0.9147	0.9162	0.9177
1.4	0.9192	0.9207	0.9222	0.9236	0.9251	0.9265	0.9279	0.9292	0.9306	0.9319
1.5	0.9332	0.9345	0.9357	0.9370	0.9382	0.9394	0.9406	0.9418	0.9429	0.9441
1.6	0.9452	0.9463	0.9474	0.9484	0.9495	0.9505	0.9515	0.9525	0.9535	0.9545
1.7	0.9554	0.9564	0.9573	0.9582	0.9591	0.9599	0.9608	0.9616	0.9625	0.9633
1.8	0.9641	0.9649	0.9656	0.9664	0.9671	0.9678	0.9686	0.9693	0.9699	0.9706
1.9	0.9713	0.9719	0.9726	0.9732	0.9738	0.9744	0.9750	0.9756	0.9761	0.9767
2.0	0.9772	0.9778	0.9783	0.9788	0.9793	0.9798	0.9803	0.9808	0.9812	0.9817
2.1	0.9821	0.9826	0.9830	0.9834	0.9838	0.9842	0.9846	0.9850	0.9854	0.9857
2.2	0.9861	0.9864	0.9868	0.9871	0.9875	0.9878	0.9881	0.9884	0.9887	0.9890
2.3	0.9893	0.9896	0.9898	0.9901	0.9904	0.9906	0.9909	0.9911	0.9913	0.9916
2.4	0.9918	0.9920	0.9922	0.9925	0.9927	0.9929	0.9931	0.9932	0.9934	0.9936

(continued)

(cont.)

x	.00	.01	.02	.03	.04	.05	.06	.07	.08	.09
2.5	0.9938	0.9940	0.9941	0.9943	0.9945	0.9946	0.9948	0.9949	0.9951	0.9952
2.6	0.9953	0.9955	0.9956	0.9957	0.9959	0.9960	0.9961	0.9962	0.9963	0.9964
2.7	0.9965	0.9966	0.9967	0.9968	0.9969	0.9970	0.9971	0.9972	0.9973	0.9974
2.8	0.9974	0.9975	0.9976	0.9977	0.9977	0.9978	0.9979	0.9979	0.9980	0.9981
2.9	0.9981	0.9982	0.9982	0.9983	0.9984	0.9984	0.9985	0.9985	0.9986	0.9986
3.0	0.9986	0.9987	0.9987	0.9988	0.9988	0.9989	0.9989	0.9989	0.9990	0.9990
3.1	0.9990	0.9991	0.9991	0.9991	0.9992	0.9992	0.9992	0.9992	0.9993	0.9993
3.2	0.9993	0.9993	0.9994	0.9994	0.9994	0.9994	0.9994	0.9995	0.9995	0.9995
3.3	0.9995	0.9995	0.9995	0.9996	0.9996	0.9996	0.9996	0.9996	0.9996	0.9997
3.4	0.9997	0.9997	0.9997	0.9997	0.9997	0.9997	0.9997	0.9997	0.9997	0.9998
3.5	0.9998	0.9998	0.9998	0.9998	0.9998	0.9998	0.9998	0.9998	0.9998	0.9998
3.6	0.9998	0.9998	0.9999	0.9999	0.9999	0.9999	0.9999	0.9999	0.9999	0.9999
3.7	0.9999	0.9999	0.9999	0.9999	0.9999	0.9999	0.9999	0.9999	0.9999	0.9999
3.8	0.9999	0.9999	0.9999	0.9999	0.9999	0.9999	0.9999	0.9999	0.9999	0.9999
3.9	1.0000	1.0000	1.0000	1.0000	1.0000	1.0000	1.0000	1.0000	1.0000	1.0000
4.0	1.0000	1.0000	1.0000	1.0000	1.0000	1.0000	1.0000	1.0000	1.0000	1.0000

Major Exchanges Trading Futures and Options

Agrarische Termijnmarkt Amsterdam	ATA
American Stock Exchange	AMEX
Australian Options Market	AOM
Belgian Futures & Options Exchange	BELFOX
Bolsa de Mercadorias y Futuros, Brazil	BM&F
Chicago Board of Trade	CBOT
Chicago Board Options Exchange	CBOE
Chicago Mercantile Exchange	CME
Coffee, Sugar & Cocoa Exchange, New York	CSCE
Commodity Exchange, New York	COMEX
Copenhagen Stock Exchange	FUTOP
Deutsche Termin Börse, Germany	DTB
European Options Exchange	EOE
Financiële Termijnmarkt Amsterdam	FTA
Finnish Options Market	FOM
Hong Kong Futures Exchange	HKFE
International Petroleum Exchange, London	IPE
Irish Futures & Options Exchange	IFOX
Kansas City Board of Trade	KCBT
Kobe Rubber Exchange	KRE
Kuala Lumpur Commodity Exchange	KLCE
London Commodity Exchange	LCE
London International Financial Futures & Options Exchange	LIFFE
London Metal Exchange	LME
London Securities and Derivatives Exchange	OMLX
Manila International Futures Exchange	MIFE
Marché à Terme International de France	MATIF
Marché des Options Négociables de Paris	MONEP
MEFF Renta Fija and Variable, Spain	MEFF
Mercado de Futuros y Opciones S.A., Argentina	MERFOX
MidAmerica Commodity Exchange	MidAm
Minneapolis Grain Exchange	MGE

(continued)

(cont.)

Montreal Exchange	ME
New York Cotton Exchange	NYCE
New York Futures Exchange	NYFE
New York Mercantile Exchange	NYMEX
New York Stock Exchange	NYSE
New Zealand Futures & Options Exchange	NZFOE
Osaka Grain Exchange	OGE
Osaka Securities Exchange	OSA
ÖTOB Aktiengesellschaft, Austria	ÖTOB
Pacific Stock Exchange	PSE
Philadelphia Stock Exchange	PHLX
Singapore International Monetary Exchange	SIMEX
Stockholm Options Market	OM
Swiss Options & Financial Futures Exchange	SOFFEX
Sydney Futures Exchange	SFE
Tokyo Grain Exchange	TGE
Tokyo International Financial Futures Exchange	TIFFE
Toronto Stock Exchange	TSE
Vancouver Stock Exchange	VSE
Winnipeg Commodity Exchange	WCE

Glossary of Terms

Accrued Interest The interest earned on a bond since the last coupon payment date.

American Option An option that can be exercised at any time during its life.

Amortizing Swap A swap in which the notional principal decreases as time passes in a predetermined way.

Arbitrage Trading strategy that involves taking advantage of the fact that two or more securities are mispriced relative to each other.

Arbitrageur Individual who does arbitrage.

Asian Option An option with a payoff dependent on the average price of the underlying asset during a specified period.

Asked Price *See* Ask Price.

Ask Price The price at which a dealer is offering an asset for sale.

Asset-or-nothing Call Option An option that provides a payoff equal to the asset price if the asset price is above the strike price, and provides zero payoff otherwise.

Asset-or-nothing Put Option An option that provides a payoff equal to the asset price if the asset price is below the strike price, and provides zero payoff otherwise.

As-you-like-it Option *See* Chooser Option.

At-the-money Option An option in which the strike price equals the price of the underlying asset.

Average Price Call Option An option giving a payoff equal to the greater of zero and the amount by which the average price of the asset exceeds the strike price.

Average Price Put Option An option giving a payoff equal to the greater of zero and the amount by which the strike price exceeds the average price of the asset.

Barrier Option An option whose payoff depends on whether the path of the underlying asset has reached a barrier (i.e., a certain predetermined level).

Basis The difference between the spot price and the futures price of a commodity.

Basis Point When used to describe an interest rate, a basis point is one hundredth of one percent (0.01 percent).

Basis Risk The risk to a hedger arising from uncertainty about the basis at a future time.

Bear Spread A short position in a put option with strike price X_1 combined with a long position in a put with strike price X_2, where $X_2 > X_1$. (A bear spread can also be created with call options.)

Beta A measure of the systematic risk of an asset.

Bid-ask Spread The amount by which the ask price exceeds the bid price.

Bid-offer Spread *See* Bid-ask Spread.

Bid Price The price at which a dealer is prepared to buy an asset.

Binary Option Either a cash-or-nothing option or an asset-or-nothing option.

Binomial Model A model in which the price of an asset is monitored over successive short periods of time. In each short period it is assumed that only two price movements are possible.

Binomial Tree A tree representing how an asset price can evolve under the binomial model.

Black–Scholes Model A model for pricing European options on stocks, published by Fischer Black and Myron Scholes in 1973.

Black's Model An extension of the Black–Scholes model, published in 1976, for valuing European options on futures contracts.

Board Broker The individual who handles limit orders in some exchanges. The board broker makes information on outstanding limit orders available to other traders.

Bond Option An option in which a bond is the underlying asset.

Bootstrap Method A procedure for calculating the zero-coupon yield curve from market data.

Bull Spread A long position in a call with strike price X_1 combined with a short position in a call with strike price X_2, where $X_2 > X_1$. (A bull spread can also be created with put options.)

Butterfly Spread A position that is created by taking a long position in a call with strike price X_1, a long position in a call with strike price X_3, and a short position in two calls with strike price X_2, where $X_3 > X_2 > X_1$ and $X_2 = 0.5(X_1 + X_3)$. (A butterfly spread can also be created with put options.)

Calendar Spread A position that is created by taking a long position in a call option that matures at one time and a short position in a similar call option that matures at a different time. (A calendar spread can also be created using put options.)

Callable Bond A bond that contains provisions allowing the issuer to buy it back at a predetermined price at certain times during its life.

Call Option An option to buy an asset at a certain price by a certain date.

Cap *See* Interest-rate Cap.

Capital Asset Pricing Model A model relating the expected return on an asset to its beta.

Caplet One component of an interest-rate cap.

Cap Rate Rate determining payoffs in an interest-rate cap.

Cash-or-nothing Call Option An option that provides a fixed predetermined payoff if the final asset price is above the strike price, and provides zero payoff otherwise.

Cash-or-nothing Put Option An option that provides a fixed predetermined payoff if the final asset price is below the strike price, and provides zero payoff otherwise.

Cash Settlement Procedure for settling a futures contract in cash, rather than by delivering the underlying asset.

Cheapest-to-deliver Bond The bond that is cheapest to deliver in the Chicago Board of Trade bond futures contract.

Chooser Option Option in which holder has the right to choose whether it is a call or a put at some point during its life.

Class of Options *See* Option Class.

Clean Price of Bond Quoted price of the bond. The cash price paid for the bond (or dirty price) is calculated by adding the accrued interest to the clean price.

Clearinghouse Firm that guarantees the performance of the parties in an exchange-traded derivatives transaction. (Also referred to as a clearing corporation.)

Clearing Margin Margin posted by clearinghouse member with the clearinghouse.

Collar *See* Interest-rate Collar.

Combination Position involving both calls and puts on the same underlying asset.

Commission Brokers Individuals who execute trades for other people and charge a commission for doing so.

Commodity Futures Trading Commission Body that regulates trading in futures contracts in the United States.

Commodity Swap Swap in which cash flows depend on the price of a commodity.

Compound Option An option on an option.

Compound Option Model Model that treats the equity of a company as an option on the company's assets.

Consumption Asset Asset held for consumption rather than investment.

Contango Situation in which futures price is above the expected future spot price.

Continuous Compounding A way of quoting interest rates. It is the limit as the assumed compounding interval is made smaller and smaller.

Control Variate Technique Technique that can sometimes be used for improving the accuracy of a numerical procedure.

Convenience Yield A measure of the benefits from owning an asset that are not obtained by the holder of a long futures contract on the asset.

Conversion Factor Factor used to determine the number of bonds that must be delivered in a Chicago Board of Trade bond futures contract.

Convertible Bond Corporate bond that can be converted into a predetermined amount of the company's equity at certain times during its life.

Convexity A measure of the curvature in the relationship between bond prices and bond yields.

Cornish-Fisher Expansion Approximate relationship between the fractiles of a probability distribution and its moments.

Cost of Carry Storage costs plus cost of financing an asset less the income earned on the asset.

Coupon Interest payment made on a bond.

Covered Call Short position in a call option on an asset combined with a long position in the asset.

Credit Risk The risk that a loss will be experienced because of a default by the counterparty in a derivatives transaction.

Currency Swap Swap in which interest and principal in one currency are exchanged for interest and principal in another currency.

Day Count Convention for quoting interest rates.

Day Trade Trade that is entered into and closed out on the same day.

Deferred Swap An agreement to enter into a swap that will start in the future. Also called a forward swap.

Delta The rate of change of the price of a derivative with the price of the underlying asset.

Delta Hedging A hedging scheme that is designed to make the price of a portfolio of derivatives insensitive to the price of the underlying asset for small changes in the price of the underlying asset.

Delta-neutral Portfolio Portfolio with a delta of zero so that there is no sensitivity to small changes in the price of the underlying asset.

Derivative Instrument whose price depends on or is derived from the price of another asset.

Diagonal Spread Position in two calls in which both the strike prices and times to maturity are different. (A diagonal spread can also be created with put options.)

Differential Swap Swap in which a floating rate in one currency is exchanged for a floating rate in another currency, with both rates being applied to the same principal.

Discount Instrument An instrument such as a Treasury bill that provides no coupons.

Discount Rate Annualized dollar return on a Treasury bill or similar instrument expressed as a percentage of the final face value.

Dividend Cash payment made to the owner of a stock.

Dividend Yield The dividend as a percentage of the stock price.

Down-and-in Option Option that comes into existence when the price of the underlying asset declines to a prespecified level.

Down-and-out Option Option that ceases to exist when the price of the underlying asset declines to a prespecified level.

Duration A measure of the average life of a bond. It is also an approximation to the ratio of the proportional change in the bond price to the absolute change in its yield.

Duration Matching A procedure for matching the durations of assets and liabilities in a financial institution.

Dynamic Hedging A procedure for hedging an option position by periodically changing the position held in the underlying assets. The objective is usually to maintain a delta-neutral position.

Early Exercise Exercise prior to the maturity date.

Efficient-market Hypothesis A hypothesis that asset prices reflect relevant information.

Embedded Option Option that is an inseparable part of another instrument.

Equity Swap Swap in which return on an equity portfolio is exchanged for either a fixed or a floating rate of interest.

Eurocurrency A currency that is outside the formal control of the issuing country's monetary authorities.

Eurodollar Dollar held in a bank outside the United States.

Eurodollar Futures Contract A futures contract written on a Eurodollar deposit.

Eurodollar Interest Rate Interest rate on a Eurodollar deposit.

European Option Option that can be exercised only at the end of its life.

EWMA Exponentially weighted moving average.

Ex-dividend Date When a dividend is declared, an ex-dividend date is specified. Investors who own shares of the stock on the ex-dividend date receive the dividend.

Exercise Price The price at which the asset may be bought or sold in an option contract. (Also called the strike price.)

Exotic Option A nonstandard option.

Expected Value of a Variable The average value of the variable obtained by weighting the alternative values by their probabilities.

Expiration Date End of life of a contract.

Exponential Weighting Weighting scheme in which the weight given to an observation depends on how recent it is. The weight given to an observation t time periods ago is λ times the weight given to an observation $t - 1$ time periods ago, where $\lambda < 1$.

Extendable Bond Bond whose life can be extended at the option of the holder.

Extendable Swap Swap whose life can be extended at the option of one side.

FASB Financial Accounting Standards Board.

Financial Intermediary Bank or other financial institution that facilitates the flow of funds among different entities in the economy.

Floor *See* Interest-rate Floor.

Floor-ceiling Agreement *See* Interest-rate Collar.

Floorlet One component of a floor.

Floor Rate Rate in an interest-rate floor agreement.

Foreign Currency Option Option on a foreign exchange rate.

Forward Contract Contract that obligates the holder to buy or sell an asset at a predetermined delivery price at a predetermined future time.

Forward Exchange Rate Forward price of one unit of a foreign currency.

Forward Interest Rate Interest rate for a future period of time implied by the rates prevailing in the market today.

Forward Price The delivery price in a forward contract that causes the contract to be worth zero.

Forward-rate Agreement Agreement that a certain interest rate will apply to a certain principal amount for a certain time period in the future.

Forward Swap *See* Deferred Swap.

FRA *See* Forward-rate Agreement.

Futures Contract Contract that obligates the holder to buy or sell an asset at a predetermined delivery price during a specified future time period. The contract is marked to market daily.

Futures Option Option on a futures contract.

Futures Price The delivery price currently applicable to a futures contract.

Gamma The rate of change of delta with respect to the asset price.

Gamma-neutral Portfolio Portfolio with a gamma of zero.

Geometric Average The nth root of the product of n numbers.

Hedge A trade designed to reduce risk.

Hedger An individual who enters into hedging trades.

Hedge Ratio Ratio of size of position in hedging instrument to size of position being hedged.

Historic Volatility Volatility estimated from historical data.

Implied Repo Rate Repo rate implied from the price of a Treasury bill and a Treasury bill futures price.

Implied Volatility Volatility implied from an option price using the Black–Scholes or similar model.

Index Amortizing Swap *See* Indexed Principal Swap.

Index Arbitrage Arbitrage involving a position in the stocks comprising a stock index and a position in a futures contract on the stock index.

Indexed Principal Swap Swap in which principal declines over time. The reduction in the principal on a payment date depends on the level of interest rates.

Index Futures A futures contract on a stock index or other index.

Index Option An option contract on a stock index or other index.

Initial Margin Cash required from a futures trader at the time of the trade.

Interest-rate Cap An option that provides a payoff when a specified interest rate is above a certain level. The interest rate is a floating rate that is reset periodically.

Interest-rate Collar A combination of an interest-rate cap and an interest-rate floor.

Interest-rate Floor An option that provides a payoff when an interest rate is below a certain level. The interest rate is a floating rate that is reset periodically.

Interest-rate Option An option dependent in some way on the level of interest rates.

Interest-rate Swap An exchange of a fixed rate of interest on a certain notional principal for a floating rate of interest on the same notional principal.

In-the-money Option Either (a) a call option in which the asset price is greater than the strike price or (b) a put option in which the asset price is less than the strike price.

Intrinsic Value For a call option, this is the greater of the excess of the asset price over the strike price and zero. For a put option, it is the greater of the excess of the strike price over the asset price and zero.

Inverted Market Market in which futures prices decrease with maturity.

Investment Asset Asset that some people hold for investment purposes.

IO Interest only. A mortgage-backed security in which the holder receives only interest cash flows on the underlying mortgage pool.

Kappa *See* Vega.

Kurtosis A measure of the fatness of the tails of a distribution.

Lambda *See* Vega.

LEAPS Long-term equity anticipation securities. These are relatively long-term options on individual stocks or stock indices.

LIBID London interbank bid rate. The rate bid by banks on Eurocurrency deposits (i.e., the rate at which a bank is willing to lend to other banks).

LIBOR London interbank offer rate. The rate offered by banks on Eurocurrency deposits (i.e., the rate at which a bank is willing to borrow from other banks).

Limit Move The maximum price move permitted by the exchange in a single trading session.

Limit Order Order that can be executed only at a specified price or a price more favorable to the investor.

Liquidity Premium Amount by which forward interest rates exceed expected future spot interest rates.

Local Individual on the floor of an exchange who trades for his or her own account rather than for someone else.

Lognormal distribution A variable has a lognormal distribution when the logarithm of the variable has a normal distribution.

Long Hedge Hedge involving a long futures position.

Long Position Position involving the purchase of an asset.

Lookback Option Option whose payoff depends on the maximum or minimum of the asset price achieved during a certain period.

Maintenance Margin When the balance in a trader's margin account falls below the maintenance margin level, the trader receives a margin call requiring the account to be topped up to the initial margin level.

Margin Cash balance (or security deposit) required from a futures or options trader.

Margin Call Request for extra margin when the balance in the margin account falls below the maintenance margin level.

Market Maker A trader who is willing to quote both bid and offer prices for an asset.

Marking to Market The practice of revaluing an instrument to reflect the current values of the relevant market variables.

Maturity Date End of the life of a contract.

Mean Reversion The tendency of a market variable (such as an interest rate) to revert back to some long-run average level.

Modified Duration A modification to the standard duration measure so that it more accurately describes the relationship between proportional changes in a bond price and absolute changes in its yield. The modification takes account of the compounding frequency with which the yield is quoted.

Monte Carlo Simulation A procedure for randomly sampling changes in market variables in order to value a derivative.

Mortgage-backed Security A security that entitles the owner to a share in the cash flows realized from a pool of mortgages.

Naked Position Short position in a call option that is not combined with a long position in the underlying asset.

No-arbitrage Assumption Assumption that there are no arbitrage opportunities in market prices.

Nonsystematic Risk Risk that can be diversified away.

Normal Backwardation Situation in which the futures price is below the expected future spot price.

Normal Distribution The standard bell-shaped distribution of statistics.

Normal Market Market in which futures prices increase with maturity.

Notional Principal Principal used to calculate payments in an interest-rate swap. The principal is "notional" because it is neither paid nor received.

Numerical Procedure Method of valuing an option when no formula is available.

OCC Options Clearing Corporation. *See* Clearinghouse.

Offer Price *See* Ask Price.

Open Interest Total number of long positions outstanding in the market. (Equals the total number of short positions.)

Option The right to buy or sell an asset.

Option-adjusted Spread Spread over Treasury curve that makes the theoretical price of an interest-rate derivative equal to the market price.

Option Class All options of the same type on a particular stock.

Option Series All options of a certain class with the same strike price and expiration date.

Order-Book Official *See* Board Broker.

Out-of-the-money Option Either (a) a call option in which the asset price is less than the strike price or (b) a put option in which the asset price is greater than the strike price.

Over-the-counter Market Market in which traders deal by phone. The traders are usually financial institutions, corporations, and fund managers.

Parallel Shift Movement in the yield curve in which each point on the curve changes by the same amount.

Par Value Principal amount of a bond.

Par Yield The coupon on a bond that makes its price equal the principal.

Payoff The cash realized by the holder of an option or other derivative at the end of its life.

Plain Vanilla Term used to describe a standard deal.

PO Principal only. A mortgage-backed security in which the holder receives only principal cash flows on the underlying mortgage pool.

Portfolio Immunization Making a portfolio relatively insensitive to interest rates.

Portfolio Insurance Entering into trades to ensure that the value of a portfolio will not fall below a certain level.

Position Limit Maximum position a trader (or group of traders acting together) is allowed to hold.

Premium Price of an option.

Prepayments Repayment of principal earlier than scheduled.

Principal Par or face value of a debt instrument.

Program Trading A procedure in which trades are automatically generated by a computer and transmitted to the trading floor of an exchange.

Protective Put A put combined with a long position in the underlying asset.

Pull-to-par A phrase describing the fact that a bond's price must revert to its par value at maturity.

Put–call Parity Relationship between price of a European call option and price of a European put option when they have the same strike price and maturity date.

Put Option Option to sell an asset for a certain price by a certain date.

Puttable Bond Bond in which the holder has the right to sell it back to the issuer at certain predetermined times for a predetermined price.

Puttable Swap A swap in which one side has the right to terminate early.

Rebalancing The process of adjusting a trading position periodically. Usually the purpose is to maintain delta neutrality.

Repo Repurchase agreement. A procedure for borrowing money by selling securities to a counterparty and agreeing to buy them back at a slightly higher price later.

Repo Rate Rate of interest in a repo transaction.

Reset Date Date in a swap when the floating rate for the next period is set.

Reversion Level Level to which the value of a market variable (e.g., an interest rate) tends to revert.

Rho Rate of change of the price of a derivative with the interest rate.

Rights Issue Issue to existing shareholders giving them the right to buy new shares at a certain price.

Risk-free Rate Rate of interest that can be earned without assuming any risks.

Risk-neutral Valuation Valuation of an option or other derivative assuming the world is risk neutral. Risk-neutral valuation gives the correct price for a derivative in all worlds, not just in a risk-neutral world.

Risk-neutral World World where investors are assumed to require no extra return on average for bearing risks.

Scalper Trader who holds positions for a very short period of time.

Scenario Analysis Analysis of the effects of alternative possible future movements in market variables on the value of a portfolio.

SEC Securities and Exchange Commission.

Series of Options *See* Option Series.

Settlement Price Average of the prices at which a contract trades immediately before the bell signalling the close of trading for a day. The settlement price is used in mark-to-market calculations.

Short Hedge Hedge in which a short futures position is taken.

Short Position Position in which the trader has sold shares that he or she does not own.

Short Rate Interest rate applying to a riskless investment made for a very short period of time.

Short Selling Selling in the market shares that have been borrowed from another investor.

Short-term Risk-free Rate *See* Short Rate.

Sigma *See* Vega.

Simulation *See* Monte Carlo Simulation.

Specialist Individual responsible for managing limit orders on some exchanges. The specialist does not make the information on outstanding limit orders available to other traders.

Spot Interest Rate *See* Zero-coupon Interest Rate.

Spot Price Price for immediate delivery.

Spread Transaction Position in two or more options of the same type.

Step-up Swap Swap in which principal increases with time in a predetermined way.

Stock Index Index monitoring the value of a portfolio of stocks.

Stock Index Futures Futures on a stock index.

Stock Index Option Option on a stock index.

Stock Option Option on a stock.

Stop-limit Order Combination of a stop-loss order and a limit order.

Stop-loss Order Order that is executed at the best available price once there is a bid or an offer at this price or a less favorable price.

Stop Order *See* Stop-loss Order.

Storage Costs Costs of storing a commodity.

Straddle A long position in a call and a put with the same strike price.

Strangle A long position in a call and a put with different strike prices.

Strap A long position in two call options and one put option with the same strike price.

Stress Testing Test of the impact of extreme market moves on the value of a portfolio.

Strike Price The price at which the asset may be bought or sold in an option contract. (Also called the exercise price.)

Strip A long position in one call option and two put options with the same strike price.

Swap An agreement to exchange cash flows in the future according to a prearranged formula.

Swaption Option to enter into an interest-rate swap in which a specified fixed rate is exchanged for a floating rate.

Synthetic Option Option created by trading the underlying asset.

Systematic Risk Risk that cannot be diversified away.

Terminal Value Value at maturity.

Term Structure Curve relating interest rates to maturity.

Theta Rate of change of price of option or other derivative with the passage of time.

Time Decay *See* Theta.

Time Value Value of an option arising from the time left to maturity. (Equals an option price's price minus its intrinsic value.)

Transactions Cost Cost of carrying out a trade. (Equal to commissions plus the difference between the price obtained and the midpoint of the bid-offer spread.)

Treasury Bill Short-term non-coupon-bearing instrument issued by the government to finance its debt.

Treasury Bill Futures Futures contract on a Treasury bill.

Treasury Bond Long-term coupon-bearing instrument issued by the government to finance its debt.

Treasury Bond Futures Futures contract on Treasury bonds.

Treasury Note *See* Treasury Bond. (Treasury notes have maturities less than 10 years.)

Treasury Note Futures Futures contract on Treasury notes.

Tree Representation of the evolution of the price of a market variable for the purposes of valuing an option or other derivative.

Triple Witching Hour Term given to the time when stock index futures, stock index options, and options on stock index futures all expire together.

Underlying Variable Variable on which price of an option or other derivative depends.

Unsystematic Risk *See* Nonsystematic Risk.

Up-and-in Option Option that comes into existence when the price of the underlying asset increases to a prespecified level.

Up-and-out Option Option that ceases to exist when the price of the underlying asset increases to a prespecified level.

Uptick Increase in price.

Value at Risk Loss that will not be exceeded at some specified confidence level.

Variation Margin Extra margin required to bring balance in the margin account up to the initial margin when there is a margin call.

Vega Rate of change in the price of an option or other derivative with volatility.

Vega-neutral Portfolio Portfolio with a vega of zero.

Volatility Measure of the uncertainty of the return realized on an asset.

Warrant Option issued by a company or a financial institution. Call warrants are frequently issued by companies on their own stock.

Wild Card Play The right to deliver on a futures contract for a period of time after the close of trading at the closing price.

Writing an Option Selling an option.

Yield Return provided by an instrument.

Yield Curve *See* Term Structure.

Zero-coupon Interest Rate Interest rate that would be earned on a bond that provides no coupons.

Zero-coupon Yield Curve Plot of zero-coupon interest rate against time to maturity.

Zero Curve *See* Zero-coupon Yield Curve.

Index